CLASSICAL PRESENCES

General Editors

LORNA HARDWICK   JAMES I. PORTER

CLASSICAL PRESENCES

The texts, ideas, images, and material culture of ancient Greece and Rome have always been crucial to attempts to appropriate the past in order to authenticate the present. They underlie the mapping of change and the assertion and challenging of values and identities, old and new. Classical Presences brings the latest scholarship to bear on the contexts, theory, and practice of such use, and abuse, of the classical past.

Milton and the Metamorphosis of Ovid

MAGGIE KILGOUR

OXFORD
UNIVERSITY PRESS

Great Clarendon Street, Oxford OX2 6DP

Oxford University Press is a department of the University of Oxford.
It furthers the University's objective of excellence in research, scholarship,
and education by publishing worldwide. Oxford is a registered trade mark of
Oxford University Press in the UK and in certain other countries

© Maggie Kilgour 2012

The moral rights of the author have been asserted

First published 2012
First published in paperback 2014

All rights reserved. No part of this publication may be reproduced,
stored in a retrieval system, or transmitted, in any form or by any means,
without the prior permission in writing of Oxford University Press,
or as expressly permitted by law, by licence or under terms agreed with the appropriate
reprographics rights organization. Enquiries concerning reproduction
outside the scope of the above should be sent to the Rights Department,
Oxford University Press, at the address above

You must not circulate this work in any other form
and you must impose this same condition on any acquirer

Published in the United States of America by Oxford University Press
198 Madison Avenue, New York, NY 10016, United States of America

British Library Cataloguing in Publication Data

Data available

Library of Congress Cataloging in Publication Data

Data available

ISBN 978–0–19–958943–2 (Hbk)
ISBN 978–0–19–871712–6 (Pbk)

*For Brian, Sole partner and sole part of all these joyes
and Nell, musa iocosa mea*

Contents

Preface	ix
Acknowledgements	xxi
Note on Editions	xxii
Introduction: Milton and the Renaissance Ovids	1
Milton's Ovidian art	1
Some other Renaissance Ovids	13
Ovid and Virgil	19
Beyond the *Metamorphoses*	28
Portrait of the artist as a young devil	35
1. Choosing Ovids (1)	49
Mastering the arts of allusion	49
First flowers	54
Comus and the *Translatio Ovidii*	74
2. Choosing Ovids (2)	97
More Ovids	97
Rereading Ovid's rapes	111
Poet of the year	115
It's about time	126
Milton and the passing of time	139
Masquing revolution	149
3. Reflections of Narcissus	165
Forms of change	165
Ovid's original	175
Renaissance Narcissi	184
Milton's original copy	196
Falling, in love	213
4. Self-Consuming Artists	229
Milton Narcissus	229
Envy and emulation	231

Ovidian *invidia*	242
Milton and the arts of envy	251
Falling poets	264
Sin and her originals	272
Conclusion: Last Words	**285**
The once and future Milton	285
Ovid's bad readers	287
The author as reader	292
The anxiety of reception	297
Reading *Samson Agonistes*	298
A phoenix too frequent	306
'The last of me or no I cannot warrant'	315
Go Little Book	**319**
Bibliography	329
Index	365

Preface

Every thing must have a beginning...and that beginning must be linked to something that went before. The Hindoos give the world an elephant to support it, but they make the elephant stand upon a tortoise. Invention, it must be humbly admitted, does not consist in creating out of void, but out of chaos; the materials must, in the first place, be afforded: it can give form to dark, shapeless substances, but cannot bring into being the substance itself... Invention consists in the capacity of seizing on the capabilities of a subject, and in the power of moulding and fashioning ideas suggested to it.[1]

Given the fact that *Paradise Lost* tells the story of the origins of all things, it is not surprising that readers have often been interested in tracing its sources. As prefaces to critical studies also often provide a narrative of their origins, I feel that I should begin with something about my own beginnings. This book has been a protean project, which has taken different shapes before settling into its final form. It started with a rather simple love of both Milton and Ovid, and a desire to get the two of them together as much as possible. One basic problem I faced from the start, however, was that of trying to understand how Milton read Ovid. The range of reading practices during the Renaissance means that this is not self-evident. Increasingly, moreover, I found myself thinking about a larger question: why does figuring out how Milton reads Ovid *matter*? What does it tell us about Milton? Ovid? Even ourselves?

Scholars of the Renaissance have of course always been fascinated by the role that classical culture played in the astonishing outburst of creative energy in this period. In literature especially, studies of imitation and allusion have returned us to thinking about individual artists' relations to their models. Thomas Greene's influential work argued that these relations were deeply ambivalent, a complex mixture of admiring emulation and envious rivalry.[2] For ambitious

---

[1] Mary Shelley, 'Introduction [1831]', in *Frankenstein; or, The Modern Prometheus*, ed. D. L. Maconald and Kathleen Scherf (Plymouth, 1999), 356.
[2] Thomas M. Greene, *The Light in Troy: Imitation and Discovery in Renaissance Poetry* (New Haven, 1982).

artists, influence is always anxiety provoking; the past is both a resource and a burden, a means of and impediment to creating something new and original. For Greene, Renaissance imitation was driven by a sense of historical difference, as artists became aware of their great distance from an origin to which they could never return. The classical world was itself a kind of paradise lost, a glorious and perfect world changed, as in Spenser's *Complaints*, into a barren wasteland of ruins.

Much of the eloquence of Greene's powerful reading comes from his own sense of distance from an irretrievable past. For Greene, reading Renaissance imitations in the modern world 'underscores even more cruelly our cultural solitude',[3] showing the great gulf between us and the ancients. That gulf can seem even wider today than when Greene was writing. Greene's model, like Harold Bloom's concept of *The Anxiety of Influence*, has been enormously influential, and for good reason. It speaks to an important dimension of our relation to our past. But it is not the whole relation. Greene's figure for historical solitude is Virgil's Aeneas, simultaneously cut off from and weighed down by the past. This reading recalls the Romantic image of the melancholy Virgil, himself severed from a Homeric source of authentic originality.[4] I am not sure such a figure would have made sense to a Renaissance critic like Scaliger, who saw Virgil as superior to his primitive source.[5] Given the belatedness of the study of Greek in Europe, Renaissance translations of Homer were frequently filtered through the much better-known Virgil, who shaped readers' expectations of epic norms.[6] The later copy influenced the understanding

---

[3] Greene, *The Light in Troy*, 53.

[4] On this interpretation of Virgil, see Gian Biagio Conte, *The Poetry of Pathos: Studies in Virgilian Epic* (Oxford, 2007), 24–7 especially.

[5] Julius Caesar Scaliger, 'Homeri et Vergilii loca. Caput III', in *Sieben Bücher über die Dichtkunst*, ed. and trans. Gregor Vogt-Spira [*Poetics Libri Septem*], 5 vols. (Stuttgart-Bad Cannstatt, 1998), iv. 64–307.

[6] Work on the Renaissance Homer itself has been somewhat belated, but is now enjoying a vigorous renaissance thanks especially to the work of Jessica Wolfe; see her 'Spenser, Homer, and the Mythography of Strife', *Renaissance Quarterly*, 58/4 (2005), 1220–88. See also Tania Demetriou, '"Essentially Circe": Spenser, Homer, and the Homeric Tradition', *Translation and Literature*, 15/2 (2006), 151–76; and Sarah Van Der Laan, 'Milton's Odyssean Ethics: Homeric Allusions and Arminian Thought in *Paradise Lost*', *Milton Studies*, 49 (2009), 49–76. At the 2009 meeting of the Renaissance Society of America Leah Whittington also presented a superb paper on the Virgilianizing of Homer: 'Raffaele Maffei Volterranno's Latin Translation of the *Odyssey* and Renaissance Literary Imitation'.

of the earlier model. Moreover, while Virgil suggests a nostalgic backward-looking model for imitation, in which the past is an increasingly receding source (Eurydice vanishing from Orpheus' view, the shades of Creusa and Anchises eluding Aeneas' embrace), a different example was available in Ovid, who grabbed the past and hurled it into the present and future, freeing it 'for a continual process of poetical and political reinvention'.[7]

Like Milton, Ovid is interested in origins. The *Metamorphoses*, like *Paradise Lost*, explains the origins of everything. In the *Metamorphoses* and *Fasti*, Ovid adopts the role of the etiological poet, who describes the beginnings of different phenomena, customs, and practices, including his own art.[8] But he also makes us think about the problem of imagining such beginnings. The *Fasti* especially gives us multiple versions of the genesis of a single phenomenon, thus both feeding and frustrating the desire for knowledge of sources. In Ovid, as in Mary Shelley, no beginning is absolute; all forms of creation are really re-creation. In *Metamorphoses* 1, therefore, Ovid's world is made not *ex nihilo*, but through the ordering of an already existing chaos by an unknown god.

Moreover, this opening scene is a statement of Ovid's own poetic origins. He too creates out of the materials of others: Homer, Hesiod, Empedocles, Euripides, Theocritus, Callimachus, Apollonius, Ennius, Lucretius, Cicero, Gallus, Propertius, Tibullus, Catullus, Horace, Virgil—to name only the more famous ones whose presences we are able to trace.[9] All classical authors are deeply allusive; as I noted, even Homer, who should be the *ne plus ultra* of all referentiality, was read in the Renaissance through Virgilian allusions. Classical writers commonly used 'double allusions', in which they simultaneously alluded to both an early work and its later imitation to draw attention to their own genealogies.[10] As Richard Thomas notes also, 'All Roman

---

[7] K. Sara Myers, 'The Metamorphosis of a Poet: Recent Work on Ovid', *Journal of Roman Studies*, 89 (1999), 196.

[8] See especially K. Sara Myers, *Ovid's Causes: Cosmogony and Aetiology in the Metamorphoses* (Ann Arbor, 1994).

[9] See the commentary on *Metamorphoses* 1 in Alessandro Barchiesi's edition of *Ovidio: Metamorfosi* I–II, trans. Ludovica Koch, (Milan, 2005), 136–7 especially.

[10] See Philip Hardie, 'The Speech of Pythagoras in Ovid *Metamorphoses* 15: Empedoclean *Epos*', *Classical Quarterly*, NS 45/1 (1995), 208; also Richard F. Thomas's discussion of 'window reference' in *Reading Virgil and his Texts: Studies in Intertextuality* (Ann Arbor, 1999), 130–2.

literature, from its very beginning, situates itself within the Greek tradition and almost immediately confronts its own evolution at the same time.'[11] Augustan poets, appearing comparatively late on the scene, are especially self-conscious about their rewriting of the past.[12] But Ovid makes his debts and relation to tradition not just the basis but also the subject of his work. Many readers would have known the Elder Seneca's account of Ovid's appropriation of a Virgilian phrase: 'non subripiendi causa, sed palam mutuandi, hoc animo ut vellet agnosci' ('with no thought of plagiarism, but meaning that his piece of open borrowing should be noticed', *Suasoriae*, 3. 7).[13] Ovid wants his audience to witness his miraculous transformation of others and marvel at his creation *non ex nihilo*. Ovid's scenes in which he claims divine inspiration from the gods are themselves derivative: they are modelled mostly on Callimachus's *Aita* fr. 1—a scene which in turn copies the opening of Hesiod's *Theogony*. So too at the very moment in which Ovid asserts his poetic freedom and immortality—the rousing climax of the *Metamorphoses* in the egotistic 'vivam' ('I will live', 15. 879)—he cheekily knows that readers will hear the echo of Ennius, of Horace's recent ode 3. 30, and of his own earlier self in *Amores* 1. 15.[14] The assertion of originality is highly conventional. The poetic ego is not alone; as Stephen Hinds notes, such claims to authority depend on the poet's relation to past writers.[15] Ovid delights in this paradox, and

---

[11] *Reading Virgil*, 4.

[12] As well as Thomas, *Reading Virgil*, see especially Gian Biagio Conte, *The Rhetoric of Imitation: Genre and Poetic Memory in Virgil and Other Latin Poets* (Ithaca, NY, 1986); Stephen Hinds, *Allusion and Intertext: Dynamics of Appropriation in Roman Poetry* (New York, 1998); Alessandro Barchiesi, *La traccia del modello: Effetti omerici nella narrazione virgiliana* (Pisa, 1984); and Barchiesi, *Speaking Volumes: Narrative and Intertext in Ovid and Other Latin Poets*, ed. and trans. Matt Fox and Simone Marchesi (London, 2001).

[13] Quotations from Seneca's *Suasoriae* are cited from *Declamations*, trans. M. Winterbottom, 2 vols. (Cambridge, Mass., 1974), ii. Also cited in Hinds, *Allusion and Intertext*, 22.

[14] Regius' edition cites Horace, and also the end of the *Georgics*, suggesting that this is a conventional way of ending a work; the note is reprinted in the Heinsius edition. Pontanus, following Scaliger, notes the parallel with the endings of Virgil, Horace, Statius, and Lucan as well as *Amores* 1. 15. 41–2. Ennius' famous claim 'volito vivos per ora virum' was quoted by Cicero in *Tusculan Disputations* 1. 34; see Karl Galinsky, *Ovid's* Metamorphoses: *An Introduction to the Basic Aspects* (Berkeley and Los Angeles, 1975), 24.

[15] Hinds also points out the paradox of the gesture: the classical poet's claim of primacy was authorized by precedents that also undermined it (*Allusion and Intertext*, 52–4).

embraces the challenge posed by the restrictions of copying earlier works, turning what might seem weakness into strength. As Karl Galinsky pointed out, his role model is the Ulysses of the *Ars Amatoria* 2. 128, who 'Ille referre aliter saepe solebat idem' ('often would he tell the same tale in other words').[16] The poet shows the extent of his skill by creating variation in repetition, difference in apparent likeness. For Ovid, belatedness is a source of power, as imitation is the path to innovation and liberation.

Ovid's debts to the past were often noted in Renaissance editions, which, as well as including moral and stylistic commentaries, identified parallels with other classical, and sometimes modern, texts.[17] Thus even when readers were not themselves able to catch allusions, annotations made Ovid's intertextual creativity visible for all to see— and to copy. As Colin Burrow notes, Ovid 'frequently influences the ways in which writers think about their own activity as imitators and

---

[16] Galinsky, *Ovid's* Metamorphoses, 4.

[17] The amount of attention paid varies between texts and editions: editions of the *Metamorphoses* tend to have fewer intertextual notes than the *Ibis*, for example. Of editors of the epic, Regius tends to be the most attentive to literary allusions. Sometimes, however, parallel passages are presented simply to explain a word use and do not therefore necessarily suggest an intertextual relation; so at *Metamorphoses* 1. 3, after noting the general conventions behind the opening lines, Regius annotates 'adspirate' with *Aeneid* 2. 385: 'adspirat primo Fortuna labori' ('Fortune favours our first effort'). Yet even such references could have reminded readers that language and meaning is produced by a system of prior practices, whose existence makes intelligibility possible. The practice of charting Ovid's sources and influences is certainly evident already in the 13th-century 'Vulgate' commentary on Ovid, which Frank Thomas Coulson has studied in depth. Coulson points out that the '"Vulgate" is remarkably sensitive to what might be termed Vergilian influences on Ovid's style and choice of dramatic movement' ('Ovid's Transformations in Medieval France (ca. 1100–ca. 1350)', in Alison Keith and Stephen James Rupp (eds.), *Metamorphosis: The Changing Face of Ovid in Medieval and Early Modern Europe* (Toronto, 2007), 58). See also his 'The *Vulgate* Commentary on Ovid's *Metamorphoses*', *Medievalia*, 13, Ovid in Medieval Culture, ed. Marilynn R. Desmond (1989 for 1987), 29–61. Criticism of other Roman authors, especially Virgil, had always been highly conscious of their use of allusions. Macrobius, for example, spends a good amount of time in *Saturnalia* 5–6 discussing Virgil's treatment of his sources, and Renaissance editions of Virgil commonly included parallels between Virgil and Homer. Concerned with the specific mechanisms of imitation, Roger Ascham complained, however, that such listing of passages in a 'heape' 'with no farder declaring the maner and way, how the one doth follow the other, were but a colde helpe, to the encrease of learning'. *The Scholemaster*, in *English Works*, ed. William Aldis Wright (Cambridge, 1904; repr. 1970), 267.

revivers of pagan antiquity'.[18] His metamorphosis of the past was a helpful example for later artists working with the classical tradition. The chance to retell Ovid gave them an opportunity to display their own Ovidian powers by putting a new spin on old stories. So Louis Martz suggests that 'Ovid's great poem, by its constant transmutation of epic materials, has helped to show Milton many ways in which he might transcend the Aonian mount'.[19] Ovid gives Milton a push up the hill, generously inviting and even provoking further rewriting.[20] By the time Milton arrived on the scene, moreover, Ovid had been worked over by almost every serious writer and painter. While studying Ovid closely, Milton was equally attentive to the reworkings of his great precursors: Dante, and especially his English ancestors, Shakespeare and Spenser. While noting their individual adaptations, Milton responds also to the fact that Ovid stands for a chain of continuing and metamorphic creativity.[21]

Using Ovid as an image for classical sources thus gives us a different perspective on Renaissance imitation and reception. Ovid undermines the illusion of a single pure source, as double allusions and multiple scenes of creation dissipate the idea of 'originality'. For Renaissance writers, Ovid cannot represent a single end point, a grand original to whom they look back with longing and trepidation. The Ovidian line between past and present is not a direct genealogical descent from classical fathers to Renaissance sons, nor is it an Oedipal

---

[18] 'Re-embodying Ovid: Renaissance Afterlives', in Philip Hardie (ed.), *The Cambridge Companion to Ovid* (Cambridge, 2002), 313.

[19] Louis Martz, *Poet of Exile: A Study of Milton's Poetry* (New Haven, 1980), 211.

[20] In the Middle Ages he had even invited dialogue, as writers continued the exchange of letters of the *Heroides*, including, in the case of Baudri of Bourgueil (1046–1130), letters to and from the exiled Ovid himself; see Ralph Hexter, 'Ovid in the Middle Ages: Exile, Mythographer, Lover', in Barbara Weiden Boyd (ed.), *Brill's Companion to Ovid* (Leiden, 2002), 422–4.

[21] Other critics have noted how different Renaissance authors also thematize the act of reception in their works, in ways that complicate Greene's description. Daniel Javitch argued that Ariosto 'regularly imitates texts that are themselves imitative and, moreover, he refers to their prior models in his imitations' ('The Imitation of Imitations in *Orlando Furioso*', *Renaissance Quarterly*, 38/2 (1985), 217). By refusing to privilege any single source as 'the beginning', Javitch argues, Ariosto creates a democratic literary system of equals; he reduces the power of the past while also acknowledging that his own work is 'the latest, but not the last, contribution' to an 'ongoing history of rewriting' (ibid. 235). In her fine recent essay, Tania Demetriou has shown that Spenser also uses what she calls 'a mannered textuality' or 'layered allusion' through which he makes explicit the tradition of reception and announces his own remaking of classical works ('"Essentially Circe"', 152).

agon between autonomous individuals severed by the abyss of time in which authority lies in the distant past.[22] It is a convoluted and messy—sometimes quite incestuous and even, as the example of Virgil and Homer shows, reversible—chain of mediation. Since Burckhardt, there has been a tendency to assume that the Renaissance recovery of the past helped produce a new type of 'individual' identified with unified autonomous subjectivity. Greene's emphasis on distance and historical solitude reinforced the detachment of the Renaissance subject, defined in opposition to a lost source. In many ways, Milton looks like the epitome of this Renaissance ego, set off from others, often apparently out of place in his own time. His Satan seems the archetypal Oedipal poet who, aspiring to be an 'autonomous, original author', struggles with the anxiety of influence.[23] Ovid too has been seen as the poet of ego whose great epic ends with the assertion of his own independence, as he projects himself into eternity with a triumphant 'vivam' ('I will live', *Met.*, 5. 879). My reading of the two authors and their meetings, however, suggests a different model for both authority and selfhood. In his grappling with Ovid, Milton is not an autonomous Bard, but a man who thinks through, and against, others. His work is full of dialogue and debate. Thomas De Quincey rather fancifully and provocatively described the relation between Milton and Ovid as 'the wedding of male and female counterparts'.[24] While I do not want to replace one familial model—that of father–son succession—with another—marriage—nor to push De Quincey's analogy into absurdity, I think Milton's relation to Ovid is similar to his ideal of marriage as the happy coming together of 'most resembling unlikeness, most unlike resemblance' (*Tetrachordon*, in *Works*, iv. 86),

---

[22] Heather James also questions some of Greene's assumptions about Renaissance writers' relations to the past; see 'Shakespeare, the Classics, and the Forms of Authorship', *Shakespeare Studies*, 36 (2008), 80–9. James argues that in the gathering of *sententiae* authority was transferred from the individual authors collected to the process of collecting the past. Such practices therefore worked to undermine the integrity and authority of the classical tradition.

[23] David Quint, *Origin and Originality in Renaissance Literature: Versions of the Source* (New Haven, 1983), 211.

[24] 'Orthographic Mutineers', in *The Collected Writings of Thomas De Quincey*, ed. David Masson, 14 vols. (1890; repr. New York: AMS Press, 1968), xi. 449. The full quote is this: 'Ovid was the great poetic favourite of Milton; and not without a philosophic ground: his festival gaiety, and the brilliant velocity of his *aurora borealis* intellect, forming a deep natural equipoise to the mighty gloom and solemn planetary movement in the mind of the other,—like the wedding of male and female counterparts. Ovid was, therefore, rightly Milton's favourite' (449).

a coupling which balances likeness and difference, proximity and distance, and which requires constant negotiation.

My book traces the changing role of Ovid through Milton's poetry. The Introduction opens with the question of how Milton might have read Ovid and discusses some of the meanings Ovid had for Renaissance writers. I argue further for the importance of adding the exilic works and *Fasti* to the 'Renaissance Ovid', and show Ovid's central role in the development of Elizabethan literature. The first three chapters are concerned with the role of Ovid in Milton's representations of the origins of his own poetry; the last two turn to consider how Ovid affects his consideration of the end of both his poetic career and his life.

The first pair of chapters examines Milton's use of Ovid in his early works, in which he is studying and imitating Ovid carefully. I suggest that Milton became increasingly attentive to revisions of Ovid by earlier writers. While I begin by noting close parallels and specific verbal echoes from Ovid's writing, I show that these references indicate that, aided especially by the example of the Elizabethans, the young Milton has a surprisingly keen grasp of the broader patterns and concerns of Ovid's works. In Chapter 1, I begin with some of the Ovidian elements in the early Latin works and then turn to 'On the Death of a fair Infant dying of a Cough' and *Comus*. I argue that as he moves into English, Milton uses Ovid to enter into the poetical debates among the Elizabethans over the directions of English poetry. In Chapter 2, I position Milton also in relation to major trends of Caroline Ovidianism, represented by both the libertine poets and the court masques. Given the role of Ovid in courtly self-representation, I suggest that rewriting Ovid drew Milton inevitably into political debates. I return to the Latin works and *Comus* to look particularly at the moments when Milton reworks Ovid's *Fasti*. Drawing on recent scholarship on Ovid's poetic calendar, I argue that the poem's experimentation with genre and its preoccupation with the poetics and politics of time spoke to the concerns of sixteenth- and seventeenth-century English writers. As well as playing a crucial role in Milton's poetical development, Ovid is bound up in his political awakening. He helps Milton see that to write poetry is to engage with questions of freedom that are as much religious and political as poetical.

The next two chapters turn to *Paradise Lost*, arguing that the failure of the Revolution deepened Milton's reading of Ovid.

I consider especially some of the ways in which *Paradise Lost* uses the act of revision to explore its central problems. By working within traditions, with stories and figures whose fates are already well known, Milton is able to explore the limits of freedom and change. Literary allusions demonstrate the problem of free will and determination. Chapter 3 focuses on the uses of Narcissus in *Paradise Lost*. While many critics have examined Ovid's story as a model for Eve's creation and the birth of Sin, I suggest that the tale underlies all the figures in the poem, and informs Milton's understanding of the origins of creativity itself. I discuss Ovid's story and its role in Renaissance art and poetry where it becomes a means of exploring the relations between self-knowledge, desire, and art. The tale encourages later artists also to reflect on their own mirroring of Ovid. While readers frequently assume that Milton's fall is caused by narcissism, I argue that Milton represents it as a failure of creative revision, which may be traced through the coupling of Adam and Eve. In Chapter 4, I discuss the consequences of this failure for the poet himself. Like Ovid, Milton fills his work with characters who are doubles for himself. Through the figures of Satan, Sin, as well as the different artists who are alluded to throughout *Paradise Lost*, Milton suggests how the fall has wounded his own creativity. For Milton, evil is a version of the poet's creative imitation, which has degenerated into sterile copying fuelled by the force of envy, which is the traditional enemy and self-destructive double of all creativity. In the figure of the narrator especially, Milton shows how the desire to create is never fully separate from the drive to destroy.

These two antithetical impulses seem especially difficult to disentangle in *Samson Agonistes*, on which I focus in the Conclusion. I look at Milton's drama in relation to Ovid's final exilic poetry, in which he is concerned with the interpretation and future reception of his works. At the end of his life Milton tried to control the future by arranging his final works to present a narrative of his own developing and achieved promise. At the same time, *Samson* offers a troubling conclusion to Milton's work and life. The vehement critical disagreements over the meaning of this poem are anticipated by the tragedy itself, which internalizes and problematizes its own reception. Milton thus returns to the questions of revision which he faced in his early works, in order to imagine himself as part of the tradition which later readers and writers will interpret and rework. In a brief *envoi*, I therefore read the Ovidian epistle 'Ad *Joannem Rousium*, Oxoniensis Academiae

Bibliothecarium', the last poem in Milton's 1673 reissue of his 1645 *Poems*, as Milton's submission to a future in which it is his turn to be read and recreated by others. It is fitting that the last lines of Milton's poem rework Ovid's hope for immortality in *Amores* 1. 15. Milton's career comes full circle, as the act of authorial self-fashioning is always continued in the process of reception.

While I am inevitably concerned with broader questions of imitation and intertextuality, not to mention textual and authorial identity, this study is primarily an exercise in practical criticism that explores a specific relation between two very distinct authors. What interests me is the creative tension and power that comes from Milton's thinking about and through Ovid, and through the writers who anticipate and influence his creative revision. It would seem wrong to try to trace an orderly genealogy of descent from a poet fascinated by incest; what follows is not a study of 'the logical succession of the history of ideas' but one of 'the far less linear history of the imagination'.[25] This has been a bit of a challenge methodologically in terms of choosing the sources to be discussed. I have tried to let them choose themselves, keeping close to the main lines on the family tree—authors whose importance for Milton and whose debts to Ovid have been noted—and not getting overly distracted by faint family resemblances. Following the twisting connections between Ovidian motifs in both Ovid himself and his imitators has also been a challenge in terms of structure. The nature of this project demanded at certain times a tripartite form: in the central chapters, I begin first by examining a set of problems or questions in Ovid, and then give evidence of how these were recognized by other writers and artists, before turning to Milton. By looking carefully at Ovid's works and their impact, I have tried to resist the temptation of 'Generalising about Ovid'[26] or his meaning for later writers. But there are times, therefore, when Milton disappears from view for longer stretches. If some of these excursi seem too extensive, I invite the reader to follow the venerable critical practice of judicious skimming. I hope that my principle of selection is not too mysterious and that the side journeys aid the goal as a whole; after all, Ovid teaches that 'Grata mora venies; maxima lena mora est' ('delay

---

[25] Leonard Barkan, *The Gods Made Flesh: Metamorphosis & the Pursuit of Paganism* (New Haven, 1986), 172. Like anyone working on Ovid's legacy I am deeply indebted to Barkan's book.

[26] See Stephen Hinds, 'Generalising about Ovid', *Ramus*, 16 (1987), 4–31.

will enhance your charm: a great procuress is delay', *Ars*, 3. 752). And all roads, ultimately, lead to Milton.

Above all, I hope to show why understanding Milton's relation to Ovid still matters to us. For Milton, and for us, thinking through the past can be creative, stimulating, and transformative. There is a polemic in this book therefore, concerning the dynamic nature of traditions and our own relation to the past. Milton's Ovid is not the embodiment of 'The Classical Tradition'—a compendium of fixed myths—but part of the dynamic process of reception in which we too are engaged as part of our own ongoing self-creation.

In writing on such a subject I am especially conscious of the question of intellectual indebtedness and of my own origins. There are many, many debts here, not adequately reflected in my discussion or notes. I have learned much from conversations with, not to mention the work of, others. I am particularly grateful for the generous readings and judicious comments on parts of this work by Philip Hardie, Stephen Hinds, Noel Sugimura, Jennifer Lewin, and Heather Dubrow. At McGill, my equally Ovidianly obsessed colleague Jamie Fumo gave me crash courses on the Middle Ages and helped me through some of the trickier sections. Her brilliant work on Ovid and Chaucer has enriched my thinking as well as that of many others. I owe much also to conversations with Alessandro Barchiesi, John Creaser, Martin Dawes, Andrew Escobedo, Ken Gross, Heather James, Edward Jones, John Leonard, Raphael Lyne, Charles Martindale, Stella Revard, William Shullenberger, Sarah Van der Laan, Andrew Wallace, and John Watkins. Thanks also to the Northeastern Milton Seminar, especially Tom Luxon and Laura Lunger Knoppers, for their stimulating responses to Chapter 1; and to Paul Stevens, Host of Hosts, and the members of the Canada Milton Seminar VI for inviting me to present some of this research and for offering such enthusiastic and pointed discussion. Over the years, I was lucky enough to be able to study Latin with the infamous Reginaldus Foster, from whom I learned so much more than Latin. I received support from the SSHRC to begin this project and from McGill's Internal SSHRC to help finish it. I have had a wonderful team of RAs who tracked down difficult references for me and slogged through some fairly tedious assignments with grace and cheer: David Anderson, Martin Dawes, Leon Grek, Meredith Donaldson, and the beady-eyed Tara Murphy. A special medal should go to Janine Harper, whose truly heroic patience and precision kept me from too much fatal *error*. I am thankful also for the care, kindness, and good cheer of Hilary O'Shea, Taryn Campbell, Tessa Eaton, Jackie Pritchard, and Andrew Hawkey at OUP who graciously guided me through the labyrinth of publication. *Nec tibi cura canum fuerit postrema* (Virgil, *Georgics*, 3. 404): through the process of writing, Nell, spirit of Ovidian play, was a constant source of inspiration. My greatest debt in this work, however, and indeed in everything I do is to Brian Trehearne. Our conversations—especially on completely unrelated topics—helped refine, focus, but also expand my thinking, and brought so much delight as well as knowledge into my life.

These friends need not fear, however, that I will trace my errors to them. This is my book. I even hope there may be something original or at least new in it—though I will not presumptuously suggest, as did the medieval commentator on Ovid, Arnulf of Orleans, that: 'Et si eas bene fecit, immo si quid habent ueri uatum presagia, uiuam cum Ouidio' ('For if he has done his work well, if the sayings of the prophets have any truth, I shall be immortalized along with Ovid').[27] But if there is anything here that is original, it is because of my conversations with such scholars and friends, and with, above all, the two authors I have been lucky enough to spend time with.

Maggie Kilgour

---

[27] Text and translation quoted from Coulson, 'Ovid's Transformations in Medieval France', 47.

Acknowledgements

An earlier version of Chapter 3 appeared as '"Thy perfect image viewing": Poetic Creation and Ovid's Narcissus in *Paradise Lost*', *Studies in Philology*, 102 (2005), 307–39.

An earlier version of Chapter 4 appeared as 'Satanic Envy and Classical Emulation', in Louis Schwarz and Mary Fenton (eds.), *Their Maker's Image: New Essays on John Milton* (Selinsgrove, Pa.: Susquehanna University Press, 2011), 46–62.

An earlier version of parts of the conclusion appeared as 'New Spins on Old Rotas: Virgil, Ovid, Milton', in Helen Moore and Philip Hardie (eds.), *Classical Literary Careers and their Reception* (Cambridge: Cambridge University Press, 2010), 179–96.

Note on Editions

All citations of *Paradise Lost* are taken from *Paradise Lost*, ed. Barbara K. Lewalski (Malden, Mass.: Blackwell, 2007); the other works, including Latin poetry and translations, are cited from *John Milton: Complete Shorter Poems*, ed. Stella Revard, trans. Lawrence Revard (Malden, Mass.: Blackwell, 2009). Passages from Milton's English and Latin prose are drawn from *The Works of John Milton*, ed. Frank Allen Patterson, 20 vols. (New York: Columbia University Press, 1931–40), cited throughout as *Works*. In some places, translations have been slightly modified. Citations from the Milton *Variorum* are from Merritt Y. Hughes (gen. ed.), *A Variorum Commentary on the Poems of John Milton*, 4 vols. (New York: Columbia University Press, 1970–5), i: *The Latin and Greek Poems*, ed. Douglas Bush, and *The Italian Poems*, ed. J. E. Shaw and A. Bartlett Giamatti; and ii: *The Minor English Poems*, ed. A. S. P. Woodhouse and Douglas Bush.

Spenser's minor works are cited from *The Poetical Works of Edmund Spenser*, ed. J. C. Smith and Ernest De Sélincourt (London: Oxford University Press, 1948). For *The Faerie Queene*, I have used *The Faerie Queene*, ed. A. C. Hamilton (3rd edn., London: Longman, 1977). Quotations from Shakespeare's plays are taken from *The Riverside Shakespeare*, ed. G. Blakemore Evans (Boston: Houghton Mifflin, 1974), while excerpts from his poetry are from *The Complete Sonnets and Poems*, ed. Colin Burrow (Oxford: Oxford University Press, 2002). References to Dante's *Commedia* use *The Divine Comedy*, trans. Charles S. Singleton, 6 vols. (Princeton: Princeton University Press, 1970).

Citations to Renaissance editions and translations of the *Metamorphoses* are taken from:

Ex Metamorphoseon Libris XV. Electorum Libri Totidem, ed. Jacobus Pontanus (Antwerp, 1618; facs. edn. *The Renaissance and the Gods*, ed. Stephen Orgel, 55 vols. (New York and London, 1976), xxiv).

Metamorphoseos libri moralizati, with Commentaries by Raphael Regius, Petrus Lavinius, and Others (Lyons, 1518; facs. edn. *The Renaissance and the Gods*, ed. Stephen Orgel, 55 vols. (New York and London, 1976), iii).

Sabinus, Georgius, *Metamorphosis seu fabulae poeticae* (Frankfurt, 1589; facs. edn. *The Renaissance and the Gods*, ed. Stephen Orgel, 55 vols. (New York and London, 1976), xiv).

For the purposes of accessibility, however, basic citations of Ovid are from the Loeb Classical Library Series: *Metamorphoses*, ed. G. P. Goold, trans. Frank Justus Miller, 2 vols. (2nd edn., London: W. Heinemann, 1916); *Heroides and Amores*, ed. G. P. Goold, trans. Grant Showerman (London: W. Heinemann, 1947); *The Art of Love, and Other Poems*, ed. G. P. Goold, trans. J. H. Mozley (London: W. Heinemann, 1957); *Ovid's Fasti*, ed. G. P. Goold, trans. Sir James George Frazer (London: W. Heinemann, 1959); *Tristia; Ex Ponto*, ed. G. P. Goold, trans. Arthur Leslie Wheeler (2nd edn., London: W. Heinemann, 1988). Citations of Virgil are from *Virgil*, ed. G. P. Goold, trans. H. Rushton Fairclough, 2 vols. (rev. edn., Cambridge, Mass.: Harvard University Press, 1999). Unless otherwise noted, translations are from these editions, with occasional small changes for poetic licence.

Introduction

Milton and the Renaissance Ovids

THE ARGUMENT

How might Milton have read Ovid and how does that reading contribute to our understanding of both writers? The critics who have looked closely at the two have very different understandings of the relation. I argue that Milton studied Ovid carefully but was also attentive to the creative adaptations of Ovid by earlier poets, especially the Elizabethans. I suggest that for these writers, moreover, Ovid was more than just his epic. Including the final works, especially the exilic poetry, reveals a more complex and ambiguous figure, whose art and life stimulate questions about poetry and change.

MILTON'S OVIDIAN ART

Since Deborah Milton reported that Ovid's *Metamorphoses* was one of her father's favourite works,[1] scholars have been fascinated by the paradox of the Puritan poet's fondness for a pagan writer whose moral and poetic vision seems in many ways the complete opposite of his own. Many commentators and critics have noted the numerous echoes of and allusions to Ovid throughout Milton's works.[2] While *Paradise Lost* draws upon the entire classical tradition, Ovid, often

---

[1] See Samuel Johnson, *Lives of the English Poets*, ed. Arthur Waugh, 2 vols. (London, 1906; repr. 1977), i. 107.
[2] See especially Davis P. Harding, *Milton and the Renaissance Ovid* (Urbana, Ill., 1946); Douglas Bush, *Mythology and the Renaissance Tradition in English Poetry* (New York, 1963), 260–97; Charles Martindale, *John Milton and the Transformation of Ancient Epic* (Totowa, NJ, 1986); Martz, *Poet of Exile*; Richard J. DuRocher, *Milton and Ovid* (Ithaca, NY, 1985); and Mandy Green, *Milton's Ovidian Eve* (Farnham, 2009).

read as the encyclopedia of that tradition, seems to have provided a particularly vivid set of motifs and figures that stimulated Milton's imagination. But Milton's transformation of his pagan subtext into Christian poetry seems in many ways the most magisterial example of Ovidian metamorphosis. On the surface the two writers could hardly be more different. Ovid is the compiler of a work often treated as a bible of classical religion; Milton is the poetizer of the Christian Bible. Ovid is notoriously the poet who represents a 'rhetorical' self,[3] a prophet of postmodern subjectivity, while Milton often appears to be 'the most monumentally unified author in the canon' who stands on 'the threshold of modern subjectivity'.[4] As we'll see, Ovid is associated with different kinds of 'error', while Milton presents an image of unwavering rectitude; where Ovid is light and frivolous, Milton projects a 'Certain Severity', a 'Mind not Condescending to Little things'.[5] Ovid is the poet of unlicensed and often violent sexuality; Milton is the poet of chastity and married love. Ovid's universe is overseen by a motley bunch of amoral gods who interact with humans mostly to abuse them; Milton's is governed by an all-powerful Father and his compassionate Son who comes to earth to redeem mankind. Yet, as Richard DuRocher rightly observed, 'Milton and Ovid are inextricably bound up together'.[6] Still, the same can be said of Dante's Paolo and Francesca. Given that Milton's works often focus on pairs whose relation ranges from the intimacy of Adam and Eve to the opposition of the Son and Satan, it seems sensible to ask what kind of coupling this might be. While critics have often cited De

---

[3] See Richard Lanham's use of Ovid as the image for the 'rhetorical man' that developed in the Renaissance (*The Motives of Eloquence: Literary Rhetoric in the Renaissance* (New Haven, 1976), 3–5). The association of Ovid with the representation of a fragmentary self runs through criticism from at least Hermann Fränkel's description of 'the phenomena of insecure and fleeting identity, of a self divided in itself or spilling over into another self' (*Ovid: A Poet between Two Worlds* (Berkeley and Los Angeles, 1945), 99), to Lynn Enterline's image of the Ovidian violated body, *The Rhetoric of the Body from Ovid to Shakespeare* (Cambridge, 2000), and Georgia Brown's evocation of a disintegrating Elizabethan world, *Redefining Elizabethan Literature* (Cambridge, 2004).

[4] Mary Nyquist and Margaret W. Ferguson, 'Preface', in Mary Nyquist and Margaret W. Ferguson (eds.), *Re-Membering Milton: Essays on the Texts and Traditions* (New York, 1987), p. xii; Kathleen M. Swaim, 'Myself a True Poem: Early Milton and the (Re)formation of the Subject', *Milton Studies*, 38 (2000), 69.

[5] Jonathan Richardson, *Explanatory Notes and Remarks on Milton's Paradise Lost*, in Helen Darbishire (ed.), *The Early Lives of Milton* (London, 1932), 212.

[6] DuRocher, *Milton and Ovid*, 9.

Quincey's description of the relation between Milton and Ovid as 'a wedding of male and female counterparts', not all have seen it as a happy or lasting union.[7] Critics have differing ways of describing the relation between this odd couple and of understanding how Milton read Ovid, and, indeed, what 'Ovid' meant to Milton. How we understand that relation both depends upon and produces rather different 'Miltons'; it gives us different models, too, for how and why poets rewrite the past.

Many critics have believed that Ovid was mediated to Milton through the allegorical tradition which emerged in the late Middle Ages and was made infamous by the *Ovide moralisé*. It had a surprisingly long life, partly through the influence of the schools, where it continued to coexist happily with the newer humanist emphasis in which Ovid became primarily a teacher of rhetoric.[8] Its presence is felt in both Golding's and Sandy's translations, and in Milton's figure of Sin. The first major study of the relation between the two poets, Davis Harding's 1946 *Milton and the Renaissance Ovid*, thus assumes that the Renaissance Ovid was allegorical, as was Milton's. Harding's assumptions have been quietly influential and have recently been given new ground in John Mulryan's 1996 study *'Through a Glass Darkly': Milton's Reinvention of the Mythological Tradition*.[9] Mulryan argues that Milton read Ovid through the allegorical tradition disseminated through the encyclopedias, commentaries, dictionaries, *Florilegia*, and handbooks common at this time.[10] In such works,

---

[7] 'Orthographic Mutineers', in *The Collected Writings of Thomas de Quincey*, ed. David Masson, 14 vols. (1890; repr. New York, 1968), xi. 449. For critical citations of the passage, see DuRocher, *Milton and Ovid*, 64; Green, *Milton's Ovidian Eve*, p. x; and Elizabeth Sauer, 'Engendering Metamorphoses: Milton and the Ovidian Corpus', in Goran V. Stanivukovic (ed.), *Ovid and the Renaissance Body* (Toronto, 2001), 208.

[8] The shift from morality to style in practices of reading Ovid under the influence of humanism has been well traced; see for example DuRocher, *Milton and Ovid*, 20–38; D. C. Allen, *Mysteriously Meant: The Rediscovery of Pagan Symbolism and Allegorical Interpretation in the Renaissance* (Baltimore, 1970), 163–99; Madelaine Doran, 'Some Renaissance "Ovids"', in Bernice Slote (ed.), *Literature and Society* (Lincoln, Nebr., 1964), 44–62; Clark Hulse, *Metamorphic Verse: The Elizabethan Minor Epic* (Princeton, 1981); and Lee T. Pearcy, *The Mediated Muse: English Translations of Ovid, 1560–1700* (Hamden, Conn., 1984).

[9] John Mulryan, *Through a Glass Darkly: Milton's Reinvention of the Mythological Tradition* (Pittsburgh, 1996).

[10] Mulryan thus claims that 'Milton never read his authors "straight"; Renaissance editions of Vergil, Ovid and Homer are filled with learned annotations, introductions and appendices' (ibid. 6). At the same time, the number of plain editions was increasing; see Ann Moss, *Ovid in Renaissance France: A Survey of the Latin Editions*

stories were commonly detached from their original context, and treated as self-contained episodes or *sententiae*, so that Ovid appears mostly as a group of independent myths.[11]

To see Ovid through this tradition then is to define him primarily as a resource book of stories, a tool-kit for would-be artists, full of individual and essentially autonomous myths to be pulled apart, interpreted, and reassembled freely. This reading of Ovid also has the advantage of explaining the potential conflict between the Christian subject of *Paradise Lost* and its pagan subtexts by explaining it away: Milton receives an Ovid who has already been taken apart and thoroughly reconciled with Christian values through allegorical interpretation, a tradition of reading with which, Harding argues, Milton is himself in sympathy.

A very different perspective was taken in DuRocher's 1985 study *Milton and Ovid*, which, as its title succinctly states, is mostly interested in the unmediated relation between the two authors themselves. While knowledgeable of Renaissance traditions of interpretation and the important role that Ovid played in the critical debates of the time, DuRocher sees the relation between authors in broadly Bloomian terms as an agon between a strong poet and his precursor. Where

---

of Ovid and Commentaries Printed in France before 1600 (London, 1982), 37–9 especially. Moss speculates that the growth of unannotated editions occurred because dictionaries took over the role of the Latin commentaries. She notes, however, that as annotations disappeared in the editions of Latin works, they increased in translations: 'Perhaps it was felt that vernacular readers needed preliminary guidance on how to understand the fables, whereas the more homogeneous public for the Latin editions, well schooled in reading the fables as moral *exempla* by their humanist teachers, could be left to cope intelligently with the text of the *Metamorphoses* plain and unadorned' (ibid. 38).

[11] The Bible was also commonly read in such a way; Locke complained of the decontextualization of passages, saying that most people read the Scriptures 'chop'd and minc'd' into 'Piece-meal' ('An Essay for the understanding of St. Paul's Epistles', in *The Works of John Locke*, 3 vols. (London, 1714); iii. 103–4; cited from Dayton Haskin, *Milton's Burden of Interpretation* (Philadelphia, 1994), p. xiii). Mary Thomas Crane has argued further that the practice of Renaissance commonplace books, such as Milton's, encouraged the tendency to encounter the classical past in bits; see *Framing Authority: Sayings, Self, and Society in Sixteenth-Century England* (Princeton, 1993). On the implications of the practice of collecting *sententiae* for Renaissance ideas of authority and the author see also James, 'Shakespeare, the Classics, and the Forms of Authorship', 80–9. Charles Martindale cautions that, as most readers encountered Ovid as fragments, critics should not presume their knowledge of any particular story's larger context ('Shakespeare's Ovid, Ovid's Shakespeare: A Methodological Postscript', in A. B. Taylor (ed.), *Shakespeare's Ovid*: The Metamorphoses *in the Plays and Poems* (Cambridge, 2000), 198–215).

Harding and Mulryan's Milton reflects tradition, DuRocher's breaks free from its shackles; as DuRocher proclaims: 'The crucial question of my study is how one fiercely independent poet, overtly skeptical of glosses and commentaries, incorporated and adapted the *Metamorphoses* within his epic.'[12]

There is something extremely attractive about this heroic single combat model, which has a long and distinguished lineage, going back to at least Longinus' description of Plato's creative wrestling match with Homer.[13] It upholds the popular image of Milton, free thinker, poet of independence and originality, a Milton for whom a Catholic system of allegorical interpretation might well be intrinsically suspect. Positioning Milton as the allegorists' successor asserts his continuity with medieval practices and traditions;[14] DuRocher makes him a Renaissance humanist who breaks from the recent past to rediscover the meaning of the ancients on his own. Drawing on Thomas Greene's influential study of Renaissance imitation, DuRocher describes the relation between the two writers as a form of what Greene calls 'dialectical imitation' or *aemulatio*, a close encounter between the two individuals themselves, typical of Renaissance creative engagements with the classical past.[15] DuRocher's reading importantly restores the integrity of the *Metamorphoses*, which he sees not as a series of isolated episodes, but as a narrative whole.[16] His

---

[12] DuRocher, *Milton and Ovid*, 19.

[13] Longinus, 'On the Sublime'. in *Aristotle: The Poetics; 'Longinus': On the Sublime; Demetrius: On Style*, ed. and trans. W. Hamilton Fyfe and W. Rhys Roberts (Cambridge, Mass., 1932), 169.

[14] As Mulryan has done elsewhere; see *Milton and the Middle Ages* (Lewisburg, Pa., 1982).

[15] See DuRocher, *Milton and Ovid*, 36–7 especially. I will return to *aemulatio* in Ch. 4.

[16] Raphael Lyne also argues that readers of the 16th century showed interest in the *Metamorphoses* as a unified work (*Ovid's Changing Worlds: English Metamorphoses, 1567–1632* (Oxford, 2001), 35–8 and 45–6 especially. Even T.H., author of the appalling 1560 *Fable of Ouid treting of Narcissus*, noted that 'Hys tales doe Ioyne, in suche a godly wyse, | That one doth hange vpon anothers ende' ('The moralization of the Fable. In Ouid of Narcissus', in *The Fable of Ovid Treting of Narcissus* (London, 1560), Early English Books Online, B1ʳ). Such readings were not unique to the Renaissance; M. L. Stapleton argues that while 12th-century teachers were still chopping up Ovid to fit Aristotelian categories, a poet like Guillaume IX was able to grasp and creatively adapt Ovid's larger poetic project (*Harmful Eloquence: Ovid's Amores from Antiquity to Shakespeare* (Ann Arbor, 1996), 76). While, in Renaissance debates over genre, some theorists argued that Ovid's episodic narrative was too disjointed to be considered an epic, others used his poem an example of the ideal creation of unity

approach heralds a turn apparent in other admirable studies of the use of Ovid by Renaissance poets: Jonathan Bate's *Shakespeare and Ovid* and Syrithe Pugh's *Spenser and Ovid*, for example, also foreground the exchange between individual artists. Especially since Leonard Barkan's magisterial *The Gods Made Flesh* showed the centrality of Ovidian metamorphoses to Renaissance aesthetics, we have become aware of how artists and writers of the time read Ovid's work individually and creatively, often politically—though sometimes just plain pornographically—with interests quite different from those of the commentaries and the schoolroom. Habits of reading may be shaped by education and cultural context but (as I teach my students) they are not completely determined by them.

The differences between Harding and DuRocher, then, demonstrate one fundamental problem in any examination of Milton and Ovid. If Renaissance ways of reading Ovid differ from ours, they also differ from each other. The plurality of reading practices possible at this time makes choosing Milton's Ovid difficult. How do we read Milton reading Ovid? Was Milton's Ovid allegorized, in bits and pieces, or 'the thing itself', a unified whole? Which Ovid do we choose? Let alone which Milton—the allegorist or the humanist? '[C]opiaque ipsa nocet', as Ovid says in *Fasti* 5. 6: the choice is a killer.

At the same time, Harding's and DuRocher's readings share some basic assumptions and therefore also some conclusions. While DuRocher's Milton is indeed more original in his use of his pagan sources than Harding's and Mulryan's, he is finally, and surprisingly, one whose understanding of Ovid does not ultimately stray far from that of the allegorists who make pagan forms reveal Christian truths. DuRocher's model, like those of Greene and Bloom, is an essentially competitive one, in which the later poet attempts to surpass and correct the earlier—'to soar | Above th' *Aonian* Mount' (*PL*, 1. 14–15). For DuRocher, however, the individual agon is essentially a conflict between

---

out of diversity, thus indicating their sense of the ultimate coherence of the separate pieces. The complexity of the situation is suggested by Moss, who notes how students were encouraged to take the epic apart for entries for their commonplace books so that 'one almost suspects that it was better known to the average student in the form of extracts than as a continuous narrative' (*Ovid in Renaissance France*, 40). But on the previous page, she cites the French writer Peletier du Mans, who in his *Ars poetique* (1555) used Ovid as the master for creating a coherent and unified narrative, 'une narracion perpetuele', or *carmen perpetuum* (ibid. 39). Different readers clearly read in different ways.

pagan and Christian values, a conflict that is ultimately contained and controlled. DuRocher's Milton needs Ovid because of 'the insufficiency of scripture and the Judeo-Christian culture generally to supply images and material for his poem'.[17] Yet the poem's use of Ovidian figures also shows the inadequacy of pagan fictions when compared to Christian truths. While Milton bravely confronts the temptations that pagan subtexts offer, the result of 'the heroic, at times perilous struggle between poetic fiction and Christian truth' seems a foregone conclusion as inevitably 'Ovidian allusions signal the superiority of the inclusive Christian mythos'.[18] The agon is won before it begins, overdetermined from the start by the certainty that Christianity will trump anything Ovid might offer. In DuRocher's reading, Milton puts his pagan precursor firmly in his place, identifying him primarily with fallen beings, especially the great shape-shifter Satan.

Harding and DuRocher thus agree that Milton read Ovid as a Christian, concerned with the vexed relationship between Christianity and its pagan past. Milton is a humanist who wants to convert Ovid's epic to a Christian purpose, either through the tools developed by the allegorists or by staging a new battle in which, as in the Nativity Ode, Christ will tidily dispose of classical copies. The Christian writer revises to correct pagan error. They also both take for granted that the best way to trace the reception of Ovid is primarily by examining the reworkings of his mythological tales, almost entirely derived from the *Metamorphoses*.

While these assumptions are clearly true—Milton is a Christian, he loved the *Metamorphoses* and its fantastic stories—in isolation I think they become distorting. They do not do justice to Ovid as a poet and they underestimate Milton as a reader. DuRocher is clearly much more interested in Ovid than Harding was, but his Ovid dwindles to a rather shrunken figure, reduced to pagan error, and manipulated to his own undoing by an unmoved and controlling, and also rather mechanical, Milton. In fact, while DuRocher sees Ovid and Milton as intimately bound together, his reading backs up those of critics who have suggested that Milton ultimately distances himself from his pagan counterpart. He assumes a profound division between Milton and Ovid that is then replicated in Milton himself, in whom poetry and Christian truth are fundamentally opposed, often in ways that

---

[17] DuRocher, *Milton and Ovid*, 10.   [18] Ibid. 218, 204.

put good poetry on the side of not only the pagans but also the devils.[19]

Mandy Green's 2009 book, *Milton's Ovidian Eve*, gives us a rather different Milton and Ovid.[20] She builds on DuRocher's attention to the allusions that cluster around Eve, who she argues is at the centre of Milton's Ovidianism. Eve's Ovidianism was interpreted negatively, of course, by many earlier readers who assumed that references to figures like Narcissus and Proserpina indicated her fallibility or even foreshadowed the fall. For Elizabeth Sauer, too, the identification of Ovid and the female is part of Milton's self-construction as a Christian *vates*; Sauer argues that 'Ovidian language and scenes of metamorphoses that pervade Milton's poems and prose works are projected onto the unruly, demonic, and the feminine, which constructs "the other".'[21] In Sauer's reading, therefore, De Quincey's marriage ends in a divorce that enables Milton to preserve his purity. For Green, in contrast, Milton's identification of Ovid with Eve shows the centrality of both Ovid and Eve to the aims of *Paradise Lost*. Green believes that describing Milton's relation as primarily competitive and corrective is reductive; she suggests instead that Milton invokes and transforms Ovid in imaginative and shifting ways to build the complex character of Eve. The relation she describes between poets is thus not one of opposition—in which Christian truth faces pagan falsehood, or masculine wholeness and stability faces feminine hybridity and instability—as Milton draws freely and creatively on Ovid's materials.

The Ovid and Milton who emerge through Green's study are thus quite different from those of Harding and DuRocher. By focusing on Eve, Green implicitly suggests that Milton reads Ovid not as a pagan but as the poet of love and desire, famous for his sympathetic portrayal of female psychology and whose exploration of questions of the body, sexual identity, and power has been of much interest recently to

---

[19] In the same year in which DuRocher's book appeared, Charles Martindale noted the inadequacy of the assumption that Milton is 'at once illustrating the benighted errors of paganism and showing how they pre-echo the Christian truth. That would be to ignore the curious edginess of Milton's relationships with the ancients, the evident sense of tension and strain' (*John Milton and the Transformation*, 76).

[20] Although Green's book appeared when this book was virtually finished, I have revised in places to take her fine readings into account. While we have different foci and approaches, we share many of the same concerns and goals.

[21] 'Engendering Metamorphoses', 219.

both classical and Renaissance scholars. Such an Ovid seems an appropriate source for Milton to turn to in thinking about Eve and gender relations in the poem. Green's Milton is erotic, aesthetic, and also remarkably flexible: he is a sensitive reader who does not just impose his own Christian authority on his source.

The strength of Green's insightful discussion is this attention to the nuances in the dialogue between two very subtle and complex authors. But as a result of the focus on Eve and gender relations, the issue of poetic relations remains underdeveloped. Green does not consider Eve in the larger context of Milton's more general Ovidianism. While she notes that the shape-shifting Satan has seemed Ovidian to many readers, she just sets this point aside, claiming that Eve is 'the more profoundly Ovidian of the two'.[22] But that kind of begs the question of what 'Ovidian' means for Milton. Ovidianism is not confined to Eve. Other critics have noted how Ovid's figures and language shape not only Satan, but also Adam, the narrator, the Father, and the Son. Nor is Ovidianism simply the appropriation of Ovidian stories. In his important discussion of Ovid in *John Milton and the Transformation of Ancient Epic* (1986), Charles Martindale argued that 'we must be careful not to restrict Ovid's influence on Milton to supposedly verbal "allusions" or imitations', as 'Ovidian feeling is diffused throughout large parts of *Paradise Lost*'.[23] Inviting critics to search for diffused Ovidian feeling might seem to be asking for trouble: it is sometimes too easy (certainly for me) to trace everything back to Ovid, a writer who in the Renaissance generally seems to be everywhere and therefore sometimes nowhere. But Martindale is right, and finding a way to account for and discuss that feeling without being washed away by it seems essential to understanding what Ovid meant to Milton.

Considering further the parallels discussed by Green moves us in that direction. Green takes us through a number of Ovidian figures with whom Eve is identified: most notably Narcissus, Daphne, Flora, Pomona, Venus, and Pyrrha. She argues that Milton yokes these 'discrete episodes . . . into fruitful collaboration'.[24] However, as Philip Hardie notes, in Ovid those episodes are *not* discrete: 'Ovidians have long been alert to the intratextual connections between "discrete

---

[22] *Milton's Ovidian Eve*, p. vii.
[23] *John Milton and the Transformation*, 159, 191.
[24] *Milton's Ovidian Eve*, 53.

episodes" in the *Metamorphoses*, and Milton's allusive practice might just as well be taken as evidence of how he read Ovid's poem as of the fusion in *Paradise Lost* of what he read as separate episodes.'[25] In other words, Green seems to be missing a rather crucial element of Milton's reading of Ovid. Far from viewing the *Metamorphoses* as a series of chopped up independent tales that he then stitches together, Milton picks up and builds on some of the thematic and formal patterns which give Ovid's apparently amorphous epic its unity. Thinking about the relations among these stories can help us understand further how and why Milton is drawn to Ovid.

There are actually many interconnections between these specific tales; Hardie himself has focused on how the story of Narcissus echoes that of Daphne and foreshadows others like those of Philomela and Scylla.[26] In some way or another, however, all are part of Ovid's ongoing reflections on the nature, origins, and purpose of artistic creation itself. To say that, though, is not actually to say very much, as almost *all* stories in Ovid are at some level explorations of the creative process. Recent classical critics have paid particular attention to Ovid's 'self-conscious muse', tracing the way in which throughout his works he foregrounds himself and his art.[27] The *Amores*, *Metamorphoses*, *Fasti*, and *Tristia* begin with scenes of creation, which include those of their own making. As I will discuss further, the stories of Daphne, Narcissus, and Flora—to take three of Green's parallels—are all *aitia*, stories of beginnings, which provide different versions of the origins of art. Eve's particular association with such Ovidian figures thus suggests how, as Diane McColley noted, 'Eve embodies and performs a great many properties and processes that Milton elsewhere attributes to poetry itself, or to himself as poet.'[28] In other words, through both Eve and Ovid, Milton is able to reflect upon what it means for him to be a poet.

---

[25] Review of Green in *Milton Quarterly*, 45/2 (2011), 128–30; quotation from 129.

[26] 'Approximative Similes in Ovid. Incest and Doubling', *Dictynna: Revue de poétique latine*, 1 (2004), 1–30. I will return to these links in Chs. 3 and 4.

[27] See especially Stephen Hinds, *The Metamorphosis of Persephone: Ovid and the Self-Conscious Muse* (Cambridge, 1987); Philip Hardie, *Ovid's Poetics of Illusion* (Cambridge, 2002); Gianpiero Rosati, *Narciso e Pigmalione: Illusione e spettacolo nelle* Metamorfosi *di Ovidio* (Florence, 1983); Garth Tissol, *The Face of Nature: Wit, Narrative, and Cosmic Origins in Ovid's* Metamorphoses (Princeton, 1997); and Joseph B. Solodow, *The World of Ovid's* Metamorphoses (Chapel Hill, NC, 1988).

[28] Diane McColley, 'Eve and the Arts of Eden', in Julia M. Walker (ed.), *Milton and the Idea of Woman* (Urbana, Ill., 1988), 103.

Introduction 11

My basic assumption is therefore that Milton reads Ovid, above all, as a poet. In this context it is easier to see some of the concerns that bring the two very different authors together. Like Ovid, Milton is deeply interested in creation, which is the subject of his epic, as well as much of his early verse.[29] *Paradise Lost* presents multiple stories of creation: the building of Pandemonium in Book 1, the generation of Sin in Book 2, the making of Eve in Book 4, the begetting in Book 5 of the Son who then makes the world in Book 7, and the origins of Adam in Book 8. The invocations make the making of the poem itself part of Milton's subject, both a consequence and microcosm of the universal story he tells. Milton takes being a creator seriously: for him, to write poetry is to engage with questions of freedom that are as much religious and political as poetical.[30] His thinking about poetry is indistinguishable from his thinking about a God who is a creator. By creating copies of himself, God makes creatures who are themselves also creators. By writing the poem, Milton proves that he is made in God's image. The creation story of Genesis is placed at the centre of *Paradise Lost* as the centre and source of the poet's own creative power. As DuRocher and others have noted, however, in retelling his original Milton turns to *Metamorphoses* 1.[31] The anxious invocation to that book, with Milton's plea for guidance lest he meet the fate of Bellerophon or Orpheus, suggests the poet's concern about imitating the sacred original that is the source of his own creativity. The tentativeness of the invocation, however, disappears in the scene itself, in which Ovidian embellishment fleshes out the stark skeleton of Genesis. As Michael Lieb describes it, the poetry explodes in 'an exuberance of detail that is reinforced by a verse symphonic and bounteous

---

[29] See especially Michael Lieb, *The Dialectics of Creation: Patterns of Birth & Regeneration in* Paradise Lost (Amherst, Mass., 1970); Regina M. Schwartz, *Remembering and Repeating: On Milton's Theology and Poetics* (Chicago, 1993); and Janet Adelman, 'Creation and the Place of the Poet in *Paradise Lost*', in Louis Martz and Aubrey Williams (eds.), *The Author in his Work: Essays on a Problem in Criticism* (New Haven, 1978), 51–69.

[30] As John Creaser's recent magnificent analysis of Milton's prosody reveals; see '"Service is Perfect Freedom": Paradox and Prosodic Style in *Paradise Lost*', *Review of English Studies*, 58 (2007), 268–315.

[31] The parallels between the two episodes are listed, though not discussed, by DuRocher, in *Milton and Ovid*, 222. For a brief but perceptive discussion of the relation between the two scenes of creation, see John W. Velz, 'Ovidian Creation in Milton and Decreation in Shakespeare', in Werner Schubert (ed.), *Ovid: Werk und Wirkung: Festgabe für Michael von Albrecht zum 65* (Frankfurt, 1999), 1035–46.

in its effects. The entire account reverberates with a sense of excitement, a sense of energy being released and exulting in its own volition. All creatures glory in the creation and instinctively celebrate the creative act.'[32] Ovid, who Renaissance commentators claimed was himself imitating Genesis here, mediates the Bible to Milton and helps him to transform the sparse biblical scene into one whose richness manifests and celebrates the conjunction of divine and human creativity.[33] This is not to say, however, that Ovid is just a buffer to protect the poet from the formidable influence of God, the ultimate precursor of all creators. When Milton remakes Ovid, he is able to think about his own imitation of God's original creativity.

Moreover, the opening scene of the *Metamorphoses* establishes two connected patterns that demonstrate aspects of creativity with which Milton is also concerned. As I have noted already, for Ovid all creation is re-creation: in *Metamorphoses* 1, Ovid's world, like the poem itself, is not made *ex nihilo*. Moreover, even in Book 1, the world has to be made *twice*. The grand finale of the opening scene of creation, the human race, quickly degenerates into barbarism; almost entirely destroyed by the horrified Jove, it is remade out of the stones thrown by Deucalion and Pyrrha. As the stones soften into human form, they are compared to figures emerging from a sculptor's block of marble (1. 404–6), an image that anticipates the animation of Pygmalion's statue. The very start of the poem therefore shows a process of transferral in which an original creation by an anonymous deity—'quisquis fuit ille deorum' ('whoever of the gods it was', 1. 32)—is repeated in and replaced with the creativity of individual humans. The repetition of such scenes of creation throughout Ovid's works suggests a world that must be constantly made anew and transformed by human artists.

In Milton, all human creativity is fundamentally revisionary as it is an extension and replication of God's original act.[34] The world must be repeatedly remade, as Milton himself reimagines Ovid. But *Metamorphoses* 1 tells us something perhaps even more important about the nature of creation. In Ovid, the formation of the world is followed

---

[32] *The Dialectics of Creation*, 56–7. See generally his splendid description of the scene, 56–63. Lieb's exuberance here shows his own participation in the chain of creativity.
[33] See also Green, *Milton's Ovidian Eve*, 53.
[34] See also Schwartz, *Remembering and Repeating*, 74; and Lieb, *The Dialectics of Creation*, 56–78.

soon after by its near annihilation in the flood—a scene that Milton will use in *Paradise Lost* 11 to tell his version of the biblical catastrophe. Ovid's juxtaposition of scenes within the first book reveals how, throughout his works, creation is intimately linked to destruction. For Milton, therefore, as we will see shortly, Ovid is a means for understanding the central problem of *Paradise Lost*: how good can create evil.

SOME OTHER RENAISSANCE OVIDS

In his reading of Ovid, Milton is not completely 'original'. Milton's Ovid, like our Ovid, cannot be detached from the traditions that have shaped him through time. As I will discuss further in Chapter 1, the early poems show Milton to be a good humanist who read original sources closely. At the same time, however, he was also studying other forms of interpretation and reworking that were available, looking for models for the revision of the past. As I have already suggested and will elaborate in Chapters 1 and 2, Milton had a variety of 'Ovids' from which to choose. He certainly was familiar with the Renaissance commentaries and handbooks discussed by Harding and Mulryan. These themselves were hardly homogeneous; as Mulryan demonstrates, the allegorical tradition contains richer and more varied creative mythologizing than we often suppose. As Ann Moss has also argued, allegorical readings were marked by their rather wild inconsistency and often incoherence. Allegorists were not interested in compiling 'a dictionary of symbols from ancient literature, whose meanings are invariable and fixed'; allegorizing Ovid was 'essentially an exercise in metaphorical thinking' that afforded the opportunity for 'a type of mental exercise akin to that involved in appreciating the technical and verbal virtuosity admired in the French vernacular writers of the period. The unexpected links made between the most disparate of objects and situations have the same sort of sophisticated and often inconsequential wit.'[35] Allegorists typically throw out a

[35] Moss, *Ovid in Renaissance France*, 25, 26. Moss suggests that the method of the humanists was actually more inhibiting for creative expression: the humanists tended to organize parallel readings in genealogical lines of source influence, thus imposing a rigid linearity on the relation between works. See also Moss's edited selections of *Latin*

wide range of completely contradictory possible interpretations without suggesting that readers might need to choose between them; their role is to open up possibilities of meaning, not to resolve them systematically. In that respect, the interpretations of the allegorists created a stimulating environment for the practice of the poets.[36]

At the same time, it is not the same as the practice of the poets, which, I believe, provides the most fruitful context for understanding Milton's reading and rewriting of Ovid.[37] Milton would have known that Ovid had been a remarkable source of inspiration for other artists, both verbal and visual. From the start, Ovid had given Renaissance artists a kind of aesthetic jolt. He provided the images and language through which painters, sculptors, and poets could both create and explore art.[38] As Leonard Barkan showed, the idea of metamorphosis stimulated thinking about the potentially liberating, though also dangerous, power of the imagination to transmute reality and remake the world. Ovidian metamorphosis was a way of imagining the transformative power of both desire and art, a power that could be both good and evil. For Barkan, 'what most essentially characterizes the Renaissance is a metamorphic aesthetics', derived

---

Commentaries on Ovid from the Renaissance (Signal Mountain, Tenn., 1998), 105, 144. Other critics have also noticed the fragmenting tendency of humanist reading practices; see Crane, *Framing Authority*; Hulse, *Metamorphic Verse*, 247; and DuRocher, *Milton and Ovid*, 23. Richard Halpern nicely describes the humanists as reducing Ovid to 'harmless, inert atoms' (*The Poetics of Primitive Accumulation: English Renaissance Culture and the Genealogy of Capital* (Ithaca, NY, 1991), 47). As Lynn Enterline suggests, such treatment of Ovid seems appropriate given that 'dismemberment informs Ovid's reflections not only on corporeal form, but linguistic and poetic as well' (*The Rhetoric of the Body*, 1).

[36] See also Angela Maria Fritsen, 'Renaissance Commentaries on Ovid's *Fasti*', Ph.D. diss. (Yale University, 1995), 117–22. The medieval *accessus ad auctores* which also framed Ovidian works for readers, treating the work in terms of fixed categories (title, author, subject matter, intention, utility, and the branch of philosophy to which the work belonged), also tended to be rather free-wheeling, offering different possible meanings between which readers might (or might not) choose. Some Ovidian *accessus* have been usefully discussed and translated by Alison G. Elliott, 'Access ad Auctores: Twelfth-Century Introductions to Ovid', *Allegorica*, 5 (1980), 6–47.

[37] See also Charles Martindale, *Redeeming the Text: Latin Poetry and the Hermeneutics of Reception* (Cambridge, 1993), who suggests that poets are generally better guides to understanding the meaning of their precursors than the commentators and critics.

[38] See especially Barkan, *The Gods Made Flesh*; and Paul Barolsky, 'As in Ovid, So in Renaissance Art', *Renaissance Quarterly*, 51/2 (1998), 451–74. I will return to this especially in Ch. 3.

largely from Ovid, and itself transformed through writers such as Dante and Petrarch.[39]

The example of the Italian writers whose use of Ovid helped set the Renaissance in motion would be extremely important for Milton. However, as Milton would also have known, Ovid played a particularly key and practical role in England and its own, rather belated, Renaissance. It is only a slight exaggeration to say that Ovid is almost single-handedly responsible for English literature. One could trace this back to medieval authors such as Chaucer (who in turn got it from Dante), but writings of the 1560s–1590s especially derive their energy from new Ovidian encounters.[40] Elizabethan writers found their subjects, honed their wit, invented genres, and justified their obsessions about sex and art through Ovid. Ovid's works were at the centre of debates on erotic desire, debates on poetry itself, and, especially, debates on the relation between desire and the imagination. Adapting Ovid was often a means of commenting on the (usually deplorable) state of English poetry. Critics who attacked the immorality of poetry inevitably evoked his bad example, noting in particular that he turned theatres into pick-up joints; defenders used allegorical readings of Ovid to insist on poetry's moral function.[41] In his *Complaints* especially, Spenser turned to Ovidian forms to lament the current neglect of art; Marlowe's Ovidian digression in *Hero and Leander* 1. 385–484 explains the origins of the denigration

---

[39] Barkan, *The Gods Made Flesh*, 242.
[40] See especially Lyne, *Ovid's Changing Worlds*; also Caroline Jameson, 'Ovid in the Sixteenth Century', in J. W. Binns (ed.), *Ovid* (London, 1973), 210–42; Brown, *Redefining Elizabethan Literature*; R. W. Maslen, 'Myths Exploited: The Metamorphoses of Ovid in Early Elizabethan England', in Taylor (ed.), *Shakespeare's Ovid*, 15–30; and Liz Oakley-Brown, 'Translating the Subject: Ovid's *Metamorphoses* in England, 1560-7', in Roger Ellis and Liz Oakley-Brown (eds.), *Translation and Nation: Towards a Cultural Politics of Englishness* (Cleveland, 2001), 48–84. Bush includes an annotated list of translations (c.1475–1600) and adaptations (c.1475–1680) (*Mythology*, 311–39). See also Stuart Gillespie and Robert Cummings's very handy 'A Bibliography of Ovidian Translations and Imitations in English', *Translation and Literature*, 13/2 (2004), 207–11.
[41] See Mary Ellen Lamb, 'Ovid and *The Winter's Tale*: Conflicting Views toward Art', in William R. Elton and William B. Long (eds.), *Shakespeare and Dramatic Tradition: Essays in Honor of S. F. Johnson* (Newark, Del., 1989), 69–87. James D. Mulvihill also notes the opposition between 'Ovid the sensualist and Ovid the spiritual lover' in debates of the time ('Jonson's *Poetaster* and the Ovidian Debate', *Studies in English Literature, 1500–1900*, 22 (1982), 242).

of poetry.[42] Almost every genre shows traces of his works: lyric poetry looks back to his erotic verse (reworked through Petrarch), and complaints were influenced by the *Heroides*.[43] Masques and drama generally draw on Ovidian stories and scenes, which are especially appropriate for a highly self-conscious theatre that constantly probes the boundary between illusion and reality. Ovid provides both form and content for the hugely popular new genre of the epyllion.[44] The major Elizabethan poets fought with each other through and over Ovid, responding to and rivalling each other's adaptations often within weeks of circulation. As I will discuss further in Chapter 1, they developed alternative and competing versions of Ovid. So Georgia Brown notes that 'the competition for supremacy among professional Elizabethan authors is played out as a battle over Ovid's inheritance'.[45] Writers were hailed as the new Ovid as, appropriately, 'Pythagorean metempsychosis, as expounded in the fifteenth book of the *Metamorphoses*, becomes a figure for the translation of one poet into another'.[46] Daniel and Chapman were described as English Ovids, while William Alexander gushed at Drayton's reworking of the *Heroides* as *Englands Heroicall Epistles*: 'OVIDS Soule revives in DRAYTON now.'[47] Most famously, Francis Meres turned Shakespeare into Ovid reborn when he observed: 'as the soule of *Euphorbus* was thought to live in *Pythagoras*: so the sweete wittie soule of *Ovid* lives in mellifluous and hony-tongued *Shakespeare*, witnes his

---

[42] See also Cyril Tourneur's Spenserian diatribe, *The Transformed Metamorphosis* (1600). As I will discuss further in Ch. 2, epyllia especially represent the degeneration of art as a form of Ovidian metamorphosis which they both denounce and often exemplify.

[43] On the role of the *Heroides* see especially Raphael Lyne, 'Writing Back to Ovid in the 1560s and 1570s', *Literature and Translation*, 13 (2004), 143–64.

[44] See Hulse, *Metamorphic Verse*; William Keach, *Elizabethan Erotic Narratives: Irony and Pathos in the Ovidian Poetry of Shakespeare, Marlowe, and their Contemporaries* (New Brunswick, NJ, 1977); and Brown, *Redefining Elizabethan Literature*, 102–9.

[45] *Redefining Elizabethan Literature*, 84.

[46] Jonathan Bate, *Shakespeare and Ovid* (Oxford, 1993), 3.

[47] William Alexander, 'To Michael Drayton', in *Englands Heroicall Epistles*, qtd. in Lyne, *Ovid's Changing Worlds*, 152. On Drayton's reworking of Ovid, see ibid. 42–97. The prefatory material to John Gower's 1640 translation of the *Fasti* repeatedly claims that the translator was Ovid reborn, beginning with the invitation: 'ON this book, Reader, lay thy hand and swear, | Ovid himself is Metamorphos'd here' ('Upon the ingenious translation of Ovids *Fasti*, intituled, *The Romane Calendar*', in *Ovids Festivalls, or Romane Calendar. Translated into English verse equinumerally* (Cambridge, 1640), Early English Books Online, ¶4ᵛ).

Venus and *Adonis*, his *Lucrece*, his sugred Sonnets among his private friends, &c'.[48]

The range of things that artists could and did do with Ovid obviously complicates any assumption that the relation between Ovid and Milton is an unmediated encounter between two great geniuses separated by the abyss of time. For Milton, to call up Ovid meant to invoke not only a classical past, but also the recent metamorphoses of that past into a native, *Englished*, tradition, identified in particular with his most formidable precursor. Transplanting Ovid onto English soil had become a means of establishing both individual authorial identity and a new English literature.[49] The process is made explicit in the works themselves: the first epyllion, Thomas Lodge's *Scillaes Metamorphosis* (1589), traces the movement of Ovidian forms through the journey to Britain of the seagod Glaucus (whose hybridity reflects that of the epyllion genre). Similarly, John Weever's *Faunus and Melliflora* (1600) mythologizes the coming of satire (satyrs) to England.[50] As we will see in Chapters 1 and 2, Milton will draw on these narratives in *Comus*, in which he imagines the immigration of another Ovidian figure to Britain. For Milton, rewriting Ovid was a way of engaging not only with the classical tradition distant in time and space, but also with a newer tradition developing closer to home. Paradoxically, to be Ovidian was to claim one's place as an English writer.

The reason for Ovid's centrality in this process begins no doubt simply in the school system of the sixteenth and seventeenth centuries, in which Ovid had an important role.[51] Like other classical authors, Ovid was translated and re-translated by young boys, who

---

[48] *Palladis Tamia: Wits Treasury: Being the Second Part of Wits Common Wealth* (1598; facs. edn., New York, 1973), Oo^v–Oo2^r.

[49] See also Lyne, *Ovid's Changing Worlds*, 5.

[50] The writers draw on the classical model of 'Importing the Muses', which Ovid himself uses for the coming of Aesculapius to Rome at the end of the *Metamorphoses*; I take the phrase from Hinds, *Allusion and Intertext*, 52–63.

[51] Ovid's role in Renaissance pedagogy is discussed by T. W. Baldwin, *William Shakspere's Small Latine & Lesse Greeke*, 2 vols. (Urbana, Ill., 1944), ii. 497–55; see also Bate, *Shakespeare and Ovid*, 19–32; and Enterline, *The Rhetoric of the Body*, 19–27, 164–6. On Ovid's place in earlier curricula see especially the works of E. H. Alton, 'The Medieval Commentators on Ovid's *Fasti*', *Hermathena*, 44 (1926), 119–51; and (with D. E. W. Wormell) 'Ovid in the Medieval Schoolroom', *Hermathena*, 94 (1960), 21–38; and 95 (1961), 76–82. See also James H. McGregor, 'Ovid at School: From the Ninth to the Fifteenth Century', *Classical Folia*, 32/1 (1978), 29–51; Ralph Hexter, *Ovid and Medieval Schooling: Studies in Medieval School Commentaries on Ovid's* Ars

thus acquired an intimate knowledge of his habits of thought. Humanist pedagogy generally assumed that poetic and indeed personal development proceeded through imitation: where we post-Romantics tend to assume that influence is anxiety-provoking and inhibiting, for Milton, and other writers of the time, encountering the minds of others through translation and adaptation could be liberating. Renaissance poets found their own voices by trying on those of others, playing with different perspectives, seeing the world through others. Learning to think as another was ideally the first step in learning to think for oneself, just as imitation ideally led to the discovery of the writer's own voice.[52] Most often, Ovid taught students how to argue. His poetry was useful for illustrating and teaching the art of persuasion; it showed men how to seduce a mistress or plead with a potential patron. The Ovid who told the same story in many ways helped young men develop the art of *copia*, verbal abundance and eloquence.[53] As we will see shortly, the poet of *ingenium*, presented by Sandys as 'ROMANVS POETARVM INGENIOSISSIMVS',[54] was associated especially with the 'wit' which writers of the time wanted to display.

Amatoria, Epistulae ex Ponto, *and* Epistulae Heroidum (Munich, 1986); and Stapleton, *Harmful Eloquence*, 43–9.

[52] On imitation generally see G. W. Pigman III's seminal essay 'Versions of Imitation in the Renaissance', *Renaissance Quarterly*, 33 (1980), 1–32. Jean-Claude Carron notes further that 'One imitates not in order to copy others, or to overtake them on their own ground, but rather to become oneself, to achieve self-recognition. Identification—but with oneself—was the goal' ('Imitation and Intertextuality in the Renaissance', *New Literary History*, 19/3 (1988), 570). Renaissance education could of course be stultifying or worse; *Titus Andronicus* is often read as a nightmare version of humanist education in which the imitation of Ovid is carried out with enthusiastic and bloody literalism. But at its best such practices were, as Joel B. Altman describes them, 'exercises in sympathetic imagination', in which the student 'was taught to imagine himself in circumstances utterly unlike his own and to see with eyes other than his own' (*The Tudor Play of Mind: Rhetorical Inquiry and the Development of Elizabethan Drama* (Berkeley and Los Angeles, 1978), 53, 45).

[53] See also Enterline, *The Rhetoric of the Body*, 25. On *copia*, see Terence Cave, *The Cornucopian Text: Problems of Writing in the French Renaissance* (Oxford, 1979). The many resonances of the word, which joins together military power, sexual potency, and verbal agility, all come into play in the reception of Ovid, as does the awareness that *copia* can become mere copying without variation. See further Ch. 3.

[54] See the frontispiece of George Sandys, *Ovid's Metamorphosis Englished, Mythologized, and Represented in Figures*, ed. Karl K. Hulley and Stanley T. Vandersall (Lincoln, Nebr., 1970), 11. While *ingenium* also commonly means 'character', 'talent' or even just broad 'skills', in Ovid the meanings seem synonymous. Brown also notes how 'In the 1590s, the *Metamorphoses* came to epitomize literary creativity through its association with the metamorphic power of wit as writers acknowledge a parallel

Ovid was so deeply ingrained in the minds of Elizabethan writers that for them, as Michael Holahan says of Spenser, 'to write poetry was to use him'.[55] Unwittingly, and with consequences they could not have foreseen and hardly desired, the pedagogues had facilitated a highly congenial marriage of minds. Ovid's interests mirrored those of the young men of the time, especially those who became writers. He spoke to poets obsessed with the relation between sex and poetry—making sex into poetry, using (or trying to use) poetry to get sex, and constantly probing the complex interchange between imaginative and sexual fancy. For artists in the process of creating a new literary tradition, at a time when Protestantism looked suspiciously at the imagination, Ovid provided, as we might say, great copy.

OVID AND VIRGIL

> I often think it's comical—fal, lal, la!
> How nature always does contrive—fal, lal, la!
> That every boy and every gal,
> That's born into the world alive,
> Is either a little Liberal,
> Or else, a little Conservative!
> Fal, lal, la![56]

As I suggested earlier, moreover, Ovid's response to his own belatedness was helpful for the writers who arrived even later on the literary scene. By alluding to so many earlier works, Ovid offered a package deal through which Renaissance writers met, certainly sometimes without knowing it, other ancient texts and ultimately each other. Or, to choose a perhaps more appropriate metaphor for this particular poet, reading Ovid is a bit like sex: intercourse with him means intercourse with all the authors he has known. Still, there is one Ovidian partner who stands out among the rest: his most immediate

---

between the principle of transformation and the literary imagination' (*Redefining Elizabethan Literature*, 39).

[55] 'Ovid', in A. C. Hamilton (ed.), *The Spenser Encyclopedia* (Toronto, 1990), 522.
[56] 'Song—Private Willis', in W. S. Gilbert, *Iolanthe: Or, The Peer and the Peri* (London, 1911), 2. 9–15.

and potentially inhibiting precursor, Virgil.[57] Perhaps I might posit a preliminary attraction for Milton in particular. Ovid stands in the same relation to Virgil as Milton does to Shakespeare: they work in the shadow of powerful predecessors, whose works also were hailed instantly as embodiments of their nation's culture. It's enough to awaken any anxiety of influence, even in sublime egotists such as Ovid and Milton. Yet both writers manage to find their own path to originality. Milton had the added advantage of Ovid's example to help him overcome that other arch-Ovidian: Shakespeare.

Given Shakespeare's identification as an Ovidian writer, however, one might have expected Milton to look to Ovid's source, Virgil, as his guide. Certainly there are many ways in which Virgil appears a more appropriate model for Milton. As is often noted, the young Milton burst on the scene in 1645 with a volume that seems carefully crafted to present himself as a Virgilian poet. Many critics have focused on the Virgilian elements in his works.[58] But our understanding of Ovid and Virgil is often framed by overly schematic thinking. Despite our awareness of the complex negotiations that take place between texts and their sources, Renaissance scholars still tend to posit the two writers as antitheses. Virgil is seen as the serious poet of hard work and social duty; Ovid the frivolous poet of light loves and individual pleasure. My assertion that Elizabethan writers looked to Ovid to create a new English literature may therefore have seemed rather odd; it is usually assumed that Virgil is the exemplary poet of nationhood. Ovid seems the poet who stands *against* nationhood and empire.[59]

---

[57] Ovid's revision of the *Aeneid*, especially in the last books, has been much discussed; see especially Hinds, *Allusion and Intertext*, 104–22; Solodow, *The World of Ovid's* Metamorphoses, 110–56; and Tissol, *The Face of Nature*, 177–91.

[58] See especially Martz, *Poet of Exile*, 31–59; and Richard Neuse, 'Milton and Spenser: The Virgilian Triad Revisited', *English Literary History*, 45/4 (1978), 606–39. Even John K. Hale, one of the most perceptive recent critics of Milton's debt to Ovid, associates Ovid's influence with an early stage of Milton's development that he outgrew as he developed 'towards Virgil and autonomy together' (*Milton's Languages: The Impact of Multilingualism on Style* (Cambridge, 1997), 33–7, 41–3; quotation from 43). Gordon Campbell and Thomas Corns's recent biography of Milton, *John Milton: Life, Work, and Thought* (Oxford, 2008), also stresses his Virgilianism; Ovid's name does not even appear in their index.

[59] See especially Patrick Cheney, *Marlowe's Counterfeit Profession: Ovid, Spenser, Counter-Nationhood* (Toronto, 1997).

Contrasted in this way, the two writers are also frequently treated as the sources of antithetical poetical traditions. In Renaissance debates over epic, Virgil is the exemplar of the unified and contained narrative, Ovid the ancestor of digressive and potentially endless romance. Renaissance writers are thus often drafted by critics onto one team or another: so Spenser, for example, has often been staked out on the Virgilian side, lined up against the Ovidians, Shakespeare and Marlowe.[60] The fortunes of the two poets and their supporters have fluctuated with revolutions in taste and politics. Very often, as for the example in the second half of the nineteenth century, this scheme has worked in favour of Virgil, poet of *gravitas* and empire, and against Ovid, the apolitical flibbertigibbet.[61] In the mid-twentieth century, Ronald Syme's revolutionary attack on Augustus, to whom Virgil's fortunes have too often been unfortunately tied, slowly led to a turning of the tables.[62] Ovid became an admirable anti-authoritarian, in contrast to toady Virgil, the justifier of a protofascist status quo.[63] Recent work on the Renaissance politics of classical allusions has therefore tended to assume that sixteenth- and seventeenth-century

---

[60] For Spenser and Virgil see John Watkins, *The Specter of Dido: Spenser and Virgilian Epic* (New Haven, 1995); and Patrick Cheney, *Spenser's Famous Flight: A Renaissance Idea of a Literary Career* (Toronto, 1993). For Marlowe and Ovid, see Cheney, *Counterfeit Profession*.

[61] Gilbert Murray illustrates the most extreme view of Ovid as an aesthete detached from the real world: 'He was a poet utterly in love with poetry ... He strikes one as having been rather innocent and almost entirely useless in this dull world which he had not made and for which he was not responsible, while he moved triumphant and effective through his own inexhaustible realm of legend' ('Poesis and Mimesis', in *Humanist Essays* (repr. London, 1964), 78–92; 85–6). It is telling that Murray saw Milton similarly, suggesting that Milton's 'imagined world is almost nothing to him but a place of beauty, a sanctuary and an escape' (ibid. 84). Both passages are cited by Martindale (*John Milton and the Transformation*, 154, 196).

[62] *The Roman Revolution* (Oxford, 1939; repr. 1951).

[63] As a victim of a political system, also, Ovid has been recently romanticized into the archetypical rebellious artist persecuted by the authority he challenged. So David Malouf's fictional 1970s Ovid sets himself up as an anti-Augustus, proclaiming: 'I too have created an age. It is coterminous with his, and has its existence in the lives and loves of his subjects. It is gay, anarchic, ephemeral and it is fun. He [Augustus] hates me for it' (*An Imaginary Life: A Novel* (New York, 1978), 26). As Richard Helgerson argues in his defence of the 'stable centred self' adopted by Renaissance poets such as Ben Jonson and, he claims, Milton, 20th-century readers tend to be readier to appreciate mobile, playful, authors who are self-conscious of their own role-playing than to value those who present themselves as sincere and 'grounded on a serious, centred self' (*Self-Crowned Laureates: Spenser, Jonson, Milton, and the Literary System* (Berkeley and Los Angeles, 1983), 40; see also 44–9).

writers used Ovid against the Virgilian orthodoxy that supported the authority of Elizabeth and the Stuarts.[64] Such a premiss might solve the riddle of Milton's fondness for Ovid: one might speculate that the Milton who sought to free verse from the bondage of rhyme and who wrote that 'Poëtas equidem verè dictos & diligo & colo... illorum etiam plerósque tyrannis esse scio inimicissimos' ('Now poets who are truly so called, I love and reverence... Besides, I know that most of them, are the sworn foes of tyrants', *Defensio Secunda*, in *Works*, vii. 76–8) identified with a rebellious artist whose art was seen as challenging the Augustan order with which the Stuarts identified.[65]

If we stick to this scheme, Ovid's revision of Virgil appears an act of what we might rather loosely call subversion. Where Virgil closes off, Ovid opens up: a poet not of closure but disclosure, especially of the mystifications of ideology. Ovid disperses the models of narrative, personal, and political unity that Virgil's work seems to uphold. He acts as a centrifugal force disrupting the centripetal and stabilizing suction of power, and reveals a self and world that is fleeting and fragmented. Ovid's revision of Virgil moreover becomes part of a revolutionary undoing of authority, both political and poetical, in which Ovid frees himself from the spectre of Virgil by overturning a monolithic and rigid ideology.

The practice of organizing authors as contrasting types, *synkrisis*, was common in both classical and Renaissance criticism.[66] It goes back to the differentiation between Homer and Hesiod, and forward at least to the opposition between Shakespeare and Milton. It is especially useful for asserting the superiority of one writer over the

---

[64] For Heather James, Renaissance poets see Virgil and Ovid 'as Prince of Poets and Lord of Misrule' (*Shakespeare's Troy: Drama, Politics, and the Translation of Empire* (Cambridge, 1997), 30). While James recognizes the complexity of the two poets themselves, she argues that Virgil was generally read as straight panegyric, in contrast to Ovid who was 'a counter-authority and master of impropriety' (ibid. 27).

[65] On the use of Augustan imagery by the Stuarts see Craig Kallendorf, *The Other Virgil: 'Pessimistic' Readings of the* Aeneid *in Early Modern Culture* (Oxford, 2007), 138–43.

[66] See Philip Hardie, 'Contrasts', in S. J. Heyworth et al. (eds.), *Classical Constructions: Papers in Memory of Don Fowler, Classicist and Epicurean* (Oxford, 2007), 141–73.

Introduction

other, and thus reinforces a combative model for poetic relations. But such unnaturally tidy antitheses are also obviously reductive, and create the illusion of a fixed opposition in what is necessarily a more fluid and shifting relation.[67] Both Ovid and Virgil are more ambiguous than such a scheme allows, and their legacies also more varied. Ovid's political views are unclear enough to enable classicists today to read the *Metamorphoses* and *Fasti* as straight panegyric, and the exilic verse as embarrassingly ingratiating flattery of the *princeps*.[68] Virgil's relation to power has also been increasingly interrogated, slowly freeing him from the clutches of Augustus. Readers since the Second World War have become sensitive to the two (and more) voices that divide the *Aeneid* and which still can divide classicists.[69] The poem's sympathies seem torn between the winners of history and the losers, those destroyed by a progress whose values are called into question at crucial moments.

Critics have begun to wonder also whether earlier readers noted Virgil's ambivalence and whether it affected their understanding of the relation between the two poets. Moreover, studies of Renaissance artists suggest more tangled and interconnected lines of affiliation. John Watkins's superb study of Spenser's Virgilianism in *Faerie Queene* 1–3 suggests that in the later books Virgil is crowded out by other influences, including Ovid, while Syrithe Pugh has argued convincingly for the centrality of Ovid to *all* of Spenser's works.[70]

---

[67] Gian Biagio Conte notes the limitations of 'this questionable agonistic vision of the literary tradition': 'This method of proceeding sets up a sort of competition which puts two distinct literary entities face to face, without considering that they are immersed in a unitary but differentiated cultural flow, without considering that there are intermediaries which continually transform their meaning (that is, make them change position in the literary system, in the spectrum of cultural values)' (*The Poetry of Pathos*, 189, 203).

[68] As we will see in Ch. 2, these debates took off with research on the *Fasti*, which in turn has led to new readings of the *Metamorphoses*. Myers's excellent review article of work on Ovid in the 1990s is extremely helpful for synthesizing the political debate, at least up until 1999; see 'The Metamorphosis of a Poet', especially 196–200.

[69] See Adam Parry, 'The Two Voices of Virgil's *Aeneid*', *Arion*, 2/4 (1963), 66–80; and R. O. A. M. Lyne, *Further Voices in Vergil's* Aeneid (Oxford, 1987). On the debates between the 'pessimistic' and 'optimistic' readings of Virgil, see S. J. Harrison (ed.), *Oxford Readings in Vergil's* Aeneid (Oxford, 1990), 1–20.

[70] Watkins, *The Specter of Dido*, 175; Pugh, *Spenser and Ovid* (Aldershot, 2005). Like James's excellent study of Shakespeare, Pugh's reading identifies her author's Ovidianism too readily with anti-Virgilianism. See also Hulse's discussion of Spenser as 'The quintessential Ovidian poet of Elizabethan England' (*Metamorphic Verse*, 243); and M. L. Stapleton, *Spenser's Ovidian Poetics* (Newark, Del., 2009).

Theresa Krier has astutely analysed the subtle interplay of both Virgil and Ovid in Spenser, while Raphael Lyne has shown that 'Spenser seems to play upon the intertextuality between Ovid and Virgil, and on his ability to see through Ovid to Virgil'.[71] I will suggest that Spenser is not playing alone. Shakespeare's relation to Virgil has also attracted attention. While Meres's identification of Shakespeare with Ovid has stuck, Margaret Tudeau-Clayton argues that in the early seventeenth century 'Shakespeare' was more often 'the culturally constructed figure of the ideal, absolute poet, the English/British equivalent to the received paradigm of Virgil'.[72] Yet it is not clear that all readers saw Virgil as the perfect poet who embodied a national ideal. Craig Kallendorf has recently demonstrated that for Renaissance writers, including both Shakespeare and Milton, the ambiguities in Virgil opened up the possibility of critiquing rather than simply supporting authority, power, and empire.[73] What 'Virgil' could mean changes further when one remembers that Renaissance editions of his work included poems such as the 'Culex' and highly Ovidian 'Ciris'.

To see Ovid and Virgil as antitheses thus oversimplifies a complex situation. As classicists have long recognized, terms like 'pro-' and 'anti-Augustan' are too rigid for the ways in which all writers, indeed subjects, under Augustus responded to his pervasive ideology.[74]

---

[71] Lyne, *Ovid's Changing Worlds*, 121; Theresa M. Krier, *Gazing on Secret Sights: Spenser, Classical Imitation, and the Decorums of Vision* (Ithaca, NY, 1990). For Spenser's mixing of sources, see also Colin Burrow, 'Spenser and Classical Traditions', in Andrew Hadfield (ed.), *The Cambridge Companion to Spenser* (Cambridge, 2001), 217–36. James notes Spenser's sophisticated negotiation of 'diplomatic relations between the Vergilian and the Ovidian traditions' (*Shakespeare's Troy*, 30).

[72] *Jonson, Shakespeare and Early Modern Virgil* (Cambridge, 1998), 4. Tudeau-Clayton's argument itself indicates how 'Virgil' could mean different things. If you define Virgil generically, as the poet of the epic, he is difficult to line up with Shakespeare. If you define Virgil, as she does, as a cultural icon whose meaning is nationhood, then the two seem similar. While this latter definition is too reductive—certainly when Milton grapples with what Virgil or Shakespeare 'means', he thinks of more than this—it suggests some of the problems here.

[73] Kallendorf, *The Other Virgil*.

[74] See Duncan F. Kennedy's important '"Augustan" and "Anti-Augustan": Reflections on Terms of Reference', in Anton Powell (ed.), *Roman Poetry and Propaganda in the Age of Augustus* (London, 1992), 26–58; in relation to Ovid's works, see A. R. Sharrock, 'Ovid and the Politics of Reading', *Materiali e discussioni per l'analisi dei testi classici*, 33 (1994), 97–102; Alessandro Barchiesi, *The Poet and the Prince: Ovid and Augustan Discourse* (Berkeley and Los Angeles, 1997) and *Speaking Volumes: Narrative and Intertext in Ovid and Other Latin Poets*, ed. and trans. Matt Fox

Moreover, the oppositional schema potentially gives us a too mechanical model for Ovid's revisionary process. It becomes simply writing against tradition: subversion as mere reversal. Ovid seems a Marxist of the Grouchoian school: whatever Virgil is for, Ovid is against it. His imagination becomes deeply reactionary, his creativity a rather mechanical process of turning old forms upside down. Such wit, clever as it may be, is essentially dependent on the system it appears to mock. Ovid's playfulness can thus seem a superficial naughtiness that reinforces dominant norms. William Keach notes how young Elizabethan law students at the Inns of Court used Ovid to rebel safely in 'piquant anti-authoritarianism', even as they prepared themselves happily for conservative careers.[75] As we will see more later, Ovidian change sometimes looks like no change at all.

This is not to deny that Ovid could be a political model and even force, but rather to suggest that seeing him simply as an anti-Virgil limits his political potential. Poetically as well the Virgil–Ovid binarism seems a revolving door of opposition that leads to a dead end. In Satan, Milton will show the inhibiting effects of imitation when it becomes mere parody.[76] More helpful models appear in the work of critics such as Stephen Hinds who argues that Ovid is 'one of Virgil's most sympathetic and perceptive readers', and Richard F. Thomas who notes that 'Ovid's intertextuality has a collaborative effect; he brings out what was already there in Virgil'.[77] As Hinds and Thomas suggest, the relation between Virgil and Ovid is not one of the static opposition between two fixed positions but a dynamic relation of interdependence. Milton does not need to choose between these two alternatives, but can adapt the dialogue between them as a model for

and Simone Marchesi (London, 2001), 76, 80; and Myers, 'The Metamorphosis of a Poet', 197–8. I will return to this in more detail in Ch. 2.

[75] Keach, *Elizabethan Erotic Narratives*, 32.
[76] See below, Ch. 3.
[77] Hinds, 'Generalising about Ovid', 16; Thomas, *Virgil and the Augustan Reception* (Cambridge, 2001), 80. Thomas's representation of revision might be compared to the 'embellishment' Gerald L. Bruns ascribes to manuscript culture in general: 'embellishment is an art of disclosure as well as an art of amplification. Or, rather, amplification is not merely supplementation but also interpretation: the act of adding to a text is also the act of eliciting from it that which remains unspoken' (*Inventions: Writing, Textuality, and Understanding in Literary History* (New Haven, 1982), 55–6). Myers notes how criticism increasingly sees Ovid's relationship to the past as 'a truly intertextual dialogue involving reinterpretation of his tradition rather than reductive parody' ('The Metamorphosis of a Poet', 191; see also 194).

his own relation to his sources. As Gian Biagio Conte notes, relationships between texts are always 'relations of transformation' which go in two directions.[78] To a large degree, however, the relation between Virgil and Ovid is and must be created by Ovid—for the simple reason that Virgil himself was unaware of it, just as Shakespeare lacked the happy foreknowledge that Milton was following hot on his heels. As Virgil's role in the shaping of Homer shows, coming second can be an advantage: Ovid has the power to form the meaning of his own source, to write his own *aition*.[79] It is a lesson he, of course, had learned from watching Virgil, who, as Joseph Farrell noted, 'uses allusion to create his own vision of [literary] history, to make the past anew, to call into being the tradition to which he wishes to be heir'.[80] As Thomas notes, therefore, 'The Ovid/Virgil antithesis that is the basis of all subsequent polarizations is itself an Ovidian construction that is created by monumentalizing and stabilizing the Virgilian original, which is then open to subversion.'[81] Ovid needs to forge the illusion of an antithetical Virgil to create a space for his own voice. But the act of construction produces a relation that is convoluted and shifting. While, on the one hand, Ovid defines himself against Virgil, on the other, as Stephen Hinds suggests, he copies moments in which Virgil seems most Ovidian and so makes the *Aeneid* 'a hesitant precursor of the *Metamorphoses*'.[82] Seen in this light, the relation

---

[78] *The Poetry of Pathos*, 197.

[79] The lesson was passed on to one of Ovid's earliest imitators, Seneca the Younger, who noted 'condicio optima est ultimi: parata verba invenit, quae aliter instructa novam faciem habent' ('he who writes last has the best of the bargain; he finds already at hand words which, when marshaled in a different way, show a new face' (*Ad Lucilium Epistulae Morales*, trans. Richard M. Gummere, 3 vols. (Cambridge, Mass., 1953), ii. 79. 6; cited in Hinds, *Allusion and Intertext*, 41).

[80] Joseph Farrell, *Vergil's* Georgics *and the Traditions of Ancient Epic: The Art of Allusion in Literary History* (New York, 1991), 17. Charles Martindale also notes that Virgil reveals how 'Authors elect their own precursors, by allusion, quotation, imitation, translation, homage, at once creating a canon and making a claim for their own inclusion in it' ('Introduction: "The Classic of All Europe"', in Charles Martindale (ed.), *The Cambridge Companion to Virgil* (Cambridge, 1997), 2). See further Hinds's discussion of Statius' 'Do-it-yourself' canon formation (*Allusion and Intertext*, 123–9).

[81] Thomas, *Augustan Reception*, 156. Garth Tissol suggests that Ovid's subversion deliberately drew attention to the inadequacy of the reductive and simplified readings of the *Aeneid* by Roman contemporaries who saw the poem as a celebration of Augustus' *auctoritas*; see *The Face of Nature*, 179.

[82] Hinds, *Allusion and Intertext*, 106. See also Hinds's discussion of the ways in which 'Ovid thematizes his intertextual dialogue with his epic predecessor' (ibid. 112).

between the writers is continuous, not antithetical. Moreover, their traditional associations might be completely reversed, as Ovid brings out other possible ways of reading Virgil. Hinds suggests that Ovid creates the impression that 'In Virgil these myths are fragmented, scattered, unresolved: not until Ovid's own poem are they gathered into perfection and system.'[83] Ovid makes Virgil into a poet of fragmentation and uncertainty; it is Ovid himself who is the creator of unity and order and closure. While critics tend to identify Ovid with openness, the conclusion of the *Metamorphoses* gives his epic a much more triumphant and closed ending than the disquieting and rushed end of the *Aeneid*.[84]

As we'll see further, Ovid's shaping of Virgil is noted in Milton's own reworking of Ovidian figures. Moreover, the problems with the conventional contrast between Ovid and Virgil enable us to look again at Milton's role in the mythologizing of his difference from Shakespeare. The depiction of Shakespeare in 'L'Allegro' as 'fancies childe' who is found warbling 'his native Wood-notes wilde' (133–4) was central in the still forceful myth of Shakespeare as the 'natural' or 'original' genius contrasted with Milton's more studied and learned personality.[85] The relegation of his precursor to the simple natural world of 'L'Allegro' allows the young Milton to define himself and stake out his own 'penseroso' territory. But the creation of the illusion of contrast also enables him to sustain a continuing dialogue with his English predecessor, whose transformed voice is heard in so many of the finest moments of *Paradise Lost*.[86]

---

[83] Ibid. 106.

[84] On the closure of the *Metamorphoses*, see also David Scott Wilson-Okamura, 'Errors and Ovid and Romance', *Spenser Studies*, 23 (2008), 222–4. Alessandro Barchiesi, however, argues that the multiplication of closural devices at the end of Ovid's epic undermines the sense of closure—a strategy we will see also at work in *Samson Agonistes* in Ch. 5; 'Endgames: Ovid's *Metamorphoses* 15 and *Fasti* 6', in Deborah H. Roberts, Francis M. Dunn, and Don Fowler (eds.), *Classical Closure: Reading the End in Greek and Latin Literature* (Princeton, 1997), 181–208.

[85] The tradition of pairing them as opposites was firmly entrenched by Coleridge, who claimed that 'Shakespeare was all men, potentially, except Milton' (qtd. in Joseph Anthony Wittreich (ed.), *The Romantics on Milton: Formal Essays and Critical Asides* (Cleveland, Oh., 1970), 194). See also ibid. 270, 277.

[86] See Paul Stevens, *Imagination and the Presence of Shakespeare in* Paradise Lost (Madison, 1985).

BEYOND THE *METAMORPHOSES*

For Milton, therefore, Ovid was a means of absorbing past sources, and for reflecting on his own transformation of the past. For Renaissance artists, as for most readers before and after, 'Ovid' seems synonymous with 'metamorphosis'. He is the great poet of change, who has inspired thinking about change that is poetical, philosophical, scientific as well as political. Still, this identification is frequently used to reinforce his reduction to the *Metamorphoses*. Critics have therefore generally assumed that for Milton Ovid means almost exclusively his epic; Harding, DuRocher, Green, and indeed most critics, all tend to focus automatically on this work.

There are good reasons for this assumption. The *Metamorphoses* was undoubtedly hugely important: it is *Ovidius maior*, the Bible of the poets, a work whose influence in general has been constant and ubiquitous. Nowhere too was it more inspiring than in the Renaissance. It has thus been easy to assume that although (like many other susceptible young lads) the young Milton was seduced by the erotic Ovid, as he matured he left behind his dalliance with lighter forms and feelings. The retraction that follows 'Elegia 7' suggests that Milton abandoned a youth of simultaneous poetic and erotic 'error' ('Haec ego mente', 1. 3) as he turned to more serious aspirations and to the higher genre of epic. By the time he writes *Paradise Lost*, therefore, he is studying only the *Metamorphoses*, which his daughter also singles out as one of his three favourite works.[87]

Sensible as this assumption is, I believe that it has also limited our understanding of Milton's engagement with his precursor. For Renaissance writers, Ovid is more than just the *Metamorphoses*. All of Ovid's works, especially those omitted by the conventional story of Milton's poetic development—i.e. the *Fasti* and the exilic verse—were read and exerted more influence than we usually recognize. As we will see, Milton's works suggest that he saw them all as an interrelated *carmen perpetuum*. As the individual episodes of the *Metamorphoses* reflect upon each other, the individual works comment on each other. When we add the other

---

[87] Johnson, *Lives*, i. 107. On this traditional reading of Milton's development, see especially E. K. Rand, 'Milton in Rustication', *Studies in Philology*, 19/2 (1922), 109–35; Bush, *Mythology*, 265; and Harding, *Milton and the Renaissance Ovid*, 43, 56.

works into the mix, our sense of what 'Ovid' meant to Renaissance writers and especially Milton is metamorphosed.

As a whole, Ovid's work seems to fall into two distinct stages: pre-exilic and exilic. The early erotic poetry, with its recurrent theme of the immortality of art (see especially *Amores* 1. 15), leads up to the grand climax of the *Metamorphoses*, which leaves the poet on top of his art and even the world, prophesying his triumph over time and change. This image of the poet has been influential; it echoes throughout the exploration of immortality of Shakespeare's sonnets, and at the end of the *Shepheardes Calender*, when Spenser too moves from time to eternity. Focusing on Ovid's last epic words gives us an attractive image of the godlike artist whose art conquers all; the poet confident and assured of his powers—as Milton often appears to be. Ovid might well have liked to have suspended his own career at this moment of triumphant achievement. But this is only half the story—and readers knew that the ending was not so happy. In terms of careers, Virgil and Ovid again seem opposites.[88] Where Virgil's writing appears to evolve naturally through its tripartite structure towards its epic triumph, Ovid's trajectory looks like one of sad decline, in which, after the premature poetic climax of the *Metamorphoses*, the poet's powers peter out in the rather dismal verse from exile. The letters from the Black Sea, written to his wife and friends (and, as we will see later, some enemies) in Rome, describe the horrors of Tomis and beg the Emperor for forgiveness. Ovid repeatedly complains about the effect of exile on his creative powers. He laments that his 'ingenium' has been worn away by hardship, and fears that he is devolving from an urbane and witty Roman into a barbaric demi-Gete. He complains that his writing is becoming monotonous in its subject, for the exiled poet can only write of one single subject: his own sad fate.[89]

---

[88] It is generally assumed that the Virgilian *rota* was the dominant model for poetic development in the Renaissance, a model that was ultimately linear and teleological. Recent critics have suggested that other poetic career models were available at this time, including an Ovidian one, and also that the Virgilian *rota* itself provided a problematic model; see Cheney, *Counterfeit Profession*; Joseph Farrell, 'Ovid's Virgilian Career', *Materiali e discussioni per l'analisi dei testi classici*, 52 (2004), 41–55; and the essays by Michael Putnam, 'Some Virgilian Unities', and Maggie Kilgour, 'New Spins on Old Rotas: Virgil, Ovid, Milton', in Moore and Hardie (eds.), *Classical Literary Careers and their Reception*, 17–38 and 179–98.

[89] For the impact of exile on his *ingenium*, see *Tristia*, 3. 14. 33 and *Ex Ponto* 4. 2. 15; see also *Tristia*, 1. 1. 39–44 and *Ex Ponto*, 3. 9. 37–42.

Poetry that constantly announces its own inadequacy does not sound inspiring or even promising for the potential reader. But this Ovid has also been extremely important for shaping the meaning of 'Ovid' because later artists have been constantly drawn to these works. They played a fundamental role in the broader reception of Ovid as well. This is again in part simply because of their prominence and placement in curricula. Like most of Ovid's works, the exilic poetry was taught in the Middle Ages; by the sixteenth and seventeenth centuries the *Tristia* in particular was a standard school text in England. At Milton's school, St Paul's, it was probably taught in the third form, the year *before* students encountered the *Metamorphoses*.[90] The letters from exile were used to introduce students to the writing of epistles and the arts of rhetorical persuasion, and then to the writing of poetry more generally. If, as Donald Clark says, 'The writing of verse began with the reading of Ovid in the Fourth Form', Ovid, and especially the exilic verse which the boys knew well by then, was at the base of their own experience of writing poetry.[91] Here too, the texts chosen for instruction may have struck a chord with their pupils; the topic of exile and alienation probably had as much appeal

---

[90] See Donald Lemen Clark, *John Milton at St. Paul's School: A Study of Ancient Rhetoric in English Renaissance Education* (New York, 1948), 110–24. It is impossible to be absolutely sure of this, as the records of St Paul's were destroyed in the fire. But Clark's theoretical curriculum, based on those of comparable schools of the time and that of St Paul's at the end of the 17th century, is plausible. Both he and Baldwin conclude that Milton read the *Tristia*, then the *Metamorphoses* and *Heroides*, and *then* Virgil—a nice overturning of poetic succession which meant that Virgil was read through Ovid rather than vice versa. See Clark, *John Milton at St. Paul's School*, 206; and Baldwin, *William Shakspere's Small Latine & Lesse Greeke*, ii, 421. This seems likely given the curricula set out by John Brinsley, William Kempe, and Charles Hoole, which outline a progression which begins with the *Tristia* (called *De tristibus*), and then proceeds in following years to the *Metamorphoses* and then *Aeneid*; see Brinsley, *Ludus Literarius: Or, the Grammar Schoole* (London, 1612); Kempe, *The education of children in learning declared by the dignitie, vtilitie, and method thereof* (London, 1588); and Hoole, *A new discovery of the old art of teaching schoole in four small treatises* (London, 1661). The sequence is clearly meant to build from the simplest to most difficult. Thomas Elyot however advocated using Virgil at all levels, noting that 'there is not that affect or desire whereto any child's fantasy is disposed, but in some of Virgil's works may be found matter thereto apt and propise' (*The Booke Named the Governor*, ed. S. E. Lehmberg (London, 1962), 31). On Renaissance curricula in general, see Peter Mack, *Elizabethan Rhetoric: Theory and Practice* (Cambridge, 2002), 11–47.
[91] Clark, *John Milton at St. Paul's School*, 199. Harding casually remarks that 'schoolboys of Milton's day must have been almost as familiar with the *Tristia* as they were with the *Catechism*' (*Milton and the Renaissance Ovid*, 31).

for students then as it has today.[92] Moreover, exile is a protean theme, adaptable to spiritual, psychological, and social situations. Ovid's poems could be read through a recognizable classical-Christian tradition of exilic writings.[93] Renaissance humanists saw their alienation from the classical past through Ovid's exile: Petrarch also yearned for Ovid's Rome.[94] Ovid's last works have always appealed to readers who were themselves exiled in one way or another: Dante, Petrarch, Du Bellay (who inverts Ovid's situation by making Rome his place of exile), and Spenser, whose *Complaints* draw both on Ovid and Du Bellay's reworking.[95] For the generation of Elizabethan schoolboys

---

[92] In the 19th century, Ovid's letters were still set as exercises especially relevant and helpful for homesick boarding-school boys; see Andrew Walker, 'Introduction', *Ramus*, 26 (1997), 2.

[93] On the classical/Christian topos of exile and its relation to Ovid, see Margaret Ferguson, 'The Rhetoric of Exile in Du Bellay and his Classical Precursors', Ph.D. diss. (Yale University, 1974); Jo-Marie Claassen, *Displaced Persons: The Literature of Exile from Cicero to Boethius* (London, 1999); Raphael Lyne, 'Love and Exile after Ovid', in Hardie (ed.), *Companion to Ovid*, 288–300; Dorothy M. Robathan, 'Ovid in the Middle Ages', in Binns (ed.), *Ovid*, 191–209; Jeremy Dimmick, 'Ovid in the Middle Ages: Authority and Poetry', in Hardie (ed.), *Companion to Ovid*, 264–87; Michael Dewar, '*Siquid habent veri vatum praesagia*: Ovid in the 1st–5th Centuries A.D.', in Boyd (ed.), *Brill's Companion to Ovid*, 383–412; and Hexter, *Ovid and Medieval Schooling*, 83–99.

[94] See Burrow, 'Re-embodying Ovid', 301, and 308–9. Hexter, in 'Ovid in the Middle Ages', notes a similar nostalgia in earlier, especially Carolingian, writers (417–18). For Greene, exile from the past is the fundamental experience of the Renaissance humanist—an image that reworks Burckhardt's picture of the homeless and peripatetic scholar.

[95] For an excellent overview, see Lyne, 'Love and Exile after Ovid'. Scholars are beginning to note the influence of the exilic work on individual authors. For some examples of early reception, see Alessandro Barchiesi and Philip Hardie, 'The Ovidian Career Model: Ovid, Gallus, Apuleius, Boccaccio', in Moore and Hardie (eds.), *Classical Literary Careers and their Reception*, 59–88. Michael A. Calabrese discusses its impact on Chaucer and medieval writers more broadly; see *Chaucer's Ovidian Arts of Love* (Gainesville, Fla., 1994), 12–21 especially. For Dante, see Michelangelo Picone, 'Ovid and the *Exul Immeritus*', in Teodolinda Barolini and Wayne H. Storey (eds.), *Dante for the New Millennium* (New York, 2003), 389–407; and Janet Levarie Smarr, 'Poets of Love and Exile', in Madison U. Sowell (ed.), *Dante and Ovid: Essays in Intertextuality* (Binghamton, NY, 1991), 139–51, who shows also the importance of the last verse for Boccaccio. Matthew McGowan notes the role of the exilic poetry in Poliziano, who wrote a lament for the exiled Ovid (translated and printed, along with similar verse by Scaliger, in Saltonstall's translation of the *Tristia*); see 'Ovid and Poliziano in Exile', *International Journal of the Classical Tradition*, 12/1 (2005), 25–45. Syrithe Pugh argues for the presence of the exilic poetry in Spenser and also Raleigh (*Spenser and Ovid*, 152 and 180 especially). On Spenser see also Richard A. McCabe, *Spenser's Monstrous Regiment: Elizabethan Ireland and the Poetics of Difference* (Oxford, 2002); and Stapleton, *Spenser's Ovidian Poetics*, 41–73. Du Bellay's

who, finding themselves well educated but unemployed, turned to writing, Ovid's exile mirrored their own social marginalization. Ovid helped seventeenth-century writers such as Herrick and Vaughan frame their experience of the Civil War.[96] As we will see further, Ovid's elegiac poetry of exile echoes throughout Milton's career: in the early 'Elegia 1', 17–24, Milton playfully compares his own pleasant rustication with Ovid's bleaker relegation; the final works draw more sombre parallels between his own situation and that of the exiled Ovid.[97]

One can easily imagine that for other writers the spectacle of the great writer losing his powers before their very eyes would be chilling. For many writers, Ovid's story is that of the artist crushed under tyrannical power. As critics have increasingly noted, however, Ovid himself is the source of this myth of poetic degeneration which the

---

response to Ovid in *Les Regrets* has been long noted; see Geneviève Demerson, 'Joachim Du Bellay et le modèle ovidien', in R. Chevalier (ed.), *Colloque Présence d'Ovide* (Paris, 1982), 281–94. Richard F. Hardin notes also how Racine's letters during his 'post-graduate rustication' are 'full of echoes of the *Tristia*, suggesting Racine in the provinces may have felt himself another Ovid among the Goths' ('Ovid in Seventeenth-Century England', *Comparative Literature*, 24 (1972), 57). In the modern world in which alienation seems the universal condition, Ovid's last poetry has seemed eerily prescient, and given him a new life as the poet of exile and alienation; see Hardie, *Poetics of Illusion*, 326–37; Duncan F. Kennedy, 'Recent Receptions of Ovid', in Hardie (ed.), *Companion to Ovid*, 320–35; and Barchiesi, *The Poet and the Prince*, 1–4. There has been a remarkable number of recent fictional renditions of Ovid's exile: Malouf, *An Imaginary Life: A Novel*; Christoph Ransmayr, *The Last World: A Novel with an Ovidian Repertory*, trans. John Woods [*Die letzte Welt*] (New York, 1990); and Antonio Tabucchi, *Dreams of Dreams and The Last Three Days of Fernando Pessoa*, trans. Nancy J. Peters [*Sogni di sogni e Gli ultimi tre giorni di Fernando Pessoa*] (San Francisco, 1999).

[96] For Herrick, see Syrithe Pugh, *Herrick, Fanshawe and the Politics of Intertextuality: Classical Literature and Seventeenth-Century Royalism* (Farnham, 2010), 21–38 and 57–83. Burrow, in 'Re-embodying Ovid', suggests that the interest in Ovid as figure of exile increased in England after the turn of the 17th century. Two translations of the *Tristia* appeared in the years leading up to the war: Wye Saltonstall's in 1633 and Zachary Caitline's in 1639. Saltonstall also published the first English translation of *Epistulae ex Ponto* (1639), dedicated to the Ovidian wit and Royalist Sir John Suckling. Though we don't know the date of composition, Aston Cokayne's play representing Ovid's last days, *The Tragedy of Ovid* (published in 1662), seems likely to have been written during his own 'exile' in the Interregnum.

[97] Milton's early interest in and identification with the exiled Ovid has been long noted; see especially Rand, 'Milton in Rustication', 109–35; and James Holly Hanford, 'The Youth of Milton: An Interpretation of his Early Development', in Eugene S. McCartney (ed.), *Studies in Shakespeare, Milton and Donne* (London, 1925), 109. See also Sauer, 'Engendering Metamorphoses', 217. An identification is implied but never developed in Martz, *Poet of Exile*.

Introduction 33

quality and complexity of the verse belies.⁹⁸ The first English translator of the *Fasti*, John Gower, marvelled at Ovid's achievement in such circumstances: '(O admirable Wit | And even beyond my thought!) amid his pain | And misery his Muse did sing again' ('Clio's complaint for the death of OVID', in *Ovids Festivalls*, B6ʳ). Ovid himself proclaims, 'ingenio tamen ipse meo comitorque fruorque: | Caesar in hoc potuit iuris habere nihil' ('my mind is nevertheless my comrade and my joy; over this Caesar could have no right', *Tristia*, 3. 7. 47–8). Despite its pretence of abjection, the final poetry is Ovid's self-exegesis, through which he attempts to regain some control over his own fate and future. The constant complaints of decline, themselves rhetorically slanted to achieve their goal ('Bring me back to Rome and I'll stop writing such dreadful stuff'), are crafted with typical care. As recent critics have demonstrated, the final poetry is in fact a powerful conclusion to Ovid's career that gives his poetry a new and unifying shape. His career comes full circle: after experimenting with the epic in the *Metamorphoses*, Ovid returns to his first source of poetry, the elegy. The themes of the erotic verse reappear, though typically metamorphosed: the frustrated sexual desire of the erotic verse becomes the longing for home and the unresponsive mistress is replaced by the *princeps*.⁹⁹ In his last works, the poet

---

⁹⁸ There has been much interesting and important work reassessing the last poetry; see especially Betty Rose Nagle, *The Poetics of Exile: Program and Polemic in the* Tristia *and* Epistulae Ex Ponto *of Ovid* (Brussels, 1980); Harry B. Evans, *Publica Carmina: Ovid's Books from Exile* (Lincoln, Nebr., 1983); Gareth D. Williams, *Banished Voices: Readings in Ovid's Exile Poetry* (Cambridge, 1994) and *The Curse of Exile: A Study of Ovid's* Ibis (Cambridge, 1996); Stephen Hinds, 'Booking the Return Trip: Ovid and *Tristia* 1', *Proceedings of the Cambridge Philological Society*, 31 (1985), 13–32, and 'After Exile: Time and Teleology from *Metamorphoses* to *Ibis*', in Philip Hardie, Stephen Hinds, and Alessandro Barchiesi (eds.), *Ovidian Transformations: Essays on the* Metamorphoses *and its Reception* (Cambridge, 1999), 48–67; R. J. Dickinson, 'The *Tristia*: Poetry in Exile', in Binns (ed.), *Ovid*, 154–90; and E. J. Kenney, 'The Poetry of Ovid's Exile', *Proceedings of the Cambridge Philological Society*, 11 (1965), 37–49. Georg Luck's analysis demonstrated there is no technical difference between the early and later verse: see 'Notes on the Language and Text of Ovid's *Tristia*', *Harvard Studies in Classical Philology*, 65 (1961), 243–61. However as Hinds points out, it is too facile to therefore assume that the poet doth protest too much in order only to prove his own continuing strength; Ovid's 'exile books grow into their trope: "decline" becomes decline, and none of the newly appreciated virtuosity in Ovid's framing of his suffering should be allowed to devalue the suffering thus framed' (*Allusion and Intertext*, 90).

⁹⁹ See Kenney, 'The Poetry of Ovid's Exile'; Nagle, *The Poetics of Exile*, 21–2, 56, 61, 70; Dickinson, 'Poetry in Exile', 159; P. A. Rosenmeyer, 'Ovid's *Heroides* and *Tristia*:

revises himself. With characteristic cunning, Ovid has made himself his own first rewriter, showing readers how he can be remade into new forms.[100] He is also his own first interpreter. The experience of exile changes everything, including the meaning of his own earlier works. As Stephen Hinds points out, 'Ovid argues that the *Metamorphoses* needs to be quite literally revised to take account of the sudden "metamorphosis" of the author's own fortunes.'[101] By speaking as if from beyond the grave, the poet aspires to control his own posthumous poetic life, claiming the right to have the last word. The poet takes charge of his life and art once again, giving his career—a career which, like that of Milton, was derailed by external circumstances over which he had no control—the illusion of authorial organization.

As we will see in more detail in Chapter 5, Ovid's final poems are thus marked by a concern with reading and reception. In many ways they helped shape the interpretation of his works, changing the ways in which later writers could understand the metamorphic poet. In Greene's reading, the *Metamorphoses* represented to Petrarch 'the relative wholeness of Roman mythography, with its visual and rhetorical clarity, its calm impersonality, its security within nature, its accommodations with suffering, its refusal of psychologistic paradox, and its capacity for repose'—all of which seemed so distant from the later poet's 'turbulent egoism, the problematic divisions and restless intensities of a voice pathetically in quest of its own integrity'.[102] For readers who knew the exilic work especially, however, the situation was more complex. Philip Hardie argues that Petrarch read the *Metamorphoses* as 'a poem that is *already* obsessed with disruption, exile, privation and division' and which thus is the mirror image of

---

Voices from Exile', *Ramus*, 26 (1997), 29–56; Williams, *Banished Voices*; and Barchiesi, *The Poet and the Prince*, 34–43.

[100] Ovid's technique of self-revision was clearly picked up by the author of the 13th-century pseudo-Ovidian poem De Vetula. The poem purports to be written by the exiled poet and left on his tomb as his last word and legacy. It offers a further retrospective on the poet's career and one final dazzling metamorphosis: conversion to Christianity. See Dorothy Mae Robathan (ed.), *The Pseudo-Ovidian* De Vetula (Amsterdam, 1968).

[101] 'After Exile', 48. See also Hinds, 'Booking the Return Trip'; and Elena Theodorakopoulos, 'Closure and Transformation in Ovid's *Metamorphoses*', in Hardie, Hinds, and Barchiesi (eds), *Ovidian Transformations*, 142–61.

[102] Greene, *The Light in Troy*, 131. James notes how Greene's reading paradoxically makes 'Ovid's poem of change . . . relentlessly stable' ('Shakespeare, the Classics', 82).

'that landscape of privation and linguistic shadowing through which he represented his own relationships'.[103] When they looked back to Ovid, Renaissance writers did not always look back from their own temporal, or even real, exiles to past glory but to a world in which exile was already the fundamental experience.

PORTRAIT OF THE ARTIST AS A YOUNG DEVIL

The final exilic works influenced the later metamorphosis of Ovid in another important way. They draw attention to the peculiarly intimate relation between the poet's life and his art. In exile, the stories he told earlier come true. The poet himself now presents himself as one of the heroines of the *Heroides*, who writes letters to an unresponding object of desire. He is equally one of his own transformed characters; as he notes: 'inter mutata referri | fortunae vultum corpora posse meae' ('my fortune's face can now be reckoned among those metamorphosed figures', *Tristia*, 1. 1. 119–20).[104] Through retrospect his early work acquires a prophetic quality; he identifies especially with tragic figures such as Actaeon (*Tristia* 2. 103–8), Phaethon, and Icarus (*Tristia*, 3. 4. 21–30).[105] Ovid defends himself by separating

---

[103] Hardie, *Poetics of Illusion*, 80.
[104] Abraham Cowley thus observed that Ovid 'is himself, methinks, like one of the *Stories* of his owne *Metamorphosis*' ('The Preface: Of the Author', in *The English Writings of Abraham Cowley*, ed. A. R. Waller (Cambridge, 1905), 7).
[105] Perhaps sensing the connection, Thomas Hall's school text, based on an explication of the story of Phaethon, included also a translation of *Tristia* 1. 1; see *Phaetons folly, or, The downfal of pride* (London, 1655), Early English Books Online, F8ʳ–H3ʳ. The link between Ovid and Actaeon appears in many commentaries on the *Metamorphoses*; see Sandys, *Ovid's Metamorphosis*, 151. As Amy Richlin notes, in general: 'The muted victims, the artists horribly punished by legalistic gods for bold expression—Marsyas, and especially Arachne—read like allegories of Ovid's experience' ('Reading Ovid's Rapes', in Amy Richlin (ed.), *Pornography and Representation in Greece and Rome* (New York, 1992), 176). Charles Segal also points out: 'It is a sad and ironical tribute to the truth of the insights implicit in the Metamorphoses [*sic*] that Augustus' decree of banishment, coming suddenly and irrevocably, is in the same spirit of sudden, cruel transformation as many of the myths of the poem. The dominant theme of the poem, abrupt, radical, irreversible change at the hands of strange, impetuous deities, is curiously prophetic of the poet's own fate. Ovid, like Daphne or Actaeon or Dryope or Scylla, falls victim to a great power invading and shattering his life' (*Landscape in Ovid's* Metamorphoses: *A Study in the Translation of a Literary Symbol* (Wiesbaden, 1969), 94.

his art and life into parallel worlds—'vita verecunda est, Musa iocosa mea' ('my life is moral, my muse is gay', *Tristia*, 2. 354). But his last poetry shows a more troubling blurring of the boundaries between fantasy and reality. Much of his description of life in Tomis, including his vivid description of his journey by sea, is based on literary sources.[106] The poetry of exile is the climax of Ovid's lifelong exploration of illusion, and especially the insistent drive of the imagination to realize its own fantasies.[107] While the story of Pygmalion tempts us with the imagination's power to make dreams come true, the story of Narcissus, who mistakes shadow for reality, reminds us of its dangers.

The intimacy between creator and creations is reinforced by the fact that, because of the last works, the figure of Ovid himself became a central part of his compelling story. The general mythology that surrounds him is almost indistinguishable from the other myths he passed on.[108] Many Renaissance editions of Ovid's works included a potted biography of the poet based on the exilic poetry.[109] As the only source of information about the poet, these works became authoritative and so enabled Ovid to shape his own image. Such biographies also meant that readers often read Ovid's poetry through his life, and knew from the start his dismal fate, exiled 'among the Goths' as Shakespeare's Touchstone puts it (*As You Like It*, 3. 3. 9). The general outline of Ovid's life was therefore well known, but also frustratingly

---

[106] See Hinds, 'Booking the Return Trip'. Some critics therefore rather ingeniously argued that Ovid's exile was itself merely a literary fiction he invented as an interesting premiss for his poetry; see especially A. D. Fitton Brown, 'The Unreality of Ovid's Tomitian Exile', *Liverpool Classical Monthly* 10.2. (1985): 18–22.

[107] On the theme of illusion in Ovid generally see Hardie, *Poetics of Illusion*. Hardie notes the importance of the story of Ceyx and Alcyone in *Metamorphoses* 11. 410–748, in which even false dreams and shades prove true, an episode which is replayed in Ovid's own life in *Tristia* 1 (ibid. 272–92; see also Tissol, *The Face of Nature*, 72–84). As Hardie also points out, recent novelistic treatments of Ovid's exile are especially drawn to the relation between his fictions and life (*Poetics of Illusion*, 326–37).

[108] Hexter notes that the story of Ovid's exile was influential even during times when the poetry itself was relegated to obscurity (*Ovid and Medieval Schooling*, 83).

[109] Biographies were also included in medieval editions which began with an *accessus ad auctores*; see Fausto Ghisalberti, 'Mediaeval Biographies of Ovid', *Journal of the Warburg and Courtauld Institutes*, 9 (1946), 10–59. Biographies also introduce many translations; see Sandys's, which ends with a translation of *Tristia* 1. 6 (*Ovid's Metamorphosis*, 12–16); and also John Gower's 1640 translation of the *Fasti*, *Ovid's Festivalls*, A^r–B4^v. Gower's biographical account, 'The Life, Works, and Approof of OVID, *Gathered out of his own works and the relations of divers faithfull Authours*', and his prefatory materials generally, are full of passages from the exilic verse.

sketchy, especially in regard to the exact cause of his banishment. While, as we will see further in Chapter 4, readers have always naturally loved to speculate, our sole source of information is Ovid himself who said only that his crime was connected to 'carmen et error' ('a poem and a blunder', *Tristia*, 2. 207). According to Ovid's account in *Tristia* 2, the *carmen* was his early erotic poetry which, he complains, had unjustly offended the *princeps*. Ironically, the creator was destroyed by his own creations, as he wryly imagines when he writes his own epitaph in *Tristia* 3. 3. 73–4: 'hic ego qui iaceo tenerorum lusor Amorum | ingenio perii Naso poeta meo' ('Here do I lie, light verse-maker of tender Loves, Naso the poet destroyed by my own genius'). His *ingenium* not only did not protect him, as he had crowed at the end of the *Metamorphoses*, it ruined him. If at the end of the *Metamorphoses* poetry gets Ovid to the stars, at the end of his life, it has brought him to Tomis.

Ovid is less forthright, however, in terms of revealing the nature of his *error*, saying only that it was innocent, and hinting that he, like Actaeon, saw something he should not have.[110] The term *error* in its many senses, however, has seemed appropriate for a poet who makes wandering, delay, and digression the source of erotic and narrative pleasure. As Ovid teaches in the *Ars Amatoria*: 'Grata mora venies; maxima lena mora est' ('delay will enhance your charm: a great procuress is delay', 3. 752). A similar principle of narrative errancy is evident in the *Metamorphoses*, in which the progression of stories is like that of the river Maeander which 'ambiguo lapsu refluitque fluitque | occurrensque sibi venturas aspicit undas' ('flows back and forth upon in doubtful course and, turning back on itself, beholds its own waves coming on their way', 8. 163–4). Ovid's *carmen* **est** *error*, as it appears to meander, circling around its central themes and figures. If Ovid inspires later erotic romances he is also a model for the genre of romance, with its complex and errant structure.[111]

---

[110] See *Tristia* 2. 103–10. As Alessandro Barchiesi notes, Ovid's error has a literary source, as line 109 'me malus abstulit error' ('my ruinous mistake ravished me away') echoes Virgil's *Eclogues* 8. 41, in which the love-maddened Damon cries: 'ut vidi, ut perii, ut me malus abstulit error' ('As I saw, how was I lost! How a fatal error swept me away'); see *Speaking Volumes*, 101. On the question of Ovid's mysterious error, see Peter Green, 'Carmen et Error: πρόφασις and αἰτία in the Matter of Ovid's Exile', *Classical Antiquity*, 1/2 (1982), 202–20.

[111] See also Pugh, *Spenser and Ovid*, 47–57. On romance and narrative error, see Patricia A. Parker's seminal *Inescapable Romance: Studies in the Poetics of a Mode*

Many critics have thought, however, that Ovid's *ingenium* led his *carmen* into a another kind of *error*. According to a famous story told by the Elder Seneca, Ovid's friends asked him to cut three of his lines; in return, he asked to be allowed to choose three which they could not touch. Of course the lines they wanted to cut and those he insisted on saving were the same. Only two of these are known for sure: 'Semibovemque virum semivirumque bovem' ('the man half bull and the bull half man', *Ars Amatoria* 2. 24), and 'Et gelidum Borean egelidumque Notum' ('freezing north wind and de-freezing south', *Amores* 2. 11. 10). The lines epitomize Ovid's fascination with paradoxes, his interest in creating figures that are both rhetorically and imagistically double and through which he can run ideas backwards and forwards to create complex systems of verbal and logical identification. For Seneca, however, this kind of excessively contrived wit is self-defeating; he draws the obvious moral from the story: 'Ex quo adparet summi ingenii viro non iudicium defuisse ad compescendam licentiam carminum suorum sed animum' ('It is clear from this that the great man lacked not the judgement but the will to restrain the licence of his poetry', *Controversiae*, 2. 2. 12). Quintilian similarly thought Ovid was simply 'nimium amator ingenui sui' ('unduly enamoured of his own wit').[112] The artist was too narcissistically in love with his own wit to restrain it when necessary. While Ovid's rhetorical skill was admired and imitated by humanists, he was the focus of a Renaissance anxiety about the dangers of uncontrolled rhetoric and wit.[113] Even Ovid's Renaissance advocate, Cintio, admitted that he 'troppo di sè medesimo si compiacque, tale che i suoi componimenti sono, come campi di verdissime biade, più del convenevole morbide e lussurianti. Il che ha fatto che più ingegnoso egli si scopre che grave, più licenzioso che osservato, e più copioso che diligente' ('was too pleased with himself, so that his works are like

---

(Princeton, 1979). As Parker notes, Ovid and later writers are also drawing out elements in Virgil which in turn originate in Homer.

[112] Quintilian, *The Institutio Oratoria of Quintilian*, trans. Harold Edgeworth Butler, 4 vols. (London, 1920), iv. 50–1. Quintilian of course also uses many examples from Ovid as models of successful rhetoric.

[113] Heather James, however, notes that this association of Ovid could also be used positively as a model for poetic licence and freedom of speech ('Ovid and the Question of Politics in Early Modern England', *English Literary History*, 70/2 (2003), 343–73). James argues that Ovid offers a model for political subversion as 'the voice of unfettered poetic imagination' (ibid. 366). See further Ch. 2.

fields of the greenest growth, inappropriately soft and luxuriant. This is what has made him seem more ingenious than profound, more licentious than law-abiding, more copious than careful').[114] Ovid showed that unrestrained copiousness leads to sterility; as in the case of Narcissus, who realized that *copia me inopem fecit*, Ovid's plenty made him poor.[115]

Ovid's works themselves, however, constantly return to stories in which creativity becomes self-destructive. The image of the river Maeander that I cited earlier as a figure for the errant narrative is part of a simile that describes the labyrinth built by the artist Daedalus to house the man-eating minotaur.[116] Like the labyrinth, Ovid's art houses many hybrid figures who embody rhetorical paradox: centaurs, fauns, the monstrous Scylla and her fishy suitor Glaucus. The poet of metamorphoses is drawn to figures who are trapped between two identities, ripped in two literally like Marsyas or the dying Hercules, or, like Medea and Althaea, torn between conflicting desires and loyalties that divide them psychologically. Moreover, as recent studies of Ovid's self-conscious art have noted, through artist figures such as Daedalus he creates surrogates of himself.[117] This

---

[114] Giovambattista Giraldi Cintio, *De' romanzi delle commedie e delle tragedie*, 2 vols. (Milan, 1864), i. 163; see also Hulse, *Metamorphic Verse*, 249. In *The Face of Nature*, Tissol discusses such attacks on Ovid's lack of artistic self-control and offers a spirited defence.

[115] As Tissol notes, Dryden especially attacked Ovid's 'Conceits and Jingles' which he dismissed as 'only glittering Trifles and so far from being Witty, that in a serious Poem they are nauseous, because they are unnatural'. The story of Narcissus is a prime example of the problem with Ovidian wit: 'Wou'd any Man who is ready to die for Love, describe his Passion like *Narcissus*? ... If this were Wit, was this a Time to be witty, when the poor Wretch was in the Agony of Death? ... On these Occasions the Poet shou'd endeavour to raise Pity: But instead of this, *Ovid* is tickling you to laugh. *Virgil* never made use of such Machines' (*The Poems and Fables of John Dryden*, ed. James Kinsley (London, 1962), 527; qtd. in Tissol, *The Face of Nature*, 11). I'll come back to this episode in Ch. 3. On this 18th-century characterization of Ovidian wit, see also David Hopkins, 'Dryden and Ovid's "Wit out of Season"', in Charles Martindale (ed.), *Ovid Renewed: Ovidian Influences on Literature and Art from the Middle Ages to the Twentieth Century* (Cambridge, 1988), 167–90. As Ovid had been essential to the formation of Elizabethan poetics, he was also, as Hopkins puts it, prominent in late 17th-century debates over 'the role which verbal and imaginative exuberance and playfulness might properly play in dramatic, heroic, and lyric poetry' (168).

[116] On the sinister side of the Maeander (grandfather of the incestuous Byblis) as an image of narrative and erotic reflux, see Micaela Janan, 'The Labyrinth and the Mirror: Incest and Influence in *Metamorphoses* 9', *Arethusa*, 24 (1991), 243.

[117] Eleanor Winsor Leach, 'Ekphrasis and the Theme of Artistic Failure in Ovid's *Metamorphoses*', *Ramus*, 3 (1974), 102–42; Valerie Merriam Wise, 'Flight Myths in

inclusion of authorial doubles in poetry is also not new with Ovid—one can trace it through Homer, where the ingenious fiction-maker Odysseus is the poet's counterpart, and Virgil, as well as many others. But Ovid again multiplies prior practice in a way that both foregrounds and transforms the tradition. With a few exceptions (most notably, if arguably, Pygmalion), Ovid's artists meet notoriously nasty ends: Philomela, Arachne, Orpheus, Niobe, and Marsyas are only the most obvious examples. While Daedalus escapes, the artist who designs the murderous labyrinth loses his son Icarus. Through such figures, Ovid explores the proximity between the creative and destructive urges. In some cases, as in those of Arachne and Marsyas, human creativity seems punished specifically for its hubristic presumption to divine powers. The artists are themselves trying to be as gods. But if Arachne's art arrogantly challenges that of Minerva, it also rivals that of Ovid, with which it has often been compared. Eleanor Leach therefore suggests that Ovid's tragic artists serve as scapegoats to contrast with and foreground the poet's own creative triumph.[118] Like his gods, Ovid preserves his own authority by denying his artists success. The creator is different from his creatures: while they are degraded by metamorphoses, through the *Metamorphoses*, he is finally raised to the stars.

However, the relation between author and these doubles is more complex, especially in the later works where these figures are transformed from opposites into analogues of the poet's own fate. If, in the earlier works, the tragic artists are mirror images whose dismal ends make Ovid's success shine more brightly in contrast, in the last works Ovid sees his face in their mirror. The exiled poet is himself the last in the line of tragic creators destroyed by their own creations. For later writers, Ovid himself can be a sobering double who shows the

---

Ovid's *Metamorphoses*: An Interpretation of Phaethon and Daedalus', *Ramus*, 6 (1977), 44–59; Donald Lateiner, 'Mythic and Non-Mythic Artists in Ovid's *Metamorphoses*', *Ramus*, 13 (1984), 1–30; William S. Anderson, 'The Artist's Limits in Ovid: Orpheus, Pygmalion, and Daedalus', *Syllecta Classica*, 1 (1989), 1–11; Byron Harries, 'The Spinner and the Poet: Arachne in Ovid's *Metamorphoses*', *Proceedings of the Cambridge Philological Society*, 36 (1990), 64–82; Patricia J. Johnson, *Ovid before Exile: Art and Punishment in the* Metamorphoses (Madison, 2008); and Solodow, *The World of Ovid's* Metamorphoses.

[118] 'Ekphrasis and Artistic Failure'. It is also possible, however, to see such figures as ironizing or undermining the final words of the *Metamorphoses*; see Theodorakopoulos, 'Closure and Transformation', 144.

dangers of errant art. Upon leaving the circle of the thieves, whose endless metamorphoses recall those of Ovid, Dante feels the need to exercise particular caution: 'e più lo 'ngegno affreno ch'i' non soglio, | perché non corra che virtù nol guidi' ('I curb my genius more than I am wont, lest it run where virtue does not guide it', *Inferno*, 26. 21–2). The need for restraint, especially of 'ingegno', at this specific point seems appropriate, as Dante is also just about to meet the eloquent and persuasive Ulysses, the archetypal wanderer and storyteller with whom Ovid identifies.[119]

As we will see further in Chapter 4, in *Paradise Lost* Milton similarly foregrounds artist figures: Mulciber, the maker of Pandemonium; Satan, author of all our woe; God, creator of all things; his Son who makes the world; Adam and Eve, who sing spontaneous hymns to God; and especially the narrator himself. Such figures enable him to represent different forms of creativity, including his own. The striking doubling between Satan and the poet especially has been long noted.[120] As also long noted, Satan is associated with Ovidian figures; moreover, he is a shape-shifter who, like Ovid's characters, is self-divided, torn by 'hateful siege | Of contraries' in which 'all good to me becomes | Bane' (9. 121–3). It is tempting therefore to agree with DuRocher, who sees Satan as a version of the erring Ovidian poet. As DuRocher notes further, there are places in which Satan even sounds rather like the exiled Ovid.[121] By making Satan in Ovid's image, Milton seems to be separating himself from his precursor and once more putting Ovid in his place: in exile, now revealed by Christianity to be the state of hell. In casting Ovid into hell, moreover, Milton defines his own place as the Christian poet,

---

[119] See above, p. xiii. As often noted, Ulysses is also a double for Dante himself; see especially Teodolinda Barolini, *The Undivine Comedy: Detheologizing Dante* (Princeton, 1992), 48–73. I argue elsewhere that Dante is aware of Ovid's creation of authorial figures; see 'Dante's Ovidian Doubling', in Maggie Kilgour and Elena Lombardi (eds.), *Dantean Dialogues: Essays in Memory of Amilcare Iannucci* (forthcoming in 2012).

[120] See especially William G. Riggs, *The Christian Poet in* Paradise Lost (Berkeley and Los Angeles, 1972), 15–45; William Kerrigan, *The Prophetic Milton* (Charlottesville, Va., 1974), 125–87; Neil Forsyth, *The Satanic Epic* (Princeton, 2003), 118–20, 268–89; and Stephen Fallon, *Milton's Peculiar Grace: Self-Representation and Authority* (Ithaca, NY, 2007), 203–36.

[121] *Milton and Ovid*, 123. DuRocher astutely connects Satan's contrast between heaven and hell with Ovid's contrast between Tomis and Rome in *Tristia* 3. 4. 51–8, 3. 8. 35–42, and 4. 1. 99–107.

who alone can prophesy a final return home, imagined now as the restoration of not Rome but an even more eternal city, paradise.

For DuRocher, Satan and Ovid are contrasted with the narrator of *Paradise Lost*. DuRocher argues that both Ovid and Satan assert a fantasy of 'rhetorical self-generation'.[122] In contrast, the narrator repeatedly acknowledges his dependence on his Muse. Yet, as I have suggested, Ovid draws attention to his use of earlier sources. Moreover, as DuRocher is aware, Milton's narrator has an Ovidian prototype. As many critics have noted, Ovid's self-conscious and obtrusive narrator was a model for Milton and many other writers.[123] It is again usually assumed that the most influential narrator is the speaker of the *Metamorphoses*, or perhaps the mock-didactic teacher of the *Ars*, who was a fertile figure in the Middle Ages and Renaissance, inspiring Courtly Love, and later libertine verse. But Ovid bequeaths other contradictory voices as well. M. L. Stapleton has shown how the voice of the hapless *desultor amoris* of the *Amores* provided a very different model for later writers from that of the cocky *magister artis* of the *Ars*.[124] Ovid presents further narrative egos in the obtrusive but not entirely confident nor reliable narrator of the *Fasti*[125]— who makes the poet of the *Metamorphoses* seem the model of self-effacement—and in the speaker of the exilic verse. The narrator of the *Metamorphoses* has often been described as ironically, even callously, detached from his narrative; the narrator of the exilic poetry, however, is completely identified with the story he is telling. Apollonius of Rhodes and Virgil had already made the narrator a subjective presence in the text;[126] in the exilic verse Ovid makes the narrator the subject of the story. Presenting himself as the epic hero of his own

---

[122] *Milton and Ovid*, 163.
[123] See ibid. 162–75 especially; see also Martz, *Poet of Exile*, 232–44. John M. Fyler shows the influence of Ovid on Chaucer's unreliable narrator, and argues that of all Ovid's legacies to medieval poetry, 'probably the most important is his self-conscious, obtrusive narrator, who refuses to be a clear medium for the poem he recites' (*Chaucer and Ovid* (New Haven, 1979), 19). On the general impact of Ovid's narrator on Renaissance literature, see Robert M. Durling, *The Figure of the Poet in Renaissance Epic* (Cambridge, Mass., 1965).
[124] *Harmful Eloquence*.
[125] See Newlands, *Playing with Time*, 51–86.
[126] See Conte, *The Poetry of Pathos*, 49–57. The effects of these subjective presences are quite different: where Apollonius asserts poetic authority by self-introjection, Ovid calls it into question.

poetry, a Ulysses and Aeneas, he anticipates the self-presentation of Dante.

In the range of voices that he presents, the protean Ovid therefore left to later writers a 'poetic consciousness of the narrative ego and its possibilities'.[127] As I will discuss in Chapter 4, traces of the exiled Ovid in the narrator of *Paradise Lost* foreground Milton's concerns with the dangers of his own creativity. Moreover, the Ovidian doubling of artist figures in *Paradise Lost* complicates what might otherwise be a straightforward moral combat between the forces of good and evil. Clearly when characters have names like 'Satan' and 'God' the reader is given a strong hint as to which side they stand on; there really should be no moral suspense. Yet by making Satan attractive, a mirror image of the poet himself, Milton exercises our moral and imaginative faculties. Like the *Metamorphoses*, *Paradise Lost* shows a world which depends on the simultaneous establishment and dissolution of divisions and asks us to make the difference. The poem both insists that good and evil are absolutely opposed and yet makes it difficult to tell the two apart. As Romantic readings of Milton's secret affinity with Satan suggest, Milton never gets completely away from his diabolical double. Regina Schwartz notes that while Milton sets up a division between 'Satanic destruction and Adamic recreation' he dramatizes 'their complex interaction, to show how difficult it is to keep them separate, how the very drives that inspire revenge and destruction also inspire the narrator's ambition to overcome destruction in order to create'.[128]

For Milton, the complexity of the relation between good and evil derives fundamentally from the fact that good produces evil, creation creates destruction. This may be the greatest Ovidian paradox in Milton's world. Throughout his works, Ovid is fascinated by the process in which one thing can become its opposite. Classical literature is full of heroic monster-slayers who turn into versions of the monsters they slew; in Ovid, moreover, even innocent victims can turn into merciless murderers. In *Metamorphoses* 13. 439–575 the

---

[127] Stapleton, *Harmful Eloquence*, 42–3. The complex internal narrators in the *Metamorphoses* and *Fasti*, as well as the speakers of the *Heroides*, provide further opportunities for exploration. On the inner voices of the *Metamorphoses* especially see Gianpiero Rosati, 'Narrative Techniques and Narrative Structures in the *Metamorphoses*', in Boyd (ed.), *Brill's Companion to Ovid*, 272–304.

[128] *Remembering and Repeating*, p. xii. Neil Forsyth also discusses at length the sinister relation between good and evil in *The Satanic Epic*.

noble Hecuba, whose entire family has been destroyed, becomes possessed by the desire for revenge and turns first into a child-murderer, and then into a savage dog. The terrifying degradation as much as suffering of this sympathetic figure haunts Shakespeare's Titus Andronicus, Lucrece, and Hamlet.[129] The related story of the raped Philomela (also replayed in *Titus* and alluded to in *The Rape of Lucrece*) shows further how artistic ingenuity can become deadly. Ovid's own end made this even clearer. In *Ars* 1. 34 he protested his poem's innocence: 'inque meo nullum carmine crimen erit' ('there will be no sin in what I sing').[130] But the play on *carmen/crimen* shows he is a liar, as it contains the truth that his own life later will reveal. After all, there is literally (and I mean literally) *crimen* in *carmine*.[131]

The pun is typical of Ovid's use of wordplay and paradox to challenge moral and logical categories by making words synonymous with their opposite; so too in the *Metamorphoses*, Althaea, who must murder her son to appease the shades of her brothers, is 'inpietate pia' ('pious in impiety', 8. 477).[132] These rhetorical transformations have even more obvious counterparts in Ovid's tales of humans turned into new forms.[133] In thinking about such extreme changes of state it seems impossible to avoid tracing the second state back into the first,

---

[129] See *Titus Andronicus*, 1. 1. 136–41, and 4. 1. 20–1; *Hamlet*, 2. 2. 502–18; *The Rape of Lucrece*, 1450–6. As Jonathan Bate notes, Erasmus's endorsement of this particular episode as a good model for the creation of emotion out of *copia* made it especially appealing to Shakespeare and other writers (*Shakespeare and Ovid*, 20). The fact that Seneca had also singled out the scene as an example in which Ovid's uncontrolled wit went too far may have made it even more attractive.

[130] I am grateful to the anonymous reader who generously suggested this witty way of reproducing the Latin pun in English. On this kind of wordplay in Ovid see Frederick Ahl, *Metaformations: Soundplay and Wordplay in Ovid and Other Classical Poets* (Ithaca, NY, 1985).

[131] A point made by Sharrock ('The Politics of Reading', 112), based on a suggestion from Hinds.

[132] See also the stories of Myrrha (*Metamorphoses*, 10. 321–3), and Procne, who claims 'scelus est pietas in coniuge Tereo' ('piety is a crime to such a husband as Tereus', 6. 635). Medea tricks the daughters of Pelias so that: 'his, ut quaeque pia est, hortatibus inpia prima est | et, ne sit scelerata, facit scelus' ('Spurred on by these words, as each was filial she became first in the unfilial act, and that she might not be wicked did the wicked deed', 7. 339–40). While Ovid rather ostentatiously skirts the story of Oedipus, he presents Thebes (Statius and Dante's infernal city) as a place where all paradoxes jumble together: 'ultusque parente parentem | natus erit facto pius et sceleratus eodem' ('son shall avenge parent on parent, filial and accursed in the selfsame act', 9. 407–8).

[133] See further Ahl, *Metaformations*; and Tissol, *The Face of Nature*, 12, 52–61.

in which, we assume, it was already present. Althaea's impiety must somehow already be a property of her *pietas*.[134] We look for causes of the new state in the old one. Similarly, critics of the *Metamorphoses* have often wanted to argue that Ovidian changes are in fact continuous: the clarification of a previously existing essence.[135] In this they may not be that different from the allegorists who also worked to try to create a rational link between before and after states. For Golding, Daphne's original desire for chastity is fulfilled by her transformation into the laurel, associated with that virtue.[136] The first metamorphosis, that of the sacrilegious and savage Lycaon, seems good evidence for this assumption, as Lycaon clearly was a beast all along.[137] This is the kind of metamorphosis Milton will identify with Satan who, in Book 10, 'will become the serpent he already is'.[138] Yet most of the changes in Ovid's poem frustrate the expectations that this episode encourages:[139] the transformation of Dryope into a flower, for example, seems completely arbitrary.

The random nature of these transformations is a source of terror. Identity in Ovid seems too fluid and vulnerable to possession and invasion—so different too from the image projected by the stable Milton. The shocking transformation of Hecuba shows what Martha Nussbaum calls 'the fragility of goodness', its ability to turn into

---

[134] This is certainly the reading Shakespeare gives the line when he adapts it in one of his most Ovidian plays, *Titus Andronicus*, as 'cruel, irreligious piety' (1. 1. 130). This kind of Ovidian paradox, which juxtaposes moral opposites, was extremely popular in both Latin and English writings of the Renaissance.

[135] The argument especially of Solodow in *The World of Ovid's* Metamorphoses.

[136] So Golding observes that in Daphne: 'A myrror of virginitie appeere untoo vs may, | Which yeelding neyther untoo feare, nor force, nor flatterye, | Doth purchace everlasting fame and immortalitye' ('Epistle', in *Shakespeare's Ovid: Being Arthur Golding's Translation of the* Metamorphoses, ed. W. H. D. Rouse (Carbondale, Ill., 1961), ll. 68–70). Sandys also says that '*Daphne* is changed into a never-withering tree, to shew what immortall honour a virgin obtaines by preserving her chastity' (*Ovid's Metamorphosis*, 74). I'll return to this reading in Chs. 1 and 2.

[137] Golding's translation makes this explicit: 'So is he made a ravening Woolf: whose shape expressely drawes | To that the which he was before: his skinne is horie graye, | His looke still grim with glaring eyes, and every kinde of waye | His cruell hart in outward shape dooth well it self bewraye' (1. 276–9). As one of my anonymous readers pointed out, in Latin the repetition of 'eadem', the same, four times in these lines (Ovid, *Met.*, 1. 238–9) makes the point that nothing has changed even more strongly.

[138] William C. Carroll, *The Metamorphoses of Shakespearean Comedy* (Princeton, 1985), 35.

[139] As argued by William S. Anderson in 'Lycaon: Ovid's Deceptive Paradigm in Metamorphoses 1', *Illinois Classical Studies*, 14 (1989), 91–101.

evil.[140] Like Ovid's hybrid figures and verbal paradoxes, however, these abrupt changes of form also challenge us to imagine something almost unimaginable. Similarly, the unpredictability of the sequence of events in the *Metamorphoses*—its structural errancy—provides a narrative analogue for a non-causal and anti-deterministic model for relations and sequence, one in which freedom and rupture may be possible. Ovid introduces the possibility of breaking the chain of fate to imagine new realities.

In *Paradise Lost*, Milton tackles a fall that is as radical as anything in Ovid: the metamorphosis of good into evil. Milton, moreover, has to preserve a difference between before and after states; otherwise, he risks implying that good was evil to begin with, and that creativity is essentially indistinguishable from the forces of destruction.[141] The difficulty of differentiation is woven into the very language of the poem itself. The world of innocence is described in words that already speak of the future yet to come. Like that of Ovid, Milton's language yokes together opposites, as single words—'wanton', 'error'—contain diametrically opposed fallen and unfallen meanings. Commenting on the presence of the morally loaded and Ovidian 'error' in the Eden of *Paradise Lost* 4. 239–40 ('With mazie error under pendant shades | Ran Nectar . . . ') Christopher Ricks explains that 'The evil meaning is consciously and ominously excluded. Rather than the meaning being simply "wandering", it is "wandering (not error)".'[142] As in Milton's infamous double negatives, positive and negative forms are simultaneously invoked. The difference between the conflicting meanings reminds us of the absolute barrier between past and present states. The world now is completely different from that lost world. Yet the

---

[140] See Nussbaum's moving reading of Euripides' *Hecuba* as a grim confrontation with the inability of innocence to sustain itself in the face of evil (*The Fragility of Goodness: Luck and Ethics in Greek Tragedy and Philosophy* (rev. edn., Cambridge, 2001), 397–421). Nussbaum's reading is extremely relevant for Ovid, whose debt to Euripides is apparent in this episode as elsewhere.

[141] Bloom argues that discontinuity is essential also for Milton's relation to the past: 'The identity of past and present is at one with the essential identity of all objects. This is Milton's "universe of death" and with it poetry cannot live, for poetry must leap, it must locate itself in a discontinuous universe, and it must make that universe (as Blake did) if it cannot find one. Discontinuity is freedom' (*The Anxiety of Influence: A Theory of Poetry* (New York, 1973), 39).

[142] *Milton's Grand Style* (Oxford, 1963), 110. See also John Leonard's discussion of 'Self-Contradicting Puns in *Paradise Lost*', in Thomas N. Corns (ed.), *A Companion to Milton* (Oxford, 2001), 393–410.

collision equally tells us what we all know to be true: that world will become this one. The language reminds us that this is a story in which the end is known from the very beginning. There can be no narrative suspense; as Dr Johnson noted, 'what is not unexpected, cannot surprise'.[143]

Milton goes out of his way to make things worse: he further reduces the suspense and heightens foreboding by throwing in classical allusions that remind us of the world produced by the fall. We know all too well what is going to happen.[144] Intertextuality assumes the force of fate: Eve's sinister similarities to the Ovidian Narcissus make the fall seem inevitable from the very start.[145] However, while Ovidian forms help Milton to imagine how good became evil, they also suggest that the chain of causality and foreshadowing might have been broken, that the story might indeed have been rewritten and given another ending. The real challenge in the poem is not to tell us what happened (which we all know) or to explain its causes (which Milton makes in fact more difficult than other writers and exegetes had done), but to stimulate us to break free from our own foreknowledge and to imagine other possibilities. Milton has to convince us that our lives might have been and perhaps might yet become something completely different.

In *Paradise Lost* especially Ovidian forms are not pagan subtexts used to flesh out the bare bones of the Genesis story and prove the general superiority of Christian myth, but a crucial part of Milton's use of his own act of creation to explore the limits of change and freedom. For Milton, and other writers, the Renaissance Ovid was more than just the author of a pagan Bible, or the supplier of handy stories and phrases, or even the source of good tips on how to get

---

[143] Johnson, *Lives*, i. 126.

[144] Dayton Haskin suggests further how contemporary habits of reading the Bible personally as a story about the reader's life could be similarly predetermining in ways that were restrictive as much as consoling: by identifying 'with a story that has already been written' a reader might feel 'that his course has been plotted and that he knows how his own personal story is to come out' (*Milton's Burden*, 18).

[145] Green also notes how 'too often the meaning of an allusion has been determined in advance because of a distorting over-emphasis on its proleptic function. Critics have been eager to alert the reader when a simile, borrowed episode or oblique allusion seems to draw Eve into a web of implication from whose inexorable sequel she cannot escape' (*Milton's Ovidian Eve*, 19). But because of this, 'it is possible to overlook others that lead in a different direction or, more interestingly, are placed under considerable tension' (ibid. 20; see also 179–80).

girls. He is a poet who generated (though not Parthenogenetically) a complicated and interconnected group of questions about poetry and change, and who stimulated the creation of new forms of art both bound to and cut off from the past. The spokesman for artistic immortality, who proclaims the glorious power of rhetoric and art, he also reveals poetry's devastating failure to move its audience. He gave artists a way of making and thinking about art, its purposes and perils, and of imagining the creativity that comes from the constant process of reworking traditions and the past. He raised questions about the boundary between fantasy and reality, suggesting the marvellous, but also dangerous, power of the imagination to make its dreams come true. Creating a world of verbal paradoxes that is populated with figures who are physically double or psychologically divided, he helped later writers confront the irresolvable contradictions of human experience. By remaking Ovid, artists created themselves, while also ensuring that Ovid would, as he prophesied at the end of the *Metamorphoses*, survive, transmuted into new works. Perhaps Milton achieved the greatest metamorphosis of all when he remade Ovidian materials into a narrative for thinking about the fall of man and the English Revolution. Even in an 'age too late' (*PL*, 9. 44) the human imagination can call into being new and wondrous forms.

1

Choosing Ovids (1)

THE ARGUMENT

In this chapter I show how in his early poetry Milton shapes his beginnings through exchanges with Ovid and the Elizabethan Ovidians. The echoes in Milton's Latin elegies suggest that Milton is already engaging seriously with themes that connect all of Ovid's works. Moreover, as he begins writing English verse Milton is still influenced by Ovid's techniques, while also studying earlier English adaptations of Ovid, particularly those of Shakespeare and Spenser. Attentive to the central role that Ovid played in Elizabethan debates over the form and direction of English poetry, Milton unites different Ovids to make his own place in an emerging English literary tradition.

MASTERING THE ARTS OF ALLUSION

Given Ovid's inspiring influence on Renaissance art it is not surprising to see the young Milton 'playing with Ovid'.[1] The many references to Ovid's works throughout Milton's early Latin elegies show a familiarity and desire to experiment with the entire spectrum of Ovid's poetry.[2] As I noted earlier, from the beginning, Milton seems

---

[1] See John K. Hale, 'Milton Playing with Ovid', *Milton Studies*, 25 (1989), 3–19.
[2] Many of these are noted in the *Variorum*; see especially i. 6–21 and the notes to individual poems. I am much indebted to Stella Purce Revard's discussion of the broader classical subtexts for Milton's Latin poems (*Milton and the Tangles of Neaera's Hair: The Making of the 1645 Poems* (Columbia, Mo., 1997), 8–31); and to John K. Hale, 'Artistry and Originality in Milton's Latin Poems', *Milton Quarterly*, 27/4 (1993), 138–49; as well as his *Milton's Languages*. While I disagree with many of

to have been especially drawn to the exilic verse, which provides him with models for his own rustication in 'Elegia 1', and his tutor Thomas Young's 'exile' in Germany in 'Elegia 4'.[3] There are also echoes of Ovid's early erotic works, which suggest a neat correspondence between the two youthful poets. 'Elegia 5', which celebrates the coming of spring in lush images that link natural fertility and creativity, captures particularly well an Ovidian spirit of careless rapture. Milton employs various Ovidian tricks and figures to set the scene: from the rhetorical 'Fallor?' ('Am I tricked?', 5), a noted Ovidian signature which Milton uses elsewhere in the elegies, to the figures of Zephyr (2) and Philomela (25). The presence of the hybrid Sylvanus, 'Semicaperque Deus, semideusque caper' ('a half-goat god and a half-god goat', 122) is a further Ovidian touch, invoking a number of precedents, including *Metamorphoses* 14. 515 and *Fasti* 4. 752, as well as Ovid's general fascination with figures that are physically or psychologically double. Most of all, it recalls Ovid's infamous line 'Semibovemque virum semivirumque bovem' ('the man half-bull and the bull half-man', *Ars Amatoria*, 2. 24), which as I mentioned earlier Seneca had used to illustrate the worst excesses of Ovid's overblown and uncontrolled wit.

Many of these references involve specific verbal echoes, through which Milton plays with Ovid's style and rhetoric. But this is not a superficial form of recreation in either sense: as John Hale has suggested, 'For the meeting of selfhood and poetry in composition, this playing with Ovid had a most liberating and educative impact upon Milton.'[4] Experimenting with Ovid allowed him to try on different voices, genres, and points of view to see how far they could take him as a poet. Moreover, this play indicates Milton's remarkable engagement with Ovidian ideas from the very start. The description of the half-goat god in 'Elegia 5' shows Milton picking up on Ovid's interest in not only hybrid figures but also verbal structures that involve repetition and inversion, and which go in two directions at once. Ovid's 'Fallor' is typical of Ovid's self-presentation as a

---

the conclusions of Jeanne Addison Roberts's 'Anxiety and Influence: Milton, Ovid, and Shakespeare', *South Atlantic Review*, 53/2 (1988), 59–75, I found her close reading of the Ovidian elements of 'Elegia 1' stimulating.

[3] See *Variorum*, i. 47; Revard, *Milton and the Tangles*, 222 n. 34; Burrow, 'Re-embodying Ovid', 315; and Ralph Condee, 'The Latin Poetry of John Milton', in J. W. Binns (ed.), *The Latin Poetry of the English Poets* (London, 1974), 58–92.

[4] Hale, 'Milton Playing', 7. See also his *Milton's Languages*, 34–7.

narrator whose authority is at times a bit shaky. It highlights his favourite theme: the relation between art, illusion, and error.[5] In Milton's 'Elegia 5' and 'Elegia 7', 'Fallor' also appropriately introduces questions concerning the source of poetic inspiration.[6] In 'In proditionem Bombardicam' it frames the typical Ovidian paradox 'cum pietate scelus' (4).[7] In several poems Milton uses another common Ovidian tic, 'nec mora' ('without delay').[8] As we will see further, like Ovid, Milton is particularly interested in the delights but also dangers of *mora*, delay. Moreover, here the phrase announces other Ovidian elements: in 'Elegia 7' it marks the poet's falling in love (69); in 'In quintum Novembris' it leads to the flight of the Ovidian allegorical figure of Fama (208). In 'Elegia 3' (35), it leads to a dream vision that climaxes rather shockingly with an echo of *Amores* 1. 5. 26. (I'll return to this moment shortly.) The exilic 'Elegia 4' plays wittily and subtly on Ovid's exile verse, beginning with the address to the letter as messenger, a moment with several parallels in Ovid.[9] Echoing *Tristia* 3. 8. 1–4, Milton asks the letter to take the chariot of Medea (the heroine of Ovid's lost play, as well as a character in the *Metamorphoses* and *Heroides*), or that which took Triptolemus to Scythia. The direction thus reverses the trajectory of Ovid's epistles, as Germany takes the place of Scythia. Milton presents himself as one of Ovid's friends who is writing to him; the emphasis on Young as Milton's teacher suggests that their relation is modelled on that of Ovid to his female poetic protégée Perilla, to whom *Tristia* 3. 7 is addressed. Like Ovid in barbaric Scythia, Young is surrounded by dangers and signs

---

[5] See Hardie, *Ovid's Poetics of Illusion*, 321–2 especially. The *Variorum* notes that the phrasing was picked up as an Ovidian mannerism by other writers (i. 17, 97 n. 5).

[6] 'Elegia 5' opens by suggesting that poetic inspiration comes from nature itself, as the poet asks: 'Fallor? an & nobis redeunt in carmina vires, | Ingeniumque mihi munere veris adest?' ('Am I tricked, or does strength, too, come back to my songs? | My genius present by a gift of spring?', 5–6). In 'Elegia 7' the poet's powers seem to come from the girls whose eyes dazzle him so much that he wonders: 'Fallor? an & radios hinc quoque Phoebus habet' ('Am I wrong or does Phoebus get his beams | from there [the girl's eyes] as well?', 56). Even Apollo, Sun and god of poetry, seems to derive his power from love.

[7] The full couplet is: 'Fallor? an & mitis voluisti ex parte videri, | Et pensare malâ cum pietate scelus' ('did you—or am I mistaken?—wish to appear forgiving, | to balance out your crime with twisted honor?', 3–4).

[8] The *Variorum* notes that this Ovidianism was also taken up by Renaissance writers (i. 72 n. 35).

[9] *Variorum*, i. 80–1; see especially *Tristia* 1. 1, 3. 7. 1; and *Ex Ponto* 4. 5. See also below Ch. 5 and 'Go Little Book'.

of war: 'Te tamen intereà belli circumsonat horror' ('war's horror sounds all around you', 83).[10] The parallels enable Milton also to play implicitly on the difference between the two situations: Milton assures Young that he has a protector more powerful and merciful than Augustus—God—who will in the end guarantee his return home. Such passages and others suggest that as Milton learns to master Ovid's verbal tricks he experiments with the major themes that unify his work. Ovid, with the Ovidian Young, is Milton's teacher, to whom he is paying subtle tribute.

Moreover, Milton seems to be studying Ovid's arts of allusion to aid his own general revision of classical sources. In some passages, Milton combines an Ovidian reference with a Virgilian one, or uses a 'double allusion', imitating phrases in which Ovid imitates Virgil. Let's look again at Milton's treatment of Ovid's signature hybrid figure in 'Elegia 5'. The *Variorum* notes that the first line in the couplet, which describes 'Sylvanusque suâ Cyparissi fronde revinctus, | Semicaperque Deus, semideusque caper' ('Sylvanus also, crowned with his own Cypress, | a half-goat god and a half-god goat', 121–2), recalls Virgil's *Georgics* 1. 20.[11] As I noted, however, the couplet is completed by an especially resonant Ovidian phrase. The effect of the combination is to give a Virgilian character an Ovidian form. Milton has out-Ovided Ovid by creating a hybrid poetics that yokes together Virgil and Ovid in a single couplet—in which Virgil fittingly falls in the epic hexameter and Ovid the pentameter.[12] Ovidian excess and Virgilian restraint are coupled in a fruitful tension. Elsewhere Milton invokes the poets through a double allusion that reveals a dynamic debate between the two, which he then enters. His claim in 'Elegia 6' that 'Carmen amat Bacchum, Carmina Bacchus amat' ('Song loves Bacchus; Bacchus loves songs', 14) looks back to *Fasti* 5. 345 ('Bacchus amat flores'), which in turn reworks *Georgics* 2. 113 ('Bacchus amat colles'). Milton's echo reveals the intertextual chain in which *colles* is replaced by *flores*, which then gives way to *carmen*. In each case, the object of Bacchus' affection is used to make a statement of

---

[10] See for example *Tristia* 5. 3. 11: 'nunc procul a patria Geticis circumsonor armis' ('now far from my country I am surrounded by the clash of Getic arms').

[11] 'et teneram ab radice ferens, Silvane, cupressum' ('and you, Silvanus, with a young uprooted cypress in thy hand').

[12] Roberts suggests that Milton draws generally on Ovid's own exploitation of the elegiac couplet's alternating lines to reflect conflict ('Anxiety and Influence', 59); here, however, it also enables him to contain apparently opposing poetic forces.

poetic vision. In Virgil, 'Bacchus loves hills' is first of all simply a way of explaining why grapes need to be planted on slopes, rather than on easier plains. But it ties into the larger concerns of Virgil's poem in which the arts of agriculture, the cultivation of land through hard work, are analogous to the poet's own arts.[13] As a response to Virgil's georgic world of endless work, Ovid's celebration of a year revolving around holidays in the *Fasti* formulates a different model for poetry.[14] Ovid's god therefore prefers a softer and easier life; he loves the more domesticated forms of nature—not open hills, but flowers. Ovid is drawing here on the traditional link of flowers with the arts of poetry/poesy, an association which Milton makes explicit by turning *flores* into *carmen*. While Virgil's Bacchus inspires poetry of hard work, that of Ovid and Milton produces the poetry of holidays.

Milton's use of repeated verbal patterns and figures of speech and thought thus shows sensitivity to key Ovidian themes and rhetorical figures that run through all of Ovid's works. He is attentive also to the nuances of Ovid's relation to Virgil.[15] His own art, like that of Ovid, begins in dialogue with others, which mirrors his exchange with Young.[16] Moreover, in 'Elegia 4', 29–32, Milton transforms a famous Virgilian claim of originality, 'primus ego in patriam mecum, modo vita supersit, | Aonio rediens deducam vertice Musas' ('I first, if life but remain, will return to my country, bringing the Muses with me in triumph from the Aonian peak' (*Georgics*, 3. 10–11), into a statement of intellectual indebtedness and gratitude to his sources:

> Primus ego Aonios illo praeeunte recessus
> Lustrabam, & bifidi sacra vireta jugi,

---

[13] Virgil's description thus also allows him to tame a dangerous god who, as he will remind us later in the same book, can lead his followers to madness and death (*Georgics*, 2. 455–7). Here instead Bacchus is transformed into a farmer, who turns even a difficult landscape into something fruitful.

[14] For Ovid's reply to Virgil, see especially Elaine Fantham, 'Ceres, Liber and Flora: Georgic and Anti-Georgic Elements in Ovid's *Fasti*', *Proceedings of the Cambridge Philological Society*, 38 (1992), 39–56. I return to the significance of holidays for both Ovid and Milton in Ch. 2.

[15] The figure of *Fama* in 'Elegia 4' and 'In quintum Novembris', also looks back to Ovid's rewriting of Virgil's figure from *Aeneid* 4; see Harding, *Milton and the Renaissance Ovid*, 53; and Philip Hardie, 'Christian Conversions of Fama', in *Rumour and Renown: Studies in the History of Fama* (Cambridge, 2011), 429–38.

[16] See also Hale, 'Artistry and Originality', who notes how the themes of relationship and especially friendship unite the Latin poems as a whole.

> Pieriosque hausi latices, Clioque favente,
> Castalio sparsi laeta ter ora mero.

> ('I journeyed by his lead first on Aonian paths,
> and the sacred glens of the twin-peaked mountain.
> I drank the Pierian springs with Clio's favor and splashed
> my joyful lips three times with pure Castalia')

The young poet does not claim to be the first to lead the Muses to a new land, but acknowledges how his teacher has led him to poetry. Thomas Greene notes how poets use allusion to create myths about their origins: 'When... intertextuality becomes self-conscious, it tends to become etiological.'[17] Through his revision of the past, Milton shapes his own poetic beginnings.

FIRST FLOWERS

While Milton's early use of Ovid in the Latin verse begins in simple rhetorical appropriations it shows that he quickly became familiar with Ovid's habit of thought, and grasped the larger concerns of his poetry. Moreover, the presence of Ovid can be felt as Milton moves from Latin into the terrain of English verse.

Milton's earliest English poem, 'On the Death of a fair Infant dying of a Cough', seems generally an exercise in forms of metamorphosis. One of the oddest transformations is that of the ostensible subject of the poem—a dead infant—into a dizzying array of figures: a flower (1), Primrose (2), Spirit (38), Starr (43), Astraea (50), Youth (53), truth (54), and one 'of the golden-winged hoast' (57). There is a striking discrepancy between the explicit bluntness of the title and the periphrastic poem. If it weren't for the title it could be difficult to figure out the exact occasion of the work; there is nothing resembling a cough, or for that matter an infant, in the poem itself. The domestic context of the title, with its attention to precise details, disappears in a flurry of images that build to create a scene of cosmic dimensions stretching from earth to heaven and back again. While commemorative poems of this time typically use inflated imagery to enhance the

---

[17] *The Light in Troy*, 18.

dignity of their subjects, not all the machinery in this hurly-burly seems to be appropriate or to invest the occasion with dignity. In particular, the opening representation of the infant's death as the result of her attempted rape by a personified Winter seems jarringly grotesque and out of keeping with both the subject and the rest of the poem. The metamorphosis of a dead infant into an object of desire involves a wit even Ovid might have found extreme. As Jackson I. Cope notes drily, rape 'is scarcely appropriate as consolation to the mother of a dead infant'.[18] Nor, one might add, is it an obvious metaphor for the cause of death, which, the title makes quite clear, was in reality a *cough*. However, this metamorphosis of a cough into a botched cosmological seduction scene is important to understanding Milton's development as a poet: it suggests some of the questions he was thinking about at this stage and also the writers he was thinking through. The poem shows Milton's origins as a poet out of the metamorphosis of Ovid.

Milton seems to have recognized that 'On the Death of a fair Infant' was not an unadulterated success; he decided not to include it in his 1645 *Poems*, which was designed to display his maturation and discovery of vocation.[19] When he later chose to publish the poem in the revised 1673 edition, he may have intended it to be read as it most often is: as an interesting if immature stage of his career, in which one can glimpse signs of the greater works to come.[20] It pushes the topic of premature death, a subject which preoccupies Milton in many of his early works, to an extreme, celebrating an infant who dies

---

[18] 'Fortunate Falls as Form in Milton's "Fair Infant"', *Journal of English and Germanic Philology*, 63 (1964), 662.

[19] On the coherence of this volume and its presentation of Milton's 'rise' as a poet, see especially Martz, *Poet of Exile*, 31–59; and John K. Hale, 'Milton's Self-Presentation in *Poems . . . 1645*', *Milton Quarterly*, 25/2 (1991), 37–48.

[20] The few critics who have bothered much with it at all generally treat it in this way. Hugh N. MacLean sees Milton's attempt in this poem to transform pagan imagery to create a Christian meaning as preparation for the synthesis of the 'Nativity Ode', another poem about an infant's birth in which death, while not instantaneous, is present ('Milton's Fair Infant', *English Literary History*, 24 (1957), 296–305; see 298–9 especially). In the grappling with premature death Milton already seems to be gesturing towards 'Lycidas' and 'Epitaphium Damonis'. For Cope the poem is a trial run for *Paradise Lost*: the story of the fall of innocence through pride and its ultimate redemption ('Fortunate Falls'). For Donald Cameron Allen the poem is, more broadly, 'a vivid indication of the poet's mature technique' (*The Harmonious Vision: Studies in Milton's Poetry* (Baltimore, 1954), 47).

almost as soon as she is born.[21] In the 1673 volume he presented it as one of his earliest works, written 'anno aetatis 17'. While it is now commonly thought that Milton actually wrote the poem at 19, his retrospective dating of it aligns it with a group of other poems he also dated as from this year: 'Elegia 2', 'Elegia 3', 'In Obitum Praesulis Eliensis', and 'In quintum Novembris'.[22] While the rest of these works are in Latin, they share with 'On the Death of a fair Infant' the poet's growing sense of his vocation against the background of the consciousness of mortality. While death threatens the poet's career it also propels it: the elegy is a standard form of poetic apprenticeship which enables the young man to consider how he might achieve the spiritual and poetical immortality he already desires. The movement upwards in all these poems towards a vision of paradise (represented satirically in 'In quintum Novembris' as Satan's foiled attempt to send James I to heaven by gunpowder), though conventional in the elegy, also reflects the eager young poet's aspirations to poetic flight. Thus 'On the Death of a fair Infant' concludes with the image of the child returned to heaven and a promise to the mother of immortal rewards that is really intended for the ambitious poet himself:

> Think what a present thou to God hast sent,
> And render him with patience what he lent;
> This if thou do he will an off-spring give,
> That till the worlds last-end shall make thy name to live. (74–7)

---

[21] While other writers—notably Virgil and Spenser—represent early death frequently, Milton seems determined to imagine a death even more premature than previously imagined. In fact, the one possible degree further—death *before* birth—appears in 'An Epitaph on the Marchioness of Winchester', in which 'The haples Babe before his birth | Had burial, yet not laid in earth, | And the languisht Mothers Womb Was not long a living Tomb' (31–4). The traditional womb/tomb rhyme encapsulates the paradoxical collapsing of birth and death—a paradox that Milton will explore again in *Paradise Lost* 2, in which he narrates the birth of death itself. As we will see further, like Ovid, Milton is fascinated from early on by moments in which a creative act becomes destructive.

[22] While the error might have been that of a compositor, the care Milton took with this volume makes it likely that it was his own decision to make this one of his earliest, and therefore most immature, poems. Noting Milton's obsessive though questionable self-dating, Edward Le Comte suggests that the 1673 poems were presented to emphasize the young poet's precocious development (*Milton's Unchanging Mind: Three Essays* (Port Washington, NY, 1973), 5–68). For Le Comte, this was part of Milton's preoccupation with time, to which I return in the next chapter.

As Edward Le Comte noted, Milton's poem 'sets the lifelong pattern of starting with mortality and ending with immortality'.[23] Despite his youth, Milton is already preoccupied with the transcendence of death and time through art. But the cause of death—the choking of air in a cough—suggests his fears that his first early attempts at 'inspiration' will themselves prove artistically fatal.

The poem also shows that, as Milton begins writing English poetry, he is reading and studying a range of English works. The *Variorum* notes the different sources and traditions that have been spotted in the poem.[24] As in the Latin poetry, Milton seems to be playing with different models. However, while in the Latin poetry it is possible to trace sources through precise verbal echoes, identifying specific models here seems a dicier project.[25] Many of the images and conventions used are widespread, as if Milton were absorbing a kind of homogenized tradition. The opening conceit is evocative partly because it seems to include so many possible sources. The child is first addressed as:

> O Fairest flower no sooner blown but blasted,
> Soft silken Primrose fading timelesslie. (1–2)

As an image of premature death, the flower is everywhere in the classical and Renaissance tradition. The diction too—the use of alliteration to express paradox, here the meeting of two antithetical states (birth and death) in a single instant—is ubiquitous in English poetry. In general, however, there is something a little old-fashioned, specifically Elizabethan, about the language and style of the poem. The rhyme royal and final alexandrine could suggest that Milton is already under the influence of Spenser and the Spenserians, especially the Fletchers.[26] It might be possible to catch an echo of Spenser's 'Januarye Eclogue' in the first lines:

---

[23] Ibid. 14.
[24] *Variorum*, ii, pt. 1, 119–35.
[25] On the problems of distinguishing allusion from 'accidental confluence, inevitable between poets dealing with a shared or related language' see Thomas, *Reading Virgil and his Texts*, 116; and Hinds, *Allusion and Intertext*, 17–51. Charles Martindale also notes places where Milton tends to draw on an entire tradition (*John Milton and the Transformation of Ancient Epic*, 4–6).
[26] This line of influence has been frequently noted; see Hanford, 'The Youth of Milton', 96–9. The *Variorum* also notes further parallels with Du Bartas and Donne that suggest Milton's attention to 'modern' English poetry generally (ii, pt. 1, 120–1).

> My timely buds with wayling all are wasted:
> The blossome, which my braunch of youth did beare,
> With breathed sighes is blowne away and blasted. (38–40)

Given both Milton's subject and his own concerns at this time with his future, it seems plausible that he was attentive to this eclogue, in which Spenser, at the start of his career, faces the spectre of an early end (though one not quite as early as that of this barely alive infant).[27]

But these Spenserian elements are combined with something quite different that erupts with the striking turn at the end of the first stanza. In the first four lines, Milton compresses the death of the child into images that convey her compressed life. In the fifth line, however, Milton abruptly shifts from static 'timeless' description to dynamic narrative, to a world of time and activity, full of the quickly shifting images that will dominate the rest of the poem. For the next two and a half stanzas, too, the poem becomes a dramatic mini-epyllion in which the event of the title is represented through an allegorical scene. The description of the infant as 'Summers chief honour if thou hadst out-lasted | Bleak winters force that made thy blossome drie' (3–4) springs to life and action. While winter first enters the poem as part of the background, and as a symbol for death, it takes on a life of its own when it is transformed from a season into a personified character with deadly designs on the infant. The sudden turn propels the poem in a rather unexpected direction, into a scene of a badly bungled rape. The infant becomes the innocent victim of Winter's unwanted desire:

> For he being amorous on that lovely die
>   That did thy cheek envermeil, thought to kiss
> But kill'd alas, and then bewayl'd his fatal bliss.
>
> For since grim Aquilo his charioter
> By boistrous rape th'Athenian damsel got,
> He thought it toucht his Deitie full neer,
> If likewise he some fair one wedded not,
> Thereby to wipe away th' infamous blot,

---

[27] As was pointed out to me during a discussion of a version of this chapter at the Northeastern Milton Seminar, Milton's echo involves a clever redefinition of Spenser's 'blown'. Where in Spenser 'blowne away' is synonymous with 'blasted', Milton uses 'blown' to mean 'born', thus turning synonyms into antonyms—which then collapse back into identity as the infant's birth coincides with death.

Of long-uncoupled bed, and childless eld,
Which 'mongst the wanton gods a foul reproach was held.

So mounting up in ycie-pearled carr,
Through middle empire of the freezing aire
He wandered long, till thee he spy'd from farr,
There ended was his quest, there ceast his care.
Down he descended from his Snow-soft chaire,
   But all unwares with his cold-kind embrace
Unhous'd thy Virgin Soul from her fair biding place. (5–21)

Another influence seems to have possessed the poem, as Ovid announces his presence in Milton's first English poem rather aggressively, and perhaps indelicately. As David Daiches notes, the scene clearly shows 'echoes of Ovid and Ovid's way of handling mythological stories'.[28] It seems a spin-off from Ovid's story of the rape of Orithyia by Boreas (*Met.*, 6. 682–713). In Milton's poem, Boreas, to whom Milton refers as Aquilo, is made the charioteer of Winter.[29] Observing his employee's marriage, Winter feels it is time to get a wife for himself. The plot follows the predictable Ovidian pattern in which a god's descent into the world is destructive, as divine desire leads to human metamorphosis or death.

Such scenes are of course ubiquitous in Ovid, whose *Metamorphoses* has been described as 'an epic of rape'.[30] Even more distressingly, Ovid makes rape a principle of creativity. Ovid's rapes often lead to the foundation of new forms: the birth of poetry in Daphne (*Met.*, 1. 452–567) and Philomela (6. 424–674), of Europe in Europa (2. 833–75, 6. 103–7), of the Republic in Lucretia (*Fasti*, 2. 685–856). As Lynn Enterline also notes, Ovidian tales create a disturbing 'alliance between rape and poetry'.[31] Such scenes were as problematic for

---

[28] *Milton* (London, 1957), 24–5.
[29] Milton's choice of name for the character may suggest he is recalling Horace's famous *Odes* 3. 30.1, in which 'Aquilo impotens' is one of the hostile forces against which Horace triumphantly asserts his own immortality.
[30] Segal, *Landscape in Ovid's* Metamorphoses, 93.
[31] *The Rhetoric of the Body*, 20. The question is whether Ovid critiques or complies with—even enjoys—the violence against women he describes. Enterline argues that Ovid contests the alliance of art and sexual violence; he is sympathetic to violated women who, she suggests, become subjects as they become objects and so offers 'a critique of the systematic violence and subordination embedded in patriarchal culture' rather than 'a mere repetition or perpetuation of it' (ibid. 33). Amy Richlin claims, however, that 'if the *Metamorphoses* lays bare a cruel cosmos, it does so voluptuously'; she believes Ovid enjoys the spectacle of female pursuit and fear ('Reading Ovid's

earlier readers as they are for modern ones. Medieval commentators and teachers had tried to chasten Ovid generally, reading the erotic poems as anti-erotic didactic.[32] As Mark Amsler notes, for perhaps obvious reasons, 'Ovid's rape narratives were the objects of some of the strongest mastering allegorical readings in the later Middle Ages.'[33] The stories were allegorized as *aitia* of natural or divine forces. Moreover, rape was read as an allegory of rapture; sexual desire, as the desire for spiritual transcendence.[34] For Pierre Bersuire, the story of Apollo and Daphne shows 'wisdom's desire for purity and spiritual virginity that transcends the body'.[35] Whereas in Ovid rape is usually the cause of the metamorphosis of a higher (human) into a lower (natural) form, in the allegorical tradition the direction is reversed.

For Cope, this mode of interpreting Ovid provides the key to understanding the erotic scene in 'On the Death of a fair Infant': 'The rationale for this unpromising metaphor will emerge only in later stanzas, where one discovers that if the narrative originates in the Ovidian text, the significance originates in the Christian commentaries.'[36] He argues that Milton is following the method of the allegorists to absorb stories of erotic violence into a moralized poetics. The apparent indecorum in the poem vanishes if rape is sublimated

---

Rapes', 176). For her, therefore, rape is the 'essence' of Ovid's point of view throughout his works (ibid. 162). Richlin's argument approaches the old attacks on the shallowness of Ovid's wit from a feminist perspective, in which he is seen as witty at women's expense especially. If, as Richlin argues, 'the pornographic is that which converts living beings into objects' (ibid. 158), then metamorphosis is pornography. Yet as she also suggests, the question of pornography is closely allied to the problem of the relation between fantasy and reality—the central question of Ovidian poetics which might in fact be used to interrogate the nature of pornography rather than be condemned as an expression of it.

[32] On the continuation of this practice in the pedagogy and writing of the 1500s see Edward Paleit, 'Sexual and Political Liberty and Neo-Latin Poetics: The *Heroides* of Mark Alexander Boyd', *Renaissance Studies*, 22/3 (2008), 351–67.

[33] 'Rape and Silence: Ovid's Mythography and Medieval Readers', in Elizabeth Robertson and Christine M. Rose (eds.), *Representing Rape: Medieval and Early Modern Literature* (New York, 2001), 92.

[34] Such interpretations were supported by Plato's use of the story of Ganymede in *Phaedrus* 255c; see Hulse, *Metamorphic Verse*, 79; and Edgar Wind, *Pagan Mysteries in the Renaissance* (2nd edn., London, 1968), 154.

[35] Amsler, 'Rape and Silence', 79; see the commentary in Moss, *Latin Commentaries on Ovid from the Renaissance*, 89.

[36] 'Fortunate Falls', 662.

into apotheosis, just as the infant is transfigured in the second part of the poem from a small child to a principle of cosmic order.[37]

Such an interpretation would seem to be confirmed by Milton's use of the (of course very common) Latin verb *rapere* in the other poems he claimed were written in the same year.[38] While, in 'Elegia 2', Milton notes simply that 'Ultima praeconum praeconem te quoque saeva | Mors rapit' ('that last beadle of beadles, cruel Death, took you too', 3–4), in the other elegies, the verb is used to suggest that death is the transition to a higher state: the heroes in the Lowlands in 'Elegia 3' are 'ad aethera raptos' (11) and the Bishop of Ely describes his joyful ascent through death:

> Hanc ut vocantem laetus audivi, citò
> Foedum reliqui carcerem,
> Volatilesque faustus inter milites
> Ad astra sublimis feror:
> Vates ut olim raptus ad coelum senex
> Auriga currus ignei.

('When I happily heard her calling, I quickly
left my filthy prison
and was carried high and blessed to the stars
among winged soldiers.
So once the old priest was taken to heaven,
a fiery chariot's driver', 'In Obitum Praesulis Eliensis', 45–50)

Transforming sexual violation into spiritual ascent is one way in which Milton could use a poet of rape to create a poetry that celebrates the power of chastity.[39] Many of his early poems are written about virgins. Milton frequently shows the reward of chastity to be ascent to heaven, although sometimes, as in the case of the infant, the

---

[37] Reading the poem in the context of this Ovidian tradition, Cope sees it as a version of the fortunate fall which he also finds in *Paradise Lost*; for Cope the poem concludes with 'a triumphant paean of promise'; 'it turns the apparent prematurity of "death" into the instrument of triumph over death' ('Fortunate Falls', 671).

[38] *Rapere* has a range of meanings: its most basic sense is to seize and carry off, though this meaning also has connotations of violence and the use of force (as in pillage).

[39] Many writers have discussed the importance of chastity in Milton's early works; see especially William Kerrigan, *The Sacred Complex: On the Psychogenesis of* Paradise Lost (Cambridge, Mass., 1983), 26–37; and William Shullenberger, *Lady in the Labyrinth: Milton's* Comus *as Initiation* (Madison, NJ, 2008), 175–202.

arrival seems a little on the early side.[40] For Milton, moreover, chastity is not just the subject of poetry, it is its origins: in 'Elegia 6' he argues that the poet who restrains his natural appetites will rise to a supernatural vision of the secrets of heaven and hell (55–76). In imagining the apotheoses of his subjects Milton therefore also figures his own elevation through sexual restraint.

I will say more about the relation between Ovidian rape and Miltonic chastity in the next chapter. But there seems to me a difference between the conventional use of *rapere* in the Latin verse and the use of a particularized Ovidian scene of rape in 'On the Death of a fair Infant'. There is equally a tension between the erotic description in the first part of the poem and the mystical ascent of the end. A similar disjunction appears in a subtler form at the end of 'Elegia 3', which superimposes Lancelot Andrewes's entrance into paradise onto Ovid's famous description in *Amores* 1. 5. 26 of his afternoon of fabulous sex with Corinna—a rather different method of entering paradise![41] The chaste apotheosis of the Bishop sits oddly on this archetypal example of the 'Ovidian fantasy of ravishment'.[42] Similarly, in 'In Obitum Praesulis Eliensis' the Bishop's rapturous ascent to the stars is modelled on the disastrous trip of Phaethon in *Metamorphoses* 2—a 'rapture' that leads to premature death. The Ovidian subtexts of these poems aren't quietly laid to rest by Christian appropriation. They stick out slightly, just as in 'On the Death of a fair

---

[40] Stephen Fallon also notes other early poems in which the young Milton claims that the rewards for a chaste life will be 'rapt flight' (*Milton's Peculiar Grace*, 52). Fallon shows the ambiguity of rapture in *Paradise Lost*, which he links to the poet's own claims for authority: 'To be seized or "rapt" is a signature boast *and* fear for Milton' (ibid. 209). For a very different and provocative reading of rape and ravishment in Milton, see Katherine Eggert's *Showing Like a Queen: Female Authority and Literary Experiment in Spenser, Shakespeare, and Milton* (Philadelphia, 2000), 22–50.

[41] The layers may be even more complex, however: Stephen Hinds has argued that Ovid overlays a scene of seduction on a landscape associated in Roman poetry with divine epiphany ('Generalising about Ovid', *Ramus*, 16 (1988), 4–11). If Milton recognizes the conventional features Ovid is adapting, he could be either restoring them to their original sacred meaning or, as he will later, continuing Ovid's interest in the fluidity between the spiritual and the sensual.

[42] Heather James, 'The Poet's Toys: Christopher Marlowe and the Liberties of Erotic Elegy', *Modern Language Quarterly*, 67/1 (2006), 121. James argues that Marlowe especially is fascinated by such moments 'in which the body goes slack while the mind ranges in the zodiac of its own capricious wit' (ibid.). As we will see later in this chapter, the example of Marlovian Ovidianism is relevant, especially given the importance of Marlowe's translation of the *Amores*.

Infant' the opening allegorical scene seems to clash with and resist the Christian conclusion.

While most critics have seen the poem as divided and ultimately damaged by the incompatibility of the pagan and Christian traditions,[43] I think that the tension is fruitful and stems from a rather different source. The poem shows different types of Ovidianism vying for attention. It clearly demonstrates Milton's familiarity with Ovid and, equally, with allegorical ways of treating Ovid. However, it also shows that Milton was studying the English writers who had adapted Ovid's works. E. M. W. Tillyard noted in passing that the poem seems 'in the tradition of the Ovidising Elizabethans, of poems like *Hero and Leander* and *Venus and Adonis*'.[44] 'On the Death of a fair Infant' suggests that, in the same year that the adolescent Milton was trying his hand at one type of compact epic in 'In quintum Novembris', he experimented with another kind in this compressed epyllion which looks back to his English predecessors.

While I suggested a Spenserian analogue for the poem's opening, the language simultaneously points us in a rather different direction, towards Milton's most important and formidable Ovidian precursor. Since Todd, critics have noted the Shakespearian, or pseudo-Shakespearian, echo under the flower image:

> Sweet rose, fair flower, untimely plucked, soon vaded,
> Plucked in the bud, and vaded in the spring (*The Passionate Pilgrim*, 10. 1–2)[45]

Like other poems in *The Passionate Pilgrim*, this poem is not now considered to have been written by Shakespeare; the volume was published as his in order to cash in on the enormous popularity of *Venus and Adonis*.[46] I obviously have no idea what Milton thought about the work's attribution (there had been doubts early on), but it is likely that he knew the poem. A faint Shakespearian strain is present

---

[43] Allen suggests that the disjunction is a deliberate reflection of the unbridgeable gap between the pagan and Christian visions (*The Harmonious Vision*); MacLean, however, sees the lack of synthesis as itself due to Milton's poetic immaturity ('Milton's Fair Infant').

[44] *Milton* (rev. edn., London, 1930), 19; see also Cleanth Brooks and John Edward Hardy, *The Poems of Mr. John Milton: The 1645 Edition with Essays in Analysis* (New York, 1951), 240.

[45] See *Variorum*, ii, pt. 1, 128.

[46] On the publication and reception history of the volume, see Burrow (ed.), *The Complete Sonnets and Poems*, 74–81.

in his own opening stanza, which may explain the pun on the word 'die' in line 5—the die of the infant's cheek attracts winter and so she must *die*.[47] The strain becomes stronger and more specific when we move from description into action and the scene of attempted rape. If the first verse of the poem opens with an echo of a Shakespearian copy, it closes with lines that come closer to the original itself. The stanza ends when Winter falls in love with the infant and 'thought to kiss | But kill'd alas, and then bewayl'd his fatal bliss' ('On the Death of a fair Infant', 6–7). Killing kisses of fatal bliss are all over Renaissance love poetry, and poets did not need Ovid or anyone else to teach them that desire gets you into trouble. Still, the wording is suggestively similar to that of Shakespeare's Venus, who complains that the boar that murdered Adonis 'thought to kiss him, and hath killed him so' (*Venus and Adonis*, 1110). In the mythological tradition, the boar was commonly identified with Winter, Milton's cradle robber. Milton's scene seems to offer a sped-up and stripped-down version of Shakespeare's poem.[48]

For a young poet interested in turning Ovid into English, Shakespeare's poem would have been an obvious model.[49] As the publication of *The Passionate Pilgrim* indicates, *Venus and Adonis* had been both hugely popular and generative—for better or worse it stimulated the imaginations of Shakespeare's contemporaries.

---

[47] With her usual superb ear, Jennifer Lewin also picked out the Shakespearian rhythms in this line, pointing out to me that 'For he being amorous on that lovely die' echoes Titania's description of her votress's death in childbirth: 'But she, being mortal, of that boy did die' (*A Midsummer Night's Dream*, 2. 1. 135). Both passages unite generation and destruction; Milton's substitution of 'amorous' for 'mortal' seems especially clever in its reinforcement of eros as a deadly force. If we return also to the 'blown/blasted' relation which I traced to Spenser, there is another Shakespearian echo; shocked by the (apparently) mad Hamlet, Ophelia cries out at 'That unmatch'd form and stature of blown youth | Blasted with ecstasy' (*Hamlet*, 3. 1. 159–60). Perhaps my point is simply that it is hard for anyone writing English at this time not to write Shakespeare.

[48] It could even be considered a gloss on Venus' complaint to Death that, in hitting Adonis, he missed his mark: 'Thy mark is feeble age, but thy false dart | Mistakes that aim, and cleaves an infant's heart' (941–2). It also recalls broadly Shakespeare's other epyllion, *The Rape of Lucrece*: 'No man inveigh against the withered flower, | But chide rough winter that the flower hath killed' (1254–5).

[49] Roberts suggests, if somewhat indirectly, a relation between *Venus and Adonis* and 'Elegia 1'. Her reading, however, turns Milton himself into a version of Adonis who flees from the sensuality of London (and Ovid) to the safety of chaste Cambridge; she argues therefore that 'Milton is rejecting Ovid even as he imitates him' ('Anxiety and Influence', 68).

While not the first epyllion, it propelled the vogue for the genre, and for Ovidianism in general. Shakespeare shows not only how to transform Ovidian plots, taking his from *Metamorphoses* 10, but also how to turn Ovid's use of wit and paradox into English. There are other reasons why this poem might have been an appropriate model for a young poet declaring his poetical ambitions, eager to enter into the network of relations that bound classical and English writers.[50] Shakespeare presented *Venus and Adonis* to the public as 'the first heir of my invention';[51] it was the poem in which 'he announced himself as a poet',[52] rather than a mere playwright. The volume opened with an Ovidian epigraph that suggested Shakespeare's intention to establish himself as a serious writer: 'vilia miretur vulgus; mihi flavus Apollo | pocula Castalia plena ministret aqua' ('Let what is cheap excite the marvel of the crowd; for me may golden Apollo minister full cups from the Castalian fount', *Amores*, 1. 15. 35–6). As Ovid helped Shakespeare, Shakespeare helps Milton enter the English literary scene. At the same time, his Shakespearian source gives him the chance to reflect on his uncertainty as well as ambition. Like 'On the Death of a fair Infant', *Venus and Adonis* raises the spectre of prematurity and early death. From the start, Adonis is described as 'unripe' (128, 524) and 'too green' (806); he warns Venus:

> Who plucks the bud before one leaf put forth?
> If springing things be any jot diminished
> They wither in their prime, prove nothing worth. (416–18; see also 523–5)

The story of an early end anticipates Milton's self-consciousness about his own beginnings and about his art in general.

Ovid's tale is well chosen for both Shakespeare's and Milton's poetic self-fashionings. Traditionally, the story of Adonis, like that

---

[50] A different echo in the concluding consolation to the mother in 'On the Death of a fair Infant' 74–7 may suggest Milton's ambition here. Cyril Tourneur's *The Transformed Metamorphosis* (1600), also written in rhyme royal, laments the decay of English poetry after the death of Spenser but prays to the Muses: 'be your heart from despaire wonne: | Your wombe may bring forth such another sonne' (D5ʳ). Citations from Tourneur's poetry are taken from *The Transformed Metamorphosis* (London, 1600), Early English Books Online. Tourneur uses Ovidian images of transformation to describe the fall of English art; Milton here is beginning to present himself as its reviver.

[51] Burrow (ed.), *Complete Poems and Sonnets*, 173.

[52] A. C. Hamilton, '*Venus and Adonis*', in Philip C. Kolin (ed.), *Venus and Adonis: Critical Essays* (New York, 1997), 153.

of Persephone, was an *aition* of seasonal change: killed by the boar which symbolizes winter, Adonis is reborn every spring, renewed by nature.[53] As I noted earlier, however, the image of the flower is itself a conventional image for poetry/poesy. Like other stories of young men turned into flowers, including that of Hyacinthus to which Milton alludes in 'On the Death of a fair Infant' 22–8, Ovid's story shows the origins of art. Venus promises that the dead boy will live on:

> luctus monimenta manebunt
> semper, Adoni, mei, repetitaque mortis imago
> annua plangoris peraget simulamina nostri.

('My grief, Adonis, shall have an enduring monument, and each passing year in memory of your death shall give an imitation of my grief', *Met.*, 10. 725–7)

Venus's language (*monimenta*, *imago*) suggests how Ovid has characteristically transformed a story originally about *nature* into one about *art*. Like the end of the *Metamorphoses* as a whole, the story offers the promise of immortality through art. But, like so many other Ovidian stories, it also suggests that art originates in destructive and deadly desire.

Later commentaries tended to focus on the myth of Venus and Adonis as a simple moral tale that shows how sensual desire is incompatible with heroic action and leads to death. Until fairly recently, Shakespeare's epyllion was read frequently as part of this tradition of allegorizing Ovid.[54] But Shakespeare's revision of the original complicates the situation. His Adonis rejects Venus' advances. Sex may lead to death but in this case, chastity does as well—a message that *The Rape of Lucrece* will drive home. It hardly seems fair or to give one much of a choice.[55] Moreover, by uncoupling Ovid's couple, Shakespeare puts a fundamental schism at the centre of the poem. Eros, the traditional force that brings together opposites,

---

[53] Sandys recounts the Phoenician rituals associated with Adonis (*Ovid's Metamorphosis Englished, Mythologized, and Represented in Figures*, ed. Hulley and Vandersall, 492–3). Northrop Frye read this seasonal myth as the context for 'Lycidas' ('Literature as Context; Milton's *Lycidas*', in *Fables of Identity: Studies in Poetic Mythology* (New York, 1963), 119–29). I think Milton would have been less interested in the mythic pattern, however, than in its use by other writers.
[54] See Hamilton, '*Venus and Adonis*', 141–2.
[55] See also Clark Hulse, 'Shakespeare's Myth of Venus and Adonis', *PMLA* 93/1 (1978), 95–105, 95 especially.

is made the source of division. Ovid's lovers are turned into antagonists locked in an irreconcilable argument.

The fact that Shakespeare's poem is largely made up of debate shows its origins in the humanist pedagogical practice of arguing different points of view, a practice that, as his early Prolusions indicate, helped form Milton. A favourite set topic was the superiority of marriage and procreation to chastity.[56] For a country ruled by a Virgin Queen in which, however, virginity was associated with Catholicism, the topic was particularly fraught.[57] Moreover, as Jeff Shulman has shown, 'the great Renaissance debate of eros and chastity' was also one of the central themes of poetry and drama in the late sixteenth century.[58] Shulman suggests that for Elizabethan writers the terms of the discussion were shaped by Ovid's exploration of the psychological tension between the desire for relatedness and personal change and the impulse towards autonomy and stasis.[59] While Shakespeare's comedies come out in favour of marriage and procreation, in *Venus and Adonis* the positions are pushed to exaggerated alternatives, as the frantically flexible Venus is constantly grabbing at the rather static (not to mention statuesque) Adonis, who, like Greta Garbo, only wants to be left alone. Neither of these options is completely attractive. The passion of the overripe and somewhat frenetic Venus is described repeatedly with animalistic, predatory imagery; it is easy to believe that she might consume any lover.[60] Still, Adonis' rather puritanical adherence to chastity has not appealed much to recent critics who have seen in

---

[56] Baldwin, *William Shakspere's Small Latine & Lesse Greeke*, ii. 339–40; and *On the Literary Genetics of Shakespeare's Poems & Sonnets* (Urbana, Ill., 1950), 183–6.

[57] I return to the role of Elizabeth in debates over chastity in Ch. 2.

[58] 'At the Crossroads of Myth: The Hermeneutics of Hercules from Ovid to Shakespeare', *English Literary History*, 50/1 (1983), 98. See also his 'Ovidian Myth in Lyly's Courtship Comedies', *Studies in English Literature*, 25/2 (1985), 249–69.

[59] 'At the Crossroads of Myth' and 'Ovidian Myth in Lyly's Courtship Comedies'. Shulman argues that both Ovid and Shakespeare (and, he claims, Lyly) successfully reconcile these two impulses, which other Elizabethan writers see as incompatible. As I suggest here, the comedies may show that Shakespeare can unite these drives when he wants to, but in *Venus and Adonis* he is interested in what happens in the face of fundamental antitheses.

[60] While recent critics have been kinder to her, Donald Cameron Allen famously reduced her to 'a forty-year-old countess with a taste for Chapel Royal altos' ('On Venus & Adonis', in *Elizabethan and Jacobean Studies Presented to Frank Percy Wilson in Honour of his Seventieth Birthday* (Oxford, 1959), 101).

him narcissistic self-love, and denial of life.[61] As we will see in more detail in Chapter 3, later epyllia link him with Narcissus and Hermaphroditus, who also try to evade sexual intercourse.

By reimagining the couple as antagonists, moreover, Shakespeare recalls another central Ovidian myth: the story of Daphne in *Metamorphoses* 1 which establishes the pattern of hunted virginity. Like Shakespeare's Adonis, Daphne prefers hunting to love; her wish to remain chaste leads to her transformation into the laurel tree and the symbol of poetry. One of the most influential myths in the Renaissance,[62] this tale was often interpreted as showing that immortality is won through the preservation of chastity, a reading that may have influenced Milton's developing belief that chastity generates great poetry.[63] Moreover, as later writers recognized, Ovid's story mythologizes the beginnings of love elegy.[64] It links the origins of poetry not to rape, but to chastity and frustrated sexual desire; Apollo fails to get the girl but gains the laurel tree instead. The myth was at the centre of Petrarch's poetics, in which sexual desire is really the longing for poetic immortality, and the pursuit of sex is a way to get poems.[65] As we will see further, Petrarch's Ovidianism, like his poetics generally, was extremely influential in England. He provided a model for internalizing and psychologizing Ovidian stories of metamorphosis, in

---

[61] Especially Coppélia Kahn, 'Self and Eros in *Venus and Adonis*', in Kolin (ed.), Venus and Adonis: *Critical Essays*, 181–202.

[62] See Christine Rees's fine study of 'The Metamorphosis of Daphne in Sixteenth- and Seventeenth-Century English Poetry', *Modern Language Review*, 66 (1971), 251–63; also Mary E. Barnard, *The Myth of Apollo and Daphne from Ovid to Quevedo: Love, Agon, and the Grotesque* (Durham, NC, 1987).

[63] See Sandys, *Ovid's Metamorphosis*, 74, as well as Sara Sturm-Maddox, *Petrarch's Metamorphoses: Text and Subtext in the* Rime sparse (Columbia, Mo., 1985), 35–6.

[64] On Ovid's story as an *aition* of love elegy, see W. S. M. Nicoll, 'Cupid, Apollo, and Daphne (Ovid, *Met.* 1. 452ff)', *Classical Quarterly*, 30 (1980), 174–82; and Hardie, *Poetics of Illusion*, 45–50. Rees notes also how the story crystallized themes central for English Renaissance writers: 'the conflict of virginity and love, love and art, art and nature...the tension between transience and permanence, gain and loss' ('The Metamorphosis of Daphne', 251).

[65] Hardie, *Poetics of Illusion*, 70–81; Sturm-Maddox, *Petrarch's Metamorphoses*; John Freccero, 'The Fig Tree and the Laurel: Petrarch's Poetics', *Diacritics*, 5/1 (1975), 34–40; Gordon Braden, 'Beyond Frustration: Petrarchan Laurels in the Seventeenth Century', *Studies in English Literature, 1500–1900*, 26/1 (1986), 8. Hardie notes how for both Ovid and Petrarch 'the story of Daphne functions as an *aition* for the textuality of desire. In Ovid's erotic world desire never exists apart from texts'; transformed into *tenuis liber* (*Met.*, 1. 549), Daphne is not only 'thin bark' but also 'a slim book' (*Ovid's Poetics of Illusion*, 50).

order to make them allegories of the writer's experience. In this, of course, he was copying the Ovid of the exilic poetry. Most of all, he set the terms for love relations that English writers first copied and then, inevitably, rebelled against.[66]

Shakespeare's reading of Ovid's stories, however, locates the origins of poetry in neither Ovidian sexual violence nor Petrarchan chastity, but in the clash between antitheses. The two characters present opposing attitudes towards the body, sexuality, and especially poetry. The poem is a kind of singing match between two voices: that of the bodily and verbally licentious Venus, and that of the physically and rhetorically self-controlled Adonis. Moreover, the conflicting poetic visions suggest alternative ways of Englishing Ovid; as Heather Dubrow suggests, 'Venus stands for the amoral eroticism so common in the mythological narratives of Ovid himself, while Adonis represents the pieties of the *Ovide moralisé*. The tension between Venus and Adonis is in effect also a tension between two possible ways of imitating and adapting Ovid, two potential metamorphoses of the *Metamorphoses*: the amoral, Italianate narrative and the pious commentary on human follies.'[67] The allegorical Ovid is indeed present in the poem, though not, as earlier critics had argued, as its interpretative key but as one side of the central argument. As a poet, Shakespeare is born from the duel between two versions of Ovid.

I suspect, however, that in presenting these different voices Shakespeare is thinking less of the *Ovide moralisé*, an easy target for ridicule by the 1590s, and more of an Ovidianism much closer to home and his own interests: Spenser's use of the story of Venus and Adonis in *Faerie Queene* 3. 6. As I noted earlier, Elizabethan writers studied each other's adaptations of Ovidian themes and figures. Critics have long suggested that Shakespeare's epyllion was partly provoked by the publication of the 1590 *Faerie Queene*, which stimulated Shakespeare to attempt his own Ovidian counterbid for poetic immortality.[68]

---

[66] See especially Heather Dubrow, *Echoes of Desire: English Petrarchism and its Counterdiscourses* (Ithaca, NY, 1995).

[67] *Captive Victors*, 48. Mary Ellen Lamb notes a similar conflict between Ovidian artist figures in *The Winter's Tale* ('Ovid and *The Winter's Tale*', 69-87).

[68] On the relation between the two versions of Venus and Adonis, see Ellen Aprill Harwood, '*Venus and Adonis*: Shakespeare's Critique of Spenser', *Journal of the Rutgers University Library*, 39 (1977), 44-60; and Judith Anderson, '*Venus and Adonis*: Spenser, Shakespeare and the Forms of Desire', in Jennifer C. Vaught (ed.), *Grief and Gender: 700-1700* (New York, 2003), 149-60. Perhaps even more tellingly,

In her recent treatment of Spenser's use of Ovid, Syrithe Pugh argues that Spenser is drawn to Ovid because of his need to redeem sexual desire as a central part of human nature. As Pugh notes, Spenser wants to imagine a way in which one can write poetry and still get the girl, as satisfied love leads to heroism and great poetry. She argues that he finds his model in Ovid's valuation of heterosexual desire. Following Brooks Otis, she sees Ovid as 'the West's first champion of true, normal, even conjugal love'.[69] She argues therefore that, in Book 3 especially, 'Spenser has repositioned Ovid at the heart of the epic enterprise, and love at the heart of his ethics.'[70] Britomart proves the compatibility of desire and heroism, thus reconciling eros and chastity. Ovid is used to imagine what seems the most unOvidian subject possible: that of chastity.[71]

Appealing as this reading is, to argue that Spenser, or anyone, finds in Ovid an unproblematic model for marital bliss seems overly optimistic. Like the allegorists, Pugh wants to make Ovidian values compatible with later beliefs. As she notes, however, Spenser's own revision of the end of Book 3, as well as the later books of *The Faerie Queene*, suggest a darker reading of Ovidian marriage.[72] Pugh cites Ovid's exilic letters to his wife and his devoted stepdaughter Perilla as evidence of happy familial relations. But the context is suggestive: with only a few exceptions (Deucalion and Pyrrha, Baucis and Philemon), whose stories stand out for their singularity, happy marriages in Ovid are shattered by death or separation: the unity between Ceyx and Alcyone is glimpsed briefly just at the moment it is broken (*Met.*, 11. 410–748); the bliss of Cephalus and Procris is ruined by a pun (7. 694–862); Atalanta and Hippomenes are destroyed by their own sexual desires (10. 560–707—a tale told by Venus to Adonis). The one happy marriage in the *Heroides*, that of Laodamia and Protesilaus, is

---

A. C. Hamilton reads Shakespeare's couple as his version of Acrasia and Guyon ('*Venus and Adonis*', 146–7).

[69] Cited in Pugh, *Spenser and Ovid*, 167.
[70] Ibid. 149.
[71] This had been done more crudely, of course, by the generations of schoolteachers who presented the *Heroides* especially as a lesson on chastity; Edward Paleit notes that in Thomas Cooper's 1578 *Thesaurus Linguae Romanae & Britannicae*, almost half of the examples from classical writers to illustrate *pudicitia* come from Ovid ('Sexual and Political Liberty and Neo-Latin Poetics', 356).
[72] *Spenser and Ovid*, 149. Pugh connects the change with Spenser's turn to Ovid's last verse and a preoccupation with the theme of exile and alienation. Yet Ovid's exilic poetry, with its echoes of his early work, makes clear that exile is always an integral part of the love relation: love always involves a lack.

represented after Protesilaus has left for Troy and his fated death (*Heroides*, 13), while all that we know about Ovid's third and successful marriage was written after he and his wife were separated forever.[73] Marital happiness may be Ovid's goal, but it is never attained. Against that distant ideal is a world in which desire is manifested repeatedly as uncontrollable violence: rape.

The fact that Ovid does not offer a solution for Spenser's problem does not, however, mean that Spenser did not find Ovid's exploration of eros stimulating. Pugh's and Otis's reading reminds us how the varied experiences and contradictions in Ovid's work spawn a number of legacies, just as different experiences of love generate different poetics. Book 3 of *The Faerie Queene* includes alternative forms of both eros and Ovidianism jostling together. The story of the impregnation of the sleeping Chrysogone by the rays of the sun (3. 6. 3–27) transforms *the* classic Ovidian scene—the rape of a helpless nymph—into a tale of immaculate conception. It thus incorporates allegorical readings of Ovidian rape as ravishment. For the next generation, Chrysogone's daughters, Belphoebe and Amoret, however, the dominant form of Ovid is Petrarchism with the threat of physical rape. The difference between generations might suggest a decline in Ovidianism which Shakespeare seems to hasten, and Spenser to redirect. It is often assumed that in Book 3 Spenser is attacking the tradition of Petrarchan love, which has bound Amoret to a false image in which desire can only be imagined as destructive, and sexual union as rape.[74] Spenser's vision of chaste married love frees desire by destroying a false image of chastity produced by Petrarchan discourse. Moreover, Pugh argues that for Spenser the Petrarchan tradition distorted not only the love experience but also the meaning of Ovid; Britomart's quest therefore involves 'Rescuing Ovid from the Ovidian Tradition',[75] to replace a false image of Ovidian desire with its true counterpart. If the source of Petrarchan poetry is the isolated and impenetrable Laura, Spenser's figure for the origin of his art is the Garden of Adonis, in which the eternal coupling of the central

---

[73] The echoes of the *Tristia* and *Ex Ponto* that Pugh and Laura J. Getty have noted in Spenser's prenuptial *Amoretti* may therefore have a more ominous significance; see Pugh, *Spenser and Ovid*, 167; and Getty, 'Circumventing Petrarch: Subreading Ovid's *Tristia* in Spenser's *Amoretti*', *Philological Quarterly*, 79/2 (2000), 293–314.

[74] See Thomas P. Roche's influential discussion in *The Kindly Flame: A Study of the Third and Fourth Books of Spenser's* Faerie Queene (Princeton, 1964), 77–88.

[75] Pugh, *Spenser and Ovid*, 145.

pair, Venus and Adonis, is the principle of both sexual and poetic generation. The vision of endless metamorphosis in the Garden is tied to a Spenserian Ovidianism in which poetry is born not out of thwarted desire, but through satisfaction in which chastity and eros are reconciled.

In *Venus and Adonis*, Shakespeare responds to Spenser's rescue mission by launching a counterattack that recalls the other side of Ovid, a side which is, of course, equally 'true'. Here, Shakespeare's Ovid is the *genius* not of married love but of perverse sexuality that leads to death—the guardian spirit, say, of *Titus Andronicus*. Like Milton, Shakespeare shows us that there are different ways of adapting Ovid. He does so to insist that they, like Venus and Adonis themselves, are completely incompatible. What Spenser hath brought together, Shakespeare pulls asunder, separating the two figures so that they become opposing principles that can never be united. In Venus, Spenser's idealization of Ovidian desire is cynically reduced to bestial 'nature'. Shakespeare turns Spenser's goddess into a version of the giantess Argante who, in *Faerie Queene* 3. 7, woos young men by whipping them up onto her horse. He thus anticipates the readers who have found Spenser's Venus a somewhat sinister and devouring figure.[76] In opposition, however, Adonis is a version of chastity that has become sterile and as deadly as desire itself. His premature death is an *aition* that explains why desire is forever doomed to frustration. As Venus prophesies, from now on all experiences of love 'shall be fickle, false, and full of fraud, | Bud and be blasted in a breathing-while' (*Venus and Adonis*, 1141–2)—not to mention forever alliterative. The story of *Venus and Adonis* narrates the origins of an experience of love irreconcilable with Spenser's ideal and explains the beginning of the poetics founded on and expressive of such desire: Petrarchan love poetry. Shakespeare thus seems to bring Spenser's poem back full circle to the House of Busirane. Spenser's attempt to free himself from Petrarchan conventions seems only to have led to their re-entrenchment.[77] In this, Shakespeare is cannily prescient of

---

[76] See especially Harry Berger's 'Actaeon at the Hinder Gate: The Stag Party in Spenser's Gardens of Adonis', in Valeria Finucci and Regina M. Schwartz (eds.), *Desire in the Renaissance: Psychoanalysis and Literature* (Princeton, 1994), 91–119.

[77] Whether Spenser himself manages to critique Petrarchism or simply reproduces it is debated. Dubrow suggests the impossibility of escaping the diacritical nature of Petrarchism which contains its own counterattack (*Echoes of Desire*).

many of Spenser's followers, whose poetry tended to polarize chastity and sexual desire once more.[78]

With the alliterative end of Shakespeare's poem, and the creation of a flower that is described as Adonis' offspring (1177–8, 1183), we also seem to come to the beginning of Milton's, with its infant primrose who will become immortal. Like Shakespeare, Milton writes a myth of his own origins as a poet, through the juxtaposition of two types of Ovidianism. However, where Shakespeare imagines the two types as irreconcilable, Milton tries to unite them, and to make himself the product of the successful coupling of the central resources of English poetry. The Ovidianisms of Spenser and Shakespeare are equally part of Milton's poem: in fact, the opening lines, which seem to point at once towards *The Shepheardes Calender* and *The Passionate Pilgrim*, delicately balance the two sources in a single image.[79]

The result of this poetic union, however, is still itself premature. Milton's fears of his own poetic 'unripeness' were not unfounded. The poem's central transformation of a cough into a rape suggests Milton's uncertainty about his poetic voice, as well as his ability to handle sexual desire both poetically and, no doubt for a 17- or even 19-year-old, personally. The exclusion of this poem from the 1645 volume enabled Milton to make the more unified 'Nativity Ode' the grand and confident announcement of his own poetic nativity, his entrance into English poetry and self-proclamation as a serious and Virgilian poet ready to march forward to epic glory. His inclusion of 'On the Death of a fair Infant' in the 1673 edition, only a few pages after the 'Nativity Ode', gives us an alternative version of his early beginnings that expresses his uncertainty about what kind of poet he would become—or, indeed, if he would be able to become one at all.

---

[78] The *Variorum* notes the Fletchers' role in the fossilization of Spenser's figures (ii, pt. 3, 776).

[79] The mixing of models is typical of epyllia of the 1590s. Thomas Edwards's ghastly *Cephalus and Procris* is both a copy of *Venus and Adonis* and a tribute to Spenser (1595; repr. 1882, Literature Online). Edwards finds a common territory between the two English poets, making Cephalus reject Aurora not to remain chaste but to be faithful to his wife (309–16 especially), and adding a fairy episode that recalls that both writers are creators of fantasy worlds of fairies (482–610). Henry Purcell's operatic treatment of *A Midsummer's Night Dream* as *The Fairy Queen* also suggests how other adapters mixed the two. (As part of the continuing practice of mixing voices, David Garrick's adaptation of Shakespeare's play is padded with lines from 'L'Allegro'.)

But in these experiments with different forms of Ovid, we can see Milton in the making.

COMUS AND THE *TRANSLATIO OVIDII*

The addition of 'On the Death of a fair Infant' to the story of Milton's poetical coming of age allows us to see his first claim to be an English writer who enters into the tradition through Ovid. Its presence can also help us understand the Ovidianism of *Comus*. Placed last in the English works in the 1645 as well as 1673 *Poems*, Milton's masque seems the climax of the first stage of his poetic self-preparation. It has often been interpreted as the definitive turning point in his development: the point at which he fully realized his vocation as an epic writer. Dr Johnson called it 'the dawn or twilight of *Paradise Lost*'.[80] Epic elements underlie the masque structure, hinting at Milton's future aspirations. The Lady is a version of the typical epic questor, whose journey is impeded by evil forces. The model of the *Odyssey* is recalled in the figure of Circe's son Comus, while parallels with *Faerie Queene* 2 and 3, the books of Temperance and Chastity, are also obvious. The outlines of Milton's future epics are visible: the debate between Comus and the Lady rehearses *in parvo* the confrontation between good and evil in his epic *Paradise Lost* and, perhaps even more closely, in *Paradise Regain'd*. Even the Ovidianism of the masque seems epic; allusions to key stories from the *Metamorphoses*—Circe (50–3), Narcissus and Echo (230–43), Apollo and Daphne (661–2)—suggest that Milton has abandoned the Ovid of the love elegies in favour of the epic writer whose theme of transformation suits the masque's form and subject. Taking as part of its subject the transition from adolescence to maturity, *Comus* dramatizes Milton's development as a poet, his readiness for the big time.[81]

The opening of the poem draws attention to Milton's aspirations to originality. In his first speech, the Attendant Spirit recounts the story of Comus, son of Bacchus and Circe. By telling the tale of a god new

---

[80] *Lives of the English Poets*, ed. Waugh, i. 115.
[81] See especially William Shullenberger, who shows how Milton's masque makes its subjects: not only the Lady, who is transformed through trial, but Milton himself for whom the process also serves as an initiation rite (*Lady in the Labyrinth*).

to the classical pantheon,[82] the Spirit is able to claim that he is revealing 'What never yet was heard in Tale or Song' (44). The line sticks out, partly because of its boldness, but also because it sets up an odd echo chamber. Post-1667 readers of the poem cannot help but hear this as a proleptic echo of Milton's claim to tell 'Things unattempted yet in Prose or Rhime' (*PL*, 1. 16). Moreover, both passages echo 'cosa non detta in prosa mai né in rima' of Ariosto, who is himself echoing Boiardo.[83] This kind of claim is however quite common in classical and later literatures: John Weever opens his epyllion, *Faunus and Melliflora*, by saying he will tell the story of 'Faire *Melliflora*, amorous, and yong, | Whose name, nor story, neuer Poet sung' (131–2).[84] The assertion of originality is a conventional way of expressing the self-consciousness of the poet, both anxious to create things anew and aware that other people and, in Milton's case later, one's own earlier self, have been there already.

Moreover, this claim to newness is immediately followed by the placement of the story in relation to a long tradition. While Comus may be a new addition to the genealogy of the pagan gods, his mother is one of the oldest and most infamous of classical figures, as the Spirit indicates when he observes: 'Who knows not *Circe* | The daughter of the Sun?' (50–1). We move from the unknown to the familiar, as the rhetorical 'Who knows not?' calls attention to the reworking of old material. The gesture is a variation on what in classical poetry David Ross calls 'an Alexandrian footnote', a moment which highlights the status of the story as one passed down so that, as Stephen Hinds says, 'the hinted "footnote" underlines the allusiveness of the verses, and intensifies their demand to be interpreted *as* a system of allusions'.[85]

---

[82] See Stephen Orgel's discussion of the evolution of Comus from allegorical to dramatic figure (*The Jonsonian Masque* (Cambridge, Mass., 1965), 152–8).

[83] Lodovico Ariosto, *Orlando Furioso*, ed. Cesare Segre (Milan, 1976), 1. 2. 2. (Modern English translations of Ariosto make the relation here between source and later copy even more complex, as they often sound as if they were copying Milton.) On Ariosto's general practice of imitating works that are themselves imitative, see Javitch, 'The Imitation of Imitations in *Orlando Furioso*', 215–39.

[84] Citations of *Faunus and Melliflora* are taken from John Weever, *Faunus and Melliflora*, ed. Arnold Davenport (Liverpool, 1948). The *Variorum* notes Horace, *Odes*, 3. 1. 2–4 (ii, pt. 3, 863); but for similar claims see also Lucretius, *De Rerum Natura*, 4. 1; Propertius, *Elegies*, 3. 1. 1–4; and especially the famous and very relevant opening of Virgil's *Georgics* 3, recalled by Milton in 'Elegia 4' (29).

[85] David O. Ross, *Backgrounds to Augustan Poetry: Gallus, Elegy and Rome* (Cambridge, 1975), 78; Hinds, *Allusion and Intertext*, 2.

The poet draws attention to his relation to his sources, as well as to the function of allusion itself. The direct reference here seems to be to three signature moments in Spenser's works in which Spenser is particularly self-conscious about his art. At these points, he emphasizes either poet figures like Colin Clout ('Poore *Colin Clout* (who knowes not *Colin Clout*?)', *FQ*, 6. 10. 16. 4), or figures associated with poetic origins: Rosalind, the source and potential end of the poetry of *The Shepheardes Calender* ('Of Rosalend (who knowes not Rosalend?)', 'August Eclogue', 141), and, finally, Arlo-Hill, on which Spenser's last poetic vision occurs (*'Arlo-hill* (Who knowes not *Arlo-hill*?)', *Mutabilitie*, 7. 6. 36. 6). The phrase draws a circle around the poet's works and career, asking us to treat it as a linked whole concerned with the sources of creation. At the same time, it points outside that insular circle to Spenser's sources. John Hollander and James Nohrnberg trace it to *Fasti* 2, where Ovid tells the story of one of his many artist and authorial figures, Arion: 'quod mare non novit, quae nescit Ariona tellus?' ('What sea, what land knows not Arion?', 83).[86] In fact, Ovid uses this formula also in *Ars Amatoria* 1. 335–6: 'cui non defleta est Ephyraeae flamma Creusae, | et nece natorum sanguinolenta parens?' ('Who has not bewailed the flames of Creusa of Ephyre, and the mother [Medea] stained with her children's blood'), in which he winks at his own lost *Medea*. Similarly, in *Metamorphoses* 15. 319, he gives us a not too subtle nudge towards a story he had told earlier in the epic: 'cui non audita est obscenae Salmacis undae?' ('Who has not heard of the ill-famed waves of Salmacis?'). Certainly the reader of the story of Hermaphroditus in *Metamorphoses* 4 has! In Ovid, as in Spenser, the formula has the effect of calling attention to moments in which the author is talking with and about himself and particularly to key stories with which he identifies. At the same time, as usual, Ovid is talking with someone else, as he has appropriated for a more self-referential purpose a form that had been used by Virgil to dismiss old chestnuts: 'quis aut Eurysthea durum | aut inlaudati nescit Busiridis aras? | cui non dictus Hylas puer' ('Who knows not pitiless Eurystheus, or the altars of detested Busiris? Who has not told of the boy

---

[86] See John Hollander, *Melodious Guile: Fictive Pattern in Poetic Language* (New Haven, 1988), 177–8; and James Nohrnberg, *The Analogy of* The Faerie Queene (Princeton, 1976), 76 n. 195.

Hylas?', *Georgics*, 3. 4–6).[87] As Virgil suggests, stories that are too well known can dwindle into hackneyed clichés.

The Spirit's line thus foregrounds the problem of novelty for a writer who is claiming his place in a long line of literary descent. As the echoes here suggest, the masque has a dense literary genealogy. These woods are full of voices, making any attempt at source study problematic: the *Variorum* has twenty-nine pages on possible sources, citing especially Marino, Fletcher, Peele, Jonson, Carew, and, above all, Spenser and Shakespeare.[88] For Angus Fletcher, the astonishing assimilation of these works makes *Comus* 'a transcendental pastiche'.[89] Milton's masque is a celebration of his own reading and study of classical and contemporary works, as he enters a metamorphosing and still fairly new literature. The gathering together of sources is suggested by the focus on movement in the poem. There are no native peoples in the woods that form the boundary between England and Wales: the Lady and her brothers come from England, Comus comes from Europe, the Attendant Spirit comes from heaven, even the landscape itself comes from elsewhere, as the resident water nymph Sabrina is descended from the Trojan Brute. As I noted earlier, Elizabethan epyllia such as Lodge's and Weever's use the movement of classical figures in space as well as time to figure their own appropriation of old material. Milton's text also draws attention to its transplanting of classical sources into the English landscape. He had done this earlier in his mini-masque *Arcades*, in which the speaker calls classical waters into the English land where 'A better soyl shall give ye thanks' as 'Here ye shall have greater grace' (101, 104). At the same time as he gathers foreign sources, writing for the Dowager Duchess of Derby 'allowed him to place himself in the long line of staunch Protestant writers she patronized, most notably Spenser',[90] shaping the family tree that would bear fruit in *Comus*.

---

[87] I am grateful to Stephen Hinds for reminding me of this Virgilian source, as well as noting the formula in *Ars Amatoria*.

[88] Woodhouse and Bush note that 'The texture of *Comus*—like that of most of Milton's verse—suggests that his memory was stored not only with the ancient classics but with much English and foreign poetry of the Renaissance' (*Variorum*, ii, pt. 3, 765; see generally 755–84).

[89] *The Transcendental Masque: An Essay on Milton's* Comus (Ithaca, NY, 1971), 201–3.

[90] Barbara Kiefer Lewalski, *The Life of John Milton* (Malden, Mass., 2000), 58.

Among all the voices in the masque, the Ovidianism is both oddly palpable and elusive; while Carey finds twenty-eight echoes and analogues to Ovid, many more Ovidian elements seem to enter second-hand, through authors who themselves reworked Ovid. Most discussions of *Comus*' Ovidianism, however, have focused on the villain, the shape-shifter Comus, son of the archetypal transformer Circe. In Comus, Ovidian metamorphosis has become a negative force that blocks higher aspirations. The masque clearly draws on allegorical or Neoplatonic readings of Circe as a symbol of a material world which turns men into beasts. The idea of degradation is reinforced by Comus' genealogy, which maps familial onto moral descent: the passing from mother to son is a further degeneration of an already degenerate line.[91] We are in a world of moralized, even allegorized, metamorphosis operating on a vertical scale: you can move up, like the chaste and virtuous Lady, or down, like the licentious and vicious Comus. In general, masques tend to be structurally and morally dualistic: Milton's masque seems relentlessly so with its endless debates and sets of contrasting characters. Even more than Venus and Adonis, Comus and the Lady represent opposing principles that cannot be reconciled: at the end, they head off in different directions.

The opposition between the journeys of Comus and the Lady suggests different routes that poets might take in importing classical traditions to English soil. On the one hand, there is the path of Comus, a pagan god who, for reasons known only to himself, has moved into a wood in Wales. Leading men astray from their quests and turning them into beasts, he hints at the possibility of regression to a licentious pagan past (a possibility that, at the level of religion, is tied to the threat of return to the wrong kind of Roman tradition:

---

[91] The concern with descent seems replicated in critical debates over the origins of Milton's Circe. While many critics argued that Milton's image of Circe recalls Ovid's sinister enchantress and her later allegorization, Leonora Leet Brodwin wanted to trace Milton's Circe back to Homer, a purer and more original source, and so dissociate Milton from a later hermeneutics that lent itself to 'easy moralizing' ('Milton and the Renaissance Circe', *Milton Studies*, 6 (1974), 23). See the response by Judith E. Browning, 'Sin, Eve, and Circe: *Paradise Lost* and the Ovidian Circe Tradition', *Milton Studies*, 26 (1990), 135–57. As in other examples of this sort, I do not see this as an either-or case: the relation between Homer and Ovid's figures is itself part of the context.

Catholicism).[92] On the other, there is the progress of the Lady, who is only passing through the woods as she moves with her family from England to Wales. While she is an Odysseus figure, her journey to a new land recalls more directly the epic and imperial progression of Aeneas, a fact that is made clearer as she is aided by Sabrina, the end of the Trojan line.[93] The two main characters themselves suggest opposing poetic but also moral paths and lines of descent: a regressive if pleasurable one that degrades, and a progressive and virtuous one that elevates.

Given the Virgilian parallels, it seems plausible to imagine these opposites as two separate family trees: a Virgilian line that produces (via Spenser) the Lady and Sabrina, and an Ovidian line which leads to the shape-shifting Comus.[94] Yet the Virgilian elements have themselves been transformed through a clever and highly Ovidian move. While Sabrina, as a descendant of Troy, is Virgilian in origins, Milton shapes her into a figure associated with metamorphosis, just as at times in the *Metamorphoses* Ovid made Virgil seem '*pre-Ovidian*'.[95] The Virgilian *translatio imperii* embodied in Sabrina is trumped by her Ovidian metamorphosis into a river to become a *translatio Ovidii*.[96] Turned into a figure of transformation, she offers an alternative to Comus and Circean change. With Comus, metamorphosis

---

[92] The relation between the masque and Laud's reforms, seen by many as first steps on the slippery slope to Catholicism, has been the subject of much discussion; see especially David Norbrook, 'The Reformation of the Masque', in David Lindley (ed.), *The Court Masque* (Manchester, 1984), 94–110; Leah Marcus, *The Politics of Mirth: Jonson, Herrick, Milton, Marvell, and the Defense of Old Holiday Pastimes* (Chicago, 1986); and Achsah Guibbory, *Ceremony and Community from Herbert to Milton: Literature, Religion and Cultural Conflict in Seventeenth-Century England* (Cambridge, 1998). See further Ch. 2.

[93] Political readers could note how the Virgilian subtext might be used to justify the English colonization of Wales that is part of the original occasion.

[94] Stanley Fish's reading draws out the Virgilian elements (*How Milton Works* (Cambridge, Mass., 2001), 173–7); see also John Watkins, '"A Goddess among the Gods": Virgil, Milton, and the Woman of Immortal Voice', in Jennifer Lewin (ed.), *Never Again Would Birds' Song Be the Same: Essays on Early Modern and Modern Poetry in Honor of John Hollander* (New Haven, 2002), 11–34.

[95] Hinds, *Allusion and Intertext*, 119.

[96] While Ovid has several figures who turn into rivers, the closest Ovidian precedent for Sabrina in fact comes from a moment in which he rewrites the *Aeneid*, turning it into the story of a persecuted female exile. *Fasti* 3. 543–656 tells the story of Dido's sister Anna, who is forced to flee Carthage after the death of Dido. She lands in Rome, where she is treated hospitably by Aeneas but persecuted by the jealous Lavinia. Warned by her sister's ghost (as Hector had warned Aeneas in *Aeneid* 2), she flees once more, to be taken (*rapere*) by the river and transformed into its nymph,

leads downwards to bondage and stasis; with Sabrina, it elevates and liberates, freeing both the Lady and, ultimately, Milton's poetic vision.

In these conflicting types of transformation Milton, like Shakespeare in *Venus and Adonis*, juxtaposes opposing ways of reading and adapting Ovid. The seducer Comus recalls the Ovid of Elizabethan erotic verse and especially epyllia, with their endless scenes of seduction. This is the rhetorical Ovid, in whom, as critics of rhetoric have always feared, 'deer Wit, and gay Rhetorick' (*Comus*, 790) are merely means of seduction. While in Petrarch sex is a pretence for poetry, here poetry looks like just a means to get sex. This kind of poetry is always supposed to have a bad effect on its readers, as Francis Beaumont perversely flaunts when he claims that the reader of his 1602 epyllion *Salmacis and Hermaphroditus* will 'turne halfe-mayd with reading it' (A4^r).[97] Comus' noted resemblance to his mother Circe (*Comus*, 57) connects him with the danger of gender confusion; he is himself a kind of Salmacis, who blurs the boundaries between the sexes as well as other categories.[98] His arts degrade human nature; they surpass those of his mother (63) who simply transforms men into animals, as he makes his victims unnatural Ovidian hybrids, animal in face and human still in body (69–72). On the other side, the Lady and her brothers, with their clear-cut sense of a world neatly divided between antithetical forces, guided by abstractions such as Faith, Hope, and Chastity, seem to live in an older world of allegorical and moralized Ovidianism—the tradition which tries to impose order on Ovidian metamorphosis and its confusion of categories.

These two broad forms of Ovidianism, moreover, seem to line up with the parts given to Spenser and Shakespeare, authors whose presences in the masque have also long been noted and discussed.[99]

---

the goddess Anna Perenna. I discuss the importance of the *Fasti* for *Comus* in the next chapter.

[97] 'The Author to the Reader', in *Salmacis and Hermaphroditvs* (London, 1602), Early English Books Online.

[98] Comus also resembles Thomas Peend's Hermaphroditus who is much more like his mother (*The Pleasant Fable of Hermaphroditus and Salmacis* (London, 1565), Early English Books Online, A4^r). The blurring of gender roles in Milton's characters in the masque has been much discussed; see especially Richard Halpern, 'Puritanism and Maenadism in *A Mask*', in Margaret Ferguson, Maureen Quilligan, and Nancy J. Vickers (eds.), *Rewriting the Renaissance: The Discourses of Sexual Difference in Early Modern Europe* (Chicago, 1986), 90–2.

[99] See especially Stevens, *Imagination and the Presence of Shakespeare in Paradise Lost*; Maureen Quilligan, *Milton's Spenser: The Politics of Reading* (Ithaca, NY, 1983);

Their roles in the poem are quite different, and suggest Milton's identification with Spenser, his proclaimed 'original', who shared his concern with temperance and chastity, and his greater ambivalence towards Shakespeare, who so often appears as his opposite. The two poets enter the poem in strikingly different ways. Spenser's presence is frank and up front: it is felt mostly through characters (explicitly Sabrina), imagery, and the overall moral vision of the poem with its commitment to the virtue of chastity. Spenser sets the plot, especially as the freeing of the Lady by Sabrina replays Britomart's rescue of Amoret in *Faerie Queene* 3. Many critics have therefore seen *Comus* as basically a Spenserian work informed by a poetics of chaste sexuality. While Spenser is invited in and honestly announces his presence, Shakespeare seems to sneak in at the level of language, through sometimes elusive echoes or broad parallels.[100] The debates on virginity recall Shakespeare's *Venus and Adonis*; the threat of rape, the representation of the Lady, and her defiant assertion that 'Thou canst not touch the freedom of my minde' (663) recall also Shakespeare's *Rape of Lucrece*, with its heroine's claim, 'Immaculate and spotless is my mind' (1656). Other echoes are largely from Shakespeare's most Ovidian plays: in particular, *A Midsummer's Night Dream* and *The Tempest*.[101] While Spenser acts as a moral principle that propels the plot, Shakespeare enters in the form of rhetoric that works against the Spenserian narrative drive. Even more, while Spenser is clearly linked to the good characters, critics often find Shakespearian elements strongest in Comus himself.[102] Similarly, in *Paradise Lost*, critics have argued that Shakespearian language—like Ovidian figures—is most often used to figure fallen and even infernal consciousness.[103] Shakespeare thus seems identified with a degraded,

---

Fletcher, *The Transcendental Masque*, 142–3; and John Guillory, *Poetic Authority: Spenser, Milton, and Literary History* (New York, 1983), 19 and 68–93. Guillory notes also how critics too often pit the sources against each other as 'mutually exclusive alternatives' (ibid. 73), between which the reader must choose.

[100] An alternative reading might, of course, grant greater weight to Shakespeare on the grounds that his subtle entrance reflects Milton's subconscious identification: Milton is of Shakespeare's party without knowing it.

[101] As Guillory notes, these works are the ones in which Shakespeare most directly explores the power of the imagination and the nature of art (*Poetic Authority*, 75).

[102] See Stevens, *Imagination and the Presence*, 13. As we'll see later, and as the opening of 'On the Death of a fair Infant' with its simultaneous echoes of both Spenser and Shakespeare should lead us to expect, this division is far less true than assumed.

[103] As Stevens shows, however, this assumption is also highly questionable (ibid.).

infernal poetics, which can only imagine desire as blasted and rapacious, and which preys on the chastity which both Milton and Spenser defend.

While this representation of the character of Shakespeare's poetry is obviously hardly fair—nor even vaguely accurate—it serves a purpose here. The division works to foreground Milton's likeness to Spenser while asserting his difference from Shakespeare, as Milton did in 'L'Allegro' with his famous representation of the warbling 'fancy's child'—the kind of native poet who just might be at home in a remote wood in Wales. The battle lines of sources seem to be forming, and the Spenserian plot to preserve chastity beats the Shakespearian attempt to take it. The defeat of Comus is imagined in Spenserian terms: in a compressed rerun of the conclusion of *Faerie Queene* 3, the Lady is saved by a Spenserian figure. John Guillory therefore suggests that, in the end, Spenser saves Milton from Shakespeare.[104] As Spenser's Britomart rescues Amoret from a false form of Ovidianism, Spenser's Ovidianism helps Milton counter the evil Ovid, Shakespeare. Sabrina, transformed into the goddess of the river, suggests a Spenserian line of adapting Ovid. If the epyllion degrades readers, Spenser's metamorphic verse has an elevating effect on its audience: Spenser's goal is to 'fashion a gentleman' ('Letter to Raleigh', in Hamilton, *FQ*, 737). In the end Spenser and Milton stand victorious together as part of a tradition of cleaned up, moral, and Christianized Ovid that expels the bad influence of Shakespeare, the rotten branch of the family tree.

Milton thus seems to be carefully constructing a version of literary history into which he can project himself. As he moves into English poetry, Ovid is still a major influence, but so are the English writers who had experimented with ways of Englishing the Latin poet. Milton surveys the possibilities offered by the previous generation, and chooses his line of descent to announce the kind of poet he wants to be.

Yet the conclusion of *Comus* shows that the choice is not as clearcut as one might assume. The terms of the central debate are themselves never resolved, nor is a winner clearly announced. In the printed version of the text, the masque ends by breaking free from the overly schematic dualisms and debates which divide the poem.

---

[104] *Poetic Authority*, 90. I think one might equally argue that Milton saves Spenser from Shakespeare, given that the Lady is herself a version of Spenser's Britomart, who is now the rescued rather than the rescuer.

Sabrina herself, whose name, the Severn, puns on 'sever', divides the Lady from Comus while offering other forms of reconciliation. As a human who is also part of nature and a supernatural force, she is a hybrid: human, river, goddess, foreigner, and now part of the English landscape, a real literary mutt who is Virgilian/Ovidian/Spenserian and now Miltonic.[105] Yet while she ends the deadlock between opposites, she does so by sending them off in opposite directions. Moreover, she is part of a genealogy that is marked by familial strife and violence—in her case, suicide.[106] The epilogue shifts to a higher sphere, as the Attendant Spirit imagines leaving behind both the woods and even the courtly world which traditionally marks the masque's telos and limits, to move upwards to a paradise inhabited by a very different couple who represent a new generation.

Up until this point, the Attendant Spirit has himself been part of the masque's antithetical structure. He is the reverse of Comus: a force for elevation who comes to earth to help the virtuous attain 'the Palace of Eternity' (14). His descent and re-ascent frame the action of the whole. His opening speech describes the world of the masque as one of stable and antithetical categories, a moralized hierarchy divided into clearly separate spheres in which abstract 'Regions milde of calm and serene Ayr' (4) float high 'Above the smoak and stirr of this dim spot, | Which men call Earth' (5–6). There's no difficulty here telling which way is up: the Spirit imagines his descent as a coming down in the world which will 'soil these pure Ambrosial weeds | With the rank vapours of this Sin-worn mould' (16–17). His puritanical attitude towards the world seems rather severe and even snobby. At the end, however, both he and the paradise from which he came seem to have changed. As he returns to his original form and home he suddenly switches poetic form. While he speaks first and throughout in blank verse, for his final speeches he turns to the rhyming couplets

---

[105] As part of her dual nature she seems to bring together different forms of metamorphosis; while there are clearly Christological resonances in her ability to walk on water (896–7), she also resembles Ovid's Circe, who skims the surface with dry feet (*Met.*, 14. 49–50).

[106] Milton's revision of Sabrina's murder into suicide both gives her choice over her fate and also emphasizes the self-destructive nature of the line of Troy; as Richard A. McCabe notes, Spenser's 'History of Britain' shows how 'children turn against parents and parents against children' (*The Pillars of Eternity: Time and Providence in The Faerie Queene* (Blackrock, 1989), 106).

which earlier had been used by Comus.[107] Many critics have noted a Shakespearian effect here, with particular parallels to the speeches of Ariel and Puck.[108] Richard Neuse argues therefore that the Spirit has turned 'into the aeriel spirit who has discovered, or recovered, the playful sense of boundless possibility characteristic of the poetic imagination'.[109] This may seem a change for the better, but it does complicate matters. Who is who here? While Stanley Fish argues that the masque moves towards the differentiation of figures who are at first hard to tell apart (Comus and the Spirit take similar disguises),[110] it seems to me to work in the reverse: from a situation of clear antithesis to one of more complex mixing, in which the act of discrimination is both more difficult and more urgent. The cosmos of the play has loosened up as the Spirit's vision of paradise has changed through the course of the action. While the heaven from which the Spirit came at the opening was part of a rigidly dualistic order, the heaven to which he returns is a much richer, more embodied, and layered place.[111] Coming down to earth required simply leaving one world for its opposite; returning means passing through different gardens in which the sensual world is not abandoned but lifted to a higher form.

While the opening dualistic cosmos looked back to the Neoplatonic tradition, the concluding vision seems based on a different model, or rather models. The spirit rises through 'the Gardens fair | Of *Hesperus*' (981–2) in which

> young *Adonis* oft reposes,
> Waxing well of his deep wound

---

[107] The shift in poetic form actually takes place during the Spirit's invocation of the Spenserian Sabrina (867), significantly suggesting that Comus' language is needed to call up Spenserian figures. The two opposites need to come together. See also Shullenberger's gorgeous description of how 'With the invocation of Sabrina...a new kind of poetry makes its presence felt in the *Maske*, a poetry of "secure delight" and "unreproved pleasures free" ('L'Allegro', 91, 40), of sensory and generative fullness that absorbs and transforms the figural and metrical dynamism displayed by Comus. This poetry celebrates the regenerate senses as portals of discovery of the sublime and the world embraced by the senses as irradiated by a world yet to come' (*Lady in the Labyrinth*, 249).

[108] See *Variorum*, ii, pt. 3, 976; and Quilligan, *Milton's Spenser*, 216–17.

[109] 'Metamorphosis and Symbolic Action in *Comus*', in *Critical Essays on Milton from ELH* (Baltimore, 1969), 100.

[110] *How Milton Works*, 146–8 especially.

[111] Shullenberger also discusses the contrast between the opening and closing visions, showing how they emerged through Milton's revisions of the performance text in which the two speeches were originally one (*Lady in the Labyrinth*, 274–6).

> In slumber soft, and on the ground
> Sadly sits th' *Assyrian* Queen. (999-1002)

The placement of the couple here is often read as a final bow to Spenser, which reconfirms the affinity between the two poets' visions of poetic and sexual generation. The figures of Venus and Adonis also show that, although Milton's masque is limited by the fact that his subject is at present a young virgin, chastity is not an end in itself. The poet looks forward to the Lady's future of chaste marriage, imagined in the Spenserian terms compatible with Milton's ideals. Yet Shakespeare's reply to Spenser is not so easily exorcized from this allusion.[112] The delicate Shakespearian echo in 'spangled sheen' in the next line (1003, recalling *A Midsummer Night's Dream*, 2. 1. 29) might tip the balance in his direction, given the general Shakespearian lilt of the final speech.[113]

In fact, the concluding vision of paradise, and specifically the image of Venus and Adonis, allows Milton to yoke together Spenser and Shakespeare, as he had tried to do in 'On the Death of a fair Infant', and as in 'Elegia 5' 121-2 he had joined Virgil and Ovid. Invoking a scene that points back to both writers, he does not give us the grounds to tell them apart, or to say whose or which Venus and Adonis this is. The boundaries between the visions overlap. The conjunction here may partly suggest that Ovid's figures themselves have become too common to let us privilege any one source: they are now simply part of the landscape of English literature. But it also may make us consider the likeness between the two English sources as well as the differences. I have said that Britomart's rescue of Amoret at the end of Book 3 of *The Faerie Queene* is often interpreted as an attack on Petrarchan Ovidianism, with its focus on unrequited sterile passion, in the name of Spenser's Ovidian poetics of chaste marriage. But the Petrarchan tradition is the frequent target also of epyllia, especially Shakespeare's.[114] Despite their differences, both poets are trying to

---

[112] Despite the *Variorum*'s attempt to warn us off: 'It is against confusion with the type of treatment exemplified by Shakespeare's *Venus and Adonis*...that Milton seeks to guard' (ii, pt. 3, 984).

[113] I discuss further the problems of disentangling the two sources in *Comus* generally in '*Comus*'s Wood of Allusion', *University of Toronto Quarterly*, 61/3 (1992), 316-33.

[114] Brown discusses the anti-Petrarchism of epyllia generally; see *Redefining Elizabethan Literature*, especially 129-31, 139-41, and 154-5. See also Enterline's discussion of Marston and Shakespeare (*The Rhetoric of the Body*, 125-78);

reinvent Ovid in order to imagine new forms of poetry and of love itself.[115]

In this, of course, they were not alone but part of the generation who turned to Ovid for inspiration. A third prominent member of this generation is also invoked by Milton's allusion to Venus and Adonis: Marlowe. Though we don't know the date of composition of Marlowe's *Hero and Leander*,[116] it seems to open by wittily putting Spenser—and possibly even Shakespeare—in his place. The narrator notes the description on Hero's dress that shows:

> a grove,
> Where Venus in her naked glory strove
> To please the careless and disdainful eyes
> Of proud Adonis that before her lies. (1. 11–14)[117]

The story of Venus and Adonis is reduced to a cheap scene of seduction, just a piece of clothing on one of the central characters. In Marlowe, Ovid's story has already become a pornographic cliché, one that can be tossed nonchalantly into the background on which he will draw a completely different pair of Ovidian lovers.[118]

Hulse, *Metamorphic Verse*, 35–92; and Keach, *Elizabethan Erotic Narratives*, 119–34, 138–43.

[115] Spenser's relation to other Ovidian writers of his generation seems ambivalent. Keach's discussion of the Elizabethan literary scene opposes Spenserian poetics to the epyllion tradition generally, arguing that, while writers of epyllia enjoy unresolved Ovidian contradictions and tensions, Spenser seeks harmony. Keach notes however the changes in the later books of *The Faerie Queene*, which reflect the mood of the 1590s (*Elizabethan Erotic Narratives*, 220–32). Hulse, moreover, generally places Spenser in a less oppositional role to the epyllion writers, noting shared properties and concerns (*Metamorphic Verse*, 242–78). M. L. Stapleton also treats Spenser as part of the Ovidianism of the time (*Spenser's Ovidian Poetics*, 36–7). Shulman's description of the aims of Shakespeare and Lyly seems well suited also for Spenser: they use 'the figures of Ovidian fable to define an ideal of chastity that incorporates sensuality, one that stresses the fruitfulness of our most personal metamorphoses' ('At the Crossroads of Myth', 98).

[116] Marlowe clearly read the first instalment of *The Faerie Queene*; he famously reworked 1. 7. 32 in 2 *Tamburlaine* 4. 3. 119–24. See *The Plays of Christopher Marlowe*, ed. Roma Gill (London, 1971). But he died three weeks after Shakespeare's poem was registered. It is possible that he saw the poem earlier, but he also may well have written *Hero and Leander* even earlier, when at Cambridge.

[117] Citations from Marlowe's poetry are taken from *Marlowe's Poems*, ed. L. C. Martin (New York, 1966).

[118] Burrow notes that the practice of reducing the central figures of earlier writers and, inversely, enlarging their marginal details was typical of Elizabethan Ovidianism

In some ways, Marlowe is the most Ovidian of the Elizabethans. His translation of Ovid's *Amores* as *All Ovid's Elegies. By Christopher Marlowe* had identified the two authors.[119] John Roe points out that 'Marlowe is probably the quintessential Ovidian poet among his contemporaries for reasons which are both compelling and yet a little disquieting. He reproduces Ovid's remarkable imaginative scope, and he revels in his freedom to do pretty much what he likes in his poem. Metamorphosis means for him mercurial inventiveness.'[120] For Marlowe, Ovid is the source of creative liberty. Few critics have considered his influence on *Comus* or on Milton more generally.[121] There are passages in *Comus*, however, that recall *Hero and Leander*, especially the seduction scene and debates over chastity, although again these are so much a part of the Elizabethan landscape that it is hard to single out a particular voice.[122] The most interesting parallel, though, comes at the very end of the Spirit's final speech. From his vision of sensual pleasure the Spirit comes back down to earth to offer us a moral:

(*Complete Sonnets*, 17). Milton similarly takes Sabrina, a peripheral figure in Spenser, and makes her a central force of transformation.

[119] See Patrick Cheney, *Marlowe's Counterfeit Profession: Ovid, Spenser, Counter-Nationhood* (Toronto, 1997), 50.

[120] John Roe, 'Ovid "Renascent" in *Venus and Adonis* and *Hero and Leander*', in Taylor (ed.), *Shakespeare's Ovid*, 42. See also Keach on the importance of Marlowe, especially his translations of the *Amores*, in shaping English Ovidianism (*Elizabethan Erotic Narratives*, 25–31).

[121] In his edition of Marlowe's poems, however, L. C. Martin claimed in passing that 'the young Milton was greatly impressed by *Hero and Leander* and that even the author of *Paradise Lost* had not forgotten it' (*Marlowe's Poems*, 13–14). Martin noted also that Milton's nephew and student Edward Philips praised Marlowe, especially for his 'clean and unsophisticated wit' (qtd. ibid. 14). Nicholas McDowell argues also for the centrality of Marlowe's story of a drowned youth in Milton's 'Lycidas' ('"Lycidas" and the Influence of Anxiety', in Nicholas McDowell and Nigel Smith (eds.), *The Oxford Handbook of Milton* (Oxford, 2009), 112–35).

[122] Like Comus, Leander is a 'bold sharp sophister' (*Hero and Leander*, 1. 197), who sees chastity as miserliness, a wilful hoarding of the self (1. 231–48). As in Milton, the argument is a perversion of the parable of the talents that was central to Elizabethan writers and Milton. A more telling echo, however, is Milton's revision of Marlowe's 'illit'rate hinds' (*Hero and Leander*, 2. 218), as part of Leander's speech condemning the hard-hearted rejecters of love, as 'unleter'd Hinds' (*Comus*, 174), the Lady's description of Comus' rabble. I am not sure that this echo contributes deeply to the meaning of the specific passage (though it may), but it shows that Milton had Marlowe's language and poems very deep in his memory.

> Mortals that would follow me,
> Love vertue, she alone is free,
> She can teach ye how to clime
> Higher than the Spheary chime;
> Or if Vertue feeble were,
> Heav'n it self would stoop to her. (1018–23)

The poem seems to end on a Spenserian note with the assertion that there is indeed care in heaven; the *Variorum* therefore, following Merritt Hughes, cites *Faerie Queene* 3. 8. 29: '"See how the heauens of voluntary grace, | And soueraine fauour towards chastity, | Doe succour send to her distressed cace: | So much high God doth innocence embrace" (*F. Q.* 3. 8. 29). And one might add the great opening of *F. Q.* 2. 8: "And is there care in heaven?"'[123] But, while the sentiment sounds highly Spenserian, some resonances in the language create a countermovement. The *Variorum* cautiously notes a resemblance to a passage in *Hero and Leander*. The scene recalled is appropriate for Milton's concerns: it shows chastity under siege both from outside, as Leander woos Hero with Comus-like rhetoric, and from inside, as the girl becomes aware of her own stirring desire.[124] Torn, Hero

> Strove to resist the motions of her heart.
> And hands so pure, so innocent, nay such
> As might have made Heaven stoop to have a touch,
> Did she uphold to Venus, and again
> Vow'd spotless chastity, but all in vain. (*Hero and Leander*, 1. 364–8)[125]

Hero is in the traditional situation of the Ovidian heroine, divided between conflicting impulses. As it is clearly crazy to expect Venus to protect chastity, the lines anticipate Hero's final capitulation to desire.

---

[123] See *Variorum*, ii, pt. 3, 990.
[124] See Shullenberger's reading of *Comus* as the Lady's confrontation with her own emerging sexuality (*Lady in the Labyrinth*, 109–41).
[125] See the *Variorum*, which qualifies the note: 'Whether or not Milton remembered Marlowe's "stoope", the contrast is rich in significance' (ii, pt. 3, 990). The *Variorum* does not note another similar image in *Hero and Leander*. Leander argues that virginity dies with the individual: 'But this fair gem, sweet in the loss alone, | When you fleet hence, can be bequeath'd to none. | Or if it could, down from th' enamell'd sky | All heaven would come to claim this legacy' (1. 247–50). According to the narrator, such a descent would confuse the categories of heaven and earth, thus causing chaos to come again. Milton imagines a more beneficial exchange.

Milton's yoking together of Spenser and Marlowe in his last lines seems rather odd. Marlowe's own premature death has too often encouraged his relegation to the sidelines of English literary history, an ur-Shakespeare whose Ovidianism, like his mighty line, was perfected by his greater successor.[126] In Stephen Greenblatt's influential reading he is the antithesis of Spenser.[127] Yet he may introduce a further alternative to the forms of courtship imagined by Shakespeare and Milton. The situation of *Hero and Leander* is the highly conventional one of sexual pursuit and, ultimately, the taking of chastity. But Marlowe's couple does not fall completely into their expected roles. While Hero, paradoxically Venus' nun, plays the role of the coy mistress, she herself desires Leander; while he acts like a typical rake, he is unsure of what to do when he first finds himself in her bed. Their union is not impeded by the conventional forbidding father, but by their own inexperience. Marlowe draws on the *Heroides*, in which the lovers equally desire each other, but are aware that what keeps them apart is less the Hellespont than their own imagined fears.[128] Like the other letters in the *Heroides*, the exchange between Hero and Leander is concerned with the power of the imagination and delay to thwart but also increase desire. While the couple complains about the delays that keep them apart, they also constantly dream of a meeting, as Leander says, 'ubi dulce morari est' ('where tarrying is sweet', *Heroides*, 18. 209). As they know, the drawing out of their courtship allows them to enjoy the imagined anticipation and heightens the pleasure of the final consummation.[129]

---

[126] Both Marlowe's and Shakespeare's roles in refining the iambic pentameter that Milton uses primarily for the *good* characters in *Comus* and throughout *Paradise Lost* are too easily overlooked.

[127] *Renaissance Self-Fashioning: From More to Shakespeare* (Chicago, 1980), 222. But see Hulse, who points out some suggestive similarities between the two writers (*Metamorphic Verse*, 10–11).

[128] Marlowe also seems to find inspiration in Ovid for his famous description of Neptune's attempted rape of Leander. In *Heroides* 19. 129–50, Hero chides Neptune for keeping the lovers apart. She reminds him that he too has been a lover, and complains that gods shouldn't bully boys: 'turpe deo pelagi iuvenem terrere natantem' ('tis shame for the god of the sea to terrify a swimming youth', 19. 145). Marlowe's Neptune has clearly taken this rebuke to heart.

[129] On Marlowe's use of narrative and erotic 'tantalization' see Fred B. Tromly, *Playing with Desire: Christopher Marlowe and the Art of Tantalization* (Toronto, 1998). The narrative principle of delay becomes even more pronounced in Chapman's continuation of Marlowe's poem which, trying to postpone the inevitable, produces a remarkable series of digressions and complications.

By choosing these Ovidian lovers, Marlowe makes innocent, reciprocal, and ultimately satisfied sexual desire the subject of his poetry. Critics, however, have been divided on his couple, and have wondered how ideal or indeed reciprocal the relation is. Gazing at Hero's naked body, Leander is compared to 'Dis, on heaps of gold fixing his look' (2. 326), a simile which makes him a miser and her his loot. At the end of the poem, moreover, the two lovers experience their union in very different ways. Leander enters gleefully into 'the orchard of th' Hesperides' (2. 298), the paradise invoked in a rather different form in Milton's Spirit's journey; in contrast, Hero is embarrassed and worries about what will happen when day comes. Even when coupled intimately, men and women remain divided in their experiences.[130] Moreover, the final climax is represented as a form of 'strife', a key word in the poem. As she finally gives in to Leander and her own desires, Hero 'trembling strove; this strife of hers (like that | Which made the world) another world begat | Of unknown joy' (2. 291–3). Some critics read this scene positively, as showing an alliance between individual and cosmic principles of creative friction rather like that in Spenser. Harry Levin sees the union of the lovers as 'a resolution of the antithesis, which runs through Marlowe's work, between creative and destructive energies. The strife, by its very striving, is metamorphosed into its opposite, which is love.'[131] John Leonard suggests antithetically that strife reveals the warlike aspects of Leander's campaign against Hero. As Leonard also points out, while the lovers may desire each other equally, they do not do so at the same time. Hero's reluctance attracts Leander; her willingness, and assumption of a more aggressive role, causes him to lose, shall we say, interest.[132]

---

[130] A reverse division of the interpretation of sexual intercourse along gender lines is apparent at the end of Thomas Peend's 1565 *The Pleasant fable of Hermaphroditus and Salmacis*. Where Salmacis experiences their merging as the triumphant union of lovers, Hermaphroditus and the narrator see it as emasculation and loss of self (A8^{r-v}). I'll return to the figure of the hermaphrodite in Ch. 3.

[131] Harry Levin, *The Overreacher: A Study of Christopher Marlowe* (Boston, 1964), 144. Gordon Braden argues also that what appears to be opposition turns out to be 'actually intimate cooperation toward a fairly simple end by a fairly roundabout way' (*The Classics and English Renaissance Poetry: Three Case Studies* (New Haven, 1978), 144).

[132] John Leonard, 'Marlowe's Doric Music: Lust and Aggression in Hero and Leander', *English Literary Renaissance*, 30/1 (2000), 55–76. Leonard argues that the 'rapture' of the final climax is hard to differentiate fully from rape. Leonard also notes how the image of Venus striving to attract Adonis' attention (*Hero and Leander*,

The final lines that describe the coming of dawn focus not on the advent of light, or other motifs expected in an aubade, but on the dark figure of 'ugly Night' who 'Dang'd down to hell her loathsome carriage' (2. 332, 334). While we do not know how Marlowe intended to finish the poem—or if indeed he intended to do so at all—the last image reminds us that this is another tale in which desire leads to death. The end thus brings us back to the beginning, which ominously foreshadows Leander's drowning by setting the scene 'On Hellespont, guilty of true love's blood' (1. 1).

The ambiguity of the poem suggests the difficulty of imagining a completely new kind of love relationship that can be free of conventions. It also suggests one thing Marlowe shares with Shakespeare and Spenser: the failure to represent a happy and enduring union between a man and a woman. Shakespeare's epyllion treats such a union as a myth that never existed.[133] Even his comedies, propelled through courtship towards marriage, end when we get there. Similarly, while Spenser's *Faerie Queene* looks forward to an ideal of chaste marriage, all unions in the poem are postponed to the future: Una and Redcrosse, Britomart and Artegall, and, above all, Arthur and the Faerie Queene. Neither Britomart nor any other knight ever sees the Garden of Adonis.

The garden where the visions of Spenser, Shakespeare, and Marlowe all flourish together is therefore not the end of the Spirit's journey. There is another still further up in which:

> farr above in spangled sheen
> Celestial *Cupid* her fam'd Son advanc't,
> Holds his dear *Psyche* sweet intranc't
> After her wandring labours long,
> Till free consent the gods among
> Make her his eternal Bride,
> And from her fair unspotted side
> Two blissful twins are to be born,
> Youth and Joy; so *Jove* hath sworn. (1003–11)

12–4) is recalled at key points by Milton in *Paradise Lost* ('Marlowe's Doric Music', 65 n. 22).

[133] Heather James, 'Shakespeare and Classicism', in Patrick Cheney (ed.), *The Cambridge Companion to Shakespeare's Poetry* (Cambridge, 2007), 210.

Milton goes beyond the Elizabethans—including Spenser (whose Cupid and Psyche appear *in* the Garden of Adonis with Venus and Adonis)—and indeed beyond Ovid himself as the story of Cupid and Psyche does not appear in his works. It is a late myth, appearing first as an inset narrative in Apuleius' *The Metamorphosis*, or *Golden Ass*, a work which, as its title suggests, is in dialogue with Ovid.[134] As E. J. Kenney has noted, Apuleius' Psyche 'at the crucial moment of decision, is portrayed as an Ovidian heroine, a conflation of Althaea, Byblis, Hypermestra and Myrrha'.[135] Moreover, the description of Cupid's palace to which Psyche comes at the opening of Book 5 (believing that she is about to die) echoes Ovid's ekphrasis of the Palace of the Sun at the opening of *Metamorphoses* 2 to which Phaethon comes.[136] By using this as background (literally) for his new figures, Apuleius recalls Ovid's first and perhaps most famous story of premature death: that of the doomed son who plunges to his death when he tries to take over the chariot of his father. Apuleius turns a story of broken filial succession into one of marital union and, in so doing, claims his own partnership with Ovid.

For Milton too the final couple figures his relation to his sources as both a succession from parent to child and a happy erotic union.[137]

---

[134] See Apuleius, *Cupid & Psyche*, ed. E. J. Kenney (Cambridge, 1990), 23–4, 29–30, and *passim*. Alison Keith and Stephen James Rupp summarize some of the main points of Apuleius' exchange with Ovid ('After Ovid: Classical, Medieval and Early Modern Receptions of the *Metamorphoses*', in *Metamorphosis: The Changing Face of Ovid in Medieval and Early Modern Europe*, 23–6). See also Barchiesi and Hardie, 'The Ovidian Career Model: Ovid, Gallus, Apuleius, Boccaccio', in Moore and Hardie (eds.), *Classical Literary Careers and their Reception*, 59–88. Mary Zimmerman's inclusion of Apuleius' myth in her popular stage adaptation of *Metamorphoses* draws on some of the relations between the two works, while also noting the crucial difference: 'Almost none of these stories have completely happy endings. | This is different' (*Metamorphoses: A Play* (Evanston, Ill., 2002), 76).

[135] *Cupid & Psyche*, 19. As we'll see in the next chapter, Milton's Lady also recalls some of these figures.

[136] See Kenney's notes (ibid. 137–42). Zimmerman's organization of the tales makes the connection between the two clear as well. In her staging, the story of Phaethon, interpreted on stage through the presence of a 'therapist' as illustrating 'the dangers of premature initiation' (*Metamorphoses: A Play*, 63), is immediately followed by that of Psyche which shows how 'The soul wanders in the dark until it finds love' (ibid. 76). I'll return to the story of Phaethon in Ch. 4 especially.

[137] In this respect, he is drawing on the occasion of the performance, which looks forward to the succession of the future Lord of the family (the Elder Brother) and the fulfilment of the Lady's chastity in marriage.

The lineage of Venus and Cupid counters the image of matriarchal inheritance with which the masque opened—Circe and Comus—so that the transforming and effeminizing power of Circe is itself transformed into a redemptive love which leads the son to go above his parent. Filial descent becomes ascent, anticipating the reciprocal up/down striving of the concluding lines. We rise above the figures of Venus and Adonis (an ambiguous model for happily married love at the best of times) to the next generation, and to Milton himself, who places a different kind of couple in his highest paradise. Erotic desire itself is reimagined, as Cupid is transformed from the sadistic tyrant of *Faerie Queene* 3.12 into an example of domestic happiness. The image here is a kind of sketch for the much more extended examination of ideal married love in *Paradise Lost*, in which Milton replies to Shakespeare by showing that fulfilled sexual desire is not a myth, but part of our original and innocent nature.

The figure of the struggling Psyche is an appropriate model for the Lady, and for Milton himself around this time. He returned to her soon after in *Areopagitica*, using her task of separating out kinds of seeds to represent the soul's endless struggle to tell good from evil (*Works*, iv. 310). In *Areopagitica*, where Milton is concerned with individual freedom of thought, the isolated Psyche is an image for differentiation. But in *Comus*, she is part of a couple and stands for the power of and need for union. In Apuleius' story, Psyche loses her husband when she is persuaded by her envious sisters that he is a monster who will devour her; through suffering she learns that in union with another she is not consumed but strengthened. Though she endures trials on her own, her ultimate goal is not individuation but relation, and she is dependent on higher forces outside of herself for the completion of her tasks.[138] Her story is thus appropriate for the Lady, who must understand that chastity does not mean the sterile autonomy of Adonis. It is equally so for the other Lady, Milton, as he makes himself through the many sources out of which he creates his new vision.[139] The masque shows that autonomy

---

[138] As Kenney notes, the story was commonly read as showing the inadequacy of human action on its own without the invention of divine grace (*Cupid & Psyche*, 19).

[139] I will return to the common identification of Milton, known as 'The Lady of Christ's', with the Lady in the next chapter.

and dependence are not mutually exclusive, but reciprocally sustaining.[140]

Psyche is part of another courtship plot, one that moves through trial, delay, and strife to reunion. Her story is thus broadly similar to that of Spenser's Amoret and Scudamour. In Milton, however, we only see Cupid and Psyche after the courtship is over. But marriage is not, as it is in Shakespeare's plays, 'The End' of the story. The poem and couple projects itself forward in time and space in the announcement of the future birth of twins, 'Youth and Joy' (1011).[141] It thus pushes us forward to imagine something new that is just beginning to take shape: Milton's poetic vision itself. There may be some competitive strife in this glimpse of the generation still to come—where Spenser's Cupid and Psyche (like Apuleius') have one child, Pleasure, Milton's have to have *two*. But the image of twins concludes the transformation of the patterns of doubling and antithesis that run through the poem. A single child might give a neater sense of closure, of resolution of differences through synthesis, like the hermaphrodite which ends the 1590 *Faerie Queene*. Instead, we are asked to think again about other ways of imagining the relation between two things. If the figures recall Spenser's twins, Amoret and Belphoebe, they do so by contrast.[142] While Amoret and Belphoebe clearly stand for antithetical experiences of desire, the connection between the terms *Youth* and *Joy* is not instantly apparent. They are obviously not antitheses nor (I sure hope) are they identical. They are an odder pair than 'L'Allegro' and 'Il Penseroso', whose asymmetry we have become acclimatized to. Twins themselves play different roles in

---

[140] As will be clearer in the next chapter, I therefore disagree with John Rumrich's description of the final vision as one of 'lofty autonomy' (*Milton Unbound: Controversy and Reinterpretation* (Cambridge, 1996), 94). My claim that Milton uses allusions to create an alternative model of identity to that of the autonomous self of Satan has been in some respects anticipated by Paul Stevens, in 'Discontinuities in Milton's Early Public Self-Representation', *Huntington Library Quarterly*, 51/4 (1988), 263–4. Stevens's argument, however, is confined to Milton's use of biblical allusions.

[141] On the openness of the ending in relation to Milton's own presentation of his new poetics, see especially Guillory, *Poetic Authority*, 93; and Colin Burrow, *Epic Romance: Homer to Milton* (Oxford, 1993), 287–8.

[142] Milton could also, as Roy Flannagan suggests, take the idea of twins from the *Symposium*, where Diotima says that spiritual procreation produced Wisdom and Virtue (*The Riverside Milton* (Boston, 1998), 113). Still, this also seems to me a very different kind of couple.

literary traditions: while they are great generators of comic plotting, as any reader of classical literature knows, they can be a source of destructive strife. The unexpected and ambiguous couple here suggests an attempt to imagine a new and open model for relations, both erotic and literary, that is not one of absolute antithesis followed by complete synthesis. The conclusion of the masque thus balances closure and open-endedness. The teleological thrust of the narrative, reinforced by its different images of journeying and translation, is answered by a corresponding resistance of teleological finality as the masque rises to heaven only to end by coming back to earth. The mixing of elements of Spenser and Marlowe in the last lines itself gently echoes the final image of the reciprocal and creative striving between high and low forces, ascending and descending to meet each other. The energies behind the poem are no longer opposed, as they first appeared, but are part of a single exchange, something rather like a dance.

2

Choosing Ovids (2)

THE ARGUMENT

This chapter doubles back to look again at Milton's early Ovidian experiments in two further contexts. I look first at two forms of seventeenth-century Ovidianism: libertine poetry and the court masque. I suggest, moreover, that Milton was aware of the political significance of Ovid's poetry, and, in particular, of his calendar, the Fasti. While this work has long been overlooked by Renaissance scholars, it contributed to the meaning of the Renaissance Ovid and provides an important Ovidian subtext for Milton's grappling with contemporary problems in both his Latin verse and Comus. Like Ovid, Milton is particularly interested in time as a poetical, political, as well as personal question.

MORE OVIDS

In looking back to earlier English Ovidianism Milton seems, as he often does, a bit out of step with his own time, a kind of 'last Elizabethan'.[1] At the same time, his interest in the classics and his English predecessors does not necessarily mean he was unaware of developments in his own time, or inattentive to the new ways in which Ovid was being used by others who were writing during the years of his own poetic apprenticeship. In fact, Milton seems very conscious of contemporary poetical forms.

---

[1] Helgerson, *Self-Crowned Laureates*, 231. Helgerson argues that Milton should be seen as part of his own milieu; see especially 187–9.

In the late sixteenth and early seventeenth centuries, the English Ovid underwent further metamorphoses. The feverish burst of inspired creativity of the 1590 Ovidian vogue quickly exhausted itself, generating a backlash by the end of the century. The rapid rise and fall of the Elizabethan Ovid is encapsulated by John Weever's 1600 *Faunus and Melliflora*, which, as I noted earlier, narrates the coming of Ovidian forms to England. However, it also foresees their further transformation as a process of literal, literary, and even moral descent, as Virgilian *translatio* turns into Ovidian metamorphosis. As in *Comus*, immigration is imagined as dynastic succession, which is a central theme in the poem. As Comus is the son of the Ovidian Circe, Weever's Faunus is the son of the Ovidian Picus.[2] Weever thus suggests that the poetry of England gives birth to new, younger gods who require new stories, and to a new form, the epyllion itself. The opening situates the action just after the moment when Jove 'Deposde his Syre *Saturnus* from the throne' (3).[3] The timing seems a bit unlucky, given that the overthrow of Saturn marks the end of the Golden Age. But filial rebellion at first appears as progress. Faunus is an improvement on his misogynistic and rather puritanical father, who warns him off both love and poetry: 'Nymphes are like Poets, full of wit, but poore' (567); 'Looke not (my boy) at wit, and Poetrie' (570). The father tries to stunt his son's growth, and to prevent him from becoming an Ovidian wit and lover.

The poem thus reflects the recent attempts in England to break free from older traditions of poetry and love in order to establish new forms of verse.[4] Weever is acutely aware, however, that he arrives late

---

[2] Weever clearly draws on Ovid's story in *Metamorphoses* 14, in which Circe turns Picus into a woodpecker when he rejects her advances because of his love of his wife Canens. But, like so many Ovidian figures, Picus comes from Virgil; in *Aeneid* 7 he is the ancestor of the Latins who inhabit Italy when the Trojans arrive. In Virgil, however, Picus is the son of Saturn and *married* to Circe. Ovid's changes foreground the role of metamorphosis in the genealogy of Rome and contribute to his presentation of Circe as a darker figure than she had been in Homer. Weever adds further twists. His Picus is a misogynist rather than an example of marital fidelity and happiness, and the figure of Circe is completely eliminated. Instead, Venus is the source of Picus' transformation, so that desire becomes a sinisterly metamorphic force.

[3] Citations from Weever's poem are taken from *Faunus and Melliflora*, ed. Davenport.

[4] See also Brown, *Redefining Elizabethan Literature*, 124–5.

in relation to other experiments with Ovid.[5] He takes sides in the battle of competing Ovidianisms, using Marlowe together with Spenser to transform and correct Shakespearian models in order to show the possibility for reciprocal and innocent sexual passion. According to Weever, Ovid and Shakespeare got the whole story wrong. It turns out that Adonis really wasn't killed by the boar (which Faunus actually kills) but died of love for Melliflora; moreover, Venus was really in love with Faunus. As in Marlowe's *Hero and Leander*, Shakespeare simply provides Weever with a handy background against which a better form of love can emerge. Having disposed of Shakespeare's lovers, Weever foregrounds a pair of Marlovian innocent and inept lovers who, after some contrived mishaps and a long authorial digression to delay the action, are finally united in mutual and apparently simultaneously pleasurable strife: 'He giues, she takes, and nothing is denide, | She his, he her loue's force and valor tride. | And still they striue' (*Faunus and Melliflora*, 1001–3). Like Spenser and Marlowe, Weever tries to imagine a desire that can be both innocent and sexually fulfilling. Eros and chastity seem reconciled at last, as the lovers run off together. Their playful courtship leads to a happy ending, in which requited love is rewarded in marriage and procreation.

However, while Faunus himself breaks free from the misogynistic and philistine past and finds freedom and marital happiness, he leaves a sinister legacy for both love and poetry. There are other forces at work in the story to undo the happiness of the couple and to bring Weever's fanciful myth up against the hard reality of his own time. Picus' diatribe against poetry reflects the English anti-Ovidianism of the end of the century, which drew on the traditional fear that poetry inflames desire. The suspicion of sexuality voiced by Picus at the beginning of the poem erupts more destructively at the end in the form of Diana who, angry at the happy marriage, turns the couple's child into a monstrous satyr. The fully human Faunus becomes the father of Ovid's half-goat Faunus. From that point, the story abruptly regresses into a Shakespearian *aition* explaining why love is always miserable and the sexes forever opposed (653–72). The conflict

---

[5] See also William Keach's fine reading of the poem in *Elizabethan Erotic Narratives*, 162–89. Keach argues that Weever's work marks a new stage in which imitation becomes more self-conscious and even 'mannerist' in its borrowing. As he notes, most critics tend to see the poem as either a parody or a slavish pastiche of earlier works.

between eros and chastity erupts once more in the quarrel between Venus and Diana which occupies the last part of the poem. Diana sets her race of satyrs/satires out to destroy love:

> As we may see within oure Faërie land:
> The Satyres ierking sharp fang'd poesie,
> Lashing and biting *Venus* luxurie. (1072–4)

In retaliation, Venus attacks satires, contriving that

> all the Satyres then in England liuing
> Should sacrifisde be in the burning fire,
> To pacifie so great a goddesse ire. (1673–5)

In Weever's version of *translatio*, satyrs come to England along with the Trojan Brute. As the classical past moves to the English present, the fanciful world of myth slides into contemporary controversies. Weever's poem was published right after the 1599 Bishops' Ban on erotic and satiric verse, as a result of which Marlowe's translation of the *Amores* had been publicly burned.[6] Publishing a hybrid satiric/erotic poem at such a time was obviously rather daring, if not plain crazy. But as well as commenting on the increasing prudishness and philistinism that were inhibiting English poetry from the outside, Weever's poem also suggests that its development was being corroded from within. Innovation had rapidly fossilized into a new conformity. Unable to invent new forms, writers either churned out feeble copies of Marlowe and Shakespeare or turned to destroying the creations of others through satire and parody. Despite the efforts of a few—notably Drayton and Chapman—to create a sober, even Neoplatonic Ovid to arrest the decline, generic experimentation and subversion lapsed into parody, the generation of monstrous, hybrid forms of poetry.[7]

---

[6] Keach notes the witty dig in Weever's *aition* at the ban on satirical works: 'The ecclesiastical authorities behind the 1599 censorship of satire ... are here shown to be the secret agents of Venus's revenge' (*Elizabethan Erotic Narratives*, 185). See Keach generally for the relation between the ban and Weever's work.

[7] See also William Barksted's 1607 *Mirrha, the Mother of Adonis* which self-consciously narrates the 'prequel' to Shakespeare's epyllion, while concluding with a confession of inadequacy: 'His song was worthie merit (*Shakspeare* hee) | sung the faire blossome, thou the withered tree | *Laurell* is due to him, his art and wit | hath purchast it, *Cypres* thy brow will fit' (*Mirrha, the Mother of Adonis: or, Lustes Prodegies* (London, 1607), Early English Books Online, E1ʳ). As Weever suggests, the decline of poetry is associated particularly with the death of Spenser, and bewailed

This did not, however, lead to an abandonment of Ovid as a model, but rather to his re-invention. For the most part, the young poets of Milton's generation turned away from Elizabethan mythological Ovidianism and towards the witty poet of erotic and rhetorical skill. The debate between eros and chastity was detached from a narrative structure, and recreated in the form of the seduction poem, which allowed poets to show off their own Ovidian powers of persuasion, by inventing increasingly elaborate ways to convince the chaste lady to sleep with them. As the prototype for seventeenth-century libertines, Ovid generated a new legacy of literary seducers, rakes, and sometimes even rapists.

This Ovidian line of descent has its own complicated family tree. While influenced by Ben Jonson, who took many as his 'sons', writers of this generation claimed Shakespeare as their ancestor: Davenant encouraged rumours that his famous godfather was his real father, and in his 1632 portrait Suckling clutches a First Folio to proclaim his inheritance. But they drew their Ovidianism most directly from that of Donne. Like others of his generation, Donne had tried to break from Petrarchan Ovidianism and return to Ovid's original spirit as a source of inspiration for creating new forms of experience and especially desire.[8] Rejecting Ovid's myths, he used Ovid to explore his own sexual and personal instability. He adapted the theme of Ovidian change as a way of thinking about personal mutability and, especially, of representing the fluctuation of desire, both sexual and spiritual, that was for him a source of endless fascination and terror. For the next generation, Donne was the great liberator who had freed others to explore new territory and to discover new ways of thinking and feeling. Thomas Carew thus praised Donne for purging 'The Muses' garden' by banishing the mythological figures taken from the *Metamorphoses* with which weak poets used to 'stuffe their lines, and swell

---

in verse that identifies Ovidian and Spenserian complaint; see *Faunus and Melliflora*, 1063–4.

[8] See especially J. B. Leishman, *The Monarch of Wit: An Analytical and Comparative Study of the Poetry of John Donne* (5th edn., London, 1962), 55–66; M. L. Stapleton, '"Why Should They Not Alike in All Parts Touch?" Donne and the Elegiac Tradition', *John Donne Journal: Studies in the Age of Donne*, 15 (1996), 1–22; and R. D. Bedford, 'Ovid Metamorphosed: Donne's *Elegy XVI*', *Essays in Criticism*, 32/3 (1982), 219–362.

the windy Page' ('An Elegie upon the death of the Deane of Pauls, Dr. John Donne', 24, 67).[9]

The entwined presences of Ovid and Donne are especially evident in Carew's seduction poem 'A Rapture', which offers an alternative to Milton's vision of heavenly coupling at the end of *Comus*. Like Milton, Carew tries to imagine a brave new world of happy sexual relations that have broken free from inhibiting social and poetic conventions. For Carew, however, paradise itself is simply a metaphor for sex. Wittily drawing on Donne's vision of physical and spiritual coupling in 'The Extasie', Carew imagines a form of rapture attained when the lovers will fly to 'Loves Elizium' (2) and, merging totally, 'in their sweet extasie expire' (54). For Carew, frank and open sexuality, not chastity, will take the couple to a higher realm, in which they will join other lovers who, through sensual pleasure, have risen beyond the limits of this world. In Carew's symbolic garden, therefore, traditional myths of chastity are reimagined as ones of sexual gratification. Lucrece, Daphne, and Laura are all now happily united with the men who had pursued them unsuccessfully in life. The lovers have even transcended the conventional sexual roles that had repressed them—in which men ask and women deny—as the women now chase after the men. Both sexes seem equally gratified, and there is even an element of gender equalizing: by breaking free of her bark, Daphne has been transformed from a mere symbol of poetry into a poet herself who 'sings inspired Layes, | Sweet Odes of love, such as deserve the Bayes, | Which she her selfe was' (137–9). Rapture thus is the meeting of equals in a physical union that is mutually satisfying.

For Carew, the only obstacles to this paradise of sexual bliss are human customs, above all 'The Gyant, Honour' (3), that keep men and women apart. By representing these impediments as allegorical figures, Carew suggests that they are merely figments of the imagination. By making love, the lovers will strike a blow for freedom and break the illusory bonds that now 'fetter your soft sex with Chastitie' (152). This argument is typical of the libertine use of the antithesis between custom and nature; it is invoked also by Ovid's Myrrha, who justifies her incestuous passion by comparing it to the uninhibited acts of animals (*Met.*, 10. 324–35), and denounces society's laws as 'invidia iura' (10. 331), invidious laws that inhibit natural impulses.

---

[9] Citations are from *The Poems of Thomas Carew with his Masque* Coelum Britannicum, ed. Rhodes Dunlap (Oxford, 1949).

In his divorce tracts, Milton will similarly condemn the manmade customs that pervert the true relation between the sexes and inhibit both domestic and political freedom—one reason why his critics denounced him as a libertine. In *The Doctrine and Discipline of Divorce*, Milton makes custom a hideous monster from Ovidian myth who joins with error to destroy truth: it is 'no other, then that swoln visage of counterfeit knowledge and literature'; 'a meer face, as Eccho is a meere voice, [that] rests not in her unaccomplishment, until by secret inclination, shee accorporat her selfe with error, who being a blind and Serpentine body without a head, willingly accepts what he wants, and supplies what her incompleatnesse went seeking. Hence it is, that Error supports Custome, Custome count'nances Error. And these two betweene them would persecute and chase away all truth and solid wisdome out of humane life' (*Works*, iii, pt. 2, 367, 368).[10]

Carew's argument reminds us that, as Heather James has shown, Ovid's poetic licence offered writers a heady model for potentially subversive freedom of thought and speech.[11] Ovidianism becomes a means of imagining a new world order, freed from the shackles of inhibiting and artificial traditions. In some ways, therefore, Carew's concerns and goals are similar to those of the young Milton. But Carew's appeal to nature is undercut by his own use of Ovid. The Ovid of the libertines is Ovid the role-player, for whom everything is art, and there is no nature. Carew's poem draws attention to and delights in its own artifice. The rational and urbane demystifier of the tyranny of custom and liberator of human nature is itself a role he tries on for purpose of seduction. Under this mask lurk traces of the sophistic seducer who will use any philosophical argument in order to persuade his mistress into bed. The imperious opening, 'I will enjoy thee now my *Celia*' ('A Rapture', 1)—copied from the beginning of

---

[10] See also *The Judgment of Martin Bucer, Concerning Divorce*, in *Works*, iv. 18. Milton also attacks custom in his religious and political pamphlets; see *The Reason of Church-Government Urg'd against Prelaty*, in *Works*, iii, pt. 1, 272. The note on 'The Verse' added to later editions of *Paradise Lost* complains that the fashion for rhyme shows how modern poets have been 'carried away by Custom, but much to thir own vexation, hindrance, and constraint to express many things otherwise, and for the most part worse then else they would have exprest them' (in Lewalski, *Paradise Lost*, 10).

[11] 'Ovid and the Question of Politics in Early Modern England', 343–73.

Donne's 'Elegy 19'—is picked up later in the image of the speaker as a bee who will 'rifle all the sweets, that dwell | In my delicious Paradise, and swell | My bagge with honey' (59–61) and gather all his 'ravisht sweets' (75) as he wanders through the garden, 'Deflowring the fresh virgins of the Spring' (58). 'Deflowring' is very clever here, and in the extended metaphor the poet is only a bug after all.[12] But in this sexual fantasy, rapture seems to slide back into something that looks rather more like mere rape. The poet who demystifies old fables about the nature of love is just another fabler, one who presents a new myth of egalitarian, reciprocal, and natural love in order to disguise his more rapacious appetites.[13]

Like most seduction poems, moreover, Carew's breaks off before the imagined consummation. The poet is left forever asking, in increasingly ingenious ways, for entrance to the Hesperides. At the same time, the poet seems quite happy on the outside, where he is able to enjoy his fantasies freely and to display his potent genius so impressively. Where in Marlowe fantasy and delay heighten the pleasure of consumption, here they replace it. William Kerrigan and Gordon Braden have noted the prevalence at this time of poems which argue or imply that actual sexual consummation is disappointing. Kerrigan and Braden suggest therefore that far from overturning Petrarchan conventions, the libertines revived 'repressed Petrarchism in a libertine world' by finding new ways to avoid consummation.[14] As Heather Dubrow also shows, anti-Petrarchism was itself a creation of Petrarchism, or, as she Miltonically puts it, 'new anti-Petrarchism is but old Petrarchism writ large'.[15] Libertine desire seeks its own frustration, preferring the pleasure of the chase and of writing about it to real union with another. Edmund Waller's treatment of Apollo's dash after Daphne seems similar to that of Petrarch, for whom the object of the pursuit is not the beloved, but poetry and fame; Waller's

---

[12] I'll return to the use of insects as images for types of poets in Ch. 4.

[13] The ending of the poem also leaves the gender relations that the poet wants to dissolve firmly in place. As often noted, the last word of the poem, 'Whores' (166), jars with the overall unruffled urbanity of the voice. The speaker's self-presentation as a truth-teller who reveals the nature that custom tries to hide makes it possible to read the final word as his true opinion of women's nature—if he can be bothered to have one.

[14] 'Milton's Coy Eve: *Paradise Lost* and Renaissance Love Poetry', *English Literary History*, 53/1 (1986), 37.

[15] *Echoes of Desire*, 267.

Apollo 'catch'd at Love, and fill'd his arms with bays' ('The Story of Phoebus and Daphne, Applied', 20).[16]

As Braden and Kerrigan observe, for libertine poets, the break for freedom from poetic conventions was only on the surface, as rebellion led to the reinstatement of the original order—Petrarchism—in a new form. Using Ovid, moreover, poets could play at licentiousness and revolution while never challenging a status quo that afforded them so many delicious opportunities for rebellion. For Caroline poets, Ovidian poetic licence was a means of reinforcing, rather than challenging, the authority of the King.

The resemblance between the rhetoric of Comus and that of the Caroline poets might suggest therefore that Milton's masque is an attempt to define himself against the popular poetics of the time. Drawing on the resources of Elizabethan poets, he exposes the morally suspect, aesthetically sterile, and politically reactionary literary culture of the 1630s. Urging the Lady to relax and seize the day, appealing to nature over mere custom, and offering a form of 'rapture' and release through the transgression of boundaries, Comus clearly sounds like a libertine. But the liberty he promises leads to imprisonment.[17] The libertine Comus is an Ovid who has been co-opted for a decadent art, ingenuity that, masquerading as subversion, stifles innovation. While, like Weever's Faunus, Comus is part of the new generation of gods, he is a derivative figure, a throwback to a classically based poetics that is not going anywhere. In contrast, the end of the masque presents us with a dynamic dynasty in which familial descent is transformed into progress, and even literal ascent. Where Carew demystifies myth, reducing paradise to sexual pleasure by emptying it of spiritual significance, Milton restores it, imagining a rapture that is both sensual and moral. He converts Ovid from libertinism and rape to a vision of chaste and transformative sexual relations.

However, there is a more dangerous and complex form of contemporary Ovidianism also invoked by *Comus*: that of the court masques, in which Ovidian stories and themes were used explicitly

---

[16] Cited from *The Poetical Works of Edmund Waller and Sir John Denham with Memoir and Critical Dissertation*, ed. Revd George Gilfillan (Edinburgh, 1857).

[17] See especially Roger B. Wilkenfield's study of images of confinement in *Comus*, 'The Seat at the Centre: An Interpretation of *Comus*', repr. in *Critical Essays on Milton from ELH*, 123–50.

to celebrate monarchical power. The masque genre generally is preoccupied with contrasting forms of metamorphosis: in the antimasque, the possibility of moral degeneration, and, in the masque proper, the social and spiritual reformation that is facilitated by the transcendent authority of the King.[18] In masques, a moralized Ovid was used for purposes that were both aesthetically and politically conservative.

In court masques, moreover, the seductive Ovid was transformed into the source of chaste desire that supported the authority of the King. At court the dangerous eroticism of the libertines was restrained, at least officially; as one court wit observed: 'We keep all our virginities at court still, at least we lose them not avowedly.'[19] The presiding example was the King himself, who 'in matter of personal morality... was not far from the position of his puritan subjects', nor, one might add, far from that of the young Milton: he was 'strict and serious', abstemious, 'chaste and even prudish'.[20] In the years of Charles's personal rule especially (1629–40) the King and Queen encouraged 'a fashionable cult of Platonic Love as a benign representation and vindication of royal absolutism' in which '[t]heir marriage was idealized in Neoplatonic and pastoral terms as the stimulus for reforming Jacobean debauchery and current Cavalier licentiousness.'[21] Masques such as Townshend's *Tempe Restored* (1632), Carew's *Coelum Britannicum* (1634), and Davenant's *Temple of Love* (1635) idealized the couple's pure love as the basis of national and indeed cosmic order.[22] In Townshend, the King and Queen

---

[18] Anyone saying anything about the masque is indebted to Stephen Orgel's *The Illusion of Power: Political Theater in the English Renaissance* (Berkeley and Los Angeles, 1975), which redirected interest to the neglected form.

[19] Cited from Thomas N. Corns, 'The Poetry of the Caroline Court', *Proceedings of the British Academy*, 97 (1998), 60.

[20] Kevin Sharpe, *Criticism and Compliment: The Politics of Literature in the England of Charles I* (Cambridge, 1987), 13.

[21] Barbara Kiefer Lewalski, 'Milton's *Comus* and the Politics of Masquing', in David Bevington and Peter Holbrook (eds.), *The Politics of the Stuart Court Masque* (Cambridge, 1998), 296. On Charles's Neoplatonic politics of chastity see also Sharpe, *Criticism and Compliment*; Erica Veevers, *Images of Love and Religion: Queen Henrietta Maria and Court Entertainments* (Cambridge, 1989); and Maryann Cale McGuire, *Milton's Puritan Masque* (Athens, Ga., 1983), 130–5.

[22] For the influence of these masques on *Comus*, see Lewalski, 'Milton's *Comus*'. As Martin Butler shows, these masques were no more homogeneous than the poets themselves, but in general they worked to justify Charles's authority as it both expanded and was questioned ('Reform or Reverence? The Politics of the Caroline Masque', in J. R. Mulryne and Margaret Shewring (eds.), *Theatre and Government under the Early Stuarts* (Cambridge, 1993), 118–56).

reform Circe herself, who represents not only the passions but also the arts; in Carew, their virtue transforms the court, the country, and even the heavens themselves.

The chaste love of the married monarchs is also at the centre of Ben Jonson's 1631 masque *Chloridia: Rites to Chloris and her Nymphs*. The masque opens with a vision of a pastoral paradise that is threatened when Cupid rebels and literally raises hell, carrying off Jealousy, Disdain, Fear, and Dissimulation—forces associated with Petrarchan love and invoked by libertines as false phantasms inhibiting free love—in order 'to trouble the gods' (129–30).[23] Typically, however, the subversive forces of the antimasque pose no real threat to order; they vanish when Juno, goddess of marriage, appears, and are replaced by the figure of Chloris, the image of content married love. The presentation of Chloris, played by a heavily pregnant Henrietta Maria, suggests the presence of desire that is barely restrained and certainly not adequately covered by the Queen's deep décolletage.[24] As Thomas Corns notes, 'the highly charged eroticism of Caroline wedded chastity'[25] was meant to make visible the fertility of the royal marriage that would guarantee the succession. The masque shows the metamorphosis of subversive eroticism that threatens the social order into chaste and fruitful desire that supports it.

While the name Chloris is fairly common in pastoral poetry of the time,[26] it comes originally from the story in Ovid's *Fasti* 5. 183–354.

---

[23] Citations from Jonson's masques are taken from *Ben Jonson: The Complete Masques*, ed. Stephen Orgel (New Haven, 1969). Veevers notes how the action allegorizes the shaky beginnings of the royal marriage, and celebrates the couple's achievement of marital happiness that secured the peace of the realm (*Images of Love and Religion*, 127).

[24] Jones's sketches of the costumes are reproduced in Stephen Orgel and Roy Strong, *Inigo Jones: The Theatre of the Stuart Court, Including the Complete Designs for Productions at Court for the Most Part in the Collection of the Duke of Devonshire Together with their Texts and Historical Documentation*, 2 vols. (London, 1973), ii. 441–8.

[25] Corns, 'Poetry of the Caroline Court', 62. Corns and Ann Baynes Coiro both note however the tension established by these images of barely controlled eroticism, and especially of female fertility and power; see Ann Baynes Coiro, '"A ball of strife": Caroline Poetry and Royal Marriage', in Thomas N. Corns (ed.), *The Royal Image: Representations of Charles I* (Cambridge, 1999), 26–46.

[26] See for example, 'Aprill', 121 of Spenser's *Shepheardes Calender*; William Smith's 'CHLORIS, OR THE COMPLAINT of the passionate despised Shepheard'; and Edmund Waller's 'To Chloris, upon a favour received'. Chloris is usually a virgin, though, in Waller, war frightens her into compliance. For Lovelace's and Rochester's further parodic use of this figure, see Ch. 5. In William Percy's 1603 play, "The Faery Pastorall, or Forrest of Elves," Chloris is the fairy queen.

Like most Ovidian stories, the tale begins with sexual violence, as the nymph Chloris is raped by Zephyr. As in other stories, rape is the basis for generation. Unusually, however, this rape victim is positively transformed, as Chloris, now married to Zephyr, becomes Flora, the goddess of the flowers. Moreover, Chloris' transformation brings colour and creativity into the world, which, until this time, 'unius... ante coloris erat' ('before had been of but one colour', 5. 222)—lines which Jonson quotes as the motto of his masque. The story of the origins of the goddess of flowers is thus, like so many Ovidian tales, one about the origins of art itself.

As his notes show, Jonson had read the *Fasti* carefully and prided himself on his knowledge of Roman rites and customs.[27] Flora was a popular Roman cultic figure whose story was well known in the Renaissance. It was also known, however, that her rites were especially popular with prostitutes; according to some myths, she herself was originally a prostitute who bought her own deification with a generous legacy.[28] In Ovid she is a figure of potentially licentious female sexuality, who is contrasted with Vesta, the more dignified Roman goddess of chastity. But Ovid's Flora looks remarkably respectable: she is a 'contented married woman' who represents satisfied and creative desire.[29] In this respect she is a good model for Jonson's Chloris. Moreover, as Carole Newlands and Alessandro Barchiesi have shown, Flora is Ovid's 'poetic alter ego',[30] whose free and easy attitude towards life epitomizes the *carpe diem* spirit of elegiac poetry (*Fasti*, 5. 351-4). Like Ovid, she is a master metamorphoser: she shows the poet her garden, which consists of the young men whom she has turned into flowers—Narcissus, Adonis, Hyacinthus, Crocus—as Ovid turned them into stories in the *Metamorphoses*. Flora's role as an image for the transformative artist—an alternative also to the debasing

---

[27] See also Jonson's notes to *Hymenaei, or the Solemnities of Masque and Barriers at a Marriage*, in *The Complete Masques*, 514-23. I'll return to the larger antiquarian use of the *Fasti* shortly.

[28] This version was recounted in the scholar Thomas Godwin's widely used school text, *Romanae Historiae Anthologia: An English Exposition of the Romane Antiqvities, Wherein Many Romane and English offices are parallel'd, and divers obscure phrases explained* (London, 1614), Early English Books Online, A3ᵛ.

[29] Carole E. Newlands, *Playing with Time: Ovid and the Fasti* (Ithaca, NY, 1995), 108.

[30] Ibid. 110; see also Barchiesi, *The Poet and the Prince*, 133-40; and Maggie Kilgour, 'Eve and Flora (*Paradise Lost* 5.15-16)', *Milton Quarterly*, 38/1 (2004), 1-17.

Circe—was recognized by Poussin, who painted several versions of the triumph of Flora to represent the powers of art.[31]

Ovid's story of Flora is thus an *aition* and celebration of his own poetics. In Jonson's version however, the story celebrates not the poet but the King. It is used to show how Charles's authority derives from the chastity of his marriage. Jonson therefore changes the means of change: in his version Chloris is not transformed into Flora by rape; instead 'in a general council of the gods [she] was proclaimed goddess of the flowers' (5-6).[32] It is all remarkably civilized, as Jonson deals with the problem of rape by simply eliminating it altogether. Zephyr, Ovid's rapist, appears in the masque as a 'plump boy' (26) representing inspiration. This revision of the plot is hardly surprising, given that the role of Chloris was played by the Queen. But Jonson's bowdlerization eliminates not only sex but real transformation. Even Chloris' name does not change, thus reinforcing the image of the royal couple as the embodiment of a changeless ideal of chastity. As the masque tames desire, it also domesticates Ovid, reducing him to the rule of law, presided over by monarchical authority. Through the power of the King, Ovid can be transformed into the advocate of chastity, continuity, and stasis.

In Jonson, and the court masque generally, Milton might have found a model for his own attempt to remake Ovid.[33] He shared the King's moral values, and there are aspects of the royal marriage

---

[31] See *The Triumph of Flora* (1627) and *The Realm of Flora* (1631); Poussin referred to the latter as 'Primavera'. Both represent the goddess surrounded by the human figures she has transformed into flowers. See also Thomas Worthen, 'Poussin's Paintings of Flora', *Art Bulletin*, 61/4 (1979), 575-88. Other painters have used Ovid's story for aesthetic statements. Discussing Botticelli's use of the story of Flora in his *Primavera*, Paul Barolsky claims that 'in a very deep sense, Botticelli's picture is about the origins of poetry' ('Botticelli's *Primavera* and the Poetic Imagination of Italian Renaissance Art', *Arion*, 3rd series, 8/2 (2000), 32). Spenser recognized that Flora's garden was the image for the source of poetic inspiration; he draws on it for his depiction of his own creative source, the Garden of Adonis, as a place which contains young men transformed into flowers (see *Faerie Queene* 3. 6. 45 and *Fasti* 5. 222-9).

[32] A similar glossing over of rape occurs in *Hymenaei*, where the bride is described as 'rap[ed]' from her mother (418). In his commentary, Jonson explains that this is just a metaphor: 'The bride was always feigned to be ravished *from her mother's bosom*' in ritual commemoration of the original rape of the Sabines (ibid. 522). In the *Shepheardes Calendar*, E.K.'s note on the story of Chloris similarily omits the rape, noting only that Zephyr: 'coueting her to wife, gaue her for a dowrie, the chiefedome and soueraigntye of al flowers and green herbes, growing on earth' (434).

[33] McGuire also notes how *Comus* 'superficially resembles dramas that grew out of the tradition' at court (*Milton's Puritan Masque*, 137).

which resonate in Milton's ideal of chaste sexuality. Puritans increasingly implied, however, that the court language of chastity masked sensuality; in the 1651 *Pro Populo Anglicano Defensio* Milton would attack both Charles and his masques for licentiousness, claiming that in the theatre the King 'mulieres petulantur amplecti, et suaviari, qui virginum et matronarum papillas, ne caetera dicam, attrectare in propatulo consueverat' ('would wantonly embrace and kiss women, and handle virgins' and matrons' breasts, not to mention the rest', *Works*, vii. 236). But that is 1651. It is not clear how the young Milton viewed the court and King. The fact that he wrote a masque itself often surprises readers. While early critics read *Comus* as a fairly conventional endorsement of aristocratic rule, many scholars of the 1980s and 1990s assumed that Milton wrote a 'reformed masque' that turned the forms of expression that traditionally supported court power against themselves.[34] Recently, however, Gordon Campbell and Thomas N. Corns have argued that there is no firm evidence of any radicalism in Milton's early work, including *Comus*.[35] In the absence of any authorial comments on the subject, Milton's works are open to conflicting interpretations; the timing of the development of Milton's political awareness is not self-evident.[36] At the same time, it seems clear that by agreeing to write in a courtly genre, Milton was forced 'to situate himself in the culture wars that intensified in the

---

[34] See especially David Norbrook's seminal essay 'The Reformation of the Masque', in Lindley (ed.), *The Court Masque*, 94–110; Marcus, *The Politics of Mirth*, 169–212; McGuire, *Milton's Puritan Masque*; and Lewalski, 'Milton's *Comus*'.

[35] *John Milton: Life, Work, and Thought*; see 82–5 especially. As well as citing evidence from Milton's poetry they note that the publisher of the 1645 *Poems*, Humphrey Moseley, published court poets including Carew (ibid. 182); moreover, in his *Erotopaignion, or The Cyprian Academy* (1647), the young Royalist writer Robert Baron quotes liberally from Milton as well as Waller, Suckling, Lovelace, and Shakespeare—as if these are all the same kinds of poets in whose company he places himself (ibid. 187). The letter from Sir Henry Wotton attached to the first editions of *Comus* implies also that a copy of the masque was bound with the poetry of Milton's classmate Thomas Randolph, a coupling that suggests that Milton was seen as a similarly courtly poet. As Coiro also argues, there are many ways in which 'the pre-eminent poet of Charles I is John Milton' ('"A ball of strife"', 38).

[36] The problems with pinpointing Milton's political beliefs at this stage are laid out succinctly by Annabel Patterson in '"Forc'd fingers": Milton's Early Poems and Ideological Constraint', in Claude J. Summers and Ted-Larry Pebworth (eds.), *'The Muses Common-Weale': Poetry and Politics in the Seventeenth Century* (Columbia, Mo., 1988), 9–22. At the Canada Milton Seminar VI (May 2010), Nicholas McDowell gave a paper, 'How Laudian was the Young Milton?', which showed the difficulty of assessing the issue on the evidence of style and genre especially.

early 1630s', and in which he would soon submerge himself for a good part of his life.[37] The choice of chastity as a subject, understandable in terms of his own beliefs, brought into the open his relation to court ideology. If, as William Shullenberger argues, the character Comus forces the Lady to think through things that she had accepted unquestioningly, the masque *Comus* seems to do something similar for Milton.[38] Milton's poetic experimentation with Ovid leads to his gradual discovery that to be a poet is to enter territory that is political as well as poetical. But that is actually not surprising, as we will see by turning to Ovid's own poetry: first, briefly, the erotic verse, and then, at greater length, the source of Jonson's *Chloridia*, the *Fasti*.

REREADING OVID'S RAPES

As I discussed in Chapter 1, Ovid's fondness for rape scenes has always troubled readers. Such episodes are the most extreme examples of Ovid's reputed indifference to, or, even worse, apparent enjoyment of, human suffering. While medieval commentators and teachers solved the problem by reading such scenes as *aitia* of natural or divine forces, the stories were also read politically. Pierre Bersuire thus claimed that Jupiter was 'superbus vel eciam quilibet malus dominus vel protervus' ('a proud or indeed any evil or oppressive ruler').[39] Similarly, George Sandys comments that the violation of innocents proves 'how difficult it is, even for the most chast, to prevent the traines, and insolent lust of Great ones'.[40]

As Charles Martindale observes, the central goal of the allegorists was 'to make Ovid relevant to contemporary concerns'—as critics of course still do.[41] In general, literary criticism of the last forty years has been much preoccupied with the relations between art and power. Bersuire and Sandys's arguments have been revived by critics such as

---

[37] Lewalski, 'Milton's *Comus*', 296.
[38] *Lady in the Labyrinth*, 170-2. I say 'something similar' as it seems impossible to imagine Milton accepting anything without question at any stage.
[39] *Reductorium Morale, Book 15: Ovidius Moralizatus: De Formis Figurisque Deorum*, ed. Joseph Engels (Utrecht, 1966), 12; qtd. in Amsler, 'Rape and Silence', 75.
[40] *Ovid's Metamorphosis: Englished, Mythologized, and Represented in Figures*, ed. Hulley and Vandersall, 289.
[41] *John Milton and the Transformation*, 162.

Charles Segal, who suggests that Ovid's stories of rape reflect the 'sense of the helplessness and vulnerability of the individual in the vast Roman *imperium*'.[42] Much recent work has examined Ovid's relation to Augustan systems of power, looking at his 'profound engagement with the regime's whole programme, his insistent probings of the very underpinnings of its authority'.[43] Still, as I noted in my introduction, critics debate the nature of Ovid's politics as much as Miltonists debate those of the young Milton. It is possible to read both the *Metamorphoses* and the *Fasti* as panegyrics on Augustan rule; moments in the exilic verse also sound like sycophantic pleading. As Stephen Hinds notes, 'Every passage ever written by Ovid about Augustus admits of a non-subversive reading: but that is not in itself a refutation of Ovidian subversion.'[44] While it is tempting, therefore, to try to figure out which one is the 'true' or 'intended' meaning, interpretation needs to begin with acknowledging that the poetry enables both meanings, and that the ambiguity is itself significant.

Ambiguity, however, does not mean detachment. In Augustus' Rome, there was no aesthetic realm segregated from public life. As Andrew Wallace-Hadrill says, 'Augustus was too demanding to allow anyone's world to remain insulated from politics. Aggressive and uncompromising, this intruder inserted himself into every corner of Roman life and consciousness, transforming it in the process.'[45] He made all activities political, subject to public scrutiny and legislation. Most importantly for Ovid, beginning in 18 BC, Augustus extended his authority into the realm of sexuality through a series of laws that restricted who could marry whom, and which provided incentives for aristocrats who married and had children, while penalizing those who were unmarried or barren. Through this programme of sexual reform, Augustus shaped an idea of *Romanitas* with which he claimed to return to the customs and morals of the early Republic. He set himself as an example, stressing his own happy marriage to Livia (without drawing attention to their previous marriages or the fact that

---

[42] *Landscape in Ovid's* Metamorphoses, 93.
[43] Myers, 'The Metamorphosis of a Poet: Recent Work on Ovid', 197.
[44] 'Generalising about Ovid', *Ramus*, 16 (1988), 25. See also Barchiesi, *Poet and the Prince*, 251–2.
[45] 'Time for Augustus: Ovid, Augustus and the *Fasti*', in Michael Whitby, Philip Hardie, and Mary Whitby (eds.), *Homo Viator: Classical Essays for John Bramble* (Bedminster, 1987), 223.

they had no children). While traditionally the Iulii were said to descend from Venus, Augustus emphasized equally his relation with Vesta, chaste goddess of the hearth, taking over the role of Pontifex Maximus of the Vestal Virgins in 12 BC.

By intruding into the erotic, however, Augustus claimed power over the realm traditionally seen as the subject not only of princes but also of poets. He identified also with Apollo, god of poetry; Servius passed down the story in which the god was Augustus' real father.[46] Ovid's tale of Daphne draws attention to the link between god and *princeps*. As Apollo embraces the laurel tree he predicts its association with political power, and especially Augustus (*Met.*, 1. 560–5).[47] The episode thus uneasily identifies the origins of elegy and Augustan authority. Moreover, the god's appropriation of the transformed girl mirrors the *princeps*' transformation of both desire and poetry into political matters.

In such a context, Ovid's love poetry is indeed inherently political, though not necessarily subversive. Still, Ovid's views on sex stand out starkly from those of Augustus, and his account in the *Tristia* suggests that his exile was provoked partly by his implicit violation of Augustus' programme in his verse. Where Augustus tried to control sexuality with laws, Ovid frequently represents passion as a force that cannot be legislated; in the great impotence poem of *Amores* 3. 7, the poet cannot control his own body. At the very beginning of the *Metamorphoses* even Augustus' Apollo, returning triumphant from his conquest of the Python, falls prey to the power of eros and is transformed from a warrior into a lover. Ovid's many stories of rape and incest show that desire is savage and antisocial. Attempts to

---

[46] On this tradition, see Paul Zanker, *The Power of Images in the Age of Augustus* (Ann Arbor, 1988), 48–53; and Karl Galinsky, *Augustan Culture: An Interpretive Introduction* (Princeton, 1996), 213–24.

[47] The political reference of the tale and its direct reference to Augustus was clear to commentators, though its meaning was variously interpreted. Jacobus Bononiensis sees the story as allegorizing Augustus' chaste life: the myth is 'perhaps alluding to the ever-constant and more-than-conjugal love that bound Augustus Caesar to Livia Drusilla' (qtd. in Moss (ed. and trans.), *Latin Commentaries on Ovid from the Renaissance*, 38). See also Sandys, *Ovid's Metamorphosis*, 73–4. The reading is somewhat perverse given that Apollo is not a devoted husband but a desperate if unsuccessful rapist. As Bononiensis notes, moreover, Augustus' marriage may have been ever-constant but it was not fruitful in a more practical way: Livia failed to produce an heir. In the light of the difficulties of Augustan succession, the *princeps*'s reputed chastity inevitably has an ironic aspect.

restrain it always backfire as it perversely feeds on obstacles: 'quod licet, ingratum est; quod non licet acrius urit' ('What one may do freely has no charm; what one may not do pricks more keenly on', *Amores*, 2. 19. 3), because 'nitimur in vetitum semper cupimusque negata' ('We ever strive for what is forbid, and ever covet what is denied', 3. 4. 17). The lover of the *Amores* is made keener by the various porters, rivers, and husbands who block his success. As the narrator of Shakespeare's *Venus and Adonis* knows, 'An oven that is stopped, or river stayed, | Burneth more hotly, swelleth with more rage' (331–2).[48]

This fundamental principle is, however, completely overturned by the premiss of Ovid's didactic *Ars Amatoria*. Responding to Virgil's *Georgics*, Ovid reduces desire to an art, comparable to farming.[49] The poem's tone is infamously urbane and reasonable, as the *magister amoris* presents himself as a know-it-all guide who offers a three-step programme for getting, keeping, and dumping a lover. Rape itself is simply part of the acceptable courtship strategy: 'Vim licet appelles: grata est vis ista puellis: | Quod iuvat, invitae saepe dedisse volunt' ('You may use force; women like you to use it; they often wish to give unwillingly what they like to give', 1. 673–4). It is in fact a good old Roman custom, as Ovid points out by using the story of the rape of the Sabines as a model for picking up girls in theatres (1. 101–34).

Read as a handbook of rhetorical persuasion, the *Ars* was later influential in the development of the conventions of courtly and Petrarchan love, against which, as we saw, Elizabethans were reacting.[50] But there is something rather funny (in both senses) about the whole premiss. John Fyler assumes both that the poem is meant to mock attempts to tame desire and also that Chaucer read it that way.[51] The narrator's technique certainly didn't help courtly lovers attain their remote mistresses. In *Metamorphoses* 1, Apollo follows

---

[48] T. W. Baldwin notes the ubiquity of this idea (*William Shakspere's Small Latine & Lesse Greeke*, ii. 433–6). For other examples of this kind of paradox, see also *The Rape of Lucrece* (645–6), as well as Marlowe's *Hero and Leander* 2. 139–45.

[49] On the relation between the two works, see the seminal essay of Eleanor Winsor Leach, 'Georgic Imagery in the *Ars Amatoria*', *Transactions and Proceedings of the American Philological Association*, 95 (1964), 142–54.

[50] See especially Andreas Capellanus, *The Art of Courtly Love*, trans. John Jay Parry (New York, 1969).

[51] *Chaucer and Ovid*, 13. Michael Stapleton sees Shakespeare's Venus as a version of Ovid's *praeceptor amoris* ('Venus as Praeceptor: The *Ars Amatoria* in *Venus and Adonis*', in Kolin (ed.), Venus and Adonis: *Critical Essays*, 309–21). Other scenes of

the instructions offered by Ovid in the *Ars*, only to end up originating elegiac frustration.[52] As I noted, moreover, Ovid claims that the *Ars* was the work that, by appearing to advocate adultery, outraged Augustus. If it did so, however, it may be less for its morals than for the fact that the *magister* looks rather like Augustus himself: someone who intrudes into Romans' private lives, claiming that love can be controlled, reduced to a system and a set of laws. The poem makes poet and *princeps* doubles of each other, rivals for authority over the subjects of imaginative and erotic fancy.[53]

POET OF THE YEAR

In recent years, however, much discussion of Ovid's relation to Augustus has focused on a different didactic work, the *Fasti*, and on the politics of not only sexuality but also temporality.[54] The poem

---

female erotic instruction add further twists to Ovid's premises. In Francis Beaumont's *Salmacis and Hermaphroditvs* (1602), Salmacis tries to teach Hermaphroditus how to woo girls; while she conducts her lesson he runs away (*Salmacis and Hermaphroditvs*, 715–34, E1ʳ). In Weever's *Faunus and Melliflora*, the Nymphs try to teach Faunus how to woo by using mythological examples consisting almost entirely of rapists.

[52] The link between *Metamorphoses* 1 and the *Ars* was recognized in the *Ovide moralisé* where Apollo was shaped as a courtly lover; see Amsler, 'Rape and Silence', 78. Apollo's amatory ineptness was not universally recognized, however; in his edition, Regius enthusiastically identifies the rhetorical tropes used by Apollo, praising them as the perfect tricks for wooing women. (I hope he had difficulty getting dates.) Regius' commentary is handily reprinted in Moss, *Latin Commentaries*, 39–45.

[53] See also *Amores* 1. 15. 32–3: 'carmina morte carent. | cedant carminibus reges regumque triumphi', which Marlowe translates as 'Verse is immortal, and shall ne'er decay, | To verse let kings give place, and kingly shows'. I am not of course implying that Ovid is any more original in pairing the ruler and poet than he is in his creation of authorial doubles generally. The inherent tension in the position of the poet—who is dependent on the ruler, and yet has the godlike power to make his superior immortal—runs throughout classical poetry. See especially the opening of *Georgics* 3, in which Virgil imagines building a shrine for the triumphant Octavian at the centre of which is a statue of the poet, 'victor ego' ('I, a victor', 17). Poet and *princeps* vie for the centre of the poet's art.

[54] As well as Barchiesi, *Poet and the Prince*, and Newlands, *Playing with Time*, see especially Wallace-Hadrill, 'Time for Augustus'; the essays in *Arethusa*, 25/1 (1992) devoted to the *Fasti*; Mary Beard, 'A Complex of Times: No More Sheep on Romulus' Birthday', *Proceedings of the Cambridge Philological Society*, 33 (1987), 1–15; J. C. McKeown, '*Fabula Proposito Nulla Tegenda Meo*: Ovid's *Fasti* and Augustan Politics',

proceeds through the year, beginning in January and ending unfinished in June, interrupted presumably by Ovid's exile. It describes the movements of the stars and recounts events associated with particular holidays, explaining the origins of constellations and the different rituals that punctuate the human year. Ovid explains the reasons for the order of the months and offers us theories of the origins of their names. If, in writing the art of love, Ovid mirrored Augustus' sexual reforms, in poeticizing the year, Ovid explicitly recalled Augustus' recent revision of the Julian calendar by which he had extended his control into the dimension of time itself. Once read as a straightforward celebration of Augustus, Ovid's poetic calendar now seems to many readers a deeply ambivalent, if not altogether subversive, attempt to replace Augustus' vision of Rome with the poet's own: Augustan time with Ovidian time.[55]

While Augustus claimed to be simply representing the workings of nature with greater scientific accuracy, critics have noted the political implications of his reorganization of time. The calendar is a means of expressing political identities, the characteristics and values that bind a nation through time as well as space. Augustus took a very mixed and irregular group of rituals and holidays, many of which were actually foreign in origin, and redefined them, foregrounding days associated with the imperial family, and making the cycle of the year tell a linear story leading from Aeneas to himself. Downplaying some of the older, popular festivals, including that of the somewhat disreputable Flora, he focused instead on celebrations, like those associated with the goddess of the hearth and chastity, Vesta, which made the experience of the rhythms of time express his own vision of Roman history, culture, and values.[56]

---

in Tony Woodman and David West (eds.), *Poetry and Politics in the Age of Augustus* (Cambridge, 1984), 169–87; and Denis Feeney, '*Si licet et fas est*: Ovid's *Fasti* and the Problem of Free Speech under the Principate', in Powell (ed.), *Roman Poetry and Propaganda in the Age of Augustus*, 1–25. On the context more broadly see also Denis Feeney, *Caesar's Calendar: Ancient Time and the Beginnings of History* (Berkeley and Los Angeles, 2007).

[55] For a survey of some of the positions and consideration of the evidence see Elaine Fantham, 'Ovid's *Fasti*: Politics, History and Religion', in Boyd (ed.), *Brill's Companion to Ovid*, 197–233. Geraldine Herbert-Brown, *Ovid and the* Fasti: *An Historical Study* (Oxford, 1994), is the most vehement defender of the pro-Augustan reading of the poem.

[56] See especially Beard, 'Complex of Times'; and Wallace-Hadrill, 'Time for Augustus'.

Augustus' reform of time was one of his most successful and thorough ways of controlling the lives and experiences of others— and not only, of course, during his own lifetime. It enabled him to expand even further his control over territory traditionally subject to, or at least of, poets. As I noted earlier, time is a constant preoccupation in all of Ovid's works, related to the theme of metamorphosis.[57] In this too, Ovid is hardly original; time is one of the oldest subjects of poetry, as it meditates on its own meaning when confronted by the force that seems to mock all human aspiration. For artists, art offers the hope of transcending time, by transforming the transient into the permanent. The end of the *Metamorphoses*, as Ovid moves from timeless myth into Roman history and the speech of Pythagoras, draws attention to the problem of 'tempus edax rerum' (15. 234) and 'edax ... vetustas' (15. 872), the devourer of all things. But it offers the poet the consolation that he will escape this destructive force through the power of art.

The *Fasti*, however, takes a different approach to the problem of temporality. With its first word, 'Tempora' (1. 1), Ovid tackles time head on by turning it into the poem's and poet's subject. The enemy of human creativity becomes a vehicle for it. While the narrator of the *Fasti* at first presents himself as the simple recorder of natural time who will tell us 'quod ... ex ipsis licuit mihi discere fastis' ('what I have been allowed to learn from the calendar itself', 1. 289), by the end of the poem he is greeted by Juno as 'o vates, Romani conditor anni' ('O poet, author of the Roman year', 6. 21). Time is art, the creation of the poet. Through his choice of form and metre, the poet controls the reader's experience of the passing of time and displays his own superb mastery of tempo. Romans generally considered the self-contained elegiac couplet, which emphasizes the end of every metrical unit, unsuited to continuous narrative.[58] Cheekily, Ovid tells the story

---

[57] For larger discussions of the theme throughout Ovid's work, see the three essays on 'Time' in Hardie, Barchiesi, and Hinds (eds.), *Ovidian Transformations*: Denis Feeney, '*Mea Tempora*: Patterning of Time in the *Metamorphoses*', 13–30; Andrew Zissos and Ingo Gildenhard, 'Problems of Time in *Metamorphoses* 2', 31–47; and Hinds, 'After Exile', 48–67.

[58] On the form and its English analogue, see L. P. Wilkinson, *Ovid Surveyed: An Abridgement for the General Reader of* Ovid Recalled (Cambridge, 1962), 9–13. See also E. J. Kenney, 'Ovid's Language and Style', and John F. Miller, 'The *Fasti*: Style, Structure, and Time', both in Boyd (ed.), *Brill's Companion to Ovid*, 27–89 and 167–96.

of time in a metre that tends to delay it—creating a double movement of action and stasis that allows him both to move forward with the passing of the year and also to rein it in.

The tension between the dynamic narrative drive forward, which gains further momentum as it is harnessed to the natural turning of the year, and the delaying involution of the couplet is indicative of a general doubleness central to Ovid's elegiac calendar. It was written around the same time as his epic *Metamorphoses*; like Milton's 'L'Allegro' and 'Il Penseroso', the two are 'companion poems' which comment upon each other.[59] The *Fasti* realizes the fantasy of rising above the stars that concludes the epic, by presenting the poet's encounters with celestial figures. Traditionally, however, epic and elegy are seen as expressing contrasting sets of values and visions of the good life: the epic upholds the pursuit of national duties; elegy celebrates the individual, identified with the world of love, set off from and frequently at odds with society. The two genres therefore promote antithetical visions of the proper way to spend time. The epic, associated with the god Mars and *arma*, arms, is concerned with not only war but also history and the future; as the genealogy of *Aeneid* 6. 756 ff. suggests, epic is built around procreation and the continuing movement from fathers to sons that extends succession through time. In contrast elegy, governed by Venus and *amor*, frees eros from its procreative purpose and offers an appealing escape from temporality, usually imagined in terms of erotic and aesthetic suspense. So Ovid tells the sun to slow down, 'O lente currite noctis equi!' ('Run softly, steeds of night!', *Amores*, 1. 13. 40)—lines that Marlowe's Faustus will cry in despair to stop the clock that ticks him to damnation (*Doctor Faustus*, 5. 2. 135). The poet's choice of genre is thus inevitably bound up with issues of politics and ideology.[60]

Like other Augustan poets, Ovid frequently foregrounds his generic choices in his poetry. Each of the three books of the *Amores* opens with a scene in which Ovid gives a different explanation of why he has chosen elegy over epic or tragedy. Moreover, both within and between the *Metamorphoses* and *Fasti*, the difference between elegy

---

[59] For further discussion of the relation between the two works, see especially Hinds, *The Metamorphosis of Persephone*.

[60] The work of Gian Biagio Conte on classical genre has been especially important; see *The Rhetoric of Imitation; Genres and Readers: Lucretius, Love Elegy, Pliny's Encyclopedia* (Baltimore, 1994); and *Latin Literature: A History* (Baltimore, 1994), 1–10.

and epic is simultaneously invoked and challenged.[61] The *Metamorphoses* is a very different kind of epic from that of Virgil; it absorbs other genres and styles in ways that will be suggestive for *Paradise Lost*.[62] The *Fasti* is also an experiment that draws attention to its own innovation. Like the *Amores*, it opens with a conventional scene of generic choosing, in which Ovid invokes to dismiss the quintessential epic subject (and first word of the *Aeneid*), *arma*: 'Caesaris arma canant alii: nos Caesaris aras, | et quoscumque sacris addidit ille dies' ('Let others sing of Caesar's wars; my theme be Caesar's altars and the days he added to the sacred roll', 1. 13–14). However, Ovid's subject is not the expected elegiac *amor* but a more complex term: *ara*, altar. Unlike *amor*, *ara* is not antithetical to *arma*—in fact, these *arae* are also Caesar's (1. 13) and temples are commonly built to commemorate war. As Hinds notes, therefore, the *Fasti* is 'a rather epic kind of elegy'.[63] Ovid's first divine informant, the ancient indigenous Janus, who is 'biformis' ('of double shape', 1. 89), gives us an image of the hybrid poem that combines the epic teleological drive forward with the elegiac impulse to make time stand still.[64]

---

[61] In *Genres and Readers*, Conte notes the tension in Augustan poetry between upholding and putting pressure on generic norms; see also the two brilliant essays by Stephen Hinds in *Arethusa*, 25/1 (1992): '*Arma* in Ovid's *Fasti*: Part I: Genre and Mannerism', 81–112; and '*Arma* in Ovid's *Fasti*: Part 2: Genre, Romulean Rome and Augustan Ideology', 113–53. The fluidity between genres is important, too, for understanding the relation between epic and romance, often treated as antitheses. The title of Colin Burrow's fine study *Epic Romance* may seem a witty Ovidian paradox, but it reflects the traditional interdependence of the two genres which define each other. See also David Scott Wilson-Okamura, 'Errors about Ovid and Romance', *Spenser Studies*, 23 (2008), 215–34, who argues that the modern reification of the difference between epic and romance is itself partly based on the misleading bifurcation of Virgil and Ovid that I discussed in the Introduction.

[62] It is important to remember, however, that Renaissance theories of epic tended to be unusually Virgil-centric. For Roman writers the epic tradition was not unified, but had two main models, going back to Hesiod and Homer. In the *Metamorphoses*, the language of Ovid's opening claim that he will write a single song that stretches from the beginning of time to the present indicates his desire to merge the two traditions: the idea of a continuous narrative, which in Rome was exemplified by Ennius, and the Callimachean programme of short, independent works; see Barchiesi (ed.), *Ovidio: Metamorfosi I–II*, trans. Koch, i. 142–5.

[63] '*Arma* in Ovid's *Fasti*: Part 1', 82. See also his '*Arma* in Ovid's *Fasti*: Part 2'; and Barchiesi, *Poet and the Prince*, 16–39.

[64] On Janus as a figure for Ovid's poetics, see especially Philip Hardie, 'The Janus Episode in Ovid's *Fasti*', *Materiali e discussioni per l'analisi dei testi classici*, 26 (1991), 47–64; and Alessandro Barchiesi, 'Discordant Muses', *Proceedings of the Cambridge Philological Society*, 37 (1991), 1–21.

Ovid's works thus introduce the possibility of reconciling elegy and epic. This experiment with generic mixing will be recalled in Renaissance re-evaluations of epic heroism, such as those of Spenser, whose *Faerie Queene* embraces both 'Fierce warres and faithfull loues' (1. Pr. 1. 9), and Milton, who in *Paradise Lost* 9. 13–41 dismisses the classical epic of war, and places love and poetry itself at the centre of his heroic vision. Such a new form requires, however, that both traditional elegy and epic be reimagined. The *Fasti*'s treatment of *amor* is therefore strikingly different from that of Ovid's other works. With some notable exceptions to which I will return, sexuality in the *Fasti* is less violent and uncontrollable than in the *Metamorphoses*. It is organized around a pattern of 'sexual comedy' formed by three parallel scenes of thwarted rape (one of which involves the comic and inept Faunus). In other tales, like that of Flora, rape leads to a positive transformation and the acquisition of new and greater powers.[65] In Ovid's version of the assassination of Caesar, Vesta herself becomes a kind of rapist who, rather than let Caesar be murdered, snatches ('rapere', *Fasti*, 3. 701) him up to heaven, turning rape into rapture. Moreover, in the poem as a whole, the goal of the poet's desire is not a girl but transcendence through knowledge. Ovid's former patroness, Venus, is therefore metamorphosed into a Lucretian principle of cosmic generation (see especially *Fasti* 4. 91–132). Elegy itself literally raises the poet to the sky, where he encounters the gods and the stars themselves directly and reaches a state of rapture in which he can claim 'est deus in nobis' ('There is a god within us', *Fasti*, 6. 5).

As Venus is transfigured, the god of war and epic, Mars, appears 'disarmed' by the elegiac form and becomes the subject of several comic love stories.[66] However the poem also shows the difficulty of

---

[65] Amy Richlin complains that in fact the rapes in the *Fasti* are 'a mixed bag' but admits that most can be read happily ('Reading Ovid's Rapes', 169). See ibid. 169–72 generally. On the sexual comedy of the poem, see Barchiesi, *Poet and the Prince*, 239–46, who notes that these repeated scenes of folk festivities suggest a popular alternative to Augustan ritual.

[66] Hinds, '*Arma* in Ovid's *Fasti*: Part 1'; Barchiesi, *Poet and Prince*, 53–65. See especially *Fasti* 3. 1–3, and then 171–2, where Mars lays aside his helmet (though he holds on to his spear). Like Milton, Ovid dissociates himself from the epic that glorifies violence; instead, he draws on the philosophical epic, in which heroism is achieved through knowledge. In *Fasti* 1. 295–308, echoing Lucretius' tribute to Epicurus in *De Rerum Natura* 1. 62–79, he contrasts those who try to reach heaven through brute strength (the image here is of the giants who piled mountains on top of

domesticating the erotic and martial passions. Mars' warrior nature returns in May, the month of the carefree elegiac Flora, when the god suddenly enters re-armed and dangerous. The god's appearance temporarily darkens the light mood of spring, producing a cacophony which catches the poet off guard: 'fallor, an arma sonant? non fallimur, arma sonabant: | Mars venit et veniens bellica signa dedit' ('Do I err, or was there a clash of arms? I err not, there was a clash of arms. Mars comes, and at his coming he gave the sign of war', *Fasti*, 5. 549–50). The initial effect of this entrance is to break the book in two, dividing the world of war and heroic action from that of love and poetry itself.[67] However, Ovid surprises us by revealing that these two apparent extremes are in fact intimately related, as Flora explains that not only did she transform Narcissus and Hyacinth into flowers, but 'Mars quoque . . . per nostras editus artes' ('Mars, too, was brought to the birth by my contrivance', 5. 229). In Ovid's bizarre story of the origins of Mars, Flora provides Juno with a magic flower which enables her to give birth alone to Mars. The elegiac goddess of flowers, who is, as I noted earlier, Ovid's 'poetic alter-ego',[68] produces a new version of the god of epic—as Ovid himself is attempting to do.

Ovid's generic experiment and transformation of Venus and Mars had particular significance for Romans. While love and war are traditionally seen as antithetical, both gods are part of the foundations of Rome: Venus as the mother of Aeneas, and Mars as the father of Romulus and Remus. They played a central role in Augustan imagery. The union of Venus and Mars has long been a subject of poetry and art, going back at least to the song of Demodocus in Homer's *Odyssey* 8, which Ovid retells in *Metamorphoses* 4. 169–89. In later allegorical readings, the coupling of these two gods was seen as the marriage of love and strife through which the universe was created.[69] Aurelian Townshend's masque *Albion's Triumph* (1632), in which Charles's imperial force is softened by the love of Henrietta Maria, draws upon this traditional reading. However, Spenser's representation in the

---

each other) with the philosophers who through knowledge of the stars rise to immortality. This conventional opposition between different ways to heaven is of course also central to Milton, although in *Paradise Lost* 8 Adam will be told that knowledge of heavenly motions is not necessary for his ascent to God.

[67] Newlands, *Playing with Time*, 104–10.
[68] Ibid. 110.
[69] See Wind, *Pagan Mysteries in the Renaissance*, 81–96; and Wolfe, 'Spenser, Homer, and the Mythography of Strife', 1263–5.

Bower of Bliss of the disarmed Verdant who, enchanted by Acrasia, 'in lewd loues, and wastfull luxuree, | His dayes, his goodes, his bodie he did spend' (*Faerie Queene*, 2. 12. 80. 7–8), offers a more sinister interpretation of the meeting as the emasculation of manly virtue by feminine desire.[70]

For Romans also, Rome's double inheritance is a paradox; after all, Aeneas must renounce *amor* to found *Roma*.[71] In *Fasti* 2. 685–852, Ovid shows the conflict between these two inheritances of Rome through another story associated with its origins: that of Lucretia, whose rape by the tyrant Tarquin the Proud was the foundational myth of the Roman Republic. For Romans, Lucretia embodied the ideal Roman matron who would rather die than lose her virtue. Moreover, her rape precipitated the overthrow of monarchy and aristocratic lawlessness and the establishment of a republic based on the defence of chastity. By foregrounding chastity, therefore, Augustus proved that he was not a tyrant but the restorer of the values of the Republic.[72] Critics note that Ovid eroticizes the story and focuses on personal suffering, shifting attention from Rome to Lucretia herself. As we will see, a similar move is often noted in Shakespeare's version. The redirection of interest might seem a sign

---

[70] Visual treatments of Venus and Mars make the polarization even more obvious. Veronese's painting, at the Metropolitan Museum in New York, shows an armed Mars embracing a gracefully naked Venus, whose breast seems to be squirting milk. A horse representing both erotic and military passions is safely tied up in the background; in the foreground, Cupid, on his very best behaviour, is playfully tying the couple together with a soft pink ribbon. The scene conveys nicely the tempering of passions and bringing together of opposite principles into a fruitful union. However, in Botticelli's more famous picture in London, an alert and clothed Venus watches over a naked and debauched Mars, whose armour and, most sinisterly, phallic lance have been appropriated by a group of demonic-looking fauns.

[71] On the literal and symbolic opposition of these two words, see Newlands, *Playing with Time*, 14.

[72] Charles I's emphasis on chastity was similarly read as proving his benign use of power. The dedication of Henry Cary's 1638 translation of Virgilio Malvezzi's *Romvlvs and Tarqvin*, published near the end of the period of personal rule, used the story of Lucrece to defend the King as both loving husband and benevolent ruler. Cary claims: 'if contraries doe best appeare, when most directly opposed; how can CHARLES *the Gratious* be better drawn to the Life, than by the description of TARQUIN the *Proud*? How can the unparallel'd, CHARLES *the Chaste*, bee better portraited, than by the deciphering of TARQUIN *the foule Ravisher*? How can the happiness your *Majesties* Realms enjoy (and long may they enjoy it) under your *Majesties* blessed Government, better appeare, than by making knowne what Miseries and Slavery the *Romans* endured under the Rule of TARQUIN the *Tyrant*?' (*Romvlvs and Tarqvin* (London, 1638), Early English Books Online, A1^{r-v}).

of Ovid's lack of interest in politics, his general aesthetic withdrawal from the political into an elegiac world that is particularly fitting for a poem written in elegiac metre. However, Carole Newlands has shown that Ovid's story is not just shaped by generic conventions but is *about* generic conventions and how they inform our relations to the world and each other. The two central characters live in different poetic universes. The warrior Tarquin embodies the world of the epic, while the spinning Lucretia represents 'not only the archetypical female virtues of chastity and thrift, but the qualities of an elegiac poem'.[73] Rome's schizophrenic legacy seems to split the poem apart, as the realms of war and love revert into incompatible oppositions embodied in these human counterparts of Mars and Venus.

Newlands argues that the episode might express Ovid's fear that 'love elegy... cannot enter the public arena and the world of heroic action without being destroyed or significantly altered'.[74] Inversely, it also shows what happens when the epic invades the sphere of elegy: when rulers enter the bedrooms of the nation, as Augustus was himself doing. Ovid's stories of the rapes of Rhea Silvia (*Fasti*, 3. 11–48) and the Sabines (3. 187–234) further trouble Augustan ideology by showing that Rome is founded through repeated acts of rape. The tales of 'sexual comedy', which Ovid invents, contrast strikingly with the historical stories of Rome, which involve sexual violation. The poem is therefore not a withdrawal from politics but an intervention in them, in which the demystifying poet exposes the incoherence and violence at the basis of Roman culture. The ideology of chastity is a convenient veil for a society which originates in and is sustained by rape, in which, by invading the private lives of its people, the *princeps* not only repeats but expands Rome's founding principles.

By writing the story of Lucretia in elegiac metre, moreover, Ovid fights back, restoring the tale to the sphere to which it belongs, and asserting the values of love and the individual. Yet the episode equally shows the problems of turning from the Roman epic to the traditional elegy as an alternative source of values. The rapist Tarquin is referred to as 'hostis ut hospes' ('a foe as guest', *Fasti*, 2. 787) and 'amans hostis' ('lover foe', 2. 805), paradoxical images which draw on the tradition of love elegy itself. As Ovid shows comically in the *Amores*,

---

[73] *Playing with Time*, 171.   [74] Ibid. 172.

in Roman elegy, love is a form of warfare waged through endless paradox.[75] When the lover is a *miles amoris*, love is not an alternative to war, but the internalization of war in the individual. *Roma* and *Amor* are truly mirror images, as Ovid's Tarquin and Lucrece are bound up with each other.[76] As the story of Daphne suggests, elegy is itself a product of Augustus' power as much as Ovid himself is.[77]

By writing the calendar, or in fact by writing any poetry at all, Ovid necessarily enters into a debate with Augustus about Rome and the place of both love and poetry in its culture. On the one hand, then, the *Fasti* seems Ovid's answer to Augustus, an assertion of the poet's powers over his traditional subjects: desire, time, and poetry itself. Foregrounding the repressed figure of Flora and popular holidays of innocent sexuality, as well as the indigenous Janus, he presents a vision of Roman time that is older than that of Augustus. By joining together elegy and epic Ovid seems to offer an inclusive alternative to the binary system on which Roman ideology was founded that opposed chastity and sexuality, Mars and Venus, war and desire, epic and elegy, but which then blurred the differences between them

---

[75] As well as Hinds, '*Arma* in the *Fasti*: Part 1', 92, see especially Gian Biagio Conte's 'Love without Elegy: The *Remedia amoris* and the Logic of Genre', *Poetics Today*, 10/3 (1989), 441–69.

[76] As we'll see, this sense of the doubling between opposites is continued in Shakespeare's version of the story. Syrithe Pugh argues that in *Faerie Queene* 2, the heroic and erotic are similarly imagined as deadly twins: Acrasia's 'way of life is a simple inversion, and therefore a reflection of Guyon's, its apparent opposite, and her ethical valuation of the passions identical to his own' so that 'what appears to be the very opposite of Guyon's Roman chastity, is in fact a form of it' (*Spenser and Ovid*, 92, 103).

[77] The links between the two stories of Daphne and Lucretia make this clear, and indicate how a reading of the *Fasti* contributes to our understanding of the *Metamorphoses*. The story of the origins of elegy is paired with the foundation of the Republic, as in both *aitia* men appropriate silenced women as their symbols. After Daphne's metamorphosis, Apollo claims her as his tree, and 'factis modo laurea ramis | adnuit utque caput visa est agitasse cacumen' ('The laurel waved her new-made branches, and seemed to move her head-like top in full consent', *Met.*, 1. 566–7). Similarly, Brutus turns Lucretia into a symbol for Republican values. Here too the story ends when the silenced woman seems to stir to confirm her possessor's speech: 'illa iacens ad verba oculos sine lumine movit | visaque concussa dicta probare coma' ('At these words, even as she lay, she moved her lightless eyes and seemed by the stirring of her hair to ratify the speech', *Fasti*, 2. 845–6). In neither case is assent directly given, but rather assumed by the hardly disinterested viewers. Both scenes show the use of women by men for ideological purposes. Perhaps more chillingly, they suggest that Augustus' appropriation of elegiac and Republican discourse impedes anyone from speaking back effectively or freely.

through false resolutions and harmony. Yet the other hand holds the obvious paradox: any alternative may be itself absorbed into the system, creating a new binarism that perpetuates what it challenges.[78]

Perhaps this is one reason why the *Fasti* is so evasive about choice of any kind. The narrator includes multiple explanations for phenomena without deciding between them. While this is typical of aetiological verse, it is telling that here even the gods cannot agree on the origins of things. In Book 6, as the poem approaches its abrupt end, three goddesses offer competing versions of the origins of the month of June. The situation has an ominous subtext that reminds the poet that choice can be disastrous: 'perierunt iudice formae | Pergama' ('Pergamum was ruined by him who adjudged the prize of beauty', 6. 99–100). Troy fell because of Paris' choice among the three goddesses. The poet is understandably reluctant to choose, as he knows that 'copiaque ipsa nocet' ('the very abundance of choice is harmful', 5. 6). '[C]opiaque ipsa nocet' is a characteristic and resonant Ovidian paradox, related to the more famous complaint of Narcissus in *Metamorphoses* 3, 'inopem me copia fecit' (3. 466), to which I will return in the next chapter. But the scene suggests the darker mood that creeps in as the work approaches its abrupt standstill halfway through the year. The hesitant voice of the narrator in this poem provides a striking contrast with Ovid's confident self-representations as the cocky *magister* in the *Amores*, or the triumphant conqueror of time at the end of the *Metamorphoses*.[79] Whereas the *Metamorphoses* ends with the resounding conclusion which asserts victory over time, the *Fasti* confesses the real limitations of his powers. Time moves too quickly for the poet to keep up: 'Tempora labuntur, tacitisque senescimus annis, | et fugiunt freno non remorante dies' ('Time slips away, and we grow old with silent lapse of years; there is no bridle that can curb the flying days', 6. 771–2). For Newlands, the poem's final openness reflects Ovid's resistance of the ideological drive towards narrative and political completion and the resolution of contradictions; the *Fasti* remains irreducibly double.[80] But the incomplete year's abrupt ending also reminds us vividly of the *princeps*' very

---

[78] See especially Barchiesi, *Poet and the Prince*, 84. For Barchiesi, Ovid's generic experiment is therefore interested less in trying to combine the two genres than in showing the difficulty of creating a dialogue between them (ibid. 66–7).

[79] See Carole Newlands, 'Ovid's Narrator in the *Fasti*', *Arethusa*, 25/1 (1992), 33–54; and *Playing with Time*, 51–86.

[80] *Playing with Time*, 209–36.

real powers—and indeed of Augustus' own sinisterly creative vision. The *princeps* controlled time, desire, and ultimately even poetry itself. With a remarkably fine sense of poetic justice, Augustus sent Ovid to a frozen land, arrested in a state of primitive barbarism. One of the great horrors of Pontus for Ovid was that it was cut off from seasonal change and variety; the state of exile is an unending winter in which even the protean force of water hardens and 'stare putes, adeo procedunt tempora tarde' ('one would think that time stood still, so slowly does it move', *Tristia*, 5. 10. 5).[81] For Ovid, the *princeps* had found a way to stop time permanently. It was a sobering example for later writers who found their poetic visions in conflict with political power.

IT'S ABOUT TIME

I have discussed Ovid's calendar at length partly because it is generally his least known work. Until recently, it has not been very popular, even among classicists.[82] Furthermore, Renaissance scholars have tended to assume with Ann Moss that 'The fables of the *Fasti* do not seem to have stirred any imaginative response. The Middle Ages

---

[81] Gareth D. Williams also notes how 'the timelessness of his living death is itself reflected in the frozen immobility of his Stygian landscape and in the monotone of his emotionally frozen persona' ('Ovid's Exilic Poetry: Worlds Apart', in Boyd (ed.), *Brill's Companion to Ovid*, 356). Ovid seems cut off from the seasonal change which fuels his verse, as the sad memories of springtime in Rome in *Tristia* 3. 12 underline.

[82] On the poem's critical fortunes, see Newlands, *Playing with Time*, 1–3. Even Hermann Fränkel, one of the driving forces behind the 20th-century re-evaluation of Ovid, suggested that 'to versify and adorn an almanac was not a sound proposal in the first place' (*Ovid: A Poet between Two Worlds* (Berkeley and Los Angeles, 1969), 148). Yet poetic calendars were, of course, respectable classical and Renaissance genres; see Feeney, 'Mea Tempora'. John Gower, the first English translator of Ovid's calendar, was clearly aware of this tradition, and praised Ovid's achievement: 'Divers Poets before *Ovid* assayed this work *Fasti*, as *Ennius, Livius, Andronicus*, and others. But *Ovid* a long time after diligently turning over all the ancient Calendars and Monuments of the Pontifies, and other old Annals which perteined to religious rites and ceremonies, and reducing the *Romane* yeare into a more exact order, with an exquisite observation of the Cosmical, Heliacal, and Acronicall rising & setting of all the fixed Constellations, composed this memorable Poeme with much labour and study' ('The Life, Works, and Approof of Ovid, Gathered out of his own works and the relations of divers faithfull Authours', in *Ovids Festivalls, or Romane Calendar: Translated into English verse equinumerally*, B2ᵛ).

had left no tradition of interpreting them, and the Renaissance commentaries on the whole restrict themselves to abstracting and expatiating on geographical, astronomical, and historical data. It does not seem to occur to them that the *Fasti* might be imitated.'[83] But recent work has shown that in Italy the *Fasti* became of great interest in the late quattrocento.[84] In Florence, Poliziano made it the centre of his 1481-2 lectures, which influenced the paintings of Piero di Cosimo and of Botticelli, while discussions in the Roman Academy under Pomponio Leto were instrumental in the publication of two rival commentaries.[85] John F. Miller has shown too how it did inspire European imitations in the form of Christianized calendars which narrated the feasts of the liturgical year.[86] Recalling Ovid's calendar, and in some cases engaging with it quite intensely, these works also asserted the superiority of Christian customs over their pagan antecedents. Ovid's calendar continued to be a model during the Reformation, as Protestants envisioned their own versions of rituals and time.

In England there is evidence of a parallel and perhaps even greater interest. Though lamentably lacking an English teacher of the calibre of Poliziano, the *Fasti* was a common school text in the sixteenth and seventeenth centuries. At Wolsey's school at Ipswich, for example, it

---

[83] Moss, *Ovid in Renaissance France*, 18. Moss notes, however, that compared to other Ovidian works, the number of editions (some unannotated) increased in the 1500s.

[84] Certainly it was read earlier in Europe as well. *Fasti* 1. 307 is recycled verbatim in a 12th-century love lyric on the nature of desire discussed by Peter Dronke in *Medieval Latin and the Rise of European Love-Lyric*, 2 vols. (rev. edn., Oxford: Clarendon Press, 1968), ii. 456, l. 157. As Dronke notes, the poem mixes a range of Ovidian sources, though Dronke is unaware of the citation of the *Fasti* (i. 232-8). Given the medieval poem's attempt to reconcile earthly and heavenly love, however, the presence of the *Fasti*, cited as an image of spiritual ascent, is extremely suggestive.

[85] See Fritsen, 'Renaissance Commentaries on Ovid's *Fasti*'. Poliziano's lecture notes have been published in *Commento inedito ai Fasti di Ovidio*, ed. Francesco Lo Monaco (Florence, 1991). Poliziano's student Michael Verinus called the *Fasti* 'illius divini vatis liber pulcherrimus' ('the most beautiful book of the divine *vates*', qtd. in Wind, *Pagan Mysteries in the Renaissance*, 114 n. 5). Over time, the *Fasti* has attracted a peculiar group of fans, including Blake.

[86] John F. Miller, 'Ovid's *Fasti* and the Neo-Latin Christian Calendar Poem', *International Journal of the Classical Tradition*, 10/2 (2003), 175. Frederick A. de Armas has studied its use in Spain; see 'Ovid's Mysterious Months: The *Fasti* from Pedro Mexía to Baltasar Gracián', in Frederick A. De Armas (ed.), *Ovid in the Age of Cervantes* (Toronto, 2010), 56-73; and 'Sancho as Thief of Time and Art: Ovid's *Fasti* and Cervantes' *Don Quixote* 2', *Renaissance Quarterly*, 61/1 (2008), 1-25.

was studied in the seventh form as an alternative to the *Metamorphoses*, and was read along with Horace's *Epistles* in a year of study which focused on 'Verse composition and Latin letter writing. Turning verse to prose and prose to verse.'[87] But while we therefore know that many English students knew the *Fasti*, we do not know how they read it. It is often assumed that earlier writers used the poem mainly as a sourcebook for information on Roman ritual, in the same way that the *Metamorphoses* was once thought to have been treated primarily as an encyclopedia of classical myth.[88] As we will see shortly, the *Fasti* was of some interest to English antiquarians. But could some readers have seen the significance of Ovid's generic experimentation? Were they aware of the political implications of Ovid's examination of time and desire, and did it seem relevant to their own situations? If so, how might this expand our ideas of the meaning of Ovid at this time?

It is easy to imagine some general things that might have made the *Fasti* relevant to the Elizabethan experience. Like Ovid, sixteenth-century English writers were obsessed with genres, and with generic experimentation. Renaissance Italian critical theory tended to reinforce generic distinctions and hierarchies. But for English writers who were themselves increasingly members of a relatively mobile middle class, mixed genres promised liberation from the restraint of old hierarchical systems. Ovid provided models for generating exciting new poetic forms that suggested a new way of seeing and arranging

---

[87] Qtd. in Clark, *John Milton at St. Paul's School*, 117. Thomas Elyot assumed that both the *Metamorphoses* and *Fasti* were 'necessary for the understanding of other poets' (*The Book Named The Governor*, ed. S. E. Lehmberg (London, 1962), 32). The *Fasti* continued to be a regular part of the curriculum, often in rotation with the *Metamorphoses*. In his 1848 edition of the *Fasti*, Thomas Keightley praised its variety and claimed that 'There is not, perhaps, in the whole compass of classical literature a work better calculated to be put into the hands of students' (qtd. in Wilkinson, *Ovid Surveyed*, 119).

[88] Vives includes it in his curriculum, 'for the better knowledge of mythology' (cited from Baldwin, *William Shakspere's Small Latine & Lesse Greeke*, i. 196). Elyot refers readers to '*De fastis*, where the ceremonies of the Gentiles, and specially the Romans, be expressed', though he warns them that Ovid has no other moral or pedagogical use (*The Governor*, 32). In the early 20th century, the tendency to read the poem for historical information was unfortunately entrenched by the work of James Frazer, whose eccentric editions turned it into an anthropological textbook on Roman ritual, a kind of proto-*Golden Bough*; see Sir James George Frazer, *Fastorum Libri Sex: The Fasti of Ovid*, 5 vols. (London, 1929), and his more succinct Loeb edition.

the world.⁸⁹ With its diffuse and errant narrative structure, the *Metamorphoses* was an appealing alternative to the unified *Aeneid* that was the model epic for many theorists. In terms of structure as well as subject it inspired the epyllion with its proliferation of digressions. But the highly self-conscious generic mixing of the *Fasti* also finds a surprising progeny in the epyllion tradition, in which writers often foreground hybrid Ovidian figures—Glaucus, Scylla, Hermaphroditus, Faunus—as figures of the form itself.

Even more particularly, however, one might suspect that the *Fasti*'s treatment of time would have caught the attention of writers of the period. As Ricardo J. Quinones has shown, the Renaissance marked an intensification of the desire to transcend time through the power of human art.⁹⁰ In *Metamorphoses* 15, readers found both a haunting image of the consuming force of mutability and an inspiring assertion of the transcendent power of poetry. It was therefore invoked repeatedly in English poetry, not only to demonstrate time's ruthless power but also to affirm the ultimate triumph of art.

Studies of Spenser have therefore noted the particular importance of this climactic book, which is recalled throughout the different *Complaints*. In an influential essay, Michael Holahan interpreted Spenser's revision of Pythagoras' speech in the *Mutabilitie Cantos* as his repudiation of an Ovidian model of time. According to Holahan, in his final vision, Spenser moves beyond the limits of the pagan world, which can only imagine time as endless natural change, to find stability in Christian eternity. Pythagorean flux is transformed through 'a saving metamorphosis which redeems the destructive circularity of fortune's wheel'.⁹¹

However, Ovid offers Spenser other models for transforming time. References to the *Fasti* appear especially at moments when the poet reflects upon time and poetry. In both the *Shepheardes Calender* and *Mutabilitie Cantos*, the representation of time as a calendar recalls

---

⁸⁹ On this liberating aspect of Ovid in general, see especially James, 'Ovid and the Question of Politics'; Maslen, 'Myths Exploited', 36–52.
⁹⁰ *The Renaissance Discovery of Time* (Cambridge, Mass., 1972).
⁹¹ Michael Holahan, '*Iamque opus exegi*: Ovid's Changes and Spenser's Brief Epic of Mutability', *English Literary Renaissance*, 6 (1976), 264. For Spenser's use of Pythagoras' speech see also Angus Fletcher, *The Prophetic Moment: An Essay on Spenser* (Chicago, 1971), 92–106; Nohrnberg, *The Analogy of the* Faerie Queene, 84–5; and William P. Cumming, 'The Influence of Ovid's *Metamorphoses* on Spenser's "Mutabilitie" Cantos', *Studies in Philology*, 28/2 (1931), 241–56.

Ovid's poem broadly.[92] The *Mutabilitie Cantos*' exploration of Ovidian change is prefaced by an *aition* focused on the figure of Faunus and based on one of the scenes of 'sexual comedy' in the *Fasti*.[93] Spenser also remembers Ovid's calendar in the 'October' eclogue of the *Shepheardes Calender* in which Piers and Cuddie debate the kinds and powers of poetry. While Piers urges Cuddie to turn from pastoral and 'sing of bloody Mars, of wars, of giusts' (39), he also insists that love can raise the 'mynd aboue the starry skie' (94). The eclogue ends with an emblem taken from *Fasti* 6. 5–6 in which Ovid claims that elegy has made him a god: 'est deus in nobis; agitante calescimus illo; | impetus hic sacrae semina mentis habet' ('There is a god within us. It is when he stirs that our bosom warms; it is his impulse that sows the seeds of inspiration').

Like Ovid also, Spenser experiments formally with the control of tempo and the mixing of rest and action. The independent eclogues of the *Shepheardes Calender*, like Ovid's retarding elegiac couplets, are swept up into a narrative by the passing of the year. Similarly, in *The Faerie Queene*, the self-enclosed Spenserian stanza, with its tendency to revolve around itself, is summoned to action by epic narrative.[94] The formal hybridity becomes a means of reaching a vision that, as Piers suggests, includes both heroic action and love. The most successful figure for this union is in Book 3, the book of Chastity, in which Britomart's quest is propelled by love. At the centre of this book, the Garden of Adonis is guarded by a figure whose very nature embodies the poem's own formal and thematic doubleness: 'Old *Genius* the porter of them was, | Old *Genius*, the which a double nature has' (3. 6. 31. 8–9). While there are obviously prototypes for

---

[92] See further, Pugh, *Spenser and Ovid*, 18–20, 250–61. Michael Holahan notes the parallels between *Mutabilitie* and the *Fasti* briefly ('Iamque opus exegi', 263–4). Elsewhere, he suggests the presence of the *Fasti* in Spenser's 'Epithalamium' ('Ovid', in Hamilton (ed.), *The Spenser Encyclopedia*, 522).

[93] See Richard N. Ringler, 'The Faunus Episode', in A. C. Hamilton (ed.), *Essential Articles for the Study of Edmund Spenser* (Hamden, Conn., 1972), 289–98; especially 293–4. Ringler, however, only sees the comparison with the episode of Faunus and Omphale in *Fasti* 2.303–58; he is not aware that the episode is part of a pattern that unites Ovid's poem as a whole.

[94] Patricia A. Parker also notes how formal tension reflects both generic and moral conflicts in the poem: '*The Faerie Queene* seems to be exploring the implications of this opposition [between epic and lyric] in its very form—narrative in its forward, linear quest and yet composed out of lyric stanzas that, like the enchantresses within it, potentially suspend or retard' (*Literary Fat Ladies: Rhetoric, Gender, Property* (London, 1987), 66).

this figure in medieval literature, Spenser's Genius inherits much of the nature and indeed function of Ovid's Janus.[95] As the opposite of the false Genius who guards the gate to the Bower of Bliss, Genius is himself part of a pattern of oppositions in the poem, by means of which readers, like knights, learn to differentiate between true and false images. Yet, like Ovid's Janus, he also offers a possible alternative to a destructive binary system that produced a conflict at the end of Book 2, where the meeting of Venus and Mars, replayed as the opposition between Acrasia and Guyon, led to the destruction of the Bower of Bliss. Genius' double nature reflects the nature of the Garden of Adonis in which the antithetical forces of Book 2 come together. Moreover, in this vision Spenser imagines the metamorphosis of the destructive enemy of all creativity, 'wicked *Tyme* who with his scyth addrest | Does mow the flowring herbes and goodly things, | And all their glory to the ground downe flings' (3. 6. 39. 3–5). While the Garden includes this destructive figure who wreaks his worst on the flowers of poesie, it also embraces the rhythms of temporality: 'There is continuall spring, and haruest there | Continuall, both meeting at one tyme (3. 6. 42. 1–2)'.[96] In the Bower of Bliss, like many elegiac spaces, time is walled out; here it is absorbed into the poet's vision and transformed, so that it appears finally, as Kenneth Gross argues, as 'a relation, a precarious relational unity, rather than as a creature or personification in its own right. This more mobile, labile form of time ... undoes that work of mind by which time is the reified object of fear.'[97] The revelation of time as a human construct and process means that the poet can turn it into the source of his own art.

---

[95] On the medieval and Renaissance sources of the figure, see D. T. Starnes, 'The Figure Genius in the Renaissance', *Studies in the Renaissance*, 11 (1964), 234–44; three essays by Edgar C. Knowlton: 'The Allegorical Figure Genius', *Classical Philology*, 15/4 (1920), 380–4, 'Genius as an Allegorical Figure', *Modern Language Notes*, 39/2 (1924), 89–95, and 'The Genii of Spenser', *Studies in Philology*, 25 (1928), 439–56; and Jane Chance Nitzsche, *The Genius Figure in Antiquity and the Middle Ages* (New York, 1975). The parallel with the Roman Janus has however also been noted by several critics; see especially Nohrnberg, *The Analogy of* The Faerie Queene, 440, 529–30.

[96] On the inclusion of time in this canto and in the fabric of the Spenserian stanza see Kenneth Gross, 'Shapes of Time: On the Spenserian Stanza', *Spenser Studies*, 19 (2004), 27–35, as well as *Spenserian Poetics: Idolatry, Iconoclasm, & Magic* (Ithaca, NY, 1985), 189. See also Theresa Krier, 'Time Lords: Rhythm and Interval in Spenser's Stanzaic Narrative', *Spenser Studies*, 21 (2006), 1–19.

[97] 'Green Thoughts in a Green Shade', *Spenser Studies*, 24 (2009), 363.

Like that of Spenser, Shakespeare's concern with time has been linked to his Ovidianism. Elements of *Metamorphoses* 15 echo throughout the sonnets' examination of the battle between art and mutability.[98] Shakespeare was also interested in the Lucrece story, to which he alludes in *Cymbeline, Macbeth,* and *Julius Caesar,* and which he retells at length in his *Rape of Lucrece*. We do not know for sure, however, whether he read the version of Livy or Ovid, nor, if the latter, how much of the entire work he read.[99] However, his handing of the story in *Lucrece* indicates a sophisticated engagement with Ovid's story, and indeed the entire calendar, that is consistent with his general response to Ovid. Like Ovid, Shakespeare doubles the victor and victim, as well as Tarquin and Brutus. While both versions seem to retreat from the story's political implications, they press the contradiction of a situation in which the violation of privacy generates an ultimately ambiguous political transformation. Moreover, the most striking difference between the two accounts, Shakespeare's transformation of Ovid's mute heroine into a fountain of *copia*, gives Shakespeare room for inspired Ovidian invention and rhetoric. Ovid's 'haec te victoria perdet' ('This victory will ruin thee', *Fasti*, 2. 811) becomes 'A captive victor that hath lost in gain' (*Lucrece*, 730). The language shows Shakespeare at his most unrestrainedly Ovidian: paradox and antithesis run riot. The relentless and rather aggressive foregrounding of these devices does not create a world in which opposites are held in balance, but rather one in which the characters are themselves contradictions.[100] Self-conflict is expressed further by the frequent use of verbal repetition and echoing which binds the antagonists to each other as it divides each from him/herself. So

---

[98] Bate, *Shakespeare and Ovid,* 85.
[99] Partly on the basis of the curriculum, Baldwin claimed that he used Ovid (*William Shakspere's Small Latine & Lesse Greeke,* ii. 424; see also 427–8). In *Roman Shakespeare: Warriors, Wounds, and Women* (London, 1997), Coppélia Kahn argues for Shakespeare's familiarity with Ovid's poem as a whole, suggesting that Lucrece is described through terms that recall Vesta (32–5, 44 n. 5).
[100] Heather Dubrow describes the governing figure of the poem as *syneciosis*, which, with characteristic colour, Puttenham calls the figure of 'crosse copling': which 'takes me two contrary words, and tieth them as it were in a paire of couples, and so makes them agree like good fellowes, as I saw once in Fraunce a wolfe coupled with a mastiffe, and a foxe with a hound'. The animal models are telling for Shakespeare's poem which as Dubrow notes, 'produces unions that at best seem in urgent need of a marriage counselor' (*Captive Victors: Shakespeare's Narrative Poems and Sonnets* (Ithaca, NY, 1987), 81).

before the rape Tarquin 'for himself himself he must forsake' (157), and 'he himself himself confounds' (160); afterwards it is Lucrece's turn, as the rape 'made herself herself detest' (1566).[101] The technique here is similar to one in Ovid, which Garth Tissol aptly describes as 'self-cancelling repetition',[102] in which a single word is repeated twice to convey antithetical meanings and to suggest the transformation and sometimes even annihilation of identity. So Niobe is described after the loss of her children: 'quantum haec Niobe Niobe distabat ab illa' ('how different now was this Niobe from that Niobe', *Met.*, 6. 273).[103] Ovid uses this verbal doubling to show the self's alienation from itself through syntactical as well as literal objectification. Shakespeare assimilates an Ovidian mannerism, and applies it to increase the tensions in Ovid's tale and to create a world in which a 'forced league doth force a further strife' (689). The Ovidian pun here also makes opposites synonymous, as 'league', sexual union, generates a strife that, in contrast to that between Hero and Leander, is unambiguously destructive.[104]

Lucrece is traditionally paired with *Venus and Adonis*, which Richard Lanham called its 'Ovidian twin sister'.[105] Both between and within the poems, Shakespeare explores models of coupling. The companionlike pairing between Shakespeare's two poems contrasts starkly with the antithetical partnerships that each depicts. Both poems revolve around the conventional debate between eros and chastity, painted in stark colours of red and white. But both poems also represent the central antitheses through responses to

---

[101] For a further discussion of this kind of rhetoric in Shakespeare and its relation to Ovidian formulations, see Eric Langley, *Narcissism and Suicide in Shakespeare and his Contemporaries* (Oxford, 2009), 1–52.

[102] *The Face of Nature*, 58; see also Philip Hardie's discussion of Ovid's repetition of proper names or nouns 'to express the internal division or self-alienation of an individual' (*Ovid's Poetics of Illusion*, 251–5; quotation from 251). I will return to this type of Ovidian rhetoric in Ch. 5.

[103] See Tissol, *Face of Nature*, 57.

[104] John Leonard argues that the representation of Lucrece and Tarquin recalls Marlowe's lovers to bring out the darker side of that erotic relation ('Marlowe's Doric Music', 71).

[105] *The Motives of Eloquence*, 95. D. C. Allen compared the pairing to that of 'L'Allegro' and 'Il Penseroso' ('Some Observations on *The Rape of Lucrece*', *Shakespeare Survey*, 15 (1962), 91); their Ovidian sources also link them to Ovid's 'companion poems', the *Metamorphoses* (source of *Venus and Adonis*) and *Fasti*. While Shakespeare's two poems were not actually published together till 1709, their dialogue with each other seems to have been evident to many early readers.

time. As Colin Burrow notes, 'Time and how you spend it also is an important element in the moral argument' of *Venus and Adonis*.[106] While the arguments seem relatively clear-cut here and divided between the two characters (Venus wants to make love and Adonis wants to hunt), in *Lucrece*, the treatment of time becomes more complex, as Shakespeare makes it part of the poem's form and structure. The poem is an examination of the role of Ovidian *mora*, delay, in both erotic and poetic desire. Everything is drawn out.[107] Like Ovid and Spenser, Shakespeare has chosen a verse form that tends to slow down narrative: rhyme royal, also the basic form of Milton's 'On the Death of a fair Infant' (and a form that is often considered 'Spenserian'). The long-windedness of both central characters slows things down further; by comparison, Ovid's version is concise and even zippy.[108] The formal tension held together in Spenser's hybrid stanza here explodes to create the schizophrenic universe that erupts in Ovid's version. Tarquin's self-debating delays the rape, which is itself fast and brutal. After the moment of decisive action, however, the centre of slowness is Lucrece herself, whose Ovidian complaints, including that against Time (925–1001), prolong the poem. It is not surprising then that she passes time and finds refuge in contemplating a work of art: the tapestry of the story of Troy. Lucrece seems to be trying to suspend time and change; when Tarquin first looks at her asleep, she appears like 'a virtuous monument' (391).

To the predatory Tarquin, the sleeping Lucrece seems to embody the perfect reconciliation of opposites that transcends strife: 'O modest wantons, wanton modesty! | Showing life's triumph in the map of

---

[106] *Complete Sonnets and Poems*, 31. As Burrow notes, the important question for the poet himself is: 'Is reading an erotic poem a proper way to spend time? Is writing one a proper way to advance a poetic career? The pressure to be serious, to use time well, runs through the poem' (ibid. 32). Such questions, as we'll see, were even more pressing for the young Milton and may again help explain his attraction to this poem.

[107] Shakespeare's treatment should be seen in comparison especially with Spenser's representation of the temptations of erotic dalliance to impede the epic quest. The importance of delay in erotic pleasure partly accounts for its role as a formal structure in romance plotting. For a brilliant exposition of the significance of deferral as a narrative principle, see Parker, *Inescapable Romance*, as well as her *Literary Fat Ladies*.

[108] Kenney discusses the effect of Ovid's elegiac couplet on narrative in this episode: 'the total effect is inescapably staccato; the narrative unfolds in a series of stills, so to say, rather than in a continuous sequence' ('Ovid's Language', 51).

death, | ... As if between them twain there were no strife, | But that life lived in death, and death in life' (401–2, 405–6). Ironically, this quality leads to her rape and inner self-division. Ovid's story of Lucretia is framed by references to the rape of Philomela and its fearful legacy of familial violence (*Fasti*, 2. 623–30, 853).[109] In Shakespeare's version the two stories are also linked. Lucrece herself sees the similarity, crying 'Come, Philomel, that sing'st of ravishment: | Make thy sad grove in my disheveled hair' (1128–9), and her complaint merges with the song of the nightingale: 'By this, lamenting Philomel had ended | the well-tuned warble of her nightly sorrow' (1079–80).[110] In both stories, the innocent victim perpetuates the violence she suffered. Paradoxically Lucrece tries to restore her original wholeness by self-objectification and suicide. Her blood spills out from her wound in the red and black rivers symbolizing her purity and contamination (1737–50). She leaves a divided legacy, foreseen also in the 'strife' between her husband and father, who make grief a competition (1791–2). Shakespeare's Rome, like Ovid's, is divided by its own unsustainable myths of wholeness. Lucrece is the embodiment of a culture built not only on rape but also suicide and whose future is intestine war.[111] At the same time, the transformation of Lucrece's chaste body from an image for the transcendence of opposites into a site of self-destructive contradiction once more shows the unsustainability of Spenser's dream of happy unions; in Shakespeare's Ovidian epyllia, all leagues are forms of deadly strife.

The *Fasti* is thus part of the Elizabethan battle over English poetry that takes place through Ovid. The poets put forward contrasting

---

[109] In the first passage, Philomela is banished from the celebration of the Caristia, which celebrates the family; in the second, Ovid uses the rhetorical tic 'Fallimur' ('Do I err?') to note the slow return of spring and of the swallow, Procne, chased by her husband Tereus. Newlands reads the connection between Philomela and Lucrece as part of Ovid's treatment of 'the repetitive pattern of sexual violence which lies at the core of Rome's founding myths' (*Playing with Time*, 162–3).

[110] Shakespeare's identification of Lucrece with Hecuba (*Lucrece*, 1447 ff.) explores a further connection between Ovidian characters.

[111] Both Dubrow, *Captive Victors*, and Kahn, *Roman Shakespeare*, thus see the poem as part of Shakespeare's larger critique of Roman culture. As Ian Donaldson shows, from Augustine on, Lucrece's suicide had been seen by Christians as motivated by pride (*The Rapes of Lucretia: A Myth and its Transformations* (Oxford, 1982), 21–39 especially. It was therefore another popular subject for school debates, which Donaldson shows are recalled by Shakespeare's poem (ibid. 38, 40–1).

ways of experiencing and representing time.[112] However, there is another front to this battle which needs consideration. The *Fasti*'s reminder that time is a political as well as poetical issue had a particularly timely relevance for English writers in the sixteenth and seventeenth centuries. The debate over Gregory XIII's plans to reform Augustus' calendar dramatically raised the question of who had the authority to decide the course of time. Britain ultimately refused to adopt the 1582 calendar on the grounds that it was foreign and Roman.[113] This defiance of papal power seems a logical extension of the Reformation into the realm of time—though it had the paradoxical effect of preventing temporal reform and keeping the British literally stuck in the old foreign and Roman time of Augustus. (Talk about all roads leading to Rome.)

As in Augustan Rome, therefore, the calendar was central in the creation of a national identity, offering a specifically English form of time, detached from the power of the Pope and Rome.[114] Moreover, the experience of English time changed internally through the

---

[112] More, I think, could be said about the relevance of the *Fasti* to Shakespeare's treatment of time in his last plays, especially *The Winter's Tale*, with its evocation of the stories of Flora and Proserpina. Here he moves beyond the vision of the *tempus edax rerum* of *Metamorphoses* 15 and the sonnets, to one in which, as Bate notes, 'Time is a Chorus chatting to the audience and playfully breaking the rules of dramatic illusion' (*Shakespeare and Ovid*, 227). This new vision of time enables the play's final transformation, in which art becomes nature.

[113] While Elizabeth was surprisingly keen on following the Pope's changes, the calendar was opposed on the grounds of its papal origins; see J. D. North, 'The Western Calendar—"Intolerabilis, Horribilis, et Derisibilis": Four Centuries of Discontent', in G. V. Coyne et al. (eds.), *Gregorian Reform of the Calendar: Proceedings of the Vatican Conference to Commemorate its 400th Anniversary, 1582–1982* (Vatican City, 1983), 75–113; see esp. 94–107. Debates continued through the 1600s and were revived briefly in 1645—the year of the publication of Milton's *Poems*—and again in 1699, when the British once more rejected the reform as evidence of the Pope's 'pretended *Supremacy*, not only over Churches and Kingdoms, but even the Celestial Motions' (Michael Hoskin, 'The Reception of the Calendar by Other Churches', in Coyne et al. (eds.), *Gregorian Reform of the Calendar*, 258). It was not until 1752 that, through the energetic intervention of Lord Chesterfield, the English calendar was synchronized with that of most of the Continent.

[114] The presence of this debate in Spenser's *Shepheardes Calender* has been noted; see especially Alison Chapman, who reads the *Calendar* as Spenser's creation of an alternative Anglican model of English time to counter that of the Pope ('Marking Time: Astrology, Almanacs, and English Protestantism', *Renaissance Quarterly*, 60/4 (2007), 1257–90). She compares this national calendar to Spenser's project to create a new kind of 'English' poetry. But despite the *Calendar*'s attempt to present an archaic, 'original' English, it is closely engaged with classical and also French, and therefore Catholic, works.

sixteenth and seventeenth centuries. Previously tied to natural and ecclesiastical cycles, marked by irregular feast days, many of which were of suspiciously Roman (in both senses) origins, the English calendar was increasingly regularized to express, as David Cressy puts it, 'a mythic and patriotic sense of national identity'. During this period there emerged 'a new national, secular and dynastic calendar centring on the anniversaries of the Protestant monarch'.[115] This temporal reformation pleased Puritans who denounced the celebration of saints' days as popish. However, it also increased royal authority, as by making her birthday and accession day national holidays, Elizabeth tied time to herself. Syrithe Pugh suggests that late sixteenth-century readers of the *Fasti* might have seen the similarity between Augustus' rewriting of the religious calendar and Elizabeth's use of time to express her control over her country.[116] Continuing debates within England over the proper celebration of Protestant rituals—the question of holidays and sabbatarianism which heated up in the seventeenth century—show that the monarch's vision was contested. In an influential study, Richard Helgerson argues that the period involved a battle between monarch and people over representing the nation that was fought through the mapping of the country in space.[117] But the war was also waged over time.

While changing the way in which time was experienced, moreover, Elizabeth surrounded herself with images that denied change. Like Augustus and later Charles I, she used chastity as part of her personal and political iconography. She drew on a symbolic correspondence between her physical chastity—the impenetrability of her body—and national security—the impenetrability of the island. As she aged, she increasingly used chastity to assert her remote self-sufficiency and difference from her subjects, and to present herself as an eternal virgin.[118] Even in the 1590s, royal iconography presented her as 'Semper eadem', always the same; late paintings depict her as an

---

[115] *Bonfires and Bells: National Memory and the Protestant Calendar in Elizabethan and Stuart England* (London, 1989), pp. xi–xii.
[116] Pugh, *Spenser and Ovid*, 18.
[117] *Forms of Nationhood: The Elizabethan Writing of England* (Chicago, 1992).
[118] See Susan Frye, *Elizabeth I: The Competition for Representation* (New York, 1993), esp. 86–147; Philippa Berry, *Of Chastity and Power: Elizabethan Literature and the Unmarried Queen* (London, 1989); and John King, 'Queen Elizabeth I: Representations of the Virgin Queen', *Renaissance Quarterly*, 43/1 (1990), 30–74.

eternally springlike virgin, caught in suspended animation through the painter's art.[119] In images at least, Elizabeth managed to stop the clock; after her death, Raleigh described her as 'a lady whom time had surprised'.[120]

Literary representations of the Queen as an image of such unchanging and unattainable desire drew on the Petrarchan tradition of Ovidianism. In adapting Ovid, therefore, Shakespeare and Spenser were not just facing each other: they both had a powerful rival in the Queen herself. And in rescuing Ovid from the Petrarchan literary tradition, they also were potentially challenging the appropriation of that tradition to support monarchical power.[121] By the 1590s, of course, the contradictions inherent in the situation were increasingly apparent. While in the *Shepheardes Calender* Spenser may have seen chastity as a source of power that confirmed his own Protestant values, by Book 3 of *The Faerie Queene*, the Queen's chastity was clearly incompatible with his belief in chaste marriage; it was also a liability for national stability.[122] Given the concerns of the time, Shakespeare's representation of chastity in his epyllia also has an inherently political edge. In Shakespeare, chastity, not erotic desire, tries to suspend time, as both Adonis and Lucrece are associated with a desire for timelessness, a chastity that leads to stasis and death. The polarization in both epyllia of red and white—the colours whose coupling the Tudors had made a symbol of their own authority—suggests a divided country, built on a fragile paradox that was

---

[119] Roy Strong, *Gloriana: The Portraits of Queen Elizabeth I* (New York, 1987), 147–8. Augustus' portraits similarly showed no signs of ageing; as Alessandro Barchiesi notes, 'the emperor lives beyond the reach of change; his image, always the same, inviolable and spread everywhere in thousands of copies, guarantees stability' ('Endgames: Ovid's *Metamorphoses* 15 and *Fasti* 6', 195).

[120] Qtd. in William Blissett, 'Spenser's Mutabilitie', in Hamilton (ed.), *Essential Articles for the Study of Edmund Spenser*, 258.

[121] Pugh thus sees Spenser's Ovidian ideal of marriage aimed at the Queen's Petrarchan Ovidianism (*Spenser and Ovid*, 167–80).

[122] As often noted, the *Calender* was written around the time when Elizabeth was considering marriage with the Duc d'Alençon; Pugh suggests that Spenser celebrates chastity in order to dissuade Elizabeth from a foreign alliance that might undermine English insularity (*Spenser and Ovid*, 29). In *The Faerie Queene*, however, her lack of issue had itself become an issue. As Richard McCabe notes, 'a virgin queen is a sterile queen automatically excluded from the vibrant cycles of sexual perpetuity upon which the poem so often insists' (*The Pillars of Eternity*, 131). McCabe argues that Spenser's preoccupation with time made him especially sensitive to Elizabeth's mortality.

beginning to collapse; at the end of *Venus and Adonis*, red and white come together in the boar's 'frothy mouth bepainted all with red, | Like milk and blood being mingled both together' (901-2).

For Elizabethan writers, then, Ovid's response to Augustus' claim of authority over desire and time—his shaping of Rome as a truly eternal city of unchanging moral rectitude—had resonances for their own situation. Moreover, further developments in the battle over time made it equally relevant for writers of the seventeenth century, including Milton.

MILTON AND THE PASSING OF TIME

Like Spenser and Shakespeare, Milton is constantly preoccupied with time.[123] Many of his first poems are tied to specific days of the year and the ritual celebration of time (Christmas in the 'Nativity Ode', the feast of the Circumcision in 'Upon the Circumcision', Easter in 'The Passion', 5 November in the Gunpowder Plot poems, his own birthday in 'How soon hath Time'), or draw attention to the passing of time.[124] In his early works, the timing of his career is a concern; he believes that being a great poet takes time, but is also anxious to display his talent and notes with some alarm his tendency to procrastinate.[125] He was under external pressure as well from a middle-class culture whose values would have been recognizable to any Roman: 'duty and a sense of civic mission, an uncompromising and

---

[123] See also Quinones, *Renaissance Discovery*, 444-93; and Amy Boesky, '*Paradise Lost* and the Multiplicity of Time', in Corns (ed.), *A Companion to Milton*, 380-92.

[124] Ann Baynes Coiro finds Milton's choices of subjects telling: 'That Milton's first great poem would be inspired by Christmas is in itself significant, for Christmas was a holiday objectionable to puritans, who saw it as pagan and superstitious and who were particularly uneasy with the drunken sexual roistering that accompanied its celebration. Christmas was ceremonial, papist and decadent, associated with the Stuart court, which had long upheld the practice of festival, and associated, inevitably, with the Virgin Mother and thus with Catholicism' ('"A ball of strife"', 35). In 'How Laudian was the Young Milton?', however, McDowell argues that these subjects themselves are not proof of political allegiances.

[125] See especially the 1633 'Letter to a Friend' in which he says he is 'somtyme suspicious of my selfe, & doe take notice of a certaine belatednesse in me' (*Works*, xii. 322).

sustained commitment to public ideals'.[126] As Quinones notes, in his later works especially Milton resists such pressures: 'Against the stern rigors of Puritanical consciousness and relentless high seriousness he suggests the virtues of small talk, easiness, the casual moments of pleasure, the unimplored visits of the Muse. These attempts to relax severity are part of a more fundamental vision, at the very core of his major works, that literally stands in opposition to the temporal pressures of the modern world, pressures, he felt, which would force man to abdicate his spiritual nature.'[127] But for the young poet, such resistance must have been difficult.[128] The meeting of past, present, and future in the 1629 'Ode on the Morning of Christ's Nativity', which constantly jumps between the first Christmas morning, Christmas 1629, and the apocalypse, suggests both Milton's attempt to represent the entrance of eternity into the world of time, and also his early problems with time management. Learning to master time through his experimentation with different metres, the apprentice poet was drawn to forms such as rhyme royal and the Latin elegiac couplet, which tend to draw out the tempo.[129] His early works show a constant self-consciousness about his own use of time, which made it easy for him to be attentive to temporality as a philosophical, poetical, and ultimately political concern.

As I showed in Chapter 1, echoes in the Latin works indicate that Milton had read the *Fasti*. These allusions in themselves of course

---

[126] Swaim, 'Myself a True Poem', 92. Anthony Low has discussed the transmission of Roman values through Virgil's *Georgics* in the 16th century (*The Georgic Revolution* (Princeton, 1985)).

[127] *Renaissance Discovery*, 502. See especially the sonnets published in the 1673 *Poems*, '*Lawrence* of virtuous Father vertuous Son', and '*Cyriack*, whose Grandsire'. 'Prolusion 7' also praises the joys of 'otium' as necessary for great work (*Works*, xii. 248). Among the few works Milton never published are his school exercises urging early rising and denouncing sloth.

[128] Northrop Frye suggests that the 'simultaneous pull in Milton's life between the impulse to get at his poem and finish it and the impulse to leave it until it ripened sufficiently... must have accounted for an emotional tension... of a kind that we can hardly imagine' (*The Return of Eden: Five Essays on Milton's Epics* (Toronto, 1965), 9).

[129] Rhyme royal seems to enable both movement and stasis, as the two opening interlocking couplets propel the stanza forward towards a slowing down achieved through the final two rhyming couplets. Milton's use of an alexandrine for the final line reinforces the sense of lingering in closure. The structure of the Petrarchan sonnet seemed also to have attracted Milton, as the involution of the envelope rhyme and repetition of sounds produces a slower pace than the freer Shakespearian alternative.

do not tell us what Milton made of Ovid's calendar. Like other readers of the time, Milton could have seen the poem partly as a source of information on Roman rituals and customs. Ovid's poem could have provided him with the information on Roman holidays in 'Prolusion 6', *Exercitationes nonnunquam Ludicras Philosophiae studiis non obesse* (*That sometimes sportive exercises are not prejudicial to philosophical studies*), in which he reminds his audience: '*Romani* sua hâbuere Floralia, Rustici sua Palilia, Pistores sua Fornacalia, nos quoque potissimum hoc tempore rerum & negotiorum vacui, *Socratico* more ludere solemus' ('The Romans had their festival of flowers, the farmers their shepherds' feast, the bakers their oven fête; we also especially at this time, free from affairs and business, are accustomed to make sport in the Socratic manner', *Works*, xii. 238). If he had recalled the *Fasti* for this information, it might account for his reference to the Vestal flame, in which he cites *Fasti* 6. 292 in order to playfully correct Ovid, who appears here, as usual, guilty of 'errorem' (232).

Yet these casual references may indicate a deeper engagement with Ovid's poem. Milton's topic here, the praise of holidays, was assigned to him as a university exercise. It is therefore unwise to rush to identify it with his own beliefs. And it would be paradoxical to take such an exercise, a variation on the *encomium morae*, too seriously. Still, the argument he makes comes back in a more serious form in his description of marriage in *Tetrachordon*, where he claims: 'No mortall nature can endure either in the actions of Religion, or study of wisdome, without somtime slackning the cords of intense thought and labour... We cannot therefore always be contemplative, or pragmaticall abroad, but have need of som delightfull intermissions, wherin the enlarg'd soul may leav off a while her severe schooling; and like a glad youth in wandring vacancy, may keep her hollidaies to joy and harmles pastime' (*Works*, iv. 85–6). The early assignment also allows him to experiment further with seeing things from an Ovidian point of view. His choice of paradox and oxymoron as the governing structures of his contradictory subject, in which 'me jocos hodie seriò laudaturum' ('I am about to speak seriously to-day in praise of jocularity', *Works*, xii. 216), allows him to display his delight in puns and paradox. Mary Ann Radzinowicz suggests that Milton's use of oxymoron here is 'the expression of a compulsion to fuse experience into a unity without suppressing its paradoxical sense of literal variety'.[130] Milton insists that the poet must be *both* Allegro and Il Penseroso: 'quia vix queat ullus belle & lepide jocarí, nisi & serio agere prius addidicerit' ('because hardly anyone can jest delightfully and charmingly, unless he has also first learned to act seriously', *Works*, xii. 224). The witty paradox allows him to overcome the restrictions of the traditionally either/or argument form of the school debate by taking a more inclusive view. As John Hale reminds us, this Prolusion was delivered as part of a 'salting', an annual feast of misrule, which Hale compares to the Saturnalia. Like Michaelmas, the occasion of *Comus*, a salting is a ritualized and ultimately contained subversion of authority. But, as Hale notes, the occasion also opens the possibility for experimentation: 'For this one night, Milton is Lord of Misrule':[131] for one night Milton played the part of Comus. He seems to have enjoyed it.

An evocation of a similar holiday spirit appears in 'Elegia 5', which captures generally 'the sensuous world of Ovidian myth'.[132] Moreover, the elegy presents a simultaneous regeneration of spring, desire, the imagination, and myth itself; as William Shullenberger argues, the poem imagines not only the springtime of the year but 'a springtime of mythology itself, as if it's just beginning, and as if something entirely new might be made of it'.[133] Like Weever, Milton sees a world in which new myths are waiting to be born. While the mood is broadly Ovidian, Ovid's calendar seems specifically recalled through Milton's exploration of the movement of 'Tempus' ('Elegia 5', 1). Natural time is made a source of artistic inspiration, as 'Ver mihi, quod dedit ingenium, cantabitur illo' ('The spring will be sung of with the genius that it gave me', 23). As in the *Fasti*, elegy raises the poet to the sky 'mihi mens liquidi *raptatur* in ardua coeli' ('My mind is whirled off in the clear sky's heights', 15, emphasis added). Here *rapere* is used again clearly to describe a spiritual rapture achieved through inspiration in which the poet rises to a vision of the cosmos:

---

[130] ' "To Play in the Socratic Manner": Oxymoron in Milton's *At a Vacation Exercise in the Colledge*', *University of Hartford Studies in Literature*, 17/3 (1985), 1–11; 1. On Milton's wit here see also John K. Hale, *Milton's Cambridge Latin: Performing in the Genres, 1625–1632* (Tempe, Ariz., 2005), 215.

[131] *Milton's Cambridge Latin*, 206.

[132] Martindale, *John Milton and the Transformation*, 180.

[133] 'Milton's Pagan Counter-Poetic: Eros and Inspiration in Elegy 5', unpublished keynote address (Milton at Mufreesboro, 2009), 10. I am grateful for being able to use this superb reading of the poem.

> Perque vagas nubes corpore liber eo.
> Perque umbras, perque antra feror penetralia vatum,
> Et mihi fana patent interiora Deûm.
> Intuiturque animus toto quid agatur Olympo,
> Nec fugiunt oculos Tartara caeca meos.

('Free of
my body, I go through wandering clouds.
I am borne through shades and caves, the holy sanctums of poets,
and the inmost shrines of the gods are open to me.
My spirit envisions what happens in all Olympus—
Nor does murky Tartarus escape my vision', 16–20)

In the sky, the poet meets Apollo who later, as Phoebus, will control the movement of the day, calling nature to rise from sleep. The scene of ascent is densely allusive, recalling a variety of classical sources. Stella Revard suggests the model of Callimachus' 'Hymn to Apollo',[134] but the Roman poets who had adapted Callimachus—Virgil, Lucretius, and of course Ovid—are equally present here.[135] There is an Ovidian sense of a drawing-together of resources to generate a new poetics. The landscape is populated by Ovidian figures, especially Faunus, who, as in the *Fasti*, appears as a harmless and inept lover (127–30).

If the hybrid Faunus recalls the *Fasti*, he also mirrors the general doubleness of Milton's poem. As Revard notes, the poem undergoes a generic metamorphosis, beginning as a hymn and ending as a love elegy.[136] In the process, the two genres are combined into a new kind of celebration in which the poet's creativity is driven not by chastity but by desire. The initial inspired ascent supposedly 'liber corpore' leads to a vision of embodied ecstasy, in which the speaker returns to wander the earth. He brings with him Apollo, who is greeted by the earth as a longed-for lover (55–74). Earthly sensuality is evoked but tempered; while the earth is described as 'lasciva' (95), her meeting with Apollo is represented as an epithalamium (61–72). In this world, Vesta is present (102), as well as Zephyr, husband of Flora (2, 69), and

---

[134] *Milton and the Tangles*, 18. Revard also notes its debt to the pagan *fasti* tradition generally, although she does not cite Ovid (64).

[135] Callimachus' 'Hymn' was extremely generative: it is a source for both the story of Apollo in *Metamorphoses* 1 and the appearance of Janus in *Fasti* 1; see Hardie, 'The Janus Episode'.

[136] *Milton and the Tangles*, 24.

Hymen, god of marriages (105–8). The poem celebrates a world that is both spiritual and sensual as, by leaving the earth and body, the speaker is able to return to them.

The poem's treatment of space is mirrored in its presentation of time. The temporal movement seems to combine contrary paces that reflect the young poet's own divided impulses at this stage—his desire to get ahead and to hold himself back. Like Ovid, Milton works to control the reader's as well as his own experience of time. The elegiac couplet itself, with its yoking together of epic action (the hexameter line) and elegiac delay (the pentameter, which shapes the couplet as a self-contained unit), creates a double tempo that is developed further through the poem as a whole. The poem begins with rapid flight and ascent; the speaker is in a hurry, bursting with energy, seizing the time by the first line and getting to heaven by line 11. Phoebus similarly calls the world to action in the morning (49–52). But his progress is slowed down by the arrival of the loving earth, who tells him to take a rest from his journey (93–4). Paradoxically, the rest of nature 'ruunt' (96), rushes, to follow her example of slowing down. While the speaker hurries at the start to get to heaven, at the end he tells us that the gods themselves prefer to come to earth: 'Dii quoque non dubitant caelo praeponere sylvas, | et sua quisque sibi numina lucus habet' ('Likewise the gods do not doubt their preference for the woods | instead of heaven; each grove gets its god', 131–2). He prays that this situation continue ('Et sua quisque diu sibi numina lucus habeto', 'Long may each woodland have its god', 133). The repetition of line 132 in line 133 contributes to the slowing down of the end of the poem. In the last lines, the speaker, like Ovid's elegiac lover in *Amores* 1. 13, asks the Sun to delay his journey to prolong pleasure: 'Tu saltem lentè rapidos age Phoebe jugales | Quà potes, & sensim tempora veris eant' ('Phoebus, at least drive your fast teams as slowly as | you can, that springtime may leave gradually', 137–8).[137] Action finds completion in rest.

Like 'Prolusion 6', 'Elegia 5' expresses a vision of time and its use which temporarily assuages Milton's anxiety about his own tendency to delay. It transforms Ovidian erotic delay into the self-preparation Milton felt necessary for greatness. Not only do *mora* and *amor* go

---

[137] The general tempo was noticed by Ralph Condee, who thought 'Elegia 5' one of the finest of Milton's Latin elegies, but also found it 'a static poem' ('The Latin Poetry of John Milton', 67–9).

together, as delay enhances both erotic and poetical pleasure, but Milton suggests that by delaying the poet achieves the higher vision in which he is able to balance spiritual and the material desires.[138] As Shullenberger argues, the poem presents the possibilities of the imagination transforming life on earth, pressing us 'towards a radically different social order and libidinal economy than one founded on repression and self-denial... in which desire would be recognized and celebrated, not as a threat to society and its projects, but as its very source and renewal'.[139] The conclusion looks forward to the final vision of *Comus*, in which heaven and earth strive to come together, and, beyond that, the innocent yet sensual Eden of *Paradise Lost*.[140] As the *Fasti* had demonstrated, the elegy can be a route to a transcendent vision of a transformed heaven, and also earth.

But the placement of 'Elegia 5' in the sequence of the 1645 *Poems* suggests that this resolution is only temporary. In the elegies that follow, the united impulses seem to undergo a sudden and violent divorce. 'Elegia 6', in which Milton first explicitly identifies chastity as the source of creativity, seems to support the conventional opposition between elegy and epic. As in 'L'Allegro' and 'Il Penseroso', Milton considers alternative forms of poetry and where they might lead him. The examples of poets such as Ovid show that 'Carmen amat Bacchum, Carmina Bacchus amat' ('Song loves Bacchus; Bacchus loves songs', 'Elegia 6', 14). As I noted in

---

[138] A more famous version of this strategy is Milton's 'covnant with any knowing reader' in the 1642 *Reason of Church Government Urg'd against Prelaty*, in which he asks that: 'I may go on trust with him toward the payment of what I am now indebted, as being a work not to be rays'd from the heat of youth, or the vapours of wine, like that which flows at wast from the pen of some vulgar Amorist, or the trencher fury of a riming parasite, nor to be obtain'd by the invocation of Dame Memory and her Siren daughters, but by devout prayer to that eternall Spirit who can enrich with all utterance and knowledge, and sends out his Seraphim with the hallow'd fire of his Altar to touch and purify the lips of whom he pleases: to this must be added industrious and select reading, steddy observation, insight into all seemly and generous arts and affaires' (*Works*, iii, pt. 1, 240-1). The very fact that Milton has not written anything much yet demonstrates the self-restraint that guarantees that he eventually will. See also 'Prolusion 7', in which he defends his own apparent slowness, claiming to seek real wisdom rather than quick fame, and suggests that in this way he will eventually acquire the knowledge of the universe that will allow him to conquer time and live forever ('hoc est, Auditores, omni aetati quasi vivus interesse, & velut ipsius temporis nasci contemporaneus', 'This means, my hearers, to reside in every age as if alive, to be born as though a contemporary of time itself', *Works*, xii. 266).

[139] 'Milton's Pagan Counter-Poetic', 21.

[140] See Revard, *Milton and the Tangles*, 26.

Chapter 1, the line echoes Ovid's statement of his poetics in *Fasti* 5. 345—in which Flora herself tells the poet that 'Bacchus amat flores'—as well as Ovid's source, *Georgics* 2. 113, 'Bacchus amat colles'. The Virgilian and Ovidian versions become themselves part of a generic choice that Milton must make to define himself as an author, and as a person. While the elegiac poet, like Ovid, can have a free and easy life of flowers, banquets, and wine, the epic writer must control his natural appetites through temperance and chastity (55–64). Self-denial, however, brings its rewards; the elegiac poet enjoys the pleasures of nature and the belly, but the epic poet achieves a supernatural vision of 'adulto sub Jove caelum' ('heaven under adult Jove', 55) and 'sancta...superum consulta deorum' ('the gods' sacred plans', 57): 'Diis etenim sacer est vates, divûmque sacerdos | Spirat & occultum pectus, & ora Jovem' ('For to the gods the poet's holy, the gods' own priest. | His secret heart and mouth both breathe out Jove', 77–8). The poem thus retracts the promise of 'Elegia 5' in which, as in the *Fasti*, elegy led to a vision of the divine. Now only *epic* wins that higher vision. Milton echoes the *Fasti* only to detach himself from Ovid's holiday world and to announce a choice of a different generic path that requires hard work and sexual self-denial but which will lead eventually, we know, to *Paradise Lost*.[141] He seems to abandon Ovid to turn to Virgil, whose own reputed chastity, as well as his poetry, makes him a more appropriate role model.[142]

However, the poem that follows, 'Elegia 7', is a dizzying backslide into Ovidian poetry, in a story based on that of Apollo in

---

[141] Shullenberger notes also that 'Elegia 5' was written, astonishingly, in the same year as the 'Nativity Ode'. He reads the two as in 'a dialectical relation to one another', in which both poems offer dreams of imagining new myths and restoring a Golden Age: 'the Nativity Ode through eschatological self-abnegation, exemplified and made possible by the sacrifice of Christ, the Elegy through the imagination's awakening recognition that the world it inhabits is the one it makes for itself out of what the natural world offers as a gift and a challenge' ('Milton's Pagan Counter-Poetic', 1, 10). For Shullenberger, therefore, the 'Nativity Ode' shows Milton shutting down the possibility of a marriage between heaven and earth that will not be reopened until the Romantics.

[142] Gordon Campbell argues that the young Milton identified with Virgil partly because he was known as 'Parthenon'; see 'Milton and the Lives of the Ancients', *Journal of the Warburg and Courtauld Institutes*, 47 (1984), 234–8. For Renaissance critics, Virgil's chastity extended to his style, which was often characterized by its *castitatas* and *frugalitas*; see Tudeau-Clayton, *Jonson, Shakespeare and Early Modern Virgil*, 169.

Metamorphoses 1.[143] The poet of chastity becomes the contentedly wretched slave of love, who begs Cupid, 'Deme meos tandem, verùm nec deme furores, | Nescio cur, miser est suaviter omnis amans' ('Take passions from me—or don't—since for some reason | every lover is happily miserable', 99–100). In turn, this poem is followed by a re-conversion in the 'Retraction' that follows, in which Milton detaches himself from his earlier playfulness: 'Haec ego mente olim laevâ, studioque supino | Nequitiae posui vana trophaea meae' ('At that time with capricious thoughts and idle learning | I set up these vain trophies of my folly', 1–2) After a period of Ovidian 'error' (3), Milton appears to find stability. For Barbara Lewalski, the moment dramatizes Milton's 'conversion from Ovid to Plato' and is key to the volume as a whole, which defines him 'as *vates*, not Cavalier lyricist', and even 'a new kind of reformist poet'.[144] Yet, as other critics have noted, there is something incomplete about the repeated scenes of vocational choosing that are staged throughout the 1645 *Poems*. While individual poems seem to reach temporary resolutions, the volume as a whole suggests a lack of closure.[145] While with hindsight we assume that Milton took the penseroso path, his 'companion poems' themselves do not explicitly show the moment of decision. The simple fact that 'L'Allegro' and 'Il Penseroso' are always printed and read together as a single unit creates a both/and rather than either/or situation: the poems themselves both posit choice and suspend it. While in 'Elegia 6' the young poet seems to choose epic he is, after all, still writing an elegy.[146] The volume is, as he described it later, inherently double: 'Gemelle cultu simplici gaudens liber, | Fronde licet geminâ' ('Double book, happy in a single cover, | granted a twin leaf', 'Ad *Joannem Rousium*, Oxoniensis Academiae Bibliothecarium', 1–2). While the opening of the English section of the 1645

---

[143] The sense of regression is reinforced by the fact that the poet's conversion to love was the classic scene for the *openings* of collections of love elegies; see for example Propertius, *Elegies*, 1. 1, as well as Ovid's opening scene of generic choosing in *Amores* 1. 1. As he comes to an end, Milton seems to start all over again.

[144] *The Life of John Milton*, 228, 227.

[145] William Kerrigan suggests that while Milton 'hoped to conclude his youth with a gesture of great finality, abandoning one sort of life in the act of embracing another', he never managed to achieve such closure (*The Sacred Complex*, 20). Or, as Richard Helgerson put it, 'Like the middle class, Milton is always rising and never getting anywhere' (*Self-Crowned Laureates*, 270).

[146] Revard argues therefore that in the poem 'Milton recognizes the claim of both kinds of poetry' (*Milton and the Tangles*, 121; see also 126).

Poems with the echoes of Virgil's 'Eclogue 4' in the Nativity Ode seems to present Milton's own poetic nativity as Virgilian, the second Latin section opens with 'Elegia 1', which places the poet back in an Ovidian world of love, art, and exile.

In the *Poems*, moreover, the elegies are immediately followed by a group of completely different and short poems on the Gunpowder Plot, which treat the subjects of time and holidays from a new perspective. They build towards the longer poem printed separately a few pages later, 'In quintum Novembris'. Supposedly written in the same year as 'On the Death of a fair Infant', this mini-epic, like the English poem, shows the young poet's eagerness for generic experimentation, as well as the influence of the Spenserian Fletchers, specifically, Phineas Fletcher whose *The Apollonyists* on the Gunpowder Plot has been seen as a subtext in *Paradise Lost*.[147]

As critics have noted, the fact that Milton wrote six poems on this topic would seem to reflect some interest in a day which had an important and contested place in the English calendar. As David Cressy notes, a recent event had quickly become part of the national year and myth. While not an official holiday, in many parts of England it took on Saturnalian characteristics, becoming 'a day of indulgence, of drinking and festivity' and even, 'a day of mischief'—as it would later become more generally.[148] It was seen as an anniversary of God's deliverance of the nation from the evil that for Protestants was incarnated in Catholicism. The day took on further significance in the first years of Charles's reign, when Milton was writing, as fears increased that the King was not going to fight against the evils of Catholicism but, seduced by his foreign bride, spread them.

'In quintum Novembris' is a compact *aition*, explaining how this day became part of the national holiday schedule. The celebration originates in the rescue of the King from a nefarious (and of course Roman) plot. Campbell and Corns read the poem as a conventional endorsement of the King.[149] The poem's political conservatism seems supported by its allusions to Virgil: James is described as 'pius' (1), the English are 'Teucrigenas populos' ('Teucer's | children', 2), and *Fama*

---

[147] See especially David Quint, *Epic and Empire: Politics and Generic Form from Virgil to Milton* (Princeton, 1993), 271–81.
[148] *Bonfires and Bells*, 147, 145.
[149] *John Milton, Life, Work and Thought*, 35.

is a central figure.[150] As John Hale shows, however, the poem is also full of Ovidian references; in particular, he points out specific verbal echoes of as well as broader parallels with the *Fasti*.[151] For Hale, moreover, the poem is evidence of Milton's 'political awakening'.[152] He notes that by the end of the poem, 'the king has faded out of the blessedness: the emphasis has shifted onto the Lord, and then to the people in their folk-rites. The crisis as narrated has changed the emphasis.'[153] A subterranean coup occurs: the King is subtly removed from the English calendar, which becomes representative only of the people. Milton's poetical experiments with Ovid, time, and holidays have led him to play with monarchical deposition.

MASQUING REVOLUTION

The trial run at usurping authority in 'In quintum Novembris' continues in *Comus*, in which, as many critics have noted, the King's power has no role in the resolution of the plot. Nor does that of the Earl of Bridgewater, for whom the masque was written.[154] The power to free the Lady comes entirely from figures associated with poetry itself: the Attendant Spirit and Sabrina. The duel between Ovidian voices merges with a contest between sources of authority, in anticipation of Milton's later writings in which 'the poet moves into the place formerly reserved for the ruler, appropriating as he does so the ancient forms that once stood for imperial power'.[155]

Like the *Fasti*, *Comus* reflects a conflict between ruler and poet over desire, time, and, in Milton's case, Ovid himself. As I argued earlier, there are many forms of Ovid jostling together in Milton's masque: the Spenserian, Shakespearian, Marlovian, libertine, courtly, and no

---

[150] See also *Variorum*, i. 167–8, and the notes to the poem.
[151] *Milton's Cambridge Latin*, 163–82. Hale, however, too quickly dismisses the readings of the *Fasti* which would suggest that Ovid's poem is particularly appropriate for the purpose he describes.
[152] Ibid. 168.
[153] Ibid. 183. Philip Hardie shows further how the poem minimizes the King's role and makes the figure of a divinely controlled *Fama*, identified with the voice of the people, the foiler of the plot; see *Rumour and Renown*, 429–38.
[154] See Revard, *Milton and the Tangles*, 153–6; Marcus, *Politics of Mirth*, 178–85.
[155] Helgerson, *Forms of Nationhood*, 61.

doubt others. While the amorous Comus recalls the *magister* of the *Ars*, his powers and the general theme of metamorphosis point towards Ovid's epic. However, Ovid's significance is complicated further by the echoes of the *Fasti* in two important passages early in the masque. I noted in Chapter 1 that the Spirit's opening 'Alexandrian footnote', 'Who knows not *Circe* | The Daughter of the Sun?' (50–1), sends us back not only to Spenser, but beyond that to Ovid, including *Fasti* 2. 83. Shortly afterwards, the Lady appears. Lost in the woods, she asks and answers her own rhetorical question, which begins with Ovid's favourite 'fallor', now Englished:

> Was I deceiv'd, or did a sable cloud
> Turn forth her silver lining on the night?
> I did not err, there does a sable cloud
> Turn forth her silver lining on the night. (221–4)

As Bishop Hurd first noted, the circular phrasing specifically parallels another rhetorically self-conscious moment in Ovid: 'fallor, an arma sonant? Non fallimur, arma sonabant' ('Do I err, or was there a clash of arms? I err not, there was a clash of arms', *Fasti*, 5. 549), which announces the entrance of the warlike Mars into the flowery world of Flora.[156]

In using these formulae, Milton may simply be remembering and recycling handy tricks he learned at school without any interest in their original context. As Martindale cautions, not all verbal parallels are meaningful; some allusions may even be 'mere will-o'-the wisps that have led the amazed interpreter from his way into bogs and mires'.[157] As I suggested in Chapter 1, however, such forms can also be the means through which poets sketch their own literary descent. There are other reasons for thinking that these verbal parallels show that Milton remembered Ovid's poetic calendar when he wrote his masque. Like the *Fasti*, *Comus* is concerned with the ritual organization and control of time. Sabrina especially is associated with ritual practices, as we are told that 'the Shepherds at their festivals | Carrol her goodness lowd in rustick layes, | And throw sweet garland wreaths into her stream | Of pancies, pinks, and gaudy Daffadils' (848–51). The masque was written for and performed on the feast of

---

[156] See *Variorum*, ii, pt. 3, 890.
[157] Martindale, *John Milton and the Transformation*, 4.

Michaelmas.[158] As 'In quintum Novembris' indicates, holidays were serious matters in the seventeenth century. Under the Stuarts, conflict over time became focused on the question of religious holidays, and especially the keeping of the Sabbath. Puritans insisted that the 'holy day' be spent in prayer or reading the Bible, newly available in English. In contrast, the King encouraged spending the day playing games, arguably less because of the health benefits of innocent recreation than for the purpose of keeping the lower classes happily occupied and even stupefied in their spare time. To the Puritans, this seemed to encourage drunken and licentious behaviour unfit for a godly Protestant nation. They increasingly attacked games as pagan and popish, targeting especially the rites of May and the maypole. In response to such agitation, James I issued the *Book of Sports*, saying how important and indeed godly it was to play games on Sunday; the debate became even more vigorous under Charles, who reissued the book in 1633, an act which has been seen as providing an important context for *Comus*.[159]

The conflict over holidays makes it worth looking a bit more closely at the *Fasti*'s use by antiquarians at this time, as there is more at stake here than a simple curiosity about the customs of other countries and times. Ovid's work provided a model for early comparative archaeologists interested in the nature and origins of English practices. Moreover, antiquarians debated the relation between Roman and English customs. For some the relation was simply one of curious analogy, showing that completely different cultures develop similar practices because of universal human needs. Thomas Godwin drew attention to the likenesses between Roman and English practices in his 1614 *Romanae Historiae Anthologia: An English Exposition of the Romane Antiqvities, Wherein Many Romane and English offices are parallel'd, and divers obscure phrases explained*. Similarly, Thomas Hobbes made a list of parallels between English and Roman holidays, observing that the Romans have 'their Procesion of *Priapus*; wee our fetching in, erection, and dancing about *Maypoles*'.[160] ('Erection' is a very naughty noun, however, given that the customs he identifies are

---

[158] Critics have noted references to liturgy of the day in the masque; see William B. Hunter, 'The Liturgical Context of Milton's *Comus*', *English Language Notes*, 10 (1972), 11–15; and Marcus, *Politics of Mirth*, 201–3.
[159] See especially Marcus, *Politics of Mirth*.
[160] *Leviathan, or The Matter, Forme, & Power of a Common-Wealth Ecclesiasticall and Civill* (London, 1651); repr. *Hobbes's Leviathan Reprinted from the Edition of*

the most controversial.) Milton's argument in 'Prolusion 6' similarly suggests that a universal human need for time off from labour produces an inevitable resemblance between otherwise different cultures. However, Milton's inclusion of the example of the Floralia, which Puritans believed was the pernicious source of May Day,[161] is puzzling: while it is possible that he is simply unaware of or uninterested in such issues, or is unperturbed by the current implications of an innocent analogy, he could be adopting a provocatively conservative position. Still, he seems to suggest that there is simply a casual resemblance between past and present practices. In his typically chaotic and unfinished *Remaines of Gentilisme and Judaisme* (1686), however, John Aubrey makes the connection genealogical. Aubrey draws heavily on Ovid's poem because he believes that British practices can be traced back to the Roman past. The early Christian habit of absorbing pagan elements stuck: 'In the Infancy of Christian Religion it was expedient to plough (as they say) with the heifer of the Gentiles: (i) to insinuate with them, and to let them continue and use their old Ethnick Festivals, which they new named with Christian names, *e.g.* Floralia, they turnd into ye Feast of St. Philip and Jacob, etc. The Saturnalia into Christmas.'[162] For Aubrey, therefore, the *Fasti* is not just an *aition* of Roman ritual, but also one of English custom itself.

Antiquarian investigation into the nature of early English customs was fuelled by the same desire to define national identity that was at the centre of the rearrangement of the calendar, and was equally fraught.[163] The Society for Antiquities (founded in 1586) was closed in 1607 when King James expressed concern that investigations into

---

1651, introd. W. G. Pogson Smith (Oxford, 1909), 518. Qtd. in Marcus, *Politics of Mirth*, 155.

[161] Marcus notes how those who wanted to suppress May Day cited the infamous reputation of the Floralia among the Romans themselves (*Politics of Mirth*, 151–2). William Prynne glosses his attack on the licentiousness of English holiday practices with notes from the *Fasti* (*Histrio-Mastix. The Players Scovrge, or, Actors Tragaedie, Divided into Two Parts* (London, 1633), Early English Books Online, Hh, Hh2; see also Pugh, *Herrick, Fanshawe and the Politics of Intertextuality*, 48.

[162] John Aubrey, *Remains of Gentilisme and Judaisme*, ed. James Britten (1881; repr. Nendeln, 1967), 6. According to Aubrey, therefore, All Souls' Day originated in the Feralia and Harvest in Lamas. Aubrey's syncretic impulse is not all that different from that of Frazer, who in his notes on the *Fasti* makes 'St. George's Day (April 23) . . . the modern equivalent of the Parilia' (21 April)—thus conveniently identifying England's birthday with Rome's (*Fasti*, p. 415).

[163] On this subject see Graham Parry's excellent *The Trophies of Time: English Antiquarians of the Seventeenth Century* (Oxford, 1995). Parry includes a chapter on

the origins of English customs, especially law, might limit royal prerogative.[164] (Indeed, John Selden's investigations would turn in that direction; they suggested that the original form of government in Britain had been an assembly, which was definitely not what the absolutist Stuarts wanted to hear.) By the 1650s, antiquarianism became an almost entirely Royalist preoccupation; its goal was to hold on to the customs, and often the buildings, which first the Reformation and then the Civil War had destroyed. Laud's earlier encouragement of such activities also indicates their role in the increasing tension between Puritans and Anglicans.[165] English customs became especially controversial in the context of the religious debates over the relation between England and Rome. Puritans insisted that the Reformation meant a complete break with all aspects of the Roman past, which should therefore be destroyed. Anglicans, however, emphasized the continuity between past and present, encouraging the kind of links with the Roman world forged by Aubrey.[166] Even when read just as a handbook of Roman rituals, the *Fasti* had an intrinsically political significance for controversies over the nature and origins of English customs.

It is not surprising, then, to find the *Fasti* invoked by a poet like Robert Herrick, who supported Anglican ceremonies.[167] Many critics have sensed a broad connection with Ovid's poetic calendar.[168] Herrick's *Hesperides* is imagined both as a place and as 'my eternall

---

John Weever, author of *Faunus and Melliflora*, whose last work, published in 1633, was on British funeral monuments.

[164] Fritsen notes how in 1468, similarly, the Roman Academy was closed down by the Pope for being politically subversive; it reopened ten years later when it was able to prove it had an orthodox religious purpose (*Renaissance Commentaries*, 210).

[165] See Parry, *Trophies of Time*, 17–18.

[166] On this debate, see especially Guibbory, *Ceremony and Community*; and Kevin Sharpe, *The Personal Rule of Charles I* (New Haven, 1992), 328–45.

[167] On Herrick's 'ceremonialism', see Guibbory, *Ceremony and Community*, 79–118.

[168] Most, however, have simply noted an interesting but casual resemblance. Leah Marcus imagines Herrick as Ovid 'creating his record of traditional festivals from the banishment of Dean Prior as Ovid had revised the *Fasti* during his exile in barbarous Tomis' (*Politics of Mirth*, 142). A. B. Chambers also sees this as simply an interesting parallel between similar sensibilities ('Herrick and the "Trans-shifting of Time"', *Studies in Philology*, 72 (1975), 114). Graham Parry speculates, however, that the relation could be one of influence: 'Herrick's habit of looking at life as a round of rituals and observances may well have been conditioned by an admiration for Ovid's *Fasti*' (*Seventeenth-Century Poetry: The Social Context* (London, 1985), 170). Syrithe Pugh is the first critic to discuss the verbal echoes and parallels of the *Fasti* as evidence

Calender' ('*To his worthy Kinsman, Mr.* Stephen Soame', 10), whose announced subject is '*Times trans-shifting*' ('*The Argument of his Book*', 9).[169] His vision of time is one centred, as in Ovid, on ceremonies and rituals, many described in terms of Roman practices and figures, and there is a holiday mood that seems shaped in part by the spirit of Ovid's calendar.

Herrick's general Ovidianism has been of some interest recently, particularly for critics looking at his politics. For Syrithe Pugh, Herrick's use of allusions from Ovid's exilic and erotic verse especially shows his defiance of an increasingly dominant Puritan ideology which, like that of Ovid's Augustus, focused on sexual purity.[170] As she notes, in the 1640s, new laws, 'Like Augustus' law...brought sexual behaviour under direct state control for the first time'.[171] By drawing on Ovid's erotic poetry, Herrick resists the legislation of desire; at the same time, he tames it, presenting himself as a remarkably innocent Ovid who vindicates the chaste eroticism of the court against Puritan charges of licentiousness.[172] In answer to the growing Puritan demand that England break from its Roman past, Herrick insists that pagan and Christian morals are compatible and can be joined together in a unified vision. He proclaims the importance of ceremony as a means of creating a community that extends in time as well as space and which may therefore include Ovid himself. Herrick might well appear therefore to have found in the *Fasti* a model for his response to Puritanism. However, while Ovid challenges the ruler's claim over time, Herrick supports it, putting his Ovidian revolution at the service of a King whom he identifies with Augustus. His Ovid, like that of the libertines and Jonson, is clearly on the side of monarchical power.

---

of a conscious appropriation that is central to Herrick's poetry (*Herrick, Fanshawe and the Politics of Intertextuality*, 39–56).

[169] Citations are from *The Poems of Robert Herrick*, ed. L. C. Martin (London, 1965).

[170] *Herrick, Fanshawe and the Politics of Intertextuality*, 21–38, 57–83.

[171] Ibid. 23.

[172] Kerrigan and Braden note how Herrick uses Ovid to create 'the fullest record we possess of the actual practice of poetic sexual fantasy as programmatic chastity' ('Milton's Coy Eve', 35). On Herrick's general self-presentation as '*Ovidius redivivus*' see Pugh, *Herrick, Fanshawe and the Poetics of Intertextuality*, 7. As Pugh notes, the prominence of Herrick's nose in the striking bust engraved on his volume's frontispiece wittily displays his identification with 'Naso' (17–18).

While politically the two authors end up on opposite sides, poetically, the young Milton and Herrick have much in common, including their appreciation of Ovid.[173] The traces of the *Fasti* in *Comus* might indicate that, like Herrick, Milton is also drawing on its subversive potential, although to make an argument antithetical to Herrick's and to transfer monarchical power to the poet.[174] The occasion, Michaelmas, allows him an opportunity for Saturnalian subversion. In many ways the antithesis between the Lady and Comus seems to reflect the growing religious and political tensions that would eventually pull the country apart. Their positions are defined partly through their opposing visions of how to spend time: while Comus urges the Lady to enjoy herself and the present, she restrains her powers for future higher rewards. Moreover, the Lady's spirited defence of the value of the 'holy dictate of spare Temperance' (767) against what she calls Comus' 'swinish gluttony' (776) invokes the generic conflict between the epic teetotaller and the elegiac wine-drinker of 'Elegia 6'. The Lady's epic journey is threatened by the elegiac Comus, who brings it to a standstill. The generic choice of the early poems has thus become explicitly a political one, in which choosing a type of poetry becomes a statement of what side one is on. The different forms of Elizabethan Ovidianism discussed in Chapter 1 become politicized when recruited to the different sides. Through the libertine Comus, Shakespeare is summoned to support aristocratic power, while, through the Lady and Sabrina, Spenser is enlisted for a Protestant poetics that protests against aristocratic excesses.[175]

The difference between the two characters is reflected also in their choice of Ovidian figures. Holding the Lady alone in his palace, the villain boasts that he has complete control over her fate:

---

[173] Alan Rudrum perceptively compares the aesthetics of Herrick's 'Delight in Disorder' to Milton's description of Eve's hair in *Paradise Lost* 4. 304–6 ('Royalist Lyric', in N. H. Keeble (ed.), *The Cambridge Companion to Writing of the English Revolution* (Cambridge, 2001), 184).

[174] Carole Newlands argues that the first English translation of the *Fasti*, by John Gower, published in 1640, reflects the debates over the nature of royal authority which were heating up in the years before the Civil War ('The Other John Gower and the First English Translation of Ovid's *Fasti*', *Hermathena*, 177–8 (2004–5), 251–66).

[175] On Spenser's appropriation by militant Protestantism, see David Norbrook, *Poetry and Politics in the English Renaissance* (London, 1984), 195–234.

> Nay Lady, sit; if I but wave this wand
> Your nervs are all chain'd up in Alabaster,
> And you a statue; or as *Daphne* was
> Root-bound, that fled *Apollo*. (659–62)

While most readers assume that the Ovidian model for Comus and the Lady is Circe and Ulysses, Comus sees them as Apollo and Daphne. His identification with Apollo makes a certain sense; he is, after all, son of Circe, 'daughter of the Sun' (51). Still, the specific myth he invokes seems peculiar, especially if we have in mind allegorical interpretations in which Daphne's metamorphosis represents the triumph of chastity. Comus is threatening to give the lady exactly what she wants, and to turn her into what she already is, which seems rather to defeat his apparent purpose of seduction.[176] Perhaps, like his libertine counterparts, he is not really interested in sex at all, but in a different kind of power. While in *Metamorphoses* 1, Daphne herself asks to be changed to escape Apollo, Comus is an Apollo who takes charge of her transformation, claiming her as his creation and symbol. His identification with Apollo therefore has a further significance, as, like Augustus and many Renaissance rulers and popes, the Stuarts used the god of poetry as part of their own iconography.[177] Like the King, Comus appropriates both Ovidian figures and chastity itself. Milton therefore has to simultaneously rescue Ovid from the hands of the supporters of the new Augustus and also save his ideal of chastity from an invasive aristocratic ideology which used it to justify the King's absolute power. Like Spenser redefining Elizabeth's virginity, Milton must rescue chastity not only *by* but also *from* chastity.[178]

---

[176] Richard J. DuRocher, who reads Ovid's story as demonstrating the sublimation of Apollo's lust into 'a chaste unconsummated union', thus considers Comus' boast 'vain, if not ludicrous', and a demonstration of his perverse appropriation of Ovidian myth (*Milton and Ovid*, 52).

[177] See Revard, *Milton and the Tangles*, 64–90. Revard traces Milton's use of Apollo from 'Elegia 5' through the 'Nativity Ode' especially as evidence of his developing political awareness.

[178] McGuire, *Milton's Puritan Masque*, 130–66, and Lewalski, 'Milton's *Comus*', thus read *Comus* as an attack on the courtly vogue for chastity. Katherine Eggert notes also the significance of the image of the Virgin Queen for Milton's poem. She argues that the Lady recalls the 'specifically Elizabethan cult of virginity', which was invoked nostalgically by critics of the Stuart court (*Showing Like a Queen*, 177). Where Elizabethan virginity meant 'morality, patriotism, and pure Protestant faith', the chastity of Charles and Henrietta Maria smacked too much of Catholicism, and

The Lady's use of Ovidian language and figures seems to offer an alternative model for chastity that is independent of monarchical power. She rejects metamorphosis altogether, offering an image of virtuous and impenetrable immobility. She vigorously dismisses Comus' myth and claim to power:

> Fool do not boast,
> Thou canst not touch the freedom of my minde
> With all thy charms, although this corporal rinde
> Thou haste immanacl'd. (663–6)

While Comus imagines the couple as Apollo and Daphne, the Lady suggests that a better model might be Tarquin and Lucretia, especially mediated through Shakespeare, whose heroine insists that 'Though my gross blood be stained with this abuse, | Immaculate and spotless is my mind. | That was not forced' (1655–7).[179] Behind both figures one can hear the voice of the exiled Ovid who proclaims his inner freedom from Augustus' power: 'ingenio tamen ipse meo comitorque fruorque: | Caesar in hoc potuit iuris habere nihil' ('my genius is nevertheless my comrade and my joy; over this Caesar could have no right', *Tristia*, 3. 7. 47–8). Other Ovidian elements reinforce the Lady's autonomy and inner freedom. Let's come back to the Ovidian rhetoric of her opening speech:

> Was I deceiv'd, or did a sable cloud
> Turn forth her silver lining on the night?
> I did not err, there does a sable cloud
> Turn forth her silver lining on the night. (*Comus*, 221–4)

Milton brilliantly intuited that this Ovidian formula is the perfect form for the Lady's integrity: the verbal circularity creates the image of an unmoving, unified, even impenetrable chastity. The Lady is so self-sufficient that she knows the answer to her own question

---

was undermined by the immorality associated with court and the practice of masquing itself. Eggert thus argues that 'Milton resurrects queenly virginity because for him, it signifies a sufficient defense against a similarly unjust and degraded monarchy' (ibid. 179). I suspect, however, that Milton is becoming more critical of all royal forms of virginity, reading Elizabeth's manipulation of the virtue through Spenser and Shakespeare.

[179] Further echoes of Shakespeare's poem appear in the younger brother's denunciation of Opportunity (401), which Lucrece sees as the servant of Time and Night (*Lucrece*, 932–3).

immediately and needs no help from outside of herself. The odd echo effect created by the lines is then continued as she next sings to the nymph Echo for help. An echo is of course literally a repetition of something already said: the speaker receives his answer by hearing his own words bounced back at him.[180] Echo's status here is ambiguous: does the Lady think of her as a separate character, or is she still talking to herself, assured that once more the answers to her own questions will come from within?

The Lady's rhetoric is backed up by her choice and use of Ovidian references. The story of Echo is famously paired by Ovid with that of Narcissus in *Metamorphoses* 3. The Lady clearly has Ovid's version in mind, as in her song she reminds us of the other half of the story, describing her brothers as '*a gentle Pair | That likest thy* Narcissus *are*' (236–7). As we will see further in the next chapter, Narcissus is one of Ovid's most popular figures in sixteenth-century literature, and in art generally. However, the fact that the Lady describes *both* boys as Narcissus is unusual: it suggests that the boys are mirror images of each other. The Lady seems to choose Ovidian myths that invoke a world of endless self-images, of copies and reflections, which exclude anything outside the self. Through both her rhetoric and these figures she builds a shield against otherness which mirrors the shield of chastity which the Elder Brother believes protects her (447–52).[181]

The name of 'The Lady' has made it hard not to identify the heroine with Milton himself, known at school as 'the Lady of Christ's'. Her rousing last speech (756–99) seems a fitting climax of Milton's

---

[180] On the use of echo as a device, see John Hollander, *The Figure of Echo: A Mode of Allusion in Milton and After* (Berkeley and Los Angeles, 1981); and Joseph Loewenstein, *Responsive Readings: Versions of Echo in Pastoral, Epic, and the Jonsonian Masque* (New Haven, 1984). John Clapham's 1591 Latin poem *Narcissus* retells the story omitting the figure of Echo, but using an Echo song to suggest Narcissus' self-love (*Narcissus: Siue amoris iuuenilis et praeipue philautiae breuis atque moralis descriptio*; cited from Charles Martindale and Colin Burrow, 'Clapham's *Narcissus*: A Pre-Text for Shakespeare's *Venus and Adonis*?', *English Literary Renaissance*, 22/2 (1992), 147–76). Milton inversely omits a literal echo song, but uses the figure of Echo to draw attention to other kinds of echoes in the Lady's speeches.

[181] The repetition in lines 221–4 create the kind of mirroring effect that is apparent in other rhetorical techniques through which English authors reproduced Ovid. Eric Langley notes that the phrase 'himself himself', which I discussed in relation to *The Rape of Lucrece*, suggests 'the mirrored surface of Ovid's pool'; moreover, 'the neat economy of a single word in tight repetition discloses the self-enclosed and self-perpetuating dynamic of narcissistic fascination' (*Narcissism and Suicide*, 1). For the Lady and Narcissus, see Ch. 3.

own early exploration of chastity as not only the subject but also the very source of poetry. Inspired by chastity to restrained eloquence, she brandishes the 'Sun-clad power of Chastity' (782) to defy the alternative Sun, Apollo. Arguing for the young Milton's religious radicalism, Guibbory claims that the Lady's vocabulary of sexual purity identifies her specifically with Puritans who figured their rejection of Anglican ceremonialism as spiritual chastity.[182] Her physical and psychological self-containment seems to make her 'Milton's exemplar of the autonomous ethical self of progressive Reformation culture'.[183] She shows the transference of chastity from a symbol of the authoritarian monarch, set off from his or her subjects by his purity and power, to the self-determining individual with which Milton himself is so often identified. Yet some readers have found her a bit of snob.[184] There is something narcissistic too in the Lady's attraction to images of likeness and identity; the 'series of protective enclosures' she imagines in her Echo song 'evoke the narcotic womb-world of Comus's mother Circe'.[185] Her resemblance to Lucrece may be disturbing, given that Lucrece's chastity is ultimately suicidal. As Shullenberger observes, her paralysis and final stony silence suggest that 'As a self-completing virtue, chastity may be at risk of setting itself apart and fixing its own enduring status as a living but frozen icon.'[186] While in the 1642 *Apology for Smectymnuus* Milton claims that the poet who aspires to greatness must be chaste and himself 'a true poem' (*Works*, iii, pt. 1, 303), the Lady, like the

---

[182] *Ceremony and Community*, 166–71.

[183] Shullenberger, *Lady in the Labyrinth*, 170. For a fuller discussion of the political, religious, and philosophical significance of chastity/virginity in relation to developing ideas of 'the autonomous liberal self', see John Rogers, 'The Enclosure of Virginity: The Poetics of Sexual Abstinence in the English Revolution', in Richard Burt and John Michael Archer (eds.), *Enclosure Acts: Sexuality, Property, and Culture in Early Modern England* (Ithaca, NY, 1994), 238.

[184] The Lady's reference to 'loose unleter'd Hinds' (174) has especially seemed an expression of disdain for the lower classes; see Patterson, 'Forc'd Fingers', 17. As noted on p. 87, n. 122, these lines also echo Marlowe, and may therefore convey simultaneously her distaste for a 'lower', i.e. erotic, form of Ovidian poetics.

[185] Shullenberger, *Lady in the Labyrinth*, 126. Stephen Orgel is especially suspicious of the Lady's 'solipsism', seeing her as 'literally singing to herself' in the Echo song ('The Case for Comus', *Representations*, 81 (2003), 41, 40). He notes the masque's obsession with duplication—from the pairing of the Attendant Spirit and Comus, to the final twins—which suggests a world in which everyone looks like someone else.

[186] *Lady in the Labyrinth*, 235. See his general discussion of the Lady's silence (ibid. 226–79).

monumental Lucrece or statuesque Adonis, may go too far. While Comus arrests the Lady's journey, there is something static about her character that suits his purposes; she is the perfect Daphne for his Apollo.[187] Fittingly, when the Lady sings to Echo, it is Comus who answers. It may be significant therefore that her rhetorical question to herself in lines 221–4 recalls *Fasti* 5. 549, which announces the rather loud entrance of Mars into the merry month of May, which up until this point has been devoted to Flora.[188] While Mars's entrance suggests an opposition between Mars and Flora, as I argued earlier, that antithesis itself turns out to be an illusion, as Flora created Mars. Ovid's lines reflect how the Lady and Comus, like Tarquin and Lucrece, have a more complicated relation than first appears. While Comus claims to be able to create the Lady, the Lady has equally created Comus.

In fact, while the Lady sees Comus as her enemy, he immediately sees her as his partner, whom he will make his 'Queen' (265).[189] Where she sees opposition he sees resemblance. The contrasting perspectives are indicative of their characters in general. The Lady, like her Elder Brother, sees the world in the rigid black and white terms that were typical of a Puritan 'rhetoric of division and opposition, an insistence on a purity that is understood as necessitating the exclusion of polluting, contaminating elements'.[190] Comus seems subversive precisely because he disturbs such categories; as Stephen Orgel says, he shows dramatically how difficult it is to tell good from evil.[191] Where the Lady separates, he wants to bring things together, uniting even human and animal in his transformed figures, and, like Herrick, mixing English and Roman customs. Ironically, however, in taking such a role, he reinforces the dualistic structure of the masque.[192]

---

[187] Fish argues that it is precisely this quality in the Lady that makes her Milton's ideal of virtue (*How Milton Works*, 140–84).

[188] John Hollander also noted this parallel, and suggested that Milton is comparing Comus to the god of war. *The Figure of Echo*, 52–6. I think the analogy is less direct but still significant.

[189] The Shakespearian subtext of his next words 'Hail forren wonder' (265) suggests their intimate relation further: they echo Ferdinand's first vision of Miranda, his future wife, in *The Tempest* 1. 2. 422–8.

[190] Guibbory, *Ceremony and Community*, 85.

[191] 'The Case for Comus', 35.

[192] Shullenberger notes too how Comus speaks in 'the either/or habit of compartmentalizing experience that belies the fluidity and energy he claims to speak for' (*Lady in the Labyrinth*, 159).

The masque however ends with an alternative model for the union of antithetical forces. In contrast to the reformable Circe of Townshend's *Tempe Restored*, Comus is ultimately impervious to change. It is instead the steadfast Lady who is transformed, undergoing, as Shullenberger has shown, an initiation into a new stage of development. Her faith in her own freedom and independence proves to be naive, as she is liberated only through the intervention of others. Moreover, her own words show that she has already been penetrated by Ovidian thought and rhetoric. As DuRocher notes, the Lady's first speech is 'characteristically Ovidian, in which an isolated female character reveals her wavering personality through a long, torturous soliloquy (169–228), as do Myrrha, Bibylis [sic], Medea, among others'.[193] This is obviously a somewhat disturbing bunch of role models for a nice young girl. Shullenberger argues, however, that the Lady's evocation of these figures enables her to confront such potential scenarios, and in doing so to redeem tragedy. Allusion enables her to encounter evil without becoming it; the logic here is similar to that of *Areopagitica* in which Milton will say that reading also enables us to safely 'see and know, and yet abstain' (*Works*, iv. 311). But allusions play a further role in the Lady's growth, as she 'begins to figure out who she is by reading her own situation in relation to classical stories'.[194] The employment of the redundant form of *Fasti* 5. 549 in the Lady's opening speech (221–4) both reflects her self-involvement and, by echoing Ovid, breaks out of it. Her goal is like that of Psyche, who, as I argued in Chapter 1, achieves individuation as she becomes aware of her dependence on others.

Unlike the 'fair Infant' or Shakespeare's Adonis, the Lady is able to grow up. Moreover, the Lady's transformation, like that of Ovid's Chloris/Flora, leads to the metamorphosis of the world.[195] The opposition between the Lady and Comus is at the centre of the rigidly hierarchical world in which the masque begins, in which higher and lower realms are sharply divided as good and evil. The division is typical of the masque form, and paradoxically compatible with both an aristocratic ideology based on the innate superiority of an upper

---

[193] *Milton and Ovid*, 51. If we move beyond the *Metamorphoses*, moreover, there are further relevant models in the *Heroides*.
[194] Shullenberger, *Lady in the Labyrinth*, 140; see also 141.
[195] See Shullenberger's discussion of the transformation of community in initiation rituals and the masque (*Lady in the Labyrinth*, 251–79).

class, as well as a Puritan rhetoric of moral absolutes. In the early version performed at Ludlow in 1634, the opening hierarchy is reaffirmed at the end. The Spirit ends the Michaelmas holiday, sending the revellers back to their appointed roles and social stations: 'Back shepheards, back, enough your playe | till next sunshine holy daye';[196] he returns the children to their parents and then presents the closing moral. The revised ending, however, leaves behind this dualistic system to rise to an alternative world in which hierarchies are fluid and dynamic, and high and low beings are part of a single movement. We glimpse a new model not only for relationships between the sexes, and, as I argued in the last chapter, between authors, but for cosmic and social order, one that anticipates the dynamic chain of being between heaven and earth that Milton shows us in *Paradise Lost*. The poet imagines a revolutionary change in the order of things.

By arguing that Milton's reading of the *Fasti* played a role in Milton's understanding of Ovid and his working through to this vision, I am not trying to make it or Ovid the cause of Milton's dawning political awareness. I do want to show, however, that the Renaissance Ovid is not simply a poet of the pure aesthetic or of retreat into a fantasy world, but one whose poetry and life show that poetry cannot escape the world it inhabits. The *Fasti* especially opened up questions that were intensely personal to Milton but which, in the context of larger debates, could not remain just private matters. Ovid was an important figure generally for Milton during this period in which he was working through what it means to be a poet, and debating what kind of poet he would be. The masque is a hybrid form, through which Milton was able to review his own earlier generic choices and to explore their larger implications. In this, I think that Ovid's experimentation with 'a rather epic kind of elegy'[197] was as provocative for him as it had been for Spenser. Milton's move into extended narrative, not to mention drama, involved an ambitious leap from the earlier short poems. Drawing together epic, lyric, and drama, the masque offered him the possibility for the

---

[196] *Bridgewater Maske*, in Revard (ed.), *Complete Shorter Poems*, 879–80. On the political differences between the two endings see Patterson, 'Forc'd Fingers'. For a different reading of the relation between the two endings, see Shullenberger, *Lady in the Labyrinth*, 174–6.
[197] Hinds, '*Arma* in Ovid's *Fasti*: Part 1', 82.

generic experimentation that he extends further in his rather elegiac kind of epic, *Paradise Lost*, to imagine a world which is both erotic and chaste, and in which love motivates the highest form of action: poetry itself.[198]

The masque generally was a form intended to reconcile conflicting political interests, representing and enacting the unity of the nation and the interdependence between ruler and subjects. In England, however, as Puritans became suspicious of court extravagance and popish rituals, masques—with links also to the Catholic mass—came instead to symbolize the growing gulf between Charles and his subjects. Rather than healing conflicts, they deepened them.[199] Milton, however, glimpses the unifying potential of the genre. It is hard not to see the debates in *Comus* as prophetic of the hardening of political conflicts into irresolvable oppositions. In hindsight we see Milton's future choice, and the regicide mediated through metaphor. But that future was not yet evident to many, including Milton himself. And in the final speech there is also a faintly visible sketch of a different possibility: a world that might still have been transformed through an imaginative rather than bloody revolution.

---

[198] On Milton's absorption of other forms, see Barbara Kiefer Lewalski, Paradise Lost *and the Rhetoric of Literary Forms* (Princeton, 1985).

[199] Martin Butler notes therefore how Charles wasted an important political opportunity for representing and forging trust ('Reform or Reverence?', 152).

3

Reflections of Narcissus

THE ARGUMENT

Like Comus, Paradise Lost *is structured around contrasting forms of change which suggest different ways of transforming sources. In this chapter, I focus particularly on Milton's rewritings of the story of Narcissus, which, like so many Ovidian tales, explores creativity and its relation to desire. For later artists, moreover, the figure of Narcissus offers a means of reflecting on their own copying of Ovid. For Milton, versions of Narcissus both point towards the fall, and help readers to imagine an alternative story and model for creative change.*

FORMS OF CHANGE

There is something both inevitable and weird about leaping from *Comus* to *Paradise Lost*. At the edge of *Comus*, Milton's epic seems just around the corner—one garden up, second door to the right, as it were—and yet also unimaginably far away. The two works are separated by a gulf of time and experience. In the years following *Comus*, Milton's personal life was notoriously full of upheaval, during which he had first-hand evidence of the difficulty of relations between men and women. He made choices which for many years meant abandoning poetry entirely for politics. His country changed its government and then changed back again. The two works thus seem like before and after versions of Milton's hopes: if in the early works he worries that he is too early, in the later works, he fears he may be too late.

These tumultuous events seem to have given Ovidian stories and themes even greater meaning for Milton. The failure of political change made him especially attentive to the theme of change that is central in Ovid's works and which has become in many ways synonymous with his legacy. Ovidian creativity is inspired by change, beginning with his own transformation of earlier works. It is often assumed that Renaissance writers associated Ovid with the form of change found in Pythagoras' speech in *Metamorphoses* 15: endless flux. For Christians, such mutability is a consequence of the fall; it marks our exile from a God who is imagined as an unmoved mover. However, Pythagoras' vision is actually very different from the other kinds of transformation in the poem. As Leonard Barkan notes, in the stories of humans turned into new forms, change paradoxically ends change.[1] Change takes different shapes in Ovid's other works: the erotic verses explore the different ways that desire transforms lovers—destructively, as in the case of Medea, or more creatively, like the lover of the *Ars* who learns new skills to woo his mistress. The control of natural, seasonal change is the topic of the *Fasti*; in the final verse, exile is the new name for change.[2] For Renaissance writers, Ovid could mean forms of change that included growth, development, expansion, as well as imaginative and even personal freedom.

Change is certainly a constant preoccupation in all of Milton's works. In 'Elegia 5' he explores natural change, in 'Elegia 7' the changes caused by erotic desire. In the elegies on early death, he explores death as the great transformer that brings about the 'heavy change' of the world ('Lycidas', 37), but which also results in the translation of the dead: the apotheosis of the Bishop of Ely ('In obitum Praesulis Eliensis') and of Charles Diodati ('Epitaphium Damonis'); the metamorphosis of the drowned Edward King into

---

[1] *The Gods Made Flesh*, 78–93. As Myers notes, aetiological stories generally involve the fixing of forms in a final state of being (*Ovid's Causes*). Colin Burrow notes the tension in the *Metamorphoses* between 'the poem's closed metamorphic tales about human beings on the one hand, and on the other the unclosed, unending, changeful universe in which they take place' ('Spenser and Classical Traditions', in Hadfield (ed.), *The Cambridge Companion to Spenser*, 230). On this tension and its significance for later artists, see further my 'Changing Ovid', in Keith and Rupp (eds.), *Metamorphosis: The Changing Face of Ovid in Medieval and Early Modern Europe*, 267–83.

[2] On the connection between exile and change in Ovid and Renaissance art see also A. Bartlett Giamatti, *Exile and Change in Renaissance Literature* (New Haven, 1984); and Harold Skulsky, *Metamorphosis: The Mind in Exile* (Cambridge, Mass., 1981).

'the Genius of the shore' ('Lycidas', 183); as well as the transformation of the fair infant into symbols ('On the Death of a fair Infant'). In the 1645 *Poems*, the theme of change climaxes in *Comus*, which, as I argued, uses its Ovidianism to imagine transformations that are psychological, moral, literary, and potentially political.

As Joseph H. Summers notes, in *Paradise Lost*, Milton is 'the celebrator of change'.[3] Eden is a garden and, like all gardens, a place of growth. Adam and Eve are dynamic characters who, even in the brief time we see them before the fall, develop.[4] They live in a world of 'ceaseless change' (5. 183). The reciprocal rising and falling at the end of *Comus* is part of the natural rhythm of a universe in which, as Raphael tells them, 'one Almightie is, from whom | All things proceed, and up to him return' (5. 469–70).[5] All created things are in motion, evolving into something else, so that, Raphael continues:

> time may come when men
> With Angels may participate, and find
> No inconvenient Diet, nor too light Fare:
> And from these corporal nutriments perhaps
> Your bodies may at last turn all to Spirit,
> Improv'd by tract of time, and wingd ascend
> Ethereal, as wee, or may at choice
> Here in Heav'nly Paradises dwell. (5. 493–500)

Here, time is not the conventional antithesis of eternity, but the path to it; a world of transformation does not mark our separation from God but rather is the path back up to him. Through their conversations with each other and with Raphael, Adam and Eve, like the garden, grow and develop towards this goal. Adam thanks Raphael for guiding him upwards:

> Well hast thou taught the way that might direct
> Our knowledge, and the scale of Nature set

---

[3] *The Muse's Method: An Introduction to* Paradise Lost (London, 1962), 86. See generally his seminal discussion of change in *Paradise Lost* (ibid. 71–86).

[4] On the significance of the analogy between the growing garden and Adam and Eve see also Barbara Kiefer Lewalski, 'Innocence and Experience in Milton's Eden', in Thomas Kranidas (ed.), *New Essays on* Paradise Lost (Berkeley and Los Angeles, 1971), 86–117.

[5] Summers notes how 'falling' is therefore part of the world of innocence: 'Both flight and song are made possible only by alternating motion: the wings and notes must fall as well as rise for ascension' (*Muse's Method*, 82).

> From center to circumference, whereon
> In contemplation of created things
> By steps we may ascend to God. (5. 508–12)

God himself authorizes the hope of such an ascent, when he announces to the angels that he is about to create:

> Another World, out of one man a Race
> Of men innumerable, there to dwell,
> Not here, till by degrees of merit rais'd
> They open to themselves at length a way
> Up hither, under long obedience tri'd,
> And Earth be chang'd to Heav'n, & Heav'n to Earth,
> One Kingdom, Joy and Union with end. (7. 155–61)

God is very clear about the differences here: he draws attention to the fact that he is inventing a different species—something new that did not exist before—and that this new being will live in a new place separate from heaven. The pointed spatial terms *here* and *there* reiterate the distance and enforce a hierarchy in which the new race occupies a specific and inferior place. Yet, the differences seem to foreshadow, if rather obscurely, a final reunion, in which *here* will become *there* through a reciprocal metamorphosis.

The natural movement of all things towards God and eternity might imply, however, that, as Spenser's *Mutabilitie Cantos* suggest, earthly flux will ultimately be superseded by heavenly stasis. But Milton's heaven is a place of lively activity in which the angels dance, sing, go places (as does God himself, though ubiquity makes this easier), fight battles, hold different jobs. They are able to change sexes (1. 423–4). Activity, individuality, and 'change delectable' (5. 629) are a part of Milton's vision of the highest spiritual life. The angels normally pass time

> In song and dance about the sacred Hill,
> Mystical dance, which yonder starrie Spheare
> Of Planets and of fixt in all her Wheeles
> Resembles nearest, mazes intricate,
> Eccentric, intervolv'd, yet regular
> Then most, when most irregular they seem,
> And in thir motions harmonie Divine
> So smooths her charming tones, that Gods own ear
> Listens delighted. Eevning now approach'd

(For wee have also our Eevning and our Morn,
Wee ours for change delectable, not need) . . . (5. 619–29)[6]

The dance of the angels is compared to the movement of the stars which, as the *Fasti* shows, is the traditional means of measuring time. In heaven, time has become a dance in which also change is 'delectable', a source of pleasure. Change makes choice and therefore freedom possible.

Like *Comus*, however, *Paradise Lost* includes different kinds of change. As Wendy Olmsted notes, it 'is a metamorphic epic par excellence, delineating a war between a force which transforms good into evil and one that turns evil into good'.[7] As the Elder Brother in *Comus* suggests, Milton identifies evil with 'eternal restless change' that is self-destructive as 'evil on it self shall back recoyl, | . . . Self-fed, and self-consum'd' (*Comus*, 596, 593–7). Like his counterpart Comus, Satan represents a type of change that is inimical to development and progress.[8] Evil fixes what was once fluid and moving. Hell is bounded by a frozen wasteland, and policed by the petrifying force of Medusa who stands guard 'with *Gorgonian* terror' (*PL*, 2. 611). In a bizarre ritual punishment, the devils are intermittently dragged to this spot by the Furies, by whom they are forced temporarily to 'pine | Immovable, infixt, and frozen round' (2. 601–2). Raphael tells Adam of a dynamic chain of endless metamorphoses leading from and back to heaven; in contrast, Satan's agents Sin and Death construct a bridge that binds earth to hell 'with Pinns of Adamant | And Chains they

---

[6] Compare Milton's active heaven with Cowley's more conventional one in *Davideis* which is placed above the stars and in which there is 'no twilight': 'No circling *Motion* doth swift *Time* divide; | Nothing is there *To come*, and nothing *Past*, | But an *Eternal Now* does always last' (*The English Writings of Abraham Cowley*, ed. A. R. Waller (Cambridge, 1905), Book 1, p. 251).

[7] 'On the Margins of Otherness: Metamorphosis and Identity in Homer, Ovid, Sidney, and Milton', *New Literary History*, 27/2 (1996), 178.

[8] On Satan's rejection of change, see especially John Creaser, '"Fear of change": Closed Minds and Open Forms in Milton', *Milton Quarterly*, 42/3 (2008), 161–82; also Schwartz, *Remembering and Repeating*. Joseph B. Solodow notes how in Ovid metamorphosis can be 'a symbol of the person's inability to grow, develop, alter' (*The World of Ovid's* Metamorphoses, 189). Similarly, Burrow notes that many of Spenser's Ovidian characters are marked by 'a failure to move forwards'; metamorphosis therefore 'frequently signifies a reluctance to participate in the processes of striving and moving and living and breeding which represent the central principles of Spenser's poem' ('Spenser and Classical Traditions', 229). See also Quilligan, *Milton's Spenser*, 115–24.

made all fast, too fast they made | And durable' (10. 318–20). Evil uses change to end change, as:

> The aggregated Soyle
> *Death* with his Mace petrific, cold and dry,
> As with a Trident smote, and fix't as firm
> As *Delos* floating once; the rest his look
> Bound with *Gorgonian* rigor not to move. (10. 293–7)

As I suggested in Chapter 1, in *Comus*, the opposing kinds of metamorphosis are identified with different ways of adapting Ovid. In thinking about change generally, Milton draws on his own transformation of past sources. Imitation is a metamorphic process which creates difference from alikeness; according to Roger Ascham it involves '*dissimilis materiei similis tractatio*; and also, *similis materiei dissimilis tractatio*, as *Virgill* followed *Homer*' ('dissimilar material treated similarly and also similar material dissimilarly treated').[9] Classical and Renaissance theorists of imitation constantly stressed the danger of simply copying the ancients without changing the past material; as G. W. Pigman summarizes, 'The emphasis on transformation is complete; what's gathered must become something different.'[10] Milton's contemporary Abraham Cowley repeats a commonplace when he denigrates 'exact *Imitation*; which being a vile and unworthy kind of *Servitude*, is incapable of producing any thing good or noble'.[11]

For Milton, such servitude is not just poetical, as the textual transformation of the past is connected to questions of political and religious reformation.[12] The political significance of imitation is explicit in his 1649 *Eikonoklastes*, commissioned by the new government to respond to the wildly popular *Eikon Basilike* which had been published immediately after Charles's execution and which purported

---

[9] Roger Ascham, *The Scholemaster*, in *English Works*, ed. William Aldis Wright (Cambridge, 1904; repr. 1970), 267; cited in Stapleton, *Spenser's Ovidian Poetics*, 26.
[10] Pigman, 'Versions of Imitation in the Renaissance', 7. See also Greene, *The Light in Troy*, 28–53.
[11] 'Preface to Pindarique Odes', in *The English Writings of Abraham Cowley*, ed. Waller, 156.
[12] Wyman H. Herendeen suggests that Milton's *Accedence Commenc't Grammar*, probably composed in the 1640s, shows a similar alertness to the political function of grammatical change ('Milton's *Accedence Commenc't Grammar* and the Deconstruction of "Grammatical Tyranny"', in P. G. Stanwood (ed.), *Of Poetry and Politics: New Essays on Milton and his World* (Binghamton, NY, 1995), 295–312).

to represent the King's intimate musings in his last days. While Milton clearly suspects the work's spurious authorship (it is not clear if Charles had in fact any role in its composition), it suits his purpose to treat it as a reflection of the King's character. Like a demonic commentator, Milton goes tenaciously through the text line by line, demolishing 'Charles's' argument and rhetoric.[13] To discredit the King, Milton opens by showing that one of Charles's supposedly personal prayers was in fact 'a Prayer stol'n word for word from the mouth of a Heathen fiction praying to a heathen God; & that in no serious Book, but the vain amatorious Poem of Sr *Philip Sidneys Arcadia*; a Book in that kind of worth and witt, but among religious thoughts, and duties not worthy to be nam'd; nor to be read at any time without good caution; much less in time of trouble and affliction to be a Christians Prayer-Book' (*Eikonoklastes*, in *Works*, v. 85–6). Such a theft, he complains, is both an offence against God, and 'a trespass also more than usual against human right, which commands that every Author should have the property of his own work reservd to him after his death as well as living' (88). This invasive violation of the rights of his subjects epitomizes the King's real crime against the nation: 'to undermine our Liberties, and putt Tyranny into an Art' (69). But his borrowings equally show his inadequacy as an artist: he was 'forc'd to robb Sr. *Philip* and his Captive Shepherdess of thir Heathen orisons, to supply in any fashion his miserable indigence, not of bread, but of a single prayer to God' (89). Charles is guilty of a failure of imagination, which causes him to become a plagiarist of others' wits. As Achsah Guibbory suggests, for Milton, the King's 'lack of creative spirit' reveals the nature of his politics: 'imitation and repetition are the appropriate literary modes for royalist Anglicans who value continuity, tradition, and the preservation of ties with the past.'[14] Charles's copying of others shows the stagnation of an entrenched ideology that works to prevent change and which, as

---

[13] John Creaser's characterization of the Milton of the prose as 'an intellectual Rottweiler, belligerent and fiercely unable to let go' ('"Fear of change"', 173) fits well here.

[14] 'Charles's Prayers, Idolatrous Images, and True Creation in Milton's *Eikonoklastes*', in Stanwood (ed.), *Of Poetry and Politics*, 288. On Milton's presentation of Charles as a bad author, see also Richard Helgerson, 'Milton Reads the King's Book: Print, Performance, and the Making of a Bourgeois Idol', *Criticism*, 29/1 (1987), 1–25; and Fallon, *Milton's Peculiar Grace*, 154–60.

I argued in Chapter 2, draws on a vocabulary of chastity and timelessness to do so.[15]

Eikonoklastes thus makes explicit the conflict in *Comus* between King and poet as competing figures of authority, and now literally rival authors. Political differences take the form of poetical ones. The monarch is a double of the poet from whom Milton distinguishes himself in order to assume his rightful role as an Apollo figure. Milton presents himself as 'puritan, public servant, well-wisher to the commonwealth, and truth-teller', while crafting Charles as a 'liar, poseur, plagiarist, hypocrite, traitor, tyrant, fool'.[16] Moreover, the two authors are differentiated by the way they use the past: while the first is transformative and liberating, the second is stagnant and oppressive. While Milton rethinks traditional forms, Charles reproduces the past to prevent change.[17] To a certain extent, Milton's aggression is a

---

[15] Milton also chides the King for making 'the Closest Companion of these his solitudes, William Shakespeare' (*Eikonoklastes*, in *Works*, v. 84). Noting how Milton was struck by Charles's love of Shakespeare, Nigel Smith argues that at this time in his life Milton believed that 'the love of Shakespearean language becomes part of a negative world of idolatrous worship, bondage to custom, and slavery to tyrants' (*Is Milton Better Than Shakespeare?* (Cambridge, Mass., 2008), 93). As we will see further in Ch. 5, however, Milton's early reading of Shakespeare is sensitive to how poets may be at the mercy of their later readers/interpreters.

[16] Campbell and Corns, *John Milton: Life, Work, and Thought*, 226. As Corns especially has shown, Milton also pares his style to distance himself from the elaborate rhetoric of *Eikon Basilike*; see his *The Development of Milton's Prose Style* (Oxford, 1982), 69–79, 83–100. See also Helgerson's discussion of Milton's self-representation as an iconoclast who smashes the idols of the King in 'Milton Reads the King's Book'. As Helgerson notes, however, as a poet, Milton is not completely comfortable with this role, as his own poetry 'participates in the system of values that in *Eikonoklastes* he so violently spurns' (ibid. 15). See also Guibbory, 'Charles's Prayers', 285.

[17] Milton himself may have drawn on a related passage in Sidney later. Pamela defies the tyrant Cecropia who scorns God, warning her: 'that the time will come, when thou shalt knowe that power by feeling it, when thou shalt see his wisedome in the manifesting thy ougly shamelesnesse, and shalt onely perceiue him to have bene a Creator in thy destruction' (Philip Sidney, *The Countesse of Pembrokes Arcadia*, ed. Albert Feuillerat (Cambridge, 1969), 3. 10. 5). Compare with Abdiel to Satan: 'Then who created thee lamenting learne, | When who can uncreate thee thou shalt know' (*PL*, 5. 894–5). For Milton, the difference between types of imitation is ultimately one of divine grace; in *Eikonoklastes* he explains that 'It is not hard for any man, who hath a Bible in his hands, to borrow good words and holy sayings in abundance; but to make them his own, is a work of grace onely from above' (*Works*, v. 264). This may help explain Milton's example of the Byzantine tyrant Andronicus Comnenus, who had constantly read Paul's epistles 'and by continual study had so incorporated the phrase & stile of that transcendent Apostle into all his familiar Letters, that the imitation seemed to vie with the Original' (ibid. 361). According to Milton, a tyrant may be able to reproduce his model but cannot create something new of his own.

response to the overwhelming popularity of Charles's work, which clearly shook both the poet and the new government. The 1644 *Areopagitica* had imagined a great nation in the midst of a process of exciting transformation, in which a people who embrace change throw off the shackles of repression and regression to wrestle with a protean Truth who 'may have more shapes than one' and who leads them forward to the further 'reforming of Reformation' (*Works*, iv. 348, 340). Five years later, in *Eikonoklastes*, he is already worried that 'the People, exorbitant and excessive in all thir motions, are prone ofttimes not to a religious onely, but to a civil kinde of Idolatry in idolizing thir Kings' (*Works*, v. 68). Seduced by the powers of a Comuslike King, 'begott'n to servility, and inchanted with these popular institutes of Tyranny... [they] hold out their eares with such delight and ravishment to be stigmatiz'd and board through in witness of thir own voluntary and beloved baseness' (*Works*, v. 309). They prefer fakes to reality, tradition to innovation; like Satan, they resist change. The concerns were to be confirmed in 1660 when the 'reforming of Reformation' Milton praised in *Areopagitica* (*Works*, iv. 340) was brought to a halt by a people who had had, they decided, more than enough of Reformation.

For Milton, therefore, the problem in *Paradise Lost* is how to create change. As I have suggested, for many sixteenth- and seventeenth-century English writers, Ovid offered the possibility of imagining an alternative literary and even possibly world order. For Milton, however, the imitation of Ovidian figures also suggests the impediments to radical change.[18] As I noted in the Introduction, to many readers Ovidian subtexts have seemed to predetermine the story's ending by making the fall seem inevitable. Most ominously, the account of Eve's creation in Book 4 is modelled closely on the story of Narcissus. Since the rise of Christianity especially, narcissism has seemed clearly a pretty bad thing. Medieval allegorists and Renaissance commentators read Narcissus as the epitome of the sins of self-love, vanity, and pride. As George Sandys notes, Narcissus became also a type of the rebel angels: 'But a fearfull example we have of the danger of selfe-love in the fall of the Angells; who intermitting the beatificall vision, by reflecting upon themselves, and admiration of their owne

---

[18] The problem of imagining change poses an interesting technical as well as philosophical challenge for visual artists adapting Ovid, who have to find ways of conveying movement and transformation in a static medium.

excellency, forgot their dependence upon their creator. Our *Narcissus*, now a flowre, instructs us, that wee should not flourish too soone, or be wise too timely, nor overlove, or admire our selves.'[19] Narcissism causes the fall of the angels, and the repeated falls of other rash and proud persons. Neoplatonists similarly used the story as an allegory of the soul's entrapment in the unreal, shadowy world of matter which, like Circe and her son Comus, impedes the soul's journey home to its celestial origins.[20] To a post-Freudian world alarmed by the social and economic consequences of unrestrained individualism, Ovid's figure is equally suspect as the epitome of a modern solipsistic and self-absorbed subject.[21]

The use of Ovid in this key scene doesn't look good. It makes Eve appear fallen from her beginning, doomed by her inherent narcissism. The presence of narcissism in the story of Sin's creation in Book 2 further overshadows Eve's narrative in Book 4. It tempts us with the likeness between the two stories. However, for Milton, Ovid's tale of Narcissus both explains the origins of the fallen world of slavish copies, and provides a means of imagining that

---

[19] Sandys, *Ovid's Metamorphosis Englished, Mythologized, and Represented in Figures*, ed. Hulley and Vandersall, 160–1. Similar readings appear throughout Renaissance handbooks and dictionaries of mythology; see Mulryan, *Through a Glass Darkly*, 38–9. On the relevance of this reading for Eve's awakening, see also Parker, *Inescapable Romance*, 114–16, 122–4.

[20] See especially Plotinus, 'On Beauty', *Enneads*, 1. 8, in *The Essential Plotinus: Representative Treatises from the Enneads*, ed. Elmer O'Brien (New York, 1964), 42; and Marsilio Ficino, *Commentary on Plato's Symposium on Love*, trans. Sears Reynolds Jayne (2nd edn., Dallas, 1985), 140–1. See also Louise Vinge, *The Narcissus Theme in Western European Literature up to the Early 19th Century* (Lund, 1967), 37–41 and 267. The story thus epitomizes Ovid's epic as a whole, at least as interpreted by Arnulf of Orléans, who wrote that the author's intention was 'nos ab amore temporalium immoderato revocare et adhortari ad unicum cultum nostri creatoris, ostendendo stabilitatem celestium et varietatem temporalium' ('to call us back from the intemperate love of worldly things and encourage us to the one worship of our creator by showing the permanence of heavenly things, while emphasizing the flux of the temporal', qtd. in Frank Coulson, 'Ovid's Transformations in Medieval France (ca. 1100–ca. 1350)', in Keith and Rupp (eds.), *Metamorphosis: The Changing Face of Ovid in Medieval and Early Modern Europe*, 48).

[21] Readers today still tend to be rather puritanical about narcissism, as Freud's influential appropriation of Narcissus as the epitome of regressive psychology and sexuality gave new life to a myth that already had a bad reputation. Julia Kristeva reworked Freud's figure as the model of modern subjectivity in *Histoires d'amour* (Paris, 1983), while in his critiques of modern consumerism, Christopher Lasch used Narcissus as the perfect image of the modern ego; see especially *The Culture of Narcissism: American Life in an Age of Diminishing Expectations* (New York, 1979).

things might have been, and perhaps still might be, different. To understand Milton's transformative revisions, however, I'd like first to go back to Ovid's story, and then trace some of its later reworkings.

OVID'S ORIGINAL

Neoplatonic readings of Ovid's episode are not as far-fetched as they might appear, as the story plays on a number of Platonic paradigms. It begins by foregrounding not self-love but self-knowledge, associated with the Delphic command 'know thyself', invoked by Socrates in *Phaedrus* 230a and usually identified with the Socratic method. For Golding, the story thus reveals the meaning of the *Metamorphoses* as a whole, which is to teach the reader 'too know himself as neerly as he can'.[22] But Ovid himself seems to have found this precept rather ridiculous, or at least paradoxical. He had made fun of it in *Ars Amatoria* 2. 500–1, where Apollo appears to the *magister* and tells him that all lovers should know themselves, which, he explains, means simply that they should know how to use their best features to get girls.[23] In the *Metamorphoses*, the blind seer Tiresias more ominously prophesies that Narcissus will have a long life 'si se non noverit' ('If he ne'er know himself', 3. 348). The meaning of the prophecy and its relation to the episode is not immediately evident. Allegorical readings often see Narcissus' fate as the consequence of his *lack* of self-knowledge.[24] But Ovid is suggesting the exact

---

[22] 'To the Ryght Honorable and Singular Good Lord, Robert Erle of Leycester', 570, in *Shakespeare's Ovid*, ed. Rouse. See also 461, where he says Ovid teaches us 'Our selves too know our owne estate'.

[23] See also Ovid's advice to women (*Ars*, 3. 771 ff.). The joke here is partly on Apollo, who in the *Metamorphoses* is such a hapless lover. Philip Hardie shows how Apollo's solipsistic self-knowledge in the *Metamorphoses* leads into the story of Narcissus (*Ovid's Poetics of Illusion*, 46–7).

[24] Sandys puzzles over the phrase: 'As strange as obscure; and seeming contradictory to that Oracle of *Apollo: To know a mans selfe is the chiefest knowledge*. The lacke hereof hath ruined man: but having it must needs ruine our beautifull *Narcissus*: who only is in love with his owne perfections' (*Ovid's Metamorphosis*, 156). Schoolboys seem to have appreciated the fable's subversion of proverbial wisdom; in a school play of 1601, Narcissus's mother, Lyriope, ponders in gloriously bilingual doggerel: 'I bethinke at Delph, | One Phibbus walls is written: Knowe thyselfe. | Shall hee not know himselfe, and so bee laught on, | When as Apollo cries, gnotti seauton?' (*Narcissus: A Twelfe Night Merriment Played by Youths of the Parish at the College*

opposite, as Narcissus' fate is the fulfilment of Tiresias' prediction. The story thus turns self-knowledge into self-love and, ultimately, self-destruction. For Ovid, self-knowledge produces self-division rather than unification, and finally leads to the self-estrangement of metamorphosis.[25]

Other Platonic elements are present as well. As the Neoplatonic interpretations suggest, Narcissus' fate is a reversal of Plato's parable of the cave: a turning to the world of matter and shadows. Elements in the scene recall especially the *Phaedrus* and *Symposium*, dialogues which deal with knowledge, desire, and art.[26] In Ficino's reading of the *Symposium*, Narcissus is invoked as the opposite of Socrates: 'It was undoubtedly in order that Socrates might avoid such a death [that of Narcissus] that Diotima led him from the Body to the Soul, from this to the Angel, and from this back to God.'[27] Where Narcissus descends into the world of the body and shadows, Socrates is led gradually from shadowy types to truth. But at the same time, Ovid's Narcissus seems to fulfil Socratic ideals of not only knowledge but also desire. His story literalizes the love described in the *Phaedrus*, in which the lover 'loves, yet knows not what he loves; he does not

---

of S. John the Baptist in Oxford, A.D. 1602 (1602), Literature Online, 10). John Clapham's 1591 *Narcissus. Siue amoris iuuenilis et praeipue philautiae breuis atque moralis descriptio* deals with the ambiguity by simply reversing Ovid; Love tells Narcissus that he will *not* know himself ('Narcisse, haud noveris ipse', 149; cited from Martindale and Burrow, 'Clapham's *Narcissus*', 147–76). For other examples, see Vinge, *The Narcissus Theme*, 85, 127, and 132.

[25] Hardie suggests one parallel for Ovid's treatment here: 'In tragedy obedience to the Delphic precept leads to knowledge but not to salvation; in the later stages of the genre the dilemmas of the tragic protagonist may become a deliberate challenge to the intellectualist ethic of a Socrates: Medea acts in full self-knowledge of what she does' ('Lucretius and the Delusions of Narcissus', *Materiali e discussioni per l'analisi dei testi classici*, 20–1 (1988), 86–7). Ovid's general debt to tragedy is well known; Ingo Gildenhard and Andrew Zissos show the relation of Ovid's tale of tragic self-knowledge to the story of Oedipus in particular: 'Ovid's Narcissus (*Met.* 3. 339–510): Echoes of Oedipus', *American Journal of Philology*, 121/1 (2000), 129–47; see also Hardie, *Ovid's Poetics of Illusion*, 165–6. The narcissistic side of self-knowledge is also stressed in some 16th-century versions of Narcissus, as writers urge independence but recognize its antisocial potential; so Sir John Davies tells the reader that 'the Diuell mockes our curious braine, | When *know they selfe* his oracle commands'; 'Looke in thy *Soule*, and thou shalte *beauties* find, | Like those which drownd *Narcissus* in the floud' (*Nosce Teipsum* (London, 1599), Early English Books Online, B2ᵛ, L4ᵛ). See also Langley, *Narcissism and Suicide*, 43.

[26] See also Shadi Bartsch's discussion of the tale in relation to the *Phaedrus*' examination of 'eros, reflection, and self-knowledge' (*The Mirror of the Self: Sexuality, Self-Knowledge, and the Gaze in the Early Roman Empire* (Chicago, 2006), 84).

[27] Ficino, *Commentary on Plato's Symposium on Love*, 141.

understand... not realizing that his loved is as it were a mirror in which he beholds himself'.²⁸ Narcissus' famous complaint that 'inopem me copia fecit' (*Met.*, 3. 466) echoes Socrates' story of the origins of love in the conjunction of Poverty and Plenty in the *Symposium* 203b; here the meeting of opposites produces death. His longing to be split in half reverses Aristophanes' fable of the first humans who, divided as punishment by Jove, are constantly seeking their other halves. Ironically, it is because Narcissus cannot be divided that he is divided from his love; in his case, death is the great reuniter, as he notes: 'duo concordes anima moriemur in una' ('we two shall die together in one breath', *Met.*, 3. 473)—a parody also of romantic notions of love in death put forward in *Phaedrus* 256e. Ovid is clearly pushing Platonic formulations to absurdity. The result is both witty and provocative, and certainly might support Richard A. Lanham's belief that for Ovid, 'Plato's conception of love remained fundamentally narcissistic'.²⁹ The play continues through a cluster of interconnected stories in Books 3 and 4, which explore the paradox through which *eros* can make two become one.³⁰ The story of Narcissus is recalled in that of Pyramus and Thisbe, in which the lovers, kept apart by a wall, are united by death; so Pyramus cries 'una duos... nox

---

[28] *Phaedrus*, 255d; cited from *The Collected Dialogues of Plato*, ed. Edith Hamilton and Huntington Cairns (2nd edn., Princeton, 1963). Like Ovid, Socrates links desire and fantasy, as the lover 'fashions for himself as it were an image' (ibid. 252d) of the beloved. Plotinus' reading of the myth of Narcissus reworks the *Phaedrus*; see Stephen Bann, *The True Vine: On Visual Representation and the Western Tradition* (Cambridge, 1989), 117–18. Philostratus also senses a link between the two passages as he incorporates the landscape of the *Phaedrus* into his revision of Ovid's scene; see Dora Panofsky, 'Narcissus and Echo: Notes on Poussin's *Birth of Bacchus* in the Fogg Museum of Art', *Art Bulletin*, 31/2 (1949), 120 n. 33.

[29] *The Motives of Eloquence*, 48. According to Lanham, Ovid offers Renaissance writers the possibility of a mutable and playful 'rhetorical self' that is fundamentally antithetical to Plato's ideal of an essential and fixed identity. (Lanham is clearly on the Ovidian side.) Lanham's opposition is an alternative version of the traditional Ovid/Virgil antitheses between open and closed models of narrative and indeed selfhood. As I have been suggesting, however, to treat Ovid as simply the poet of flux is to ignore other aspects of his work; his poetry, like Milton's, acknowledges the desire for closure as well as a commitment to openness.

[30] Ovid's version of the union of Venus and Mars, trapped together in Vulcan's net, is also part of this pattern. The theme returns later in stories of incest and in the tale of Ceyx and Alcyone, in which the wife pleads with her husband not to leave her, and to 'animasque duas ut servet in una' ('save two lives in one', *Met.*, 11. 388). For later writers, Ovid will be particularly associated with the paradox of the couple who are 'two-in-one' (Hardie, *Ovid's Poetics of Illusion*, 25), which will be at the centre of Milton's poem.

perdet amantes' ('One night two lovers die', *Met.*, 4. 108; my translation still misses the witty one-two punch of the Latin). The momentum of Platonic parody continues in the story of Salmacis and Hermaphroditus, also told in *Metamorphoses* 4, which shows the recovery of the original unity in Aristophanes' fable through the dissolution of sexual difference. Through these stories, Ovid examines the puzzling combination of alienation and intimacy in desire. While desire is drawn to likeness, it requires difference for satisfaction.[31] It thrives on obstacles, as Ovid repeatedly notes in his *Ars*. Narcissus knows himself by discovering that he cannot 'know' himself; what keeps the lovers apart is the fact that they are the same, a situation recalled later in the stories of incest.[32]

For Ovid, moreover, desire is always stimulated by deception and illusion.[33] Like other episodes in which bodies are transformed into flowers, Ovid's myth is about the origins and nature of artistic creation. Here, too, the presence of Plato offers a framework. For Plato, art is a double illusion of the cave, as it is a copy of a material world which itself is the mere shadow of reality. The story of Narcissus

---

[31] The identification of desire with lack is of course made by Socrates himself in *Symposium* 200b–201. Charles L. Griswold Jr., *Self-Knowledge in Plato's* Phaedrus (New Haven, 1986), notes how the dialogue form, with its focus on interaction with another, is central to the theme of self-knowledge in the *Phaedrus*. In the *Charmides* 169a, Socrates says that knowledge also must have an object different from itself, and cannot be completely reflexive: 'there is nothing which has an inherent property of relation to self rather than to something else'; see also Bartsch, *The Mirror of the Self*, 27.

[32] See especially the story of Myrrha, who, lusting after her father, notes the irony of her situation: 'quia iam meus est, non est meus, ipsaque damno | est mihi proximitas: aliena potentior essem' ('since he's mine, he is not mine and my very closeness dooms me; if I were farther off I'd be better off', *Met.*, 10. 339–40). I'll return to the theme of incest in relation to the interlinking of episodes later in this chapter.

[33] See especially Hardie, *Ovid's Poetics of Illusion*, 143–72; and Rosati, *Narciso e Pigmalione*. The erotic verse shows that deception is essential to love. To win a girl you must deceive her (see, for example, *Ars* 1. 487–90). Deception is further justified as women are themselves false; therefore, the lover must 'Fallite fallentes' ('Deceive the deceivers', 1. 645). But lovers themselves like to be lied to, as in *Amores* 1. 4. 69–70, where Ovid begs his girlfriend to lie to him about sleeping with her husband. In fact, by playing roles, one can make them come true: 'Saepe tamen vere coepit simulator amare, | Saepe, quod incipiens finxerat esse, fuit'; 'Fiet amo verus, qui modo falsus erat' ('Yet often the pretender begins to love truly after all, and often becomes what he has feigned to be'; 'one day will the love be true which now was false', *Ars*, 1. 615–16, 618). As the story of Narcissus shows, in love the difference between truth and illusion seems especially questionable (a point made further in the story of the lovers Ceyx and Alcyone, in which false dreams tell the truth).

demonstrates the danger of art's mimetic ability, which leads to the confusion of shadow and substance. While art copies nature it also transforms it; like metamorphosis itself, it turns 'real substances into empty, fleeting images'.[34] The boundary between reality and fantasy is as absolute and as insubstantial as the surface of the water which both creates Narcissus' beloved and keeps him from him; as he complains: 'minimum est, quod amantibus obstat' ('it's a tiny thing that blocks our love', 3. 453).[35] At the centre of the story therefore is the power of illusion. The boy's desire is founded on a double error, a simultaneous confusion of self and other as well as that of image and reflection. He mistakes his reflection for a real person who he imagines is other than himself: 'spem sine corpore amat, corpus putat esse, quod umbra est' ('He loves an unsubstantial hope and thinks that substance which is only shadow', 3. 417).[36] The narrator tries to call out to Narcissus and warn him that what he loves 'imaginis umbra est' ('is but the shadow of a reflected form', 3. 434). The deluded boy is infatuated with the shadow of a shadow; desire draws him further and further from reality into the cave of images and the illusory world of art. Furthermore, this rather Platonic warning about the danger of falling in love with a mere copy of a copy creates the impression that the narrator has forgotten that Narcissus is himself simply a fiction, an *umbra*, created by the author. The speaker replicates his character's error, and so demonstrates further the power of illusion to persuade us of its reality. Erotic and creative fancy make something

---

[34] Barkan, *The Gods Made Flesh*, 51.

[35] Like many classical writers, Ovid is fascinated with water. This is partly because the paradoxical insubstantiality and power of water make it the perfect image for both desire and poetry. It keeps the lovers apart in *Amores* 3. 6; it is also of course the medium through which Leander reaches Hero, but which also divides them forever (see *Heroides* 18 and 19, especially 18. 125–6, which includes the 'una duos', one-two, paradox I noted in *Metamorphoses* 4. 108: 'Ei mihi! Cur animis iuncti secernimur undis, | unaque mens, tellus non habet una duos?' ('Ah me! why are we joined in soul and parted by the wave; two beings of one mind, but not of one land?').

[36] I believe the vocabulary of the episode supports a reading of *umbra* in line 417 rather than *unda*, which some manuscripts give; on the critical debates, see Rosati, *Narciso e Pigmalione*, 4. The most common Renaissance editions—those of Regius, Sabinus, and Heinsius—have *umbra*, a decision reflected in both Golding's and Sandys's translations. While *umbra* means shadow, as well as shades of the dead, it also means reflection and 'image'; it is connected to *imago* and *simulacra*, words Ovid uses in this episode and throughout his epic in connection with art. See also Solodow, *The World of Ovid's* Metamorphoses, 204–9.

out of nothing.[37] The story thus sets up a central theme that will be continued in later tales such as those of Pygmalion and his statue, Cephalus and Procris, and Ceyx and Alcyone,[38] and will be central to Ovid's later presentation of his own story as one in which his fictions became real.

In Book 3, the relation between illusion and reality is complicated further by the fact that, from the start, the boy seems to be a work of art. Gazing at himself in the water, Narcissus becomes a statue: 'adstupet ipse sibi vultuque inmotus eodem | haeret, ut e Pario formatum marmore signum' ('He looks in speechless wonder at himself and hangs there motionless in the same expression, like a statue carved from Parian marble', 3. 418–19). Metaphor foreshadows metamorphosis, so that the transformation of Narcissus seems the inevitable consolidation of the character's essential nature.[39] Paradoxically, therefore, as a shadow Narcissus is more substantial; made a work of art, he is transformed from an ephemeral human being into a thing of permanence. While from a Platonic perspective, art is a mere *imaginis umbra*, a reflection of a reflection, for Ovid it alone is real and substantial. Art gives stability and permanence to the transient flux of life. The episode thus looks forward to the end of the poem, in which Ovid claims a similar transformation for himself: when his body dies, he will live on in his 'parte... meliore' ('better part', 15. 875), his poetry. The Platonic treatment of the danger of

---

[37] Later versions of the scene enjoy finding further ways of representing art's powers of deception. In *Imagines* 1. 23, Philostratus describes a painting of Narcissus. The hyperrealistic representation encourages the viewer, as well as a lone bee, to experience the boy's confusion: 'The painting has such regard for realism that it even shows drops of dew dripping from the flowers and a bee settling on the flowers—whether a real bee has been deceived by the painted flowers or whether we are to be deceived into thinking that a painted bee is real, I do not know' (*Philostratus: Imagines; Callistratus: Descriptions*, trans. Arthur Fairbanks (London, 1931), 91–3). See also Callistratus' 'On the Statue of Narcissus', in which the water tries to outdo the statue (*Descriptions* 5, in *Philostratus: Imagines*, 390–5). The theme of illusion is of particular interest in the 17th century especially in mannerist writers; see Vinge, *The Narcissus Theme*, 210–12.

[38] For the importance of the latter as a story of the power of the imagination, see especially Tissol, *The Face of Nature*, 72–84, and Hardie, *Ovid's Poetics of Illusion*, 272–92.

[39] This dimension is picked up by Shakespeare in *Venus and Adonis* 211–14, where Venus' accusation that Adonis is as hard as a statue is fulfilled by his final change, and in *The Rape of Lucrece* 391, where the sleeping Lucrece's appearance 'like a virtuous monument' anticipates her transformation into a Roman icon.

images turns upon itself and calls into question any simplistic division between substance and shadow, original and copy.

Narcissus does not remain, moreover, in a state of confusion. Ovid is unusual in giving Narcissus' story two distinct stages. While Narcissus, like Actaeon, acts at first 'inprudens' ('Unwittingly', 3. 425) of his error, he eventually recognizes his mistake, crying: 'iste ego sum: sensi, nec me mea fallit imago' ('Oh, I am he! I have felt it, I know now my own image', 3. 463). The original sensual mistake is corrected by reason and the boy finally does indeed know himself, freeing himself from the world of the cave. He now has a moment of choice, and deliberates: 'quid faciam? roger anne rogem? quid deinde rogabo? | quod cupio mecum est: inopem me copia fecit' ('What shall I do? Shall I be wooed or woo? Why woo at all? What I desire, I have; the very abundance of my riches beggars me', 3. 465-6). Soliloquy is the perfect form of conversation for the speaker who is both subject and object of his own desire. The monological question and answer here create a convoluted echo chamber. The speech pushes to a rather ludicrous extreme the dramatic form which Ovid uses with characters such as Medea, Scylla, and Byblis for great effect, to suggest a divided self, poised on a critical moment of choice.[40] The one-sided conversation provides a further unsettlingly Ovidian subtext for the first speech of the Lady in *Comus*, which, as I argued in Chapter 2, suggested the potential narcissism in her chastity. While the Lady appeals to Echo for information, Narcissus' rejection of Echo underlines his inability to enter into dialogue. Echo's status is ambiguous: she is both a character separate from Narcissus, and simply his own voice copied and thrown back to him. In other words, she exists on the boundary between self and other. As a figure of verbal reflection Echo neatly doubles the boy, and should be his perfect mate. As is often noted, Ovid is the first to pair these stories to show how they reflect each other.[41] Moreover, through Echo's intervention in his

---

[40] As John W. Veltz has shown, these moments of internal debate had an impact on drama ('The Ovidian Soliloquy in Shakespeare', *Shakespeare Studies*, 18 (1986), 1-24). The use of Ovidian examples and situations in debates at schools trained speakers and writers to turn to Ovid as a rich resource for arguments on both sides of a case, and, in drama, for characters who are torn between incompatible alternatives.

[41] Hermann Fränkel points out that the two are mirror images: 'While Narcissus was caught in the net of mere sameness and was touched by nothing but his own unsubstantial reflection, Echo is mere otherness and is herself only an unsubstantial reflection. He is too much prepossessed with his own share to share it with others, and

story, Narcissus' words briefly become part of a conversation. But the two parallel stories never come together, as Narcissus rejects dialogue for his self-enclosed monologue. As in an echo, the answer to Narcissus' question is contained in the question itself. The boy considers the alternatives—to woo or be wooed—only to realize that he doesn't need to choose. He *is* both wooer and wooed: the Ovidian paradox embodied.

In its exploration of the themes of knowledge, desire and its ability to make two one, and the power of illusion, the story of Narcissus is central to Ovid's poem and to his poetry as a whole. Narcissus' famous description of his situation—'inopem me copia fecit'—epitomizes the way in which Ovidian wit constantly strives to turn one thing into its opposite. The word *copia* itself is a key word for Ovid and his legacy. As I noted in the previous chapter, confronting all the versions of the origins of the months offered to him by squabbling deities in the *Fasti*, Ovid refuses to choose, saying 'copiaque ipsa nocet' ('the very abundance is harmful', *Met.*, 5. 6). In Ovid, *copia*—abundance, excess—is both the matter of art and also always potentially self-destructive. Narcissus' paradox is echoed shortly afterwards by Niobe, who boasts that 'tutam me copia fecit' ('My very abundance has made me safe', 6. 194). In fact, *copia* makes her vulnerable. In *Ex Ponto* 4. 10. 59, Ovid notes further how *copia* weakens the waters of Tomis: 'copia tot laticum, quas auget, adulterat undas' ('The wealth of so many waters corrupts the waves which it augments'); a further conceptual pun, given water's association with poetry and eloquence. In the *Remedia Amoris*, *copia* (with its connotations of sexual potency) in love is dangerous: 'copia tollat amorem' ('plenty destroys passion', 541).[42] For later writers, Ovid is a source of *copia*, the rhetorical skill of elaboration, which was seen as essential in the artistic process.

---

she has no self of her own which she might share' (*Ovid: A Poet between Two Worlds*, 84–5).

[42] In the *Metamorphoses*, *copia* also links stories of insatiable appetites: in *Metamorphoses* 8, *copia* cannot satisfy either *Fames* or Erysichthon (8. 792–93, 838–9); in 11. 127–9, it also fails to appease the appetites of Midas (an episode which is connected to that of Narcissus; see Tissol, *The Face of Nature*, 67–8). However, *copia* is also generated from the torn horn of the eloquent Achelous (*Met.*, 9. 85–8). As Barkan notes, the aetiology here is strikingly different from the traditional one (used in *Fasti* 5. 121–8). In Ovid's new version the cornucopia is like his own art; it 'embodies a transforming power in the real world—the power of nature's abundance' which can make 'a solid substance of what was a shifting, protean form' (*The Gods Made Flesh*, 78–9).

But he illustrates the dangers of such skills; Erasmus cites Ovid as a warning against the ostentatious indulgence of *copia* in his influential treatise *De Utraque Verborum ac Rerum Copia* 1. 3. For Dryden, the treatment of Narcissus epitomized the way in which Ovid's own *copia* was *inops*. Dryden found the wordplay distasteful and inappropriate: 'Wou'd any Man who is ready to die for Love, describe his Passion like *Narcissus*? ... If this were Wit, was this a Time to be witty, when the poor Wretch was in the Agony of Death? ... On these Occasions the Poet shou'd endeavour to raise Pity: But instead of this, *Ovid* is tickling you to laugh. *Virgil* never made use of such Machines.'[43] The episode shows Ovid becoming Quintilian's artist, 'nimium amator ingenii sui' ('unduly enamoured of his own gifts', *Institutio Oratoria*, 10. 1. 88).[44] As Rosati points out, Ovid seems to invite the identification with his character, presenting himself as 'the poet Narcissus, the poet with head bowed in admiration of his own virtuosity, who becomes excited by seeing his reflection in the astonishment of his public'.[45]

For later artists the story of Narcissus, like that of so many Ovidian figures, is read through Ovid's own fate. But it also speaks to their own situations as imitators of Ovid, aware that their own *copia* can turn into mere copying: the dry repetition of hackneyed topoi and stories raided from the classics. If the Platonic subtext shows how art copies reality, it also reminds us that art copies other art. Like all of Ovid's stories, the episode draws on a range of sources—not only Plato, but also Lucretius, Catullus, and, of course, Virgil.[46] As Philip Hardie notes, Ovid's tale is 'a subtle example of reflection and echo as mechanisms of literary *imitatio*'.[47] The central images of the story are those used in classical discussions of imitation; for Quintilian, the difference between copy and original is 'ut umbra corpore' ('as the

---

[43] *The Poems and Fables of John Dryden*, ed. Kinsley, 527; see also Tissol, *The Face of Nature*, 11.

[44] Quintilian, *The Institutio Oratoria of Quintilian*, trans. Butler.

[45] *Narcisso e Pigmalione*, 50.

[46] See Hinds, *Allusion and Intertext*, 5–10. Alison Keith notes the episode's exploitation of elegiac motifs ('Sources and Genres in Ovid's *Metamorphoses* 1–5', in Boyd (ed.), *Brill's Companion to Ovid*, 252–6). Philip Hardie discusses the exchange with Lucretius especially in 'Lucretius and the Delusions of Narcissus' and *Ovid's Poetics of Illusion*, 152–6. Hardie also suggests that Narcissus' fixation on his reflection looks back to *Aeneid* 1. 495 ff., where Aeneas stops in Carthage to gaze at his own image, carved in the temple of Juno (*Ovid's Poetics of Illusion*, 146). Like everything else, Ovid's theme of illusion is deeply Virgilian.

[47] *Ovid's Poetics of Illusion*, 152.

shadow to substance', *Institutio Oratoria*, 10. 2. 11). John Hollander has shown how Echo serves as a figure of allusion in both Ovid and later writers.[48] As we will see, Narcissus will also be a handy image for writers who are self-conscious about their own acts of copying.

RENAISSANCE NARCISSI

The poet is always a Narcissus.

(Schlegel)

All creation is essentially an exercise of Narcissism.

(Havelock Ellis)[49]

Given its concerns, it is hardly surprising that Ovid's story has been astonishingly fertile for artists. In England, the deluge of Ovidian writings in the sixteenth century begins with T.H.'s 1560 *The fable of Ovid treting of Narcissus*, and for the rest of the century, Narcissus is everywhere. As Eric Langley has suggested, he seems the epitome of the autonomous self emerging in the period, though he is often also invoked precisely to critique an ethos of self-absorbed self-interest.[50] The boy is frequently combined with similar Ovidian characters, including Adonis and Actaeon.[51] T.H. draws parallels with the story of Marsyas.[52] Most often, the story is combined with that of

---

[48] Hollander, *The Figure of Echo*; see also Gildenhard and Zissos, "Ovid's Narcissus", 144.

[49] Schlegel and Ellis qtd. from Havelock Ellis, 'The Conception of Narcissism', in *Studies in the Psychology of Sex*, 2 vols., i, pt. 2, *Eonism and Other Supplementary Studies* (New York, 1942), 369–70, 374.

[50] *Narcissism and Suicide*. R. W. Maslen also notes how the figure is used by writers such as Gascoigne and Warner to attack 'a nation of Narcissi, who have abandoned the humanist quest for self-knowledge in favour of a relentless pursuit of self-interest and mutual flattery' ('Myths Exploited', 26).

[51] In Thomas Edwards's 'Narcissus', Narcissus calls for sympathy from Adonis as well as Leander; see *Narcissvs: Aurora musae amica* (1595; repr. 1882), Literature Online, 155–75.

[52] See *The fable of Ouid treting of Narcissus*, D2^r–D3^r. A link between these two artist figures is also suggested by Sandys, who brilliantly turns Narcissus' self-fascination, 'adstupet ipse sibi vultuque' (*Met.*, 3. 418, which the Loeb flattens as 'He looks in speechless wonder at himself'), into the Ovidian 'Himselfe, himselfe distracts' (*Ovid's Metamorphosis*, 138). This resonates later in Sandys's version of Marysas' plaintive cry, 'quid me mihi detrahis?' (*Met.*, 6. 385), as 'Me from my selfe, ah why doe you distract?' (*Ovid's Metamorphosis*, 276). James Shirley's 1646 poem *Narcissvs, Or, The*

Hermaphroditus, as readers and writers saw the two stories as mirror images of each other.[53] Adapters also grasped the episode's doubling with the story of Pygmalion: where Narcissus' body becomes an image, Pygmalion's image becomes a body.[54] Versions of *inopem me copia fecit* are used to generate countless further paradoxes.[55] While Kenneth Knoespel argues that the story of Narcissus was a particular source of inspiration because its puzzles invited later writers to rewrite the tale in order to clarify or complete it, often these revisions led to further complications, and sometimes confusions.[56]

Still, it is possible to trace some clusters of uses. Writers often exploit the aetiological aspects of Ovidian myths, using them to explain how human experience became fixed in permanent forms. From the *Roman de la Rose* to Freud, the story of Narcissus is used most commonly as a parable of erotic development, to show that love begins in a narcissistic state and must be channelled outside of the self into love of another. As a variant of this, Narcissus occasionally represents an ideal and innocent chastity.[57] Milton's Lady could

---

Self-Lover picks up on this double meaning of 'distraction' when 'A new distraction fell upon the streame' ((London, 1646), Early English Books Online, B8ʳ).

[53] See Keach, *Elizabethan Erotic Narratives*, 265-6 n. 41.

[54] On the relation of the two stories, see also Rosati, *Narciso e Pigmalione*; Enterline, *The Rhetoric of the Body*, 97-8. Many writers play on the connection; see especially John Marston, whose Pygmalion 'was enamourèd | On that fair image himself portrayèd' (*The Metamorphosis of Pygmalion's Image, and Certain Satires*, 17-18; quotations from Marston are taken from *The Works*, ed. Arthur Henry Bullen, 3 vols. (1887; repr. Hildesheim, 1970)). Paul Barolsky notes that Narcissus and the linked figure of Pygmalion appear frequently in writings also on visual art, as 'tales of how the artist falls in love with his own creation', as Ovid himself was thought to have done ('As in Ovid, So in Renaissance Art', *Renaissance Quarterly*, 51/2 (1998), 453).

[55] Spenser plays on the paradox in the *Amoretti* (see especially 35. 8) and uses it as an epigram for Diggon Dauie's crushed ambition in the 'September' eclogue of *The Shepheardes Calender* 261, where E.K. notes, 'This poesie I knowe, to have been much vsed of the author' (p. 340). It is a motif also in *Venus and Adonis*, 18-20, 22. See also the popular *Willobie his Avisa, or, The True Picture of a modest Maid, and of a chast and constant wife* ((London, 1594), Early English Books Online, Q2ʳ), which tells of the unsuccessful courtship of the chaste Avisa. It still resonates (though a little feebly by this time) in the 1630s for John Cleveland who uses it to end his 'An Elegy on Ben Jonson': 'Heere IONSON lies, *whom* had I nam'd before | In that one word alone, I had paid more | Then can be now, when *plentie* makes me *poore*' (in Brian Duppa (ed.), *Ionsonus Viribvs: or, The Memorie of Ben Jonson Revived by the Friends of the Muses* (London, 1638), Early English Books Online, E2ᵛ).

[56] *Narcissus and the Invention of Personal History* (New York, 1985), pp. ix, 104.

[57] Jean Puget's 1627 *Les Amours de Narcisse* thus praises the boy and argues that his transformation into a flower is appropriate, as 'il n'est rien de plus pur que les fleurs, de mesme il n'estoit rien au monde de plus chaste que cét Amant. L'Amour

possibly be thinking of this tradition when she compares her brothers to the boy. But more often, Ovid's tale is read as a moral cautionary tale of arrested development, suggesting the danger if the Bridgewater children's innocence becomes an end in itself.[58] As Louise Vinge shows, in medieval love poetry, the story of Narcissus is often used to prove the dangers of rejecting the powers of love. The proud and unmovable lady is imagined as a Narcissus. Petrarch's Laura is thus also a Narcissus as well as a Daphne figure.[59] Chastity is represented as unnatural and selfish, and ultimately self-destructive. In *Venus and Adonis*, Venus uses the example of Narcissus to warn Adonis of the dire perils of chastity (161-2).[60] The young man of Shakespeare's *Sonnets* is a Narcissus figure who makes 'a famine where abundance

---

qu'il auoit pour soy, ne rendoit pas ses affections criminelles, parce que il y a de la iustice, & de la raison naturelle à s'aymer: de sorte qu'il viuoit dans sa passion, auec toutes les austeritez d'vne ame parfaictement chaste' ('there is nothing more pure than flowers, just as there is nothing in the world more chaste than this Lover. The Love that he has for himself does not make his affection a crime, because there is justice and natural reason in loving oneself: so that he lives in his passion with all the austerity of a soul perfectly chaste', qtd. in Vinge, *The Narcissus Theme*, 229).

[58] Stephen Orgel thus reads Milton's masque as 'a love poem' showing 'the destructiveness of unresponsiveness' ('The Case for Comus', *Representations*, 81 (2003), 41). His use of *Venus and Adonis* as an analogy to make his case (ibid. 41-2) is perceptive but ultimately misleading, as it ignores the crucial differences between the two works.

[59] See Vinge, *The Narcissus Theme*, 110-45. As we will see shortly, the tales of Daphne and Narcissus are linked in both Ovid and the later tradition. In the *Amoretti*, Spenser thus uses the story of Daphne as a warning of the sad fate of those who resist love (28. 7-12), and urges his lady not to suffer the same punishment: 'Then fly no more fayre loue from Phebus chace, | But in your brest his leafe and loue embrace' (28. 13-14). While most commentators read Daphne as a positive figure John Brinsley thought her a 'male content' (*sic*) whose troublemaking is indicated by the fact that she lived 'all alone without a husband' (*Ovids Metamorphosis translated grammatically, and also according to the propriety of our English tongue, so farre as Grammar and verse will bear* (London, 1618), Early English Books Online, L4ʳ; cited in Green, *Milton's Ovidian Eve*, 73). William Barksted also draws on the link between Narcissus and Ovid's stories of incest; his Mirrha is a version of the proud chaste lady whose rejection of love (here quite literal as the god himself courts her) leads to unnatural desires; see especially *Mirrha the Mother of Adonis*: 'I know not loue' (B1ᵛ).

[60] See also 751-68. Adonis, however, identifies with Narcissus when he claims that he is not ready for sexual experience, begging Venus: 'Measure my strangeness with my unripe years. | Before I know myself seek not to know me' (524-5). The tension between the characters thus involves also a debate between two readings of the Narcissus story: for Venus, it is a story of selfishness, for Adonis, it is about the desire for integrity.

lies, | Thy self thy foe' ('Sonnet 1', 7–8).[61] In Francis Beaumont's 1602 *Salmacis and Hermaphroditvs*, Salmacis warns the boy that if he does not give himself to her, he will meet the fate of his precursor (D4^v, E1^v). (Unfortunately, while she is lecturing him, Hermaphroditus sees his own image in Salmacis' eyes and falls in love with it.[62]) The story is used to underline the message that those who reject love are punished: in Thomas Peend's 1565 *The Pleasant Fable of Hermaphroditus and Salmacis*, Hermphroditus' narcissistic refusal of love causes him 'hym selfe to loose' (A4^r);[63] in Beaumont's version, elements from the story of Narcissus help teach through negative example that 'All creatures that beneath bright *Cinthia* be, | Haue appetite vnto society' (E3^v).

---

[61] See also Bate, *Shakespeare and Ovid*, 97–9. Clapham's 1591 *Narcissus* may have been written to persuade the Earl of Southampton to marry Burghley's granddaughter; see Martindale and Burrow, 'Clapham's *Narcissus*', 150.

[62] The scene replays the attempt by Shakespeare's Venus to win Adonis through his self-love; she tells him he may see himself in her: 'Look in mine eye-balls, there thy beauty lies' (*Venus and Adonis*, 119).

[63] Peend's assumption that the story of Hermaphrodite is one of *self-loss* is especially telling. In most literature of this time, Ovid's image of the 'semiur' (*Met.*, 4. 386) is used ambiguously. In the Renaissance Neoplatonic tradition, it appears as an image for ideal love that transcends boundaries and the making of man and woman one flesh in marriage; see A. R. Cirillo, 'The Fair Hermaphrodite: Love-Union in the Poetry of Donne and Spenser', *Studies in English Literature*, 9/1 (1969), 81–95; and Edgar Wind's *Pagan Mysteries*, 211–17 especially. William Carroll shows how the figures of Narcissus and Hermaphroditus, examples of a double identity that is 'two-in-one', appear in Shakespeare's representations of marriage also; see *Metamorphoses of Shakespearean Comedy*, 52–4. In Weever's *Faunus and Melliflora*, the climactic coupling follows closely Ovid's description of metamorphosis, while celebrating the result: 'their kisses make two bodies one' (827). Du Bartas's Adam and Eve are also 'sweet *Hee-Shee*-Coupled-One!' whom God is able to 'Make Two of One, and One of Two againe' (*Divine Weeks*, in *The Divine Weeks and Works of Guillaume de Saulste, Sieur Du Bartas*, trans. Josuah Sylvester, ed. Susan Snyder, 2 vols. (Oxford, 1979), i, 1. 6. 1051, 1054). In Bersuire, moreover, the fable of Hermaphroditus is an allegory of the meeting of Christ's two natures in the incarnation. But Dante uses the figure to describe the infernal metamorphoses of the thieves in *Inferno* 24. 46–78, and elsewhere it is mocked as the epitome of effeminization caused particularly by self-indulgence and unchastity (see Lauren Silberman, 'Mythographic Transformations of Ovid's Hermaphrodite', *Sixteenth Century Journal*, 19/4 (1988), 643–52). As I noted earlier, Peend gives us two interpretations of the figure at the end of his poem, divided along gender lines: where the female Salmacis sees their merging as the triumphal union of lovers, the male Hermaphroditus and narrator see it as emasculation and loss of self (*Hermaphroditus and Salmacis*, A8^v). The use of the figure at the end of the 1590 *Faerie Queene* to describe the reunion of Amoret and Scudamour is thus ambiguous.

Some lucky Narcissi, of course, learn their lesson and turn away from self-love in the nick of time. Spenser's Britomart moves beyond an initially Narcissistic love for Artegall, who first appears in Merlin's mirror only as the 'shade and semblant of a knight' (*FQ*, 3. 2. 38. 3), when she learns that she loves 'No shadow, but a bodie' (3. 2. 45. 7).[64] The love experience represented in the *Amoretti* suggests also a move from sterile to creative love through images of Narcissus which recreate Plato's parable of the cave as a story of psychosexual development. In Spenser, narcissism is an early but potentially dangerous stage that the lovers abandon as they rise to mutual love.

Obviously such uses of the myth are not disinterested. The speakers are trying to persuade their mistresses to be less hard-hearted and selfish—in other words, a little less chaste, please. The story is handy for purposes of seduction.[65] Moreover, the wooers are themselves frequently narcissists. The speaker of Spenser's *Amoretti* compares himself to '*Narcissus* vaine | whose eyes him staru'd: so plenty makes me poore' (35. 7–8).[66] While the chaste Lucrece might seem to be a Narcissus figure, it is Tarquin who 'poorly rich, so wanteth in his store | That, cloyed with much, he pineth still for more' (Shakespeare, *Lucrece*, 97–8).[67] Most blatantly, Beaumont's lustful Salmacis who warns Hermaphroditus to shun Narcissus' fate is herself set up as a Narcissus who not only admires her own image in the water but actually *is* the nymph of the fountain where Narcissus died (*Salmacis and Hermaphroditvs*, D1ᵛ, C3ᵛ). Given Narcissus' story, it is highly appropriate that the boy should be the model for both wooer and wooed. Lover and beloved mirror each other;[68] when Shakespeare's

---

[64] See Calvin R. Edwards, 'The Narcissus Myth in Spenser's Poetry', *Studies in Philology*, 74/1 (1977), 63–88.

[65] The story of Narcissus therefore provides further ammunition in *The Metamorphosis of Pygmalion's Image*, in which Marston uses the tale of a stony lady come to life to try to warm up his own cold mistress.

[66] Like almost everything in Spenser, this is echoed by Drayton whose beloved drowns in her own image ('Amour 9') even as the lover is Narcissus: 'In plenty, am I starv'd with penury' ('Amour 50', 11). Quotations from Drayton are from *The Works of Michael Drayton*, ed. William J. Hebel, 5 vols. (Oxford, 1961). As Raphael Lyne notes, 'Drayton's debt to Spenser is also seen in the Ovidian aspects of his work' (*Ovid's Changing Worlds*, 146): Drayton copies Spenser copying Ovid.

[67] See also the rhetoric around Venus' desire, especially *Venus and Adonis*, 19–21 and 540–6. I return to the common translation of *copia* as store later in this chapter.

[68] Maurice Scève sees how this offers the possibility for arguing for greater intimacy between the two when he tells his beloved: 'Tu es le Corps, Dame, & ie suis ton vmbre' ('You the body, & I your shadow, Lady', 376. 1; cited from *Emblems of*

Venus and Adonis kiss they unite the two parts of Narcissus' paradox: 'He with her plenty pressed, she faint with dearth, | Their lips together glued, fall to the earth' (*Venus and Adonis*, 545–6), becoming also a new Hermaphroditus: 'Incorp'rate then they seem; face grows to face' (540).

The narcissism of desire, however, also reflects a general urge for self-perpetuation and immortalization. Shakespeare urges his narcissistic young man to marry and 'Make thee another self' ('Sonnet 10', 13). In the opening sonnets in the sequence, the speaker argues that the story of Narcissus teaches the need for self-duplication through procreation rather than artistic creation: 'Look in thy glass and tell the face thou viewest | Now is the time that face should form another' ('Sonnet 3', 1–2). Through images of himself in his children the young man can live forever.[69] The alternative is oblivion: 'Die single, and thine image dies with thee' (14). However, 'Sonnet 18' begins to suggest that art is a better guarantee of self-preservation. As Ovid had asserted his immortality at the end of the *Metamorphoses*, the speaker tells the boy that 'Nor shall Death brag thou wand'rest in his shade, | When in eternal lines to time thou grow'st' (11–12). Shakespeare offers a different form of immortality to the young man, by turning him, as Ovid did Narcissus, into poetry.

For artists, creation is like desire in that it is inherently narcissistic; it is a means of preserving the artist and his subject through images. Gordon Braden suggests that Petrarch's *Canzoniere* might well be considered 'a new mode of narcissistic poetics'.[70] Petrarch is aware that in desiring Laura—who may or may not have been a real *corpus*—he also adores the fictions he himself creates and through which he hopes to achieve eternal fame. His potentially 'self-reflexive idolatry' makes him anxious.[71] At the same time, as Braden notes, this

---

Desire: Selections from the Délie *of Maurice Scève*, ed. and trans. Richard Sieburth (Philadelphia, 2003)).

[69] Ricardo J. Quinones discusses the Renaissance view of procreation as a means of conquering time; see especially his discussion of Rabelais in *The Renaissance Discovery of Time*, 187–203.

[70] Gordon Braden, *Petrarchan Love and the Continental Renaissance* (New Haven, 1999), 44. For narcissism in Petrarchan poetics see also Freccero, 'The Fig Tree and the Laurel', 34–40; Robert M. Durling (ed.), *Petrarch's Lyric Poems: The Rime sparse and Other Lyrics* (Cambridge, Mass., 1976), 31–3; and Enterline, *The Rhetoric of the Body*, 94–8.

[71] Enterline, *The Rhetoric of the Body*, 97.

helps explain why, despite their obvious limitations, Petrarchan models of desire were so compelling for later writers: Petrarchism is 'a mode that brings with it a dramatic aggrandizement of the authority of the poetic imagination'.[72] Other artists are able to explore more positive aspects of the narcissism of creativity. In *De Pictura*, Alberti famously proclaimed Narcissus to be 'the inventor of painting... What else can you call painting but a similar embracing with art of what is presented on the surface of the water in the fountain?'[73] While the analogy here is loose and undeveloped, an identification of painting with narcissism was encouraged by artists' experimentation with mirrors and their increasing interest in self-portraiture. According to Leonardo, 'ogni dipintore dipinge se': what the painter paints is himself.[74] Art is a form of self-knowledge; for Leonardo, it is in his images that the artist sees himself as an Other, and so knows himself objectively. Here again Poussin's use of Ovidian myths of creation is especially illuminating. As I noted in Chapter 2, the painter was drawn powerfully to Ovid's Flora as a figure for his own transformative powers. He was equally haunted by the story of Narcissus, which he painted four times. In one of the most famous and enigmatic of these, reproduced on the dust jacket of this book, the birth of Bacchus

---

[72] 'Beyond Frustration', 10–11. As Braden also suggests, Petrarchism leads to 'the theory for an exalted narcissism that is not entrapment but access to a higher reality' (ibid. 19) that in many ways anticipates the Romantics; see also Rosati, *Narcisso e Pigmalione*, 50.

[73] Leon Battista Alberti, *On Painting*, trans. John R. Spencer (rev. edn., New Haven, 1966), 64.

[74] On Leonardo's particular use of this idea see Martin Kemp, '"Ogni dipintore dipinge se": A Neoplatonic Echo in Leonardo's Art Theory', in Cecil H. Clough (ed.), *Cultural Aspects of the Italian Renaissance: Essays in Honour of Paul Oskar Kristeller* (Manchester, 1976), 311–23, who argues that Leonardo turns this Neoplatonic commonplace against Platonism. On the centrality of Narcissus and self-knowledge in Renaissance painting, see also Norman E. Land, 'Narcissus Pictor', *Source: Notes on the History of Art*, 16/2 (1997), 10–15; Avigdor W. G. Posèq, 'The Allegorical Content of Caravaggio's Narcissus', *Source: Notes on the History of Art*, 10 (1991), 21–31; Cristelle L. Baskins, 'Echoing Narcissus in Alberti's *Della Pittura*', *Oxford Art Journal*, 16/1 (1993), 25–33; Paula Carabell, 'Painting, Paradox, and the Dialectics of Narcissism in Alberti's *De Pictura* and in the Renaissance Theory of Art', *Medievalia et Humanistica*, 25 (1998), 53–73; and Stephen Bann, *The True Vine*, 105–56. Bann follows Kristeva in situating 'the genesis of the modern subject in the ambiguous myth of Narcissus' (ibid. 125). Carabell notes further the (Ovidian) paradox underlying this model, in which 'identity depends upon disjunctive experience' ('Painting, Paradox', 64).

is juxtaposed with the death of Narcissus, bringing together two versions of the origins of art, and linking creativity and destruction.[75]

Of course, the connection between Narcissus and the artist could be used simply to reinforce the commonplace that all artists are egotists, blinded, like poor Ovid, by self-love. For Freud, Leonardo is the prototype for the narcissistic artist. Since at least Burckhardt, Renaissance art and culture have been read as originating in a surge of egotism which produced peculiarly narcissistic personalities. In Cesare Ripa's *Iconologia* (1593), the artist's relation to his works is the essence of 'Amor di se stesso', which Ripa defines as: 'vagghegiarsi tutto nell'opere proprie con sodisfattione, & con applauso' ('to marvel at oneself in one's own work with satisfaction and applause').[76] Alciatus further makes Narcissus a type for the arrogant new scholar who believes himself to be self-sufficient and therefore rudely scorns tradition:

> Quod nimium tua forma tibi, Narcisse placebat,
> In florem, & noti est versa stuporis olus.
> Ingenii est marcor, cladesque, φιλαυτια, doctos
> Quae pessum plures datque, deditque viros:
> Qui veterum abiecta methodo, noua dogmata quaerunt,
> Nilque suas praeter tradere phantasias.

('Because your beauty was excessively pleasing to you, Narcissus, it was changed into a flower and into the well-known plant which causes insensibility. Self-love means the decay and destruction of character

---

[75] For Poussin's interest in Narcissus, see Dora Panofsky, 'Narcissus and Echo'; and especially Jonathan Unglaub, *Poussin and the Poetics of Painting: Pictorial Narrative and the Legacy of Tasso* (Cambridge, 2006), 72–81. Hazlitt commented that 'With a laborious and mighty grasp, he [Poussin] put nature into the mould of the ideal and the antique; and was among painters (more than anyone else) what Milton was among poets' (*Table Talk*, 1821; cited from Wittreich, *The Romantics on Milton*, 395). Mario Praz also noted some interesting stylistic parallels between poet and painter ('Milton and Poussin', in J. Dover Wilson (ed.), *Seventeenth-Century Studies Presented to Sir Thomas Grierson* (Oxford, 1938), 192–210). Tantalizingly, Poussin was in Rome at the time of Milton's visit. While I do not want to claim any direct connection, Poussin's complex and sustained interpretation of Ovidian myth is similar to Milton's, and suggests how Ovid offered artists fables that were relevant for exploring art's transformative powers. Poussin is a highly allusive painter, who draws attention to the process of creation. By depicting figures of ambiguous consistency, whose often chalky or marble-like flesh makes them look like cartoons or statues, he is constantly blurring the boundaries between art and life, suggesting how nature aspires to become the art objects that, in his paintings, they are.

[76] *Iconologia* (1611; repr. New York, 1976), 21; Vinge, *The Narcissus Theme*, 143.

[ingenium]; it brings and has brought to ruin many learned men, who, having cast off the procedure of the ancients, seek new doctrines and wish to hand down nothing but their own fantasies')[77]

De te fabula lector: a sobering cautionary tale for critics! Like Satan, Alciatus' egotistical scholar wants to be 'self-begot, self-rais'd' (*PL*, 5. 860), and denies his debt to previous sources. Narcissus here seems an image of what Cristelle Baskins describes as 'hermaphroditic authorial self-sufficiency'.[78] Natale Comes also reads the story as an example of human failure to acknowledge that all human talent is given by the ultimate source, God: Narcissus 'neque cognoscat se largiente Deo haec omnia habere: ille ob suam imprudentiam haec sibi facit pernitiosa' ('does not realize that he possesses all this through the generosity of God; he makes all this dangerous to himself by his folly').[79] Narcissus is thus the opposite of Psyche, who learns her dependence on divine grace. His story overlaps with other tales of pride, such as that of Niobe, and especially that of Arachne, to which I'll return at the end of the next chapter.[80]

Dante, however, sees a different possibility in the artist's egotism. R. A. Shoaf has shown how Dante uses the figure of Narcissus in the *Commedia* as part of a 'systematic meditation on narcissism and, in particular, on narcissism in art'.[81] While Dante himself appears as a potential Narcissus in *Inferno* 30, in *Purgatorio* and *Paradiso* 30 especially, the poet is transformed into a 'corrected Narcissus'.[82] He

---

[77] Andreas Alciatus, *The Latin Emblems, Indexes and Lists*, ed. Peter M. Daly (Toronto, 1985), Emblem 69.

[78] 'Echoing Narcissus', 30. For Baskins this is also specifically a 'parthenogenic, exclusively masculine creativity' (ibid. 27)—like that of Milton's Satan.

[79] *Mythologiae* (1567; repr. New York, 1976), Hhhh2^v; translation from Vinge, *The Narcissus Theme*, 146.

[80] For the link between Narcissus and Niobe see above, p. 182. As Unglaub demonstrates, Poussin's drawing of the figure of Narcissus is based partly on an engraving of one of the dead Niobids (*Poussin and the Poetics*, 76–7).

[81] R. A. Shoaf, *Dante, Chaucer, and the Currency of the Word: Money, Images, and Reference in Late Medieval Poetry* (Norman, Okla., 1983), 22. See also Roger Dragonetti, 'Dante et Narcisse ou les faux-monnayeurs de l'image', *Revue des études italiennes*, 11 (1965), 85–146; Kevin Brownlee, 'Dante and Narcissus (*Purg*. XXX, 76–99)', *Dante Studies*, 96 (1978), 201–6.

[82] Brownlee, 'Dante and Narcissus', 201; see also Shoaf, *The Currency of the Word*, 48. Laurie Churchill has suggested a similar redemption of narcissism in one of Dante's most important sources, Augustine: see '"Inopem me copia fecit": Signs of Narcissus in Augustine's *Confessions*', *Classical and Modern Literature*, 10 (1990), 373–9.

therefore is remade in the image of God who, as Robert McMahon notes, is represented as 'the Ultimate and Original Narcissist. God gazes eternally upon His Image, loving Himself, yet His self-love implies perfect self-knowledge.' As McMahon suggests also, 'the self-reflexivity of the Trinity represents Dante's transformation of Narcissus' sterile self-gazing';[83] through the poet's journey, the narcissistic base of creativity is acknowledged, purged of pride, and metamorphosed into the generative principle of the universe that moves the sun and other stars, and the poet himself. Dante's use, however, is not unique; it is part of a tradition in religious poetry in which God's relation to his images—Christ, Mary, and man—is seen as a kind of cosmic self-love.[84] Especially common in religious poetry of the seventeenth century, this reading, as we will see shortly, is central to *Paradise Lost*, in which God is the maker of images of himself.

The story of Narcissus thus provided a *copia* of images through which later artists were able to think about their own creativity, and especially their relation to the past which they were copying and transforming. It is the *locus classicus* of artistic self-reflection.[85] Many of the central ingredients of the tale are combined, albeit into

---

[83] 'Satan as Infernal Narcissus: Interpretive Translation in the *Commedia*', in Sowell (ed.), *Dante and Ovid*, 82.

[84] As Vinge shows, both Christ and Mary can be imagined as God's reflection; see for example, Pierre de Marbeuf's *Maria* (1620): 'En ce cristal tu te mires, | Grand Dieu Narcisse parfait, | Et toy-mesme en toy t'admires, | Amoureux de ton objet' ('In your mirror you admire yourself, great God, perfect Narcissus, and you admire yourself in yourself, in love with your object'; qtd. in *The Narcissus Theme*, 227). Vinge notes that in the Jesuit Jacobus Masenius' *Speculum Imaginum Veritatis Occultae* (1650), Narcissus is both those who blindly value themselves too highly and also 'quaedam imago Dei amore hominum capti atque incarnati' ('a kind of image of God who was seized with love for men and became flesh', qtd. ibid. 189). As she points out also, while the mirror can suggest vanity, in the mystical tradition it is connected to purity and wisdom and is often a symbol for the relation between God and creation (ibid. 190). In Sor Juana Inés de la Cruz's *El divino Narciso*, written in Mexico in the mid-1680s, 'The love between Narcissus and his reflection illustrates God's love for man whom he has created in his image' (ibid. 247). Vinge argues that in this period 'the reflection symbolism of mysticism makes Narcissus an image of God' (ibid. 249). While this tradition is predominantly Catholic, specifically Jesuit, in 'A Discourse of the Freedom of the Will' (published in London in 1675), the Presbyterian Peter Sterry compares God's self-knowledge to that of Narcissus; see Lee A. Jacobus, 'Self-Knowledge in *Paradise Lost*: Conscience and Contemplation', *Milton Studies*, 3 (1971), 113–14.

[85] See also Tasso's description of his hero Tancredi's first glimpse of his beloved Clorinda as an image, 'nel solitario fonte' ('in a lonely fountain', *Gerusalemme liberata*, ed. Lanfranco Caretti (Turin, 1971), 3. 22. 8), which is based on Ovid and

a rather ghastly poetic stew, in T.H.'s *The fable of Ouid treting of Narcissus*. Despite its artistic limitations, the poem sets the tone for what is to come in England. T.H.'s Narcissus is a man who, graced with great talents, abuses them by denying that they come from God. He trusts too much in his own independent powers, becoming proud and disdainful. The obsessive repetition of the word 'dysdayne', reminiscent of the cold-hearted narcissistic mistress, preserves Narcissus' association with the rejection of love.[86] What Narcissus is so proud of, however, is less his physical beauty than the fact that he has 'A passing witte aboue the ingnoraunte' (B3^v). While we are told that this in general is 'A vertue greate to them that vse it well' (C3^r), Narcissus' denial of the source of his gift leads to its degeneration into 'wandring witte' (C3^r). As T.H. translates Ovid, elements of Ovid's own fate seem to haunt the poet's mind as a hideous moral cautionary tale. Narcissus is an example of good genius gone bad: 'With good, moche good, his good therby to saue | Yet [by] his good, as sure is euel to have, | He gaynis the losse that other neuer fele' (C4^r).[87] A similar paradoxical moral is drawn by Thomas Edwards's later (but equally awful) poem *Narcissus*. The boy himself realizes that he has 'made this well my ill, this bowre my bane, | This daily good become my hourly wane' (349–50).[88] In the midst of Edwards's otherwise largely unintelligible verbiage, the figure of Narcissus generates a bit of

---

provides a model for Spenser. As Emily Wilson has recently shown, Tasso's scene stages its own use of earlier texts as a 'moment of change and recognition' ('*Quantum Mutatus ab Illo*: Moments of Change and Recognition in Tasso and Milton', in M. J. Clarke, B. G. F. Currie, and R. O. A. M. Lyne (eds.), *Epic Interactions: Perspectives on Homer, Virgil, and the Epic Tradition Presented to Jasper Griffin by Former Pupils* (New York, 2006), 273–99).

[86] Shakespeare's Adonis is also associated with disdain; see *Venus and Adonis*, 33, 241, 501. The resonances of the word are still heard in Satan's soliloquy in *Paradise Lost* 4, when he claims that he cannot repent, 'O then at last relent: is there no place | Left for Repentance, none for Pardon left? | None left but by submission; and that word | *Disdain* forbids me' (4. 79–82). While in Book 9 Satan will appear as a familiar type of Ovidian seducer, in Book 4 he is the cold lady who will not submit to another; in either case, he is trapped in conventional and antagonistic models for erotic relations.

[87] On this passage, see also Maslen, 'Myths Exploited', 21.

[88] Maslen notes T.H.'s surprisingly witty punning on the meanings of 'well' in the line: 'in this well to [sic] well he vewse' himself ('Myths Exploited', 21). The same idea, though minus the pun, appears in the *Roman de la Rose*, where Genius claims that in the fountain of Narcissus 'li sain devienant malade' ('the healthy become sick', 20392). See Guillaume de Lorris and Jean de Meun, *Le Roman de la Rose*, ed. Ernest Langlois, 5 vols. (Paris, 1914).

recognizable if feeble Ovidian punning on 'well' and 'ill', antithetical words that have two letters in common. The juxtaposition of linguistic difference and sameness reworks the confusion at the centre of the story, while compressing further the radical metamorphosis of goodness into its opposite. For T.H. and Edwards, the story shows how easily good may become evil.

Though blissfully unaware that he is at the forefront of a new vogue of literature, T.H. is nervously conscious that in showing off his own talents he could himself become an example of the very errors he wants to denounce.[89] The author is therefore careful to guard himself against charges of being too pleased with his own wit by saying that he hasn't any. Most readers think he is right. Still, his tale has its own crude cleverness, and shows a remarkable awareness of the central problems that artists of the time find in the story.[90] It brings together the themes of desire and art. The narrator is eager to differentiate himself from Narcissus. While the boy rejects not only love but also friendship and good counsel (T.H.'s reading of Echo), the narrator emphasizes his debt to Ovid and to other interpreters of Ovid.[91] In this he is typical of Elizabethans who did not try to hide their use of Ovid. While Ovid's Narcissus wants to know only himself, new versions of Narcissus enable a union of self and other, copy and original.

For T.H., however, the gap between past and present is a sign of his own inferiority. He humbles himself to his sources and to those who came before, assuming that temporal priority means authority.[92] But with its questioning of the Platonic reversal of the distinction between illusion and reality, the story of Narcissus equally authorizes a witty reversal of the relation between copy and original. While drawing on Ovid's myths in his sonnets, Shakespeare preposterously claims that

---

[89] See also Clapham's *Narcissus*, where the author sees the boy as a dangerous reflection of his own situation.

[90] Liz Oakley-Brown generously attributes the poem's unreadability to the author's struggle with translation: 'The Ovidian episode articulates the frustration of the subject caught in a translative dilemma, confounded by desire' ('Translating the Subject', 60).

[91] His knowledge of the interpretative tradition is actually fairly wide: not surprisingly, he refers to Bersuire's *Metamorphosis Ovidiana Moraliter* (thought in England to be the work of Thomas Walleys), but he has also some familiarity with Boccaccio and Poliziano.

[92] As Quintilian had of course said it did: 'Adde quod, quidquid alteri simile est, necesse est minus sit eo, quod imitatur' ('Again, whatever is like another object, must necessarily be inferior to the object of its imitation', *Institutio Oratoria*, iv, 10. 2. 11).

his beloved is the 'substance' that the myths merely shadow: 'Describe Adonis, and the counterfeit | Is poorly imitated after you' ('Sonnet 53', 5–6).[93] Similarly, while copying Ovid, Milton turns the classical myth into a pagan *umbra* of the true and original version he is telling. It had been generally assumed that many of Ovid's stories were derived from corrupted versions of the Old Testament; so Golding notes that 'What man is he but would suppose the author of this booke | The first foundation of his woorke from Moyses writing tooke?' ('To the Ryght Honorable and Singular Good Lord, Robert Erle of Leycester', 342–3). In *Paradise Regain'd*, therefore, the Son will reject the culture of the ancients, on the grounds that '*Greece* from us these Arts deriv'd; | Ill imitated' (*PR*, 4. 338–9). For Milton, Ovid copies the original story which Milton tells in *Paradise Lost*. The fiction of his own priority enables Milton to imagine a lost version of Narcissus before that of Ovid, one in which the story might have had a very different ending.

MILTON'S ORIGINAL COPY

Milton's dynamic Eden is a mythic world evolving into a real one. Its groves are '*Hesperian* Fables true, | If true, here only, and of delicious taste' (*PL*, 4. 250–1). Eden is the place of the imagination realizing itself, as Keats realized when he wrote, 'The Imagination may be compared to Adam's dream—he awoke and found it truth.'[94] Milton's use of the story of Narcissus is central to his presentation of the development of the garden and its inhabitants. While the creation of Eve is explicitly modelled on Ovid's figure, versions of

---

[93] See also Bate, *Shakespeare and Ovid*, 89. I use 'preposterous' in the sense of sequential reversal explored by Patricia Parker in *Literary Fat Ladies*, 67–96, and *Shakespeare from the Margins: Language, Culture, Context* (Chicago, 1996), 20–55. As Parker shows, the meanings of the word connect it further to concepts of delay and doubling. Her elegant examination of Shakespeare's wordplay captures his Ovidian wit at work.

[94] 'To Benjamin Bailey', in *The Letters of John Keats*, ed. Maurice Buxton Forman (rev. 4th edn., London, 1952), 67. See *Paradise Lost* 8. 310–11 where Adam describes how he comes into the garden and finds 'Before mine Eyes all real, as the dream | Had lively shadowd'. Eve's experience in Book 5 shows, however, that even in Eden, not all dreams should come true; after her dream of flying she exclaims: 'O how glad I wak'd | To find this but a dream!' (5. 92–3).

the boy are omnipresent in *Paradise Lost*. Narcissism is a cosmic force of generation emanating from God that unifies the universe of the poem. Like Dante, Milton imagines God as the arch-narcissist, who makes and admires images of himself. Creation begins with the begetting of a reflection of the Father, 'The radiant image of his Glory' (3. 63), the Son, in whom 'all his Father shon | Substantially express'd' (3. 139–40). As creator of the other angels and the world, the Son mirrors and extends his Father's creativity, making man also, as Raphael tells Adam: 'in his own Image hee | Created thee, in the Image of God | Express' (7. 526–8).

All creativity and desire is therefore essentially narcissistic, as it begins in God's self-love and the copying and multiplying of his own image. Yet it is narcissistic with a difference, as God's self-images are not exact duplications of himself, but creative copies who are individuals in their own right. Even as he expresses God 'Substantially' (3. 140), the Son is not identical with his Father.[95] The difference is crucial both theologically and poetically: if they were of the same essence so that the Son knew what his Father did, the Son's offer of self-sacrifice would be meaningless, and the dialogue between Father and Son in Book 3 might sound rather like Narcissus' debate with himself. Moreover, the difference between original and copy enables God's creatures to become themselves creators, who make independent choices and exercise free will. The fact that God makes the world in his own image means that he creates other creators: Adam and Eve are natural artists and, as we see at the opening of Book 5, even nature is inspired to join in their morning hymn of praise to the celestial originator. God beams his narcissistic nature into his creations, who fittingly beam it back at him in a cosmic mutual admiration society. The creativity of divine narcissism comes full circle when it is reflected back to God through praise first by Adam and Eve, and finally by the poet himself whose reflection on God's creative act generates his own poetic creation.

The poem thus brazenly challenges our assumptions that narcissism is evil by tracing it to a divine source. But Satan and the devils anticipate our suspicions, interpreting the circle of universal admiration as really

---

[95] This important and unorthodox distinction between the persons of the Trinity is articulated further in the discussion 'De Filio Dei' (Of the Son of God) in Ch. 5 of *De Doctrina Christiana*, in which Milton argues that while the Son is made from the substance of the Father, they do not have the same essence (*Works*, xiv. 186).

a golden chain of sycophancy. From hell, Mammon looks back to heaven as a place where angels are forced to:

> Stand in his presence humble, and receive
> Strict Laws impos'd, to celebrate his Throne
> With warbl'd Hymns, and to his Godhead sing
> Forc't Halleluiah's; while he Lordly sits
> Our envied Sovran, and his Altar breathes
> Ambrosial Odours and Ambrosial Flowers,
> Our servile offerings. This must be our task
> In Heav'n this our delight. (2. 240–7)

For Satan, God finally goes too far when he duplicates himself once more in order to increase his power; the angels now have two figures to whom they must offer 'prostration vile, | Too much to one, but double how endur'd, | To one and to his image now proclaim'd?' (5. 782–4). In heaven, moreover, the angels are condemned to admire the creations of another; hell offers them the possibility of being creative in their own right. Mammon thus argues that, free from God's influence, they 'can create' (2. 260) and make:

> Our own good from our selves, and for our own
> Live to our selves, though in the vast recess,
> Free, and to none accountable, preferring
> Hard liberty before the easie yoke
> Of servile Pomp. (2. 253–7)

Satan presents his rebellion against God as the heroic rejection of a corrupt system of narcissistic nepotism and the assertion of independence and originality.

Satan's own creativity is expressed first in the making of Sin, narrated in Book 2. As long noted, the scene draws on Ovid's story of Narcissus. In some ways, Satan seems an ingenious and perceptive adapter of Ovid's story, which he ominously turns into an *aition* of the origins not of poetry, but of Sin. The emergence of Sin from Satan's head as he contemplates rebellion combines the myth of the birth of Athena/Minerva, wisdom, with that of Narcissus, bringing to the surface the element of self-knowledge in Ovid's original that most later adaptations fumble, reverse, or simply avoid. The revision makes clear the link between Narcissus and the tales of incest in the *Metamorphoses*. Satan is so delighted with his creation that, as Sin reminds him, 'Thy self in me thy perfect image viewing' (*PL*, 2.

764), he is moved to rape her. The language here echoes the traditional descriptions of the Son as the 'radiant image' of the Father (3. 63). Imposing the relation of Father and Son onto Ovid's story, Satan tries to write God out of the picture so that he can be the original Narcissus and an alternative source of creativity. Like God, he plans to make man in his own image, as Satan admits, 'Nor hope to be my self less miserable | By what I seek, but others to make such | As I' (9. 126–8). Rather than rejecting narcissism, therefore, Satan creates an alternative form that reflects himself and not God. His rebellion is itself a form of replication, in which he becomes, in Northrop Frye's terms, 'a demonic parody'[96] of his creator. Where God creates the creating Son in his own image, Satan imagines Sin and, through her, Death. It seems appropriate that Satan's progeny are allegorical characters whose natures are pinned down by their names. Sin is Sin, Death is Death: there's not much room for character development or growth there! In building the bridge between hell and earth Satan's creatures copy the Son's creation of the world. Where God's creative energy generates new and dynamic creativity, Satan's agents inhibit it, spreading infernal stasis, as the potential of chaos is 'Bound with *Gorgonian* rigor not to move' (*PL*, 10. 297).[97] As Colin Burrow points out, moreover, Sin herself is 'the most wearisomely derivative figure in *Paradise Lost*',[98] a version of numerous hybrid figures that range from Ovid's Scylla to Spenser's Error. For a poet, sin is copying that has become drained of artistic energy and originality.

I'll return to Sin's complex originals in the next chapter. The final metamorphosis of Satan in Book 10 also draws attention to the reworking of different sources. It is based on the transformation of Cadmus in *Metamorphoses* 4. 563–603, which brings to a close the cycle of stories connected to Narcissus and the city of Thebes, the doomed home of Oedipus. The subtext is suggestive: Cadmus

---

[96] See *The Great Code: The Bible and Literature* (New York, 1982). See also Schwartz, *Remembering and Repeating*, 99–103, where she links diabolical narcissism to repetition and doubling.

[97] On this scene, see also Lieb, *The Dialectics of Creation*, 173–8, and his discussion of hell as a parody of divine creativity (ibid. 81–106).

[98] *Epic Romance*, 269. For a different reading of Sin as 'consciously derivative' see John M. Steadman, 'Tradition and Innovation in Milton's "Sin": The Problem of Literary Indebtedness', *Philological Quarterly*, 39 (1960), 101. Steadman argues that Sin shows how Milton uses 'an entire tradition, as well as the specific precedents of Ovid, Fletcher, and others, to make it convincing' (ibid. 103), but also to show his own innovations.

founded the cursed city by killing a giant snake; at the end of his life, like so many classical heroes, he becomes (or perhaps was all along?) the monster that he slew. The Ovidian episode is mediated through another important source: Dante's famous description of the transformations of the thieves into serpents in *Inferno* 24. 97–118. Back in hell, triumphing in his success on earth, Satan suddenly finds himself undergoing an unexpected change:

> His Visage drawn he felt to sharp and spare,
> His Armes clung to his Ribs, his Leggs entwining
> Each other, till supplanted down he fell
> A monstrous Serpent on his Belly prone,
> Reluctant, but in vaine, a greater power
> Now rul'd him, punisht in the shape he sin'd,
> According to his doom: he would have spoke,
> But hiss for hiss returned with forked tongue
> To forked tongue. (10. 511–19)

The figure who claims the most extreme form of originality—to be 'self-begot, self-rais'd | By our own quick'ning power' (*PL*, 5. 860–1)—is in the end just a copy of a copy of Ovid, whose fate is in turn replicated by his followers who are changed into an undifferentiated swarm of serpents.[99] As in Dante, the prolonged description of the actual moment of metamorphosis is highly Ovidian. Milton lingers on the horror with which Satan becomes aware of his unexpected and unwilled change, and his terror as he discovers his loss of voice. By appropriating the forms of others he has lost his identity completely. The drawn-out scene builds on Ovid's representation of what Joseph Solodow describes as 'in-between states', moments of extreme 'indeterminacy and shapelessness'. As Solodow claims, 'these intermediate phases are intense, vivid examples of the flux from which metamorphosis removes the character. They are the extremes of indeterminacy and shapelessness, the foil to fixity. By dwelling on movements when a figure is neither one thing nor another, when it

---

[99] The use of Dante here is especially appropriate as, despite their obvious differences, Dante and Milton both imagine evil as the failure to be open to change. As Irene Samuel says, 'fixity, the ultimate opposite to the spontaneity of life, is an exact symbol for Dante's view, and Milton's, of the end of evil. As the compulsively repeated choice becomes mechanical, purposeless, and ceaseless, it becomes the whole character, and the whole character thus becomes one fixed posture' (*Dante and Milton: The* Commedia *and* Paradise Lost (Ithaca, NY, 1966), 126). Both writers turn also to Ovidian forms for thinking about the resistance to change.

temporarily lacks identity, Ovid sharpens our sense of the permanence which metamorphosis will bring.'[100] In Milton's version, the achievement of such permanence is especially sinister, as it means the closing off of the possibility for freedom afforded by change. The metamorphosis of Satan suggests the fixing of an identity that, up until that point, was itself still evolving.[101] By foregrounding the moment of transition, moreover, Milton highlights the irony of Satan's rejection of change, and makes us see the loss of the very individuality he asserted in rebellion.

With the representation of the origins of Sin in Book 2 and the appearance of the Father's image, the Son, in Book 3, the poem begins poised between two opposing versions of Narcissus and of creativity. The presentation of the two adheres to a general pattern in the poem in which we see evil before good, the imitation before the original. It reminds readers that we know good through evil. In Dante, a similar sequencing from hell to paradise created a sense of progression from error to truth. In Milton, however, the reader can never leave Plato's cave, so that the relation is more complicated and less simply linear. Heaven and hell are clearly opposites, between which Adam and Eve must eventually choose as they evolve. The difference between these two poles creates a stable universe, structured around the opposition between good and evil. It is the basis for intelligible choices. But *Paradise Lost* is set in a world of growth and metamorphosis, in which these poles are themselves in motion. The plot explains the means by which one form turns into its opposite: how a world of generative metamorphosis became one which inhibits change. While the narrative sequence proceeds from hell to heaven, the poem works in reverse to explain how heaven turned into hell: how and when copying God went dreadfully wrong. Part of the explanation is offered through the use of the figure of Narcissus in Book 2 to show how Satan perverted divine creativity. But at the centre of the poem, Milton also has the much more difficult job of trying to convince us that copying God might have gone wondrously *right*: that in Adam and Eve a version of Narcissus different from that of Satan and yet also not identical to that of God might have

---

[100] *The World of Ovid's* Metamorphoses, 188.
[101] See also Creaser, '"Fear of change"', 163–5, who argues that the poem shows Satan's hardening; Satan still has the ability to change, but repeatedly rejects it out of fear of his own mutability.

developed. He has to make us imagine the possibility of a tale that no longer can be written, one which contradicts what we, in hindsight, know happened. It's the greatest story never told.

The outline for this spectral plot is sketched through the figures of Adam and Eve, who are suspended between the opposed poles of heavenly narcissism and its infernal copy. Although Ovid's Narcissus appears most famously, or infamously, as the explicit subtext of Eve's creation in Book 4, the story also underlies Adam's creation in Book 8.[102] In both instances, the original subtext is revised significantly with redemptive effects. Eve is a Narcissus who turns away from the watery reflection, while Adam realizes Narcissus' dream that: 'o utinam a nostro secedere corpore possem! | votum in amante novum, vellem, quod amamus, abesset' ('Oh, that I might be parted from my own body! and, strange prayer for a lover, I would that what I love were absent from me', Ovid, *Met.*, 3. 467–8). Where Plato's Aristophanes sees division as the fall from an original unity, Milton makes division central to the creative act. As I have suggested, the relation between Adam and Eve mirrors the creative process presented in Book 7, in which, following the pattern of both Genesis 1 and Metamorphoses 1, the Son separates the elements of chaos into order.[103] However, division is only the first step in a process of reunion in which the original relation is itself recreated in a new form of unity.[104] Milton's Adam and Eve begin as not only one flesh, but also one subtext, which divided becomes two new and distinct stories of creation. Like other lovers—Petrarch and Laura, Venus and

---

[102] Noting Adam's narcissism, Julia Walker argues that Adam is the real Narcissus figure, and that the passage in Book 4 is a 'false Narcissus allusion' that the reader must correct ('The Poetics of Antitext and the Politics of Milton's Allusions', *Studies in English Literature, 1500–1900*, 37/1 (1997), 164). I think it is misguided to attempt to decide the 'real' Narcissus of the text; all the figures are, in one way or another, Narcissi.

[103] A number of critics have foregrounded the role of division and divorce in Milton's idea of creativity; see R. A. Shoaf, *Milton, Poet of Duality: A Study of Semiosis in the Poetry and the Prose* (New Haven, 1985); and Sanford Budick, *The Dividing Muse: Images of Sacred Disjunction in Milton's Poetry* (New Haven, 1985). Ovid, whose account of creation also begins with the separation of elements, was associated with division in some of the commentaries, which etymologized his name as coming from 'Ovum dividens' (dividing an egg), a phrase which showed his ability to discriminate the parts of the cosmos; see Ghisalberti, 'Mediaeval Biographies of Ovid', 27–8.

[104] John Rumrich thus stresses the importance of union in Milton; see *Milton Unbound*, 122–7.

Adonis, the speaker of the *Amoretti* and his beloved—Adam and Eve are both Narcissi, who reflect each other. But this enables Milton to imagine a new kind of erotic and literary relation which consists of 'most resembling unlikeness, most unlike resemblance' (*Tetrachordon*, in *Works* iv. 86).

The physical division of the two characters is mirrored in the distance between their two accounts of their beginnings, which are split between Books 4 and 8. In both, Ovid's story becomes a means of elaborating on and expanding the story told in Genesis 1–2, which will be told also by Raphael in Book 7. Like Ovid, Milton gives us repeated versions of origins.[105] Moreover, by presenting Eve's story before that of Adam, he reverses the original sequence of creation in Genesis 2. From the beginning, the relation between original and copy is complicated: while Eve is made in Adam's image, her story, told before his, becomes the model with which readers compare his later version.

For obvious reasons, the story told in Book 4 is usually read as being all about Eve: broadly, it either exposes her inherent and fatal narcissism, or shows her development from a stage of innocent self-love into a relationship with Adam (a process that itself can be read either positively, as a turn from destructive self-absorption, or negatively, as indoctrination into patriarchal oppression).[106] Like Britomart and the speaker of the *Amoretti*, Eve moves from shadows to substances, from error and illusion to truth and reality. However, while the story clearly reveals insights into Eve's character, the fact that it is told to Adam suggests that it may be relevant for him as well.[107] For both characters, the story of Narcissus is key to their developing self-knowledge.

---

[105] Genesis itself of course offers different versions: in Genesis 1, man and woman are created at the same time; in 2, they are created in sequence. By assigning the different versions to different characters, Milton inventively transforms the narrative discrepancy that had plagued biblical exegetes into the means of exploring different perspectives.

[106] Richard J. DuRocher summarizes the main lines of debate well in 'Guiding the Glance: Spenser, Milton, and "Venus's Looking Glas"', *Journal of English and Germanic Philology*, 92/3 (1993), 325–41. See also his *Milton and Ovid*, 85–93; Kenneth Jacob Knoespel, 'The Limits of Allegory: Textual Expansion of Narcissus in *Paradise Lost*', *Milton Studies*, 22 (1986), 79–99; Diane Kelsey McColley, *Milton's Eve* (Urbana, Ill., 1983), 74; and Green, *Milton's Ovidian Eve*, 36–8.

[107] McColley suggests that the memory of Eve's creation, with its arrested fall, might have stopped Adam from falling (*Milton's Eve*, 85).

The idea of self-knowledge fascinated Milton throughout his life;[108] it is clearly highly significant for an epic in which different kinds of and means to knowledge play such a crucial role. Far from being the essentially paradoxical and tragic enterprise that it is in Ovid, self-knowledge is an important prerequisite for free will; both Adam and Eve are created to 'Govern the rest, self-knowing' (7. 510). When Adam requests a help meet, God praises him for 'knowing not of Beasts alone... but of thy self' (8. 438–9). In contrast to Narcissus' solipsistic model, however, self-knowledge in paradise is a dynamic process that emerges through dialogue and relation, as Adam and Eve learn from each other.

Plato's dialogues suggest that self-knowledge emerges through such exchanges. Aristotle claims further that self-knowledge involves others, or, more specifically, an intimate who serves as a kind of moral mirror:

> Since then it is both a most difficult thing, as some of the sages have said, to attain a knowledge of oneself, and also a most pleasant (for to know oneself is pleasant)—now we are not able to see what we are from ourselves... as then when we wish to see our own face, we do so by looking into the mirror, in the same way when we wish to know ourselves we can obtain that knowledge by looking at our friend. For the friend is, as we assert, a second self. If, then, it is pleasant to know oneself, and it is not possible to know this without having some one else for a friend, the self-sufficing man will require friendship in order to know himself.[109]

It is telling that underneath Milton's ideal of a 'help meet' who is '*another self, a second self, a very self it self*' (*Tetrachordon*, in *Works*, iv. 90) lies the traditional description of the friend, made most famous in the Renaissance by Montaigne.[110] Yet Milton also insists that

---

[108] See especially Jacobus, 'Self-Knowledge in *Paradise Lost*'; Albert W. Fields, 'Milton and Self-Knowledge', *PMLA* 83/2 (1968), 392–9; and Fields, 'The Creative Self and the Self Created in *Paradise Lost*', in Charles W. Durham and Kristin A. Pruitt (eds.), *Spokesperson Milton: Voices in Contemporary Criticism* (Selinsgrove, Pa., 1994), 153–64.

[109] *Magna Moralia*, 2. 15, in *The Complete Works of Aristotle: The Revised Oxford Translation*, ed. Jonathan Barnes, 2 vols. (Princeton, 1984), ii. 1920; see also *Eudemian Ethics*, 7. 12. For the influence of this ideal in the Renaissance, see Fields, 'Milton and Self-Knowledge', 393.

[110] Thomas H. Luxon, *Single Imperfection: Milton, Marriage, and Friendship* (Pittsburgh, 2005), has discussed in depth the significance of Milton's transformation of the classical model of friendship into the ideal of the bourgeois marriage. Heather

marriage is greater than friendship, traditionally a same-sex relation, as marriage foregrounds difference as well as likeness, in its 'most resembling unlikenes, and most unlike resemblance' (*Tetrachordon*, in *Works* iv. 86).[111] In *Paradise Lost*, moreover, the marriage between a couple who are both one and two creates a new form of the story of Narcissus and of his close relation, Hermaphroditus, a version that is different not only from Ovid's original, but from Milton's original Narcissus, God. The narcissistic relation between husband and wife is similar to that between copy and source, in which 'new self-realization can only be achieved by means of a detour through the other'.[112] The mutual reflection between and differentiation of Adam and Eve thus offers Milton a model for his own relation to his twin sources: Ovid and God. De Quincey's description of Milton and Ovid as 'the wedding of male and female counterparts' may be not so whimsical after all.[113]

In Book 4 of *Paradise Lost*, we are able to watch the original forging of the new Narcissus out of Ovid's tale. The opening already suggests the Ovidian subtext; it begins with the narrator wishing he could speak to his own characters (4. 1–5), as Ovid had tried also to reach out to his fictitious boy. As in Ovid, the intrusion shows the author's simultaneous identification with and detachment from his characters, and foregrounds the power of images to make the author himself forget the boundary between illusion and reality, especially as he describes a paradise in which myths come true. The sustained presence of the subtext keeps the relation between Milton's copy and Ovid's original in the reader's mind, and draws attention to the play between likeness and difference that occurs at different levels throughout the scene.

James also notes how Narcissus was used as an image of friendship; according to Sir John Hayward: 'This did the poets also signifie, when they fained Narcissus to be in loue with his image. For what is more like vnto vs then our own image? and whosoeuer loueth another man, what else doth he loue but his own image in him?' (cited from James, 'Ovid in Renaissance English Literature', in Peter E. Knox (ed.), *A Companion to Ovid* (Malden, Mass.: Blackwell, 2009), 440).

[111] On the significance of this passage for the scene in Book 4, see also Heather James, 'Milton's Eve, the Romance Genre, and Ovid', *Comparative Literature*, 45/2 (1993), 121–45.

[112] Carron, 'Imitation and Intertextuality in the Renaissance', 572.

[113] 'Orthographic Mutineers', 449.

The scene begins by copying Ovid closely. According to Eve, her first experience is of what appears to be narcissistic self-knowledge and infatuation with her own image. The Platonic subtext in Ovid's tale is brought to the surface in the image of the cave (4. 454). Drawn to the water, Eve takes up Narcissus' position. Illusion causes her to confuse heaven and earth, as she looks in the water and sees what she takes as 'another Skie' (4. 459). She is attracted by the shape in the water who offers her 'answering looks | Of sympathie and love' (4. 464–5). Sameness draws her to herself, suggesting to some readers her essential self-absorption, and even her desire to be God.[114]

However, at this point the plot seems to start separating itself off from the original. Where Ovid's narrator tries in vain to break through the fiction, here a voice reaches through to redirect Eve's gaze. She remembers that:

> there I had fixt
> Mine eyes till now, and pin'd with vain desire,
> Had not a voice thus warnd me, What thou seest,
> What there thou seest fair Creature is thy self. (4. 465–8)

This differs from Ovid subtly. Narcissus figures out his own predicament all by himself; Eve is helped by a voice outside of herself. This does not necessarily mean that Eve has less 'wit' than the boy and needs patriarchal authority to teach her what is good for her. It shows that, unlike the self-sufficient and self-absorbed Narcissus who rejects even his own 'Echo', Eve is able to respond to a voice outside of herself which draws her from herself. Her intelligence is further demonstrated by the fact that she recognizes that this was a determining moment, in which something else might have happened that would have given her story a very different ending.

The interruption of the voice, however, indicates the intrusion of another model into this Ovidian scene: Homer. As both Bruce Loudon and James V. Morrison have argued, in Homer such moments—which Loudon calls 'pivotal contrafactuals' and Morrison 'reversal passages'—in which we are told 'and now *x* would have occurred had not *y* intervened' introduce narrative possibilities

---

[114] See Don Parry Norford's provocative essay 'The Separation of the World Parents in *Paradise Lost*', *Milton Studies*, 12 (1978), 3–24, in which Eve is a gnostic, proto-Romantic egotist, whose narcissism is a sign of her glory.

which might have taken the story in a different direction.[115] So, for example, we are told that without the intervention of the gods in *Iliad* 2 the Greeks might well have simply left Troy, and that, in *Iliad* 5. 311–13 and 20. 288–9, Aeneas might have been killed. As Loudon shows, such moments bring a scene to a suspenseful climax and then suddenly shift direction; moreover, by entertaining alternative outcomes and even imagining events that might bring the story to a premature conclusion, 'The narrative here briefly threatens its own existence.'[116] These episodes draw attention to the question of divine determinism by treating it as a narrative problem; for Morrison, Homer uses such moments to meditate on what it means to work within a tradition in which the end is already known to both author and reader: 'Although he pulls back, Homer shows how the traditional story might have been changed.'[117]

As Loudon has further pointed out, Milton is clearly interested in this formula, which he uses ten times in *Paradise Lost* in order to 'emphasize the free will which God assigns even to Satan'.[118] In Homer, the moments of suspense open up the imagination to alternatives that fate, as well as the epic reader's knowledge of the eventual outcome, ultimately closes off. Milton's revision of Ovid's Narcissus in Book 4, however, entertains the possibility of radical change. In

---

[115] Bruce Loudon, 'Milton and the Appropriation of a Homeric Technique', *Classical and Modern Literature*, 16/4 (1996), 325; and James V. Morrison, 'Alternatives to the Epic Tradition: Homer's Challenges in the *Iliad*', *Transactions of the American Philological Association*, 122 (1992), 61. See also Loudon's 'Pivotal Contrafactuals in Homeric Epic', *Classical Antiquity*, 12/2 (1993), 181–98.

[116] 'Pivotal Contrafactuals', 185.

[117] 'Alternatives', 67.

[118] 'Milton and the Appropriation', 339. Loudon notes *Paradise Lost* 2. 722–6 (the confrontation between Satan and Death which is interrupted by Sin); 4. 990–7 (the hostile meeting of Satan and Gabriel which is stopped by God); 2. 934–8 (Satan's fall through chaos which is stopped by chance); 6. 217–29 and 669–74 (the War in Heaven which the Son ends); 4. 465–8 (Eve's lingering by the pool which is stopped by the 'voice'); 8. 311–14 (Adam's early wandering which is ended by God's appearance); 11. 668–71 (the translation of Enoch to save him from death); 3. 222–6 (the rescue of doomed Man from Sin by the intervention of the Son); 10. 616–20 (the eternal existence of paradise which is ended by the fall). While Loudon contrasts Milton's goal with that of Homer, Jessica Wolfe argues that in both Homer and Milton, such 'contrary-to-fact' moments are essential to the project of theodicy in which both poets are involved, as they indicate points at which humans have freedom of choice. Her brilliant work shows further how this Homeric structure informs Milton's scenes of deliberation, especially the intervention of the Son in Book 3; I am grateful to her for showing me parts of her manuscript, *The Razor's Edge: Homer, Milton, and the Problem of Deliberation*.

this, Milton also looks back to Ovid's strategy for dealing with the familiar Homeric material of the Trojan War near the end of the *Metamorphoses* where, as Charles Segal notes, Ovid 'replaces Homeric inevitability with a surprise ending'.[119] In the *Heroides* also, as Alessandro Barchiesi has shown, Ovid takes epic and tragic characters and follows them as they 'attempt to rewrite their own story in terms of a new and different code'.[120] While, like Eve, the women of the *Heroides* have futures that are already recorded, Ovid represents them at a stage at which they have not yet become their later selves; he is therefore able to momentarily liberate his heroines from their conventional roles. While Catullus' Ariadne is immobile (in Catullus 64 she is actually a figure on a bedspread), Ovid's is active, dynamic, 'just as if she had been let out of a prison, the prison of the static character of the Catullan ekphrasis'.[121]

The pivotal point in Eve's development marks her similar break from the confining plots of Ovid and Genesis. Unlike Narcissus, who entertains choice only to evade it, or Homeric heroes whose actions are willed by Zeus, Eve faces and makes a real choice. The boy's comic decision—woo or be wooed—becomes a more serious and substantial set of alternatives: Eve can either stay fixed on her own image, or turn towards another. God explains the option he offers:

> And I will bring thee where no shadow staies
> Thy coming, and thy soft imbraces, hee
> Whose image thou art, him thou shall enjoy
> Inseparablie thine, to him shalt beare
> Multitudes like thy self. (*PL*, 4. 470–4)

Eve might have become a copy of Narcissus; instead, like Britomart, her narcissism is channelled into a higher form of love. Unlike Ovid's Narcissus, who turned from *corpus* to *umbra*, Eve is guided from her shadow to the body whose shadow, or image, she is. Properly instructed in self-knowledge, Eve follows a path that again recalls Plato's parable of the cave as she is led from illusion to reality and to Adam.

---

[119] 'Ovid: Metamorphosis, Hero, Poet', *Helios: Journal of the Classical Association of the Southwest*, 12 (1985), 53.
[120] *Speaking Volumes*, 114.
[121] Ibid.

However, it seems to me misleading to think of this as a scene of 'correction', in which an originally negative impulse is redeemed, as it is for Britomart. The extension of the imagery of copying to describe both the couple and the act of procreation ('multitudes like thy self') suggests that narcissism is not a stage to be left behind. There is nothing inherently wrong with Eve's narcissism. Created through God's divine narcissism, the couple are brought together by their shared inheritance which their relation will not abandon but deepen and make more real. In fact, while Ovid's story is changed, it continues to provide the subtext for their relation as it develops. Adam waits for Eve 'Under a Platan' (4. 478), the tree under which, as Milton noted in 'Prolusion 7', Socrates teaches in the *Phaedrus*. As in Ovid, there are further echoes of Platonic ideas in Milton's presentation of desire and knowledge; Eve's reunion with her other half recalls Aristophanes' myth of desire, as well as Ovid's parody of that myth in the story of Hermaphroditus. When Adam speaks to Eve, he stresses their essential oneness:

> Whom fli'st thou? whom thou fli'st, of him thou art,
> His flesh, his bone; to give thee being I lent
> Out of my side to thee, neerest my heart
> Substantial Life, to have thee by my side
> Henceforth an individual solace dear;
> Part of my Soul I seek thee, and thee claim
> My other half. (4. 482–8)

Adam's first words here—'Whom fli'st thou?'—echo Narcissus' cry to his reflection: 'quo refugis?' ('Oh, whither do you flee?', Ovid, *Met.*, 3. 477).[122] At the end of Eve's story, as her own similarity to Narcissus seems to reach its end, Adam steps into his place. As the verbal echo which identifies Adam with Narcissus suggests, Milton divides Narcissus' story, as Adam was divided, giving parts of it to both partners. Division is a means of creativity and *copia*, as two new stories are generated from a single source, in order to be reunited as a new whole.

While Eve gives us the first stage of Ovid's story, Adam continues the revision in Book 8 when he narrates his own creation and education into self-knowledge. Milton reverses the sequence of events, not

---

[122] Noted also by Knoespel, 'The Limits of Allegory', 89; and James, 'Milton's Eve', 134.

only presenting Eve's story before Adam's, but also giving the second part of the Narcissus story to the character created first. In terms of 'real' chronology, however, Adam was a Narcissus before Eve, who, after all was made in his image. She is, as W. B. C. Watkins put it, 'a copy of a copy',[123] as Plato describes art. Yet Adam and Eve have clearly distinct characters, as do Milton's Father and Son.[124] Like Marlowe's Hero and Leander, and indeed most couples, the two lovers also have different memories of their courtship and union that are suggestive of the personalities Milton will develop for the newly separated halves. In this respect they are strikingly different from Du Bartas's pair who are so alike that 'hardly, one | Could have the Lover from his Love describe, | Or knowne the Bridegroome from his gentle Bride' (*Divine Weeks*, 6. 1034–6).[125] The relation between Milton's Adam and Eve involves negotiating their resemblances and differences, which each perceives differently: where Eve is intensely aware of the distinctions between herself and Adam, Adam stresses the similarities; to him she is 'Bone of my Bone, Flesh of my Flesh, my Self' (*PL*, 8. 495).[126]

One obvious difference between the two characters is that the introverted Eve seems happy and self-sufficient in her solitude, while the extroverted Adam immediately craves and seeks others. After he has named the animals and met his maker, Adam is still unsatisfied, and asks God for a partner, pointing out that 'In solitude |

---

[123] *An Anatomy of Milton's Verse* (Hamden, Conn., 1965), 68.
[124] Karen Edwards notes that in *Paradise Lost* 4. 295–6, 'The peculiar grammatical construction, "both | Not equal", insists upon the sameness of Adam and Eve even as it admits some unspecified degree of difference' ('Gender, Sex and Marriage in Paradise', in Angelica Duran (ed.), *A Concise Companion to Milton* (Malden, Mass., 2007), 149).
[125] See also Green, *Milton's Ovidian Eve*, 24–6. Du Bartas's Adam also sees the newly created Eve as his own image, 'his new-come Halfe' 'calling her his Life, | His love, his Stay, his Rest, his Weale, his Wife, | His other-Selfe, his Helpe (him to refresh) | Bone of his bone, Flesh of his very Flesh' (*Divine Weeks*, 6. 1045, 1047–50)— language that Milton's Adam will use in *Paradise Lost* 4. 481–8. What is lacking in Du Bartas's account is *Eve's* version of the relation. By giving two perspectives, Milton emphasizes difference and creates a fruitful friction between the characters.
[126] As Green suggests, Adam 'actively conceals any indication of a conflict of wills between them' (*Milton's Ovidian Eve*, 70) as if any marital strife would sully the peace of Eden. On Adam's erasure of Otherness, see also Karen L. Edwards, 'Resisting Representation: All about Milton's "Eve"', *Exemplaria*, 9/1 (1997), 244; and Burrow, *Epic Romance*, 281.

What happiness, who can enjoy alone' (8. 364–5). The newly made Eve might have answered this rhetorical question with a cheerful 'I can', but God instead offers himself as an example of the joys of autonomy. Adam immediately grasps that, while made in God's image, he is not an exact replica. The two are different, so that the comparison is inappropriate:

> Thou in thy self art perfet, and in thee
> Is no deficience found; not so is Man,
> But in degree, the cause of his desire
> By conversation with his like to help,
> Or solace his defects. No need that thou
> Shouldst propogat, already infinite;
> And through all numbers absolute, though One;
> But Man by number is to manifest
> His single imperfection, and beget
> Like of his like, his Image multipli'd,
> In unitie defective, which requires
> Collateral love, and deerest amitie. (8. 415–26)

In this dialogue, God plays the role of the Socratic questioner, who guides Adam to a self-knowledge that seems very different from that of Eve.[127] Adam's intuitive grasp of the difference between the divine and the human is quite impressive. But it also reveals his limitations and lack; his self-knowledge links him to Narcissus, as Adam too sees that his plenty makes him poor. His story thus deviates happily from Ovid's when Narcissus' wish to achieve satisfaction through self-division comes true. God agrees to create:

> Thy likeness, thy fit help, thy other self,
> Thy wish exactly to thy hearts desire. (8. 450–1)

Adam's body is opened up and, from a single part, God creates a new partner, whom Adam first addresses as the 'Sole partner and sole part of all these joyes' (4. 410). In two lines, he compresses their entire dating history with remarkable Ovidian wit. Eve began as a *part* of him but is now his *partner*; it is because he *parted* from her (he was in

---

[127] See also Lewalski's *The Rhetoric of Literary Forms*, which suggests that God's method is more truly 'open—and gracious' than that of Socrates' structured chain of dialogue (214, 123–4). Another model for Socratic dialogue emerges in the conversation with Raphael in Books 5–8.

fact taken *apart*) that he is able to *part* (share) his life with her.[128] In Plato's *Symposium*, the division of the original men is a result of hubris and produces erotic dissatisfaction; in *Paradise Lost*, it is prompted by desire and is the prelude to greater satisfaction which includes both verbal and sexual play.

In both scenes of creation, then, Adam and Eve appear in states that recall aspects of Ovid's story of Narcissus and his tragic self-knowledge. Both learn through images of themselves: Eve. In the unfallen world, an originally divine narcissistic impulse becomes the basis for dynamic self-knowledge which produces a chain of continuing creativity: God's creation of the Son, who in turn creates the world; the genesis of Adam and Eve, who are in turn the source of future generations, including the poet, who himself will produce more figures. Copying necessarily involves the introduction of difference, which in the case of Satan leads to the duplication of divine narcissism in parodic forms that restrict change and creative possibilities. In both Eve's and Adam's cases, their resemblance to the subtext of Narcissus ends initially in difference, as Milton's copy deviates from its original. Like Narcissus, Eve first makes an unconscious mistake; then, like him again, she makes it consciously (knowing she is choosing a mere shadow); *then* (with a little help) she leaves behind her image and joins Adam. The laboured clumsiness of the sequence—which has seemed to many readers an inauspicious start to marital bliss—foregrounds Eve's power of choice. Like Narcissus, Eve errs unconsciously and then consciously; unlike Narcissus, she *then* consciously chooses to correct her error.[129] In so doing, her parallel to the subtext is broken and a new story, and character, is created. Like Narcissus, Adam finds his original wholeness and self-containment dissatisfying, and asks to be divided in two. In his case, the difference between the stories is that Adam's wish comes true. Milton thus divides Ovid's single tale into two new and interesting ones that, while still separate, also come together into a new whole that is, as Adam proclaims, 'one Flesh, one Heart, one Soule' (8. 499).

---

[128] On the importance of punning on 'part' in the poem generally, see Shoaf, *Milton, Poet of Duality*, 15–23, 68–71.

[129] In fact, Adam's development is equally awkward, as it seems to take God three tries to get it right. Created first outside of Eden, Adam has to be put back to sleep and brought inside the garden; even then, he is again put to sleep and recreated with the making of Eve. Both creation scenes thus emphasize how creation for Milton, as for Ovid, is an ongoing process.

Because they have been divided from each other, Adam and Eve are able to be reunited into a new kind of Narcissus, a hermaphrodite in whom sexual and individual differences are retained.

FALLING, IN LOVE

The uses of the subtext of Narcissus reinforce one of the striking features about the relationship between Adam and Eve: unlike Hero and Leander, these lovers do not fall in love at first sight. Love takes time, as Marlowe's lovers also discover. Even in Eden, courtship is required.[130] The Ovidian *mora* which had been central to the vision of 'Elegia 5' becomes in paradise a key ingredient for marital bliss. As in the early elegy, the 'erotics of delay' informs the poem's narrative structure, as well as the prolongation of pleasure and drawing out of time before the fall.[131] At the same time, however, Eve's coyness recalls an all too familiar form of courtship, in which an initially suspiciously narcissistic lover rejects her suitor. Other Ovidian subtexts remind us of that well-known scenario, pointing towards 'such hazards of postlapsarian sexuality as wandering desires, destabilizing uncertainty about the beloved, and potential violence'.[132] In retrospect, the story is, like *Venus and Adonis*, an explanation of the origins of love's torments; the postlapsarian Adam sees the future as a relentlessly miserable series of 'innumerable | Disturbances on Earth through Femal snares, | And straight conjunction with this Sex', 'Which infinite calamitie shall cause | To Humane life, and houshold peace confound' (*PL*, 10. 896–8, 907–8). In Book 9, as the fall approaches, foreshadowing is intensified by references to 'a series of ancient stories concerning rape, metamorphosis to avoid rape, and

---

[130] Compare here too with Du Bartas, whose custom-made couple need no courtship at all; after the creation of Eve, the narrator just bursts into a celebration of the joys of marriage: 'O blessed Bond! O happy Mariage! | Which doost the match twixt Christ and us presage! | O chastest friendship, whose pure flames impart | Two Soules in one, two Harts into one Hart!' (*Divine Weeks*, 6. 1055–8). Milton's similar celebration of 'wedded love' in *Paradise Lost* 4. 750–75 comes only after we have heard of Eve's wooing and, significantly, the couple have gone to bed in their bower; it is the climax of an unfolding and developing relationship.

[131] Amy Boesky, '*Paradise Lost* and the Multiplicity of Time', in Corns (ed.), *A Companion to Milton*, 384. See also Parker, *Inescapable Romance*, 114–58.

[132] James, 'Milton's Eve, the Romance Genre', 126.

sexual jealousy'.[133] Like heavy orchestration in a suspense film, the ominous allusions alert the reader that something nasty is about to happen.

Moreover, Adam's first pursuit of the coy Eve bears a family resemblance to Apollo's doomed chase of Daphne.[134] The first 'love story' in the *Metamorphoses*, it sets the pattern for flight and pursuit that will be repeated in later tales. As Philip Hardie has also shown, the story links desire and art, specifically imitation, and so anticipates the tale of Narcissus.[135] Like the boy, Daphne wants to preserve her chastity. Moreover, she tries to be an imitation or *aemula* of Diana (Ovid, *Met.*, 1. 476). (I'll return to the importance of this word in the next chapter.) The fact that Diana is not just the goddess of chastity but also Apollo's twin makes the god's pursuit of the nymph potentially incestuous and narcissistic.

As Hardie argues, the likeness between the stories of Daphne and Narcissus, which is expanded through the poem as Ovid builds on the themes that connect his stories, identifies narrative repetition with narcissism and incest.[136] Narrative doubling is a kind of textual incest, which binds the stories closely in involuted patterns in which they ultimately begin to look the same. Micaela Janan also notes how Ovid's stories of incest (which are all of course related to each other) play out 'a nightmare of artistic self-referentiality, in which every possible choice leads to what has *already* been done'.[137] A similar repetition of the familiar appears in Milton's incestuous and derivative Sin. If marriage is the erotic analogue for an intertextuality that allows resemblance and variation, incest is the sexual form of textual self-replication. The drive to erotic and narrative sameness cuts off the possibility of the creation of something different.

For Ovid, however, the artist's task is to break through this loop by creating change; the poet is like the Ulysses of *Ars Amatoria* 2. 128,

---

[133] Smith, *Is Milton Better Than Shakespeare?*, 169. See, however, Green's reading of this foreshadowing, which is similar to mine (*Milton's Ovidian Eve*, 19–20, 174–80).

[134] See Douglas Bush, 'Ironic and Ambiguous Allusion in *Paradise Lost*', *Journal of English and Germanic Philology*, 60/4 (1961), 638; and Green, *Milton's Ovidian Eve*, 59–60.

[135] Philip Hardie, 'Approximate Similes in Ovid: Incest and Doubling', *Dictynna: Revue de poétique latine*, 1 (2004), 1–30.

[136] For Hardie, therefore, incest is 'a central figure for Ovid's own artistic practices of mimesis and *imitatio*' (ibid. 27).

[137] '"The Labyrinth and the Mirror": Incest and Influence in *Metamorphoses* 9', *Arethusa*, 24/2 (1991), 243.

whom Ovid praises for his ability to tell one story in many different ways.[138] Near the end of the *Metamorphoses* Ovid takes up the challenge of reimagining his own patterns with the story of Pomona, which as the last 'love story' in the epic mirrors that of Daphne. It starts off looking, in fact, as if it will be an exact replica of the earlier episode, bringing the epic back to where it started in Book 1. Like Daphne, Pomona is not interested in men, although she is not a huntress but a gardener, and therefore an appropriate figure for Eve. She too is sought after by a god, in this case Vertumnus, who, as his name with its root of 'vertere' (to turn) suggests, was known for his shape-shifting. In Propertius he explains his flexible nature: 'opportuna meast cunctis natura figuris: | in quamcumque voles verte, decorus ero' ('My nature suits any role: turn me to which you please, and I shall fit you well', *Elegies*, 4. 2. 21-2).[139] His protean nature marks him broadly as an Ovidian figure, though in particular he recalls the artful lover who advises in *Ars* 1. 759-61: 'Pectoribus mores tot sunt, quot in ore figurae; | Qui sapit, innumeris moribus aptus erit, | Utque leves Proteus modo se tenuabit in undas, | Nunc leo, nunc arbor, nunc erit hirtus aper' ('Hearts have as many fashions as the world has shapes; the wise man will suit himself to countless fashions, and like Proteus will now resolve himself into light waves, and now will be a lion, now a tree, now a shaggy boar').[140] As in *Metamorphoses* 1 Apollo had tried to follow Ovid's directions, Vertumnus tries to please Pomona by becoming all things. When that fails, however, he turns to storytelling as a method of courtship; taking the shape of an old woman, he tells Pomona a classic cautionary tale in which a disdainful lady, Anaxerete, rejects her passionate suitor. When the frustrated lover kills himself, the hard-hearted mistress is appropriately, if predictably, turned to stone. This familiar story does not, however, have its desired effect of softening Pomona.

---

[138] 'Ille referre aliter saepe solebat idem' ('often would he tell the same tale in other words'). Ovid's desire to challenge himself to create difference out of sameness is especially evident in the *Heroides*, where he imagines different perspectives on the experience of separation and abandonment, and in the exilic poetry with its spectre of monotony.

[139] Cited from Sextus Propertius, *Elegies*, ed. and trans. G. P. Goold (Cambridge, Mass., 1990).

[140] As M. L. Stapleton notes, this sound advice would have been particularly familiar to many English schoolboys who had been taught Latin through the 1513 translation of the *Ars*: *The flores of Ouide de arte amandi with theyr englysshe afore them: and two alphabete tablys*; *Spenser's Ovidian Poetics*, 32.

The frustrated Vertumnus takes his original shape and prepares to use a more basic Roman courting method: rape. However, violence is prevented, not through metamorphoses, but by Pomona's sudden ravishment by Vertumnus' beauty: 'inque figura | capta dei nympha est et mutua vulnera sensit' ('and the nymph, smitten by the beauty of the god, felt an answering passion', Ovid, *Met.*, 14. 770–1). Both rape and metamorphosis are avoided, replaced instead by mutual satisfaction.

Looking back on his arts of love, as well as the earlier stories of the *Metamorphoses*, Ovid seems to be making fun of his own instructions. The episode plays comically on the theme of the failure of rhetoric that will reappear in a more sinister form in the exilic verse.[141] The arts of love and the imagination do not work—what wins hearts is nature, and that old cliché, be yourself (which is actually pretty hard for a god whose nature it is to change shapes). But the episode is more serious than just self-parody, suggesting that, as we reach the end of the epic, Ovid breaks out of the pattern of frustrated and unreciprocated love.

The comparison of Eve to '*Pomona* when she fled | *Vertumnus*' in *Paradise Lost* 9. 394–5 might therefore point us towards a different story from the one that Milton ultimately tells. While the courtship of Eve begins as a conventional story of the pursuit of a narcissistic lover, it develops into a new narrative and model altogether, one that moves beyond the couples imagined by Ovid, the Elizabethans, and even the end of *Comus*. Milton suggests there was a time before the kind of love relation imagined by Ovid and his later adapters, a time when desire was innocent and deeply satisfying. By depicting an explicitly sexual union between individuals, Milton rewrites the union of Spenser's Amoret and Scudamour whom Spenser can only imagine either as joined as 'one flesh'—at the end of the 1590 *Faerie Queene* they merge into a hermaphrodite—or not united at all—in the 1596 version they miss each other altogether. More directly, the couple transforms the oppositional relation of Shakespeare's Venus and Adonis, whose story suggested that reciprocal and satisfying desire was always a myth. The distance between Shakespeare's and Milton's couples may be measured in hands. When Shakespeare's

---

[141] See generally Richard Tarrant, 'Ovid and the Failure of Rhetoric', in Doreen Innes, Harry Hine, and Christopher Pelling (eds.), *Ethics and Rhetoric: Classical Essays for Donald Russell on his Seventy-Fifth Birthday* (Oxford, 1995), 63–74.

Venus attempts to take Adonis' hand in her own, it seems to reflect the predatory nature of her desire.[142] Milton's Adam reaches out to Eve firmly but tenderly; she recalls how 'with that thy gentle hand | Seisd mine' (*PL*, 4. 488–9). The balance between gentleness and power is a delicate one that will be tipped after the fall when desire becomes predatory. Still, for a brief moment here, *rapere* has been transformed into its most down-to-earth and benign form—not rape, but simply *take*.

The 'handedness' of the couple is often remarked as the key to their relationship. Separated, they come together no longer literally as one flesh but as independent yet attached individuals. But the focus on their hands also suggests their relationship with God, whose hand is identified with the act of creation.[143] The couple reflects God's creative nature through their union. In Eden, sexual fulfilment, rather than frustration, is at the centre of all other acts of creation.[144] The couple's hands thus play a key role in the tending of the garden, through which they express their divine nature as creators (see especially 5. 211–19 and 9. 207–8). The growing garden is itself a place of endless *copia* and abundance, as Adam suggests when he asks Eve to prepare lunch for Raphael: 'goe with speed | And what thy stores contain, bring forth and poure | Abundance' (5. 313–15). 'Store' was often used as the English translation for *copia*—as may be seen when the Son creates the world with compasses taken from 'Gods Eternal store' (7. 226).[145] By tending the garden, Adam and Eve

---

[142] See 'with this she seizeth on his sweating palm' (*Venus and Adonis*, 25), which then leads her 'to pluck him from his horse' (30). She tries a more subtle tactic later, 'Full gently now she takes him by the hand' (361); but Adonis still whines: 'You hurt my hand with wringing. Let us part' (421).

[143] See Lieb, *The Dialectics of Creation*, 175 n. 7; and Mario A. DiCesare, 'Advent'rous Song: The Texture of Milton's Epic', in Ronald David Emma and John T. Shawcross (eds.), *Language and Style in Milton: A Symposium in Honor of the Tercentenary of Paradise Lost* (New York, 1967), 21, who notes 4. 364–5, 7. 224, 7. 500, 8. 470, and 9. 344–5. A similar emphasis is notable in mannerist painting, in which enlarged hands are often used to draw attention to the means of creativity.

[144] See especially the hymn to wedded love in 4. 750–75. On unfallen sexuality as a mirror of divine creativity, see further Lieb, *The Dialectics of Creation*, 71–8.

[145] So in *The Rape of Lucrece*, Tarquin is compared to Narcissus who 'poorly rich, so wanteth in his store | That, cloyed with much, he pineth still for more' (97–8); a narcissistic pattern intensified in the rape, in which 'Pure chastity is rifled of her store, | And lust, the thief, far poorer than before' (692–3). In Thomas Edwards's 'Narcissus', Narcissus puns on the word, 'Nor shall I want the meanes to grace my tale, | Abundant store of sweet perswasiue stories' (589–90). Spenser also uses store frequently to signify abundance—see for example the Garden of Adonis' 'euerlasting store' (*Faerie*

repeat the Son's originary ordering of chaos.[146] Moreover, Milton draws on a principle familiar to any gardener to epitomize the nature of Eden: nature 'by disburd'ning grows | More fruitful' (5. 319–20). A growing garden that is 'Wilde above Rule or Art' (5. 297) needs to be cut back; it requires 'hands to check | Fruitless imbraces' (5. 214–15) to make it fruitful. Without the intervention of creative human hands, the *copia* of nature would become *inops* indeed.[147] In their life together in the garden, Adam and Eve are involved in the constant battle to keep creativity from turning against itself, and turning into Satanic destruction. Through gardening and sexuality they keep recreating the world.

The courtship of Adam and Eve is thus a central part of the dynamics of the unfallen world that keep it moving towards God. Milton's revisions of Ovid allow us to glimpse this process of change away from the familiar and predictable. Yet of course the subtexts also remind us of what happened. The ambiguity of the allusions is especially evident in the comparison of Eve to '*Pomona* when she fled | *Vertumnus*' in *Paradise Lost* 9. 394–5.[148] In this reference, Eve is

---

Queene, 3. 6. 36. 4), echoed in *Paradise Lost* 7. 226's 'Eternal store'. In *Comus*, the Lady refers to Nature's 'store' (774) in her debate with Comus (see also line 720), and in *Paradise Regain'd* Satan tries to tempt the Son with nature's 'choicest store' (2. 334). As she goes to prepare lunch for Raphael, Eve puns on the different meanings of the word, thus displaying her own verbal *copia*: 'Adam, earth's hallowd mould, | Of God inspir'd, small store will serve, where store, | All seasons, ripe for use hangs on the stalk; | Save what by frugal storing firmness gains | To nourish, and superfluous moist consumes' (*PL*, 5. 321–5). It's a good reminder that some store needs storing. See also the similar pun on abundance, store, and choice in Eve's conversation with Satan before the fall: 'in such aboundance lies our choice, | As leaves a greater store of Fruit untoucht' (9. 620–1). Her own wit should remind her that both verbal and herbal plenty require choice as a means of limitation.

[146] See also Lewalski, 'Innocence and Experience in Milton's Eden', 90–5 especially.

[147] In 'Prolusion 7' the young Milton had already expressed his awareness of this paradox in relation to his own rhetorical skills: 'in his ipsa sibi officit *copia*, & rerum multitudine comprimit & coangustat expandentem se elocutionis pompam; hâc ego argumenti foecunditate nimiâ laboro, ipsae me vires imbecillum, arma inermem reddunt' ('In these the very abundance [copia] thwarts itself, and by the mass of material checks and restrains the ostentation of delivery from expanding itself. I am oppressed by this excessive abundance of evidence; the supplies themselves make me helpless; the means of defence render me defenceless', *Works*, xii. 252; emphasis mine).

[148] A similar ambiguity appears in the comparison of Eve to Ovid's Flora in *Paradise Lost* 5. 16. While Adam corresponds to the husband/rapist Zephyr, Eve has just spent the night (in one sense) with Satan; see my 'Eve and Flora (*Paradise Lost* 5. 15–16)'.

obviously Pomona, but who is her Vertumnus? So far I have been innocently assuming that her future husband Adam is. Yet there is another suitor whom she is just about to meet, and who in some ways seems better suited to Ovid's role: the shape-shifting Satan.[149] The presence of Satan in the garden introduces an alternative love story. In Books 5 and 9, Satan approaches Eve like a Petrarchan lover, who assumes his lady is narcissistic and vain, and who begs her not to view him 'with disdain' (9. 534). In both her dream and Book 9, he lays it on pretty thick, treating her as a coy mistress whom he woos as 'sovran Mistress' (9. 532), 'sole Wonder' (9. 533), and 'A Goddess among Gods' (9. 547) whom all nature wants to gaze on and adore (5. 41–7; 9. 539–42). In his speeches we glimpse the future courtly lover who sings serenades 'To his proud fair, best quitted with disdain' (4. 770).[150] By playing this role, Satan tries to turn Eve into the conventional disdainful and narcissistic lover.

Satan's story of the serpent's 'Strange alteration' (599) in 9. 571–612 looks back also to another Ovidian tale of courtship: that of Glaucus and the nymph Scylla, told at the end of *Metamorphoses* 13. Another narcissistic lady who disdains all suitors, Scylla is suddenly surprised by the smitten Glaucus, who tells her how, once a mere fisherman, he has become a god by eating a magic herb which expanded his mind as well as transforming his body. Unfortunately, however, Glaucus' new form, half human and half fish, repulses the girl, who flies in horror. The parallel with this particular Ovidian story is unsettling; as I will discuss further in the next chapter, Scylla, who in *Metamorphoses* 14 is herself made into a hybrid monster, is more famously a model for Milton's Sin. The shared subtext, like that of Narcissus, thus seems to link Eve and Sin and to point towards Eve's transformation through the fall. Yet Scylla's rejection of her amphibious suitor might equally offer Eve the possibility of an alternative conclusion to the courtship of Satan. Hindsight creates foreshadowing, as because of our foreknowledge of the story we read earlier words

---

[149] Green notes how readings of the allusion depend upon their identification of Milton's Vertumnus (*Milton's Ovidian Eve*, 162–4). While many critics treat the story as one of marital happiness, she stresses the darker aspects (ibid. 157).

[150] On Milton's rejection of Petrarchism, see also Dubrow, *Echoes of Desire*, 269–70; Ilona Bell, 'Milton's Dialogue with Petrarch', *Milton Studies*, 28 (1992), 91–120; and Kerrigan and Braden, 'Milton's Coy Eve'. Karen Edwards, 'Resisting Representation', argues that in Adam's courtship of Eve Petrarchan desire survives and is transvalued.

and allusions as leading to the fall that took place. But each moment in which things seem to take a wrong turn still *might* in fact have led to a very different conclusion. The challenge of the poem is to make us glimpse the unrealized alternatives and free up alternative meanings. Milton must work against Samuel Johnson's assertion that 'truth allows no choice',[151] by convincing us that the characters face real decisions.

In fact, Milton makes it extremely difficult to locate a cause or pinpoint the exact moment where things go wrong. While Adam's motives for eating the fruit will seem fairly simple—love for Eve— hers are more complex and mysterious. What got into her? In retrospect, Eve's creation, or her dream, could suggest the weaknesses that determine her fatal error; or, one might see Eve's idea of dividing labour as itself a dire mistake. The fact that she speaks first that morning for the first time might reveal a new and sinister ambition. In retrospect, Adam will attribute the fall to Eve's 'strange | Desire of wandring' (9. 1135–6). Yet, as Book 8 demonstrated, there is nothing inherently wrong with the couple separating, and both characters have wandered freely and innocently in Eden.[152] Eve's sensitivity to the pleasure caused by temporary absence shows her growing understanding of the role of Ovidian delay in happiness. Like that of Elizabethan schoolboys, her education seems to involve lessons from the *magister amoris*. When Eve realizes that Adam 'would intermix | Grateful digressions, and solve high dispute | With conjugal Caresses, from his Lip | Not Words alone pleas'd her' (8. 54–7), she is applying *Ars* 1. 663: 'Quis sapiens blandis non misceat oscula verbis?' ('Who but a foole that cannot iudge of blisses, | But when he speakes will with his word mixe kisses?').[153] While Eve's sudden interest in speed

---

[151] *Lives of the English Poets*, ed. Waugh, i. 120.
[152] In fact, Adam is the first wanderer in Eden. Like that of Eve, his story of creation includes a 'pivotal contrafactual' at which point it might have gone in a different direction. Waking for the second time, now in the garden, he realizes that 'Here had new begun | My wandring, had not hee who was my Guide | Up hither, from among the Trees appeer'd' (8. 311–13) to steer him towards the creation of Eve. Errancy is not ended, but redirected to become part of the erotic relationship.
[153] Translation from Thomas Heywood, *Pvblii Ovidii Nasonis De Arte Amandi: or, The Art of Love* (London, 1625), Early English Books Online, B6ᵛ, a work reprinted six times after the Restoration. On the popularity of the *Ars* generally, see M. L. Stapleton, 'Ovid the Rakehell: The Case of Wycherley', *Restoration: Studies in English Literary Culture, 1660–1700*, 25/2 (2001), 87–8. In *Heroides* 13. 118–20, Laodamia also anticipates the return of her beloved husband from Troy full of stories that he will

and efficiency on the morning of the fall seems both uncharacteristic and inimical to pleasure, it is not, therefore, necessarily suspicious; her idea may again show how the couple is growing and developing, trying new things, and even taking new roles in their relationship. They are changing as they learn from each other and from the garden. The argument between Adam and Eve before the fall seems to anticipate the battle of the sexes that erupts at the end of the book. But it could equally indicate the evolution of a relation that does not demand absolute conformity of thinking, in which tension and strife may be a means of growth—a marital version of the endlessly debating community Milton had imagined in *Areopagitica*. As Addison suggested, the disagreement may be literally quite innocent: 'It is such a Dispute as we may suppose might have happened in *Paradise*, had Man continued happy and innocent.'[154] It points towards an unfallen world in which women may speak first.

The chain of events leading up to the fall is in fact rather loose and drawn out. It is only by chance that Satan finds Eve alone. He first gets her attention simply because she is astonished to meet a talking snake. Once enticed to listen, however, she becomes entangled in his seductive rhetoric because it echoes things she has heard from other sources. As Leander had told Hero that 'Venus' nun' could paradoxically only fulfil her vows by breaking them, Satan convinces Eve that by disobeying God's taboo she will be doing exactly what a good God would want: showing initiative in helping herself ascend up the road to heaven. By eating the fruit, she seems to be cutting back the growth of Eden which, as he also told her in the dream, will be 'much more sweet thus cropt' (5. 68; see also 5. 58–9).[155] At the same time, she will achieve the immortality and knowledge which she and Adam have been encouraged to seek. Satan's argument is cunning because like

---

recount mixed with kisses, noting also that 'promptior est dulci lingua referre mora' ('more ready for report is the tongue refreshed by sweet delay', 13. 122). See also James, 'Milton's Eve', 126; Green, *Milton's Ovidian Eve*, 65–6. Kerrigan and Braden argue also that 'Eve has learned something from those moments in the libertine tradition that unexpectedly reaffirm the erotic value of modesty and withholding' ('Milton's Coy Eve', 41).

[154] *Spectator*, 351, in *The Spectator: Complete in One Volume* (London, 1877), 512.
[155] Comus makes a similar argument to the Lady (Milton, *Comus*, 728–9). Unlike Eve, the Lady remembers that natural abundance and 'store' (774) provoke human choice, or, as she calls it, 'Temperance' (767). See also *Areopagitica*, in *Works*, iv. 308–9.

everything he does it is a copy: it mimics ideas Eve has just been taught. 'And what are Gods that Man may not becomen | As they, participating God-like food?' (9. 716–17) recalls Raphael's hint that 'time may come when men | With Angels may participate, and find | No inconvenient Diet' (5. 493–5); it also echoes God's suggestion (reported by Raphael) that he hopes that men may ascend to heaven 'by degrees of merit rais'd' (7. 157). Satan offers an alternative means of metamorphosis, which will hasten the prolonged process of human development. For Eve, who has just come up with the novel notion that working separately might be more efficient, a shortcut in the long climb upwards may be appealing.

So far these errors still seem fairly innocent. Everything seems to change, however, when Satan as Petrarchan lover convinces his prey to seize the day, not to mention fruit.[156] Like Ovid's Glaucus, Eve undergoes an immediate and complete mental metamorphosis when she eats. She suddenly experiences differences as threatening, and urges Adam to eat so that they may become the same:

> Thou therefore also taste, that equal Lot
> May joyne us, equal Joy, as equal Love;
> Least thou not tasting, different degree
> Disjoyne us. (9. 881–4)

Her vow to never again leave Adam's side (9. 857–61) ominously recalls Salmacis' prayer in *Metamorphoses* 4. 371–2: 'ita di iubeatis, et istum | nulla dies a me nec me deducat ab isto' ('Grant me this ye gods, and may no day ever come that shall separate him from me or me from him'). Through Satan, the couple starts slipping into a different kind of relationship, as Eve's need for sameness seems to trigger Adam's original narcissism. Realizing immediately what Eve has done, Adam cries that he will follow her example in order to be one:

> So forcible within my heart I feel
> The Bond of Nature draw me to my owne,
> My own in thee, for what thou art is mine;
> Our State cannot be severd, we are one,
> One Flesh; to loose thee were to loose my self. (*PL*, 9. 955–9)

---

[156] See Parker, *Inescapable Romance*, 132, who contrasts this foreshortening of time with the suspense of Eden. In *Paradise Regain'd* as well, Satan will urge the Son to seize the day and opportunity.

Adam's language here identifies the fall with a narcissistic desire for total oneness between loved and beloved. This is not to say his response is unattractive—many readers have found this moment the most moving in the poem. Plato's Aristophanes would find the passionate longing for the beloved quite natural. But it is different from the kind of love that Milton was trying to convince us was possible before the fall. While in the *Symposium* division is a result of a fall from original perfection, in *Paradise Lost*, the desire to erase difference leads to the loss of another kind of perfection, one that includes difference and change.

However, as Milton separated the two stories of creation, he clearly differentiates the two stages of the fall. In Genesis, Adam and Eve fall in a single verse; in *Paradise Lost*, the two falls are temporally distinct events which also have very different causes and motives. The two parts mean that, even after Eve eats, Adam faces a moment of real and critical choice. But his alternatives are not clearly laid out. We may wonder what God might have done if Adam had not eaten—would he, as feared, have destroyed Eve and made Adam a new wife? would he have forgiven Eve because of Adam's steadfastness?—but Adam does not. He lapses into Satanic determinism, denying the possibility of even imagining other options, 'Submitting to what seemd remediless' (9. 919), as he bewails 'But past who can recall, or don undoe?' (9. 926). He forgets that he and Eve are no longer one flesh nor one story. In Book 8, Adam had told Raphael that he was able to make rational choices not swayed by passion: 'yet still free | Approve the best, and follow what I approve' (8. 610–11). The lines ominously echo a popular tag from Ovid. Torn between her loyalty to her family and love for Jason, Medea cries:

> sed gravat invitam nova vis, aliudque cupido,
> mens aliud suadet: video meliora proboque,
> deteriora sequor.

('But some strange power holds me down against my will. Desire persuades me one way, reason another. I see the better and approve it, but I follow the worse', *Met.*, 7. 19–21)

For Medea, as for Narcissus, choice is disastrous, and self-knowledge does not lead to freedom but to tragedy; she makes her fatal decision in complete awareness: 'quid faciam, video: non ignorantia veri | decipiet, sed amor' ('I see what I am about to do, nor shall ignorance of the truth be my undoing, but love itself', 7. 92–3). While in Book 8 Adam revises Medea's decision, as earlier he had rewritten Narcissus' story, in the fall he repeats it. Copying both Medea and Eve too closely, he chooses what he does not approve in full knowledge of the consequences, and so:

> scrupl'd not to eat
> Against his better knowledge, not deceav'd,
> But fondly overcome with Femal charm. (9. 997–9)

The two falls are strikingly different in tempo as well as motives. Eve's is prolonged, staged; it requires much logical debate and careful, if fatal, choosing. In contrast, Adam's is swift and passionate rather than reasoned; he entertains choice only to reject it. The stories are still therefore quite distinct. But Adam's decision reunites the halves of the subtext once more to make them parts of a single narcissistic sequence in which Eve replays Narcissus' unconscious error and Adam his conscious choice. Eve acts 'imprudens', not knowing, as she is misled by Satan. Adam, however, like Narcissus and Medea, knows exactly what he is doing. Ironically, in Book 10, Christ will tell Adam that he would not have fallen 'had'st thou known thy self aright' (10. 156). Had he known himself he would have known that he was not Eve, nor Narcissus: not a mere copy, but a created and creative original.

The sad consequence of the convergence of the two Narcissus stories is the metamorphosis of love. Myth becomes a reality that is all too familiar, as earth now replicates hell, and the lineage of Satan and Sin rather than that of heaven. The 'erotics of delay' are transformed into a darker, more ominous kind of suspense, part of the errant wandering that will take the couple out of Eden at the end of the poem and into the wilderness of history. Time becomes the familiar Ovidian 'edax rerum' ('devourer of all things', *Met.*, 15. 234) who is the accomplice of Death, as 'whatever thing | The Sithe of Time mowes down', Death is able to 'devour unspar'd' (10. 605–6). Fallen sexuality is no longer satisfying, and the argument between Adam and Eve is transformed into a full-scale battle between the sexes. As they start to make love, Adam repeats a familiar gesture: 'Her hand he seis'd' (9. 1037). But the word now missing—gently—made all the difference. Desiring to be one flesh again, the couple has become totally different, sentenced now by the Son to separate forms of labour and forever alienated from each other. The earlier discussions and differences of opinion degenerate into mutual recrimination, summed up at the end of Book 9: 'Thus they in mutual accusation spent | The fruitless hours, but neither self-condemning, | And of thir vain contest appeer'd no end' (9. 1187-9). The creative and playful puns of Eden have now themselves become a 'fruitless' sign of endless wrangling.[157] With Adam's lamentation of his sad fate in Book 10. 720 ff., the various verse of Eden turns into Ovidian complaint; Adam is the ancestor of Medea and the other heroines of the *Heroides*, as well as the exiled Ovid himself.[158] The couple slides into familiar patterns of destructive and alienated desire. We are back in the world of Shakespeare in which, as Adonis argued, desire is lust, and in which also, as the rape of Sin makes abundantly clear, sex leads to Death.[159]

In Books 10-12, however, the relation between Adam and Eve begins to be reformed. The slow process replays, now painfully, the lengthy negotiation of their original happier courtship. As often noted, Eve is the first to imagine an alternative to endless bickering, by seeking forgiveness and reconciliation. She re-establishes the possibility for constructive dialogue between the two. Her voice breaks through Adam's Narcissistic complaint, just as God's voice had earlier penetrated her watery reverie.[160] In turn, Adam grasps what is now needed, reaching out to her: 'But rise, let us no more contend, nor blame | Each other, blam'd enough elsewhere, but strive | In offices of Love, how we may light'n | Each others burden in our share of woe' (10. 958-61). In Marlowe, as I argued in Chapter 1, strife is ambiguous: it is a creative force that generates the universe, and a destructive one that exposes Hero and Leander's distance from each other. For Milton, postlapsarian humans must strive to recover God's

---

[157] See also Satan's punning in the war in heaven, Book 6, 560 ff., which in its conflation of the languages of generation and destruction indicates his abuse of *copia*.

[158] On the relation between Adam's complaint and the *Heroides* generally, see Lewalski, Paradise Lost *and the Rhetoric of Literary Forms*, 249.

[159] As Summers notes, in Book 10 Sin and Death are now transformed into a parodic version of romantic love (*Muse's Method*, 62). On the association of infernal creativity with perverse forms of sexuality see also Lieb, *Dialectics of Creation*, 133-45.

[160] Forsyth sees this crucial moment of turning as a kind of Augustinian experience of grace as 'the chance to change', in which 'what is important for Adam, too, is that the voice is outside himself, the voice of another, denied to that solitary voyeur, Satan' (*The Satanic Epic*, 299).

original creativity by turning destructive energies into creative ones, alienation into new forms of relation. We strive to turn strife itself into 'offices of Love' and cooperation.

One of the most fatal consequences of the fall for Milton, however, is the wounding of human creative powers. The reunion of the two halves of the story of Narcissus in the fall might suggest that, since then, it is impossible to imagine a different version of Narcissus; Ovid's subtext seems to determine the conclusion of the narrative after all. While Eve's creation opens up the possibilities of alternative outcomes, the foreknown conclusion of the Genesis story means that in the end they must be closed down. Milton is obviously not free to rewrite or correct the Bible in the way that he is free to redo classical myths: he is bound by the outcome both he and the reader know. Creativity is no longer free and spontaneous, but struggles against monotony and repetition. The fall explains the origins of tyranny and a King whose 'creations, like Satan's in *Paradise Lost*, are paradoxically both self-generated and derivative, sterile imitations'.[161] It brings us into the world of 1660 and a nation which preferred copies and idols to the real thing, the familiar to the new.

However, a final allusion suggests that humans may still be able to make changes. One of the first consequences of the fall is the flood, which Milton narrates at the end of *Paradise Lost* 11. As he drew on *Metamorphoses* 1 to describe the making of the world, he now turns to this book to tell of its undoing. The appearance of Ovid's story is prepared for at the beginning of the book, where Milton compares Adam and Eve to Ovid's survivors of the catastrophe, Deucalion and Pyrrha, who are also, strikingly, one of the few happily, and safely, married couples in Ovid. As brother and sister, moreover, they are mirror images of each other, and thus linked to Narcissus.[162] While the allusion comes before Milton's account of Noah's story, the flood is happening already in the couple's first quarrel, in which 'nor onely Teares | Raind at thir Eyes, but high Winds worse within | Began to

---

[161] Guibbory, 'Charles's Prayers', 293–4.
[162] Hardie notes how their likeness to each other is conveyed through verbal repetition (*Ovid's Poetics of Illusion*, 280): 'et superesse virum de tot modo milibus unum, | et superesse vidit de tot modo milibus unam | innocuos ambo, cultores numinis ambo' ('only one man was left from so many thousands, and only one woman was left from so many thousands, both innocent, both worshippers of the gods', *Met.*, 1. 325–7).

rise' (9. 1121-3). After this emotional tempest has subsided, Adam and Eve slowly make peace, and then join together again to pray to God. To describe the reunited couple, Milton now turns directly to Ovid:

> yet thir port
> Not of mean suiters, nor important less
> Seem'd thir Petition, then when th'ancient Pair
> In Fables old, less ancient yet then these,
> *Deucalion* and chaste *Pyrrha* to restore
> The race of Mankind drownd, before the Shrine
> Of *Themis* stood devout. (11. 8-14)

The scene circles back to the morning hymn of praise in Book 5, in which Adam and Eve show their likeness to God through their spontaneous creativity. But it shows the dreadful distance between that lost world and the new one they now enter. In unfallen Eden the couple are naturally poets: 'for neither various style | Nor holy rapture wanted they to praise | Thir Maker, in fit strains pronounc't or sung | Unmeditated, such prompt eloquence | Flowd from thir lips, in Prose or numerous Verse' (5. 146-50). When Adam and Eve pray after the fall, we no longer hear their prayer, and the repetition at the end of Book 10 (as Adam's suggestions to Eve in 10. 1086-92 are restated by the narrator in 10. 1098-104) indicates how easily poetry can become the uncreative repetition that Milton associates with Satan. The simple comparison to Ovid's figures itself suggests a world in which all characters and stories are becoming the same sad story. The move into a world of dreary sameness is reinforced by Michael's presentation of history, which shows how the sins of the fall are copied endlessly by later generations. Rather discouragingly, moreover, Michael explains that humans themselves cannot do anything to break the pattern of error; only Christ can bring the vicious recycling of history to an end.

Ovid, however, introduces a different possibility. As I noted much earlier, his story of Deucalion and Pyrrha shows how the original act of creation, instigated by a nameless god, has to be redone immediately by the remaking of the world by human beings themselves. In Milton, the reference thus balances and completes the Ovidian story of the creation of the world told in Book 7, so that divine creativity is seen to continue in the fallen world after all. At the end of Milton's poem, his focus is on *human* creation, an act that tells us that, despite everything, Adam and Eve can remake the world.[163] Human creativity still matters after all, as the poem itself attests. By drawing out the fall and elaborating it through Ovid's figures, Milton suggests that, as Eve's revision of Narcissus had shown, the chain might have been broken: something else might have happened that led to a different story. The poem challenges us to imagine a world different from our own, one in which narcissism is not evil, and in which men and women are actually happy together.

---

[163] See also Green, who emphasizes however the way in which Adam and Eve are therefore given a role in their own salvation (*Milton's Ovidian Eve*, 202).

4

Self-Consuming Artists

THE ARGUMENT

In this chapter, I turn to the representation of Ovidian artists in Paradise Lost. Ovidian doubles enable Milton to explore the nature of evil and its relation to the making of the poem. Satan, Sin, and figures such as the doomed Phaethon and Bellerophon are mirror images of the poet, who show how the fall has made human creativity self-destructive. For Milton, moreover, evil is a version of creative imitation which has degenerated into sterile copying fuelled by the traditional enemy and evil twin of all creativity: envy. The poem shows the narrator's struggle to detach himself from these doubles and from his own desire to destroy.

MILTON NARCISSUS

While the story of Narcissus underlies the plot of *Paradise Lost*, it also has a particular resonance for an author whose strong ego and narcissistic propensities have often been noted. Contrasting Shakespeare and Milton as fundamentally different kinds of poets, Coleridge explained that:

> Milton is the deity of prescience; he stands *ab extra*, and drives a fiery chariot and four, making the horses feel the iron curb which holds them in. Shakspeare's poetry is characterless; that is, he does not reflect the individual Shakspeare [sic]; but John Milton himself is in every line of the Paradise Lost.... In the Paradise Lost—indeed in every one of his poems—it is Milton himself whom you see; his Satan, his Adam, his

Raphael, almost his Eve—are all John Milton; and it is a sense of this intense egotism that gives me the greatest pleasure in reading Milton's works. The egotism of such a man is a revelation of spirit.[1]

Like God, Milton makes his creations in his own image. The poem justifies Milton's self-duplication as his own reproduction of God's creative narcissism. Still, not all readers have been as thrilled as Coleridge by Milton's 'intense egotism'. It is hard not to suspect Milton of making God in his own image, grandiosely expanding his own sublime ego into a universal principle of creativity.

Most readers have been especially struck by the likeness between Milton and his character Satan. There are, however, different ways of understanding this likeness between the author of the poem and the 'Author of evil' (6. 262). The Romantics assumed that the similarities exposed Milton's subconscious identification with his devil, showing that he was, as Blake famously said, 'a true poet and of the Devil's Party without knowing it'.[2] Others have assumed, however, that far from revealing the author's darker desires, these resemblances are consciously crafted by Milton so that he may distinguish himself from Satan.[3] Through the devil, the author expresses, corrects, and purges his own potential for error. Satan's role in the poem is thus rather like that of the errant and pagan Ovid himself as described by DuRocher.

As I suggested in the Introduction, however, this kind of authorial doubling is itself Ovidian. It looks back to Ovid's construction of tragic artist figures—Daedalus, Philomela, Marsyas, Arachne—whose awful ends contrast with his own brilliant triumph in the *Metamorphoses*. The relation between author and double is complicated, however, by Ovid's exilic verse, which reveals that the author himself has become the last and best example of the self-destructing nature of creativity. In adapting Ovid's practice, Milton is conscious of Ovid's

---

[1] *Table Talk* (12 May 1830, 18 August 1833), qtd. in Wittreich (ed.), *The Romantics on Milton*, 270, 277. See also ibid. 194, 199, and 222–3. Stephen M. Fallon similarly notes that 'Milton's poems can seem like halls of mirrors, with aspects of the poet peering back from virtually every character' (*Milton's Peculiar Grace*, 3; see also his discussion 203–10). See also Joseph Wittreich, '"Reading" Milton: The Death (and Survival) of the Author', *Milton Studies*, 38 (2000), 10–46; Rumrich, *Milton Unbound*, 66–7, 81.

[2] 'The Marriage of Heaven and Hell', plate 6; qtd. in Wittreich, *The Romantics on Milton*, 35.

[3] See especially Riggs, *The Christian Poet in* Paradise Lost, 17. See also the survey of interpretations in Forsyth, *The Satanic Epic*, 114–23. In Forsyth's own diabolically persuasive reading, the similarity between the forces of good and evil reveals the scandal of Christianity: good needs evil, as 'the Devil keeps God good' (ibid. 17).

own fate, which haunts both Satan and his narrator. Since the fall, the desire to create is never completely free from the impulse to destroy. With the severing of the original chain of generative narcissism, the relation between source and copy, like that between Adam and Eve, includes strife and friction. Like Adam and Eve, the poet must strive to recover God's original creativity by turning destructive energies into creative ones, alienation into new forms of relation. As we will see, Milton's representations of falling and fallen artists allow him to reflect on his own aspiration to 'soar | Above th' *Aonian* Mount' (*PL*, 1. 14–15), and to surpass and correct past authors. Moreover, through the figures of Satan and his creation, the Ovidian hybrid Sin, Milton acknowledges how his own emulation of his originals unleashes the mortal foe of all creativity, envy.

ENVY AND EMULATION

The resemblance between Milton and his diabolical double has often been noted especially in relation to pride, the sin with which Narcissus is also often associated. Satan's pride is clearly important both for the unfolding of Milton's story and for the poet's wrestling with his own nature.[4] But there is another aspect of Satan's character that is equally important for the aspiring poet. The opening of *Paradise Lost* draws attention to the fact that Satan was 'Stird up with Envy and Revenge' (1. 35), and throughout the poem Milton notes how Satan's desire for Godhead is spurred not only by pride but also by envy.[5] While most frequently pride is the deadliest of the deadly sins, envy is also particularly vicious as it is considered as the opposite of Christian charity and love.[6] For some theologians and writers, therefore, it and

---

[4] Fallon especially shows how 'The specter of Satanic pride, given substance by the convergence of Satan's story with Milton's' shadows Milton's self-representation in the invocations (*Milton's Peculiar Grace*, 206).

[5] The envy of Satan and the devils is foregrounded in *Paradise Lost* 1. 35; 2. 244; 3. 552–4; 4. Argument, 115, 502–4; 5. 662; 6. 89, 791–3, 813, 900; 7. 139; and 9. 175, 254, 264, 466.

[6] In *Purgatorio* 13, Envy is therefore scourged by examples of charity; for John Gower also 'Agein Envie is Charité' (*Confessio Amantis*, 2. 3173); see *Confessio Amantis*, ed. Russell A. Peck and trans. Andrew Galloway, 3 vols. (Kalamazoo, Mich., 2000), ii. 140. See also Anthony K. Cassell, 'The Letter of Envy: *Purgatorio* XIII–XIV', *Stanford*

not pride is the worst of all sins. In Wisdom 2: 23 infernal envy brings death into the world; St Cyprian therefore argues also that 'ENVY IS THE ROOT OF ALL WICKEDNESS' whose 'ORIGIN IS TO BE TRACED TO THE DEVIL'.[7] In *Paradise Lost*, the envy of Satan reveals an important aspect of the nature of the evil against which Milton battles in order to create the poem.

While the envy of Satan has usually been understood in the context of the Christian tradition of the vices, it also has an important part in Milton's representation of evil as the perversion of creativity. Envy is

---

Italian Review, 4/1 (1984), 7–8, esp. n. 7. This opposition between envy and Christian charity is reworked in humanist terms so that, as David Cast notes, 'envy, in the language of the humanists, is a failure of humanity, a distortion of what all human relations, at their finest, can be' (*The Calumny of Apelles: A Study in the Humanist Tradition* (New Haven, 1981), 6). Milton draws on this tradition in *De Doctrina Christiana*, where he treats envy as the opposite of love in the form of 'BENEVOLENTIA' ('good will', *Works*, xvii. 266). His prime examples are Satan and also Cain who was a proverbial figure for envy (see also *Purgatorio* 14.133). In *Paradise Lost*, the description of Cain's murder of Abel as 'th'unjust the just hath slain | For envie' (11. 455–6) reverses the formulation of Christ's sacrifice in 1 Peter 3: 18 in which 'Quia et Christus semel pro peccatis nostris mortuus est, iustus pro iniustus, et nos offerret Deo' ('For Christ also hath once suffered for sins, the just for the unjust, that he might bring us to God'). Milton draws on this verse in *Paradise Lost* 3 when, seeking volunteers to save mankind, the Father asks whether anyone will be 'just th'unjust to save' (3. 215). Cain's murderous envy of his brother in Book 11 parodies the Son's self-sacrificing love for his.

[7] St Cyprian, 'Treatise X: On Jealousy and Envy', trans. Ernest Wallis, in Alexander Roberts and James Donaldson (eds.), *Ante-Nicene Fathers*, 10 vols., v: *Hippolytus, Cyprian, Caius, Novatian, Appendix* (New York, 1919), 491–6; 491. Bacon calls envy 'the vilest affection, and the most depraved, for which cause it is the proper attribute of the devil' ('Of Envy', in *The Essays or Counsels, Civil and Moral*, ed. Brian Vickers (New York, 1999), 22). Aquinas sees Envy as a sin against the Holy Ghost (*Summa Theologica*, New Advent Online Encyclopedia, pt. 2. 2, q. 14 a. 2; see also pt. 2. 2, q. 36 a). Augustine also tentatively suggests that envy is the unpardonable sin: 'Maliciously and enviously to assail brotherly love after having received the grace of the Holy Spirit—perhaps this is the sin against the Holy Spirit, the sin which the Lord says will never be forgiven in this world or in the world to come' (*De Sermone Domini in Monte*, 1. 22. 75, qtd. in Cassell, 'The Letter of Envy: *Purgatorio* XIII–XIV', 7–8). This tradition is continued in Chaucer's Parson's Tale, in which the Parson, quoting Augustine that envy 'is "Sorwe of oother mennes wele, and joye of othere mennes harm"', claims that it goes against the 'bountee' of the Holy Spirit (*The Riverside Chaucer*, ed. Larry D. Benson (Boston, 1987), x. 485). While the Parson ranks envy below pride, he claims finally that 'Certes, thanne is Envye the worste synne that is. For soothly, alle othere synnes been somtyme oonly agayns o special vertu, | but certes Envye is agayns alle vertues and agayns alle goodnesses.' For him too, therefore, the antidote to envy is love: 'Certes, thanne is love the medicine that casteth out the venym of Envye fro mannes herte' (x. 488–9, 531); see Lynn S. Meskill, *Ben Jonson and Envy* (Cambridge, 2009), 48–9).

a central and ubiquitous topic in ancient poetry. From Pindar on, envy is represented as the antithesis and enemy of poetry: where poets produce and create, the envious consume and destroy.[8] Complaints about envy as the destroyer of true genius appear especially in times of aggressive poetical and political competition; they are therefore widespread in sixteenth-century England as well. Elizabethan writers depict themselves as constantly battling against the *invidia* rampant in a courtly world, as Spenser laments:

> Where each one seeks with malice and with strife,
> To thrust downe other into foule disgrace,
> Himselfe to raise: and he doth soonest rise
> That best can handle his deceitfull wit,
> In subtil shifts, and finest sleights deuise
> Either by slaundring his well deemed name
> Through leasings lewd, and fained forgerie:
> Or else by breeding him some blot of blame,
> By creeping close into his secrecie;
> To which him needs a guilefull hollow hart,
> Masked with faire dissembling curtesie,
> A filed toung furnisht with tearmes of art,
> No art of schoole, but Courtiers schoolery.
> ('Colin Clouts Come Home Againe', 690–702)[9]

As Lynn Meskill has recently pointed out, Elizabethan works frequently begin with exorcisms warding off the corrosive power of envy.[10] Moreover, as Spenser's outburst implies, the attack against the envy of others plays an important part in the poet's self-definition, by showing what the poet is *not*. Through depicting the *invidia* of others, the poet asserts his own moral authority as well as his creative

---

[8] Peter Walcot, *Envy and the Greeks: A Study of Human Behaviour* (Warminster, 1978); Patricia Bulman, *Phthonos in Pindar* (Berkeley and Los Angeles, 1992); and Glenn W. Most, 'Epinician Envies', in David Konstan and N. Keith Rutter (eds.), *Envy, Spite and Jealousy: The Rivalrous Emotions in Ancient Greece* (Edinburgh, 2003).

[9] See also Ronald Bond, 'Supplantation in the Elizabethan Court: The Theme of Spenser's February Eclogue', *Spenser Studies*, 2 (1981), 55–65; and '*Invidia* and the Allegory of Spenser's "Muiopotmos"', *English Studies in Canada*, 2 (1976), 144–55. Lindsay Kaplan has examined the context for the remarkable preoccupation with reputation and slander at this time (*The Culture of Slander in Early Modern England* (Cambridge, 2001), 12–33).

[10] *Ben Jonson and Envy*, 66–8. I have tried to repress my own envy of this recent fine study.

power.¹¹ In encomiastic poetry especially, the generous and creative praise of the poet is contrasted with the begrudging and destructive response of the invidious.¹² Ben Jonson begins his famous poem to Shakespeare by claiming freedom from envy, while in his other works he frequently draws attention to the envy of others.¹³ Envy is thus often projected especially onto the poet's perennial opponent, the infamously vicious critic who, unable to write himself, wrecks the work of others. This tradition begins with the figure of Momus and is still going strong in Swift's grotesque goddess Criticism.¹⁴

The relation between envy and creativity is, however, a complex one. To begin with, both are seen as originating in an aspiration for

---

[11] Most, 'Epinician Envies', 128–33; Dickie, 'Disavowal of *Invidia*'; Bulman, *Phthonos in Pindar*; Alison Keith, *The Play of Fictions: Studies in Ovid's Metamorphoses Book 2* (Ann Arbor, 1992), 127–31. The gendering of *Invidia* as female is also frequently drawn on to reinforce the difference between the male poet and his antithesis. See especially Ellen Oliensis's important reading of Horace's denunciation of the witch Canidia, 'Canidia, Canicula, and the Decorum of Horace's Epodes', *Arethusa*, 24 (1991), 107–38. As Oliensis shows, Canidia is specifically associated with the envy from which Horace always distances himself.

[12] This opposition is reworked in Melanie Klein's psychoanalytic theory in which envy is a response to the creativity of others and the opposite of gratitude; see 'A Study of Envy and Gratitude', in Juliet Mitchell (ed.), *The Selected Melanie Klein* (London, 1986), 211–29.

[13] See Meskill, *Ben Jonson and Envy*, who focuses especially on Jonson's constant representation of readers as malicious consumers from whom he must protect his works.

[14] Jonson's *Poetaster* opens with the figure of Envy, who suggests (among other things) the invidious critic; see Ian Donaldson, 'Looking Sideways: Jonson, Shakespeare and the Myths of Envy', in Takashi Kozuka and J. R. Mulryne (eds.), *Shakespeare, Marlowe, Jonson: New Directions in Biography* (Aldershot, 2006), 242 especially. The association of the critic with envy also runs through the satires of Marston. In his *Mythologiae*, Natale Conti uses Momus, the embodiment of 'criticism by fault-finders and envious people', as a foil for his own kind of criticism; he protests that 'a true sign of a wise and honourable man is that he has the kind of generous spirit that rejects the slanders of stupid, really contemptible fault-finders' (*Mythologiae*, trans. John Mulryan and Steven Brown, 2 vols. (Tempe, Ariz., 2006), 883). Swift's Goddess of the *Battel of the Books* is clearly the unholy spawn of Ovid's *Invidia*, Spenser's Envy, and Milton's Sin. She has: 'Eyes turned inward, as if she lookt only upon herself: Her Diet was the overflowing of her own *Gall*: Her *Spleen* was so large, as to stand prominent like a Dug of the first Rate, nor wanted Excrescences in forms of Teats, at which a Crew of ugly Monsters were greedily sucking; and, what is wonderful to conceive, the bulk of the Spleen encreased faster than the Sucking could diminish it' ('The Battel of the Books', in *The Writings of Jonathan Swift*, ed. Robert A. Greenberg and William B. Piper (New York, 1973), 386–7). On the legacy of envy in 19th-century ideas of critical *ressentiment*, see Lucy Newlyn, *Reading, Writing, and Romanticism: The Anxiety of Reception* (Oxford, 2000), 215–23.

greatness that is triggered by the example of others. The tradition begins with Hesiod, who notes that there are two kinds of strife, one positive, the other negative: 'One of these a man would praise once he got to know it, but the other is blameworthy; and they have thoroughly opposed spirits. For the one fosters evil war and conflict... But the other one... is much better for men. It rouses even the helpless man to work... and this Strife is good for mortals.'[15] Hesiod's opposing forms of strife are developed further in Aristotle's distinction between emulation (*zelos*) and envy (*phthonos*). Both are forms of competition, triggered by the success of another, particularly an equal: 'So too we compete with those who follow the same ends as ourselves: we compete with our rivals in sports or in love, and generally with those who are after the same things; and it is therefore these whom we are bound to envy beyond all others. Hence the saying, "Potter against potter".'[16] Aristotle's *zelos* and *phthonos* have very different aims: 'Emulation makes us take steps to secure the good things in question, envy makes us take steps to stop our neighbour having them.'[17] Christian discussions of envy draw also on this distinction. According to St John Chrysostom, 'wholesome rivalry, imitation without contention' binds us to each other and to God (1 Cor 12: 26, sect. 7).[18] Its opposite is envy, 'the root of all evils', which tears apart the unity of the body of Christ by dividing humans from each other.

Emulation is thus a form of competition or strife that makes us creative. Longinus cites Hesiod to explain how Plato's genius was fired by his rivalry with Homer. Plato's writing would have been less

---

[15] 'Works and Days', in *Hesiod*, ed. Glenn W. Most, 2 vols., i: *Theogony, Works and Days, Testimonia* (Cambridge, Mass., 2006), 87–9. As Glenn Most notes, this latter kind is 'a positive economic principle which stimulates men to emulation, rivalry, and ultimately the production and accumulation of wealth' ('Epinician Envies', 130). See also Wolfe, 'Spenser, Homer, and the Mythography of Strife', 1220–88, who notes the ambiguity of strife in Renaissance literature; as she shows, in Spenser it is primarily negative characters such as Despair and Phaedria who want to eliminate strife completely.

[16] *Rhetoric*, 2. 10, in *The Complete Works of Aristotle*, ed. Barnes, ii. 2211–12. Aristotle is citing Hesiod, who notes how 'potter is angry with potter, and builder with builder, and beggar begrudges beggar, and poet poet' (*Works and Days*, 89). Hesiod's saying was repeated frequently by English Renaissance writers; see Meskill, *Ben Jonson and Envy*, 43.

[17] *Rhetoric*, 2. 11, in *Complete Aristotle*, ii. 2212. The distinction is less clear in other writers, notably Hesiod.

[18] St John Chrysostom, 'Homily 31 on First Corinthians', New Advent Online Encyclopedia.

perfect 'had he not striven, with heart and soul, to contest the prize with Homer like a young antagonist with one who had already won his spurs, perhaps in too keen emulation, longing as it were to break a spear and yet always to good purpose. For, as Hesiod says, "Good is this strife for mankind".'[19] Here rivalry produces a creative friction that empowers later authors to become great creators themselves. In contrast, envy is passive, sterile, and consuming.[20] It is associated with inertia and melancholy; Robert Burton will see it is as a particular danger for scholars (*caveat lector*).[21] Its consuming nature is indicated through imagery of biting snakes and barking dogs (recalled in Spenser's Blatant Beast as well as Milton's Sin); it is frequently also described as gnawing, tearing, wounding, and sometimes bursting inside those who experience it.[22] St Basil thus says that '*phthonos* consuming the soul in its agony is like the vipers who come into the light of day by gnawing through the belly of their mother'[23]—an image of perversely destructive production that also anticipates Sin. While envy begins in strife and the desire to hurt someone else, it ultimately turns back on itself. So Spenser's Envy:

> feedes on her owne maw vnnaturall,
> And of her owne foule entrayles makes her meat;
> Meat fit for such a monsters monsterous dyeat. (*FQ*, 5. 12. 31. 7–9)

---

[19] Longinus, 'On the Sublime', 169.

[20] As Matthew Dickie, who has written more essays on the topic than seems healthy for any critic, suggests, '*Invidi* are not spurred to action by the sight of another's success. They are marked by torpor and inertia. They do not then try to emulate those for whom they feel *invidia*. *Invidia* gives rise to basically destructive impulses and not to emulation' ('The Disavowal of *Invidia* in Roman Iamb and Satire', *Papers of the Liverpool Latin Seminar*, 3, ed. Francis Cairns (1981), 202).

[21] Aristotle is again the origins of the connection between envy, sloth, black bile, and melancholy; see *Rhetoric*, 2. 10; and *Problems*, 30. 1, in *Complete Aristotle*, ii, 2211, 1498.

[22] See Martial's classic, 'Rumpitur Invidia', in *Epigrammata*, ed. D. R. Shackleton Bailey (Stutgardiae, 1990), 9. 97. See also Katherine M. D. Dunbabin and M. W. Dickie, 'Invidia Rumpantur Pectora: The Iconography of Phthonos/Invidia in Graeco-Roman Art', *Jahrbuch für Antike und Christentum*, 26 (1983), 7–37.

[23] 'Homily 11', qtd. in Dunbabin and Dickie, 'Invidia Rumpantur Pectora', 15. A similar image is used in Ben Jonson's *Poetaster* 5. 3. 319–21, when Horace turns on his detractor Demetrius: 'Now thou curl'st up, thou poor and nasty snake, | And shrink'st thy pois'nous head into thy bosom. | Out viper, thou that eat'st thy parents, hence'; see Ben Jonson, *Poetaster*, ed. Tom Cain (Manchester, 1995). All further references will be from this edition. I'll return to Jonson's play, which tells the story of Ovid's exile through the theme of envy, later in this chapter.

She is said to 'murder her owne mynd' (5. 12. 33. 5); according to Burton, the envious man will *'eat his owne heart'*.[24] Where emulation inspires men to great achievements, envy drives them to suicide.

As the opposite of creativity, envy is also conventionally dissociated from divinity. In the *Timaeus*, Plato claims that the creator god lacked envy because 'He was good, and the good can never have any jealousy of anything. And being free from jealousy, he desired that all things should be as like himself as they should be.'[25] Classical poets therefore prayed to gods for protection from their evil critics. As rulers were often considered divine, they were also seen as being above envy; the praise of a ruler's godlike generosity towards the creativity of others became a standard, and very convenient, part of a bid for patronage.[26] However, despite Plato's assertion, even Greek gods are often represented as showing *phthonos*.[27] When Milton's Satan tempts Eve to question God's prohibition he revives an old anxiety about divine motives: 'is it envie, and can envie dwell | In Heav'nly brests?' (*PL*, 9. 729–30). It is commonly argued, however, that when *phthonos* refers to gods it has a different meaning from when it is applied to humans.[28] This semantic difference itself suggests a fundamental disjunction between the human and the divine realms. Divine and human types of *phthonos* are related only through opposition: in Pindar especially, the *phthonos* of the gods is a principle of justice that asserts itself when humans, driven by destructive *phthonos*, try to rise above their allotted places.

Yet this distinction between divine and human *phthonos* is not always as clear-cut as it seems. Satan's question reworks the narrator's famous question in *Aeneid* 1. 11, 'tantaene animis caelestibus irae?'

---

[24] Burton, 'Aemulation, Hatred, Faction, Desire of Revenge Causes', in *Anatomy of Melancholy*, ed. Thomas C. Faulkner, 6 vols. (Oxford, 1989), i. 265–8; 266. Burton effusively praises 'Honest emulation' as *'ingeniorum cos,* as one calls it, the whetstone of wit, the nurse of wit and valour', citing in a footnote '*Aemulatio alit ingenia*' and observing further 'tis a sluggish humour not to emulate or sue at all, to withdrawe himselfe' (ibid. 267).

[25] See Plato, *Timaeus*, in *The Collected Dialogues of Plato*, ed. Hamilton and Cairns, 1151–211; 29e–30a. See also Edward B. Stevens, 'Envy and Pity in Greek Philosophy', *American Journal of Philology*, 2 (1948), 171–89.

[26] See further Matthew W. Dickie, '*Invidia Infelix*: Vergil, *Georgics* 3. 37–9', *Illinois Classical Studies*, 8 (1983), 65–79, esp. 74–9. Ronald Bond notes the use of the topos in relation to Elizabeth I ('Supplantation', 60); see also Meskill, *Ben Jonson and Envy*, 59–60.

[27] On the envious nature of Greek gods, see Most, 'Epinician Envies'.

[28] See especially Bulman, *Phthonos in Pindar*, 9, 31.

('Can resentment so fierce dwell in heavenly breasts?'), in which Virgil refers to the wrath of Juno. Satan's substitution is important in what it reveals of Satan's character and his preoccupation with divine envy especially, to which I will return later. But it also is a perceptive comment on the character of Virgil's Juno, implying that her anger is itself driven by envy. In the *Fasti*, Ovid will refer to her as 'Saturnia... invidiosa' ('Saturn's envious daughter', *Fasti*, 1. 265–6). In Ovid, moreover, all of the gods seem meanly invidious of human aspiration and creativity.[29]

A similar confusion is apparent in the relation between envy and emulation as the terms evolve in the Roman and then Renaissance traditions, and become part of discussions of imitation generally. The Latin *aemulor* includes both positive and negative forms of competition, as Thomas Cooper's definition suggests: 'With a certayne enuy and ambition to indeuour to passe & excell an other man: to folowe, or study to be like an other: to imitate or counterfaite.'[30] The term emulation is thus often used negatively. In his *De Compendiosa Doctrina*, Nonius differentiates imitation from emulation, equating the *latter* with envy: 'imitatio simplex est et livorem atque invidiam non admittit; aemulatio autem habet quidem imitandi studium, sed cum malitiae operatione' ('*imitatio* is sincere and admits neither spite nor envy; *aemulatio*, however, includes the desire to imitate, but with malice at work').[31] The distinction is repeated verbatim in the fifteenth century by Antonio da Rho, in his *De Imitationibus*

---

[29] Robert A. Kaster notes how the *invidia* of the Roman gods in general is completely different from Greek divine *phthonos*; Robert A. Kaster, '*Invidia* is One Thing, *Invidia* Quite Another', in *Emotion, Restraint, and Community in Ancient Rome* (Oxford, 2005), 84–103.

[30] *Thesaurus Linguae Romanae et Britanniae* (1565), qtd. in Bond, '*Invidia* and the Allegory of Spenser's "Muiopotmos"', 147. As Kaster suggests, part of the problem of definition may begin with the translation of Greek concepts into Latin. In Greek, *phthonos* is contrasted not only with *zelos* but also with *nemesis*, which is something like righteous indignation. In Latin, *nemesis* and *phthonos* are both expressed as *invidia*; see Kaster, '*Invidia* is One Thing'. The line between just resentment and sheer spite, noble and base forms of *invidia*, is blurred early on.

[31] Nonius Marcellus, *De Compendiosa Doctrina*, V. 437 M., ed. W. M. Lindsay, 3 vols. (Hildesheim, 1964), iii. 703; see also Pigman, 'Versions of Imitation in the Renaissance', 24. As an example of destructive *aemulatio*, Nonius cites Book 6 of the *Aeneid*, which tells of the death of Miseunus who challenged the gods with his music; in response 'aemulus exceptum Triton, si credere dignum est, | inter saxa virum spumosa inmerserat unda' ('jealous Triton—if the tale can win belief—caught and plunged him in the foaming waves amid the rocks', 6. 173–4). For Nonius, Virgil's gods express something very much like human envy.

Eloquentie.[32] In *The Purple Island*, Phineas Fletcher makes *Zelos* the offspring of *Eris* (Strife) and the embodiment of 'spitefull emulation' that '[c]ould not endure a fellow in excelling'.[33] G. W. Pigman III thus argues that Renaissance emulation, which he also refers to as 'eristic' imitation, is an irresolvably ambivalent mix of 'admiration for a model joined with envy and contentiousness'.[34] He notes that even in Hesiod 'the good, creative *eris* is not so benign as appeared at first'.[35] Longinus' wrestling match and its later derivations excuse 'violence and envy as necessary for the formation of "brilliant minds"' which thrive on the strenuous exercise of power.[36]

The slippery relation between the terms envy, emulation, and imitation suggests how hard it is to exclude envy from artistic imitation, with its inevitable mixing of identification and rivalry.[37] In other ways, envy is like creativity in general. Envy is associated with vision; *invidia* comes from *videre*, to see, and so envy is connected to the concept of the evil eye, and is often represented as looking aslant at another's good.[38] In Dante's *Purgatorio*, the envious have their eyes

---

[32] See Martin L. McLaughlin, *Literary Imitation in the Italian Renaissance: The Theory and Practice of Imitation from Dante to Bembo* (Oxford, 1995), 109.

[33] *The Purple Island, or The Isle of Man*, in *The Poetical Works of Giles Fletcher and Phineas Fletcher*, ed. Frederick S. Boas, 2 vols. (Cambridge, 1909; repr. 1968), ii. 7. 53. 1–2. See also Wolfe, 'Spenser, Homer, and the Mythography of Strife', 1226.

[34] 'Versions of Imitation', 4. For the proximity of envy and emulation generally, see also R. B. Gill, 'The Renaissance Conventions of Envy', *Medievalia et Humanistica*, 9 (1979), 215–30, esp. 221–4; and Meskill, *Ben Jonson and Envy*, 43, 62–5. On the negative aspects of emulation see also Vernon Guy Dickson, '"A pattern, precedent, and lively warrant": Emulation, Rhetoric, and Cruel Propriety in *Titus Andronicus*', *Renaissance Quarterly*, 62/2 (2009), 378. For a critique of the central role of emulation in Elizabethan culture, see Kahn, *Roman Shakespeare*, 15–17, 92–3.

[35] Pigman, 'Versions of Imitation', 16. As Pigman also wryly notes, writings on imitation tend themselves to be rather competitive, and 'often exhaust themselves in vindictive and ferocious *ad hominem* polemics' (ibid. 1).

[36] Ibid. 18, 24. Pigman suggests that 'this dark side plays an important role in preventing *aemulatio* from becoming a technical term for a particular type of imitation' (ibid. 18). Greene uses it, however, to describe the most sophisticated and ambivalent forms of Renaissance imitation; see *The Light in Troy*, 43–6. DuRocher takes it to describe Milton's relation to Ovid (*Milton and Ovid*, 36–7).

[37] For René Girard, envy is the name Shakespeare gives to what Girard calls 'mimetic desire'. Girard argues that at its most extreme, mimetic desire becomes the desire for evil (*A Theater of Envy: William Shakespeare* (New York, 1991), 296), a claim I think both Ovid and Milton would have understood.

[38] Whitney's emblem, *Inuidiae descriptio*, explains this: 'What meanes her eies? so bleared, sore, and redd: | Her mourninge still, to see an others gaine.' See Geffrey Whitney, *A Choice of Emblems*, ed. Henry Green (New York, 1967), 94. See also Ronald Bond, 'Vying with Vision: An Aspect of Envy in *The Faerie Queene*',

sewn shut so that they can learn to see again in a more charitable fashion. The envious are morally blind.[39] The link between envy and vision shows its proximity to love, associated, especially in the Platonic tradition, with the eyes.[40] However, envy is a sin that also makes us see things that are not in fact there;[41] it is thus similar to the power of the imagination.[42] Moreover, appropriately for writers, it is not just a visual but also a verbal sin. Spenser's Envy attacks the poet's wit using his own power, words, against him:

> And eke the verse of famous Poets witt
> He does backebite, and spightfull poison spues
> From leprous mouth on all, that euer writt. (FQ, 1. 4. 32. 6–8)

Envy leads to the perversion of poetic language into Sclaunder, whose speech Spenser describes:

> Her words were not, as common words are ment,
> T'expresse the meaning of the inward mind,
> But noysome breath, and poysnous spirit sent
> From inward parts, with cancred malice lind,
> And breathed forth with blast of bitter wind;
> Which passing through the eares, would pierce the hart,
> And wound the soule it selfe with griefe vnkind;
> For like the stings of Aspes, that kill with smart,
> Her spightfull words did pricke, and wound the inner part. (4. 8. 26. 1–9)

Renaissance and Reformation, 8/1 (1984), 30–8, esp. 31–2; and Meskill, *Ben Jonson and Envy*, 29–35, 44–5, and 55–8.

[39] Pietro di Dante's commentary on *Purgatorio* 13 explains the punishment through the etymology: 'Invidia facit, quod non videatur, quod expedit videre; ed ideo dicitur *invidia*, quasi *non visio*' ('Envy causes that which should be seen not to be seen. And therefore it is called *invidia*, almost as if to say, nonvision', *Inferno*, ii. 213).

[40] Bacon also notes this similarity between love and envy: 'There be none of the affections which have been noted to fascinate or bewitch, but love and envy. They both have vehement wishes; they frame themselves readily into imaginations and suggestions; and they come easily into the eye, especially upon the presence of the objects' ('Of Envy', in *The Essays*, 18). The essay after 'Of Envy' is thus, appropriately, 'Of Love'.

[41] See for example Lucretius, *De Rerum Natura*, ed. Martin Ferguson, trans. W. H. D. Rouse (2nd edn., Cambridge, Mass., 1992), 3. 74–7: 'Consimili ratione ab eodem saepe timore | macerat invidia ante oculos illum esse potentem | illum aspectari, claro qui incedit honore, | ipse se in tenebris volvi caenoque queruntur' ('In like manner and through the same fear, they are often consumed with envy that before their very eyes he is clothed in power, he is the sight of the town, who parades in shining pomp, while they complain that they themselves are wallowing in darkness and in mire').

[42] See also Hardie, *Ovid's Poetics of Illusion*, 198–9.

Sclaunder is the power of language gone wrong, just as Envy is creative energy that has become destructive.[43]

Moreover, while envy is the traditional enemy and antithesis of true poetic genius, it is also frequently noted to be a property of genius. Poets who attack the envy of others can sound suspiciously bitter and invidious themselves.[44] John Skelton's poem 'Against Venomous Tongues' seems inspired by a remarkable outburst of venom. Rabelais is often described as the epitome of good-hearted generosity. But as he denounces critics as vicious dogs in the Prologue to the *Tiers Livre*, he himself begins to bark and growl, like one of Ovid's transforming figures who lose their voice when they take new animal forms. Even Spenser is, as Richard A. McCabe observes, sensitive to his own possible 'complicity with detraction'.[45] In the famous rivalry between Jonson and Marston both poets declare themselves the innocent victims of envy and with splenetic rage denounce their opponent as motivated only by malice.[46] Jonson in particular has been frequently described as spiteful, especially towards the creative genius of Shakespeare. While this characterization of Jonson was

---

[43] See also Anne Lake Prescott, 'Sclaunder', in Hamilton (ed.), *The Spenser Encyclopedia*, 632–3; and Bond, 'The Blatant Beast', ibid. 96–8, and 'Envy', ibid. 248–9.

[44] Oliensis shows also how Horace's attacks on Canidia reveal the likeness between the opposites: 'The excoriated "other" also tends to bear an uncanny resemblance to Horace himself'; her presence reveals 'the monstrous and discordant elements within the Horatian corpus' ('Canidia, Canicula', 118, 135). See also Alessandro Barchiesi, 'Ultime difficoltà nella carriera di un poeta giambico: L'Epode XVII', in *Atti Convegno Oraziano, Nov. 1993* (Venosa, 1994), 205–20. Lucy Newlyn observes that 'When a writing subject constructs the other as envious, this produces in the writing subject itself a form of envious doubling, or mimicry', *Reading, Writing, and Romanticism*, 215.

[45] *The Pillars of Eternity*, 78. Jennifer Vaught discusses Spenser's Errour also as an image of the invidious nature of *imitatio* in 'Spenser's Dialogic Voice in Book I of *The Faerie Queene*', *Studies in English Literature 1500–1800*, 41 (2001), 71–89. Errour demonstrates that 'the ingestion and creative regurgitation of the words of others are often aggressive' (ibid. 72). See also Philip Hardie, 'Fame and Blame, Fame and Envy: Spenserian Personifications of the Word', in *Rumour and Renown*; Stapleton, *Spenser's Ovidian Poetics*, 24.

[46] As we'll see shortly, Jonson's attack on Marston is particularly prominent in the *Poetaster*. Marston attacks envy throughout his satires; see especially 'To Detraction I present my Poesy', in *The Works*, ed. Bullen, iii. 299–300. There are many other examples of invidious sounding denouncers of *invidia* among the satirists of the 1590s. The end of Weever's satiric *Faunus and Melliflora* is an attack on satire, which he claims has destroyed true poetry; while he ends insisting that he himself 'was borne to hate your censuring vaine, | Your enuions [sic] biting in your crabbed straine' (1085–6), he sounds equally crabby. Citations from Weever's poem are taken from *Faunus and Melliflora*, ed. Davenport.

partly fuelled by the idealization of Shakespeare, Lynn Meskill has recently shown that the idea of envy seems a necessary precondition for Jonsonian creativity.[47] The victims of envy are not always completely innocent, as seeing through twisted eyes, the invidious project their own vice upon others.[48]

OVIDIAN *INVIDIA*

For later artists, moreover, Ovid's work and life were particularly bound up with envy. Ovid's generative legacy might suggest that his own poetics is both derived from and encourages emulation rather than envy; he praises other poets and claims to be free from *invidia*.[49] But as Alison Keith notes, 'Ovid...seems to have been intrigued by the programmatic potential of Envy as a literary construct from the outset of his career' and 'is concerned to articulate a specifically literary challenge to Envy'.[50] The theme of envy is inseparable from his thinking about poetry. The relation, however, appears as primarily one of opposition, as he makes envy the antithesis and enemy of his art. In the *Remedia Amoris*, he complains that 'Ingenium magni livor detractat Homeri' ('Envy disparages great Homer's genius', 365), because 'Summa petit livor' ('What is highest is Envy's

---

[47] Meskill, *Ben Jonson and Envy*, esp. 1–41, 72.

[48] Meskill argues that this kind of projection is especially key to Jonson; she cites Freud's comment in 'The Uncanny': 'Whoever possesses something at once valuable and fragile is afraid of the envy of others, in that he projects onto them the envy he would have felt in their place' (*Ben Jonson and Envy*, 7 n. 23). Meskill thus suggests that Jonson's image of the envious reader 'may very well reflect the way Jonson read or misread those writers who preceded him' (ibid. 5); see also ibid. 99.

[49] Ovid pays explicit tributes to other writers in *Amores* 1. 15, 3. 9, and *Tristia* 4. 10. 41–54. His encouragement of his stepdaughter and protégée Perilla is especially remarkable. From exile, he continued to urge her to write despite the example of his fate (which he assures her she will not emulate); see *Tristia* 3. 7. The pseudo-Ovidian *Nux* draws on this representation of Ovid as a poet free from *invidia*; it points out that the suffering poet/tree might be justified in being bitter and envious but denies that he is (33). John Gower's 1640 edition of the *Fasti* insists that Ovid was admiring of and admired by all; he adapts *Tristia* 4. 10. 55: 'As I my Elders, so my Juniours me | Ador'd'; 'I others honour'd: other honoured | Me with the best; and through the world I'm read'; *Ovids Festivalls, or Romane Calendar*, B3^v, B4^v.

[50] Keith, *The Play of Fictions*, 129.

mark', 369).[51] Envy is not always so discriminating in its target, however: even the poor harmless parrot whose death is lamented in *Amores* 2. 6. 25 was destroyed by envy ('Raptus... invidia'). Like other writers, Ovid uses his own poetry to fight this pernicious monster. In *Amores* 1. 15. 1, the poet strikes back at 'Livor edax' ('biting Envy'), claiming that despite its gnawing tooth he will live on in his poetry. So in the *Remedia* he defiantly proclaims his victory: 'Rumpere, Livor edax: magnum iam nomen habemus; | Maius erit, tantum quo pede coepit eat' ('Burst thyself, greedy Envy! my fame is great already; it will be greater still, so it keeps its first good fortune', 389–90).[52]

The poet's relation to the convention becomes more complex, however, in the *Metamorphoses*, in which envy takes a new and more palpable form. In Book 2, *Invidia* is the first of the poem's four allegorical figures.[53] In many ways, Ovid's figure seems quite conventional, even predictable, especially when read backwards through later writers who drew on Ovid's vivid scene. Envy is found munching on snakes in a chilly black fogbound cave; she moves sluggishly and groans at the splendour of Minerva, who has come to summon her (2. 773–4). She is pale, squinty-eyed, with rotten teeth; venom flows from her tongue and gall from her breast, 'carpitque et carpitur una | suppliciumque suum est' ('And she gnaws and is gnawed, herself her own punishment', 2. 781–2). When she leaves her cave she tramples down the flowers in her path ('florentia proterit', 2. 791), demonstrating her devastating effect on creativity.

In Ovid, however, the absorption of this traditional figure into the pattern of self-destructive artist figures that runs through all his works enables him to expose the disturbing likeness between envy and creativity. Appearing near the end of Book 2, the story of Envy is part of the early series of creation tales that includes the making (and remaking) of the world and the story of Daphne. Ovid draws a parallel between *Invidia*'s possession of her victim and artistic

---

[51] On the convention that *invidia* 'like lightening, strikes the "peaks"', see Kaster, *Emotion, Restrain and Community*, 88, and 183 n. 15.
[52] See also *Amores*, 1. 15. 39–42.
[53] On the representation of Envy and the theme as a whole in *Metamorphoses* 2, see Keith, *The Play of Fictions*, 124–32. On Ovid's personifications generally see Tissol, *The Face of Nature*, 61–72; D. C. Feeney, *The Gods in Epic: Poets and Critics of the Classical Tradition* (Oxford, 1991), 242–7; and Hardie, *Ovid's Poetics of Illusion*, 231–8.

creation: she inspires ('inspirat', 2. 800) Aglauros, filling the girl's imagination with images. Consumed with envy, Aglauros wastes away until she becomes merely a 'signum' (2. 831): the sign or representation of envy and also, as the Loeb translation puts it, a 'statue'. Like Satan's possession of the snake in *Paradise Lost* 9. 187–90, the scene is a parodic version of inspiration. But the parody also hints that envy itself paradoxically inspires Ovid's art. The link between envy and creativity generally is made further in *Metamorphoses* 8, in which Ovid explains that the archetypal artist, Daedalus, murdered his rival out of envy: he envied ('invidit', 8. 250) his talented nephew Perdix, and to avoid being surpassed by him, 'sacraque ex arce Minervae | praecipitem misit' ('thrust him down headlong from the sacred citadel of Minerva', 8. 250–1).[54]

As Alison Keith notes, moreover, Ovid's representation of *Invidia* in *Metamorphoses* 2 is an imitation of Virgil's *Fama*, who appears in *Aeneid* 4.[55] The rewriting draws attention to the relation between *Invidia* and *Fama*, who appears explicitly in *Metamorphoses* 12. 39–66, as the last of Ovid's four allegorical figures. In Virgil, *Fama* is a double of the poet who seeks fame for himself, and whose job is to spread stories. As Philip Hardie shows, however, *Fama* is a complex figure whose meaning includes rumour as well as both good and bad fame.[56] In *Aeneid* 4, *Fama*, who reports Dido's love for

---

[54] As an artist, Daedalus seems generally to prevent his succession by a new generation. His inventions are deadly for both the young men who are trapped in his labyrinth and even his own son Icarus. On the story of Perdix, see Tissol, *The Face of Nature*, 97–105; I will return to Icarus and other figures for broken succession further below, see pp. 264–72; 309–10; 321–4.

[55] Keith, *The Play of Fictions*, 131. Jonson certainly recognized the connection between these two figures, which he positions symmetrically at the beginning and end of the *Poetaster*. The play opens with a mock exorcism of the figure of Envy, who appears brandishing vipers in the hope of working the audience up against the play. While this cartoon figure is easily defeated by the entrance of the Prologue, in the play proper the forces of envy continue to threaten poetry, and eventually destroy Ovid. At the very moment Virgil reads to Augustus his description of *Fama* as a 'monster', 'covetous . . . of tales and lies' (*Poetaster*, 5. 2. 84, 96), Lupus and Tucca, who incarnate *Invidia*, enter the scene. In a highly Ovidian move, Virgilian *Fama* brought to life turns into Ovidian *Invidia*.

[56] Hardie has followed this topic through a group of studies, most notably: *Virgil's Aeneid: Cosmos and Imperium* (Oxford, 1986), 273–80; '"Why is Rumour Here?" Tracking Virgilian and Ovidian Fama', *Ordia Prima*, 1 (2002), 67–80; *Lucretian Receptions: History, the Sublime, Knowledge* (Cambridge, 2009), 67–135; and especially *Rumour and Renown*.

Aeneas, is like Virgil himself who was the first to link the two characters. The doubling between the poet and this multi-tongued monster suggests the underside of Virgil's epic enterprise: in order to praise Rome and Augustus, he defames Dido's character. *Fama* is, as Hardie notes, the 'demonic double of the epic poet' who reveals that the poet's good fame is built on the bad fame of another.[57]

By doubling Virgil's double figure, Ovid characteristically foregrounds his own technique here in order to add further to this exploration of the darker, even predatory, dimension of poetic creativity. The appearance of *Invidia* at a moment in which Ovid is revising Virgil hints that even Ovid's creative imitation may have its own inherently spiteful side. In retrospect, Envy's avian target in *Amores* 2. 6 takes on an added significance. The parrot, as Ovid reminds us, is an 'imitatrix' (2. 6. 1), a mimic or imitator; the poet shows the perils of imitation in a poem that is an imitation of Catullus 3.[58] The imitative artist in particular seems to attract *Invidia*, not only as its victim but also as its embodiment.

Ovid's relation to envy becomes even more complex, moreover, in the exilic poetry, in which his nemesis is transformed once again. The allegorical figure now appears to take on a life of its own to destroy its creator. In *Tristia* 3. 11 Ovid begins to write poems to a nameless but powerful detractor who, he complains, persecutes him ruthlessly even in his misfortune. In *Tristia* 4, Ovid claims to be still victorious in his fight against this evil: 'nec, qui detractat praesentia, Livor iniquo | ullum de nostris dente momordit opus' ('Nor has Envy, that detractor of the present, attacked with malignant tooth any work of mine', 4. 10. 123–4). The triumphant conclusion of the *Metamorphoses*, with the poet's assurance of immortality in verse, returns occasionally.[59] But the self-confident tone becomes fainter as time progresses, and the exilic verse, and Ovid's career, ends on a bleaker note. The last poem in the *Ex Ponto*, and thus in Ovid's works as a whole, opens with the poet's defence against his unrelenting enemy: 'Invide, quid laceras Nasonis carmina rapti?' ('Envious one, why do you wound the verse of ravished Naso?', 4. 16. 1). The poem builds towards the cry:

---

[57] *Rumour and Renown*, 391.
[58] Hinds, *Allusion and Intertext*, 5.
[59] See for example *Tristia* 3. 7. 50–2, and *Tristia* 4. 10. 119–28; in *Ex Ponto* 3. 4. 93–4, Ovid also echoes the claim to vatic status of *Fasti* 6. 5.

'ergo summotum patria proscindere, Livor,/desine' ('So, Envy, cease to tear one banished from his country', 4. 16. 47–8). In the battle between envy and creativity, envy now seems to be winning.

As I noted earlier, Ovid's last works have, as he intended, influenced his reception. Because of these poems, many later commentators have assumed that envy was the cause of his mysterious exile. Thomas Lodge suspected that the angry Augustus banished '*Ovid* for envy';[60] Margaret Cavendish added that the *princeps*' motive was the famous rivalry between Virgil and Ovid: '*Ovid's* Banishment was through *Caesar's* Partial Envy to him for *Virgil's* sake, and not for any Crime, for he Banished *Ovid*, fearing he might Out-shine *Virgil*, his Flattering Favourite, and Deifier, at least, Glorifier'.[61] Early commentators believed that Ovid had a poetic rival who spread lies about his poetry and/or morals. In some versions, Ovid was accused of adultery with Augustus' wife Livia.[62] In one, Ovid spurned her advances and she, enraged by rejection, accused him to her husband. This version combines Ovid's story with two others, one Judaeo-Christian, the other classical, which were frequently interlinked and read in terms of the dangers of envy: the tales of Joseph and Bellerophon. Their stories helped commentators who wanted to turn the erotic poet into a figure of chastity. (I'll return to the latter shortly.) In another particularly nutty account, Ovid's malicious rival was Virgil himself. A tale of erotic rivalry was superimposed onto the traditional poetic rivalry: when the besotted Ovid tried to climb into Livia's bedchamber, Virgil removed a rung from his ladder and revealed the plot![63]

---

[60] Quoted in Keach, *Elizabethan Erotic Narratives*, 33.

[61] 'Letter CXLVI', in *Sociable Letters* (London, 1664), Early English Books Online, Pp 4^r. Thanks to Katie Larson for pointing out this passage to me.

[62] See the accessus in Anthonio La Penna, *Scholia in P. Ovidi Nasonis Ibin* (Florence, 1959), 3–4; and Hexter, *Ovid and Medieval Schooling*, 221. The similarity between *Livor* and Livia is extremely tempting; see Peter Green's discussion in *The Poems of Exile: Tristia and the Black Sea Letters*, ed. and trans. Peter Green (Berkeley and Los Angeles, 2005), 272 and 341.

[63] This accessus is reprinted in Hexter, *Ovid and Medieval Schooling*, 221, and discussed (along with some of the other fun theories concerning Ovid's exile) in his 'Ovid's Body', in James I. Porter (ed.), *Constructions of the Classical Body* (Ann Arbor, 1999), 335–6. As Hexter notes, the story shows 'the ongoing opposition of Ovid and Virgil. Further, if one considers the instructional context of the accessus, there is a certain justice in making Virgil and Ovid rivals for Livia the way they must have been rivals for classroom attention' (ibid. 336).

Even in less fanciful treatments, however, Ovid's downfall was frequently attributed to envy. In Jonson's *Poetaster*, Ovid (here, as more commonly rumoured, the lover of Augustus' daughter Julia) becomes the hapless victim of envy, which appears first in the prologue in an allegorical form based on *Metamorphoses* 2. The play proper, moreover, begins with Ovid himself dangerously conjuring up envy, as he writes *Amores* 1. 15, in which the poet defies *Livor*.[64] Ovid's sense of his own omnipotence proves erroneous; in the play, as in the exilic verse itself, the fictional figure becomes real, returning in the characters of Lupus, Tucca, and Crispinus, who try to ruin the Augustan poets. As Hardie notes, the play thus stages the central Ovidian pattern in which 'illusion is overtaken by a reality that destroys both it and its author.'[65] While the allegory is easily swept off stage, the real characters do some damage before they are finally foiled, as Lupus and Tucca reveal Ovid's love affair to Augustus, who promptly banishes the poet. Moreover, poetry is threatened further by the poetaster Crispinus, who slavishly follows Horace and who uses Ovidian strategies to seduce a married woman. As James D. Mulvihill notes, the play thus shows that 'to a significant degree Ovid has been the victim of unscrupulous detractors and imitators'.[66] The poet is destroyed by the twinned forces of envy and imitation.

As critics have noted, Jonson's play is an attack on Elizabethan Ovidianism, particularly that of Shakespeare, whose *Romeo and Juliet* is parodied in the parting scene between Ovid and Julia in 4.10.[67] Part also of the larger 'Poets' War' between Jonson and his sometimes collaborators, Marston and Dekker, it enables Jonson to present

---

[64] As critics have noted, Jonson uses Marlowe's translation of Ovid here, creating what Cain describes as 'a graceful if double-edged tribute to Marlowe' (*Poetaster*, 19). Jonson's conflation of Marlowe and Ovid is telling: it enables him to distinguish himself and go beyond the dead writers, even as he appropriates their language. Here envy and admiration seem particularly hard to tell apart.

[65] *Ovid's Poetics of Illusion*, 100. As Hardie suggests, Jonson punishes Ovid for being unable to tell the difference between fantasy and reality.

[66] 'Jonson's *Poetaster* and the Ovidian Debate', 254. In his poem 'On Paradise Lost' printed with the 1674 edition of the epic, Marvell confessed that he had feared that Milton might meet a similar fate; aiming especially at Dryden's plans to remake the poem into a play in rhymed couplets, he noted that he had been 'Jealous . . . that some less skilful hand | (Such as disquiet always what is well, | And by ill imitating would excell) | Might hence presume the whole Creations day | To change in Scenes, and show it in a Play' (18–22).

[67] Bate, *Shakespeare and Ovid*, 168–9; and Hardie, *Ovid's Poetics of Illusion*, 104, who notes that the scene is also based on *Tristia* 1. 3.

himself as the victim of malicious rivals.[68] Perhaps because of his own obsession with the psychologically and socially corrosive power of envy, Jonson is extremely attentive to Ovid's treatment of the figure and its relation to other Ovidian concerns. In its attack on Jonson's invidious enemies, *Poetaster* is especially indebted to Ovid's other exilic work, the *Ibis*. This bizarre poem is basically a string of extravagant and violent curses against an unnamed and unidentified enemy, whom the poet blames for his exile and who, as Gareth Williams has noted, is shaped as a figure of *invidia* incarnate.[69] In the commentaries, the oldest extant scholia on Ovid, it was also suggested that Ovid was writing against a certain 'aemulus' who invidiously used the poet's innocent verse to teach adultery.[70] Until critics like Williams began to study it in depth, the *Ibis* had been widely neglected. Ann Moss notes, however, that it was printed at least six times in Paris in the late sixteenth century; she argues that it was of great interest for Renaissance writers, who were attracted by the work's winning combination of 'sustained invective and gratuitous erudition'.[71] It was one of the first of Ovid's works translated into English (by Thomas Underdowne in 1569), and it has had an intriguing number of fans, including Poliziano.[72] The commentary tradition, some of which has been usefully collected and edited by Antonio La Penna, suggests some of the ways in which this strange poem was read. Much energy is expended simply trying to identify the poem's titular figure and target. Most of the notes then trace the

---

[68] Meskill, *Ben Jonson and Envy*, 94–109. As Meskill notes, the common assumption that Jonson represents himself only through his ideal Horace obscures his more ambivalent identification with Ovid and Ovidian poetics. The Protean Ovid provides Jonson with a rich but problematic classical source, with whom he wrestled throughout his works; as Heather James shows, 'almost every poem of *The Forrest* contains an allusion to Ovid's poetry' ('Ovid in Renaissance English Literature', in Knox (ed.), *A Companion to Ovid*, 432). See also Hardie, *Ovid's Poetics of Illusion*, 99–105.

[69] *The Curse of Exile*, 21.

[70] La Penna, *Scholia*, 3.

[71] Moss, *Ovid in Renaissance France*, 54. She notes that the translations coincide with increased polemic in the period of civil war (ibid. 55).

[72] It clearly influenced also the 15th-century commentator on the *Fasti*, Paolo Marsi; throughout his edition, Marsi rails against a detractor whom he then denounces in *Praefatio in V Librum Fastorum et contra Invidum*. See Fritsen, 'Renaissance Commentaries on Ovid's *Fasti*', 71 n. 13. Milton's early familiarity with Ovid's poem is apparent in a casual reference in 'In Obitum Praesulis Eliensis' ('On the Death of the Bishop of Ely'), 18–19, written when he was 17. It would be worth considering further the poem's inspiration of satirists like Skelton and Marston, as well as Jonson.

vast range of mythological references, pointing to other sources, and particularly directing the reader to Ovid's other works in which the tales are told more fully.[73] The commentators are also aware of and interested in the poem's place in literary traditions. Early on in the *Ibis*, Ovid himself explicitly draws attention to the fact that he is imitating Callimachus:

> Nunc quo Battiades inimicum devovet Ibin,
>   Hoc ego devoveo teque tuosque modo.
> Utque ille, historiis involvam carmina caecis:
>   Non soleam quamvis hoc genus ipse sequi.
> Illius ambages imitatus in Ibide dicar
>   Oblitus moris iudiciique mei. (55–60)

Underdowne's rough and tumble verse turns this into:

> But now as earst *Calimacbus*, [sic]
>   dyd enmy *Ibis* cursse:
> By that same meanes both thee & thine
>   I earnestly do cursse.
>
> And as he dyd, so I my verse,
>   wyll wrap in stories blynde:
> Although my selfe am neuer wont
>   to imitate this kynde.
> His trade obscure I folowing,
>   gainste *Ibys* wyll inuay,
> My customes olde and iudgement to,
>   the whyle wyll cast away.[74]

As Moss notes, the poem presents itself as an attempt to outdo Callimachus, 'in the accumulation of recondite allusion and obscure

---

[73] Explaining the meaning of the word 'Ibis' is also the source of much simple pleasure: 'Callimachus, in invidum scribens pro eius inmuniditia, eum Ibidem in libro suo appellavit, quia ibis, s. ciconia, rostro purgat posteriora et in hoc execretur' ('Callimachus, writing against an enemy [invidus] on account of his filth called him Ibis in this book since the Ibis, that is, stork, cleans its bum with its bill and so shits', qtd. in La Penna, *Scholia*, 118). The image is gleefully picked up by Jonson to describe Marston and Dekker in the 'Apologetical Dialogue' in *Poetaster*: 'these vile ibids [sic], these unclean birds, | That make their mouths their clysters, and still purge | From their hot entrails' (206–8). At the risk of sounding too invidious myself, I should point out that, while Cain assumes that Jonson found this image in Pliny (*Poetaster*, 273 n.), Ovid is clearly its source.

[74] 'Ouid his Inuective against Ibis' (London, 1577), Early English Books Online, B1^v–B2^r.

paraphrase. It is an example of how to imitate and surpass a literary model.'[75]

The poem thus originates in emulation of two kinds: the enemy's destructive emulation of Ovid and the poet's own creative emulation of Callimachus. The two types again seem opposites. Yet the relation is more complicated than this. As Stephen Hinds nicely puts it, Ibis is presented as the poet's 'evil twin': 'Ovid... makes of Ibis a kind of double of himself by wishing on his persecutor the same sufferings—and the same mythological analogies—which he himself suffers in the *Tristia*.'[76] Ovid fantasizes about making the man who copied his work copy his fate. Like Philomela and Hecuba, the innocent victim becomes the savage avenger, at least in his imagination. As we have seen, in Ovid, the transformation from one state to another generally involves a loss of or change of voice. As Ovid himself announces here, in imitating Callimachus, he abandons his own voice to take on another. Piling up an astonishing array of curses, the poet previously known for his detachment and urbanity undergoes a disturbing change. While the exilic verse as a whole laments the metamorphosis of Ovid's poetic *copia* into repetition, here *copia* is both concentrated and expanded with demonic fury, as his imagination is channelled by invective into relentless images of suffering. The poet whose verse had celebrated the act of creation now can only imagine an almost infinite list of elaborate forms of destruction. The relentless cataloguing of violence is in many ways quite fascinating, as Ovid once more rises to the challenge of generating variety out of potentially monotonous material. Some early readers admired the copious catalogues of evils as demonstrations of the fertile imagination of the 'ingeniosus poeta';[77] recent readers have tended to be more disturbed by this obsessive outpouring of venom. Gareth Williams reads the poem as the representation of 'an intense and highly charged state of mind', 'a condition of perverse obsessiveness which can never fully satisfy the sadistic relish on which it feeds'.[78] The effect seems even more unsettling as classicists since A. E. Housman have tended to assume that 'Ibis' is simply a figment of Ovid's imagination.[79] Even more, the

---

[75] Moss, *Ovid in Renaissance France*, 54.
[76] Hinds, 'After Exile', 65.
[77] Morillo, cited from Moss, *Ovid in Renaissance France*, 54.
[78] Williams, *The Curse of Exile*, 23.
[79] 'The *Ibis* of Ovid', in *The Classical Papers of A. E. Housman*, ed. J. Diggle and F. R. D. Goodyear, 3 vols. (Cambridge, 1972), iii. 1018–42.

Ibis seems an image *for* Ovid's imagination as it turns against itself in exile. In the end, the poet and his enemy seem indistinguishable; as Williams puts it, 'The avenger gradually succumbs to the irrational forces of his diseased imagination.'[80]

As the *Poetaster* suggests, for later writers Ovid was an unsettling example of the poet crushed by the envy that always feeds on creativity. Writers recalled him when they lamented their own persecution. In Guillaume de Deguileville's *Pèlerinage de vie humaine* (*c*.1330) translated by John Lydgate as *The Pilgrimage of the Life of Man* (*c*.1426), the pilgrim is attacked by Envy and her daughters, Treason and Detraction, and is unjustly thrown into prison. Here he is visited by Ovid, who comes both to offer pity for his plight and to curse his enemies for him; he quotes *Ibis* 105 (23249). For de Deguileville, who is reworking the *Roman de la Rose*, Ovid is not the poet of love who teaches his pupils how to court, but the poet of envy who teaches them how to curse.[81] As both creator and victim of envy, Ovid offers Milton a model for both Satan and the narrator, and for the complex relation between these two figures.

MILTON AND THE ARTS OF ENVY

From early on, Milton was conscious of the dangers that envy traditionally holds for an ambitious poet. When first venturing out into publication in the 1645 *Poems* he defends himself against the envy of others, quoting as his epigram Virgil's 'Eclogue 7': 'baccare frontem | Cingite, ne vati noceat mala lingua futuro' ('wreathe my brow with foxglove, lest his evil tongue harm the bard that is to be', 27–8). He is especially aware that in printing the 'Testimonia', the series of little poems written by his Italian friends as tributes to his genius, he is courting envy, though he protests that he 'nimiae laudis invidiam totis ab se viribus amolitur, sibique quod plus aequo est non attributum esse mavult' ('strives with all his powers to avoid the envy

---

[80] *The Curse of Exile*, 40.
[81] Citations are from *The Pilgrimage of the Life of Man, Englisht by John Lydgate, A.D. 1426, from the French of Guillaume de Deguileville, A.D. 1330, 1355*, ed. F. J. Furnivall (1899; repr. Millwood, NY, 1978). While the narrator is sympathetic to Ovid, however, he is not interested in cursing his enemies, but prefers to hope that justice and love will win out. Rejected as a model, Ovid disappears from the poem.

engendered by excessive praise and would not receive a higher commendation than is his by right', *Complete Shorter Poems*, 130).[82] The conventional representation of envy as the poet's greatest enemy appears in the poems as well. In 'Ad Patrem' 105–10, Milton claims to rise untouched above the aspersions of envy and calumny, and in the Italian 'Sonnet 6', he describes himself as 'd'invidio sicuro' (9). A year after the publication of the volume, Milton sends a copy to the Bodleian where he hopes it will be safe from 'invidiâ' ('Ad *Joannem Rousium*', 76). Moreover, the subject of envy is especially appropriate and useful in Milton's polemical works, in which he claims (not always convincingly) to be both free from envy and its victim. In *The Reason of Church-Government* he protests that 'neither envy nor gall hath enterd me upon this controversy' (*Works*, iii, pt. 1, 234), while in *An Apology for Smectymnuus* he notes how he has been 'bitten' by envy and the 'Alchymist of slander' (*Works*, iii, pt. 1, 301, 298).[83] In the *Doctrine and Discipline of Divorce* he presents himself furthermore as the champion of truth and bitter enemy of envy, which is the tool of those other evil monsters, 'Error and Custome': 'Who with the numerous and vulgar train of their followers, make it their chiefe designe to envie and cry-down the industry of free reasoning, under the terms of humor, and innovation; as if the womb of teeming Truth were to be clos'd up, if shee presume to bring forth ought, that sorts not with their unchew'd notions and

---

[82] See also Hale, *Milton's Languages*, 93.

[83] He presents his argument in public: 'Although I am not ignorant how hazardous it will be to do this under the nose of the *envious*, as it were in skirmish to change the compact order, and instead of outward actions to bring inmost thoughts into front. And I must tell ye Readers, that by this sort of men I have bin already bitten at; yet shall they not for me know how slightly they are esteem'd, unless they have so much learning as to read what in Greek 'Απειροκαλία [lack of taste] is, which together with *envie* is the common disease of those who censure books that are not for their reading' (*Works*, iii, pt. 1, 301, emphasis added). He complains that his 'nicenesse of Nature, an honest haughtinesse, and self-esteem either of what I was, or what I might be' has been misrepresented by 'envie' as 'pride' (*Works*, iii, pt. 1, 304). In the *Defensio Secunda*, Milton also defends himself, rather self-righteously, saying that 'immo mihi gratuler, & gratias insuper largitori munerum coelesti iterum summas agam obtigisse talem, ut aliis invidenda multò magìs, quàm mihi ullo modo poenitenda videatur' ('I may rather congratulate myself, and once again return my highest thanks to the heavenly bestower of gifts, that such a lot has fallen to me, as may be viewed, with much greater reason, as a subject of envy to others, than in any way a cause of repentance to myself', *Works*, viii. 10). See also *Pro se defensio*, in *Works*, ix. 86.

suppositions' (*Works*, iii, pt. 2, 368–9).[84] Envy is the means by which tyrants suppress virtue and greatness in others (*Eikonoklastes*, in *Works* v. 218). For Milton, it is the property of his uncreative enemies, such as Salmasius who in the 1651 *Pro Populo Anglicano Defensio* is taunted: 'Túne igitur sine sale, sine genio proclamator et rabula, bonis authoribus divexandis tantùm aut transcribendis natus, quicquam de tuo quod vivat producere te putas posse?' ('And so, you senseless witless bawling pettifogger, born only to pick good writers to pieces or transcribe them, do you really think yourself capable of writing anything that will live?', *Works*, vii. 40), and who in the *Defensio Secunda* is denounced as 'invidiae artifex' ('the artificer of envy', *Works*, viii. 58).

In *Paradise Lost*, however, the title of 'invidiae artifex' clearly belongs to Satan. Like Plato's creator, Milton's God seems above envy, as he encourages emulation so that others may be creative like him. Satan, however, experiences God's love as envy.[85] With Satan the chain of creative emulation—the proliferation of divine Narcissi—turns into envy of, and strife with, his source. The creativity of others does not inspire but enrages him. The sight of the newly made Eden, not to mention the creative happiness generated by the 'Conjugal Love' (9. 263) of Adam and Eve, fuels his desire to destroy what God can create.[86] The making of a race of inferior humans confirms his suspicion that God creates only in order to inspire envy; God made 'this Man of Clay, Son of despite . . . us the more to spite' (9. 176–7), and thus set off an endless battle in which 'spite then with spite is best repaid' (9. 178).[87] To Satan, the elevation of others means his own degradation: he complains that man was 'by our exile | Made happie' (10. 484–5).

Most of all, therefore, Satanic envy is aimed at the Son, God's creating force, who Satan feels was unjustly promoted above him. His rebellion is triggered by the Son's begetting and consolidated in

---

[84] See also *Pro Populo Anglicano Defensio*, in *Works*, vii. 6; and *Defensio Secunda*, in *Works*, viii. 222, in which he presents himself as the defender of others against envy.
[85] See especially *Paradise Lost* 1. 258–60; 4. 515–18, 524; 5. 61; as well as 9. 729–30.
[86] See *Paradise Lost* 3. 553; 4. 115; 6. 900; 9. 175, 254, 264, 466.
[87] See also *Paradise Lost* 9. 147–51 in which he bitterly complains that God made humans: 'to spite us more, | Determin'd to advance into our room | A creature form'd of Earth, and him endow, | Exalted from so base original. | With Heav'nly spoils, our spoils.'

the war in heaven in which the Son's full powers are displayed.[88] At the moment of the proclamation of the Son, Satan:

> fraught
> With envie against the Son of God, that day
> Honourd by his great Father, and proclaimd
> *Messiah* King anointed, could not beare
> Through pride that sight, & thought himself impair'd. (5. 661–5)

Envy thus sets the plot of the poem into action, as it will again in *Paradise Regain'd*, in which the recognition of Jesus as the Son of God at his baptism leaves Satan 'With wonder, then with envy fraught and rage' (1. 38).[89] For Satan 'wonder', which he feels also at first sight of the world (*PL*, 3. 552–4) and Adam and Eve (4. 363), leads only to envy and anger.[90] For that reason also, in *Paradise Lost* 6 the Son's entrance in the extravagant chariot of paternal deity, which is greeted with joy by the good angels, infuriates the devils. As Anne T. Barbeau shows, the Son's appearance is described in images of fertility which 'give precedence to Christ's creative and fostering powers'.[91] The multiple eyes of his chariot also might offer an alternative model of perception to that of Satan's invidious vision.[92] But the manifestation of the Son's creativity only deepens Satan's and his followers' resentment:

> They hard'nd more by what might most reclame,
> Grieving to see his Glorie, at the sight
> Took envie, and aspiring to his highth,
> Stood reimbattell'd fierce, by force or fraud
> Weening to prosper, and at length prevaile
> Against God and *Messiah*. (*PL*, 6. 791–6)

---

[88] See also Stella P. Revard, 'Satan's Envy of the Kingship of the Son of God: A Reconsideration of *Paradise Lost*, Book 5, and its Theological Background', *Modern Philology*, 70/3 (1973), 190–8; and Anne T. Barbeau, 'Satan's Envy of the Son and the Third Day of the War', *Papers on Language & Literature*, 13 (1977), 362–71.

[89] In Cowley's *Davideis* the action similarly begins with the 'spight' and 'Malice' of Saul, which is stirred up further by a visit of an allegorical Envy; see *Davideis*, 1. 9, 11.

[90] Elizabeth Bradburn argues that in *Paradise Lost* other responses of wonder bring spiritual regeneration; see 'Theatrical Wonder, Amazement, and the Construction of Spiritual Agency in *Paradise Lost*', *Comparative Drama*, 40/1 (2006), 77–98.

[91] 'Satan's Envy of the Son and the Third Day of the War', 364.

[92] While the origins of the chariot are clearly biblical, based on Ezekiel 1, they overlap with the conventional representations of *Fama*, which, in the form of good fame (as opposed to Rumour or infamy), is often represented as having a thousand eyes; Milton draws on this convention in 'In quintum Novembris', 187–90.

The expression of creativity inspires in Satan the need to destroy. Like other forms of envy, however, Satanic energy is ultimately self-destructive, as it 'back on it self recoiles' (9. 172). So Raphael explains to Adam:

> the evil soon
> Driv'n back redounded as a flood on those
> From whom it sprung, impossible to mix
> With Blessedness. (7. 56–9)

By refusing to acknowledge God as a creator, the devils will experience him as a destroyer; as Abdiel warns Satan: 'Then who created thee lamenting learne, | When who can uncreate thee thou shalt know' (5. 894–5).

Milton's foregrounding of the envy of Satan is central to his representation of evil as the perversion of divine creativity. Moreover, as classical writers assert their own moral authority in opposition to the spite of others, the poet of *Paradise Lost* uses Satan as his double through whom he proves his own freedom from envy. By representing Satan as invidious, Milton is able to present himself as an antithetical example of good emulation.[93] Within the poem, the envy of Satan is contrasted with the creativity of the narrator. While Satan insists that he is 'self-begot, self-rais'd' (5. 860) and produces Sin independently, the narrator emphasizes his need for the Muse and divine inspiration, and hopes that the poem reflects God and not its human author.[94] Although he writes 'In solitude', he hastens to add that he is 'not alone' (7. 28); unlike Narcissus, he lets a female figure into his world. His creativity, like that of Adam and Eve, is dependent on dialogue, first of all with his Muse. He acknowledges that his poem will fail 'if all be mine, | Not Hers who brings it nightly to my Ear' (9. 46–7). Maureen Quilligan suggests further that the poet similarly highlights his reliance on his *human* sources through allusions in order to distinguish himself from Satan. She argues that Milton acknowledges the authority of others: 'in predicating Sin's character on Errour's, he avoids making Satan's mistake: he pays due respect to *his* original, to Spenser.' Satan's invidious rivalry with his source is

---

[93] The envy of Satan is also contrasted in the poem with the *zeal* of Abdiel (another figure whose doubling of Milton is often noted), which is stressed in 5. 805, 807, 849, and 900.

[94] DuRocher, *Milton and Ovid*, 123.

contrasted with the poet's gratitude towards his which shows Milton's 'great saving humility'.[95]

Still, the acknowledgement of sources does not necessarily imply humility towards them. Poets foreground the presence of earlier sources not only to pay homage but also to assert their own superior cleverness, to criticize, and to correct past errors—as many readers assume Milton corrects Ovid. As Quilligan also notes, Milton himself is the creator of Sin who is, through the logic of the poem, 'the original of which Errour and Scylla may be presumed mere copies'.[96] While, from one perspective, Sin is a hand-me-down from Ovid and Spenser, from another, *she* is their original. Isn't Milton doing what Satan does: sneakily claiming priority over his own sources to be his own original, and to make his own maker?[97] It is not always easy to tell forms of strife apart; as Satan tells Michael, 'The strife which thou call'st evil... wee style | The strife of Glorie' (6. 289–90).

While Quilligan's Milton graciously acknowledges his sources, Dr Johnson saw a rather different author, one who, both politically and poetically pugnacious, was 'very frugal' in his praise of others, and was driven by a 'predominant desire... to destroy rather than establish'.[98] Less censorious critics have commonly described Milton as 'the most competitive of poets' whose goal is to 'overgo' his

---

[95] *Milton's Spenser*, 90. These days, of course, Milton's spiritual safety might be in the hands of editors who may or may not footnote his sources.

[96] Ibid. 87.

[97] See also the metamorphoses of the devils in Book 10, which the narrator suggests is itself the original source of all 'later' classical myths. Burrow argues that the figure of Sin embodies Milton's awareness that poets 'might mistakenly claim originality and priority for what is in fact imitation' ('Re-embodying Ovid: Renaissance Afterlives', 318).

[98] *Lives of the English Poets*, ed. Waugh, i. 69, 109. While Johnson is speaking here of Milton's radical politics, which the staunch Tory vehemently deplored, his general characterization of Milton is of an ungenerous writer who had 'a lofty and steady confidence in himself, perhaps not without some contempt for others; for scarcely any man ever wrote so much, and praised so few' (ibid. 69). For other 18th-century comments on Milton's 'malice and wickedness', see Dustin Griffin, *Regaining Paradise: Milton and the Eighteenth Century* (Cambridge, 1986), 22–3. Others however hotly defended him against what was itself seen as critical *invidia*. When William Lauder claimed that Milton was a plagiarist in *An Essay on Milton's Use and Imitation of the Moderns in his Paradise Lost* (1747), Lauder's own plagiarism and falsification of evidence was soon exposed and viciously attacked. Milton was exonerated, most notably in Robert Lloyd's 'The Progress of Envy: A Poem, in Imitation of Spenser. Occasioned by Lauder's Attack on the Character of Milton' (1751), a poem which uses its own emulation of Spenser and Milton to imagine the defeat of a highly Ovidian allegorical Envy.

sources—not only pagan writers, but also nearer contemporaries like Shakespeare.[99] As we've seen, from early on Milton had aspired to become immortal and, like Ovid, to rise above the stars. In *Paradise Lost* he announces that his aim is to 'soar | Above th' *Aonian* Mount' (*PL*, 1. 14–15) and boldly go where no poet had gone before. As I suggested earlier, claims such as 'Things unattempted yet in Prose or Rhime' (1. 16), or 'What never yet was heard in Tale or Song' (*Comus*, 44), which assert originality, also restrain it. Through their conventionality, they place the poet firmly in a network of tradition which enables his creativity. Yet they also indicate the poet's desire to push the limits of tradition. Certainly early tributes assumed that Milton was vying with the great authors of the past. In the 'Testimonia' to the 1645 *Poems*, both Salzilli and Selvaggi rank Milton as equal and perhaps superior to Homer, Virgil, and Tasso, while Samuel Barrow's prefatory poem to the 1674 edition of *Paradise Lost*, 'In Paradisum Amissam Summi Poetae JOHANNIS MILTONI' ('On the *Paradise Lost* of the most excellent poet, John Milton'), uses the war in heaven as a metaphor for Milton's own poetic battle with his pagan predecessors; as the rebel angels fled from the Son to hide 'Infernis... tenebris' ('in infernal darkness', 38), classical writers are doomed to everlasting obscurity by the appearance of the new poem.

Milton's competition with his sources is especially evident in the first books, in which he presents the fallen angels.[100] His hell is bigger than everyone else's hell. Describing the magnitude of the angels—both their numbers and their actual size—Milton is constantly drawn to comparisons that insist that the scene he imagines surpasses those in any other epic. Satan is larger than the largest of monsters (1. 192–208), and his shield and spear are also of unimaginable magnitude (1. 284–94). The number of the devils outdoes the armies of all imagined epic battles combined, 'For never since created

---

[99] Balachandra Rajan, *The Lofty Rhyme: A Study of Milton's Major Poetry* (London, 1970), 128.

[100] Other moments occur especially in describing the Garden itself. In Book 4 the narrator wants to assure us that no other garden 'might with this Paradise | Of *Eden* strive' (4. 274–5), and the couple's bower is shadier and 'More sacred and sequestered' than the 'feigned' (4. 706) ones in which Pan and Silvanus slept and '*Faunus* haunted' (4. 708). In Book 9, we are told again that the place where Satan finds Eve is a 'Spot more delicious than those Gardens feign'd | Or of reviv'd *Adonis*, or renownd | *Alcinous*, host of old *Laertes* Son' (9. 439–41). In relating the war in heaven also, Raphael is concerned with conveying the scale of the spectacle.

man, | Met such imbodied force' (1. 573–4), and the magnificence of Pandemonium makes all later monuments seem insignificant (1. 695–7, 717–22). The devils outshine all later heroes, and Satan outshines all the devils: 'Thus far these beyond | Compare of moral prowess, yet observ'd | Thir dread commander: he above the rest | In shape and gesture proudly eminent | Stood like a Towr' (1. 587–91); even his throne is brighter than all others (2. 1–2) This display of infernal power enables the poet's display of his own power and *copia*, in its sense of military might as well as imaginative energy. The devils' hopeless ambitions fuel the poet's desire to surpass his sources; their hopes to rise again, symbolized by 'Th' ascending pile' of Pandemonium (1. 222), mirror the poet's own aspiration 'to soar | Above th' *Aonian* Mount' (1. 14–15).

The building of Pandemonium allows the poet one famous opportunity to go even further and tear down the fictitious constructions of the ancients. The narrator stops the action to first tell a fable about its creator and then to take it back:

> Men call'd him *Mulciber*; and how he fell
> From Heav'n, they fabl'd, thrown by angry *Jove*
> Sheer o're the Chrystal Battlements; from Morn
> To Noon he fell, from Noon to dewy Eve,
> A Summers day; and with the setting Sun
> Dropt from the Zenith like a falling Star,
> On *Lemnos* th' *Aegean* Ile: thus they relate,
> Erring; for he with his rebellious rout
> Fell long before. (1. 740–8)

Epyllion writers who rewrote classical myths had similarly remarked that their predecessors had got it wrong. Both Marlowe and Weever playfully correct Ovid's story of Phaethon, which is also a subtext for Milton's description here. In *Hero and Leander* 1. 45–50, Marlowe had explained that the dark skins of some races were caused not by the scorching of the earth with the fall of Phaethon (as Ovid claimed in *Metamorphoses* 2. 235–6), but through Hero's draining of beauty from part of the world. Correcting Marlowe as well, Weever goes even further, explicitly announcing that '(*Ouid's* beguilde, it was not *Phaeton*)' (150): the earth was actually scorched because of the Sun's love of Mellifora.[101] The effect of this kind of cheeky authorial correction

---

[101] See also above, Ch. 2, p. 99 on Weever's 'correction' of both Ovid and Shakespeare's version of the story of Venus and Adonis. Shakespeare in turn corrects

of the past version is not, of course, to confirm the truth of the new, but to draw attention to the process of revision and to call into question the possibility of an authoritative account.

The effect of Milton's carefully crafted verse is, however, quite different. As often noted, the gorgeous lyrical passage, which suspends Mulciber's fall in mid-flight, ends with a resounding poetical thud, as the author barges in to expose the errors of the ancients.[102] The passage is intertextually dense in ways that draw attention to Milton's virtuoso mastery of language as well as past sources. As Charles Martindale notes, 'Milton aims to dazzle', as he 'engages in emulous rivalry with Homer', specifically *Iliad* 1. 589–94, in which Haephestus is hurled from heaven by Zeus.[103] But Milton also recalls Ovid's emulation of Homer in his description of the fall of Phaethon (*Met.*, 2. 321–2).[104] As Martindale notes further, the simultaneous inclusion and rejection of a story has a precedent in Lucretius' *De Rerum Natura* 391–3.[105] As Milton masters these sources, he corrects them, telling the true version that they had misleadingly copied. Like Narcissus, the ancients were trapped in illusion and Ovidian error, and so only able to glimpse dreams of '*Hesperian* fables true, | If true, here only' (*PL*, 4. 250). The correction of falsehood anticipates the Son's rejection of classical learning in *Paradise Regain'd* as 'false, or little else but dreams, | Conjectures, fancies, built on nothing firm' (4. 291–2); it is 'An empty cloud' (4. 321), as '*Greece* from us these Arts deriv'd; | Ill imitated' (4. 338–9).[106] Classical myths are, after all, mere shadows of the poet's reality. The contrast between the delicacy of the lyric fall and the weight of the authorial

---

both Marlowe and Ovid in *As You Like It* 4. 1. 89–102, when Rosalind, mocking the idea of dying for love, says Leander really died of a cramp during a nocturnal dip.

[102] See especially Forsyth, *The Satanic Epic*, 105–8, and Martindale, *John Milton and the Transformation*, 72–8.

[103] *John Milton and the Transformation*, 73, who notes especially the careful copying of the pivotal position of the words denoting descent.

[104] Milton had linked these stories in his early 'Naturam non pati senium', 23–8, in which he also uses pagan stories to discredit them: he claims that the decay of the world is as much a fiction as myths of falling gods. See David Quint, 'Fear of Falling: Icarus, Phaethon, and Lucretius in *Paradise Lost*', *Renaissance Quarterly*, 57/3 (2004), 867–70.

[105] *John Milton and the Transformation*, 74–5.

[106] See also *PR*, 4. 346–7, where Jesus asserts Christianity's poetic superiority to its precursor; the classics are 'unworthy to compare | With *Sion*'s songs, to all true tasts excelling', an idea expressed also in *The Reason of Church-Government* (*Works*, iii. 238).

intervention reinforces the opposition between pagan shadows and Christian substance. The passage separates the artist of Pandemonium from the creator of the poem, the pagan mythographers who fall from the poet of truth who rises above illusion.

In Stanley Fish's influential reading of the poem, the passage is typical of Milton's method in general, through which the poet puts not only pagan stories but also readers in their place: on the side of error.[107] Fish's account was partly a response to A. J. A. Waldock's objection to what he described as the narrator's 'running fire of belittling commentary', of 'automatic snubs, of perfunctory jabs and growls'.[108] For Waldock, such obtrusive intrusions betrayed Milton's identification with Satan, and his fear that he had made evil too appealing. Like the Romantics, Waldock was put off by what Harold Bloom described as 'Milton's meanness towards Satan, towards his rival poet and dark brother'.[109] For Fish, however, the target of corrections is not Satan but the reader. Milton creates a deliberate 'programme of reader harassment' and authorial correction which replays the story of the fall from error to ultimate redemption in the experience of reading.[110] By leading us into and out of temptation through interpretative error, the poet hopes to show us the path to salvation.

If Milton's plan was to control the reader's experience and even salvation, however, he seems sadly to have failed. As Waldock's reading indicates, many good readers have not experienced the poem according to this model. In many ways, the severity of the authorial interjection in Book 1 brings out the beauty of the error. As poetry, the false description has remarkable power. It shows that the narrator himself is able to make something out of what is, he tells us, really nothing at all. Moreover, this kind of explicit authorial intervention and correction is most pronounced in the early books of the poem.[111] It is at odds with the more subtle ways throughout the poem in which Milton teaches the reader to wrestle with the simultaneous likeness and difference between good and evil. While Fish focuses on the experience of the implied reader as the internalization of the fall,

---

[107] *Surprised by Sin: The Reader in* Paradise Lost (London, 1967).
[108] Paradise Lost *and its Critics* (Cambridge, 1964), 83, 78.
[109] *The Anxiety of Influence*, 23. Bloom is speaking specifically here of Shelley's dislike of Milton's handling of Satan.
[110] *Surprised by Sin*, 4.
[111] See *PL*, 1. 125–6, 1. 690–2, 2. 112–16, 2. 226–8, and especially 2. 380–7.

the poem itself offers the experience of the speaker who struggles against evil both outside and inside himself. The narrator himself is a more divided 'complex, even unstable personality' than Fish's account implies.[112] Like Satan, he changes over the course of the poem. In Book 1 he starts out, like the epic Ovid, confident that his epic will raise him above all others; in Book 9 too as he approaches the fall, he rejects the standard topics of classical and Renaissance epic, claiming that through 'long choosing, and beginning late' (9. 26) he has found a subject that is 'more Heroic' (9. 14) and 'higher Argument' (9. 42). However, in his last speech in Book 9, he is also worried about the effects of time and cold on his creative powers; after the fall, he is strikingly silent as if this radical change has crushed his individuality. Like Satan, who disappears around the same point, he seems to lose his voice.

As I suggested earlier, moreover, Milton's creation of a subjective narrator preoccupied with his own artistry looks back to Ovid, in particular the speaker of the last poems from Tomis. The distinct voice of the fallen narrator creates the impression that when Milton rewrites the *Metamorphoses* in *Paradise Lost* it is from the perspective of Ovid's exilic verse. There are even times when the speaker seems to mirror the experience of Ovid. While DuRocher points to the echoes of Ovid's exilic poetry in Satan's speeches,[113] the narrator also sounds like the exiled Ovid when he contrasts his past with his present. As Ovid had complained of living in a frozen world of perpetual winter in which time stands still (*Tristia*, 3. 12; 5. 10. 5), the speaker laments being cut off from the experience of seasonal change which he too has found inspiring (*PL*, 3. 40–50).[114] Both speakers—like Satan as well, of course—assert that despite fate they are unchanged; they find solace in the freedom of their imaginations. Milton's speaker finds an inner light that he asks to 'Shine inward' (3. 52), while Ovid retreats into his 'ingenium': 'ingenio tamen ipse meo comitorque

---

[112] Forsyth, *The Satanic Epic*, 97; see generally 77–113. See also Fallon's fine discussion of the combination of confidence and insecurity in Milton's character (*Milton's Peculiar Grace*, 203–36).

[113] *Milton and Ovid*, 123.

[114] With his usual contempt for anyone susceptible to changes of time or weather, Dr Johnson mocked Milton's sensitivity to the seasons, as well as 'his dread of decaying Nature, or a frigid zone', as 'fumes of vain imagination' (*Lives*, i. 97, 96). But as usual, Johnson draws attention to an aspect of Milton's self-presentation that is worth noting.

fruorque: | Caesar in hoc potuit iuris habere nihil' ('my mind [ingenio] is nevertheless my comrade and my joy; over this Caesar could have no right', *Tristia*, 3. 7. 47–8). As the speaker's voice is 'unchang'd' (*PL*, 7. 24), Ovid insists that, 'nec cum fortuna mens quoque versa mea est' ('my mind has not changed along with my fate', *Ex Ponto*, 4. 9. 90). His imagination is not exiled (4. 9. 41); through its powers he is able to leave the world of Scythia and return to Rome.[115] Yet Ovid's solace is paradoxical; not only does his poetry return him to his present (as he writes about his situation) but it also got him into this mess in the first place. As he keeps reminding his readers: 'ingenio sic fuga parta meo' ('my own wit has brought me exile', *Tristia*, 1. 1. 56). In *Tristia* 3, Ovid describes his works as his children: 'Palladis exemplo de me sine matre creata | carmina sunt; stirps haec progeniesque mea est' ('Pallas-fashion were my verses born from me without a mother; these are my offspring, my family', 3. 14. 13–14). The image looks back of course to the birth of Minerva, suggesting an ironic identification of Ovid's poetry with wisdom, but it also anticipates Milton's representation of the origins of Sin.[116] The latter parallel seems even more appropriate given that, earlier, Ovid had bitterly identified his offspring: 'Oedipodas facito Telegonosque voces' ('give them the names of Oedipus or of Telegonus', *Tristia*, 1. 1. 114). His children are parricides, creations who, like the hellhounds gathered round Sin's belly, have turned on their creator. Returning to his Muses seems, therefore, a perversely fatal attraction to the very thing that has destroyed him.[117] However, in continuing to write, Ovid hopes to turn the cause of exile into its cure: 'sic mihi res eadem vulnus opemque feret, | Musaque, quam movit, motam quoque leniet iram' ('the same object will both wound and cure me, and the Muse

---

[115] See also, for example, *Tristia* 4. 10. 103–32. In *Tristia* 4. 1. 48, he notes how through writing, 'temporis adversi sic mihi sensus abest' ('I lose the sense of evil days'). While it would be nice to find this echoed in Milton's narrator's 'evil days', the echo is really created by the translator, who appears to be surreptitiously channelling Ovid through Milton.

[116] Ovid's image was picked up by another Ovidian, Samuel Daniel, to describe the origins of his own art, that he '*Minerua*-like, brought foorth without a Mother' ('Sonnet II', in *Delia* (London, 1592), Early English Books Online, B1ᵛ).

[117] As part of his rewriting of his earlier erotic verse, Ovid reworks the familiar *odi et amo* theme into the poet's obsession with the Muses. See, for example, *Tristia*, 5. 7. 31–4, and *Tristia* 4. 1. 36 where the poet claims, 'quodque mihi telum vulnera fecit, amo' ('I love the very weapon that made my wounds'); also Williams, *Banished Voices*, 100–53.

who aroused the wrath will also soften it', *Tristia*, 2. 20–2). Although his poetry failed to persuade Augustus, Ovid claims that the cause of his fall may also be the means of redemption; what became destructive can be made creative again.

While I do not believe that Milton is consciously trying to make himself into Ovid's image, I think that his own situation inevitably calls up the shadow of the archetypal exiled poet, as had his early rustication in 'Elegia 1'. The story of Ovid's fall, which had interested the young Milton, informs the narrator's hopes and fears about the consequences of his own poetic aspirations. Like Ovid, he is attempting a reverse metamorphosis in which he turns what has become evil into good.

As many critics have noted, the narrator's anxiety about his enterprise is most apparent in the invocations in which he draws attention to his own making of his poem.[118] He seems especially uncertain when he approaches the source of his creativity in Book 3, in which also he first represents his own creator, and in Book 7, in which he describes the creation of the world. In retelling the opening of Genesis, he is imagining his own poetic origins. The opportunity to tell the true story of creation which the ancients had glimpsed only in shadows enables him to surpass his poetic sources, as he reiterates his claim that 'above th' *Olympian* Hill I soare, | Above the flight of *Pegasean* wing' (7. 3–4). The subject of the divine creativity that he emulates, however, triggers the spectre of envy. The speaker presents himself as someone who is:

> fall'n on evil dayes,
> On evil dayes though fall'n, and evil tongues;
> In darkness, and with dangers compast round. (7. 25–7)

While he claims to be the innocent victim of slander, his physical blindness links him to the traditional representations of *invidia*.[119]

---

[118] See especially Fallon, *Milton's Peculiar Grace*, 210–32; Schwartz, *Remembering and Repeating*, 60–6; and Adelman, 'Creation and the Place of the Poet in *Paradise Lost*', 51–69.

[119] While Cheryl H. Fresch's reading of Satan's envious glances as Milton's exploration of the concept of the Evil Eye seems at times overly literal, she notes how this enables Milton to acknowledge his own limited perspective; see '"Aside the Devil Turned | For Envy": The Evil Eye in *Paradise Lost*, Book 4', in Kristin A. Pruitt and Charles W. Durham (eds.), *Living Texts: Interpreting Milton* (Selinsgrove, Pa., 2000), 118–30.

Moreover, the repeated word *fall'n* has obviously ominous resonances in this poem, even when used in this apparently neutral sense. At the same time as the poet appears as the target of external forces, he entertains the possibility of his own culpability.

FALLING POETS

By presenting himself as 'fall'n', the narrator also links himself to the falling or destroyed artist figures who appear throughout *Paradise Lost*. Like Ovid, Milton creates a hall of mirrors of artist figures who seem to predict his own fate, beginning with Mulciber in Book 1. As I noted earlier, one of the subtexts for Milton's description of this false but beautiful fall is Ovid's account of Phaethon. Told in *Metamorphoses* 1-2, and thus close to the unleashing of the figure of *Invidia*, the story of Apollo's doomed son is also part of Ovid's pattern of self-destructive artists. Drawing on both Homer's story of the fall of Hephaestus as well as the related tale of Icarus told in *Aeneid* 6 and Ovid's *Amores* 2, the episode raises the question of poetic imitation and succession.[120] Like Shakespeare's Adonis, Phaethon is too young, and is therefore unable to follow in the path of his father, the god of poetry. The rash son who falls mirrors by contrast Ovid, who at the end of his epic will soar above the stars to immortality. The poet's doubling with Phaethon is even more explicit in the *Fasti*, which recreates Phaethon's catastrophic meeting with the constellations as the poet's safe encounter with the signs of the zodiac.

Ovid's tale of deadly aspiration has always been a popular one, most often serving as another warning against the dangers of pride and rash ambition.[121] Golding sees the similarity between

---

[120] Ovid is particularly indebted to Virgil's description of the doors at Cumae on which the related story of Icarus' tragic flight is engraved (*Aeneid*, 6. 14-33); see Barchiesi (ed.), *Ovidio: Metamorfosi*, trans. Koch, i. 235-40. As I noted in Ch. 1, the opening description of *Metamorphoses* I-II 2 is recalled by Apuleius in the palace of Cupid in *The Golden Ass*, where the scene of broken succession is remade into a story of marital friction and resolution.

[121] See especially Sandys, *Ovid's Metamorphosis Englished, Mythologized, and Represented in Figures*, ed. Hulley and Vandersall, 106-9. Sandys's astronomical reading also makes the common connection between Phaethon and Lucifer: the story of Phaethon is another version of the fall of the devils.

Phaethon and Narcissus and combines the stories to offer a moral for the reader:

> The use of this same booke therfore is this: that every man
> (Endevoring for too know himself as neerly as he can,
> As though he in a chariot sat well ordered) should direct
> His mynd by reason in the way of vertue, and correct
> His feerce affections with the bit of temprance
> ('To the Ryght Honorable and his Singular Good Lord, Robert Erle of Leycester', 569–73)

In Elizabethan representations of tragic falls the story of Phaethon is often invoked; it is used to characterize Shakespeare's narcissistic Richard II (*Richard II*, 3. 3. 178–9), as well as Marlowe's protagonists, and provides the epic subtext for the attempt of Spenser's Mutabilitie to storm the heavens.[122] It is a constant theme, moreover, throughout Milton's works. The tale seems especially relevant for a young poet with grand dreams of poetic flight, the kind of 'rapture' I discussed in Chapter 1, but who is equally aware of the frailty of his wings/pen. The son who tries and fails to follow the path of his father, god of poetry, demonstrates further the perils of emulation, and the fragility of poetic succession.

In the early works, however, Milton seems generally to invoke the story of Phaethon in order to assure himself that his own path to the heavens will be more successful. As in Ovid, Phaethon offers an antithesis for the rising poet. In 'In Obitum Praesulis Eliensis' ('On the Death of the Bishop of Ely'), the dead Bishop rises to eternity, joyously and safely passing through the stars and retracing the route of Phaethon. A story of a pagan fall is thus inverted when it is converted into a scene of Christian apotheosis. A similarly successful ascent is imagined for the poet himself in 'Elegia 5', in which Milton claims to be lifted to the sky where heaven and hell open up to him and he comes face to face with Apollo himself. Earth's joyful

---

[122] See especially Marlowe, 1 *Tamburlaine*, 4. 2. 49–52; 2 *Tamburlaine*, 5. 3. 230–3; *Edward II* 1. 4. 16–17; *Doctor Faustus*, 3. Chorus. 1–10. Like other artists, Marlowe combines this with the tale of Icarus; see, for example, *Doctor Faustus*, 1. Chorus. 20–2. The tale was used further as an explicit political parable in the 1650s by the Presbyterian minister Thomas Hall who interpreted it as showing '*the Nature of rash, ambitious, inconsiderate Rulers, who being inflamed with a desire of Government, aim at things above their reach, to their own ruin and downfall*' (*Phaetons folly, or, The downfal of pride*, B1^v–B2^r).

welcoming of the Sun into her arms expresses the poet's confidence in the poetic path he is on: Earth says:

> Nec me (crede mihi) terrent Semelëia fata,
>   Nec Phäetontéo fumidus axis equo;
> Cum tu Phoebe tuo sapientius uteris igni,
>   Huc ades & gremio lumina pone meo.

('Believe me, Semele's fate does not frighten me, nor
    the chariot smoking with Phaethon's horse.
As you make use of your fire more wisely, Phoebus,
    come here and lay your sunlight in my lap', 91–4)

Similarly, the memory of Phaethon does not deter the poet but spurs his flight. Though he's not literally in the chariot of the sun, at the end of the poem he directs its course, telling Apollo to drive more slowly so that he can enjoy the spring as long as possible.

The story of Phaethon also appears in Milton's early defence of poetry, 'Ad Patrem'. As the title suggests, the poem is concerned with the relations between fathers and sons, and the relation between Phaethon and Apollo shadows that of Milton and his father. The premise of the poem (which may or may nor reflect real life) is that John Milton Sr. objected to his son's dedication to poetry and possibly, depending on when the poem was written, his choice of it as a career.[123] It thus stages a version of the classic generational conflict that in *Poetaster* Jonson makes part of Ovid's story. The pretext of parental disapproval allows Milton to celebrate the power of poetry, reminding his father that it is of divine origins and has the power to conquer death and confer immortality. But the poem also suggests that this self-defence is not necessary. The conflict between father and son dissolves when Milton points out that his father is an artist too:

> Nec tu perge precor sacras contemnere Musas,
> Nec vanas inopesque puta, quarum ipse peritus
> Munere, mille sonos numeros componis ad aptos,
> Millibus & vocem modulis variare canoram
> Doctus, Arionii meritò sis nominis haeres.
> Nunc tibi quid mirum, si me genuisse poëtam
> Contigerit, charo si tam propè sanguine juncti
> Cognatas artes, studiumque affine sequamur:

---

[123] On the date of composition, see *Variorum*, i. 232–40.

> Ipse volens Phoebus se dispertire duobus,
> Altera dona mihi, dedit altera dona parenti,
> Dividuumque Deum genitorque puerque tenemus.

('So I pray, do not continue scorning the sacred muses.
Do not think them vain and poor in whose art you are skilful,
You who set a thousand notes to proper measures and learned
to tune a harmonious voice for a thousand melodies—
may you deservedly inherit Arion's name.
Why wonder now if you happened to father a poet
in me—if we, joined so close by our cherished blood,
pursue the kindred arts, affiliated studies?
Phoebus, wanting to share himself with two of us,
presented some gifts to me, and others to my father,
and we keep this partitioned god, father and son', 56–66)[124]

Milton's dedication to poetry turns out not to be a rebellion against his father after all. Moreover, his earthly father is in fact only his brother; they are both sons of Apollo, from whom they receive their joint inheritance.

The transformation of John Sr. from father to brother eliminates the possibility of Oedipal rivalry while also enabling Milton to claim that he can surpass his father while still acknowledging his debts. When Milton thanks his father for all he has given him he adds:

> Quae potuit majora pater tribuisse, vel ipse
> Jupiter, excepto, donâsset ut omnia, coelo?
> Non potiora dedit, quamvis & tuta fuissent,
> Publica qui juveni commisit lumina nato
> Atque Hyperionios currus, & fraena diei,
> Et circùm undantem radiatâ luce tiaram.

('What greater could a father give? Could Jove himself
if he had given everything (excepting heaven)?
He gave no better who entrusted our shared light,
Hyperion's chariot, the day's reins, and the crown

---

[124] Here one can see Milton's early attention to Ovid's exilic verse in the context specifically of the defence of art. The poem's argument in general echoes the self-defence of *Ex Ponto* 4. 8, in which Ovid notes the divine origins and powers of poetry (45–62), while the passage here specifically reworks his plea to Germanicus: 'non potes officium vatis contemnere vates' ('Thou canst not as a poet despise the tribute of a poet', *Ex Ponto* 4. 8. 67).

> surging with radiating light to his young son—
> even had these been safe!', 95–100)

Still, the expression of gratitude is somewhat ambiguous: if heaven is the one thing that even Jove could not give, it is the thing Milton most wants and which, he claims, he will earn for himself through poetry. Moreover, the reference to Apollo's deadly paternal gifts seems unsettling, suggesting as it does that fathers do not always give their sons the best things. (Look at Icarus too!) Phaethon's journey is recalled earlier in the poem, in Milton's description of poetry's ability to elevate us to the stars (35–40). Here again, however, the constellations that so terrified poor Phaethon are under the poet's command. Like the Bishop of Ely, the poet is a successful Phaethon whose mastery of his father's powers earns him control of the stars. As in 'Elegia 5', Phaethon provides a contrast that ensures Milton's future success: his fall to earth defines Milton's rise to the heavens. Where Phaethon was not able to assume his father's role, Milton imagines himself acknowledging his legacies from his human, heavenly, and indeed literary fathers, which lead him to rise above the stars to eternity. Moreover, the son's ascent benefits his father as well. By surpassing his father, the son is able to immortalize him; the poem ends by asserting not the poet's eternal life in his art, but that of his subject (115–20).

David Quint has argued further that in *Paradise Lost* Milton uses the figures of both Phaethon and Icarus, commonly linked in the Renaissance, to differentiate between Satan's destruction and the Son's creativity, and to represent but ultimately assuage his own 'fear of falling'. Quint notes how *Paradise Lost* offers different versions of Ovid's doomed son. In the war in heaven, a Satanic Phaethon is contrasted with and defeated by the redeemed Phaethon, the Son. The Son's reimagining of the story of the failed heir in turn becomes a model for the narrator himself, who 'claims to be a successful Icarus in his poetic flight'.[125] The poet marks out a different route to heaven from that of Phaethon: when Raphael warns Adam not to speculate about the nature of the stars, he also deters him from following the path of both Phaethon and the Ovid of the *Fasti*.

As the recurrence of Phaethon suggests, however, Milton's poetic flight is strikingly littered with fallen and falling bodies. Even in the *History of Britain*, Milton can't resist digressing to tell the weird story

---

[125] 'Fear of Falling', 875.

of Elmer, a monk of Malmsbury who claimed to be able to read the stars but 'who could not foresee, when time was, the breaking of his own Legs for soaring too high. He in his youth strangely aspiring, had made and fitted Wings to his Hands and Feet; with these on the top of a Tower, spread out to gather air, he flew more then a Furlong; but the wind being too high, came fluttering down, to the maiming of all his Limbs' (*Works*, x. 308). The theme of false ascent first appears in the early series of Gunpowder Plot poems in which the conspirators try to blow the King sky high. In *Paradise Lost*, it is continued in Satan's flight (Books 2 and 3) and also in the fate of the future inhabitants of the '*Limbo* large and broad, since calld | The Paradise of Fools' (3. 495–6) described during this journey.[126] The self-destructive nature of Satan's attempted ascent is suggested as Milton digresses to explain how those who in the future try to rise to heaven through false means will be blown to a place that contains a 'store' 'Of all things transitorie and vain, when Sin | With vanity had filld the works of men: | Both all things vain, and all who in vain things | Build thir fond hopes of Glorie or lasting fame' (3. 444, 446–9). The Limbo of Fools is a place where *copia*, store, has become destructive for those who are trapped in the narcissistic love of illusions. Appropriately, it is described at the end of Book 3, in which the Son is presented as the true pathway to heaven.

Milton's use of Phaethon and these other figures suggests that for him, as for the early Ovid, the creation of authorial doubles is a means of proving his own success. The poet rises by projecting his fear of falling onto these others. In *Paradise Regain'd*, Jesus will recognize that his relation with Satan is governed by a similar teeter-totter dynamic; as he says to his devilish double: 'Know'st thou not that my rising is thy fall, | And my promotion will be thy destruction?' (3. 201–2). As Ovid's example suggests, however, this strategy of self-definition through projection can reveal likeness as well as difference. Moreover, elsewhere in the poem, Milton's narrator acknowledges his resemblance to authorial figures who suggest vulnerability. Lamenting his blindness, the speaker seeks consolation for the loss of external light by comparing himself with the inspired classical blind bards whose fame he hopes to equal: Homer, Thamyris, Tiresias, and

---

[126] The episode draws also on Astolfo's flight to the moon in *Orlando Furioso* 34–5, in which Ariosto mocks dreams of artistic immortality.

Phineus (3. 32–6).[127] The repetition of 'equal'd' in lines 33 and 34 stresses identification and seems to head off the possibility of either rivalry or opposition: here the speaker does not soar above past models, but seeks safety by joining them. But it's mixed company. Homer's presence in this context seems straightforward and unambiguous. As the first poet, he is the pure fountain of natural art, the ideal example for the poet whose story also goes backs to the origins of all things. Tiresias, the prophet associated with sex changes and with Narcissus, is more complicated. Struck blind by the malicious Juno, he comes from a world of unjust divine forces who envy and punish mortal visionaries. The comparison might suggest that the narrator is subtly murmuring against the injustice of his own fate. But the blindness of Thamyris and Phineus is caused by their own errors, raising different questions.[128] Phineus was associated with rivalry between both fathers and sons and also humans and gods: according to different stories, he was punished with blindness either for his blinding of his sons, who had been falsely accused of adultery with their own stepmother, or for revealing the secrets of the gods. Moreover, the singer Thamyris, like many Ovidian figures, challenged the Muses to a singing match; losing it, he lost his vision and, even more terrifyingly, his genius.

The invocation that introduces the creation of the world in Book 7 calls up further artist figures who reflect on the narrator's situation. It climaxes with Orpheus, the classical poet who had interested Milton from early on in his career.[129] Here again, the classical figure is used as a contrast. As 'Lycidas' had earlier shown, the story of Orpheus reveals the limitations of classical myths. While the classical Muse

---

[127] On this passage in relation to Milton's self-presentation, see also Fallon, *Milton's Peculiar Grace*, 218–22.

[128] See the accounts of both in Natale Conti, *Mythologiae*, ii. 518–20 (the story of Thamyris appropriately comes between Niobe and Marsyas); and ii. 617–18.

[129] On Milton's interest in Orpheus, see DuRocher, *Milton and Ovid*, 64–74; and especially Rachel Falconer, *Orpheus Dis(re)membered: Milton and the Myth of the Poet-Hero* (Sheffield, 1996); and Martin Dawes, 'Milton and the Politics of Enchantment', Ph.D. diss. (McGill University, 2009). There is a common assumption that for Milton and other Renaissance writers, Orpheus is the ultimate artist figure; moreover, for Richard DuRocher, 'Orpheus is not only a lyric poet but in some sense the figure of Ovid in his work' (*Milton and Ovid*, 65). While Orpheus and his quest to conquer death through poetry haunts Milton's poetry, I see him as part of a larger cluster of questions about the poet and art generally. Ovid's Orpheus is himself a reworking of the Virgilian figure of the fourth *Georgic*, indicating again the revisionary nature of Ovid's poetic vision.

could not protect her son, the narrator has higher hopes for his Christian one: 'For thou art Heav'nlie, shee an empty dreame' (*PL*, 7. 39). The speaker reassures himself once more that pagan figures are just shadowy types of Christian reality.

However, the narrator who has 'fall'n' on hard times also remembers another classical fall which he does not wish to emulate. He asks his Muse to guide him down to earth:

> Least from this flying Steed unrein'd, (as once
> *Bellerophon*, though from a lower Clime)
> Dismounted, on th' *Aleian* Field I fall
> Erroneous there to wander and forlorne. (7. 17–20)

In some ways, Bellerophon seems a surprising figure here, replacing the more obvious examples of Phaethon and Icarus.[130] He is most famous as the rider of Pegasus, the horse of poetry, to which Milton had alluded in an early letter to Charles Diodati describing his own poetic flight: 'quid cogitem quaeris? Ita me bonus Deus, immortalitatem. Quid agam vero? πτεροφῶ, & volare meditor: sed tenellis admodum adhuc pennis evehit se noster Pegasus, humile sapiamus' ('You ask what I am thinking of? So may the good Deity help me, of immortality! And what am I doing? Growing my wings and meditating flight; but as yet our Pegasus raises himself on very tender pinions. Let us be lowly wise', *Works*, xii. 26). The young poet knows he needs to curb his aspirations. In contrast, Bellerophon, like Thamyris, was associated with human presumption and literally flying too high. In *Iliad* 6. 200–2, Bellerophon's attempt to see the stars (from which Adam will be discouraged) is an act of hubris punished by the gods with blindness and exile. In *Isthmian 7*, moreover, Pindar represents Bellerophon as an overreacher driven by *phthonos* to challenge the limitations of human nature; the poet expresses his own hope that if he accepts his station he will not be troubled by the *phthonos* of the gods. Bellerophon is thus specifically the opposite of Pindar, who adheres to an ideal of *mediocritas*.[131] In Horace's *Odes* 4. 2, Bellerophon is one

---

[130] See also Fallon, *Milton's Peculiar Grace*, 222–30.
[131] See further Stella Revard, *Pindar and the Renaissance Hymn-Ode, 1450–1700*, Medieval & Renaissance Texts & Studies 221 (Tempe, Ariz., 2001), 113–18. She argues elsewhere that the figure of Bellerophon appears indirectly in Milton's 'Ad Patrem' to show how 'the poet must walk humbly, lest he provoke the envy of the gods or the malice and spite of human beings' (*Milton and the Tangles*, 214). As Revard notes, however, in 'Olympian 13', Pindar uses Bellerophon as a positive example of the artist.

of Pindar's most characteristic figures, whom Horace recalls as he asserts his own desire 'aemulari' ('to emulate') the Greek poet both in verse and in his adherence to the middle ground.[132] While he emulates Pindar, he hopes his aspiration will not end as did the flight of Icarus (1–4). As Horace suggests, the story of Bellerophon is similar to and was often linked with those of the doomed sons Icarus and Phaethon. Yet his story is not identical to theirs. Although Bellerophon is an image for excess ambition, he is also connected to virtue and, through Pegasus, the Muses and poetic flight. Moreover, he is a chaste young man who rejects lust. The innocent victim of envy and slander, he ends up blind, wandering, and, in Petrarch's account, 'ipse suum cor edens' ('eating his heart out')[133]—as the envious are themselves described.[134] More than the young Icarus and Phaethon, Bellerophon seems an especially appropriate and potentially troubling double for the blind and alienated narrator.

SIN AND HER ORIGINALS

Like the exiled Ovid, Milton's narrator is acutely conscious of his resemblance to fallen artists, including Ovid himself. Moreover, in describing himself as 'In darkness, and with dangers compast round' (*PL*, 7. 27) the narrator shapes himself in the image of Sin who is

---

[132] Cited from Horace, *The Odes and Epodes*, trans. C. E. Bennett (rev. 2nd edn., Cambridge, Mass., 1960). On the influence of Pindar on Renaissance readings of the myth, see Revard, *Pindar and the Renaissance Hymn-Ode*, 114 n. 116.

[133] Petrarch, *De Secreto Conflictu Curarum Mearum*, in *Opere*, ed. G. Ponte (Milan, 1968), iii. 548; cited from Marianne Shapiro, 'Perseus and Bellerophon in *Orlando Furioso*', *Modern Philology*, 81/2 (1983), 116.

[134] Bellerophon appears in the *Ibis* as one of the many figures whose fate Ovid wishes on his enemy. Ovid mentions him close to the figures of Phineus and Thamyris; see *Ibis* 257–74 and the commentaries in La Penna, *Scholia*, 24–7, which note how the stories are connected through the themes of blindness, chastity, and generational conflict. The scholia also refers to a tradition in which it was not just his heart that the fallen Bellerophon ate but 'perfractis cruribus artus edisse suos' ('His legs being broken, he ate his own limbs', ibid. 24). I have not found any other references to this version, which seems influenced by the story of Erysichthon (*Met.*, 8. 877–8) and by Ovid's general fascination with forms of self-consumption, although Petrarch may have had it in mind. For more traditional summaries of the story of Bellerophon, see Fabius Planciades Fulgentius, *Fulgentius the Mythographer*, trans. Francis George Whitbread (Columbus, Oh., 1971), 82–4; and Conti, *Mythologiae*, ii. 824–8.

'With terrors and with clamors compasst round' (2. 862). Her particular terrors are, of course, her own creations, the hell-hounds who, as she explains, 'when they list into the womb | That bred them they return, and howle and gnaw | My Bowels, thir repast' (2. 798–800). Milton's Sin is imagined as perverse and self-destructive creativity that redounds upon its origins, as Ovid's poetry had turned upon him. Through her, Milton is able to examine his own art, and its relation to the origins of evil. Sin marks the place where imitation becomes sterile copying, and where Satan turned from emulating God to just envying him.[135] With Sin, literary history becomes an endless cycle of incestuously generated creatures who try to destroy their own creators, only to find themselves trapped in self-consuming parody of them. Satan is indeed the author of one kind of anxiety of influence.

As an allegorical figure, Sin can trace her ancestry broadly back to Ovid's use of allegory as a place for reflecting on his metamorphosis of abstract concepts into embodied figures, shadows into substances.[136]

---

[135] Sin's double nature is anticipated in an earlier image of perverted creativity in Milton's *Defensio Secunda*. Attacking two 'poetasters' who had defended his enemy Salmasius, Milton describes them as: 'vel duo vel unus, biformi sane specie & bicolore; Sphingémne dicam an Horatianum illud monstrum Poëticum, capite muliebri, cervice asininâ, variis indutum plumis, undique collatis membris: id profectò ipsissimum est. Rhapsodus videlicet quispiam, centonibus & pannis obsitus; unúsne an duo incertum, nam & Anonymus quoque est' ('either two or one; but there are two different shapes and colours. Shall I call it a sphinx, or that poetical monster of Horace, with a woman's head, an ass's neck, arrayed in motley plumes, and with limbs assembled from different animals? Aye, that is the very thing: that is, some rhapsodist, covered from head to foot with centos and patches; whether he is one or two is doubtful, as he also is without a name' (*Works*, viii. 76). Unable to create themselves, these ambiguous creatures are stitched together out of the bits and pieces of others, 'sine delectu, sine discrimine' ('without choice, without discrimination', *Works*, viii. 78), and are contrasted with those who are truly poets, and who Milton insists are the sworn enemies of tyrants. While the central subtext here is Horace's *Ars Poetica*, the couple who are both two and one look back to Ovid's hermaphrodite (*Met.*, 4. 373–9) and hybrid monsters.

[136] In the 1720s George Sewell noted that Ovid's figures were key for later allegory: 'Those *Shadowy Beings*, as they have been lately properly termed, which abound in *Spenser, Milton*, (and I might go back to *Chaucer*) are mostly owing to *Ovid*. Spenser, in particular is remarkable for imitating the Exuberance of our Poet in all his *Creatures of Fancy*' (*Ovid's Metamorphoses* (1724), qtd. in Colin Burrow, '"Full of the Maker's Guile": Ovid on Imitating and on the Imitation of Ovid', in Hardie, Barchiesi, and Hinds (eds.), *Ovidian Transformations*, 284). Since Dr Johnson first complained that Milton's use of allegory was 'undoubtedly faulty' in its 'ascribing effects to non-entity' (*Lives*, i. 127), critics have debated the appropriateness of the form for this particular episode. Barbara Kiefer Lewalski argues that by representing

Moreover, in fleshing out the meaning of Sin, Milton draws together a number of specific Ovidian figures. As I noted in the last chapter, the story of her origins recalls the tale of Narcissus. The description of her metamorphosis from lovely to loathsome lady looks back also to the story of Scylla told in *Metamorphoses* 13–14, as part of Ovid's retelling of the Trojan War and founding of Rome.[137] Ovid's episode is a literary *aition*, explaining the origins of the monster of *Odyssey* 12 by tracing it to a love triangle between Scylla, her suitor, Glaucus, and another dangerous female, Circe, who is in love with Glaucus.[138] As I noted in the last chapter, Ovid's failed courtship scene, in which Glaucus tells his story of metamorphosis to impress his beloved, is used also by Satan as part of his enticement of Eve. Scylla's rejection of love, however, leads unfortunately to her deformation. Her story is thus a more sinister version of that of Daphne. Spurning Glaucus, who has himself been turned into a kind of merman, Scylla is transformed by the vengeful Circe into a hybrid monster, still female on top, but below a bunch of savage dogs that gnaw on her. She tries to run from what she, like Narcissus, has not yet realized is herself, 'sed quos fugit, attrahit una' ('But what she tries to flee she takes along with her', *Met.*, 14. 63). She is one of Ovid's most terrifying stories of physical and psychological self-division: Ovidian hybridity at its most monstrous and self-destructive.

Like other Ovidian hybrids, Scylla is inspiring for the epyllion, and, in fact, the subject of the first English epyllion, Thomas Lodge's 1589 *Scillaes Metamorphosis*. In Lodge's version, Scylla is the familiar hardhearted Lady who rejects desire, and who is gratifyingly punished by

---

Sin and Death as allegorical figures Milton 'emphasizes their ontological status as concepts, lacking the reality of living beings', and so shows Satan's 'essential sterility' (*Paradise Lost and the Rhetoric of Literary Forms*, 74). See also Quilligan, *Milton's Spenser*, 119–20, 129–32; and Stephen M. Fallon, 'Milton's Sin and Death: The Ontology of Allegory in *Paradise Lost*', *English Literary Renaissance*, 17/3 (1987), 329–50.

[137] Harding, *Milton and the Renaissance Ovid*, 96–7; DuRocher, *Milton and Ovid*, 204–5. Like the other stories in these books, the tale of monstrous metamorphosis comments indirectly on Aeneas' quest; not only does Glaucus' journey roughly follow that of Aeneas, but Scylla's Ovidian self-division suggests the potential incoherence in Aeneas' character that erupts in his last action of the *Aeneid*.

[138] Ovid's revision again changes elements in the story to bring out the sinister side of Circe: where Homer's enchantress warns the Greeks about the perils of Scylla, Ovid's is the author of those perils.

being turned to stone.[139] Lodge thus uses the story to teach the familiar moral of the tale of Narcissus. As Milton also recognizes, however, Ovid himself links the two figures: Scylla's discovery of her own division as she looks in the water clearly echoes the story of Narcissus (combined with that of Actaeon): seeing the barking dogs, she at first does not know herself (*Met.*, 14. 61–3). As Hardie notes, in classical poetry she was a figure for tall tales, and 'a touchstone for poetic fictiveness'.[140] She is art that is pure illusion. As Ovid knew, moreover, Scylla was associated with licentious female sexuality which is always the dark underbelly of the chaste disdainful lady of love poetry.[141] Sandys explains that she is 'a Virgin; who as long as she is chast in thought, and in body unspotted, appears of an excellent beauty . . . But once polluted with the sorceries of Circe; that is, having rendred her maiden honour to bee deflowered by bewitching pleasure, she is transformed into an horrid monster.'[142] (One might imagine her as the Lady transformed by Comus into her opposite.) Moreover, as Charles Segal notes, Scylla is a 'monstrous version of parturition',[143] a nightmare image of fertility gone wrong. Scylla is connected generally to perverse creativity, and also to envy, which St Basil had compared to the viper devoured by its newborn young.[144] Sandys notes the association of Scylla with 'the envy of infamous women';[145] in de Deguilleville's *Pèlerinage de vie humaine*, she accompanies the allegorical figure of Envy.[146] She inspires later images for perverted creation, most notably Spenser's Errour, with her viper spawn whom she endlessly produces and consumes (*FQ*, 1. 1. 14).[147]

---

[139] As Ovid had explained, Scylla was later transformed into the dangerous rock that is proverbially paired with Charybdis (*Met.*, 14. 74) and a conventional peril to all sea travellers. Lodge omits Scylla's first transformation to make his point.

[140] 'The Self-Divisions of Scylla', *Trends in Classics*, 1 (2009), 122.

[141] See also Catullus, *Odes*, 60. 1–2, in which the poet accuses the hard-hearted Lesbia of having turned into the monstrous Scylla. If Daphne is the image of the ideal chaste virgin, Scylla may be the same figure seen from a different perspective.

[142] *Ovid's Metamorphosis*, 645.

[143] 'Ovid's Metamorphic Bodies: Art, Gender, and Violence in the *Metamorphoses*', *Arion*, 3rd series, 5/3 (1998), 31.

[144] See above, p. 236; and Hardie, 'The Self-Divisions of Scylla', 131 n. 42.

[145] *Ovid's Metamorphosis*, 645.

[146] Lydgate, *Pilgrimage*, 23050–2; see also 21328–38 where she appears as an 'Old enchaunteresse [*sic*]' (21329). For further examples of this association, see Hardie, 'The Self-Divisions of Scylla', 127–31.

[147] Cyril Tourneur's complaint on the degeneration of English verse following the death of Spenser, *The Transformed Metamorphosis* (1600), draws on imagery

Sin is thus part of a convoluted and inherently incestuous family tree. However, the most obvious classical model for her birth is that of Minerva, goddess of wisdom.[148] Milton's choice of subtext has puzzled some critics—John Mulryan wonders 'why did he give a negative twist to a basically positive myth?'[149] In the *Odyssey*, the Greek Athena is the guardian of the crafty Odysseus, and she is often associated with creativity. In the *Tristia*, Ovid notes that his birthday falls during a festival sacred to Minerva (*Tristia*, 4. 10. 13); in the *Fasti*, he invokes the goddess as his patroness: 'mille dea est operum: certe dea carminis illa est; | si mereor, studiis adsit amica meis' ('She is the goddess of a thousand works; certainly she is the goddess of song; may she be friendly to my pursuits, if I deserve it', 3. 833–4). (The tribute is diluted slightly by the fact that he promiscuously claims many other divine patrons throughout the poem.[150]) The use of the myth as a subtext for Sin seems thus to suggest further how in rewriting his sources, Satan parodies them, perverting creativity and knowledge.

Yet in Ovid, Minerva is a complicated figure. In the *Metamorphoses*, she is linked to Ovid's nemesis, *Invidia*, whom she raises in Book 2. Ovid tells us that Minerva cannot enter Envy's hideous lair nor even bear to look directly at her; Sandys interprets this to mean that they are opposites that can never meet.[151] In Renaissance art, Minerva is often represented as vanquishing Envy.[152] However, in

---

from both Ovid and Spenser to explain how artists who have been deceived by false art that 'in female shape a serpent stands' (184) so that each 'Teares vp our mothers wombe to finde hir slime: | And doth ysearch her bowells all vncleane, | For noysome filth; the poyson of our time' (B7^v, B8^v).

[148] In terms of biblical sources, critics often cite Wisdom 2: 23–5, a passage which, tellingly, links imitation, envy, and the birth of Death: 'Quoniam Deus creavit hominem inexterminabilem, Et ad imaginem similitudinis suae fecit illum. Invidia autem diaboli mors introivit in orbem terrarum: Imitantur autem illum qui sunt ex parte illius' ('For God created man incorruptible, and to the image of his own likeness he made him. But by the envy of the devil, death came into the world: And they follow [*imitor*] him that are of his side').

[149] *Through a Glass Darkly*, 239.

[150] '[C]erte dea' also recalls Aeneas's famous and resonant identification of *Venus* ('O dea certe', *Aeneid*, 1. 328), a goddess with whom Ovid identifies more frequently. Minerva is thus getting Venus' hand-me-down epithets, turned inside out to feebly mask the borrowing.

[151] *Ovid's Metamorphosis*, 62.

[152] See Jonson, 'Ode 34', in *Ben Jonson: The Complete Poems*, ed. George Parfitt (New Haven, 1975), in which he asks Athena to make the 'Gorgon Envye yield' (41). The power of Minerva to conquer envy seems to be a further message of the story of

Metamorphoses 2 Ovid sets up verbal parallels between the two figures.[153] They meet again in the story of Arachne, which demonstrates the fate of presumptuous mortals who rival their own teachers. Arachne, the goddess's 'aemula' ('rival', 6. 83), refuses to praise Minerva or even acknowledge that the goddess is the source of her skill; the girl's belligerent insistence on artistic autonomy—'consilii satis est in me mihi' ('I am quite able to advise myself', 6. 40)—anticipates Satan's denial that he was created by the Son. Arachne's arrogance and *invidia* (*phthonos*) seem justifiably to trigger divine *phthonos* in response. This is the way in which she will appear in Spenser's 'Muiopotmos', where Arachne's own inherent envy of Minerva turns her into a spider (339–52). For Spenser, the transformation simply reveals the girl's already invidious nature.

Ovid, however, tells a different story in which metamorphosis is imposed on Arachne from outside. The duel between Arachne and Minerva is a classic example of the artistic competition made famous in the singing matches of Virgil's *Eclogues*, in which poets try to outdo each other. The winner here is not clear. While Minerva's art may be divine, Arachne's creation is so perfect that 'Non illud Pallas, non illud carpere Livor | possit opus' ('Not Pallas, nor Envy himself, could find a flaw in that work', *Met.*, 6. 129–30). The syntactical parallelism here links not *Arachne* and Envy but *Pallas* and Envy as equal forces critical of human endeavours. In Ovid, it is in fact Minerva who, enraged by the girl's superb achievement, destroys Arachne's tapestry, and then hits her on the head. The maddened Arachne attempts to hang herself, at which point Minerva turns her into a spider. As in *Metamorphoses* 2, Minerva seems to create *invidia*.[154]

Ovid's story suggests that Satan may be right: the gods are envious after all. Of all Ovid's stories, that of Arachne has most commonly been evoked as a portrait of the artist himself, the 'prototype of the

---

the murder of Perdix in *Metamorphoses* 8. Minerva and Envy are linked in a single line (8. 250), but as potential opposites. The goddess is the counter of the invidious Daedalus, as she is the protector of 'ingenium', who saves Perdix, albeit by turning him into a partridge.

[153] See Keith, *The Play of Fictions*, 126; and Feeney, *The Gods in Epic*, 246.

[154] Fulgentius' reading of the story of the birth of Minerva's ward Ericthonius, also told in *Metamorphoses* 2, seems similarly to imply that Minerva produces Envy; he connects Ericthonius with Envy by identifying *tonos* as *phthonos* (*Fulgentius the Mythographer*, 76).

exiled poet' and victim of envy.[155] Barkan's *The Gods Made Flesh* begins with the figure of Arachne whose art, in contrast to the staid images of divine order propagated by Minerva, mirrors the poet's vision and anticipates the later metamorphic tradition.[156] She provides a good image for the poet as persecuted victim, destroyed by unjust political authority supported by conservative—perhaps even Virgilian?—aesthetics.

Spenser's revision of the story of Arachne is worth pausing briefly over, however, as his epyllion turns Ovid's victim into the villain of a tale about artistic rivalry. Moreover, as Ronald Bond has argued, Spenser rewrites Ovid's myth as 'an aetiology of envy'.[157] Spenser traces the origins of the sin back to the competition between Arachne and Minerva, which is the beginning also of the enmity between the butterfly and the spider. Classical and Renaissance writers commonly used contrasting kinds of insects as models to describe different forms of creativity. The bee's gathering and transformation of nectar from a variety of flowers is a common image for *imitatio*.[158] The predatory spider, which spins its web out of its own guts, is associated with a more self-contained and often sinister kind of creation; Bacon uses it to deride scholastic philosophy for solipsistically indulging in its own introverted reflections.[159] In 'The Preface: Too the Reader' in his translation of Ovid, Golding uses those two insects suggestively to describe two kinds of readers: those who will take his work 'as fragrant flowers most full of pleasant juce, | The which the Bee conveying home may put too wholesome use' and those who use

---

[155] Harries, 'The Spinner and the Poet: Arachne in Ovid's *Metamorphoses*', 65.

[156] See 1–5 especially. On the centrality of this episode to the *Metamorphoses*, see also Leach, 'Ekphrasis and the Theme of Artistic Failure in Ovid's *Metamorphoses*'.

[157] Ronald Bond, '*Invidia* and the Allegory of Spenser's "Muiopotmos"', 146.

[158] So the younger Seneca famously says: 'Apes, ut aiunt, debemus imitari' ('We should follow, men say, the example of the bees', *Ad Lucilium Epistulae Morales*, ii, 84. 3). Both Pigman and Greene discuss this tradition more generally. Greene suggests that the bee offers a non-conflictual model for copying (*The Light in Troy*, 75).

[159] See Bacon, *The Advancement of Learning*, ed. Michael Kiernan (Oxford, 2000), 24: 'This kinde of degenerate learning did chiefly raigne amongst the Schoole-men, who . . . did out of no great quantitie of matter, and infinite agitation of wit, spin out vnto vs those laborious webbes of Learning which are extant in their Bookes. For the wit and minde of man, if it worke vpon matter, which is the contemplation of the creatures of God worketh according to the stuffe, and is limited thereby; but if it worke vpon it selfe, as the Spider worketh his webbe, then it is endlesse, and brings forth indeed Copwebs of learning, admirable for the finesse of thread and worke, but of no substance or profite'.

the work like the spider which 'sucking on too poison may convert, | Through venym spred in all her limbes and native in hir hart' (163–6). The differences between types of insects also play a role in moral fables. Spenser's couple recalls the common antithesis found in the didactic tradition between the carefree grasshopper and the careful ant. This opposition would later be politicized by the defeated Royalist poets Lovelace and Cowley, for whom the grasshopper epitomizes their own Ovidian poetry and indeed their fate at the hands of the revolutionary regime.[160]

Spenser's little tale of the spider's killing of the butterfly invokes these different traditions and complicates them, as the poem gives us the terms of a moral fable and then makes it hard to figure out the moral. For one thing, it is not clear which side of this insectine war the poet is on. Readers who see the fable as an allegory of the dangers of pleasure tend to side implicitly with the spider Aragnoll; those who emphasize the poem as a story about art, remembering also that Psyche can mean soul as well as butterfly, are more sympathetic to the butterfly Clarion.[161] Like the grasshopper, and in contrast to the spider, ant, or bee, Spenser's butterfly makes nothing at all. He is not himself a producer of beautiful things, but merely their consumer, whose day is spent flitting about happily to please his carefree 'fancie' ('Muiopotmos', 158). In contrast, the spider is productive—and Aragnoll makes a pretty impressive web (357–76). Yet his artwork is also murderous. Moreover, as Ronald Bond notes, in didactic treatments, the spider is often associated with envy and detraction.[162] Aragnoll is a killer, driven by 'Enfested grudge' (354) and 'vengefull malice' (356); even more diabolically he is 'The foe of faire things, th'author of confusion, | The shame of Nature, the bondslaue of spight' (244–5).[163]

In the moral tradition, the butterfly is often identified with the ephemerality of earthly beauty. Clarion is certainly a more attractive

---

[160] See Richard Lovelace's 'The Grasse-hopper' and 'The Ant', and Abraham Cowley's 'The Grashopper'.
[161] See Judith Dundas's '*Muiopotmos*: A World of Art', *Yearbook of English Studies*, 5 (1975), 30–8. Although Dundas identifies Aragnoll as 'the life-denying impulses' and Clarion as the 'life-affirming' (36), she argues that the poem shows a world that must include both.
[162] '*Invidia* and the Allegory of Spenser's "Muiopotmos"', 149–50 especially.
[163] Franklin E. Court, 'The Theme and Structure of Spenser's *Muiopotmos*', *Studies in English Literature*, 10 (1970), 1–15, thus identifies him with Satan.

and fragile figure than the malicious spider: he is a splendid work of art in himself, whose wings are 'Painted with thousand colours, passing farre | All Painters skill' (90–1). Delightfully 'careles' (375), he seems the spirit of beauty and freedom, who represents (in miniature) the poet's highest dream of bliss:

> What more felicitie can fall to creature,
> Than to enjoy delight with libertie,
> And to be Lord of all the workes of Nature,
> To raine in th'aire from earth to highest skie,
> To feed on flowers, and weeds of glorious feature,
> To take what euer thing doth please the eie?
> Who rests not pleased with such happiness,
> Well worthie he to taste of wretchednes. (209–16)

Spenser seems unable to contain his own delight in this world of infinite variety and charm, and the fantasy of total freedom. Moreover, identified with 'change', gadding about 'careleslie' (391), and 'wauering wit' (160), Clarion is the poem's Ovidian spirit. Spenser seems to be adapting Ovid's story of Arachne but reversing the roles, drawing on the story of the innocent poet who was persecuted and crushed by poisonous envy. Given Spenser's own apparent experiences with the corrosive power of *invidia*, one could imagine that he sympathized with the exiled Ovid.[164]

Still, there are aspects of Clarion's character that might undermine his innocence. In his own little buggy way he extends his dominion over the world around him, seeing himself as 'Lord of all the workes of Nature' (211). The ethical concern with the complicity between poetry and imperialism that shadows *The Faerie Queene* seems to be already sneaking in here. Clarion begins by taking in his garden with his eyes (171), but this leads to a more direct possession and consumption as 'He casts his glutton sense to satisfie, | Now sucking of the sap of herbe most meete' (179–80). Innocent pleasure slides easily, even

---

[164] Bond's reading suggests this identification. He interprets Clarion as Spenser's desire for fame, linking the name to Calliope's announcement in *The Teares of the Muses*: 'now I will my golden Clarion rend' (463; see Bond, '*Invidia* and the Allegory of Spenser's "Muiopotmos"', 150). Spenser's self-representation as a butterfly thus attests to his growing frustration with his lack of power at court; envy had crushed his fame. Richard Helgerson similarly suggests that by the 1590s Spenser 'saw himself less as a new Virgil and more as the Ovid of the *Tristia*, abandoned by his friends for his *carmen et error*' (*Self-Crowned Laureates*, 86); see also Stapleton, *Spenser's Ovidian Poetics*, esp. 41–73.

naturally, into destruction: 'And then again he turneth to his play, | To spoyle the pleasures of that Paradise' (185-6):

> Of euerie one he takes, and tastes at will,
> And on their pleasures greedily doth pray.
> That when he hath both plaid and fed his fill,
> In the warme Sunne he doth himself embay,
> And there him rests in riotous suffisaunce
> Of all his gladness, and kingly ioyaunce. (203-8)[165]

While it is possible to dismiss this as mock moralizing, appropriate for a mock epic,[166] for Spenser this is pretty dangerous language: *spoyle, greed, riot*. Is Clarion such a completely innocent victim after all, or does his behaviour somehow generate his own downfall? The fact that this description of rampage *precedes* the poet's rhapsode on the bug's perfect life makes the question even more difficult to answer. Even the ideal and innocent world of artistic liberty seems to unleash forces of destruction. At the end, moreover, Clarion's own striving for freedom hastens his death as, caught in the spider's web, 'striuing more, the more in laces strong | Himselfe he tide, and wrapt his winges twaine | In lymie snares the subtill loupes among' (427-9).

Striving to align the two sides with moral positions seems futile. There is, however, another way of describing this insectomachia. The opposition between the two bugs lines up with the two primary poetic sources of the poem. In genre, figures, and rhetoric, this epyllion seems to point back to Ovid. But it centres on enemies rather than lovers, hatred rather than desire. Moreover, the opening and close are Virgilian. It begins with an announcement of an epic battle between two mighty forces and an echo of *Aeneid* 1. 11's famous 'tantaene animis caelestibus irae?' ('Can resentment so fierce dwell in heavenly hearts?') in 'And is there then | Such rancour in the harts of mightie men?' ('Muiopotmos', 15-16). The end reveals even more clearly the presence of Virgil; the last lines replay the abrupt flight of

---

[165] Compare also with Carew's fanciful self-representation in 'The Rapture' as a bee wandering in the garden of love who will 'rifle all the sweets, that dwell | In my delicious Paradise, and swell | My bagge with honey' (59-61) as he goes, 'Deflowring the fresh virgins of the Spring' (58); see above, p. 104. Pleasure and violence, here rape, are very close together.

[166] As Dundas does, noting that 'A riotous butterfly can scarcely merit rebuke from even the most puritanical critic' ('*Muiopotmos*: A World of Art', 33).

Turnus' shade to the underworld at the end of the *Aeneid* (12. 951–2), as Clarion's 'deepe groning spright | In bloodie streames foorth fled into the aire' ('Muiopotmos', 438–9).[167] Spenser rewrites Ovid's scene of artistic competition as a conflict between Virgilian and Ovidian aesthetics, in which a Virgilian plot propelled towards teleological closure crushes a figure of Ovidian beauty and undirected freedom; a purposeful poetics of morality finishes off an aimless and amoral flight of fancy.

By setting the two sources specifically in a tale about the origins of envy, Spenser draws attention to the supposed rivalry between the two poets.[168] The poem's ambiguity might be resolved by reading it as a dramatization and resolution of the conflict in Spenser himself which ended when he renounced Ovidian poetics—appealing as they might be—and took up the Virgilian mantle in *The Faerie Queene*. But I have already indicated that I do not believe that Spenser is of the house of Virgil alone, nor even, for that matter, the house of Ovid. He belongs to both, as do most major writers of the time. Bringing together these sources, Spenser tries to turn the strife between the two writers into creative friction and fiction.[169] If 'Muiopotmos' narrates the origins of envy, it simultaneously announces the origin of Spenser's own emulative art. The haunting of the poet by the forces of Envy, Slander, and the Blatant Beast in *The Faerie Queene* suggests, however, that Spenser's own poetics can never be free from its own dark double. Pugh notes that the abrupt ending of *The Faerie*

---

[167] Virgil is of course also a source of much Renaissance bug imagery; Spenser translated the *Culex* (which was then still part of the Virgilian canon) and the description of the bees in *Georgics* 4 is important for the didactic and later political tradition.

[168] Robert A. Brinkley thus reads Spenser's Minerva as a model for a Virgilian artist who 'silences her Ovidian rival—here not through violence but through art' ('Spenser's *Muiopotmos* and the Politics of Metamorphosis', *English Literary History*, 48/4 (1981), 673). Brinkley's reading makes Spenser an Ovidian artist who challenges the linked forces of Virgil and monarchical authority.

[169] Vernon Guy Dickson argues that Shakespeare similarly exposes the dangers of competitive rivalry and emulation in *Titus Andronicus*; see '"A pattern, precedent, and lively warrant"', 379 especially. In this reading, Shakespeare shows that Renaissance culture, steeped in emulation, fosters strife and vicious cycles of revenge in which the difference between good and evil, victim and victor, inevitably breaks down; the play contrasts its own creative imitation of past and present authors with the appropriation of Ovid by the different characters.

Queene, with the unleashing of the Blatant Beast, recalls the triumph of envy in Ovid's final exilic poem.[170]

Comparing 'Muiopotmos' and *Paradise Lost* seems an extreme example of relating big things by small. Yet with his magnification of its own emulative practice into an epic conflict, Spenser anticipates Milton's use of revision to understand the consequences of the fall for the artist. For Milton, evil is a version of the poet's creative imitation, which has degenerated into sterile copying fuelled by the traditional enemy and self-destructive double of all creativity, envy. While Satan's mission is 'out of good still to find means of evil' (1. 165), the poet, like God, seeks 'Good out of evil to create' (7. 188). I would like to say therefore that the difference between Satan and the poet lies finally in the simple fact that Satan's actions are destructive and, like envy itself, self-destructive; the poet, however, creates the poem. In exile, he refuses Ovid's temptation to curse and remains committed to imagining new worlds and other possibilities. It is sometimes hard for us to realize what an astonishing achievement the retention of imaginative creativity in such circumstances was. At the same time, however, the presentation of the narrator and his many mirror images suggests that to create is always to be, like Ovid's Scylla, divided and unable to flee the impulse to destroy. As we will see in the next chapter, this is even clearer in Milton's most critically divisive and self-destructive double: Samson.

---

[170] *Spenser and Ovid*, 242.

Conclusion

Last Words

THE ARGUMENT

In this chapter I argue that the concern with reception evident in Ovid's exilic poetry is also central to Milton's last publications, especially Samson Agonistes. The critical disagreements over the meaning of this work are anticipated by the tragedy itself, which internalizes and problematizes its own reception. Through allusions, including those to his own early works, Milton brings his poetry full circle to the relation between creativity and revision with which he began, now to imagine himself as part of the tradition which future readers and writers would interpret and rework.

THE ONCE AND FUTURE MILTON

Like that of Ovid, Milton's art has always seemed to have a peculiarly intimate and complex relation to his life. He returns constantly to himself in both his political and poetical writings, as he understands, shapes, and mythologizes his life. Moreover, as Ovid's autobiographical statements informed his reception, Milton's self-representation in his prose has influenced his. In sharp contrast to Ovid, however, Milton never seems to err. In his recent study, Stephen M. Fallon shows how Milton's self-presentation in his political writings rejects the prodigal son or Augustinian conversion narratives common to seventeenth-century autobiographies. Where other writers present themselves as fallen into redemption, Milton appears the epitome of 'precocious and continued virtue, even at times, it seems, of sinlessness', as is suggested by his claims to be free from envy and his assertion of difference from figures like the falling Phaethon.¹ He seems 'a poet of the ego' who, motivated by 'lordly certitude',² never wavered or changed from beginning to end.³ Many eighteenth-century biographies made him the 'preeminently virtuous man'.⁴ Yet as I suggested in the last chapter, in *Paradise Lost*, Milton admits his own destructive and errant side. And, as Fallon shows, even in the prose, his self-representation is conflicted. As Lorna Sage observes of Milton's self-images generally, the poet's wholeness and self-completion is a superb illusion, a work of art in itself: 'Milton has excluded muddle, failure, contingency, all the signs of the experiment he was continuously engaged in' in order to 'present himself so determinedly as a finished product'.⁵

Clearly, Milton's development was uncertain, its end not foreseen from the start. His plans, like Ovid's, were derailed by muddle, failures, and contingencies—one Civil War, three marriages, births, deaths, blindness—that he could not control. The war itself, or the punishment of regicides that followed the Restoration, easily might have prevented the fulfilment of his early promise.⁶ In many ways, he was simply lucky. In his last years he was able to make up for lost time with the publication of all his major works: the two versions of *Paradise Lost, Paradise Regain'd... To which is Added Samson*

---

[1] Fallon, *Milton's Peculiar Grace*, x. See also Haskin, *Milton's Burden of Interpretation*, xv, 29–53. On Milton's insistence on his lack of envy, see Ch. 4, 251–3.
[2] Kerrigan, *The Prophetic Milton*, 125.
[3] See also Edward Le Comte's tellingly titled *Milton's Unchanging Mind*, and more recently Fish, *How Milton Works*. For Fish, Milton's career is marked by the repetition of fixed themes, and Milton is a thinker for whom non-development and the absence of change is the highest good.
[4] Griffin, *Regaining Paradise*, 29.
[5] 'Milton's Early Poems: A General Introduction', in John Broadbent (ed.), *John Milton: Introductions* (Cambridge, 1973), 261. As Sage reminds us, 'We tend to under-rate the amount of creative energy certain artists—Milton and Joyce among them—put into shaping their lives in order to write their works. It is easy to be taken in by the illusion they project, and to treat them as distantly god-like figures in control of all the pressures and accidents of existence' (ibid. 262).
[6] The example of the precocious Cowley, who Milton claimed was one of his three favourite English authors, may have reminded Milton also that not all youthful aspirations are easily realized; in the Preface to his 1656 *Poems* Cowley confessed defeatedly that his early works were '*Promises* and *Instruments* under my own hand, whereby I stood *engaged* for more than I have been able to *perform*' (*The English Writings of Abraham Cowley*, ed. Waller, 9). In contrast to Milton, who added more juvenilia to his 1673 *Poems* to stress the unity of his career, Cowley omitted his early works from his later collection.

Agonistes, and the revised 1645 *Poems*, to which, as noted earlier, he had added poems and dates that reinforced the impression of his own early precocity, thus ensuring that his works would be seen as a coherent whole, a narrative of his rise as a poet.[7]

The gathering and publication of his works enabled Milton to reconsider and interpret his own beginning, crafting his life into a work of art. At the same time, in his last writings especially, Milton is aware of the limits and fragility of his own creative powers, and their dependence on others. His language and stories have already been shaped by writers and readers in the past, and in turn they will be remade by others in the future. As Lucy Newlyn notes, 'Anxieties experienced by writers centre as much on the future as on the past', as authors who themselves revise the past are particularly aware 'that all writing—including their own—is contingent, provisional, open to reconstruction'.[8] No author can be fully in control of his works' meaning, which will already have cultural associations and resonances of which he himself is not fully aware, and which will accrue new ones after his death. Like the early works, Milton's final writings are concerned with interpretation and reception, but now from a reverse perspective. If the poet's creativity originates in his reading and transforming of earlier writers, its survival depends on the later readers and poets who will equally interpret and use *him*.

OVID'S BAD READERS

Milton's attention to the power of future readers gives Ovid's last poetry a further relevance. As I have already suggested, Ovid's exilic verse is deeply concerned with how he will be read. While Ovid focuses on the act of writing and how it got the poet into trouble, he also reveals the dangerous effects of reading.

The power of interpretation plays a particularly central role in Ovid's long single book, *Tristia* 2, often read as his 'apologia pro

---

[7] The last years also enabled the publication of an astonishing number of prose works written at various times in his career: *Accedence Commenc't Grammar* (1669), *History of Britain* (1670), *Art of Logic* (1672), *Of True Religion* (1673), *Of Education* (1673, in the same volume as the revised *Poems*), and his personal letters and Prolusions (1674).

[8] *Reading, Writing, and Romanticism*, pp. vii, viii.

arte sua',[9] in which he defends himself to Augustus. The poem begins with an apparent expression of guilt, in which he again blames his own verses for his misfortunes:

> Quid mihi vobiscum est, infelix cura, libelli,
>   ingenio perii qui miser ipse meo?
> cur modo damnatus repeto, mea crimina, Musas?
>   an semel est poenam commeruisse parum?
> carmina fecerunt, ut me cognoscere vellet
>   omine non fausto femina virque meo:
> carmina fecerunt, ut me moresque notaret
>   iam demi iussa Caesar ab Arte mea.
> deme mihi studium, vitae quoque crimina demes;
>   acceptum refero versibus esse nocens.

('What have I to do with you, ye books, ill-starred object of my toil—I, ruined and wretched through my own genius? Why do I return to the Muses I have just denounced, the causes of my guilt? Or is one well-earned penalty not enough? Verse gave men and women a desire to know me, but 'twas no good omen for me; verse caused Caesar to brand me and my ways by commanding that my "Art" be forthwith taken away. Take away from me my pursuit and you will take away from my life also the charges against it. I lay the charge of guilt against my verse', 2. 1–10)

However, having attributed all his guilt to his poetry, Ovid proceeds to protest its innocence. His resonant claim 'vita verecunda est, Musa iocosa mea' ('my life is moral, my muse is gay', 2. 354) might seem a sensible way of distancing himself from his naughty verse. The poems may be guilty, but the poet himself is innocent. However, the radical bifurcation of art and life contradicts Ovid's constant exploration of the slippage between the two; moreover, it goes against the central premiss of the exilic verse, which is that these poems express his real character and indeed experiences. But it allows Ovid to push his argument further until finally he has cleared the poetry itself of all charges against it. Because art is separate from life, he can defend poetic licence on the grounds that 'multa licet castae non facienda

---

[9] S. G. Nugent, 'Tristia 2: Ovid and Augustus', in Kurt A. Raaflaub and Mark Toher (eds.), *Between Republic and Empire: Interpretations of Augustus and his Principate* (Berkeley and Los Angeles, 1990), 242. See also Bruce Gibson, 'Ovid on Reading: Reading Ovid. Reception in Ovid *Tristia* II', *Journal of Roman Studies*, 89 (1999), 19–37.

legant' ('the chaste may read much that they should not do', 2. 308). Poetry makes nothing happen; anyone who argues that Ovid's verse has corrupted its audience 'nimium scriptis arrogat ille meis' ('attributes too much to my works', 2. 278). If literature is dangerous it is simply because 'nil prodest, quod non laedere possit idem' ('Nothing is useful which cannot at the same time be injurious', 2. 266), and 'omnia perversas possunt corrumpere mentes | stant tamen illa suis omnia tuta locis' ('All things can corrupt perverted minds, yet all things stand harmless in their own proper places', 2. 301–2). Moral value is not intrinsic to a work, but is produced by the reader: 'sic igitur carmen, recta si mente legatur, | constabit nulli posse nocere meum' ('So then with verse: if it be read with upright mind, it will be established that it can injure nobody—even though it be mine', 2. 275–6).

The meaning of poetry thus originates not in the author but in the reader. Talk about a reader-centred theory of interpretation—and one created by the author himself! The advantage to the poet is that this abnegation of authorial power is accompanied by a shift of culpability. The source of Ovid's exile is really not bad writing at all—even the poet's licentious *ingenium* is innocuously playful, *iocosum*—but bad reading. Ovid thus impertinently insinuates that, if Augustus saw anything naughty in his writings, it reflects not the poems but the *princeps*' dirty mind.[10]

The poet thus offers the *princeps* a lesson in right reading. Reassuming the role of the didactic *magister* that he had taken in the *Ars* and *Fasti*, Ovid presents Augustus with an introduction to poetry and a survey of Roman literature. Most importantly, he demonstrates how he himself should be interpreted. Read properly, i.e. with the exiled poet thoughtfully steering us in the right direction, all of Ovid's works are really about Augustus. Ovid not only rereads his works to prove this, he also rewrites them, describing the *Metamorphoses* as a text which brings history down to 'tua... tempora, Caesar' ('your times, Caesar', *Tristia*, 2. 560). The poet thus returns to the opening of his epic, in which he promises to tell the story of the world down to 'mea... tempora' ('my time', *Met.*, 1. 4).[11] Time is in the power of

---

[10] See also Nugent, '*Tristia* 2', 250–1.
[11] Barchiesi, *Speaking Volumes*, 75.

Augustus after all, along with everything else. The story is not about the poet, but about the *princeps*, its most powerful reader.[12]

Ovid's presentation of the author/reader relation as that of poet/ruler exposes the power struggle involved in the making of meaning.[13] It is the reader, not the author, who rules. Ovid himself fluctuates between self-abnegation and assertion; he transfers all interpretative power to Augustus, but equally claims for himself the role of the authoritative reader and so 'asserts his own right to poetic authority, even over the *princeps*'.[14] *Tristia* 2 thus suggests the urgency behind Ovid's concern with revising himself and guiding future readers. The poet tries to assert his power over the meaning of his works because his exile reveals how little he really has.

The immediate effect of exile on the poet's 'publication' in *Tristia* 1. 1 shows further the poet's loss of control. Typically, Roman poets would read their works to others, thus helping to determine their reception. The opening of the volume however draws attention to the exiled poet's absence from the scene of reading of his new works. The poet sends his first volume back to Rome: 'Parve—nec invideo—sine me, liber, ibis in urbem, | ei mihi, quod domino non licet ire tuo!' ('Little book, you will go without me—and I do not envy you—to the city, whither alas your master is not allowed to go!', 1. 1. 1–2). The disclaimer of envy is belied by the tension between creator and his creatures that emerges in the poem. Ovid recalls the journeys of Phaethon and Icarus as he sends his books (libri)/sons (liberi) off to Rome,[15] warning them to avoid the high and dangerous path, as 'vitaret caelum Phaëthon, si viveret' (Phaëthon would avoid the sky if he were alive', 1. 1. 79), and 'dum petit infirmis nimium sublimia pennis | Icarus, aequoreas nomine fecit aquas' ('By seeking too lofty heights on weak wings Icarus gave a name to waters of the

---

[12] Ovid seems here to look forward to Oscar Wilde, who observed that 'It is the spectator, and not life, that art really mirrors' (Preface to *The Picture of Dorian Gray*, in *The Complete Works of Oscar Wilde*, ed. Vyvyan Holland (London, 1966; repr. 1989), 17. The paradoxical Wilde similarly insists on the rigid separation of art and life, asserting that 'All art is quite useless' (ibid. 17), but shows their indistinguishability. In many other ways, Ovid's life and art runs parallel to that of Wilde—the two aesthetes punished by the societies they first dazzled and then offended, and whose lives strangely copied their own fictions.
[13] See also Barchiesi, *Speaking Volumes*, 80.
[14] Nugent, '*Tristia* 2', 254; see also ibid. 243–4.
[15] Frederick Ahl notes the puns here: the books/sons, *libri/liberi*, are also *liberi*, free, in contrast to their author/parent (*Metaformations*, 56–7).

Conclusion

sea', 1. 1. 89–90). He is worried that his new creations will meet a similar fate. But while concerned about these 'sons', he reminds them that their 'brothers' in Rome, his other works, were parricides ('Oedipodas facito Telegonosque voces', 1. 1. 114). His relation to this new volume is also ambivalent. The book represents the poet, but also seems to have usurped his rightful place: 'tu tamen i pro me, tu, cui licet, aspice Romam. | di facerent, possem nunc meus esse liber!' ('But do you go in my stead, do you, who are permitted to do so, gaze on Rome! Would that the gods might grant me now to be my book!', 1. 1. 57–8). The poet's sending forth of his works to the place where he himself cannot go dramatizes his inability to control the fate of his works which now go out to take on a life of their own. While children are supposed to leave their parents to become independent, the classical analogue suggests that they develop by killing their parents. We seem to be back in an Oedipal relation between creators and their creatures. But it is now explicitly the reader who, like the enemy in the *Ibis*, has the power to turn the author's progeny against him.

Ovid's wish to *be* his own book recalls the end of the *Metamorphoses*, where the poet triumphantly looked forward to his own future immortality. He did not worry about the loss of his *corpus*, as he would live on in his 'parte...meliore' ('better part', 15. 875). For Ovid, despite the disclaimer in *Tristia* 2 that 'nec liber indicium est animi, sed honesta voluptas | plurima mulcendis auribus apta ferens' ('A book is not evidence of the writer's mind, but respectable entertainment; it will offer many things suited to charm the ear', 2. 357–8), the poet's spirit *is* his poetry through which he may gain eternal life. But that survival already depends on circumstances and others, as he ties his endurance to his empire: 'quaque patet domitis Romana potentia terris, | ore legar populi' ('Wherever Rome's power extends over the conquered world, I shall have mention on men's lips', *Met.*, 15. 877–8). The experience of exile makes Ovid less confident about future immortality. So in *Tristia* 4. 10. 129–32 he comes back once again to the concluding boast of the *Metamorphoses*, now to acknowledge that his immortality depends on his readers:

> si quid habent igitur vatum praesagia veri,
>   protinus ut moriar, non ero, terra, tuus.
> sive favore tuli, sive hanc ego carmine famam,
>   iure tibi grates, candide lector, ago.

('If then there be truth in poets' prophecies, even though I die forthwith, I shall not, O earth, be thine. But whether through favour or by very poetry I have gained this fame, 'tis right, kind reader, that I render thanks to thee.')

The vulnerability of the poet is exposed in the last exilic poem which, as I noted in the previous chapter, is addressed to 'Invide' (*Ex Ponto*, 4. 16). It is hardly reassuring for Ovid's future that his last imagined reader in his works is Envy itself.

Ovid could never have guessed, however, how much his posthumous survival depended on less invidious readers whose worlds and sensibilities were completely alien to his. If misreading got him into exile, it also saved him from eternal oblivion. Nor could he have imagined all the forms into which different readers have turned him: wise teacher of chaste love, licentious poet, Christian allegorist, sober teacher of the arts of persuasion, spokesman of political and poetic freedom, romantic rebel, Augustan conformist, and today, prophet of postmodernity. The many metamorphoses of Ovid dramatically demonstrate the creativity and ingenuity as well as the plain obtuseness and frequently the narcissism (and sometimes *invidia*) of later readers, their ability to make entirely new meanings from old stories, including that of Ovid himself.

THE AUTHOR AS READER

In offering the *princeps* a lesson on literature, *Tristia* 2 especially recalls Horace's writings on poetry, both his famous *Epistle* 2. 1 to Augustus and the *Ars Poetica*.[16] While Horace's works influenced Renaissance theories of poetry, Ovid's defence of his art was resonant for writers aware of the dangerous power of readers. Boccaccio draws on *Tristia* 2 in his defence of the *Decameron*, in which he argues that his tales 'e nuocere e giovar possono, sì come tutte l'altre cose, avendo riguardo all'ascoltatore' ('can both hurt and help, as can all things,

---

[16] See especially Barchiesi, *Speaking Volumes*, 79–103; Nugent, '*Tristia* 2', 249; and Jennifer Ingleheart, 'Writing to the Emperor: Horace's Presence in Ovid's *Tristia* 2', in L. B. T. Houghton and Maria Wyke (eds.), *Perceptions of Horace: A Roman Poet and his Readers* (Cambridge, 2009), 123–39.

depending on the listener').[17] Sidney follows Ovid when he claims in his *Defence* 'that whatsoever being abused doth most harm, being rightly used (and upon the right use each thing conceiveth his title) doth most good',[18] while in his Preface to his 1656 *Poems* Abraham Cowley paraphrases *Tristia* 2. 357–8, telling his readers that his love poems are not born from experience but from convention: poetry 'is not the *Picture* of the *Poet*, but of *things* and *persons* imagined'.[19] Herrick attempts to ward off attacks on his own Ovidian poetry from the growing Puritanism that, like Augustus, was cracking down on immorality, by invoking Ovid's separation of poet and poetry; *Hesperides* ends with a disclaimer that reworks *Tristia* 2. 354: '*Jocond his Muse was, but his life was chast.*'[20]

Ovidian principles are also fundamental to Milton's argument against censorship in *Areopagitica*. Like Ovid, Milton claims that the reader determines the meaning of a work: 'To the pure all things are pure, not only meats and drinks, but all kinde of knowledge whether of good or evill; the knowledge cannot defile, not consequently the books, if the will and conscience be not defil'd' (*Works*, iv. 308). Unlike Ovid, Milton does not sever a work from its source; for him a book is the soul of an author, 'the pretious life-blood of a master-spirit, imbalm'd and treasur'd up on purpose to a life beyond life' (298). However, how it is used depends on the character of the reader. But character is in turn shaped and strengthened by the act of reading. Censorship is wrong not simply because it murders the creations of authors, but more perniciously because it inhibits the freedom of the people by limiting the right to read to a select few. Milton thus expands the principles of Ovid's self-defence to transform reading into the basis of liberty. Like imitation, reading brings us into contact with the minds of others, through which we learn to think for ourselves. Even more fundamentally, it is the basis of choice and free will, through which we can safely encounter evil without

---

[17] See Janet Levarie Smarr, 'Ovid and Boccaccio: A Note on Self-Defense', *Mediaevalia: A Journal of Mediaeval Studies*, 13 (1989 for 1987), 247–55; quote and translation from 247.

[18] *An Apology for Poetry*, ed. Forrest G. Robinson (Indianapolis, 1970), 60.

[19] 'The Preface: Of the Author', in *The English Writings of Abraham Cowley*, ed. Waller, 10. Compare with *Tristia* 2. 357–8.

[20] Herrick's version also reminds us that, like so many catchy Ovidian phrases, this is borrowed from and by other writers; see Catullus 16. 5–6, and Martial 1. 4. 8.

giving in to it.[21] It is essential to informed debate and trial; it must be at the centre of a 'knowing people, a Nation of Prophets, of Sages, and of Worthies' who are not only writing but 'reading, trying all things, assenting to the force of reason and convincement' (*Areopagitica*, in *Works*, iv. 341).

The idealism of this description may be partly the result of the rhetorical context as well as Milton's early hopeful enthusiasm. It is easy to give up authority when one believes that 'all the Lords people are become Prophets' (*Areopagitica*, in *Works*, iv. 342–3), eager to determine their own fates. While the 1649 *Eikonoklastes* shows Milton's diminishing faith in the English as readers, it similarly demonstrates the vital importance of interpretation. As in *Tristia* 2, treating monarch and subject as author and reader reveals the power relation inherent in reading; Milton, however, transfers power to the subject who, through interpretation, is able to break the enchantment of tyranny and be free. Richard Helgerson thus suggests that at this stage Milton imagined that reading was the pathway to political revolution: 'The right reader, the reader who has freely exposed himself to the great number of mutually conflicting books that an uncensored press makes available, is thus a true king over himself.'[22]

In the early 'On *Shakespear*', moreover, Milton acknowledges that transferring power from the author to the reader has particular advantages for a young poet who is at the receiving end of literary history. Appearing in the 1632 edition of Shakespeare's works, Milton's first publication reflects his aspirations to poetic authority while demonstrating his dependence on his great precursor under whose auspices he appears in print. The author begins as a reader who pays homage to his source, with whom his own origins are bound up both figuratively and, in the edition, literally. Like Ben Jonson, whose 'To the Memory of My Beloved, the Author William Shakespeare, and

---

[21] See also the implicit defence of poetic licence in *Paradise Lost* 5, when Adam explains the innocence of Eve's dream: 'Evil into the mind of God or Man | May come and go, so unapprov'd, and leave | No spot or blame behind' (5. 117–19). Adam's theory is as important for Milton as it is for Eve: it justifies the poet who is able to imagine Satan and who can know evil without being evil. For Dr Johnson, however, Milton *just* managed to stay on the right side of a fine line where even thought becomes culpable: 'there are thoughts...which no observation of character can justify, because no good man would willingly permit them to pass, however transiently, through his own mind' (*Lives of the English Poets*, ed. Waugh, i. 119).

[22] 'Milton Reads the King's Book', 12.

What He Hath Left Us' also appeared in the volume, Milton seems less interested in Shakespeare himself than the question of 'what he hath left' the writers who follow. Both tributes raise questions of poetic succession. They thus take up the central theme of Shakespeare's sonnets, in which the poet is concerned with how both the young man and the poet himself may achieve immortality. Milton begins by saying that Shakespeare needs no monument in order to be remembered because he will live in his verse, a claim generally associated with Horace (*Odes*, 2. 20, 3. 30). At the end of the *Metamorphoses*, Ovid recalls Horace when he asserts that his poem will be his monument. As Marlin Blaine has pointed out, this topos was popular in sixteenth- to seventeenth-century England, and was a favourite theme of Shakespeare himself.[23] Jonson also recalls the commonplace when he says that Shakespeare is 'a monument, without a tomb, | And art alive still, while thy book doth live' ('To the Memory', 22–3).[24]

But Milton offers a different resting place and form of immortality, shaping what Blaine calls a 'reader-response myth of the monument's creation'.[25] The poet's monument is not his own works, but the reader, including Milton himself: 'Thou in our wonder and astonishment | Hast built thyself a live-long Monument' ('On *Shakespear*', 7–8). In *Paradise Lost* and *Regain'd*, 'wonder' is precisely the feeling that awakens Satan's envy (*PL*, 4. 363, 5. 661–5; *PR*, 1. 38), and it is hard to imagine that Milton's feelings for Shakespeare were completely free from that vice.[26] Moreover, astonishment is both a good and bad thing; it suggests Shakespeare's ability to evoke awe, but leaves open the possibility that his talent will simply petrify his followers, who

---

[23] Marlin E. Blaine, 'Milton and the Monument Topos: "On Shakespeare," "*Ad Joannem Roüsium*," and *Poems* (1645)', *Journal of English and Germanic Philology*, 99/2 (1990), 215–34. Blaine argues that Milton's use of the topos suggests the tension between his desire for monumental stature and his iconoclasm, especially his attraction to and distrust of the printed book.

[24] Cited from *Ben Jonson: The Complete Poems*, ed. Parfitt. As Blaine shows also, in England the convention was also associated with the Horatian Jonson, and appears in many of the tributes written after his death; see Blaine, 'Milton and the Monument Topos', 224.

[25] Blaine, 'Milton and the Monument Topos', 225. Blaine notes a precedent for this in the two epitaphs written for Sir Edward and Sir Thomas Stanley, which in the 17th century were commonly attributed to Shakespeare.

[26] On wonder and envy, see above, Ch. 4, p. 254.

are made 'Marble with too much conceaving' ('On *Shakespear*', 14). The situation has itself been anticipated by Shakespeare who, in the Sonnets, briefly worries that his art will be blocked by his own poetic and erotic rival: 'Was it the proud full sail of his great verse, | Bound for the prize of all-too-precious you, | That did my ripe thoughts in my brain inhearse, | Making their tomb the womb wherein they grew' ('Sonnet 86', 1–4): a passage that with its imagery of ships, ripeness, and aborted creation anticipates the themes of Milton's own early verse. For some critics, Milton's wording in his tribute reveals his Oedipal struggle with his literary father who seems to have already used up all the best imagery.[27] Moreover, Shakespeare's 'easie numbers' which 'flow' (10) may intimidate those whose art is 'slow-endeavouring' (9) and, like that of Milton, slow to fruition. The metaphor of flowing suggests that the relation between poet and reader is one of influence. This is the model with which Jonson concludes as he turns Shakespeare into a star shining in the darkness he left behind ('To the Memory', 75–80). But Milton offsets the potential anxiety of the influenced by shifting to a different perspective on the relation, in which the reader is not simply the passive and petrified recipient of the poet's genius. The reader is the resting place, and indeed final cause, of the poet who died in order to be read by us: 'And so Sepulcher'd in such pomp dost lie, | That Kings for such a Tomb would wish to die' ('On *Shakespear*', 15–16).

While the appearance of the poem in the Folio edition suggests that Milton needs Shakespeare in order to be published and to find his own identity, the conclusion of the poem reverses the relation to claim that Shakespeare needs Milton to be immortalized. Milton shows that, as Lawrence Lipking notes, 'The living poet always wins the day... The dead cannot choose their own monuments.'[28] The later poet gets to make his maker, and stage his own scene of origins.

---

[27] See Guillory, *Poetic Authority*, 18–19; but see also the response by Paul Stevens, who suggests that Milton celebrates Shakespeare as a source of divine wisdom ('Subversion and Wonder in Milton's Epitaph "On Shakespeare"', *English Literary Renaissance*, 19/3 (1989), 375–88). If Stevens's reading errs on the side of idealization, it rightly resists the tendency to see Milton as simply petrified by his precursor.

[28] *The Life of the Poet: Beginning and Ending Poetic Careers* (Chicago, 1981), 140.

THE ANXIETY OF RECEPTION[29]

In 1632, Milton gets to make Shakespeare's monuments in his poetry, shaping the myth of Shakespeare as he defines himself as a new poet. From early on, however, he is also aware that others will in turn do this to him. His concern with his reputation after death is at the heart of 'Mansus', written to the Italian poet and patron Giovanni Battista Manso whom he had met in Italy in 1638. Like so many qualities of the young poet, this anxiety seems premature: worrying about his future immortality when he has not yet written much to earn it looks like putting the cart well before the horse. His own preoccupation explains his elaborate praise for Manso, whom he celebrates less for his own achievements than for his support of the works of Tasso and Marino. By striving to make others immortal, however, Manso guarantees his own endurance; playing on Ovid's boast in *Metamorphoses* 15. 877–88 that he will live forever on men's lips, 'ore', Milton claims that whenever Tasso and Marino are read: 'Tu quoque in ora frequens venies plausumque virorum, | Et parili carpes iter immortale volatu' ('you will often arrive on men's lips for approval, | and journey to eternity in equal flight', 52–3). The end of the poem moves explicitly from the ostensible subject to its real concern: meditations on Milton's own situation. The young poet who wrote so many elegies is aware of his own mortality and concerned with what will happen to him after death, not only in heaven, but also on earth. He wishes that he might himself have a friend like Manso who:

> Forsitan & nostros ducat de marmore vultus,
> Nectens aut Paphiâ myrti aut Parnasside lauri
> Fronde comas, at ego securâ pace quiescam.
> Tum quoque, si qua fides, si praemia certa bonorum,
> Ipse ego caelicolûm semotus in aethera divûm,
> Quò labor & mens pura vehunt, atque ignea virtus
> Secreti haec aliquâ mundi de parte videbo
> (Quantum fata sinunt) & totâ mente serenùm
> Ridens purpureo suffundar lumine vultus
> Et simul aethereo plandam mihi laetus Olympo.

---

[29] I steal the phrase from the subtitle of Newlyn's *Reading, Writing, and Romanticism*.

('would also, maybe, craft my face from marble, wreathing
my hair with Paphian myrtle leaves or Parnassian
laurel leaves while I would lie in a restful peace.
Then if there's any faith, and sure rewards for the good,
and I—apart in heavens of celestial gods
where labor, a pure mind, and glowing virtue lead—
will see these things from some part of that hidden realm
and (as much as fate permits), with my whole mind serenely
smiling, I'll steep my face in rosy light and happily
congratulate myself with heavenly Olympus', 91–100)

Milton's vision of his own afterlife seems to confirm the self-image that dominates the early works. Self-confident and directed, he has no doubt that he is a virtuous and hard worker of pure mind, nor that those talents will earn him a place in heaven. But he also admits the limits of his own intrinsic abilities. The climax of the vision, the poet's eternal happiness, is dependent not upon his own labours but upon those of a friend, whose care will assure Milton's immortality.[30]

READING *SAMSON AGONISTES*

Milton's self-consciousness about his posthumous reputation—how his works and indeed life will be read—is especially apparent in the last pair of new poems published before his death: *Paradise Regain'd ... To which is added Samson Agonistes*. Like Milton's first published collection, his last new work is a double volume that shows his continued interest in generic experimentation. These twin poems have always seemed especially personal to Milton, forming a pair of authorial doubles through which he presents possible interpretations of his life and the choices he made. They bring together Milton's past and present through heroic figures who represent the beginning and end of his career. Both poems centre on questions of vocation and career choice; the first shows Christ searching for the path by which he may start to fulfil his destiny, and the second the means by which Samson may end his. As Thomas Corns notes, in *Paradise Regain'd* Milton's Son seems 'made in his own image, a daring, almost

---

[30] See also Hale's discussion of the theme of friendship in the Latin poems generally in 'Artistry and Originality in Milton's Latin Poems'.

impudent *imitatio Miltoni*'.[31] Like so many of Milton's early works, the poem is obsessed with time and the question of timing, as Milton revisits his own youth.[32] The action of the poem—or rather the Son's rejection of action—seems to offer a justification of Milton's own slow development. Delay is turned into a principle of redemption, through which Jesus resists Satan's temptation to precipitate action.[33] It is almost impossible not to read Samson as equally, if not even more, autobiographical, expressing the frustrated rage of the failed and blind revolutionary, betrayed by a people too weak to grasp the freedom he had offered to them. If Christ returns us to the beginning of Milton's career, the blind and alienated Samson pushes us to its conclusion. Samson seems to confirm a Johnsonian reading of Milton the Destroyer, who at the end his life, like the deranged speaker of the *Ibis*, retreats into a vicious fantasy of revenge.[34]

Nothing about the volume is straightforward, however. Like other Miltonic pairings, the combination prompts us to interpret the relation between the two works. Are they antitheses? 'Companion poems'? The juxtaposition of the two poems and heroes makes it hard not to see the Old Testament hero from a New Testament perspective and to see the poems as related typologically. But their order of presentation is provocative.[35] If *Samson* had been placed first

---

[31] Thomas N. Corns, '"With Unaltered Brow": Milton and the Son of God', *Milton Studies*, 42 (2002), 108. See also Fallon, *Milton's Peculiar Grace*, 242.

[32] Frye, *The Return of Eden*, 136; see also Gordon Teskey, *Delirious Milton: The Fate of the Poet in Modernity* (Cambridge, Mass., 2006), 166–9.

[33] See Parker, *Inescapable Romance*, 152–3, 157. A similar transformation of delay appears at the end of *Paradise Lost*. While Adam and Eve first bemoan the prolongation of time, imagining, as Adam complains, 'A long days dying to augment our paine' (10. 964), they gradually learn that the drawn-out process of history will enable the working out of redemption. The need for delay is exemplified also in the Exodus story in which the Israelites wander 'Through the wilde Desert, not the readiest way, | Least entring on the *Canaanite* allarmd | Warr terrifie them inexpert, and feare | Return them back to *Egypt*, choosing rather | Inglorious life with servitude' (12. 216–20); see also 223–6, where 'thir delay' gives them time to establish Mosaic law.

[34] Milton was driven by a 'predominant desire . . . to destroy rather than establish' (*Lives of the English Poets*, ed. Waugh, i. 109).

[35] Nothing is known, however, about the circumstances of the volume's publication, so we don't know whose decision it was to print the texts together and in this sequence. Stephen Dobranski points out that while authors at this time had little control over publication, Milton tends to pair poems; Dobranski therefore suggests a collaboration between publisher and author ('Text and Context for *Paradise Regain'd* and *Samson Agonistes*', in Mark R. Kelley and Joseph Wittreich (eds.), *Altering Eyes: New Perspectives on* Samson Agonistes (Newark, Del., 2002), 30–53). Joseph Wittreich also notes how the present order of the poems conforms to Milton's recurrent

in the volume, the two poems would have followed a neat typological sequence: we would read about the Old Testament man of action first and then move on to the new, improved New Testament story of heroic suffering. The volume itself might then suggest historical progression: Samson would be the earlier and morally inferior version of Jesus which Jesus fulfils and replaces. But *Paradise Regain'd* precedes *Samson Agonistes* in the volume. The reading experience takes us backwards in time, undercutting typology and teleology in general. Stylistically and thematically, moreover, *Samson* seems to belong to an earlier stage of Milton's career; some critics have therefore suggested that it was written much earlier.[36] At the same time, and regardless of whether or not *Samson* was actually the last thing Milton wrote, to many readers, its placement in the volume has conferred on it the status of Milton's last word, 'the culminating poem of Milton's career'.[37]

As Joseph Wittreich showed, while Samson was read as a type of Christ, in the seventeenth century, he was an extremely controversial hero.[38] Readers of Milton's poem have been equally divided over the character of the hero and the significance of his final action. Many readers have seen the drama as one of regeneration in which

---

habits of thought ('"Strange Text!" "Paradise Regain'd... To which is added *Samson Agonistes*"', in Neil Fraistat (ed.), *Poems in their Place: The Intertextuality and Order of Poetic Collections* (Chapel Hill, NC, 1986), 164–6). For other discussions of the unity of the volume, see Joseph Wittreich, *Interpreting* Samson Agonistes (Princeton, 1986), 329–85; Ann Baynes Coiro, 'Fable and Old Song: *Samson Agonistes* and the Idea of a Poetic Career', *Milton Studies*, 36 (1998), 127–8; John Shawcross, 'The Genres of *Paradise Regain'd* and *Samson Agonistes*: The Wisdom of their Joint Publication', *Milton Studies*, 17 (1983), 225–48; Balachandra Rajan, 'To which is added *Samson Agonistes*', in Balachandra Rajan (ed.), *The Prison and the Pinnacle* (Toronto, 1973), 82–110; Arthur Barker, 'Calm regained through passion spent', in Rajan (ed.), *The Prison and the Pinnacle*, 3–48; and Peter C. Herman, *Destabilizing Milton: Paradise Lost and the Poetics of Incertitude* (New York, 2005), 155–76.

[36] *Samson*'s date of composition is unknown; on the possibilities for an early dating, see especially William Riley Parker, 'The Date of *Samson Agonistes*', *Philological Quarterly*, 28 (1949), 145–66 (who argued for the early date partly to explain the hiatus in Milton's career); and John T. Shawcross, 'The Chronology of Milton's Major Poems', *PMLA* 4 (1961), 345–58. In response, see Mary Ann Radzinowicz, *Toward* Samson Agonistes: *The Growth of Milton's Mind* (Princeton, 1978), 387–407. As the subtitle of Radzinowicz's book ('The Growth of Milton's Mind') suggests, debates over *Samson*, including the time of composition, are concerned with the stages and shape of the poet's development.

[37] Coiro, 'Fable and Old Song', 124. As will be increasingly evident, I am especially indebted to this terrific essay.

[38] *Interpreting* Samson Agonistes, especially 174–238.

Samson's final act is proof of his recovery of his insight and his heroic fulfilment of God's plan.[39] Others have argued that the play marks Samson's degeneration and that Milton means us to denounce, not applaud, Samson's violent end.[40] As this suggests, it is not clear whether Samson is meant to be a model to be copied or a moral cautionary tale to be avoided. Is he a hero or a villain, a prototype for Christ or for Satan? Does Milton wish to distance himself from this double, or present him as a heroic self-image? As in *Paradise Lost*, the likeness between author and mirror image is provocatively baffling. Milton's last poem and self-representation is deeply ambiguous. If Milton is trying to control our reading of the poem in order to present a clear image of his overall achievement, he is doing a rather bad job of it.

The elusive quality of the work is increased by its allusiveness. The tragedy weaves together a wide range of sources, as it retells the story from Judges through the classical traditions that the Son had strenuously rejected in *Paradise Regain'd*. Samson bears a strong resemblance to Hercules, Ajax, and the blind Oedipus, while he himself suggests a kinship with Tantalus, who also was punished for revealing divine secrets (497–501).[41] Elsewhere I have suggested a further parallel with Virgil's hero, Aeneas, who was the model for many

---

[39] See especially Radzinowicz, *Toward* Samson Agonistes; Anthony Low, *The Blaze of Noon: A Reading of* Samson Agonistes (New York, 1974); and John Shawcross, *The Uncertain World of* Samson Agonistes (Cambridge, 2001). Most regenerative readings tend to downplay the violence as an unpleasant but necessary side-effect of spiritual growth; Michael Lieb, however, argues forcefully that Milton approves of violence as a regenerative act. Violence is not a by-product of the action, it is the main action: 'The drama is a work of violence to its very core. It extols violence. Indeed, it exults in violence' (*Milton and the Culture of Violence* (Ithaca, NY, 1994), 237).

[40] See especially John Carey, 'Sea, Snake, Flower and Flame in *Samson Agonistes*', *Modern Language Review*, 62 (1967), 395–9; Joseph Wittreich, *Interpreting* Samson Agonistes; Wittreich, *Shifting Contexts: Reinterpreting* Samson Agonistes (Pittsburgh, 2002); and Kelley and Wittreich (eds.), *Altering Eyes*. Carey's article, 'A Work in Praise of Terrorism', *The Times Literary Supplement* (6 Sept. 2002), 15–16, pushes further the arguments of his earlier work. Derek Wood provides a thoughtful summary and critique of the critical disagreements over the character of Samson during the last fifty years (*Exiled from Light: Divine Law, Morality, and Violence in Milton's* Samson Agonistes (Toronto, 2001), 3–26).

[41] On the importance of Hercules especially, see Stella P. Revard, 'The Politics of Milton's Hercules', *Milton Studies*, 32 (1995), 217–45. Hardie notes the parallels with Ajax, first pointed out by Todd; see *Rumour and Renown*, 549 n. 18.

Renaissance heroes.[42] Aeneas' metamorphosis from defeated Trojan to victorious Roman takes place through his relations with three versions of his past self—Anchises, Dido, and Turnus—just as the renewal of Samson's faith occurs through his encounters with Manoa, Dalila, and Harapha. Both heroes thus define themselves in terms of three relationships central to patriarchal order: the first between father and son, the second between husband and wife, and last, soldier and enemy. Each hero must leave behind these seductive potential selves, undergoing renewal through psychological amputation, to be reborn as a new kind of hero. Both narratives thus suggest a pattern of heroic growth and development through the conquest of their dark doubles. Yet, both heroes resist this change. Throughout the *Aeneid*, Aeneas is tempted by a desire to simply copy the past, a nostalgia that is suggested also by the poem's rewriting of Homer and, indeed, of its own episodes.[43] Milton's nephew Edward Phillips claimed that the name Samson meant 'There a second time', and Milton's hero also tends to repeat his own actions, including marriage, without change or development.[44] Moreover, the violent climactic action of both poems that should separate the hero from his counterparts potentially confirms continuing identification. When Aeneas strikes Turnus he is driven by the very anger, 'ira', that is the mark of his opponent, while Samson's slaughter of the Philistines brings his own death as he 'with these immixt, inevitably | Pulld down the same destruction on himself' (*SA*, 1657–8). By slaying their enemies, the heroes may have become them.

While both poems give us violent and troubling endings, however, Milton's climax is strikingly different from Virgil's in terms of presentation. The *Aeneid* concludes with a tense close-up on the single combat between Aeneas and his rival Turnus, which ends, as the poem does, with Turnus' violent death. In *Samson*, the final action is

---

[42] 'Heroic Contradictions: Samson and the Death of Turnus', *Texas Studies in Literature and Language*, 50/2 (2008), 201–34. On Aeneas' role in later epic see especially Philip Hardie, *The Epic Successors of Virgil: A Study in the Dynamics of a Tradition* (Cambridge, 1993); and Burrow, *Epic Romance*.

[43] See especially Quint, *Epic and Empire*, 50–65.

[44] On Samson's repetition and patterns of repetition in the poem generally see Coiro, 'Fable and Old Song', 134–6; Shoaf, *Milton, Poet of Duality*, 169–89; John Guillory, '"The Father's House: *Samson Agonistes* in its Historical Moment', in Nyquist and Ferguson (eds.), *Re-Membering Milton*, 148–76; and John Carey, *Milton: Complete Shorter Poems* (London, 1968), 335–6.

carefully kept at a distance. Samson's death occurs offstage; it is reported second-hand by the Messenger and then submitted to the Chorus and Manoa for interpretation. The immediacy and stark swiftness of Virgil's last scene, with its shockingly truncated close mimicking the sudden snuffing out of a life, is replaced in Milton by an elaborate chain of mediating voices who relay the remote action with painful slowness (as the Messenger has difficulty even saying what his message is) and then offer an extended interpretation of its meaning. From its opening, the play has been centrally concerned with questions of interpretation, as Samson struggles to understand the significance of his talents and life. With his death offstage, however, interpretation is passed from the authorial figure to the readers of the action who, like the readers of the text itself, try to make meaning out of Samson's life and death.[45] Milton thus makes the interpretation of the story part of the story; the text internalizes its own reception, offering us a reading of itself.

There are many things to tempt us to accept the interpretation offered in the poem as authoritative. Manoa and the Chorus offer the possibility of closure and the resolution of uncertainties and doubt. According to them, the drama is one of regeneration. The play starts with the hero in a state of internal division and incoherence, as Samson is unable to make sense of the difference between 'what once I was, and what I am now' (22), his transformation from liberator to slave. He is trying to understand a life that has undergone a radical metamorphosis. The Chorus also faces a problem of trying to comprehend a world of mutability. Recalling the 'Fall of Princes' tradition, they interpret Samson's 'miserable change' (340) as a 'mirror of our fickle state' (164), which causes even the greatest to fall from 'the top of wondrous glory' (167). In the end, however, they are cheered up when Samson's revolution of identity seems to come full circle and he fulfils his divine purpose; as Manoa asserts, '*Samson* hath quit himself | Like *Samson* and heroicly hath finish'd | A life Heroic' (1709–11). To celebrate this ultimate success, Manoa claims he will build a monument. The emergence of rhyme in the last

---

[45] Revard notes the parallels with the end of Seneca's *Hercules Oetaeus* in which Hercules' gory death is described and commented upon ('The Politics of Milton's Hercules', 241). However, at the end of the long narration, Seneca's apotheosized hero appears himself to confirm the truth of the story; unlike Hercules, Milton's Samson does not get the chance to tell his version. In Milton's account, the hero is ultimately unable to control his own story.

fourteen lines encourages a sense of harmony, peace, and closure. The Chorus brings the poem to a satisfying end, asserting that all doubts about Samson's life have now been resolved by the explanation of God's mysterious ways:

> All is best, though we oft doubt,
> What th' unsearchable dispose
> Of highest wisdom brings about,
> And ever best found in the close. (1745–8)

They not only tell readers what to think but how they should feel:

> His servants he with new acquist
> Of true experience from this great event
> With peace and consolation hath dismist,
> And calm of mind all passion spent. (1755–8)

The last words invoke the vocabulary of Aristotelian catharsis cited by Milton in the headnotes, so that the text comes full circle to fulfil the author's promise that tragedy raises 'pity and fear, or terror, to purge the mind of those and such like passions, that is to temper and reduce them to just measure with a kind of delight, stirr'd up by reading or seeing those passions well imitated' (*Shorter Poems*, p. 461). The conclusion thus has an authoritative ring. At times, moreover, the Chorus sounds rather like Milton, especially in their praise of Patience and the justness of God's ways (652–4, 1287–96, 293–5). Speaking in proverbial forms, they seem to anticipate a future sublimation of Milton into distilled wisdom, 'The Essential Milton', to be handed down to future generations.

At the same time, however, the final speeches contain meanings of which the speakers themselves are not fully aware, and which open up the very questions they are trying to close off. Manoa's tautological comparison of Samson to himself draws on a Renaissance commonplace, used to stress a hero's self-consistency and integrity.[46] As the reflexivity of *Comus* 221–4 expressed the Lady's chastity, the rhetoric here replicates Samson's autonomy, inscribing him as a closed circle that no longer requires or even admits interpretation.[47] As figures for

---

[46] See Hereward T. Price, 'Like Himself', *Review of English Studies*, 16 (1940), 178–81. See for example Jonson's *Poetaster*, in which Virgil applauds Caesar: 'Caesar hath done like Caesar. Fair and just' (*Poetaster*, ed. Cain, 5. 3. 130).

[47] See above, Ch. 2, pp. 157–8. There are other parallels linking the two heroes and their works. When Samson attacks Dalila as an enchantress whose 'fair enchanted

the author at different stages in his life, the young virgin and the he-man are surprisingly linked, suggesting therefore perhaps that Milton also has been found 'like himself', consistent from beginning to end, while growing in strength. However, as the Lady's self-enclosure showed how chastity might become self-destructive, here the verbal and logical redundancy, in which an anticipated simile collapses in on itself in perfect likeness (*A* is like *A*), seems suspicious in a hero who already was prone to copying his own actions. The structure is similar to that of the 'pseudo-simile' Stanley Fish associates with Satan in *Paradise Lost*;[48] it suggests that, like Satan, Samson has become what he always was. In Shakespeare, the phrase is particularly associated with Roman ideals of heroism and autonomy. Lucilius prophesies that the defeated Brutus 'will be found like Brutus, like himself' (*Julius Caesar*, 5. 4. 25), anticipating the act of suicide in which 'Brutus only overcame himself' (5. 5. 56). As in *The Rape of Lucrece*, variations of redundant and reflexive phrasing contribute to Shakespeare's general portrayal of Rome as a world of endless violence in which heroic self-assertion is self-destructive.[49] Brutus' conqueror Antony will in turn commit suicide, as 'a Roman by a Roman | Valiantly vanquish'd' (*Antony and Cleopatra*, 4. 15. 57–8).[50] As we saw in Chapter 2, moreover, this kind of repetitive rhetoric is itself typical of Ovid, who uses it 'to express the internal division or self-alienation of an individual'.[51] The

---

cup' (934) he rejects, he repeats the position of the Lady in *Comus*. John P. Rumrich discusses the similarities between Milton's two characters in relation to Milton's treatment of gender difference (*Milton Unbound*, 89–90).

[48] *Surprised by Sin*, 310–11.

[49] See Kahn, *Roman Shakespeare*. On this phrasing in relation to representations of self-slaughter especially see Langley, *Narcissism and Suicide*.

[50] On the influence on *Samson* of *Antony and Cleopatra*, see John Guillory, 'Dalila's House: *Samson Agonistes* and the Sexual Division of Labour', in Ferguson, Quilligan, and Vickers (eds.), *Rewriting the Renaissance*, 112–15; and Anne Ferry, who notes how the relation between the two is reworked through Dryden's adaptation of Shakespeare's play as *All for Love* (*Milton and the Miltonic Dryden* (Cambridge, Mass., 1968)). A central problem of Shakespeare's play is that of determining when Antony is truly 'himself' (see for example 1. 1. 42–3, 57–9; 3. 11. 7; 3. 13. 92–3, 185–6): he is divided between his Egyptian and Roman natures which are only resolved—if ever—through suicide. Shakespeare also exploits the potential humour in these tautologies in Antony's comically redundant description of the crocodile: 'It is shap'd, sir, like itself, and it is as broad as it hath breadth. It is just so high as it is, and moves with it own organs. It lives by that which nourisheth it, and the elements once out of it, it transmigrates' (*Antony and Cleopatra*, 2. 7. 42–5).

[51] Hardie, *Ovid's Poetics of Illusion*, 251; see also 'Fama in Milton', in which Hardie notes the particular relevance of Ovid's description of Ajax who kills himself 'ne

phrase which Manoa uses to reflect Samson's integrity equally suggests self-division. An Ovidian rhetoric of closure seems itself to open new questions about the nature of the hero.[52]

A PHOENIX TOO FREQUENT

Manoa's claim that '*Samson* hath quit himself | Like *Samson*' (1709–10) suggests that, by his final self-fulfilling actions, Samson has reached a realm of absolute autonomy in which he cannot be compared to anything other than himself.[53] The hero's opening metamorphosis turns out to be illusory, as he becomes himself once more. However, in the final speeches, the dead Samson is also seen to be *like* many other things, as he is transformed into a group of images which have past and future lives of which the speakers themselves are not conscious. When Manoa hears of his son's death, he is first crushed by what appears the end of all his paternal hopes:

> What windy joy this day had I conceiv'd
> Hopeful of his Delivery, which now proves
> Abortive as the first-born bloom of spring
> Nipt with the lagging rear of winters frost. (1574–7)

'Delivery' is a key word in the poem, connected to Samson's sense of himself as the liberator of his people. The wordplay here shifts it into an image of birth (see also 1504–6), only to slip once again: Samson's death is imagined grotesquely as an abortion—a collapsing of birth and death.[54] It turns Samson into a child who has prematurely died before he could be reborn, and who ends before he can begin. The striking imagery recalls Milton's own beginnings in 'On the Death of a fair Infant dying of a Cough' in which the infant was the 'Fairest

---

quisquam Aiacem possit superare nisi Aiax' ('lest any man save Ajax conquer Ajax', *Met.*, 13. 390).

[52] One might compare this with the multiplication of closural devices at the end of the *Metamorphoses*, which Barchiesi argues undermines the sense of closure; see Barchiesi, 'Endgames: Ovid's *Metamorphoses* 15 and *Fasti* 6', 181–208.

[53] One might compare this to Dante's rhyming of 'Cristo' and 'Cristo' in *Paradiso* 12. 70–5; 14. 104–8; 19. 103–8; and 32. 83–7 as an expression of divine incommensurability: no word can adequately be coupled with Christ except Christ.

[54] On the imagery here, see also Kerrigan, *Prophetic Milton*, 212–17.

flower no sooner blown but blasted' (1) by 'Bleak winters force' (4). Manoa's speech contains an allusion that he himself cannot grasp, one that is accessible only to the poet himself and the post-1673 reader.

As we will see shortly, through other such self-allusions the drama circles back to Milton's own poetic beginnings. As Milton's infant was metamorphosed into a series of cosmic figures, the dead Samson is transformed by Manoa and the Chorus. In the most dazzling passage of the poem, the hero rises 'From under ashes into sudden flame' (1691), becoming 'an ev'ning Dragon' (1692), 'an Eagle' (1695), and finally, as the fulfilment of the idea of fiery rebirth, a phoenix:

> So vertue giv'n for lost,
> Deprest, and overthrown, as seem'd,
> Like that self-begott'n bird
> In the *Arabian* woods embost,
> That no second knows nor third,
> And lay e're while a Holocaust,
> From out her ashie womb now teem'd,
> Revives, reflourishes, then vigorous most
> When most unactive deem'd,
> And though her body die, her fame survives,
> A secular bird ages of lives. (1697–1707)

Like the young Milton, Manoa and the Chorus are searching for reassurance in the face of sudden death. The phoenix is a conventional, even somewhat predictable, image for resurrection; it celebrates Samson's ascent from death into eternal life.[55] What Manoa feared was the end is now reimagined as a new beginning, as Samson's death is turned into his rebirth.

The phoenix returning to its own unchanging form seems an apt symbol to underline Samson's triumphant recovery of 'himself'. However, it also ironically moves us further *away* from Samson as, in the process of interpretation, the dead hero is metamorphosed into figures that in his absence take over the end of the text. As Anthony Low suggested, the blurring of both images and syntax in this passage makes the exact referents unclear, burying Samson further under a

---

[55] See R. Van Den Broek, *The Myth of the Phoenix According to Classical and Early Christian Tradition*, trans. I. Seeger (Leiden, 1972).

heap of figures.⁵⁶ As in 'On the Death of a fair Infant', the original subject is left behind in the process of immortalization. Moreover, the phoenix widens the gap between the readers *within* the text and the readers *of* the text as interpreters able to grasp the meaning of the action. As Hebrews, the Chorus cannot foresee that the phoenix would be appropriated by Christians as a symbol of Christ. For Milton's readers, however, this would have been a reminder that Samson was also considered a type for Christ. For those who can see the significance, Samson and the phoenix foreshadow a future and greater hero. It shifts our attention from Samson himself to Jesus, who will revise and complete Samson's story and life.

The religious symbolism of the phoenix thus points the readers towards the future and a quite different version of Samson's story. Samson becomes a shadowy type, whose life will derive its full meaning only from a later reinterpretation. At the same time, however, the wording takes the reader, though not the speakers, backwards into the literary past: to Ovid's description of the phoenix in Pythagoras' speech on eternal change in *Metamorphoses* 15. 391–407. In *Samson*, the presence of the Ovidian figure complicates further the Virgilian narrative of heroic development.

As I noted earlier, the speech of Pythagoras has been one of the most influential passages in Ovid. The philosopher's vision of flux has been frequently identified with that of the author himself, and seen as a key to the meaning of the text. While I argued against such an identification, the speech is clearly important; it offers one model for change, and builds towards the climax of the epic and the poet's emergence as the conqueror of change.⁵⁷ Interrupting the history of Rome that began with Ovid's retelling of the *Aeneid*, it is still part of Ovid's response to Virgil, in which never-ending and circular Ovidian metamorphosis replaces Virgilian *translatio* and linear progress. Moreover, as Philip Hardie has shown, Pythagoras' speech is concerned with imitation and succession; it shows the transmission of literature from Greece to Rome and specifically 'Ovid's construction

---

⁵⁶ Anthony Low, 'The Phoenix and the Sun in *Samson Agonistes*', *Milton Studies*, 14 (1980), 222.

⁵⁷ On the problems of interpreting the role of Pythagoras' speech see Colin Burrow, 'Spenser and Classical Traditions', in Hadfield (ed.), *The Cambridge Companion to Spenser*, 230; and Barchiesi, who treats the philosopher as one of the internal narrators of the poem (*Speaking Volumes*, 62–9).

of his own poetic genealogy'.[58] It is, as usual, a complicated family tree, stretching back to Empedocles, and then passing down through the various forms of Ennius, Lucretius, and Virgil. As Hardie notes further, the density of the relations is reflected by the passage's use of 'double allusions', in which Ovid simultaneously imitates both an original source and a later imitator. Thus Empedocles is invoked along with his imitators Ennius and Lucretius, who are in turn accompanied by their imitator Virgil. The complex networks of meaning draw attention to creativity as a process of repeated revision. Pythagoras' lengthy speech, so often copied by later writers and thinkers, also sets up the process of transmutation in which Ovid will be reformed into new works, and by new readers who will interpret his text in different ways. As I noted in the Introduction, Pythagorean metempsychosis was used frequently as an image for poetic succession, as writers were hailed as the reincarnation of Ovid.

The appearance of the phoenix at this particular point in the *Metamorphoses* is important in terms of Ovid's meditation on the literary tradition. As I suggested in the previous chapter, Ovid is interested in the problem of succession, which appears especially in the tragic stories of Phaethon and Icarus, sons who are unable to follow their fathers. The theme is also central in Virgil whose work is haunted by the 'son who does not survive'.[59] For both writers, the problem of broken succession was political (as it would be for the Elizabethans), connected to the failure of Augustus to establish a secure dynasty which would allow for the smooth transfer of power after his death. In *Aeneid* 6, the death of the young and promising Marcellus brings Anchises' vision of history to an abrupt halt, pointing towards Rome's uncertain future. But for Ovid especially, the question is also a poetical one, as at the end of the poem, he imagines what will happen to him after death. As an heir to the past, Ovid's phoenix is the opposite of Phaethon: he is a son of the sun who is not destroyed by fire but reborn out of it.[60] The bird is part of a series of figures for regeneration that run through the end of the

---

[58] 'The Speech of Pythagoras in Ovid *Metamorphoses* 15: Empedoclean Epos', *Classical Quarterly*, NS 45/1 (1995), 204.
[59] Quint, 'Fear of Falling', 848.
[60] Stella Revard thus notes that, in an earlier reference to the phoenix in 'Epitaphium Damonis', 'Milton takes care... to contrast the phoenix poetically with Phaethon, Apollo's fatal son, whose mismanagement of the Sun's fire scorches the earth and fells him... The very fire that kills Phaethon... wakes the phoenix to new life'

Metamorphoses, leading up to the poet's own climactic claim of immortality. At the same time, these figures look back to and comment on Virgil's account of the founding of Rome. In *Metamorphoses* 13, Aeneas is given a cup on which is engraved the death of the daughters of Orion and the birth from their ashes of the Coroni (13. 692–704).[61] The image of rebirth clearly looks forward to the rise of Rome out of Troy's ashes. Yet a more sinister form of resurrection appears earlier in the same book, when a flock of birds ascends from the pyre of Memnon. The newly born offspring kill each other in an annual ritual of perverse filial piety ('cum sol duodena peregit | signa, parentali moriturae more rebellant', 'and still, when the sun has completed the circuit of his twelve signs, they fight and die again in customary ceremony for their dead father', 13. 618–19). Not everything that returns from death is good, and perpetuation can be simply the perpetuation of destruction. The legacy of Troy will also be civil war.

Moreover, the phoenix seems a particularly static form of change. According to Pythagoras, the phoenix is the only thing that does not change forms at all, that is, in essence, always and only 'like itself': 'Haec tamen ex aliis generis primordia ducunt, | una est, quae reparet seque ipsa reseminet, ales' ('Now all these things get their life's beginning from some other creature; but there is one bird which itself renews and reproduces its own being', *Met.*, 15. 391–2). It suggests stability in the midst of flux, sameness in a process of eternal differentiation. The description of the son who 'fertque pius cunasque suas patriumque sepulcrum' ('piously bears his own cradle and his father's tomb', 15. 405) evokes the *pius Aeneas* whose journey Ovid has just retold in *Metamorphoses* 13–14. As usual, Ovid is one of Virgil's most astute readers and adapters, who here exposes the resistance to change that haunts the *Aeneid*. The phoenix, like Milton's Satan, epitomizes the kind of redundant and static change that makes real

---

(*Milton and the Tangles*, 232). The antithesis is already established in Ovid, however, where it is reinforced by the linking of the phoenix with another son of Apollo, Aesculapius, also born out of divine fire. The birth of Aesculapius at the end of *Metamorphoses* 2 counters the destruction of Phaethon at the book's beginning. Aesculapius' story is picked up in Book 15, where, along with the phoenix, he is an example of filial piety and the carrying over of the past into the present.

[61] Philip Hardie points out that the description of Aeneas' cup (*Met.*, 13. 684) is echoed by Milton in the description of Manso's cup, on which is engraved the figure of the phoenix and celestial Cupid in 'Epitaphium Damonis' 184; see 'Fama in Milton'.

change impossible. The son who *is* his own father suggests that present and future are simply copies of the past, without progression or difference. The phoenix family is a fantasy of narcissistic self-perpetuation through identical images 'like itself'.

An image of exact replication, the phoenix has, however, a surprisingly split family tree. As I noted earlier, for Christians the phoenix became an image for Christ and spiritual resurrection. In Milton's elegy for his best friend Charles Diodati, 'Epitaphium Damonis', it is used as a means of reaching the poem's conclusion with Diodati's spiritual rebirth in heaven (180–9). Milton here draws also on the phoenix's association with chastity, as does William Habington in his *Castara* sequence, written in the 1630s.[62] As a complete contradiction, the phoenix is also invoked as an image of the *coincidentia oppositorum* in the divine nature. For Queen Elizabeth, it was an apt symbol for her virginity and of her transcendence of both gender and time, which she used in connection with her motto, *Semper eadem*.[63] Elizabeth also exploited the fact that the bird was considered both male and female—a tradition Donne uses for rather different purposes in the 'Canonization' where he makes the phoenix 'riddle' (23) a figure for sexual coupling. For Donne, the bird's ambiguous gender is a source of Ovidian wit and paradox. Lactantius also enjoys playing with the impossibilities of this she/he with rather Ovidian glee:

> ipsa sibi proles, suus est pater et suus heres,
>   nutrix ipsa sui, semper alumna sibi.
> ipse quidem, sed non [eadem est], eademque nec ipsa est
>   aeternam vitam mortis adepta bono.[64]

---

[62] William Habington, *Castara* (London, 1634), Early English Books Online; see, for example, 'To Castara, A Sacrifice', B1^r; and 'To Castara, Vpon a sigh', I1^v.

[63] Strong, *Gloriana*, 82–3, 104. While, like other symbols of Elizabeth's chastity, the phoenix also drew attention to the problems created by her virginity, in *Henry VIII* 5. 4. 39–47, Shakespeare cleverly makes the bird the symbol of continuity as James becomes the phoenix born out of Elizabeth's ashes. Other rulers had also used the phoenix to stress their divinity, and to support the idea of the 'king's two bodies' which facilitated succession; see Ernst H. Kantorowicz, *The King's Two Bodies: A Study in Mediaeval Political Theology* (Princeton, 1957), 388–95.

[64] All citations are from Lactantius, *De Ave Phoenice*, ed. and trans. Mary Cletus Fitzpatrick (Philadelphia, 1933).

('She is her own progeny, her own sire, and her own heir. She is her own nurse, ever foster child to herself. She is indeed herself, yet not the same, the same and not herself, having attained life everlasting through death's boon', 167–70)[65]

The phoenix's paradoxical double nature made it a useful image for the transcendence of difference generally.

Yet the image is also frequently used negatively. In Dante the bird appears in *Inferno* 24, the Ovidian canto of the thieves, which, as I noted earlier, provides a further subtext for the final metamorphosis of Satan and the other devils. In *Inferno* 24. 103–11 the sudden dissolution and reconstitution of the thief Vanni Fucci is compared to that of the phoenix. The Ovidian allusion is reinforced in *Inferno* 25. 48–78, in which the transformation of Agnolo de' Brunelleschi draws in some detail on the metamorphosis of Hermaphroditus in *Metamorphoses* 4. 361–5. Dante's coupling of the phoenix with the hermaphrodite suggests his interest in the connections between Ovidian stories, as the bi-sexed phoenix recalls the tale of sexual union told in *Metamorphoses* 4.[66] In Dante, these complementary visions of two becoming one suggest untranscendent infernal identity. The phoenix is also linked ambiguously with the hermaphrodite in Shakespeare's 'The Phoenix and Turtle', in which the phoenix is part of the vision of a love in which the lovers have merged completely, becoming, in their 'mutual flame', 'Neither two nor one' (24, 40). While the song celebrates this complete meeting of male and female, self and other, it also shows it to be a dead end: a poem which should be an epithalamion of 'married chastity' (61) becomes a dirge for soul mates who have left 'no posterity' (59). The self-destroying nature of the phoenix therefore serves as a convenient image for the sterility of chastity in seduction poems; as Milton's classmate Thomas Randolph

---

[65] Claudian also plays up the paradoxical elements of the phoenix, although he omits its blurring of gender differences; see *Claudian*, introd. and trans. Maurice Platnauer, 2 vols. (Cambridge, Mass., 1922; repr. 1972), ii. 222–30.

[66] The link between the tales is made clear in the story of Caenis, the woman who becomes a man, told in *Metamorphoses* 12. Taunted as effeminate, 'semimari' (12. 506) by the Centaurs (who are themselves, of course, 'semihomines', 12. 536), Caenis is crushed to death and becomes 'nunc avis unica' ('now sole bird of thy kind', 12. 531). Mary Cletus Fitzpatrick suggests that Ovid's description of the hermaphrodite may have influenced later descriptions of the bi-gendered phoenix, such as that of Lactantius cited above (*De Ave Phoenice*, 21, 90). For other discussions of the bird's hermaphroditism see Van den Broek, *Myth of the Phoenix*, 360–76.

observes, 'The *Phoenix* chast yet when she dyes, | Her self with her own ashes lyes' ('A Pastorall Courtship', O3ʳ).⁶⁷

In *Metamorphoses* 15, the juxtaposition of the immortal phoenix and the poet who rises above change implies the narcissism of the artist's dream of eternal self-perpetuation. For Petrarch and Spenser, who are haunted by the spectre of Ovidian mutability in the world and themselves, the phoenix expresses but also questions their desire to transcend flux. Petrarch's *Rime sparse* 323, copied by Spenser as 'The Visions of Petrarch', describes the mutability of the world. While most beautiful ephemera are destroyed by forces outside of themselves (a lovely lady is killed by a serpent, earth destroys a poetic spring), the poet sees self-destruction at work in the phoenix who, according to Petrarch: 'volse in se stessa il becco | quasi sdegnando, e'n un punto disparse' (58–9) (in Spenser's version: 'Himselfe smote with his beake, as in disdaine, | And so foorthwith in great despight he dide', 66–7). The motive of 'sdegna/disdain', traditionally associated with the narcissism of the coldly chaste beloved, is disturbing, however. The phoenix expresses the speaker's longing to escape the world of flux, to arrest change in art, and specifically, in Petrarch's case, 'un dolce di morir desio' ('a sweet desire to die', 75). The desire for the transcendence of change and differentiation leads to self-destruction.

We clearly cannot know for certain how much or which of these meanings—if in fact any—Milton himself had in mind. Nor in turn, however, could he anticipate or control the meanings readers might import.⁶⁸ The figure is weighted down with potential but conflicting associations, between which the reader must choose in order to interpret the meaning of the final action. But it obscures rather than clarifies the nature of Samson, who is transmuted into a proliferating

---

⁶⁷ Citations of Randolph's poetry are taken from *Poems with The Mvses Looking-Glasse and Amyntas* (Oxford, 1638), Early English Books Online.

⁶⁸ As Barchiesi notes, 'one of the main problems in handling allusion is the difficulty of knowing where to stop.... intertextuality can unleash a real struggle for power by which the poetic act proliferates indeterminate meanings' (*Speaking Volumes*, 98–9). I discuss this problem further in 'Comus's Wood of Allusion', 319–20 especially. The problem of circumscribing meaning was on Milton's mind when compiling his *Art of Logic*. Here, however, he raises it only to shut it down firmly, explaining that when two things are compared: 'Warning, however, should be given that likes whether of short or full form are not to be urged beyond that quality which the man making the comparison intended to show as the same in both. Thus a magistrate is likened to a dog, yet merely in the fidelity of his guardianship' (*Works*, xi. 195). Poetical language, however, frustrates this kind of boundary policing.

series of images. The phoenix points us in opposing directions, towards the transcendence of time and difference, and towards mere repetition of the same. The description of the bird as one whose 'fame survives, | A secular bird ages of lives' (*SA*, 1706–7) echoes Ovid's claim at the end of the *Metamorphoses* that 'omnia saecula fama... vivam' ('through all the ages shall I live in fame', 15. 878–9). The language thus might suggest Samson's own achievement of Ovidian immortality—an idea that is reinforced by Manoa's plan to turn the dead man into his own monument.[69] But Milton's 'secular bird' (1707) seems bound to the endurance of 'fame' (1706) and to the repetitive cycles of human time and the world, 'saeculum',[70] and thus cut off from the spiritual resurrection of Christ. The fact that it is 'self-begott'n' (1699) brings in a different reference, recalling Satan's claim in *Paradise Lost* to be 'self-begot, self-rais'd' (5. 860), and reminding us of Satan's desire to arrest change through narcissistic self-replication. Moreover, the phoenix suggests an ideal of autonomy which, as in Shakespeare's Roman works, seems at least socially suicidal. While it generates itself, it cannot generate anything else: it knows no second or third.

The presence of this symbol is especially troubling given that, like the *Aeneid* and *Metamorphoses*, not to mention *Paradise Lost*, Milton's tragedy makes much of father–son relations. It gives a central role to Samson's kindly and loving father, Manoa, who is barely mentioned in Judges. But it ends with the rupture of succession, and a son who does not survive. Despite two marriages, Samson himself does not leave a son. In this he is clearly differentiated from his final adversary, the giant Harapha, a figure Milton not only invents but also ostentatiously claims is the father of Goliath. By making the rival Harapha the founder of a gigantic dynasty, Milton emphasizes Samson's contrasting lack of progeny. Instead, the father is his son's heir, the custodian of his memory, builder of his monument, and shaper of his career and fame. As Manoa describes Samson's legacy for future generations, Samson's future seems to lie in or at least with the past.

---

[69] See Low, who notes other uses of the phoenix to symbolize fame ('Phoenix and the Sun', 221), and also Hardie, 'Fama in Milton'.
[70] See also Kerrigan, *Prophetic Milton*, 245–6.

'THE LAST OF ME OR NO I CANNOT WARRANT'

As I noted earlier, *Samson* has struck many readers as a review of Milton's life and work, a retrospective that brings together the poet's beginnings and his ending. The sense of autobiography is encouraged by the parallels with Milton's political pamphlets.[71] Moreover, as Ann Coiro especially has noted, *Samson* is full of echoes of Milton's early poetry.[72] Like the exiled Ovid, Milton circles back to and reworks his beginning. As the old poet looks back from the perspective of his end, images of premature endings especially seem to return with renewed urgency. The imagery of shipwreck in the drama (197–200; 1044–5) recalls 'Lycidas'. Manoa's plans to take Samson's body, and 'from the stream | With lavers pure and cleansing herbs wash off | The clotted gore' (1726–8), looks back to both 'Lycidas' and the description of the watery baptism of another young suicide, Sabrina, in *Comus* (833–42). Manoa's closing claim that 'Nothing is here for tears' (*SA*, 1721) translates 'Nec tibi conveniunt lacrymae' (202) of Milton's 'Epitaphium Damonis', in which Milton first used the image of the phoenix to suggest rebirth. I have already noted the echoes of 'On the Death of a fair Infant', which suggest that, at the end of Milton's career, he remembers his own poetic beginning through an image of the destructive identification of birth and death.[73]

In Milton's last poem, as in his first English work, he is concerned with the relation between the beginnings and endings of lives. Through *Samson*, and like his hero, Milton rereads his own life in order to find a pattern, the underlying coherence to unify a life full of change, and to understand the meaning of his own achievement. Moreover, while the drama opens with the hero looking backwards to his heroic past, grappling with his transformation from hero to slave, it ends looking to the future—not only to the coming of Christ, suggested by the phoenix, but to the process of further transmutation by which Samson will be turned into 'copious Legend, or sweet Lyric Song' (1737), including of course Milton's own work. The poet

---

[71] See especially Lieb, *Milton and the Culture of Violence*, 226–63.
[72] 'Fable and Old Song'. Quint draws connections between *Samson* and Milton's early Gunpowder poems, suggesting that Milton's career 'began and ended ... with the Gunpowder Plot' (*Epic and Empire*, 281).
[73] See also Coiro, 'Fable and Old Song', 138.

returns to the situation of 'On *Shakespear*', and indeed all the early poems on dead people in which Milton shaped their and, more importantly, his own immortality. But now it is Milton who is awaiting monumentalization. For Coiro, *Samson* reflects Milton's 'anxiety about his own influence at the threshold of becoming a great dead poet himself' whose meaning is in the hands of his future readers.[74]

The concluding speeches of Manoa and the Chorus might suggest, therefore, that Milton is trying to stabilize how he will be read in the future. By returning to his origins he reveals the unity of the works as a whole and brings them to a close in a final self-gathering of climactic self-fulfilment and resolution. He includes the act of interpretation as part of the work itself to offer us, as Ovid did his readers, the authorized version of the meaning of his works and life that will be perpetuated through later generations. The poet thus becomes a version of the *magister amoris*, a didactic and controlling teacher who teaches his readers how to read him correctly, as Stanley Fish argued in regard to *Paradise Lost*.[75]

By presenting his interpretation in his own voice in *Tristia* 2, Ovid had asserted a claim to the unique and privileged position of authorial knowledge. At the same time, his situation in exile showed the limits of an author's control of his text. Milton also acknowledges his inability to have the last word and ensure his own meaning. In his poem, interpretation is offered through dramatic characters: first Samson, and then Manoa and the Chorus. The readings in the play are, however, themselves texts to be read by later interpreters, who will always see meanings that the original speakers themselves did not intend. The perspectives of Manoa and the Chorus are limited, but they also are appealing, understandable, and deeply human. The kindly father especially, who had hoped that Samson might still get his powers back, wants to bring Samson and the story to a peaceful and satisfying end in which meaning is secured. The ending interpretations suggest the author's fantasy of controlling his own monumentalization, but they also anticipate the reader's desire to wrest meaning from muddle and uncertainty, to eradicate

---

[74] 'Fable and Old Song', 126.
[75] See especially *Surprised by Sin*. Fallon notes the paradox of Fish's study of '*The Reader in* Paradise Lost': for Fish the poem is actually 'relentlessly author-centered', as 'Milton appears as the nearly omniscient and omnipotent creator and controller of our reading' (*Milton's Peculiar Grace*, 12, 11).

ambiguity and bring closure. However, the story and hero resist their attempts to contain it. As Fish argues, there is a disjunction between the Chorus' relentless effort to make sense of Samson and the hero's own disruption of tidy categories.[76] Samson himself exits in a state of 'abiding uncertainty',[77] not knowing that his end is near or what it will mean. His last words are a simple confession of his own ignorance of his fate: 'the last of me or no I cannot warrant' (*SA*, 1426).

As Samson goes off to perform a final unknown act to an audience he cannot see, Milton's works enter a future he cannot imagine. The literary climate at the end of Milton's career, with its turn to the kind of balance and closure Manoa seeks, and its reduction of conflict and difference to witty parody, probably did not cheer him much. Nor, one might think, would the fate of Ovid, who was increasingly reduced to licentious burlesque that supported the newly reborn monarchical system.[78] The libertine artist of deception and seduction was revived as the Restoration rake.[79] In Rochester especially,

---

[76] *How Milton Works*, 438–57.

[77] Ibid. 420; see also 417, 464–5. See also Barbara Kiefer Lewalski, 'Barbara Lewalski on Why Milton Matters', *Milton Studies*, 44 (2005), 13–21.

[78] The tone was set by the publication in 1651 of James Smith's smutty parody of both Marlowe and Ovid, *The Loves of Hero and Leander: A Mock Poem*, which explains the lovers' end: 'They both were drown'd, whilst Love and Fate contended; | And thus they both pure Flesh, like pure Fish ended' ((London, 1651), Early English Books Online, D3^r). (Smith is drawing on the earlier spoofs of Marlowe by Thomas Nashe in *Lenten Stuffe* ((London, 1599), Early English Books Online, G1^r–G4^v) and Jonson's burlesque puppet show in *Bartholomew Fair* 5. 4.) For another example of Ovidian parody from this period, see James Harmer, 'Reginald Forster's Burlesque Ovidian Epistle', *Translation and Literature*, 16/2 (2007), 193–204. The vogue for Ovidian parodies increased later in the 1680s with Matthew Stevenson's *The Wits Paraphrased, or Paraphrase upon Paraphrase in a Burlesque* (1680), and Alexander Radcliffe's *Ovid Travestie: A Burlesque upon Ovids Epistles* (1681). As in the late 16th century, Ovid became a means of bemoaning the degeneration of poetry itself in such a climate; see especially the anonymous *Poeta de Tristibus, or The Poet's Complaint* (1682), which enlists Milton in its lament on the neglect of art: 'What could the *Muses* more have done, | Or *Apollo* for a Son?' (*Poeta de Tristibus, or The Poet's Complaint*, ed. Harold Love, (Los Angeles, 1971), D3^r). I am not sure Milton would have been heartened much by the alternative Ovidianism of his acquaintance Peter Sterry, who tried to restore Ovid to the status of a mystical fable full of serious Christian meaning; see N. I. Matar, 'Peter Sterry and the Puritan Defense of Ovid in Restoration England', *Studies in Philology*, 88/1 (1991), 110–21.

[79] M. L. Stapleton notes the enormous popularity of Ovid's erotic verse in the years immediately following the Restoration ('Ovid the Rakehell: The Case of Wycherley'). Heywood's early 17th-century translation of the *Ars* was reprinted six times, and was later included, along with Smith's volume, in the hilariously bad and raunchy miscellany *Ovid De Arte Amandi and the Remedy of Love Englished, as also the Loves of*

Ovidian eroticism fuels a poetry in which explicitness always verges on the anti-erotic: Ovid's Chloris, who becomes Flora, goddess of flowers and Ovid's elegiac muse, is reduced to a whore ('Song: How perfect Cloris, and how free', 'To a Lady, in a Letter'), a peasant raped by a passing shepherd ('As *Chloris* full of harmless thought'), and a masturbating pigkeeper ('*Faire Cloris* in a Pigsty lay', 40).[80] The Restoration Ovid reflects a cynical view of freedom, human nature, the imagination, and sexuality that seems far from the innocence imagined as once possible in *Paradise Lost*. The sending forth of his works at the end of his life suggests, however, that, no matter how disillusioned Milton was by the failure of the Revolution, nor how dismayed by the tastes of his contemporaries, he never lost hope that reading could be the path to personal and political freedom.

Hero & Leander, a Mock-Poem, Together with Choice Poems, and Rare Pieces of Drollery (first printed in 1662, and then again in 1672, 1677, 1682, and 1684). More sober versions of Ovid's work appeared in Francis Wolferson's 1661 *The Three Books of Publius Ovidius Naso, De Arte Amandi* (1661), and, after Milton's death, in Dryden's *Ovid's Art of Love, in Three Books, Translated by Mr. Dryden, Mr Congreve, &c* (1692). Later, Dryden published other versions of Ovid's works: *Ovids Epistles* (1680) and then, in *Fables Ancient and Modern* (1700), tales from the *Metamorphoses* that became part of Samuel Garth's multi-authored 1717 edition of the epic.

[80] Citations of Rochester's poems are taken from *The Works of John Wilmot Earl of Rochester*, ed. Harold Love (Oxford, 1999). Rochester is building on other dirty uses of Ovid's figure earlier in the century which reduce Ovidian desire to masturbatory fantasy. The speaker of Richard Lovelace's auto-erotic poem 'Love made in the first Age: To Chloris' is rebuffed by the virgin, and retreats into a dream of a Golden Age of innocent sex; by the end, he is so aroused by his own imagination that no longer interested in the girl at all: 'ravish'd with these Noble Dreams, And crowned with mine own soft Beams, | Injoying of my self I lye' (10. 4–6). Citations from Lovelace's poetry are taken from *Lucasta: Posthume Poems of Richard Lovelace Esq.* (London, 1659), Early English Books Online. Narcissistic Ovidian fantasy becomes again a means of avoiding sexual union with another. Like the libertines before him, Rochester seems to find the female body and sexual union distasteful. M. L. Stapleton argues that Rochester's impotence, portrayed in his reworking of *Amores* 3. 7 as 'The Imperfect Enjoyment', suggests his sense of his own poetic lack of power ('"Thou idle Wanderer, about my Heart": Rochester and Ovid', *Restoration: Studies in English Literary Culture, 1660–1700*, 23/1 (1999), 10–30). This may explain the underlying viciousness that is barely controlled by the veneer of urbanity in Rochester's verse and which bursts out in his invective; he seems to rewrite Ovidian erotic elegy from the perspective of the poet of the *Ibis*.

Go Little Book

Milton's concern with his future is evident in another, less discussed work, which also might have a claim to be the poet's last word: 'Ad *Joannem Rousium*, Oxoniensis Academiae Bibliothecarium'. The poem first appeared in the 1673 edition of Milton's early works, where it was placed as the last of the Latin poems and was, therefore, the final poem in the volume as a whole. Chronologically, of course, it is not his last piece of writing; dated 23 January 1646 (i.e. 1647) it goes back to the period in Milton's life just after the publication of his *Poems* to no acclaim or even much apparent interest. Under attack as a polemicist and underappreciated as a poet, Milton is already sensitive to the vulnerability of his publications. It is a fitting valedictory poem for Milton's volume, his career in general, and my discussion.

As is typical of Milton's Latin writings, the poem has a wide range of classical subtexts which make the young writer part of an ongoing tradition. The general form is Pindaric, though reworked into Latin, suggesting Milton's interest in the dynamics of change and adaptation within classical (and neoclassical) literatures.[1] But like elegies 1 and 4, the situation evokes the exiled Ovid, recalling in particular *Tristia* 1. 1, in which the poet sends his book off from Tomis to Rome. Like Ovid, Milton is anxious about the fate of his work when it leaves its originator. The poem begins by looking backward nostalgically, to the volume's conception in an idyllic world in which its creator was footloose and fancy free: 'Insons populi, barbitóque devius | Indulsit patrio... | & humum vix tetigit pede' ('unconcerned with the public, uncommon, he indulged | a native lyric... | and his feet barely touched the ground', 9–10, 12). The self-representation here seems

---

[1] On the Pindaric elements especially see Revard, *Milton and the Tangles*, 237–63. On Milton's general use of classical models in the poem see *Variorum*, i. 324–31; and John K. Hale, 'The Pre-Criticism of Milton's Latin Verse, Illustrated from the Ode "Ad Joannem Rousium"', in Stanwood (ed.), *Of Poetry and Politics*, 17–34.

more playful than in the rest of the early verse, as Milton's early fantasies of poetic flight are gently mocked by a speaker who presents himself as more mature. But the description invokes not only the young poet's past naivety but also a world from which he is now cut off; as Louis Martz notes, it shows 'a state of mind, a point of view, ways of writing, ways of living, an old culture and outlook now shattered by the pressures of maturity and by the actions of political man'.[2] For Stella Revard, the poem is a farewell to this old life and the assumption of the mantle demanded by harsher times of war which are hostile to art.[3] The world has changed and the poet himself has had to grow up. He is moving from the innocent pastoral world of his youth into a harsher universe of epic conflict between monstrous harpies and the Muses, in which the country awaits a heroic champion who will:

> Almaque revocet studia sanctus
> Et relegatas sine sede Musas
> Jam penè totis finibus Angligenûm;
> Immundasque volucres
> Unguibus imminentes
> Figat Apolloneâ pharetrâ,
> Phinéamque abigat pestem procul amne Pegaséo.

('... restore wholesome learning
and the exiled Muses, now homeless
through nearly all the English lands;
and use Apollo's arrows
to impale these defiled,
winged, clawed menaces
and drive the plague of Phineas far from the river of Pegasus', 30–6)

The inflation of the occasion—the sending of a little book to a library (not the most obvious setting for an epic)—into a scene involving an epic battle with mythical monsters is of course rather comic and part of the self-mockery here. It is as if Milton is so keen to write his epic that he can't help but turn every occasion into a cosmic conflict between good and evil. But there is of course a more serious side to this imagery which reflects the poet's meditations on his future and the dangers that poetry faces in a changing world. As Milton explains, the book he is sending is a new copy to replace an original

---

[2] *Poet of Exile*, 33.   [3] *Milton and the Tangles*, 262–3.

that was lost, possibly stolen. The treatment of the original book is a sign of the current contempt for poetry, and therefore a justification of his anxiety about the future of his works as a whole. Milton speculates on the lost book's unknown fate, imagining it in a cave, or in the hands of some vulgar bookseller who cannot appreciate its value (37–42). However, he insists, there is now hope of redemption, as the book may 'Fugere Lethen, vehique Superam | In Jovis aulam remige pennâ' ('escape abysmal Lethe, | swept up to the high court | of Jove by a feathered oar', 45–6). The book is suddenly transformed into an epic hero who has been to hell and back.

In David Quint's discussion of the figures of Phaethon and Icarus in *Paradise Lost*, he notes that the image of 'remige pennâ' ('Ad Joannem Rousium', 46), which conflates rowing and flying, is densely allusive.[4] It plays on the practice in Latin poetry of describing wings as oars. In *De Rerum Natura* 6. 744, which tells of the fall of birds into the cavern of Avernus, Lucretius notes how they lose 'remigii ... pennarum' ('the oarage of their wings'). The image is also used by both Virgil (*Aeneid*, 6. 19) and Ovid (*Ars*, 2. 45) in the context of the doomed flight of Icarus.[5] It is taken up again in Dante's story of Ulysses' last voyage in *Inferno* 26, in which Ulysses remembers 'de' remi facemmo ali al folle volo' ('we made of oars wings for the mad flight', 26. 125). Milton himself will evoke this common metaphor in his description of the flight through Chaos of Satan in *Paradise Lost* 2. 941–2, when he makes his way 'half on foot, | Half flying; behoves him now both Oare and Saile'.

In 'Ad *Joannem Rousium*', the wording plunges the book and poem into a complicated network of textual relations circling around the theme of tragic fall which preoccupies Milton throughout his career. In the *Inferno* and *Paradise Lost*, the Lucretian descent to Avernus, traditionally the entrance to the pagan underworld, becomes the path

---

[4] 'Fear of Falling', see 847–57 especially.
[5] The metaphor is also implicit in *Metamorphoses* 8. 228, where 'Remigium', oars, is used to described Icarus' melting wings. The imagery connects these two stories of failed flight with that of Leander's attempt to cross the Hellespont. While Hero warns him that his arms are not as strong as a ship's oars (*Heroides*, 19. 184), when Leander sets out for his fatal journey he cries 'remis ego corporis utar' ('I shall make use of the oarage of my arms', 18. 215). The link with Icarus is explicit earlier in his letter, when Leander wishes he could fly across the channel: 'nunc daret audaces utinam mihi Daedalus alas' ('Now would that Daedalus could give me his daring wings', 18. 49). Swimming at night he notes that he is guided by the stars, but rejects the lure of the constellations, describing Hero as a better star (18. 149–70).

to hell. Furthermore, Virgil's and Ovid's adaptations of Lucretius' image conflate spatial and genealogical descent once more, identifying Lucretius' headlong plunge with the rupture of filial succession, and with the son who spatially and temporally does not follow his father.

Milton's use of the phrase here, however, stands out against the direction of these other occurrences: where other poets, including his later self, imagine a fall downwards from heaven or the heavens, he imagines a flight upwards, from hell into paradise. As I noted in the last chapter, *Tristia* 1. 1 also uses the stories of Phaethon and Icarus to imagine the sending forth of Ovid's verse from exile. For the poet destroyed by his earlier works, publication is both necessary for survival and potentially disastrous.[6] Milton imagines a more positive reaching out into the future. As Milton had used the story of Phaethon in early works as a foil to define his own future rising to the stars, he contrasts his book's journey with these tales of disastrous flights and ill-fated sons. He turns falling into rising, reversing the downward trend to imagine the recovery of continuity and establishment of succession and even future progression. The poet's deprecation of his own ambitions for poetic flight as 'humum vix tetigit pede' ('his feet barely touched the ground', 12) curbs his potentially destructive Icarian presumption. Moreover, he suggests that there exists in England a paradise from which the Muses have never been banished. Oxford is the new Delphi, home of the Muses and of Apollo, who prefers it to Delos or Parnassus (61–6). As the poet himself goes out into a new and uncertain world, he sends his creations off to a place where they can find safety: 'Quò neque lingua procax vulgi penetrabit, atque longè | Turba legentum prava facesset' ('where the indecent tongue of a commoner will not poke | and which will eagerly keep freakish mobs of readers back', 79–80). The future of the poem is assured because of the recipient of the letter, Rouse, who is:

> Aeternorum operum custos fidelis,
> Quaestorque gazae nobilioris,
> Quàm cui praefuit Iön
> Clarus Erechtheides
> Opulenta dei per templa parentis

---

[6] See above, pp. 290–1.

> Fulvosque tripodas, donaque Delphica
> Iön Actaea genitus Creusâ.

('a trusted keeper of eternal works,
a protector of a treasure still more grand
than what Ion (Erechtheus' famed descendant
born of Actaean Creusa) watched over
throughout the sumptuous shrines,
golden tripods, and Delphic offerings
of his father god', 54–60)

The sudden and ostentatious reference to Ion here seems rather surprising, however, bringing in a different though related source. His story is told in Euripides' *Ion*, to which Milton is generally seen as alluding.[7] According to Milton's daughter, Euripides was another of his favourite classical writers; moreover, in his examination of Milton's marginalia in his edition of Euripides, John Hale has noted that *Ion* is one of the most heavily annotated plays.[8] The play is also concerned with father–son relations. As the priest at the temple of Delphi, Ion is the humble servant of his father, Apollo. But he frankly seems an improvement on his father, whose thoughtless rape of Ion's mother Creusa provides one of the central dilemmas of the play as it grapples with the rather dubious morality of the gods. However, the most dominant concern of the play is that of succession. The action is generated because the marriage of Creusa and her new husband, Xuthus, is barren, causing a crisis in Athens. They seek advice from the oracle of Apollo. At the beginning of the play, Creusa does not know that Ion is her son, and he himself is completely ignorant of his parentage. This leads to a slight misunderstanding in which she almost kills him and is then almost killed herself; it takes the intervention of Athena to straighten things out. The discovery of Ion as both son of Apollo and rightful heir to Athens enables the re-establishment of what had appeared to be a broken line of succession, and brings the rejuvenation of Athens.

The story of Ion thus suggests an alternative to that of Icarus or, more precisely here, the other doomed son Phaethon, who was the subject of another play by Euripides (which unfortunately only exists

---

[7] See *Variorum*, i. 330.

[8] John K. Hale, 'Milton's Euripides Marginalia: Their Significance for Milton Studies', *Milton Studies*, 27 (1991), 23–35. As I mentioned earlier, Euripides was also an important influence on Ovid.

now in fragments).[9] Ion is a son who claims inheritance through humble service to his father, and who as a result becomes the founder of a new and powerful line.[10] Milton's compact reference to the story identifies character through lineage, drawing attention to the lines of descent: Ion is descended from Creusa ('genitus Creusâ', 60), who in turn is the daughter of Erectheus (57); on the other side of his family, he is the son of Apollo, and appears as the custodian of 'templa parentis' ('the temple of his father', 58). Revard thus suggests that the allusion anticipates the recovery of poetry by 'the true sons of Apollo': both Milton and Rouse, who restore the continuity of tradition that the war has broken.[11] Unlike Icarus and Phaethon, who tried to soar beyond the past and claim their place prematurely, these sons of Apollo together serve and preserve tradition. As Milton had made himself and his father brothers born of Apollo in 'Ad Patrem', here he makes writer and reader siblings, and equal heirs of a classical legacy which stretches back through the Roman poets to their Greek sources. Rouse becomes the ideal friend hoped for at the end of 'Mansus'. Moreover, Rouse's receiving of the letter into his library becomes a rehearsal of the more general hoped-for reception of the poet's creations in the future. Milton's political sympathies may be suggested by the fact that his ideal reader is not the traditional monarch or aristocratic patron who will protect the author from the envy of others, but a librarian.[12] He offers books 'Perfunctam invidiâ requiem' ('a rest freed from envy', 'Ad *Joannem Rousium*', 76). Moreover, while Rouse is himself a figure of the reader, he is also the means by which the poet can address more readers in the future. The librarian is the heroic guardian at the gates of immortality, monumentalizer of others: 'Sunt data virûm monumenta curae' ('to whose care | are given the glorious monuments of men', 51),[13] who takes and preserves books in order to hand them on to others.

---

[9] Euripides also wrote plays on Bellerophon (the lost *Stheneboea*) and Hippolytus (*Hippolytus*), suggesting his general interest in this pattern of tragic sons.

[10] Like all of Euripides' plays, *Ion* ends with an *aition*, here of Athenian supremacy. Ion will be the forerunner of the Ionians, while his prophesied half-brothers, Dorus and Achaeus, will generate the Dorians and Achaeans.

[11] *Milton and the Tangles*, 259.

[12] Fittingly, at the time of Charles's occupation of Oxford during the war, Rouse had also asserted his authority over the King, refusing to grant him borrowers' privileges.

[13] Revard's edition notes here the possible echo of Horace 3. 30. Certainly there is a general allusion to the monument topos discussed in the last chapter.

The entrance into the library thus enables Milton to join a community that stretches backwards into the past and forwards into the future. The allusions themselves are a means of binding times, and holding together a world that is falling apart. Milton's book becomes a part of an established society of classics, as Milton tells it: 'Illic legéris inter alta nomina | Authorum, Graiae simul & Latinae | Antiqua gentis lumina, & verum decus' ('You will be read among great names of authors there | of Greek and Latin both, | ancient visionaries of the race, and their true glory', 70–2). Its admission assures the poet that his work and life has achieved something, though he again pokes fun at his own inflated ego: 'Vos tandem haud vacui mei labores, | Quicquid hoc sterile fudit ingenium' ('At end, my labors, you are not valueless, | whatever gushed from this empty genius', 73–4). Not only is he part of the past, but he now has hope of the future, through readers who may live at better times:

> At ultimi nepotes,
> Et cordiator aetas
> Judicia rebus aequiora forsitan
> Adhibebit integro sinu.
> Tum livore sepulto,
> Si quid meremur sana posteritas sciet
> Roüsio favente.

('But our latest descendants
and a wiser age
perhaps from a sound heart will share
more balanced judgments of affairs.
Then with envy in the grave,
a reasonable posterity will know if I have any worth
with Rouse's aid', 81–7)

Rouse is the reader who keeps the poet alive for a future that may be able to appreciate him.

Like the early poems with which I began, 'Ad *Joannem Rousium*' shows the young Milton's longing to create works that, drawing on and transforming the past, will endure. The concluding dream of immortality is rather different from the one at the end of the *Metamorphoses*, which, as I have noted, so often resounds in Renaissance claims for the transcendent power of art. But it is still framed in Ovidian terms, recalling Ovid's earlier assertion in *Amores* 1. 15. 39–42:

> pascitur in vivis Livor; post fata quiescit,
> cum suus ex merito quemque tuetur honos.
> ergo etiam cum me supremus adederit ignis,
> vivam, parsque mei multa superstes erit.

('It is the living that Envy feeds upon; after doom it stirs no more, when each man's fame guards him as he deserves. I, too, when the final fires have eaten up my frame, shall still live on, and the great part of me survive my death.')

The young Ovid is aware of the power of envy, but imagines himself exempt from it and thus safe in the future. But this early claim is ironized when read through his last poem, *Ex Ponto* 4. 16, in which his reader is Envy itself. Because of Rouse, Milton hopes for a more favourable reception. At the same time, he already knows that his future is uncertain. The poet's fantasy of a 'sana posteritas', 'reasonable posterity', is held in check by the simple 'forsitan', 'perhaps'. His future survival is dependent also on the crucial if ambiguously self-contained clause 'livore sepulto': the burial of the eternal force of envy which Ben Jonson saw as 'almost consubstantial with the act of reading'.[14] As Milton knew also, Oxford was not a divinely protected haven from the Civil War; from 1642 to 1646 it had been appropriated as the headquarters of the Royalists, housing a King who fancied himself as Apollo. Even as Milton presents a fantasy in which the transmission of the text from writer to reader is simply its passing from one brother to another in an unchanging paradise, he recognizes the limits of this authorial dream.

The final note on the poem in the *Variorum* observes that 'It is interesting that Milton's last formal piece of Latin verse should end with an apparent echo of the poet of his youthful idolatry.'[15] It is even more interesting if we abandon the assumption that Ovid was simply part of an idolatrous phase of Milton's youth and see Ovid instead as part of the fabric of Milton's thought, through and with whom he explored some of the central questions of his work. Milton's early training through reading, translation, and rewriting not only made him intimate with Ovid's thought, but it equally taught him that the

---

[14] Meskill, *Ben Jonson and Envy*, 35. [15] *Variorum*, i. 331.

act of revision itself raises questions concerning creativity, freedom, and change. It also made him aware that, by entering into a dialogue with past writers, responding to and rewriting their works, he set in motion his own future revision and metamorphosis by others. He could not foresee who he would be and what he would become to later generations, who find new meanings in his work, and therefore keep him alive.

Bibliography

Adelman, Janet, 'Creation and the Place of the Poet in *Paradise Lost*', in Louis Martz and Aubrey Williams (eds.), *The Author in his Work: Essays on a Problem in Criticism* (New Haven: Yale University Press, 1978), 51–69.

Ahl, Frederick, *Metaformations: Soundplay and Wordplay in Ovid and Other Classical Poets* (Ithaca, NY: Cornell University Press, 1985).

Alciatus, Andreas, *The Latin Emblems, Indexes and Lists*, ed. Peter M. Daly et al. (Toronto: University of Toronto Press, 1985).

Allen, Don Cameron, *The Harmonious Vision: Studies in Milton's Poetry* (Baltimore: Johns Hopkins Press, 1954).

—— 'On Spenser's *Muiopotmos*', *Studies in Philology*, 53/2 (1956), 141–58.

—— 'On *Venus & Adonis*', in *Elizabethan and Jacobean Studies Presented to Frank Percy Wilson in Honour of his Seventieth Birthday* (Oxford: Clarendon Press, 1959), 100–11.

—— 'Some Observations on *The Rape of Lucrece*', *Shakespeare Survey*, 15 (1962), 89–98.

—— *Mysteriously Meant: The Rediscovery of Pagan Symbolism and Allegorical Interpretation in the Renaissance* (Baltimore: Johns Hopkins University Press, 1970).

Altman, Joel B., *The Tudor Play of Mind: Rhetorical Inquiry and the Development of Elizabethan Drama* (Berkeley and Los Angeles: University of California Press, 1978).

Alton, E. H., 'The Medieval Commentators on Ovid's *Fasti*', *Hermathena*, 44 (1926), 119–51.

—— and Wormell, D. E. W., 'Ovid in the Medieval Schoolroom', *Hermathena*, 94 (1960), 21–38; and 95 (1961), 76–82.

Amsler, Mark, 'Rape and Silence: Ovid's Mythography and Medieval Readers', in Elizabeth Robertson and Christine M. Rose (eds.), *Representing Rape in Medieval and Early Modern Literature* (Basingstoke: Palgrave, 2001), 61–96.

Anderson, Judith, '*Venus and Adonis*: Spenser, Shakespeare and the Forms of Desire', in Jennifer C. Vaught (ed.), *Grief and Gender: 700–1700* (New York: Palgrave, 2003), 149–60.

Anderson, William S., 'The Artist's Limits in Ovid: Orpheus, Pygmalion, and Daedalus', *Syllecta Classica*, 1 (1989), 1–11.

—— 'Lycaon: Ovid's Deceptive Paradigm in *Metamorphoses* 1', *Illinois Classical Studies*, 14 (1989), 91–101.

Anonymous, *Narcissus: A Twelfe Night Merriment Played by Youths of the Parish at the College of S. John the Baptist in Oxford, A.D. 1602* [online text] (1602), Literature Online, http://gateway.proquest.com/openurl?ctx_ver=Z39.88-2003&xri:pqil:res_ver=0.2&res_id=xri:lion-us&rft_id=xri:lion:ft:dr:Z100051122:1 accessed 12 Nov. 2006.

Apuleius, *Cupid & Psyche*, ed. E. J. Kenney (Cambridge: Cambridge University Press, 1990).

Aquinas, St Thomas, *Summa Theologica* [online text], New Advent Online Encyclopedia http://www.newadvent.org/summa/index.html accessed 5 May 2006.

Aristotle, *The Complete Works of Aristotle: The Revised Oxford Translation*, ed. Jonathan Barnes, 2 vols. (Princeton: Princeton University Press, 1984).

Ascham, Roger, *The Scholemaster*, in *English Works*, ed. William Aldis Wright (Cambridge, 1904; repr. 1970).

Aubrey, John, *Remains of Gentilisme and Judaisme*, ed. James Britten (London: W. Satchell, Peyton: 1881; repr. Kraus Reprint: Nendeln, Liechtenstein, 1967).

Baldwin, Thomas Whitfield, *William Shakspere's Small Latine & Lesse Greeke*, 2 vols. (Urbana, Ill.: University of Illinois Press, 1944).

—— *On the Literary Genetics of Shakespeare's Poems & Sonnets* (Urbana, Ill.: University of Illinois Press, 1950).

Bann, Stephen, *The True Vine: On Visual Representation and the Western Tradition* (Cambridge: Cambridge University Press, 1989).

Barbeau, Anne T., 'Satan's Envy of the Son and the Third Day of the War', *Papers on Language & Literature*, 13 (1977), 362-71.

Barchiesi, Alessandro, *La traccia del modello: Effetti omerici nella narrazione virgiliana* (Pisa: Giardini, 1984).

—— 'Discordant Muses', *Proceedings of the Cambridge Philological Society*, 37 (1991), 1-21.

—— 'Ultime difficoltà nella carriera di un poeta giambico: L'Epode XVII', in *Atti Convegno Oraziano, Nov. 1993* (Venosa, 1994), 205-20.

—— 'Endgames: Ovid's *Metamorphoses* 15 and *Fasti* 6', in Deborah H. Roberts, Francis M. Dunn, and Don Fowler (eds.), *Classical Closure: Reading the End in Greek and Latin Literature* (Princeton: Princeton University Press, 1997), 181-208.

—— *The Poet and the Prince: Ovid and Augustan Discourse* (Berkeley and Los Angeles: University of California Press, 1997).

—— *Speaking Volumes: Narrative and Intertext in Ovid and Other Latin Poets*, ed. and trans. Matt Fox and Simone Marchesi (London: Duckworth, 2001).

—— (ed.), *Ovidio: Metamorfosi* I-II, trans. Ludovica Koch, (Milan: Arnoldo Mondadori, 2005).

—— and Hardie, Philip, 'The Ovidian Career Model: Ovid, Gallus, Apuleius, Boccaccio', in Helen Moore and Philip Hardie (eds.), *Classical Literary Careers and their Reception* (Cambridge: Cambridge University Press, 2010), 59–88.

Barkan, Leonard, *The Gods Made Flesh: Metamorphosis & the Pursuit of Paganism* (New Haven: Yale University Press, 1986).

Barker, Arthur, 'Calm regained through passion spent', in Balachandra Rajan (ed.), *The Prison and the Pinnacle* (Toronto: University of Toronto Press, 1973), 3–48.

Barksted, William, *Mirrha, the Mother of Adonis: or, Lustes Prodegies* [online facsimile] (London: E. A[llde] for Iohn Bache, 1607), Early English Books Online, http://gateway.proquest.com/openurl?ctx_ver=Z39.88-2003&res_id=xri:eebo&rft_id=xri:eebo:image:19461 accessed 8 May 2008.

Barolini, Teodolinda, *The Undivine Comedy: Detheologizing Dante* (Princeton: Princeton University Press, 1992).

Barolsky, Paul, 'As in Ovid, So in Renaissance Art', *Renaissance Quarterly*, 51/2 (1998), 451–74.

—— 'Botticelli's *Primavera* and the Poetic Imagination of Italian Renaissance Art', *Arion*, 3rd series, 8/2 (2000), 5–35.

Bartsch, Shadi, *The Mirror of the Self: Sexuality, Self-Knowledge, and the Gaze in the Early Roman Empire* (Chicago: University of Chicago Press, 2006).

Baskins, Cristelle L., 'Echoing Narcissus in Alberti's *Della Pittura*', *Oxford Art Journal*, 16/1 (1993), 25–33.

Bate, Jonathan, *Shakespeare and Ovid* (Oxford: Oxford University Press, 1994).

Beard, Mary, 'A Complex of Times: No More Sheep on Romulus' Birthday', *Proceedings of the Cambridge Philological Society*, 33 (1987), 1–15.

Beaumont, Francis, *Salmacis and Hermaphroditvs* [online facsimile] (London: [S. Stafford] for John Hodgets, 1602), Early English Books Online, http://gateway.proquest.com/openurl?ctx_ver=Z39.88-2003&res_id=xri:eebo&rft_id=xri:eebo:image:8089 accessed 17 Aug. 2005.

Bedford, R. D., 'Ovid Metamorphosed: Donne's *Elegy XVI*', *Essays in Criticism*, 32/3 (1982), 219–36.

Bell, Ilona, 'Milton's Dialogue with Petrarch', *Milton Studies*, 28 (1992), 91–120.

Berry, Philippa, *Of Chastity and Power: Elizabethan Literature and the Unmarried Queen* (London: Routledge, 1989).

Blaine, Marlin E., 'Milton and the Monument Topos: "On Shakespeare," "*Ad Joannem Roüssium*," and *Poems* (1645)', *Journal of English and Germanic Philology*, 99/2 (1990), 215–34.

Blissett, William, 'Spenser's Mutabilitie', in A. C. Hamilton (ed.), *Essential Articles for the Study of Edmund Spenser* (Hamden, Conn.: Archon, 1972), 253–66.

Bloom, Harold, *The Anxiety of Influence: A Theory of Poetry* (New York: Oxford University Press, 1973).

Boesky, Amy, '*Paradise Lost* and the Multiplicity of Time', in Thomas N. Corns (ed.), *A Companion to Milton* (Oxford: Blackwell, 2001), 380–92.

Bond, Ronald, '*Invidia* and the Allegory of Spenser's "Muiopotmos"', *English Studies in Canada*, 2 (1976), 144–55.

—— 'Supplantation in the Elizabethan Court: The Theme of Spenser's February Eclogue', *Spenser Studies*, 2 (1981), 55–65.

—— 'Vying with Vision: An Aspect of Envy in *The Faerie Queene*', *Renaissance and Reformation*, 8/1 (1984), 30–8.

—— 'The Blatant Beast', in A. C. Hamilton (ed.), *The Spenser Encyclopedia* (Toronto: University of Toronto Press; London: Routledge, 1990), 96–8.

—— 'Envy', in A. C. Hamilton (ed.), *The Spenser Encyclopedia* (Toronto: University of Toronto Press; London: Routledge, 1990), 248–9.

Bradburn, Elizabeth, 'Theatrical Wonder, Amazement, and the Construction of Spiritual Agency in *Paradise Lost*', *Comparative Drama*, 40/1 (2006), 77–98.

Braden, Gordon, *The Classics and English Renaissance Poetry: Three Case Studies* (New Haven: Yale University Press, 1978).

—— 'Beyond Frustration: Petrarchan Laurels in the Seventeenth Century', *Studies in English Literature, 1500–1900*, 26/1 (1986), 5–23.

—— *Petrarchan Love and the Continental Renaissance* (New Haven: Yale University Press, 1999).

Brinkley, Robert A., 'Spenser's *Muiopotmos* and the Politics of Metamorphosis', *English Literary History*, 48/4 (1981), 668–76.

Brinsley, John, *Ludus Literarius: Or, the Grammar Schoole* [online facsimile] (London: [Humphrey Lownes] for Thomas Man, 1612), Early English Books Online, http://gateway.proquest.com/openurl?ctx_ver=Z39.88-2003&res_id=xri:eebo&rft_id=xri:eebo:image:6954 accessed 2 March 2010.

—— *Ouids Metamorphosis translated grammatically, and also according to the propriety of our English tongue, so farre as grammar and the verse will well beare* [online facsimile] (London: Humfrey Lownes for Thomas Man, 1618), Early English Books Online, http://gateway.proquest.com/openurl?ctx_ver=Z39.88-2003&res_id=xri:eebo&rft_id=xri:eebo:image:21687 accessed 2 March 2010.

Brodwin, Leonora Leet, 'Milton and the Renaissance Circe', *Milton Studies*, 6 (1974), 21–83.

Brooks, Cleanth, and Hardy, John Edward, *The Poems of Mr. John Milton: The 1645 Edition with Essays in Analysis* (New York: Harcourt, 1951).

Brown, Georgia, *Redefining Elizabethan Literature* (Cambridge: Cambridge University Press, 2004).

Browning, Judith E., 'Sin, Eve, and Circe: *Paradise Lost* and the Ovidian Circe Tradition', *Milton Studies*, 26 (1990), 135–57.

Brownlee, Kevin, 'Dante and Narcissus (*Purg.* XXX, 76–99)', *Dante Studies*, 96 (1978), 201–6.

Bruns, Gerald L., *Inventions: Writing, Textuality, and Understanding in Literary History* (New Haven: Yale University Press, 1982).

Budick, Sanford, *The Dividing Muse: Images of Sacred Disjunction in Milton's Poetry* (New Haven: Yale University Press, 1985).

Bulman, Patricia, *Pthonos in Pindar* (Berkeley and Los Angeles: University of California Press, 1992).

Burrow, Colin, *Epic Romance: Homer to Milton* (Oxford: Clarendon Press, 1993).

—— ' "Full of the Maker's Guile": Ovid on Imitating and on the Imitation of Ovid', in Philip Hardie, Alessandro Barchiesi, and Stephen Hinds (eds.), *Ovidian Transformations: Essays on the* Metamorphoses *and its Reception* (Cambridge: Cambridge Philological Society, 1999), 271–87.

—— 'Spenser and Classical Traditions', in Andrew Hadfield (ed.), *The Cambridge Companion to Spenser* (Cambridge: Cambridge University Press, 2001), 217–36.

—— 'Re-embodying Ovid: Renaissance Afterlives', in Philip Hardie (ed.), *The Cambridge Companion to Ovid* (Cambridge: Cambridge University Press, 2002), 301–19.

Burton, Robert, *The Anatomy of Melancholy*, ed. Thomas C. Faulkner, 6 vols. (Oxford: Clarendon Press, 1989).

Bush, Douglas, 'Ironic and Ambiguous Allusion in *Paradise Lost*', *Journal of English and Germanic Philology*, 60/4 (1961), 631–4.

—— *Mythology and the Renaissance Tradition in English Poetry* (new rev. edn., New York: W. W. Norton, 1963).

—— 'Ironic and Ambiguous Allusion in *Paradise Lost*', *Journal of English and Germanic Philology*, 60/4 (1961), 631–4.

Butler, Martin, 'Reform or Reverence? The Politics of the Caroline Masque', in J. R. Mulryne and Margaret Shewring (eds.), *Theatre and Government under the Early Stuarts* (Cambridge: Cambridge University Press, 1993), 118–56.

Calabrese, Michael A., *Chaucer's Ovidian Arts of Love* (Gainesville, Fla.: University Press of Florida, 1994).

Campbell, Gordon, 'Milton and the Lives of the Ancients', *Journal of the Warburg and Courtauld Institutes*, 47 (1984), 234–8.

—— and Corns, Thomas, *John Milton: Life, Work, and Thought* (Oxford: Oxford University Press, 2008).

Carabell, Paula, 'Painting, Paradox, and the Dialectics of Narcissism in Alberti's *De Pictura* and in the Renaissance Theory of Art', *Medievalia et Humanistica*, 25 (1998), 53–73.

Carew, Thomas, *The Poems of Thomas Carew with his Masque* Coelum Britannicum, ed. Rhodes Dunlap (Oxford: Clarendon, 1949).
Carey, John, 'Sea, Snake, Flower and Flame in *Samson Agonistes*', *Modern Language Review*, 62 (1967), 395–9.
—— (ed.), *Milton: Complete Shorter Poems* (London: Longman, 1968).
Carroll, William C., *The Metamorphoses of Shakespearean Comedy* (Princeton: Princeton University Press, 1985).
Carron, Jean-Claude, 'Imitation and Intertextuality in the Renaissance', *New Literary History*, 19/3 (1988), 565–79.
Cary, Henry, *Romvlvs and Tarqvin* [online facsimile] (London: I[ohn] H[aviland] for Iohn Benson, 1638), Early English Books Online, http://gateway.proquest.com/openurl?ctx_ver=Z39.88-2003&res_id=xri:eebo&rft_id=xri:eebo:image:12191 accessed 8 May 2007.
Cassell, Anthony K., 'The Letter of Envy: *Purgatorio* XIII–XIV', *Stanford Italian Review*, 4/1 (1984), 5–22.
Cast, David, *The Calumny of Apelles: A Study in the Humanist Tradition* (New Haven: Yale University Press, 1981).
Cave, Terence, *The Cornucopian Text: Problems of Writing in the French Renaissance* (Oxford: Clarendon Press, 1979).
Cavendish, Margaret, *Sociable Letters* [online facsimile] (London: William Wilson, 1664), Early English Books Online, http://gateway.proquest.com/openurl?ctx_ver=Z39.88-2003&res_id=xri:eebo&rft_id=xri:eebo:image:100053 accessed 16 Aug. 2009.
Chambers, A. B., 'Herrick and the "Trans-shifting of Time"', *Studies in Philology*, 72 (1975), 85–114.
Chapman, Alison, 'Marking Time: Astrology, Almanacs, and English Protestantism', *Renaissance Quarterly*, 60/4 (2007), 1257–90.
Cheney, Patrick, *Spenser's Famous Flight: A Renaissance Idea of a Literary Career* (Toronto: University of Toronto Press, 1993).
—— *Marlowe's Counterfeit Profession: Ovid, Spenser, Counter-Nationhood* (Toronto: University of Toronto Press, 1997).
Chrysostom, St John, 'Homily 31 on First Corinthians' [online text], New Advent Online Encyclopedia, http://www.newadvent.org/fathers/220131.htm accessed 12 Dec. 2006.
Churchill, Laurie, '"Inopem me copia fecit": Signs of Narcissus in Augustine's *Confessions*', *Classical and Modern Literature*, 10 (1990), 373–9.
Cintio, Giovambattista Giraldi, *De' romanzi delle commedie e delle tragedie*, 2 vols. (Milan: G. Daelli, 1864).
Cirillo, A. R., 'The Fair Hermaphrodite: Love-Union in the Poetry of Donne and Spenser', *Studies in English Literature*, 9/1 (1969), 81–95.
Claassen, Jo-Marie, *Displaced Persons: The Literature of Exile from Cicero to Boethius* (London: Duckworth, 1999).

Clark, Donald Lemen, *John Milton at St. Paul's School: A Study of Ancient Rhetoric in English Renaissance Education* (New York: Columbia University Press, 1948).

Claudian, *Claudian*, introd. and trans. Maurice Platnauer, 2 vols. (Cambridge, Mass.: Harvard University Press; London: William Heinemann, 1922; repr. 1972).

Coiro, Ann Baynes, 'Fable and Old Song: *Samson Agonistes* and the Idea of a Poetic Career', *Milton Studies*, 36 (1998), 123–52.

—— '"A ball of strife": Caroline Poetry and Royal Marriage', in Thomas N. Corns (ed.), *The Royal Image: Representations of Charles I* (Cambridge: Cambridge University Press, 1999), 26–46.

Condee, Ralph, 'The Latin Poetry of John Milton', in J. W. Binns (ed.), *The Latin Poetry of English Poets* (London: Routledge & Kegan Paul, 1974), 58–92.

Conte, Gian Biagio, *The Rhetoric of Imitation: Genre and Poetic Memory in Virgil and Other Latin Poets*, Cornell Studies in Classical Philology (Ithaca, NY: Cornell University Press, 1986).

—— 'Love without Elegy: The *Remedia Amoris* and the Logic of Genre', *Poetics Today*, 10/3 (1989), 441–69.

—— *Genres and Readers: Lucretius, Love Elegy, Pliny's Encyclopedia* (Baltimore: Johns Hopkins University Press, 1994).

—— *Latin Literature: A History* (Baltimore: Johns Hopkins University Press, 1994).

—— *The Poetry of Pathos: Studies in Virgilian Epic* (Oxford: Oxford University Press, 2007).

Conti, Natale, *Mythologiae*, trans. John Mulryan and Steven Brown, 2 vols. (Tempe, Ariz.: Arizona Center for Medieval and Renaissance Studies, 2006).

Cope, Jackson I., 'Fortunate Falls as Form in Milton's "Fair Infant"', *Journal of English and Germanic Philology*, 63 (1964), 660–74.

Corns, Thomas N., *The Development of Milton's Prose Style* (Oxford: Clarendon Press, 1982).

—— *Uncloistered Virtue: English Political Literature, 1640–1660* (Oxford: Clarendon Press, 1992).

—— 'The Poetry of the Caroline Court', *Proceedings of the British Academy*, 97 (1998), 51–73.

—— '"With Unaltered Brow": Milton and the Son of God', *Milton Studies*, 42 (2002), 106–21.

Coulson, Frank Thomas, 'The *Vulgate* Commentary on Ovid's *Metamorphoses*', *Medievalia*, 13, Ovid in Medieval Culture, ed. Marilynn R. Desmond (1989 for 1987), 29–61.

Coulson, Frank Thomas, *The 'Vulgate' Commentary on Ovid's* Metamorphoses: *The Creation Myth and the Story of Orpheus* (Toronto: The Pontifical Institute of Mediaeval Studies, 1991).

—— 'Ovid's Transformations in Medieval France (ca. 1100–ca. 1350)', in Alison Keith and Stephen James Rupp (eds.), *Metamorphosis: The Changing Face of Ovid in Medieval and Early Modern Europe* (Toronto: Centre for Reformation and Renaissance Studies, 2007), 33–60.

Court, Franklin E., 'The Theme and Structure of Spenser's *Muiopotmos*', *Studies in English Literature*, 10 (1970), 1–15.

Cowley, Abraham, *The English Writings of Abraham Cowley*, ed. A. R. Waller (Cambridge: Cambridge University Press, 1905).

Crane, Mary Thomas, *Framing Authority: Sayings, Self, and Society in Sixteenth-Century England* (Princeton: Princeton University Press, 1993).

Creaser, John, '"Service is Perfect Freedom": Paradox and Prosodic Style in *Paradise Lost*', *Review of English Studies*, 58 (2007), 268–315.

—— '"Fear of change": Closed Minds and Open Forms in Milton', *Milton Quarterly*, 42/3 (2008), 161–82.

Cressy, David, *Bonfires and Bells: National Memory and the Protestant Calendar in Elizabethan and Stuart England* (London: Weidenfeld and Nicolson, 1989).

Cumming, William P., 'The Influence of Ovid's *Metamorphoses* on Spenser's "Mutabilitie" Cantos', *Studies in Philology*, 28/2 (1931).

Cyprian, St, 'Treatise X: On Jealousy and Envy', trans. Ernest Wallis, in Alexander Roberts and James Donaldson (eds.), *Ante-Nicene Fathers*, 10 vols., vol. v: *Hippolytus, Cyprian, Caius, Novatian, Appendix* (New York: Charles Scribner's Sons, 1919), 491–6.

Daiches, David, *Milton* (London: Hutchinson University Library, 1957).

Dane, Joseph A., 'The Ovids of Ben Jonson in *Poetaster* and in *Epicoene*', *Comparative Drama*, 13/3 (1979), 222–34.

Daniel, Samuel, *Delia* [online facsimile] (London: I.C. for Simon Waterson, 1592), Early English Books Online, http://gateway.proquest.com/openurl?ctx_ver=Z39.88-2003&res_id=xri:eebo&rft_id=xri:eebo:image:181243 accessed 5 Jan. 2007.

Davies, John, *Nosce Teipsum* [online facsimile] (London: Richard Field for John Standish, 1599), Early English Books Online, http://gateway.proquest.com/openurl?ctx_ver=Z39.88-2003&res_id=xri:eebo&rft_id=xri: eebo:image:25824 accessed 8 Dec. 2010.

Dawes, Martin, 'Milton and the Politics of Enchantment', Ph.D. diss. (McGill University, Montreal, 2009).

De Armas, Frederick, 'Sancho as Thief of Time and Art: Ovid's *Fasti* and Cervantes' *Don Quixote* 2', *Renaissance Quarterly*, 61/1 (2008), 1–25.

—— 'Ovid's Mysterious Months: The *Fasti* from Pedro Mexía to Baltasar Gracián', in Frederick A. De Armas (ed.), *Ovid in the Age of Cervantes* (Toronto: University of Toronto Press, 2010), 56–73.

Demerson, Geneviève, 'Joacham Du Bellay et le modèle ovidien', in R. Chevalier (ed.), *Colloque Présence d'Ovide* (Paris: Les Belles Lettres, 1982), 281–94.

Demetriou, Tania, ' "Essentially Circe": Spenser, Homer, and the Homeric Tradition', *Translation and Literature*, 15/2 (2006), 151–76.

De Quincey, Thomas, *The Collected Writings of Thomas De Quincey*, ed. David Masson, 14 vols. (Edinburgh: Adam and Charles Black, 1890; repr. New York: AMS Press, 1968).

Dewar, Michael, '*Siquid habent veri vatum praesagia*: Ovid in the 1st–5th Centuries A.D.', in Barbara Weiden Boyd (ed.), *Brill's Companion to Ovid* (Leiden: Brill, 2002), 383–412.

DiCesare, Mario A., 'Advent'rous Song: The Texture of Milton's Epic', in Ronald David Emma and John T. Shawcross (eds.), *Language and Style in Milton: A Symposium in Honor of the Tercentenary of* Paradise Lost (New York: Frederick Ungar, 1967).

Dickie, Matthew W., 'The Disavowal of *Invidia* in Roman Iamb and Satire', *Papers of the Liverpool Latin Seminar*, 3, ed. Francis Cairns (1981), 183–208.

—— '*Invidia Infelix*: Vergil, *Georgics* 3.37–39', *Illinois Classical Studies*, 8 (1983), 65–79.

Dickinson, R. J., 'The *Tristia*: Poetry in Exile', in J. W. Binns (ed.), *Ovid* (London: Routledge, 1973), 154–90.

Dickson, Vernon Guy, ' "A pattern, precedent, and lively warrant": Emulation, Rhetoric, and Cruel Propriety in *Titus Andronicus*', *Renaissance Quarterly*, 62/2 (2009), 376–409.

Dimmick, Jeremy, 'Ovid in the Middle Ages: Authority and Poetry', in Philip Hardie (ed.), *The Cambridge Companion to Ovid* (Cambridge: Cambridge University Press, 2002), 264–87.

Dobranski, Stephen, 'Text and Context for *Paradise Regain'd* and *Samson Agonistes*', in Mark R. Kelley and Joseph Wittreich (eds.), *Altering Eyes: New Perspectives on 'Samson Agonistes'* (Newark, Del.: University of Delaware Press; London: Associated University Presses, 2002), 30–53.

Donaldson, Ian, *The Rapes of Lucretia: A Myth and its Transformations* (Oxford: Clarendon Press, 1982).

—— 'Looking Sideways: Jonson, Shakespeare and the Myths of Envy', in Takashi Kozuka and J. R. Mulryne (eds.), *Shakespeare, Marlowe, Jonson: New Directions in Biography* (Aldershot: Ashgate, 2006), 241–57.

Donno, Elizabeth Story, *Elizabethan Minor Epics* (New York: Columbia University Press, 1963).

Doran, Madelaine, 'Some Renaissance "Ovids"', in Bernice Slote (ed.), *Literature and Society* (Lincoln, Nebr.: University of Nebraska Press, 1964), 44–62.

Dragonetti, Roger, 'Dante et Narcisse ou les faux-monnayeurs de l'image', *Revue des études italiennes*, 11 (1965), 85–146.

Drayton, Michael, *The Works of Michael Drayton*, ed. William J. Hebel, 5 vols. (Oxford: Shakespeare Head Press, 1961).

Dryden, John, *The Poems and Fables of John Dryden*, ed. James Kinsley (London: Oxford University Press, 1962).

Du Bartas, Guillaume de Saluste, *The Divine Weeks and Works of Guillaume de Saluste, Sieur Du Bartas*, trans. Josuah Sylvester, ed. Susan Snyder, 2 vols. (Oxford: Clarendon Press, 1979)

Dubrow, Heather, *Captive Victors: Shakespeare's Narrative Poems and Sonnets* (Ithaca, NY: Cornell University Press, 1987).

—— *Echoes of Desire: English Petrarchism and its Counterdiscourses* (Ithaca, NY: Cornell University Press, 1995).

Dunbabin, Katherine M. D., and Dickie, Matthew W., 'Invidia rumpantur pectora: The Iconography of Phthonos/Invidia in Graeco-Roman Art', *Jahrbuch für Antike und Christentum*, 26 (1983), 7–37.

Dundas, Judith, '*Muiopotmos*: A World of Art', *Yearbook of English Studies*, 5 (1975), 30–8.

Duppa, Brian (ed.), *Ionsonus Viribvs: or, The Memorie of Ben Jonson Revived by the Friends of the Muses* [online facsimile] (London: E.P. for Henry Seile, 1638), Early English Books Online, http://gateway.proquest.com/openurl?ctx_ver=Z39.88-2003&res_id=xri:eebo&rft_id=xri:eebo:image:173154 accessed 30 Oct. 2010.

Durling, Robert M., *The Figure of the Poet in Renaissance Epic* (Cambridge, Mass.: Harvard University Press, 1965).

DuRocher, Richard J., *Milton and Ovid* (Ithaca, NY: Cornell University Press, 1985).

—— 'Guiding the Glance: Spenser, Milton, and "Venus's looking glas"', *Journal of English and Germanic Philology*, 92/3 (1993), 325–41.

Edwards, Calvin R., 'The Narcissus Myth in Spenser's Poetry', *Studies in Philology*, 74/1 (1977), 63–88.

Edwards, Karen L., 'Resisting Representation: All about Milton's "Eve"', *Exemplaria*, 9/1 (1997), 231–53.

—— 'Gender, Sex and Marriage in Paradise', in Angelica Duran (ed.), *A Concise Companion to Milton* (Malden, Mass.: Blackwell, 2007), 144–60.

Edwards, Thomas, *Cephalus and Procris* [online text] (1595; repr. 1882), Literature Online, http://gateway.proquest.com/openurl?ctx_ver=Z39.88-2003&xri:pqil:res_ver=0.2&res_id=xri:lion-us&rft_id=xri:lion:ft:po:Z200344649:2 accessed 10 Oct. 2005.

—— *Narcissvs: Aurora muae amica* [online text] (1595; repr. 1882), Literature Online, http://gateway.proquest.com/openurl?ctx_ver=Z39. 88-2003&xri: pqil:res_ver=0.2&res_id=xri:lion-us&rft_id=xri:lion:ft:po:Z200344651:2 accessed 14 Oct. 2005.

Eggert, Katherine, *Showing Like a Queen: Female Authority and Literary Experiment in Spenser, Shakespeare, and Milton* (Philadelphia: University of Pennsylvania Press, 2000).

Elliott, Alison G., 'Access ad Auctores: Twelfth-Century Introductions to Ovid', *Allegorica*, 5 (1980), 6–47.

Elyot, Thomas, *The Book Named The Governor*, ed. S. E. Lehmberg (London: Dent, 1962).

Enterline, Lynn, *The Rhetoric of the Body from Ovid to Shakespeare* (Cambridge: Cambridge University Press, 2000).

Evans, Harry B., *Publica Carmina: Ovid's Books from Exile* (Lincoln, Nebr.: University of Nebraska Press, 1983).

Falconer, Rachel, *Orpheus Dis(re)membered: Milton and the Myth of the Poet-Hero* (Sheffield: Sheffield Academic Press, 1996).

Fallon, Stephen M., 'Milton's Sin and Death: The Ontology of Allegory in *Paradise Lost*', *English Literary Renaissance*, 17/3 (1987), 329–50.

—— *Milton's Peculiar Grace: Self-Representation and Authority* (Ithaca, NY: Cornell University Press, 2007).

Fantham, Elaine, 'Ceres, Liber and Flora: Georgic and Anti-Georgic Elements in Ovid's *Fasti*', *Proceedings of the Cambridge Philological Society*, 38 (1992), 39–56.

Farrell, Joseph, *Vergil's Georgics and the Traditions of Ancient Epic: The Art of Allusion in Literary History* (New York: Oxford University Press, 1991).

—— 'Ovid's Virgilian Career', *Materiali e discussioni per l'analisi dei testi classici*, 52 (2004), 41–55.

Feeney, D. C., *The Gods in Epic: Poets and Critics of the Classical Tradition* (Oxford: Clarendon, 1991).

—— '*Si licet et fas est*: Ovid's *Fasti* and the Problem of Free Speech under the Principate', in Anton Powell (ed.), *Roman Poetry and Propaganda in the Age of Augustus* (London: Bristol Classical Press, 1992), 1–25.

—— '*Mea Tempora*: Patterning of Time in the *Metamorphoses*', in Philip Hardie, Alessandro Barchiesi, and Stephen Hinds (eds.), *Ovidian Transformations: Essays on the* Metamorphoses *and its Reception* (Cambridge: Cambridge Philological Society, 1999), 13–30.

—— *Caesar's Calendar: Ancient Time and the Beginnings of History* (Berkeley and Los Angeles: University of California Press, 2007).

Ferguson, Margaret W., 'The Rhetoric of Exile in Du Bellay and his Classical Precursors', Ph.D. diss. (Yale University, 1974).

Ferry, Anne, *Milton and the Miltonic Dryden* (Cambridge, Mass.: Harvard University Press, 1968).

Ficino, Marsilio, *Commentary on Plato's Symposium on Love*, trans. Sears Reynolds Jayne (2nd edn., Dallas: Spring Publications, 1985).
Fields, Albert W., 'Milton and Self-Knowledge', *PMLA* 83/2 (1968), 392–9.
—— 'The Creative Self and the Self Created in *Paradise Lost*', in Charles W. Durham and Kristin A. Pruitt (eds.), *Spokesperson Milton: Voices in Contemporary Criticism* (Selinsgrove, Pa.: Susquehanna University Press, 1994), 153–64.
Fish, Stanley Eugene, *Surprised by Sin: The Reader in* Paradise Lost (Berkeley and Los Angeles: University of California Press, 1971).
—— *How Milton Works* (Cambridge, Mass.: Belknap Press of Harvard University Press, 2001).
Fletcher, Angus, *The Prophetic Moment: An Essay on Spenser* (Chicago: University of Chicago Press, 1971).
—— *The Transcendental Masque: An Essay on Milton's* Comus (Ithaca, NY: Cornell University Press, 1971).
Fletcher, Phineas, *The Purple Island, or The Isle of Man*, in *The Poetical Works of Giles Fletcher and Phineas Fletcher*, ed. Frederick S. Boas, 2 vols. (Cambridge: Cambridge University Press, 1909; repr. 1968).
Forsyth, Neil, *The Satanic Epic* (Princeton: Princeton University Press, 2003).
Fowler, Don P., 'Narrate and Describe: The Problem of Ekphrasis', *Journal of Roman Studies*, 81 (1991), 25–35.
Fränkel, Hermann Ferdinand, *Ovid: A Poet between Two Worlds*, Sather Classical Lectures (Berkeley and Los Angeles: University of California Press, 1945).
Freccero, John, 'The Fig Tree and the Laurel: Petrarch's Poetics', *Diacritics*, 5/1 (1975), 34–40.
Fresch, Cheryl H., ' "Aside the Devil Turned | For Envy": The Evil Eye in *Paradise Lost*, Book 4', in Kristin A. Pruitt and Charles W. Durham (eds.), *Living Texts: Interpreting Milton* (Selinsgrove, Pa.: Susquehanna University Press, 2000), 118–30.
Fritsen, Angela Maria, 'Renaissance Commentaries on Ovid's *Fasti*', Ph.D. thesis (Yale University, 1995).
Frye, Northrop, *Fables of Identity: Studies in Poetic Mythology* (New York: Harcourt, Brace & World, 1963).
—— *The Return of Eden: Five Essays on Milton's Epics* (Toronto: University of Toronto Press, 1965).
Frye, Susan, *Elizabeth I: The Competition for Representation* (New York: Oxford University Press, 1993).
Fulgentius, Fabius Planciades, *Fulgentius the Mythographer*, trans. Francis George Whitbread (Columbus, Oh.: Ohio State University Press, 1971).
Fyler, John M., *Chaucer and Ovid* (New Haven: Yale University Press, 1979).

Galinsky, Karl, *Ovid's* Metamorphoses: *An Introduction to the Basic Aspects* (Berkeley and Los Angeles: University of California Press, 1975).

—— *Augustan Culture: An Interpretive Introduction* (Princeton: Princeton University Press, 1996).

Getty, Laura J., 'Circumventing Petrarch: Subreading Ovid's *Tristia* in Spenser's *Amoretti*', *Philological Quarterly*, 79/2 (2000), 293–314.

Ghisalberti, Fausto, 'Mediaeval Biographies of Ovid', *Journal of the Warburg and Courtauld Institutes*, 9 (1946), 10–59.

Giamatti, A. Bartlett, *Exile and Change in Renaissance Literature* (New Haven: Yale University Press, 1984).

Gibson, Bruce, 'Ovid on Reading: Reading Ovid. Reception in Ovid *Tristia* II', *Journal of Roman Studies*, 89 (1999), 19–37.

Gildenhard, Ingo, and Zissos, Andrew, 'Ovid's Narcissus (*Met.* 3. 339–510): Echoes of Oedipus', *American Journal of Philology*, 121/1 (2000), 129–47.

Gill, R. B., 'The Renaissance Conventions of Envy', *Medievalia et Humanistica*, 9 (1979), 215–30.

Gillespie, Stuart, and Cummings, Robert, 'A Bibliography of Ovidian Translations and Imitations in English', *Translation and Literature*, 13/2 (2004), 207–11.

Girard, René, *A Theater of Envy: William Shakespeare*, Odéon (New York: Oxford University Press, 1991).

Godwin, Thomas, *Romanae Historiae Anthologia: An English Exposition of the Romane Antiqvities, Wherein Many Romane and English offices are parallel'd, and divers obscure phrases explained* [online facsimile] (London: Joseph Barnes, 1614), Early English Books Online, http://gateway. proquest.com/openurl?ctx_ver=Z39.88-2003&res_id=xri:eebo&rft_id=xri: eebo:image:3342 accessed 20 Oct. 2008.

Golding, Arthur, *Shakespeare's Ovid: Being Arthur Golding's Translation of the* Metamorphoses, ed. W. H. D. Rouse (Carbondale, Ill.: Southern Illinois University Press, 1961).

Gower, John, *Confessio Amantis*, ed. Russell A. Peck, trans. Andrew Galloway, 3 vols. (Kalamazoo, Mich.: Medieval Institute Publications, 2000).

Gower, John, *Ovids Festivalls, or Romane Calendar. Translated into English verse equinumerally* [online facsimile] (Cambridge: Roger Daniel, 1640), Early English Books Online, http://gateway.proquest.com/openurl?ctx_ ver=Z39.88-2003&res_id=xri:eebo&rft_id=xri:eebo:image:25106 accessed 7 Sept. 2009.

Green, Mandy, *Milton's Ovidian Eve* (Farnham: Ashgate, 2009).

Green, Peter, 'Carmen et Error: πρόφασις and αἰτία in the Matter of Ovid's Exile', *Classical Antiquity*, 1/2 (1982), 202–20.

—— (ed. and trans.), *The Poems of Exile: Tristia and the Black Sea Letters* (Berkeley and Los Angeles: University of California Press, 2005).

Greenblatt, Stephen, *Renaissance Self-Fashioning: From More to Shakespeare* (Chicago: University of Chicago Press, 1980).
Greene, Thomas M., *The Light in Troy: Imitation and Discovery in Renaissance Poetry* (New Haven: Yale University Press, 1982).
Griffin, Dustin, *Regaining Paradise: Milton and the Eighteenth Century* (Cambridge: Cambridge University Press, 1986).
Griswold, Charles L., Jr., *Self-Knowledge in Plato's* Phaedrus (New Haven: Yale University Press, 1986).
Gross, Kenneth, *Spenserian Poetics: Idolatry, Iconoclasm, & Magic* (Ithaca, NY: Cornell University Press, 1985).
—— 'Shapes of Time: On the Spenserian Stanza', *Spenser Studies*, 19 (2004), 27–35.
—— 'Green Thoughts in a Green Shade', *Spenser Studies*, 24 (2009), 355–71.
Guibbory, Achsah, 'Charles's Prayers, Idolatrous Images, and True Creation in Milton's *Eikonoklastes*', in P. G. Stanwood (ed.), *Of Poetry and Politics: New Essays on Milton and his World* (Binghamton, NY: Medieval & Renaissance Texts & Studies, 1995), 283–94.
—— *Ceremony and Community from Herbert to Milton: Literature, Religion, and Cultural Conflict in Seventeenth-Century England* (Cambridge: Cambridge University Press, 1998).
Guillory, John, *Poetic Authority: Spenser, Milton, and Literary History* (New York: Columbia University Press, 1983).
—— 'Dalila's House: *Samson Agonistes* and the Sexual Division of Labour', in Margaret W. Ferguson, Maureen Quilligan, and Nancy J. Vickers (eds.), *Rewriting the Renaissance: The Discourses of Sexual Difference* (Chicago: University of Chicago Press, 1986), 106–22.
—— 'The Father's House: *Samson Agonistes* in its Historical Moment', in Mary Nyquist and Margaret Ferguson (eds.), *Re-Membering Milton: Essays on the Texts and Traditions* (New York: Methuen, 1987), 148–76.
H., T., *The fable of Ouid treting of Narcissus* [online facsimile] (London: [J. Tisdale for] Thomas Hackette, 1560), Early English Books Online, http://gateway.proquest.com/openurl?ctx_ver=Z39.88-2003&res_id=xri:eebo&rft_val_fmt=&rft_id=xri:eebo:image:14229 accessed 3 Sept. 2005.
Habington, William, *Castara* [online facsimile] (London: Anne Griffin for William Cooke, 1634), Early English Books Online, http://gateway.proquest.com/openurl?ctx_ver=Z39.88-2003&res_id=xri:eebo&rft_id=xri:eebo:image:3754 accessed 23 Mar. 2010.
Hale, John K., 'Milton Playing with Ovid', *Milton Studies*, 25 (1989), 3–19.
—— 'Milton's Euripides Marginalia: Their Significance for Milton Studies', *Milton Studies*, 27 (1991), 23–35.
—— 'Milton's Self-Presentation in *Poems . . . 1645*', *Milton Quarterly*, 25/2 (1991), 37–48.

—— 'Artistry and Originality in Milton's Latin Poems', *Milton Quarterly*, 27/4 (1993), 138–49.

—— 'The Pre-Criticism of Milton's Latin Verse, Illustrated from the Ode "Ad Joannem Rousium"', in P. G. Stanwood (ed.), *Of Poetry and Politics: New Essays on Milton and his World*, Medieval & Renaissance Texts & Studies 126 (Binghamton, NY: Medieval & Renaissance Texts & Studies, 1995), 17–34.

—— *Milton's Languages: The Impact of Multilingualism on Style* (Cambridge: Cambridge University Press, 1997).

—— *Milton's Cambridge Latin: Performing in the Genres, 1625–1632*, Medieval and Renaissance Texts and Studies 289 (Tempe, Ariz.: Arizona Center for Medieval and Renaissance Studies, 2005).

Hall, Thomas, *Phaetons folly, or, The downfal of pride* [online facsimile] (London: George Calvert, 1655), Early English Books Online, http://gateway.proquest.com/openurl?ctx_ver=Z39.88-2003&res_id=xri:eebo&rft_id=xri:eebo:image:111529 accessed 12 Oct. 2010.

Halpern, Richard, 'Puritanism and Maenadism in *A Mask*', in Margaret Ferguson, Maureen Quilligan, and Nancy J. Vickers (eds.), *Rewriting the Renaissance: The Discourses of Sexual Difference in Early Modern Europe* (Chicago: University of Chicago Press, 1986), 88–105.

—— *The Poetics of Primitive Accumulation: English Renaissance Culture and the Genealogy of Capital* (Ithaca, NY: Cornell University Press, 1991).

Hamilton, A. C., '*Venus and Adonis*', in Philip C. Kolin (ed.), *Venus and Adonis: Critical Essays* (New York: Garland, 1997), 141–56.

Hanford, James Holly, 'The Youth of Milton: An Interpretation of his Early Development', in Eugene S. McCartney (ed.), *Studies in Shakespeare, Milton and Donne* (London: Macmillan, 1925), 89–163.

Hardie, Philip, *Virgil's Aeneid: Cosmos and Imperium* (Oxford: Clarendon, 1986).

—— 'Lucretius and the Delusions of Narcissus', *Materiali e discussioni per l'analisi dei testi classici*, 20–1 (1988), 71–89.

—— 'The Janus Episode in Ovid's *Fasti*', *Materiali e discussioni per l'analisi dei testi classici*, 26 (1991), 47–64.

—— *The Epic Successors of Virgil: A Study in the Dynamics of a Tradition* (Cambridge: Cambridge University Press, 1993).

—— 'The Presence of Lucretius in *Paradise Lost*', *Milton Quarterly*, 29 (1995), 13–24.

—— 'The Speech of Pythagoras in Ovid *Metamorphoses* 15: Empedoclean Epos', *Classical Quarterly*, NS 45/1 (1995), 204–14.

—— *Ovid's Poetics of Illusion* (Cambridge: Cambridge University Press, 2002).

—— '"Why is Rumour Here?": Tracking Virgilian and Ovidian *Fama*', *Ordia Prima*, 1 (2002), 67–80.

Hardie, Philip, 'Approximative Similes in Ovid. Incest and Doubling', *Dictynna: Revue de poétique latine*, 1 (2004), 1–30.
—— 'Contrasts', in S. J. Heyworth et al. (eds.), *Classical Constructions: Papers in Memory of Don Fowler, Classicist and Epicurean* (Oxford: Oxford University Press, 2007), 141–73.
—— *Lucretian Receptions: History, the Sublime, Knowledge* (Cambridge: Cambridge University Press, 2009).
—— 'The Self-Divisions of Scylla', *Trends in Classics*, 1 (2009), 118–47.
—— *Rumour and Renown: Studies in the History of Fama* (Cambridge: Cambridge University Press, forthcoming in 2011).
Hardin, Richard F., 'Ovid in Seventeenth-Century England', *Comparative Literature*, 24 (1972), 44–62.
Harding, Davis P., *Milton and the Renaissance Ovid* (Urbana, Ill.: University of Illinois Press, 1946).
Harmer, James, 'Reginald Forster's Burlesque Ovidian Epistle', *Translation and Literature*, 16/2 (2007), 193–204.
Harries, Byron, 'The Spinner and the Poet: Arachne in Ovid's *Metamorphoses*', *Proceedings of the Cambridge Philological Society*, 36 (1990), 64–82.
Harwood, Ellen Aprill, '*Venus and Adonis*: Shakespeare's Critique of Spenser', *Journal of the Rutgers University Library*, 39 (1977), 44–60.
Haskin, Dayton, *Milton's Burden of Interpretation* (Philadelphia: University of Pennsylvania Press, 1994).
Helgerson, Richard, *Self-Crowned Laureates: Spenser, Jonson, Milton, and the Literary System* (Berkeley and Los Angeles: University of California Press, 1983).
—— 'Milton Reads the King's Book: Print, Performance, and the Making of a Bourgeois Idol', *Criticism*, 29/1 (1987), 1–25.
—— *Forms of Nationhood: The Elizabethan Writing of England* (Chicago: University of Chicago Press, 1992).
Herbert-Brown, Geraldine, *Ovid and the* Fasti: *An Historical Study* (Oxford: Clarendon Press, 1994).
Herendeen, Wyman H., 'Milton's *Accedence Commenc't Grammar* and the Deconstruction of "Grammatical Tyranny"', in P. G. Stanwood (ed.), *Of Poetry and Politics: New Essays on Milton and his World* (Binghamton, NY: Medieval & Renaissance Texts & Studies, 1995), 295–312.
Herman, Peter C., *Destabilizing Milton:* Paradise Lost *and the Poetics of Incertitude* (New York: Palgrave Macmillan, 2005).
Herrick, Robert, *The Poems of Robert Herrick*, ed. L. C. Martin (London: Oxford University Press, 1965).
Hesiod, *Hesiod*, ed. and trans. Glenn W. Most, 2 vols. (Cambridge, Mass.: Harvard University Press, 2006).

Hexter, Ralph, *Ovid and Medieval Schooling: Studies in Medieval School Commentaries on Ovid's* Ars Amatoria, Epistulae ex Ponto, *and* Epistulae Heroidum (Munich: Arbeo-Gesellschaft, 1986).
—— 'Ovid's Body', in James I. Porter (ed.), *Constructions of the Classical Body* (Ann Arbor: University of Michigan Press, 1999), 327–54.
—— 'Ovid in the Middle Ages: Exile, Mythographer, Lover', in Barbara Weiden Boyd (ed.), *Brill's Companion to Ovid* (Leiden: Brill, 2002), 413–42.
Heywood, Thomas, *Pvblii Ovidii Nasonis De Arte Amandi: or, The Art of Loue* [online facsimile] (London, 1625), Early English Books Online, http://gateway.proquest.com/openurl?ctx_ver=Z39.88-2003&res_id=xri:eebo&rft_id=xri:eebo:image:13998 accessed 20 Aug. 2004.
Hinds, Stephen, 'Booking the Return Trip: Ovid and *Tristia* 1', *Proceedings of the Cambridge Philological Society*, 31 (1985), 13–32.
—— *The Metamorphosis of Persephone: Ovid and the Self-Conscious Muse* (Cambridge: Cambridge University Press, 1987).
—— 'Generalising about Ovid', *Ramus*, 16 (1988), 4–31.
—— '*Arma* in Ovid's *Fasti*: Part 1: Genre and Mannerism', *Arethusa*, 25/1 (1992), 81–112.
—— '*Arma* in Ovid's *Fasti*: Part 2: Genre, Romulean Rome and Augustan Ideology', *Arethusa*, 25/1 (1992), 113–53.
—— *Allusion and Intertext: Dynamics of Appropriation in Roman Poetry* (New York: Cambridge University Press, 1998).
—— 'After Exile: Time and Teleology from *Metamorphoses* to *Ibis*', in Philip Hardie, Alessandro Barchiesi, and Stephen Hinds (eds.), *Ovidian Transformations: Essays on the* Metamorphoses *and its Reception* (Cambridge: Cambridge Philological Society, 1999), 48–67.
Holahan, Michael, '*Iamque opus exegi*: Ovid's Changes and Spenser's Brief Epic of Mutability', *English Literary Renaissance*, 6 (1976), 244–70.
—— 'Ovid', in A. C. Hamilton (ed.), *The Spenser Encyclopedia* (Toronto: University of Toronto Press; London: Routledge, 1990), 520–2.
Hollander, John, *The Figure of Echo: A Mode of Allusion in Milton and After* (Berkeley and Los Angeles: University of California Press, 1981).
—— *Melodious Guile: Fictive Pattern in Poetic Language* (New Haven: Yale University Press, 1988).
Hoole, Charles, *A new discovery of the old art of teaching schoole in four small treatises* [online facsimile] (London: J.T. for Andrew Crook, 1661) Early English Books Online, http://gateway.proquest.com/openurl?ctx_ver=Z39.88-2003&res_id=xri:eebo&rft_id=xri:eebo:image:61977 accessed 3 March 2011.
Hopkins, David, 'Dryden and Ovid's "Wit out of Season"', in Charles Martindale (ed.), *Ovid Renewed: Ovidian Influences on Literature and*

Art from the Middle Ages to the Twentieth Century (Cambridge: Cambridge University Press, 1988).

Hoskin, Michael, 'The Reception of the Calendar by Other Churches', in G. V. Coyne et al. (eds.), *Gregorian Reform of the Calendar: Proceedings of the Vatican Conference to Commemorate its 400th Anniversary, 1582–1982* (Vatican City: Specola Vaticana, 1983), 255–64.

Housman, A. E., 'The *Ibis* of Ovid', in *The Classical Papers of A. E. Housman*, ed. J. Diggle and F. R. D. Goodyear, 3 vols. (Cambridge: Cambridge University Press, 1972), 1018–42.

Hulse, Clark, 'Shakespeare's Myth of Venus and Adonis', *PMLA* 93/1 (1978), 95–105.

—— *Metamorphic Verse: The Elizabethan Minor Epic* (Princeton: Princeton University Press, 1981).

Hunter, William B., 'The Liturgical Context of Milton's *Comus*', *English Language Notes*, 10 (1972), 11–15.

Ingleheart, Jennifer, 'Writing to the Emperor: Horace's Presence in Ovid's *Tristia* 2', in L. B. T. Houghton and Maria Wyke (eds.), *Perceptions of Horace: A Roman Poet and his Readers* (Cambridge: Cambridge University Press, 2009), 123–39.

Jacobus, Lee A., 'Self-Knowledge in *Paradise Lost*: Conscience and Contemplation', *Milton Studies*, 3 (1971), 103–18.

James, Heather, 'Milton's Eve, the Romance Genre, and Ovid', *Comparative Literature*, 45/2 (1993), 121–45.

—— *Shakespeare's Troy: Drama, Politics, and the Translation of Empire* (Cambridge: Cambridge University Press, 1997).

—— 'Ovid and the Question of Politics in Early Modern England', *English Literary History*, 70/2 (2003), 343–73.

—— 'The Poet's Toys: Christopher Marlowe and the Liberties of Erotic Elegy', *Modern Language Quarterly*, 67/1 (2006), 103–27.

—— 'Shakespeare and Classicism', in Patrick Cheney (ed.), *The Cambridge Companion to Shakespeare's Poetry* (Cambridge: Cambridge University Press, 2007), 202–20.

—— 'Shakespeare, the Classics, and the Forms of Authorship', *Shakespeare Studies*, 36 (2008), 80–9.

—— 'Ovid in Renaissance English Literature', in Peter E. Knox (ed.), *A Companion to Ovid* (Malden, Mass.: Blackwell, 2009), 423–41.

Jameson, Caroline, 'Ovid in the Sixteenth Century', in J. W. Binns (ed.), *Ovid* (London: Routledge, 1973), 210–42.

Janan, Micaela, '"The Labyrinth and the Mirror": Incest and Influence in *Metamorphoses* 9', *Arethusa*, 24/2 (1991), 239–56.

Javitch, Daniel, 'The Imitation of Imitations in *Orlando Furioso*', *Renaissance Quarterly*, 38/2 (1985), 215–39.

Johnson, Patricia J., *Ovid before Exile: Art and Punishment in the Metamorphoses* (Madison: University of Wisconsin Press, 2008).
Johnson, Samuel, *Lives of the English Poets*, ed. Arthur Waugh, 2 vols. (London: Oxford University Press, 1906; repr. 1977).
Jonson, Ben, *Ben Jonson: The Complete Masques*, ed. Stephen Orgel (New Haven: Yale University Press, 1969).
—— *Poetaster*, ed. Tom Cain (Manchester: Manchester University Press, 1995).
Kahn, Coppélia, *Roman Shakespeare: Warriors, Wounds, and Women* (London: Routledge, 1997).
—— 'Self and Eros in *Venus and Adonis*', in Philip C. Kolin (ed.), Venus and Adonis: Critical Essays (New York: Garland, 1997), 181–202.
Kallendorf, Craig, *The Other Virgil: 'Pessimistic' Readings of the Aeneid in Early Modern Culture* (Oxford: Oxford University Press, 2007).
Kaplan, Lindsay, *The Culture of Slander in Early Modern England* (Cambridge: Cambridge University Press, 2001).
Kaster, Robert A., *Emotion, Restraint, and Community in Ancient Rome* (Oxford: Oxford University Press, 2005).
Keach, William, *Elizabethan Erotic Narratives: Irony and Pathos in the Ovidian Poetry of Shakespeare, Marlowe, and their Contemporaries* (New Brunswick, NJ: Rutgers University Press, 1977).
Keith, Alison, *The Play of Fictions: Studies in Ovid's* Metamorphoses *Book 2* (Ann Arbor: University of Michigan Press, 1992).
—— 'Sources and Genres in Ovid's *Metamorphoses* 1–5', in Barbara Weiden Boyd (ed.), *Brill's Companion to Ovid* (Leiden: Brill, 2002), 235–69.
—— and Rupp, Stephen James, 'After Ovid: Classical, Medieval and Early Modern Receptions of the *Metamorphoses*', in *Metamorphosis: The Changing Face of Ovid in Medieval and Early Modern Europe*, Essays and Studies 13 (Toronto: Centre for Reformation and Renaissance Studies, 2007), 15–32.
Kemp, Martin, '"Ogni dipintore dipinge se": A Neoplatonic Echo in Leonardo's Art Theory', in Cecil H. Clough (ed.), *Cultural Aspects of the Italian Renaissance: Essays in Honour of Paul Oskar Kristeller* (New York: A. F. Zambelli, 1976), 311–23.
Kempe, William, *The education of children in learning declared by the dignitie, vtilitie, and method thereof* [online facsimile] (London: Thomas Orwin for John Porter and Thomas Gubbin, 1588), Early English Books Online, http://gateway.proquest.com/openurl?ctx_ver=Z39.88-2003&res_id=xri:eebo&rft_id=xri:eebo:image:9756 accessed 2 March 2011.
Kennedy, Duncan F., '"Augustan" and "Anti-Augustan": Reflections on Terms of Reference', in Anton Powell (ed.), *Roman Poetry and Propaganda in the Age of Augustus* (London: Bristol Classical Press, 1992), 26–58.

Kenney, E. J., 'The Poetry of Ovid's Exile', *Proceedings of the Cambridge Philological Society*, 11 (1965), 37–49.
—— 'Ovid's Language and Style', in Barbara Weiden Boyd (ed.), *Brill's Companion to Ovid* (Leiden: Brill, 2002), 27–89.
Kerrigan, William, *The Prophetic Milton* (Charlottesville, Va.: University Press of Virginia, 1974).
—— *The Sacred Complex: On the Psychogenesis of* Paradise Lost (Cambridge, Mass.: Harvard University Press, 1983).
—— and Braden, Gordon, 'Milton's Coy Eve: *Paradise Lost* and Renaissance Love Poetry', *English Literary History*, 53/1 (1986), 27–51.
Kilgour, Maggie, '*Comus*'s Wood of Allusion', *University of Toronto Quarterly*, 61/3 (1992), 316–33.
—— 'Eve and Flora (*Paradise Lost* 5.15–16)', *Milton Quarterly*, 38/1 (2004), 1–17.
—— 'Changing Ovid', in Alison Keith and Stephen James Rupp (eds.), *Metamorphosis: The Changing Face of Ovid in Medieval and Early Modern Europe*, Essays and Studies 13 (Toronto: Centre for Reformation and Renaissance Studies, 2007), 267–83.
—— 'Heroic Contradictions: Samson and the Death of Turnus', *Texas Studies in Literature and Language*, 50/2 (2008), 201–34.
—— 'Satan and the Wrath of Juno', *English Literary History*, 75 (2008), 653–71.
—— 'New Spins on Old Rotas: Virgil, Ovid, Milton', in Helen Moore and Philip Hardie (eds.), *Classical Literary Careers and their Reception* (Cambridge: Cambridge University Press, 2010), 179–98.
King, John, 'Queen Elizabeth I: Representations of the Virgin Queen', *Renaissance Quarterly*, 43/1 (1990), 30–74.
Knoespel, Kenneth Jacob, *Narcissus and the Invention of Personal History* (New York: Garland, 1985).
—— 'The Limits of Allegory: Textual Expansion of Narcissus in *Paradise Lost*', *Milton Studies*, 22 (1986), 79–99.
Krier, Theresa M., *Gazing on Secret Sights: Spenser, Classical Imitation, and the Decorums of Vision* (Ithaca, NY: Cornell University Press, 1990).
—— 'Time Lords: Rhythm and Interval in Spenser's Stanzaic Narrative', *Spenser Studies*, 21 (2006), 1–19.
Lamb, Mary Ellen, 'Ovid and *The Winter's Tale*: Conflicting Views toward Art', in William R. Elton and William B. Long (eds.), *Shakespeare and Dramatic Tradition: Essays in Honor of S. F. Johnson* (Newark, Del.: University of Delaware Press, 1989), 69–87.
Land, Norman E., 'Narcissus Pictor', *Source: Notes on the History of Art*, 16/2 (1997), 10–15.
Langley, Eric, *Narcissism and Suicide in Shakespeare and his Contemporaries* (Oxford: Oxford University Press, 2009).

Lanham, Richard A., *The Motives of Eloquence: Literary Rhetoric in the Renaissance* (New Haven: Yale University Press, 1976).
La Penna, Antonio, *Scholia in P. Ovidi Nasonis Ibin* (Florence: La Nuova Italia, 1959).
Lateiner, Donald, 'Mythic and Non-Mythic Artists in Ovid's *Metamorphoses*', *Ramus*, 13 (1984), 1–30.
Leach, Eleanor Winsor, 'Georgic Imagery in the *Ars Amatoria*', *Transactions and Proceedings of the American Philological Association*, 95 (1964), 142–54.
—— 'Ekphrasis and the Theme of Artistic Failure in Ovid's *Metamorphoses*', *Ramus*, 3 (1974), 102–42.
Le Comte, Edward, *Milton's Unchanging Mind: Three Essays* (Port Washington, NY: Kennikat Press, 1973).
Leishman, J. B., *The Monarch of Wit: An Analytical and Comparative Study of the Poetry of John Donne* (5th edn., London: Hutchison, 1962).
Leonard, John, 'Marlowe's Doric Music: Lust and Aggression in *Hero and Leander*', *English Literary Renaissance*, 30/1 (2000), 55–76.
—— 'Self-Contradicting Puns in *Paradise Lost*', in Thomas N. Corns (ed.), *A Companion to Milton* (Oxford: Blackwell, 2001), 393–410.
Levin, Harry, *The Overreacher: A Study of Christopher Marlowe* (Boston: Beacon Press, 1964).
Lewalski, Barbara Kiefer, 'Innocence and Experience in Milton's Eden', in Thomas Kranidas (ed.), *New Essays on* Paradise Lost (Berkeley and Los Angeles: University of California Press, 1971), 86–117.
—— Paradise Lost *and the Rhetoric of Literary Forms* (Princeton: Princeton University Press, 1985).
—— 'Milton's *Comus* and the Politics of Masquing', in David Bevington and Peter Holbrook (eds.), *The Politics of the Stuart Court Masque* (Cambridge: Cambridge University Press, 1998), 296–320.
—— *The Life of John Milton* (Malden, Mass.: Blackwell, 2000).
Lieb, Michael, *The Dialectics of Creation: Patterns of Birth & Regeneration in* Paradise Lost (Amherst, Mass.: University of Massachusetts Press, 1970).
—— *Milton and the Culture of Violence* (Ithaca, NY: Cornell University Press, 1994).
Lipking, Lawrence, *The Life of the Poet: Beginning and Ending Poetic Careers* (Chicago: University of Chicago Press, 1981).
Loewenstein, Joseph, *Responsive Readings: Versions of Echo in Pastoral, Epic, and the Jonsonian Masque* (New Haven: Yale University Press, 1984).
Longinus, 'On the Sublime', in *Aristotle: The Poetics; 'Longinus': On the Sublime; Demetrius: On Style*, ed. and trans. W. Hamilton Fyfe and W. Rhys Roberts (Cambridge, Mass.: Harvard University Press, 1932), 118–253.

Loudon, Bruce, 'Pivotal Contrafactuals in Homeric Epic', *Classical Antiquity*, 12/2 (1993), 181–98.

—— 'Milton and the Appropriation of a Homeric Technique', *Classical and Modern Literature*, 16/4 (1996), 325–40.

Lovelace, Richard, *Lucasta: Posthume Poems of Richard Lovelace Esq.* [online facsimile] (London: William Godbid for Clement Darby, 1659), Early English Books Online, http://gateway.proquest.com/openurl?ctx_ver=Z39.88-2003&res_id=xri:eebo&rft_id=xri:eebo:image:96122 accessed 2 Aug. 2010.

Low, Anthony, *The Blaze of Noon: A Reading of* Samson Agonistes (New York: Columbia University Press, 1974).

—— 'The Phoenix and the Sun in *Samson Agonistes*', *Milton Studies*, 14 (1980), 219–31.

—— *The Georgic Revolution* (Princeton: Princeton University Press, 1985).

Luck, Georg, 'Notes on the Language and Text of Ovid's *Tristia*', *Harvard Studies in Classical Philology*, 65 (1961), 243–61.

Lucretius, *De Rerum Natura*, ed. Martin Ferguson, trans. W. H. D. Rouse (2nd edn., Cambridge, Mass.: Harvard University Press, 1992).

Luxon, Thomas H., *Single Imperfection: Milton, Marriage, and Friendship* (Pittsburgh: Duquesne University Press, 2005).

Lydgate, John, *The Pilgrimage of the Life of Man, Englisht by John Lydgate, A.D. 1426, from the French of Guillaume de Deguileville, A.D. 1330, 1355*, ed. F. J. Furnivall (London: Kegan Paul, Trench, Trübner & Co., 1899; repr. Millwood, NY: Kraus Reprint Co., 1978).

Lyne, Raphael, *Ovid's Changing Worlds: English* Metamorphoses, *1567–1632* (Oxford: Oxford University Press, 2001).

—— 'Love and Exile after Ovid', in Philip Hardie (ed.), *The Cambridge Companion to Ovid* (Oxford: Oxford University Press, 2001), 288–300.

—— 'Writing Back to Ovid in the 1560s and 1570s', *Literature and Translation*, 13 (2004), 143–64.

Lyne, R. O. A. M., *Further Voices in Vergil's* Aeneid (Oxford: Clarendon Press, 1987).

McCabe, Richard A., *The Pillars of Eternity: Time and Providence in* The Faerie Queene (Blackrock: Irish Academic Press, 1989).

—— *Spenser's Monstrous Regiment: Elizabethan Ireland and the Poetics of Difference* (Oxford: Oxford University Press, 2002).

McColley, Diane Kelsey, *Milton's Eve* (Urbana, Ill.: University of Illinois Press, 1983).

—— 'Eve and the Arts of Eden', in Julia M. Walker (ed.), *Milton and the Idea of Woman* (Urbana, Ill.: University of Illinois Press, 1988), 100–19.

McDowell, Nicholas, ' "Lycidas" and the Influence of Anxiety', in Nicholas McDowell and Nigel Smith (eds.), *The Oxford Handbook of Milton* (Oxford: Oxford University Press, 2009), 112–35.

―― 'How Laudian was the Young Milton?', unpublished paper (Canada Milton Seminar VI, 2010).
McGowan, Matthew, 'Ovid and Poliziano in Exile', *International Journal of the Classical Tradition*, 12/1 (2005), 25–45.
McGregor, James H., 'Ovid at School: From the Ninth to the Fifteenth Century', *Classical Folia*, 32/1 (1978), 29–51.
McGuire, Maryann Cale, *Milton's Puritan Masque* (Athens, Ga.: University of Georgia Press, 1983).
Mack, Peter, *Elizabethan Rhetoric: Theory and Practice* (Cambridge: Cambridge University Press, 2002).
McKeown, J. C., '*Fabula Proposito Nulla Tegenda Meo*: Ovid's *Fasti* and Augustan Politics', in Tony Woodman and David West (eds.), *Poetry and Politics in the Age of Augustus* (Cambridge: Cambridge University Press, 1984), 169–87.
McLaughlin, Martin L., *Literary Imitation in the Italian Renaissance: The Theory and Practice of Imitation from Dante to Bembo* (Oxford: Clarendon Press, 1995).
MacLean, Hugh N., 'Milton's Fair Infant', *English Literary History*, 24 (1957), 296–305.
McMahon, Robert, 'Satan as Infernal Narcissus: Interpretive Translation in the *Commedia*', in Madison U. Sowell (ed.), *Dante and Ovid: Essays in Intertextuality* (Binghamton, NY: Medieval & Renaissance Texts & Studies, 1991), 65–86.
Macrobius, *The Saturnalia*, trans. Percival Vaughan Davies (New York: Columbia University Press, 1969).
Marcus, Leah S., *The Politics of Mirth: Jonson, Herrick, Milton, Marvell, and the Defense of Old Holiday Pastimes* (Chicago: University of Chicago Press, 1986).
Marlowe, Christopher, *Marlowe's Poems*, ed. L. C. Martin (New York: Gordian Press, 1966).
―― *The Plays of Christopher Marlowe*, ed. Roma Gill (London: Oxford University Press, 1971).
Marston, John, *The Works*, ed. Arthur Henry Bullen, 3 vols. (London: John C. Nimmo, 1887; repr. Hildesheim: Georg Olms Verlag, 1970).
Martin, Christopher, 'A Reconsideration of Ovid's *Fasti*', *Illinois Classical Studies*, 10 (1985), 261–74.
Martindale, Charles, *John Milton and the Transformation of Ancient Epic* (Totowa, NJ: Barnes & Noble, 1986).
―― *Redeeming the Text: Latin Poetry and the Hermeneutics of Reception*, Roman Literature and its Contexts (Cambridge: Cambridge University Press, 1993).

Martindale, Charles, 'Introduction: "The Classic of All Europe"', in Charles Martindale (ed.), *The Cambridge Companion to Virgil* (Cambridge: Cambridge University Press, 1997), 1–18.

—— 'Shakespeare's Ovid, Ovid's Shakespeare: A Methodological Postscript', in A. B. Taylor (ed.), *Shakespeare's Ovid: The Metamorphoses in the Plays and Poems* (Cambridge: Cambridge University Press, 2000), 198–215.

—— and Burrow, Colin, 'Clapham's *Narcissus*: A Pre-Text for Shakespeare's *Venus and Adonis*?', *English Literary Renaissance*, 22/2 (1992), 147–76.

Martz, Louis Lohr, *Poet of Exile: A Study of Milton's Poetry* (New Haven: Yale University Press, 1980).

Maslen, R. W., 'Myths Exploited: The Metamorphoses of Ovid in Early Elizabethan England', in A. B. Taylor (ed.), *Shakespeare's Ovid: The Metamorphoses in the Plays and Poems* (Cambridge: Cambridge University Press, 2000), 15–30.

Matar, N. I., 'Peter Sterry and the Puritan Defense of Ovid in Restoration England', *Studies in Philology*, 88/1 (1991), 110–21.

Meres, Francis, *Palladis Tamia: Wits Treasury: Being the Second Part of Wits Common Wealth* (London: P. Short for Cuthbert Burbie, 1598; facs. edn., New York: Garland, 1973).

Meskill, Lynn S., *Ben Jonson and Envy* (Cambridge: Cambridge University Press, 2009).

Miller, John F., 'The *Fasti*: Style, Structure, and Time', in Barbara Weiden Boyd (ed.), *Brill's Companion to Ovid* (Leiden: Brill, 2002), 167–96.

Morrison, James V., 'Alternatives to the Epic Tradition: Homer's Challenges in the *Iliad*', *Transactions of the American Philological Association*, 122 (1992), 61–71.

Moss, Ann, *Ovid in Renaissance France: A Survey of the Latin Editions of Ovid and Commentaries Printed in France before 1600* (London: The Warburg Institute, University of London, 1982).

—— (ed. and trans.), *Latin Commentaries on Ovid from the Renaissance* (Signal Mountain, Tenn.: Summertown, 1998).

Most, Glenn W., 'Epinician Envies', in David Konstan and N. K. Rutter (eds.), *Envy, Spite, and Jealousy: The Rivalrous Emotions in Ancient Greece* (Edinburgh: Edinburgh University Press, 2003), 123–42.

Mulryan, John, *Through a Glass Darkly: Milton's Reinvention of the Mythological Tradition* (Pittsburgh: Duquesne University Press, 1996).

Mulvihill, James D., 'Jonson's *Poetaster* and the Ovidian Debate', *Studies in English Literature, 1500–1900*, 22 (1982), 239–55.

Myers, K. Sara, *Ovid's Causes: Cosmogony and Aetiology in the Metamorphoses* (Ann Arbor: University of Michigan Press, 1994).

—— 'The Metamorphosis of a Poet: Recent Work on Ovid', *Journal of Roman Studies*, 89 (1999), 190–204.

Nagle, Betty Rose, *The Poetics of Exile: Program and Polemic in the* Tristia *and* Epistulae ex Ponto *of Ovid*, Collection Latomus (Brussels: Latomus, 1980).

Nashe, Thomas, *Lenten Stuffe* [online facsimile] (London: N.L. and C.B., 1599), Early English Books Online, http://gateway.proquest.com/openurl?ctx_ver=Z39.88-2003&res_id=xri:eebo&rft_id=xri:eebo:image:176502 accessed 12 Sept. 2010.

Neuse, Richard, 'Metamorphosis and Symbolic Action in *Comus*', in *Critical Essays on Milton from ELH* (Baltimore: Johns Hopkins Press, 1969), 87–102.

—— 'Milton and Spenser: The Virgilian Triad Revisited', *English Literary History*, 45/4 (1978), 606–39.

Newlands, Carole E., 'Ovid's Narrator in the *Fasti*', *Arethusa*, 25/1 (1992), 33–54.

—— *Playing with Time: Ovid and the* Fasti (Ithaca, NY: Cornell University Press, 1995).

Newlyn, Lucy, *Reading, Writing, and Romanticism: The Anxiety of Reception* (Oxford: Oxford University Press, 2000).

Nicoll, W. S. M., 'Cupid, Apollo, and Daphne (Ovid, *Met.* 1.452ff)', *Classical Quarterly*, 30 (1980), 174–82.

Nohrnberg, James, *The Analogy of* The Faerie Queene (Princeton: Princeton University Press, 1976).

Norbrook, David, *Poetry and Politics in the English Renaissance* (London: Routledge & Kegan Paul, 1984).

—— 'The Reformation of the Masque', in David Lindley (ed.), *The Court Masque* (Manchester: Manchester University Press, 1984), 94–110.

Norford, Don Parry, 'The Separation of the World Parents in *Paradise Lost*', *Milton Studies*, 12 (1978), 3–24.

North, J. D., 'The Western Calendar—"Intolerabilis, Horribilis, et Derisibilis": Four Centuries of Discontent', in G. V. Coyne et al. (eds.), *Gregorian Reform of the Calendar: Proceedings of the Vatican Conference to Commemorate its 400th Anniversary, 1582–1982* (Vatican City: Specola Vaticana, 1983), 75–113.

Nugent, S. G., '*Tristia* 2: Ovid and Augustus', in Kurt A. Raaflaub and Mark Toher (eds.), *Between Republic and Empire: Interpretations of Augustus and his Principate* (Berkeley and Los Angeles: University of California Press, 1990), 239–57.

Nussbaum, Martha Craven, *The Fragility of Goodness: Luck and Ethics in Greek Tragedy and Philosophy* (rev. edn., Cambridge: Cambridge University Press, 2001).

Nyquist, Mary, and Ferguson, Margaret, 'Preface', in Mary Nyquist and Margaret Ferguson (eds.), *Re-Membering Milton: Essays on the Texts and Traditions* (New York: Methuen, 1987), pp. xii–xvii.

Oakley-Brown, Liz, 'Translating the Subject: Ovid's *Metamorphoses* in England, 1560-7', in Roger Ellis and Liz Oakley-Brown (eds.), *Translation and Nation: Towards a Cultural Politics of Englishness* (Cleveland: Multilingual Matters, 2001), 48-84.

Oliensis, Ellen, 'Canidia, Canicula, and the Decorum of Horace's Epodes', *Arethusa*, 24 (1991), 107-38.

Olmsted, Wendy, 'On the Margins of Otherness: Metamorphosis and Identity in Homer, Ovid, Sidney, and Milton', *New Literary History*, 27/2 (1996), 167-84.

Orgel, Stephen, *The Jonsonian Masque* (Cambridge, Mass.: Harvard University Press, 1965).

—— *The Illusion of Power: Political Theater in the English Renaissance* (Berkeley and Los Angeles: University of California Press, 1975).

—— 'The Case for Comus', *Representations*, 81 (2003), 31-45.

—— and Strong, Roy, *Inigo Jones: The Theatre of the Stuart Court, Including the Complete Designs for Productions at Court for the Most Part in the Collection of the Duke of Devonshire Together with their Texts and Historical Documentation*, 2 vols. (London: Sotheby Parke Bernet; Berkeley and Los Angeles: University of California Press, 1973).

Panofsky, Dora, 'Narcissus and Echo: Notes on Poussin's *Birth of Bacchus* in the Fogg Museum of Art', *Art Bulletin*, 31/2 (1949), 112-20.

Parker, Patricia A., *Inescapable Romance: Studies in the Poetics of a Mode* (Princeton: Princeton University Press, 1979).

—— *Literary Fat Ladies: Rhetoric, Gender, Property* (London: Methuen, 1987).

—— *Shakespeare from the Margins: Language, Culture, Context* (Chicago: University of Chicago Press, 1996).

Parker, William Riley, 'The Date of *Samson Agonistes*', *Philological Quarterly*, 28 (1949), 145-66.

Parry, Adam, 'The Two Voices of Virgil's *Aeneid*', *Arion*, 2/4 (1963), 66-80.

Parry, Graham, *Seventeenth-Century Poetry: The Social Context* (London: Hutchison, 1985).

—— *The Trophies of Time: English Antiquarians of the Seventeenth Century* (Oxford: Oxford University Press, 1995).

Patterson, Annabel, '"Forc'd fingers": Milton's Early Poems and Ideological Constraint', in Claude J. Summers and Ted-Larry Pebworth (eds.), *'The Muses Common-Weale': Poetry and Politics in the Seventeenth Century* (Columbia, Mo.: University of Missouri Press, 1988), 9-22.

Pearcy, Lee T., *The Mediated Muse: English Translations of Ovid, 1560-1700* (Hamden, Conn.: Archon, 1984).

Peend, Thomas, *The Pleasant Fable of Hermaphroditus and Salmacis* [online facsimile] (London: T. Colwell, 1565), Early English Books Online, http://

gateway.proquest.com/openurl?ctx_ver=Z39.88-2003&res_id=xri:eebo&rft_val_fmt=&rft_id=xri:eebo:image:20060 accessed 18 Aug. 2005.

Petrarch, Francesco, *Petrarch's Lyric Poems: The Rime sparse and Other Lyrics*, ed. Robert M. Durling (Cambridge, Mass.: Harvard University Press, 1976).

Philostratus, *Imagines*, in *Philostratus: Imagines; Callistratus: Descriptions*, trans. Arthur Fairbanks (London: W. Heinemann, 1931).

Picone, Michelangelo, 'Ovid and the *Exul Immeritus*', in Teodolinda Barolini (ed.), *Dante for the New Millenium* (New York: Fordham University Press, 2003), 389–407.

Pigman, G. W. III, 'Versions of Imitation in the Renaissance', *Renaissance Quarterly*, 33 (1980), 1–32.

Plato, *The Collected Dialogues of Plato*, ed. Edith Hamilton and Huntington Cairns (2nd edn., Princeton: Princeton University Press, 1963).

Plotinus, *The Essential Plotinus: Representative Treatises from the Enneads*, ed. Elmer O'Brien (New York: New American Library, 1964).

Poliziano, Angelo, *Commento inedito ai Fasti di Ovidio*, ed. Francesco Lo Monaco (Florence: L. S. Olschki, 1991).

Posèq, Avigdor W. G., 'The Allegorical Content of Caravaggio's Narcissus', *Source: Notes on the History of Art*, 10 (1991), 21–31.

Praz, Mario, 'Milton and Poussin', in J. Dover Wilson (ed.), *Seventeenth-Century Studies Presented to Sir Thomas Grierson* (Oxford: Clarendon, 1938), 192–210.

Prescott, Anne Lake, 'Sclaunder', in A. C. Hamilton (ed.), *The Spenser Encyclopedia* (Toronto: University of Toronto Press; London: Routledge, 1990), 632–3.

Price, Hereward T., 'Like Himself', *Review of English Studies*, 16 (1940), 178–81.

Prynne, William, *Histrio-Mastix. The Players Scovrge, or, Actors Tragaedie, Divided into Two Parts* [online facsimile] (London: E.A. and W.I. for Michael Sparke, 1633), Early English Books Online, http://gateway.proquest.com/openurl?ctx_ver=Z39.88-2003&res_id=xri:eebo&rft_id=xri:eebo:image:15744:2 accessed 25 Feb. 2010.

Pugh, Syrithe, *Spenser and Ovid* (Aldershot: Ashgate, 2005).

—— *Herrick, Fanshawe and the Politics of Intertextuality: Classical Literature and Seventeenth-Century Royalism* (Farnham: Ashgate, 2010).

Quilligan, Maureen, *Milton's Spenser: The Politics of Reading* (Ithaca, NY: Cornell University Press, 1983).

Quinones, Ricardo J., *The Renaissance Discovery of Time* (Cambridge, Mass.: Harvard University Press, 1972).

Quint, David, *Origin and Originality in Renaissance Literature: Versions of the Source* (New Haven: Yale University Press, 1983).

Quint, David, *Epic and Empire: Politics and Generic Form from Virgil to Milton* (Princeton: Princeton University Press, 1993).

—— 'Fear of Falling: Icarus, Phaethon, and Lucretius in *Paradise Lost*', *Renaissance Quarterly*, 57/3 (2004), 847–81.

Quintilian, *The Institutio Oratoria of Quintilian*, trans. Harold Edgeworth Butler, 4 vols. (London: Heinemann, 1920).

Radzinowicz, Mary Ann, *Toward* Samson Agonistes: *The Growth of Milton's Mind* (Princeton: Princeton University Press, 1978).

—— '"To Play in the Socratic Manner": Oxymoron in Milton's *At a Vacation Exercise in the Colledge*', *University of Hartford Studies in Literature*, 17/3 (1985), 1–11.

Rajan, Balachandra, *The Lofty Rhyme: A Study of Milton's Major Poetry* (London: Routledge and Kegan Paul, 1970).

—— 'To which is added *Samson Agonistes*', in *The Prison and the Pinnacle* (Toronto: University of Toronto Press, 1973), 82–110.

Rand, E. K., 'Milton in Rustication', *Studies in Philology*, 19/2 (1922), 109–35.

Randolph, Thomas, *Poems with The Mvses Looking-Glasse and Amyntas* [online facsimile] (Oxford: Leonard Lichfield for Francis Bowman, 1638), Early English Books Online, http://gateway.proquest.com/openurl?ctx_ver =Z39.88-2003&res_id=xri:eebo&rft_id=xri:eebo:image:16066 accessed 8 Nov. 2010.

Rees, Christine, 'The Metamorphosis of Daphne in Sixteenth- and Seventeenth-Century English Poetry', *Modern Language Review*, 66 (1971), 251–63.

Revard, Stella Purce, 'Satan's Envy of the Kingship of the Son of God: A Reconsideration of *Paradise Lost*, Book 5, and its Theological Background', *Modern Philology*, 70/3 (1973), 190–8.

—— *The War in Heaven:* Paradise Lost *and the Tradition of Satan's Rebellion* (Ithaca, NY: Cornell University Press, 1980).

—— 'The Politics of Milton's Hercules', *Milton Studies*, 32 (1995), 217–45.

—— *Milton and the Tangles of Neaera's Hair: The Making of the 1645* Poems (Columbia, Mo.: University of Missouri Press, 1997).

—— *Pindar and the Renaissance Hymn-Ode, 1450–1700* (Tempe, Ariz.: Arizona Center for Medieval and Renaissance Studies, 2001).

Richlin, Amy, 'Reading Ovid's Rapes', in Amy Richlin (ed.), *Pornography and Representation in Greece and Rome* (New York: Oxford University Press, 1992), 158–79.

Ricks, Christopher, *Milton's Grand Style* (Oxford: Clarendon, 1963).

Riggs, William G., *The Christian Poet in* Paradise Lost (Berkeley and Los Angeles: University of California Press, 1972).

Ringler, Richard N., 'The Faunus Episode', in A. C. Hamilton (ed.), *Essential Articles for the Study of Edmund Spenser* (Hamden, Conn.: Archon, 1972), 289–98.

Robathan, Dorothy Mae, 'Ovid in the Middle Ages', in J. W. Binns (ed.), *Ovid* (London: Routledge, 1973), 191–209.

Roberts, Jeanne Addison, 'Anxiety and Influence: Milton, Ovid, and Shakespeare', *South Atlantic Review*, 53/2 (1988), 59–75.

Roche, Thomas P., *The Kindly Flame: A Study of the Third and Fourth Books of Spenser's* Faerie Queene (Princeton: Princeton University Press, 1964).

Roe, John, 'Ovid "Renascent" in *Venus and Adonis* and *Hero and Leander*', in A. B. Taylor (ed.), *Shakespeare's Ovid: The* Metamorphoses *in the Plays and Poems* (Cambridge: Cambridge University Press, 2000), 31–46.

Rogers, John, 'The Enclosure of Virginity: The Poetics of Sexual Abstinence in the English Revolution', in Richard Burt and John Michael Archer (eds.), *Enclosure Acts: Sexuality, Property, and Culture in Early Modern England* (Ithaca, NY: Cornell University Press, 1994), 229–50.

Rosati, Gianpiero, *Narciso e Pigmalione: Illusione e spettacolo nelle* Metamorfosi *di Ovidio*, Nuovi Saggi (Florence: Sansoni, 1983).

—— 'Narrative Techniques and Narrative Structures in the *Metamorphoses*', in Barbara Weiden Boyd (ed.), *Brill's Companion to Ovid* (Leiden: Brill, 2002), 272–304.

Rosenmeyer, P. A., 'Ovid's *Heroides* and *Tristia*: Voices from Exile', *Ramus*, 26 (1997), 29–56.

Ross, David O., *Backgrounds to Augustan Poetry: Gallus, Elegy and Rome* (Cambridge: Cambridge University Press, 1975).

Rudrum, Alan, 'Royalist Lyric', in N. H. Keeble (ed.), *The Cambridge Companion to Writing of the English Revolution* (Cambridge: Cambridge University Press, 2001), 181–97.

Rumrich, John P., *Milton Unbound: Controversy and Reinterpretation* (Cambridge: Cambridge University Press, 1996).

Sage, Lorna, 'Milton's Early Poems: A General Introduction', in John Broadbent (ed.), *John Milton: Introductions* (Cambridge: Cambridge University Press, 1973), 258–97.

Samuel, Irene, *Dante and Milton: The* Commedia *and* Paradise Lost (Ithaca, NY: Cornell University Press, 1966).

Sandys, George, *Ovid's Metamorphosis Englished, Mythologized, and Represented in Figures*, ed. Karl K. Hulley and Stanley T. Vandersall (Lincoln, Nebr.: University of Nebraska Press, 1970).

Sauer, Elizabeth, 'Engendering Metamorphoses: Milton and the Ovidian Corpus', in Goran V. Stanivukovic (ed.), *Ovid and the Renaissance Body* (Toronto: University of Toronto Press, 2001), 207–23.

Scaliger, Julius Caesar, *Sieben Bücher über die Dichtkunst*, ed. and trans. Gregor Vogt-Spira [*Poetics Libri Septem*], 5 vols. (Stuttgart-Bad Cannstatt: Frommann-Holzboog, 1998).
Schwartz, Regina M., *Remembering and Repeating: On Milton's Theology and Poetics* (Cambridge: Cambridge University Press, 1993).
Segal, Charles, *Landscape in Ovid's* Metamorphoses*: A Study in the Transformation of a Literary Symbol* (Wiesbaden: Franz Steiner Verlag GMBH, 1969).
—— 'Ovid: Metamorphosis, Hero, Poet', *Helios: Journal of the Classical Association of the Southwest*, 12 (1985), 49–63.
—— 'Ovid's Metamorphic Bodies: Art, Gender, and Violence in the *Metamorphoses*', *Arion*, 3rd series, 5/3 (1998), 9–41.
Seneca the Elder, *Declamations*, trans. M. Winterbottom, 2 vols., Loeb Classical Library (Cambridge, Mass.: Harvard University Press; London: W. Heinemann, 1974).
Seneca the Younger, *Ad Lucilium Epistulae Morales*, trans. Richard M. Gummere, 3 vols. (Loeb Classical Library; Cambridge, Mass.: Harvard University Press; London: W. Heinemann, 1953).
Shapiro, Marianne, 'Perseus and Bellerophon in *Orlando Furioso*', *Modern Philology*, 81/2 (1983), 109–30.
Sharpe, Kevin, *Criticism and Compliment: The Politics of Literature in the England of Charles I* (Cambridge: Cambridge University Press, 1987).
—— *The Personal Rule of Charles I* (New Haven: Yale University Press, 1992).
Sharrock, A. R., 'Ovid and the Politics of Reading', *Materiali e discussioni per l'analisi dei testi classici*, 33 (1994), 97–102.
Shawcross, John T., 'The Chronology of Milton's Major Poems', *PMLA* 4 (1961), 345–58.
—— 'The Genres of *Paradise Regain'd* and *Samson Agonistes*: The Wisdom of their Joint Publication', *Milton Studies*, 17 (1983), 225–48.
—— *The Uncertain World of* Samson Agonistes (Cambridge: Cambridge University Press, 2001).
Shirley, James, *Narcissvs, Or, The Self-Lover* [online facsimile] (London: Humphrey Moseley, 1646), Early English Books Online, http://gateway.proquest.com/openurl?ctx_ver=Z39.88-2003&res_id=xri:eebo&rft_id=xri:eebo:image:62065 accessed 29 Aug 2006.
Shoaf, R. A., *Dante, Chaucer, and the Currency of the Word: Money, Images, and Reference in Late Medieval Poetry* (Norman, Okla.: Pilgrim Books, 1983).
—— *Milton, Poet of Duality: A Study of Semiosis in the Poetry and the Prose* (New Haven: Yale University Press, 1985).
Shullenberger, William, *Lady in the Labyrinth: Milton's* Comus *as Initiation* (Madison: Fairleigh Dickinson University Press, 2008).

—— 'Milton's Pagan Counter-Poetic: Eros and Inspiration in Elegy 5', unpublished keynote address (Milton at Mufreesboro, 2009).
Shulman, Jeff, 'At the Crossroads of Myth: The Hermeneutics of Hercules from Ovid to Shakespeare', *English Literary History*, 50/1 (1983), 83–105.
—— 'Ovidian Myth in Lyly's Courtship Comedies', *Studies in English Literature*, 25/2 (1985), 249–69.
Sidney, Philip, *The Countesse of Pembrokes Arcadia*, ed. Albert Feuillerat (Cambridge: Cambridge University Press, 1969).
Silberman, Lauren, 'Mythographic Transformations of Ovid's Hermaphrodite', *Sixteenth Century Journal*, 19/4 (1988), 643–52.
Skulsky, Harold, *Metamorphosis: The Mind in Exile* (Cambridge, Mass.: Harvard University Press, 1981).
Smarr, Janet Levarie, 'Ovid and Boccaccio: A Note on Self-Defense', *Mediaevalia: A Journal of Mediaeval Studies*, 13 (1989 for 1987), 247–55.
—— 'Poets of Love and Exile', in Madison U. Sowell (ed.), *Dante and Ovid: Essays in Intertextuality* (Binghamton, NY: Medieval & Renaissance Texts & Studies, 1991), 139–51.
Smith, James, *The Loves of Hero and Leander: A Mock Poem* [online facsimile] (London, 1651), Early English Books Online, http://gateway.proquest.com/openurl?ctx_ver=Z39.88-2003&res_id=xri:eebo&rft_id=xri:eebo:image:169733 accessed 13 Nov. 2010.
Smith, Nigel, *Is Milton Better Than Shakespeare?* (Cambridge, Mass.: Harvard University Press, 2008).
Solodow, Joseph B., *The World of Ovid's* Metamorphoses (Chapel Hill, NC: University of North Carolina Press, 1988).
Stapleton, M. L., *Harmful Eloquence: Ovid's* Amores *from Antiquity to Shakespeare* (Ann Arbor: University of Michigan Press, 1996).
—— '"Why Should They Not Alike in All Parts Touch?": Donne and the Elegiac Tradition', *John Donne Journal: Studies in the Age of Donne*, 15 (1996), 1–22.
—— 'Venus as Praeceptor: The *Ars Amatoria* in *Venus and Adonis*', in Philip C. Kolin (ed.), Venus and Adonis: *Critical Essays* (New York: Garland, 1997), 309–21.
—— '"Thou idle Wanderer, about my Heart": Rochester and Ovid', *Restoration: Studies in English Literary Culture, 1660–1700*, 23/1 (1999), 10–30.
—— 'Ovid the Rakehell: The Case of Wycherley', *Restoration: Studies in English Literary Culture, 1660–1700*, 25/2 (2001), 85–102.
—— *Spenser's Ovidian Poetics* (Newark, Del.: University of Delaware Press, 2009).
Starnes, DeWitt T., and Talbert, Ernest William, *Classical Myth and Legend in Renaissance Dictionaries: A Study of Renaissance Dictionaries in their*

Relation to the Classical Learning of Contemporary English Writers (Chapel Hill, NC: University of North Carolina Press, 1955).
Steadman, John M., 'Tradition and Innovation in Milton's "Sin": The Problem of Literary Indebtedness', *Philological Quarterly*, 39 (1960), 93–103.
Stevens, Edward B., 'Envy and Pity in Greek Philosophy', *American Journal of Philology*, 2 (1948), 171–89.
Stevens, Paul, *Imagination and the Presence of Shakespeare in* Paradise Lost (Madison: University of Wisconsin Press, 1985).
—— 'Discontinuities in Milton's Early Public Self-Representation', *Huntington Library Quarterly*, 51/4 (1988), 261–80.
—— 'Subversion and Wonder in Milton's Epitaph "On Shakespeare"', *English Literary Renaissance*, 19/3 (1989), 375–88.
Strong, Roy, *Gloriana: The Portraits of Queen Elizabeth I* (New York: Thames and Hudson, 1987).
Sturm-Maddox, Sara, *Petrarch's Metamorphoses: Text and Subtext in the* Rime sparse (Columbia, Mo.: University of Missouri Press, 1985).
Summers, Joseph H., *The Muse's Method: An Introduction to* Paradise Lost (London: Chatto & Windus, 1962).
Swaim, Kathleen M., 'Myself a True Poem: Early Milton and the (Re)formation of the Subject', *Milton Studies*, 38/1 (2000), 66–95.
Tarrant, Richard, 'Ovid and the Failure of Rhetoric', in Doreen Innes, Harry Hine, and Christopher Pelling (eds.), *Ethics and Rhetoric: Classical Essays for Donald Russell on his Seventy-Fifth Birthday* (Oxford: Clarendon Press, 1995), 63–74.
Teskey, Gordon, *Delirious Milton: The Fate of the Poet in Modernity* (Cambridge, Mass.: Harvard University Press, 2006).
Theodorakopoulos, Elena, 'Closure and Transformation in Ovid's *Metamorphoses*', in Philip Hardie, Alessandro Barchiesi, and Stephen Hinds (eds.), *Ovidian Transformations: Essays on the* Metamorphoses *and its Reception* (Cambridge: Cambridge Philological Society, 1999), 142–61.
Thomas, Richard F., *Reading Virgil and his Texts: Studies in Intertextuality* (Ann Arbor: University of Michigan Press, 1999).
—— *Virgil and the Augustan Reception* (Cambridge: Cambridge University Press, 2001).
Tillyard, E. M. W., *Milton* (rev. edn., London: Chatto & Windus, 1930).
Tissol, Garth, *The Face of Nature: Wit, Narrative, and Cosmic Origins in Ovid's* Metamorphoses (Princeton: Princeton University Press, 1997).
Tourneur, Cyril, *The Transformed Metamorphosis* [online facsimile] (London: Valentine Sims, 1600), Early English Books Online, http://gateway.proquest.com/openurl?ctx_ver=Z39.88-2003&res_id=xri:eebo&rft_val_fmt=&rft_id=xri:eebo:image:2172 accessed 26 Aug. 2005.
Tromly, Fred B., *Playing with Desire: Christopher Marlowe and the Art of Tantalization* (Toronto: University of Toronto Press, 1998).

Tudeau-Clayton, Margaret, *Jonson, Shakespeare and Early Modern Virgil* (Cambridge: Cambridge University Press, 1998).
Underdowne, Thomas, 'Ouid his Inuective against Ibis' [online facsimile] (London: Henry Bynneman, 1577), Early English Books Online, http://gateway.proquest.com/openurl?ctx_ver=Z39.88-2003&res_id=xri:eebo&rft_id=xri:eebo:image:14131 accessed 17 Feb. 2004.
Unglaub, Jonathan, *Poussin and the Poetics of Painting: Pictorial Narrative and the Legacy of Tasso* (Cambridge: Cambridge University Press, 2006).
Van Den Broek, R., *The Myth of the Phoenix According to Classical and Early Christian Tradition*, trans. I. Seeger (Leiden: E. J. Brill, 1972).
Van Der Laan, Sarah, 'Milton's Odyssean Ethics: Homeric Allusions and Arminian Thought in *Paradise Lost*', *Milton Studies*, 49 (2009), 49–76.
Vaught, Jennifer, 'Spenser's Dialogic Voice in Book I of *The Faerie Queene*', *Studies in English Literature 1500–1800*, 41 (2001), 71–89.
Veevers, Erica, *Images of Love and Religion: Queen Henrietta Maria and Court Entertainments* (Cambridge: Cambridge University Press, 1989).
Velz, John W., 'The Ovidian Soliloquy in Shakespeare', *Shakespeare Studies*, 18 (1986), 1–24.
—— 'Ovidian Creation in Milton and Decreation in Shakespeare', *Ovid: Werk und Werkung: Festgabe für Michael von Albrecht zum 65* (Frankfurt: Peter Lang, 1999), 1035–46.
Vinge, Louise, *The Narcissus Theme in Western European Literature up to the Early 19th Century* (Lund: Gleerups, 1967).
Walcot, Peter, *Envy and the Greeks: A Study of Human Behaviour* (Warminster: Aris & Phillips, 1978).
Waldock, A. J. A., *Paradise Lost and its Critics* (Cambridge: Cambridge University Press, 1964).
Walker, Julia M., 'The Poetics of Antitext and the Politics of Milton's Allusions', *Studies in English Literature, 1500–1900*, 37/1 (1997), 151–71.
Wallace-Hadrill, Andrew, 'Time for Augustus: Ovid, Augustus and the *Fasti*', in Michael Whitby, Philip Hardie, and Mary Whitby (eds.), *Homo Viator: Classical Essays for John Bramble* (Bedminster: Bristol Classical Press, 1987), 221–30.
Waller, Edmund, *The Poetical Works of Edmund Waller and Sir John Denham with Memoir and Critical Dissertation*, ed. Revd George Gilfillan (Edinburgh: James Nichol, 1857).
Watkins, John, *The Specter of Dido: Spenser and Virgilian Epic* (New Haven: Yale University Press, 1995).
Watkins, W. B. C., *An Anatomy of Milton's Verse* (Hamden, Conn.: Archon, 1965).
Weever, John, *Faunus and Melliflora*, ed. Arnold Davenport (Liverpool: Liverpool University Press, 1948).

Whitney, Geffrey, *A Choice of Emblemes*, ed. Henry Green (New York: Benjamin Blom, 1967).
Wilkenfield, Roger B., 'The Seat at the Centre: An Interpretation of *Comus*', *English Literary History*, 33/2 (1966); repr. in *Critical Essays on Milton from ELH* (Baltimore: Johns Hopkins Press, 1969), 123–50.
Wilkinson, L. P., *Ovid Surveyed: An Abridgement for the General Reader of Ovid Recalled* (Cambridge: Cambridge University Press, 1962).
Williams, Gareth D., *Banished Voices: Readings in Ovid's Exile Poetry* (Cambridge: Cambridge University Press, 1994).
—— *The Curse of Exile: A Study of Ovid's Ibis* (Cambridge: Cambridge Philological Society, 1996).
—— 'Ovid's Exilic Poetry: Worlds Apart', in Barbara Weiden Boyd (ed.), *Brill's Companion to Ovid* (Leiden: Brill, 2002), 337–81.
Willobie, Henry, *Willobie his Avisa, or, The True Picture of a modest Maid, and of a chast and constant wife* [online facsimile] (London: John Windet, 1594), Early English Books Online, http://gateway.proquest.com/openurl?ctx_ver=Z39.88-2003&res_id=xri:eebo&rft_id=xri:eebo:image:1443 accessed 14 Sept. 2010.
Wilmot, John, Earl of Rochester, *The Works of John Wilmot Earl of Rochester*, ed. Harold Love (Oxford: Oxford University Press, 1999).
Wilson, Emily, '*Quantum Mutatus ab Illo*: Moments of Change and Recognition in Tasso and Milton', in M. J. Clarke, B. G. F. Currie, and R. O. A. M. Lyne (eds.), *Epic Interactions: Perspectives on Homer, Virgil, and the Epic Tradition Presented to Jasper Griffin by Former Pupils* (New York: Oxford University Press, 2006), 273–99.
Wilson-Okamura, David Scott, 'Errors about Ovid and Romance', *Spenser Studies*, 23 (2008), 215–34.
Wind, Edgar, *Pagan Mysteries in the Renaissance* (rev. edn., Toronto: W. W. Norton & Co., 1968).
Wise, Valerie Merriam, 'Flight Myths in Ovid's *Metamorphoses*: An Interpretation of Phaethon and Daedalus', *Ramus*, 6 (1977), 44–59.
Wittreich, Joseph Anthony, *The Romantics on Milton: Formal Essays and Critical Asides* (Cleveland, Oh.: Press of Case Western Reserve University, 1970).
—— *Interpreting* Samson Agonistes (Princeton: Princeton University Press, 1986).
—— '"Strange Text!": "Paradise Regain'd... To which is added *Samson Agonistes*"', in Neil Fraistat (ed.), *Poems in their Place: The Intertextuality and Order of Poetic Collections* (Chapel Hill, NC: University of North Carolina Press, 1986), 164–94.
—— '"Reading" Milton: The Death (and Survival) of the Author', *Milton Studies*, 38 (2000), 10–46.

—— Shifting Contexts: Reinterpreting Samson Agonistes (Pittsburgh: Duquesne University Press, 2002).

Wolfe, Jessica, 'Spenser, Homer, and the Mythography of Strife', *Renaissance Quarterly*, 58/4 (2005), 1220–88.

Wood, Derek, *Exiled from Light: Divine Law, Morality, and Violence in Milton's* Samson Agonistes (Toronto: University of Toronto Press, 2001).

Worthen, Thomas, 'Poussin's Paintings of Flora', *Art Bulletin*, 61/4 (1979), 575–88.

Zanker, Paul, *The Power of Images in the Age of Augustus* (Ann Arbor: University of Michigan Press, 1988).

Zimmerman, Mary, *Metamorphoses: A Play* (Evanston, Ill.: Northwestern University Press, 2002).

Zissos, Andrew, and Gildenhard, Ingo, 'Problems of Time in *Metamorphoses* 2', in Philip Hardie, Alessandro Barchiesi, and Stephen Hinds (eds.), *Ovidian Transformations: Essays on the* Metamorphoses *and its Reception* (Cambridge: Cambridge Philological Society, 1999), 31–47.

Index

Actaeon 35, 37, 181, 184, 275
Adam 2, 9, 11, 41, 167, 197, 201–14, 216–19, 220–8, 229, 231, 253–4, 256, 268, 271
Adonis 64–8, 69, 70–3, 78, 84–6, 90 n. 132, 92, 93, 99, 108, 134, 138, 160, 161, 180 n. 39, 184, 186, 187 n. 63, 189, 194 n. 87, 196, 202–3, 216–17, 225, 264, *see also* Shakespeare, *Venus and Adonis*
aemulatio ix–x, 5–7, 231, 235–6, 238–9, 242, 250, 265, 271–3, 277, 282–3
  and Milton 255–60, 239 n. 36, 256 n.98
  see also imitation; envy
Aeneas x, xi, 43, 79, 116, 121–2, 183 n. 46, 207, 244–5, 274 n. 138, 301–3, 310
Aesculapius 17 n. 50, 310 n. 60
Aglauros 244
Ahl, Frederick 290 n. 15
Alberti 190
Alciatus, Andreas 191–2
Alexandrian footnote 75–6, 150
allegory 243, 273
Allen, Donald Cameron 55 n. 20, 63 n. 43, 67 n. 60, 133 n. 105
allusion ix–xii, xiii–xiv, 9, 75–7, 161, 184, 308–9
  Milton's use of 49–54, 255–60, 301–2, 307, 315, 325
  and predetermination xvii, 47, 173, 207–8, 213–14, 219–20, 226
  see also imitation; reception and reading
Althaea 39, 44–5, 92
Altman, Joel B. 18 n. 52
Amsler, Mark 60
Apollo 60, 65, 68, 74, 104–5, 113–14, 115 n. 52, 143, 146–7, 156–7, 159, 160, 172, 175, 214–15, 264, 265–8, 309 n.60, 320, 322–4, 326;
  see also Daphne
Apollonius of Rhodes 42

Apuleius 92–4, 264 n. 120
Aquinas, Thomas 232 n. 7
Arachne 35 n. 105, 40, 192, 230, 277–82
Ariosto, Ludovico xiv n. 21, 75, 269 n. 127
Aristotle 204, 235–6 n. 21
artist figures
  in Milton 10, 41–3, 230–1, 264, 269–72, 298–9, 301–2, 322
  in Ovid 9–10, 39–43, 183, 230, 264, 277–8; *see also* creativity; narcissism; Narcissus; poetry and political power
Ascham, Roger xiii n. 17, 170
Attendant Spirit 74–5, 77, 83–4, 87, 91, 149
Aubrey, John 152–3
Augustus 21, 24, 112–17, 124, 136, 139, 154, 156, 245–7, 288–90, 309

Bacchus 52–3, 74, 145–6, 190–1
Bacon, Francis 240 n. 40, 278
Baldwin, Thomas Whitfield 17 n. 51, 30 n. 90, 114 n. 48, 132 n. 99
Barbeau, Anne T. 254
Barchiesi, Alessandro 27 n. 84, 37 n. 110, 108, 120 n. 65, 125 n. 78, 138 n. 119, 208, 289, 306 n. 52, 308 n. 57, 313 n. 68
Barkan, Leonard xviii, 6, 14–15, 166, 179, 182 n. 42, 278
Barksted, William 100 n. 7, 186 n. 59
Barolsky, Paul 109 n. 31, 185 n. 54
Basil, St 236
Baskins, Crystelle 192
Bate, Jonathan 6, 16, 44 n. 129, 132, 136 n. 112
Beaumont, Francis 80, 187–8
Bellerophon 11, 246, 271–2, 324 n. 9
Bersuire, Pierre 60, 111
Blaine, Marlin E. 295
Blake, William 230
Bloom, Harold x, 6, 260
Boccaccio 292–3

Index

Bond, Ronald 237 n. 26, 278–9, 280 n. 165
Botticelli, Sandro 109 n. 31, 122 n. 70, 127
Braden, Gordon 90 n. 131, 104–5, 154 n. 172, 189–90, 220 n. 154
Brinsley, John 30 n. 90, 186 n. 59
Brown, Georgia 16, 18 n. 54
bugs 104, 278–80
Burckhardt, Jacob xv, 31 n. 94, 191
Burrow, Colin xiii–xiv, 32 n. 96, 86 n. 118, 119 n. 61, 134, 166 n. 1, 169 n. 8, 199, 256 n. 97
Burton, Robert 236–7
Byblis 92, 161, 181

Cadmus 199–200
Callimachus xi–xii, 119 n. 62, 143, 249–50
Campbell, Gordon 110, 148
Carew, Thomas 77, 101–7, 281 n. 166
Carey, John 78
Carroll, William C. 45, 187 n. 64
Carron, Jean-Claude 18 n. 52, 205
Cary, Henry 122 n 72
Catullus xi, 183, 208, 245, 275 n. 142, 293 n. 20
Cavendish, Margaret 246
Cephalus and Procris 70, 73 n. 79, 180
Ceyx and Alcyone 36 n. 107, 70, 177 n. 30, 180
change
  in Milton 46–7, 78, 165–73, 221
  in Ovid 28, 43–6, 166, 214–16
  and Satan 45, 169–70, 227, 310–11
Chapman, George 16, 100
Charles I 106–7, 109–11, 121–2, 137, 148, 151, 156, 170–3, 226, 326
chastity 45, 66–9, 70–3, 81–2, 87–9, 91, 99–100, 102, 130, 154, 214, 246, 275, 304–5
  and Augustus 112–13, 122–3
  and Charles I 106–7, 109–10, 122 n. 72, 156, 172
  and Elizabeth I 137–9, 156, 311
  and Milton 2, 61–2, 85, 87, 93–4, 145–7, 156–60
  and narcissism 159–60, 181, 185–9
  and phoenix 311–13
Chaucer, Geoffrey 15, 42 n. 123, 114, 232 n. 7
Chloris, see Flora

Christianity and paganism 4, 6–7, 47, 63, 259–60, 271
Cintio, Giovambattista Giraldi 38–9
Circe 74–5, 78–80, 83 n. 105, 93, 98, 106–7, 109, 150, 156, 159, 161, 174, 274–5
Clapham, John 158 n. 180, 175 n. 24, 187 n. 61, 195 n. 90
Clark, Donald 30
Claudian 312 n. 65
Coiro, Ann Baynes 107 n. 25, 110 n. 35, 139 n. 124, 300, 315–16
Coleridge, Samuel Taylor 27 n. 85, 229–30
Comus 77–80, 82–4, 98, 105, 111, 155–62, 169, 174, 275
Conte, Gian Biagio 26, 118 n. 60, 119 n. 61
Conti, Natale 192, 234 n. 14
Cooper, Thomas 238
Cope, Jackson I. 55, 60
copia 18, 38–9, 44 n. 129, 125, 132, 177, 181–3, 185, 217–18, 250, 258, 269; *see also inopem me copia fecit*
Corns, Thomas N. 20 n. 58, 107, 110, 148, 172, 298–9
Coulson, Frank Thomas xiii n. 17
courtly love 42, 114–15
courtship, forms of 89–91, 94, 99, 114, 213–17, 185 n. 55, 218–19
  in Milton 94, 210, 213–14, 216–17, 219–20, 221–2, 225–6, 264
  in Ovid 114, 215, 274
  see also delay; desire; marriage
Cowley, Abraham 35 n. 104, 169 n. 6, 170, 254 n. 89, 279, 286 n. 6, 293
Creaser, John 171 n. 13, 201 n. 102
creativity
  and destruction 36–7, 39–48, 66, 230–1, 250, 262, 264–83, 286, 288
  in Eden 217–18
  in Milton 10–13, 47, 73–4, 197, 202–3
  in Ovid xi–xiii, 10–13, 68, 107–8, 178–80, 190–1
  postlapsarian xvii, 226–8, 231, 283
  and recreation xi–xiv, 12–13, 183–4, 212 n. 130, 227–8, 309
  and Satan 197–201, 277

and Son 197, 212, 253–5
see also aemulatio; allusion; artist figures; envy; imitation; narcissism; Narcissus; poetry and political power
Cressy, David 137, 148
Cupid 91–3
custom 102–3, 252–3
Cyprian, St 232

Daedalus 39, 230, 244
Daiches, David 59
Daniel, Samuel 16, 262 n. 116
Dante xiv, 2, 31, 41, 43, 187 n. 64, 192–3, 200–1, 239–40, 306 n. 53, 312–13, 321
Daphne 9–10, 45, 59–60, 68–9, 74, 102, 104–5, 113, 124, 156–7, 160, 186, 214–15, 243, 274; *see also* Apollo; chastity
Da Rho, Antonio 238–9
Davenant, William 101, 106
Davies, John 176 n. 125
De Deguileville, Guillaume 251, 275
delay 51, 89, 104, 134, 144–5, 213, 220–1, 224, 299; *see also* courtship; desire; marriage
De Quincey, Thomas xv, 2–3, 8, 205
desire
  in Milton 73, 93, 142–7, 166, 209, 212–14, 216–17, 220–1, 225
  in Ovid 8–9, 33, 35, 59, 66, 68–9, 70–2, 89, 102, 108, 111–15, 120–4, 154, 166, 176–82, 213–14
  see also courtship; delay; incest; marriage; rape
Deucalion and Pyrrha 12, 70, 226–7
Dickie, Matthew 236 n. 20
Dickson, Vernon Guy 282 n. 170
Donaldson, Ian 135 n. 111
Donne, John 101–2, 104, 311
Drayton, Michael 16, 100, 188 n. 67
Dryden, John 39 n. 115, 183, 305 n. 50, 317 n. 79
Du Bartas, Guillaume de Saluste 187 n. 64, 210, 213 n. 131
Du Bellay, Joachim 31
Dubrow, Heather 69, 72, 104, 132 n. 100, 135 n. 111

DuRocher, Richard J. 2, 4–8, 11, 28, 41–2, 156 n. 176, 161, 203 n. 107, 230, 239 n. 36, 255, 261

Echo 158–60, 181–2, 184, 195; *see also* Narcissus
Edwards, Thomas 73 n. 79, 184 n. 51, 194–5, 217 n. 146
Eggert, Katherine 156 n. 178
Elegy, relation to epic 118–24, 145–7, 162–3
Elizabeth I 22, 137–9
Elyot, Thomas 30 n. 90, 88, 128 n. 87
emulation, *see aemulatio*
Ennius xi, xii, 119 n. 62, 309
Enterline, Lynn 2 n. 3, 13 n. 35, 59, 189
envy 272, 275, 278–80, 282–3
  and creativity 231–45
  of critics 234
  and gods 237–8
  and love 231, 240
  in Milton 231, 251–7, 263, 285–6, 295, 324–6
  in Ovid 242–51, 275–7, 292, 325–6
  Ovid as victim of 246–51
  of Satan 231–2, 253–5, 273, 283, 295
  see also aemulatio; imitation
epyllion 16–17, 58, 63, 65, 82, 87 n. 115, 98, 129, 259, 274
Erasmus 183
Ericthonius 277 n. 155
error 46, 147, 252
  and Ovid 2, 37–9, 141, 259–60
Errour 199, 241 n. 45, 255–6, 275
Euripides xi, 46 n. 140, 323–4
Europa 59
Eve 2, 8–11, 41, 47, 167, 197, 201–14, 216–28, 230–1, 237, 253, 254, 256, 274

Fallon, Stephen M. 62 n. 40, 230 n. 1, 231 n. 4, 285–6, 316 n. 75
fallor 50–1, 121, 150
Fama 244–5
Farrell, Joseph 26
fathers and sons 92, 98, 118, 265–8, 309–11, 314, 323–4; *see also* oedipal relations
Faunus 98–9, 105, 120, 129, 130, 143; *see also* Weever
Ficino, Marsilio 176

Index

Fish, Stanley 84, 260–1, 286 n. 3, 305, 316–17
Fletcher, Angus 77
Fletcher, Giles and Phineas 57, 77, 148, 239
Flora 9–10, 107–9, 116, 120–1, 124, 143, 146, 160–1, 190, 218 n. 149, 318
flowers, and poetry 53, 57, 66, 73
Forsyth, Neil 225 n. 161, 230 n. 3, 261
Fränkel, Hermann 2 n. 3, 126 n. 82, 181 n. 41
Freud, Sigmund 174 n. 21, 185, 191, 242 n. 48
friendship 204–5, 297–8, 323
Frye, Northrop 199
Fyler, John 114

Galinsky, Karl xiii
Genesis 11–12, 47, 202–3, 208, 223, 226, 263
Glaucus 17, 39, 129, 219, 222, 274; *see also* Scylla
Godwin, Thomas 108 n. 28, 151–2
Golding, Arthur 3, 45, 175, 179 n. 36, 196, 264–5, 278–9
Gower, John (c. 1330–1408) 231 n. 6
Gower, John (fl. 1628–36) 16 n. 47, 33, 36 n. 109, 126 n. 82, 155 n. 174, 242 n. 49
Green, Mandy 8–10, 28, 47 n. 145, 210 n. 127, 214 n. 134, 219 n. 150, 228 n. 164
Greenblatt, Stephen 89
Greene, Thomas M. ix–x, xv, 5–6, 31 n. 94, 34, 54, 239 n. 36, 278 n. 159
Griffin, Dustin 286
Gross, Kenneth 131
Guibbory, Achsah 159, 171, 226
Guillory, John 80 n. 99, 81 n. 101, 82

H., T. 5 n. 16, 184–5, 193–5
Habington, William 311
Hale, John K. 20 n. 58, 50, 53 n. 16, 142, 149, 323
Hall, Thomas 35 n. 105, 265 n. 123
Hamilton, A. C. 65 n. 52, 69 n. 68
Hardie, Philip 9–10, 34–5, 36 n. 107, 68, 133 n. 102, 149 n. 153, 175 n. 23, 176 n. 25, 177 n. 30, 183, 214, 226 n. 163, 244–5, 247–8, 275, 301 n. 41, 305, 308–9, 310 n. 61

Harding, Davis P. 3–7, 13, 28, 30 n. 91
Hecuba 44–6, 135 n. 110, 250
Helgerson, Richard 21 n. 63, 97, 137, 147 n. 145, 149, 172 n. 16, 280 n. 165, 294
Hercules 39, 301, 303 n. 45
hermaphrodite 94, 213, 216
Hermaphroditus 68, 76, 90 n. 130, 114 n. 51, 129, 178, 185, 187–8, 205, 209, 312
Hero, *see* Marlowe, *Hero and Leander*; Ovid, *Heroides*
Herrick, Robert 32, 153–5, 160, 293
Hesiod xi, xii, 22, 119 n. 62, 234–6, 239
Hexter, Ralph 31 n. 94, 36 n. 108, 246 n. 63
Heywood, Thomas 220, 317 n. 79
Hinds, Stephen xii, xviii n. 26, 17 n. 50, 25–7, 33 n. 98, 34, 62 n. 41, 75, 79, 112, 119–20, 162, 245, 250
Hobbes, Thomas 151
Holahan, Michael 19, 129
Hollander, John 76, 184
Homer x, xv, 5, 22, 26, 40, 74, 121, 206–8, 235, 259, 264, 269–71
Horace xi, xii, 247, 271–2, 292, 295
Housman, A. E. 250
Hughes, Merritt 88
Hulse, Clark 23 n. 70, 86 n. 115, 89 n. 127
Hyacinthus 66, 108, 121

Icarus 35, 40, 264, 268, 271–2, 290, 309, 321–4
illusion 36, 48, 178–82, 183 n. 46, 205, 247
imitation ix–xiii, 5, 9, 17–18, 25, 99 n. 5, 183–4, 195–6, 205, 264, 276 n. 149, 278, 294, 308–9
  as form of change 170–3, 195–6, 206–8, 226–8
  and envy 235, 238–9, 244–5, 273, 283
  in Milton xvii, 12, 25, 49–54, 57, 170–5, 196, 201, 205–10, 212–13, 226–8, 255–6, 273, 283 325
  in Ovid xi–xvi, 183–4, 214, 243–5, 249–50, 308–9
  of Ovid xiii–xvi, 25–6
  politics of 170–3
  and Satan 199–201
  see also *aemulatio*, envy, reception and reading

immortality and art 59 n. 129, 68–9,
    189, 246, 269 n. 127, 295, 316
  in Milton xviii, 55–7, 265–9, 271,
    294–8, 316, 325–7
  in Ovid xii, 29, 66, 120 n. 66, 264,
    291–2, 310–11
incest xviii, 102, 113, 177 n. 30, 178, 186
    n. 59, 198–9, 214
  and narrative doubling 214–15
inopem me copia fecit 39, 125, 177,
    181–3, 185, 211; *see also copia*
Ion 323–4

James, Heather xv n. 22, 22 n. 64, 24 n.
    71, 34 n. 102, 38 n. 113, 62, 91,
    103, 204 n. 111, 213, 248 n. 68
James I 148–9, 151, 152–3
Janan, Micaela 214
Janus 119, 124, 131
John Chrysostom, St 235
Johnson, Samuel 1 n. 1, 29 n. 87, 47, 74,
    220, 256, 261 n. 114, 273 n. 137,
    255–6, 294 n. 21, 299
Jonson, Ben 77, 101, 154, 234, 241–2,
    276 n. 153, 294–6, 326
  Chloridia 107–9, 111
  Poetaster 236 n. 23, 244 n. 55 247–8,
    249 n. 73, 251, 266, 304 n. 46, 317
    n. 78

Kahn, Coppélia 132 n. 99
Kallendorf, Craig 24
Keach, William 25, 86 n. 115, 87 n. 120,
    99 n. 5, 100 n. 6
Keats, John 196
Kenney, E. J. 92, 93 n. 138, 134 n. 108
Kerrigan, William 104–5, 147 n. 145,
    154 n. 172, 220 n. 154, 286
Knoespel, Kenneth 185
Krier, Theresa 24

Lactantius 311–12
Lady, in Milton 74, 78–82, 105, 111, 149,
    155–62, 181, 185–6, 304–5
  and Milton 158–9
Langley, Eric 184
Lanham, Richard 2 n. 3, 133, 177
La Penna, Antonio 248
Lauder, William 256 n. 98
Leach, Eleanor 40
Leander, *see* Marlowe, *Hero and
    Leander*; Ovid, *Heroides*

Le Comte, Edward 57
Leonard, John 90
Leonardo 190–1
Levin, Harry 90
Lewalski, Barbara Kiefer 77, 106, 110–11,
    147, 211 n. 128, 273 n. 137
Lieb, Michael 11–12, 301 n. 39
'like himself' 303–6, 310–11
Lloyd, Robert 256 n. 98
Lodge, Thomas 17, 77, 246, 274–5
Longinus 5, 235, 239
Loudon, Bruce 206–7
Lovelace, Richard 279, 318 n. 80
Low, Anthony 307–8
Lucrece 44, 102, 134–5, 138, 159–60,
    180 n. 39, 188; *see also*
    Shakespeare, *Rape of Lucrece*
Lucretia 59, 122–4, 135, 157
Lucretius xi, 120, 143, 183, 240 n. 41,
    259, 309, 321–2
Luxon, Thomas H. 204 n. 111
Lycaon 45
Lydgate, John 251, 275
Lyne, Raphael 5 n. 16, 24, 188 n. 67

McCabe, Richard A. 83 n. 106, 138 n.
    122, 241
McColley, Diane 10
McDowell, Nicholas 87 n. 121, 110 n.
    36, 139 n. 124
MacLean, Hugh 55 n. 20, 63, n. 43
McMahon, Robert 193
Macrobius, xiii n. 17
Marlowe, Christopher 21, 62 n. 42, 89,
    95, 99, 100, 104, 265
  and Ovid 87, 115 n. 53, 118,
    247 n. 64
  Hero and Leander 15–16, 63, 86–91,
    99, 114 n. 48, 133 n. 104, 159 n.
    184, 210, 213, 221, 225–6, 258
marriage xv, 59, 67, 85, 91–5, 99, 106–7,
    109–10, 112, 121–2, 138, 187 n.
    64, 213 n. 141, 302
  ideal of in Milton 2–3, 85, 92–5, 141,
    144, 204–5
  in Ovid 70–1
  and poetic relations xv–xvi, 2–3, 8,
    92–4, 205, 214
  postlapsarian 225–8
  see also courtship; desire; incest
Marston, John 85 n. 114, 185 n. 54, 188,
    234 n. 14, 241, 247, 249 n. 73

Index

Mars 118, 120–3, 124, 130–1, 150, 160, 177 n. 30
Marsyas 35 n. 105, 39–40, 184, 230
Martindale, Charles 4 n. 11, 8 n. 19, 9, 14 n. 37, 26 n. 80, 111, 142, 150, 259
Martz, Louis xiv, 320
Maslen, R. W. 184 n. 50, 194 n. 89
masque 16, 78, 105–7, 109–10, 161–3
Medea 39, 44 n. 132, 51, 76, 161, 166, 176 n. 25, 181, 223–4, 225
Meres, Francis 16–17, 24
Meskill, Lynn S. 233, 242, 248 n. 68, 326
metamorphosis of opposites 13, 43–8, 182, 195
Miller, John F. 127
Milton, Deborah 1
Milton, John
  reputation of 2–3, 256–7, 285–6
  self-presentation of 55–6, 73–4, 229–30, 285–7, 298–9, 304–5, 315–17
  and Virgil 20, 146, 301–3
  'Ad *Joannem Rousium*, Oxoniensis Academiae Bibliothecarium' 147, 252, 319–26
  'Ad Patrem' 252, 266–8, 271 n. 132, 324
  Apology for Smectymnuus 159, 252
  Arcades 77
  Areopagitica 93, 173, 221, 293–4
  Comus 17, 74–95, 105–6, 110–11, 142, 149–63, 165, 169–70, 216, 257, 304–5, 315
  De Doctrina Christiana 197 n. 95, 231 n. 6
  Defensio Secunda 22, 253, 273 n. 136
  Doctrine and Discipline of Divorce 103, 252–3
  Eikonoklastes 170–3, 253, 294
  'Elegia 1' 32, 49, 64 n. 49, 148, 263
  'Elegia 2' 56, 61
  'Elegia 3' 51, 56, 61–2
  'Elegia 4' 50, 51–4, 75 n. 84
  'Elegia 5' 50–2, 85, 142–6, 156 n. 177, 166–7, 213, 265–6, 268
  'Elegia 6' 52, 62, 145–7, 155
  'Elegia 7' 51, 146–7, 166–7
  'Epitaphium Damonis' 55 n. 20, 166–7, 310 n. 61, 311, 315
  'Haec ego mente' 28, 147
  History of Britain 269–70
  'In Obitum Praesulis Eliensis' 56, 61–2, 166–7, 248 n. 72, 265
  'In quintum Novembris' 51, 53 n 15, 56, 63, 139, 148–9, 151, 254 n. 92, 269
  'L'Allegro' and 'Il Penseroso' 145, 147
  Lycidas 166–7, 270, 315
  'Mansus' 297–8, 324
  'Nativity Ode' 7, 55 n. 20, 73, 139, 140, 146 n. 141, 147–8, 156 n. 177
  'On *Shakespear*' 294–6, 316
  'On the Death of a fair Infant dying of a Cough' 54–74, 85, 161, 167, 306–8, 315
  Paradise Lost 165–228, 253–74, 283
  Paradise Regain'd 74, 259, 269, 286–7, 298–301
  Poems (1645) 20, 55, 73–4, 147, 167, 251–2, 257
  Poems (1673) 55–6, 73–4, 287, 319
  'Prolusion 6' 141–2, 152,
  Pro populo Anglicano defensio 110, 253
  Reason of Church-Government 252
  Samson Agonistes 286–7, 298–317
  Second Defence of the People of England 22
  Tetrachordon xv–xvi, 141, 203–5
Minerva 40, 198, 243–6, 262, 275–8, 282 n. 169
mora, *see* delay
Morrison, Bruce 206–7
Moss, Ann 3 n. 10, 13, 126–7, 248, 249–50
Most, Glenn W. 235 n. 15
Mulciber 41, 258–60
Mulryan, John 3–5, 13, 276
Mulvihill, James D. 247
Myers, K. Sara xi, 23 n. 68, 25 n. 77, 112, 166 n. 1
Myrrha 44 n. 132, 92, 102, 161, 178 n. 32, 186 n. 59

narcissism
  of artists 189–96, 313
  and desire 185–9
  of God 193, 197
  of Milton 229–30
  of Ovid 38–9, 183
  of Satan 197–9, 212
  see also chastity; creativity
Narcissus 9–10, 36, 39, 68, 74, 108, 121, 125, 158, 173–5, 204 n. 111, 214, 219, 255, 259, 265, 274–5

Index

Adam and Eve as 201-13, 222-8
  in Milton 47, 158, 196-213
  in Ovid 175-84
  in Renaissance 184-96
Narcissus: A Twelfe Night Merriment 175 n. 24
narrators
  in Milton 41-3, 251, 261, 263-4, 269-73
  in Ovid 42-3, 261-3
Nashe, Thomas 317 n. 78
Neoplatonism 78, 84, 100, 106, 174-6, 187 n. 64, 190
Neuse, Richard 84
Newlands, Carole E. 108, 121, 123, 125, 135 n. 109
Newlyn, Lucy 241 n. 44, 287
Niobe 40, 133, 182, 192
Nohrnberg, James 76
Nonius 238
Nussbaum, Martha 45-6

Oedipal relations xiv-xvi, 266, 273, 291; *see also* fathers and sons; imitation
Oliensis, Ellen 234 n. 11, 241 n. 44
Olmsted, Wendy 169
Orgel, Stephen 160
Orpheus xi, 11, 40, 270-1
Otis, Brooks 70-1
Ovid
  allegorical interpretations of 3-4, 13-14, 60-1, 63, 66, 69, 71, 111, 173
  in antiquarianism 108, 128, 151-3
  and court masques 105-11
  and Elizabethans 14-19, 63, 98-100
  humanist readings of 3-6, 13-14, 18 n. 52, 38
  hybrids in 39, 48, 50, 80, 129, 274-5
  and Stuart poets 101-5
  relation of art to life 35-7, 180, 288, 321
  reputation of 2-3
  in the Restoration 317-18
  rhetoric of 18, 38-9, 44-6, 48, 132-3, 161, 181-2, 216, 305-6; *see also* *fallor*; *inopem me copia fecit*; wit
  in schools 17-19, 30-32, 127-8
  and Virgil 19-27, 29, 52-4, 79-80, 146, 177 n. 29, 183 n. 46, 244-5, 246, 274, 281-3, 308-11
  Amores xii, 29, 42, 62, 113-14, 118-19, 123-5, 243, 245, 264, 326

Ars amatoria xiii, 37, 42, 44, 114, 175, 220, 289, 321
De Vetula 34 n. 100
Fasti xi, 28, 42, 52-3, 76, 79 n. 96, 107-9, 111, 115-26, 150, 268, 276, 289
  influence of 126-39, 151-3
  in Milton 140-5, 150, 152, 155, 160-1
Heroides 16, 35, 70-1, 89, 208, 225, 321 n. 5
Ibis 248-51, 291
Metamorphoses xi-xii, 12, 28-9, 37, 40, 125, 226-7, 243-5, 276-8, 289, 291, 308-11, 314
Nux 242 n. 49
Remedia amoris 242-3
Tristia and *Ex Ponto* 28-37, 42, 51-2, 126, 157, 245-6, 261-3, 276, 287-92, 319
  influence of 30-7, 42-3
  in Milton 32, 42, 261-3

Pandemonium 258, 260
Peend, Thomas 80 n. 98, 90 n. 130, 187
Perdix 244, 277 n. 153
Petrarch, Francesco 16, 31, 34-5, 80, 104-5, 107, 114, 186, 189-90, 202, 272, 313
  and Ovidianism 68-9, 71-3, 85, 101, 138, 219, 222
Phaethon 35, 62, 92, 258-9, 264-5, 271-2, 286, 290, 309, 321-4
  in Milton 265-9
Philomela 10, 40, 44, 50, 59, 135, 230, 250
Philostratus 180 n. 37, 177 n. 28
Phineas 269-70, 272 n. 135, 320
phoenix 307-15
Picus 98-9
Pigman, G. W. III 170, 239
Pindar 233, 237, 271-2, 319
Plato 5, 147, 175-80, 183, 188, 195, 202, 204, 206, 208-10, 212, 223, 235-6, 237
Plotinus 177 n. 28
poetry, and political power xvi, 21-2, 24-5, 103, 109-15, 123-6, 148-9, 154, 162-3;
  see also creativity
Poliziano 31 n. 95, 127, 248
Pomona and Vertumnus 9, 215-16, 218-19

Poussin, Nicolas 108–9, 190–1, 192 n. 81
Propertius xi, 215
Psyche 91–4, 161, 192, 279
Pugh, Syrithe 6, 23, 31 n. 95, 70–1, 124 n. 76, 137, 138 n. 121–2, 153 n. 168, 154, 282–3
Pygmalion 12, 36, 40, 180, 185
Pyramus and Thisbe 177–8
Pythagoras 16, 117, 129, 132, 166, 308–10

Quilligan, Maureen 255–6
Quinones, Ricardo J. 129, 140, 189 n. 70
Quint, David xv, 268, 309, 315 n. 72, 321
Quintilian 38, 183–4, 195 n. 93

Rabelais 241
Radzinowicz, Mary Ann 141–2
Randolph, Thomas 110 n. 35, 312–13
rape 64, 71, 89 n. 128, 104, 113, 120, 216–7
  in Milton 55, 58–64, 73, 81, 213–14
  in Ovid 44, 59–60, 108–9, 111–12, 113–14, 120, 122–4, 135
  reception, reading
    in Milton 287, 292–9, 303–4, 315–27
    in Ovid 34–5, 287–92
Rees, Christine 68 n. 64
Regius, Raphael xii n. 14, xiii n. 17, 115 n. 52, 179 n. 36
Revard, Stella Purce 143, 147 n. 146, 156 n. 177, 271 n. 132, 303 n. 45, 309 n. 60, 320, 324
Richlin, Amy 35 n. 105, 59 n. 31, 120 n. 65
Ricks, Christopher 46
Ripa, Cesare 191
Roberts, Jeanne Addison 49 n. 2, 52 n. 12, 64 n. 49
Roe, John 87
Roman de la Rose 185, 251
Romulus and Remus 121
Rosati, Gianpiero 183
Ross, David 75
Rumrich, John 94 n. 140, 202 n. 105, 304 n. 47

Sabrina 77, 79–83, 84 n. 107, 86 n. 118, 149, 150, 155, 315
Sage, Lorna 286
Salmacis 76, 80, 90 n. 130, 114 n. 51, 187–8, 222; *see also* Hermaphroditus

Samson 298–308, 314–17
  as author figure 298–302, 316–17
Sandys, George 3, 18, 35 n. 105, 36 n. 109, 45 n. 136, 66 n. 53, 68 n. 63, 111–12, 113 n. 47, 173–4, 175 n. 24, 179 n. 36, 184 n. 52, 264 n. 121, 275–6
Satan 41, 197–201, 212, 218–22, 231–2, 251, 253–6, 260–1, 314, 321
  metamorphosis of 199–201
  and Milton 41–3, 229–31, 255–6
  and Ovid 41, 261
Sauer, Elizabeth 8
Schwartz, Regina 43, 199 n. 97
Scylla 10, 39, 129, 181, 199, 219, 256, 274–5, 283
  and envy 275
Segal, Charles 35 n. 105, 59, 111–12, 208, 275
Selden, John 153
self-knowledge 175–6, 223, 265
  in Milton 203–5, 211–12
Seneca the Elder xii, 38, 50
Servius 113
Shakespeare, William xiv, 16, 20, 22, 23–4, 27, 36, 77, 80–2, 84–5, 91, 99, 100, 122, 138–9, 155, 157, 172 n. 15, 234, 241–2, 247, 257, 265, 294–6, 297, 305–6, 312
  The Rape of Lucrece 81, 132–5, 160, 188
  Sonnets 29, 186–7, 189
  Titus Andronicus 18 n. 52, 44, 72
  Venus and Adonis 63–9, 72–4, 81, 114, 133–4, 138–9, 186, 189, 213, 216–17
Shoaf, R. A. 192
Shullenberger, William 74 n. 81, 84 n. 107, 84 n. 111, 111, 142, 145, 146 n. 141, 159, 160 n. 192, 161
Shulman, Jeff 67
Sidney, Philip 171–2, 293
Sin 3, 11, 169–70, 174, 198–9, 214, 219, 236, 256, 262, 272–6
Skelton, John 241
Smith, James 317 n. 78, 317 n.79
Smith, Nigel 172 n. 15, 213–14
Solodow, Joseph 200–1
Spenser, Edmund xiv, 19, 21, 23–4, 76–7, 80–2, 85, 89, 91, 94–5, 99, 120, 121–2, 129–31, 135, 138–9, 150, 155, 156, 233, 236, 241, 265, 313

Amoretti 185 n. 55, 186 n. 59, 188, 203
Complaints 15, 31
The Faerie Queene 69–72, 74, 81–2,
   91, 93, 138, 188, 216, 240, 280
'Muiopotmos' 277–83
Mutabilitie Cantos 76, 129–30,
   168, 265
The Shepheardes Calender 29, 57–8,
   73, 76, 109 n. 32, 129–30, 136 n.
   114, 138, 185 n. 55
Stapleton, M. L. 5 n. 16, 42, 43, 86 n.
   115, 114 n. 51, 215 n. 141, 317 n.
   79, 318 n. 80
Stevens, Paul 81 n. 103, 94 n. 140,
   296 n. 27
strife 90–1, 94–5, 99, 133–5, 225–6,
   235, 256
Suckling, John 101
Summers, Joseph H. 167, 225 n. 160
synkrisis 22–3

Tarquin, *see* Lucretia; Ovid, *Fasti*;
   Shakespeare, *Rape of Lucrece*
Tasso, Torquato 193 n. 86
Thamyris 269–71
Thomas, Richard xi–xii, 25–6
Tillyard, E. M. W. 63
time
   in Milton 139–52, 155, 224, 299
   in Ovid 115–26
   poetics of 117–18, 125–6, 129–30,
      134–6, 140
   politics of 116–17, 126, 136–9,
      148–9, 151
   in Shakespeare 132–5
   in Spenser 129–31
Tiresias 175–6, 269–70
Tissol, Garth 26 n. 81, 39 n.
   115, 133
Tourneur, Cyril 65 n. 50, 275 n. 148
Townshend, Aurelian 106, 121, 161
translatio 17, 77, 79–80
Tudeau-Clayton, Margaret 24
twins 94–5

Ulysses xiii, 41, 43, 79, 156, 214–15, 321
Underdowne, Thomas 248–9

Vaughan, Henry 32
Venus 9, 70, 72, 78, 84–6, 90 n. 132,
   134, 92–3, 99–100, 118, 120–3,
   124, 131, 177 n. 30, 186, 187 n.
   63, 189, 202–3, 216–17; *see also*
   Shakespeare, *Venus and Adonis*
Vertumnuus, *see* Pomona
Vesta 108, 113, 116, 120, 132 n.
   99, 143
Vinge, Louise 186
Virgil x–xi, xv, 19–27, 40, 42, 52–4,
   76–7, 79–80, 118–19, 143,
   146, 148–9, 183, 237–8,
   308–11, 321–2
   Aeneid 23, 244–5, 264, 281–2, 301–3,
      314, 321
   Ciris 24
   Culex 24, 282 n. 168
   Eclogues 277
   Georgics 52–4, 114
   see also Ovid, and Virgil

Wallace-Hadrill, Andrew 112
Waller, Edmund 104–5
Watkins, John 23
Watkins, W. B. C. 210
Weever, John 17, 75, 77, 98–100, 105,
   114 n. 51, 142, 187 n. 64, 241 n.
   46, 258
Williams, Gareth 248, 250–1
Willobie, Henry 185 n. 55
Wilmot, John, Earl of Rochester 317–18
Wilson, Emily 194 n. 86
wit
   in Milton 80, 141–2, 211–12
   and Ovid 18, 38–9
   wandering 194
   see also Ovid, rhetoric of
Wittreich, Joseph 300

Zimmerman, Mary 92 n. 134, 92 n. 136

Made in the USA
Middletown, DE
08 August 2017